ORGANIZATIONAL BEHAVIOR

McGRAW-HILL SERIES IN MANAGEMENT
Keith Davis and Fred Luthans, Consulting Editors

ORGANIZATIONAL BEHAVIOR
Second Edition
Fred Luthans

Professor of Management, University of Nebraska

McGRAW-HILL BOOK COMPANY

New York   St. Louis   San Francisco   Auckland   Bogotá
Düsseldorf   Johannesburg   London   Madrid   Mexico   Montreal
New Delhi   Panama   Paris   São Paulo
Singapore   Sydney   Tokyo   Toronto

Library of Congress Cataloging in Publication Data

Luthans, Fred.
Organizational behavior.

(McGraw-Hill series in management)
Includes bibliographies and index.
1. Management. 2. Organization. 3. Psychology,
Industrial. I. Title.
HD38.L92   1977   658.4   76-17071
ISBN 0-07-039130-0

ORGANIZATIONAL BEHAVIOR

4 5 6 7 8 9 0 D O D O 7 8 3 2 1 0 9

This book was set in Times Roman by Black Dot, Inc.
The editors were William J. Kane and Michael Weber;
the cover was designed by Ben Kann;
the cover photograph was taken by Charles Gatewood;
the production supervisor was Dennis J. Conroy.
New drawings were done by Danmark & Michaels, Inc.
R. R. Donnelley & Sons Company was printer and binder.

For
Kay, Kristin,
Brett, Kyle,
and
Paige

Contents

Preface

Definite progress has been made since the first edition of this book in solving the human problems of management. Yet, human problems and challenges still dominate the theory and practice of management and will probably continue to do so for the foreseeable future. The first edition was aimed at making the transition from the old human relations approach to the new organizational behavior approach. Human relations was based on some very simplistic assumptions about human behavior and offered equally simplistic, prescriptive solutions for managing people. The organizational behavior approach assumes that humans are extremely complex and that there is a need for theoretical understanding backed by rigorous empirical research before applications can be made for managing people effectively. The transition has now been completed. Human relations no longer has a dominant role in the behavioral approach to management. Few people would question that the organizational behavior approach, with its accompanying assumptions, dominates the behavioral approach to management for the present and will do so in the foreseeable future.

Now that organizational behavior has become the widely accepted approach, it has had a chance to develop and mature as an academic discipline. However, as with any other relatively new academic endeavor, there have been some "rough spots" and "sidetracks" in its development. Besides the healthy academic controversies over theoretical approach or research findings, perhaps the biggest problem that organizational behavior has had to face is an identity crisis. Exactly what is meant by *organizational behavior*? Is it an attempt to replace all of management with behavioral science concepts and techniques? How, if at all, does it differ from good old applied or industrial psychology? Fortunately, these questions have now largely been answered to the satisfaction of most management academicians, behavioral scientists, and management practitioners. Organizational behavior is directly concerned with the understanding, prediction, and control of human behavior in organizations. It represents the *behavioral* approach to management, not the whole of management. Other recognized approaches to management include process, quantitative, systems, and contingency. In other words, organizational behavior does not intend to replace the whole of management. The charge of being only old wine (applied/ industrial psychology) poured into a new bottle (organizational behavior) has also proved to be groundless. Although it is certainly true that the behavioral sciences make a significant contribution to the foundation (both theory and research) of organizational behavior, it is equally true that applied/ industrial psychology should not be equated with organizational behavior. For example, organizational structure and management processes (decision making, communication, and control) play an integral, direct role in organizational behavior but have, at most, an indirect role in applied/industrial psychology. The same is true of the many important dynamics and applications of organizational behavior. Although there will probably never be total agreement on the exact meaning and domain of organizational behavior—which is not necessarily bad, because it makes the field more exciting and dynamic—there is little doubt that organizational behavior has come into its own as a field of study, research, and application.

As did the first edition, this book provides a strong conceptual framework for the study and understanding of organizational behavior. A concerted effort has been made to include a palatable blend of both behavioral science and management. Neither behavioral science nor management is emphasized at the expense of the other. It is hoped that the reader will gain an understanding of the variables and complexities involved in organizational behavior. It is further hoped that the study of this book and the application of the techniques presented will lead to more effective management of human resources today and in the future.

The book contains five major parts: (1) an introductory foundation; (2) the major structural and process variables of formal organizations; (3) the psychological variables in human behavior; (4) the important dynamics of organizational behavior; and (5) some specific techniques and applications for human resource management. Chapters in the first part lay down a historical, behavioral science, management, and environmental foundation. The last chapter in the first part presents a specific conceptual framework for organizational behavior. The model incorporates both cognitive and behavioristic concepts and perspectives. The remaining parts and specific chapters closely follow this conceptual framework. The chapters in Part Two discuss both classical and modern organizational theory and structure and give specific attention to the management processes of decision making, communication, and control. The third part examines in depth the psychological processes of perception, learning, and motivation and is capped by a chapter on personality theory and development. Part Four, on the dynamics of organizational behavior, contains chapters on groups and informal organization, conflict, work motivation, and leadership and power. Finally, the last part has chapters on the latest application techniques for selection, job design and appraisal, applied behavioral analysis and change, and organization development.

This edition differs from the first by giving relatively less attention to management variables and relatively more attention to the dynamics and applications of organizational behavior. Specifically, in the first part the two historical chapters in the first edition have been combined into one, the chapter on scientific methodology has been incorporated into the chapter on behavioral sciences, and there are two substantially new chapters: "Approaches to Management" and "The Relevant Environment." In the second part the three chapters on structure have been reduced to two, and the two decision-making chapters have been reduced to one; the old chapter on technology has been incorporated into the environment chapter in the first part. The chapter on communication has been completely revised by taking a personal rather than a linear-information flow perspective. The introductory chapter on behavioral analysis formerly in Part Three has been incorporated into the conceptual model chapter in Part One. Old Part Four has been divided into two new parts. Part Four, on the dynamics of organizational behavior, now has a chapter specifically devoted to the dynamics of conflict and substantially new separate chapters: "The Motivation to Work" and "Leadership and Power." The final part, on applications, has three new chapters: "Selection, Job Design, and Appraisal," "Applied Behavioral Analysis and Change," and "Organization Development." In addition, of course, new research findings that have been published since the first edition have been incorporated throughout, and ideas, concepts, and research that have since proved to be invalid have been eliminated. Considerable effort has been made to update the book thoroughly so that it can stay abreast of the rapidly growing and changing field of organizational behavior.

Besides the eight completely or substantially new chapters and the expansion/modification and updating of all remaining material, much new material has been added to chapters carried over from the first edition. A few examples are the human resource model in the historical chapter, role and contingency theories in the modern organization chapter, the nominal group technique in the decision chapter, the Berlo and transactional models in the communication chapter, the feedforward concept and techniques in the control chapter, drive theories in the basic motivation chapter, and biofeedback in the personality chapter.

Other significant additions to the new edition are the short cases at the end of each chapter. These short cases have been added as a further effort to make this new edition more applications-oriented. The cases allow the reader to take the more abstract theories, concepts, and research findings discussed in the preceding chapter and analyze and apply them in a realistic organizational situation. The cases are short enough that they can be read during class. They were written to be relevant, interesting, and realistic so that they may be an effective vehicle for class discussion and debate. They may also be assigned as readings in human behavior problems and dynamics in today's organizations.

Despite the considerable additions, changes, and reorganization in this new edition, the purpose and intended audience of the book remain the same. Very little of the content of the first edition has been deleted. With all the new material in this edition, the size of the book remains about the same because much of the older material which is still relevant has been condensed rather than eliminated. This edition, like the first, is aimed at those who wish to take a totally modern behavioral approach to management. It does not assume the reader's prior knowledge of either management or the behavioral sciences. Thus, the book can be used effectively in the first or only course in four-year or two-year colleges. It may also be appropriate for the behavioral follow-up course to the more traditional introductory management course or the behavioral course in the MBA program. Moreover, the book should be helpful to practicing managers who want to understand and manage better their most important asset, their human resources.

Every author owes a great deal to others, and I am no exception. I would like to acknowledge the valuable interaction I have had with my colleagues in my area at the University of Nebraska. In particular, I would like to thank Professors Henry Albers, Richard Hodgetts, Richard Mowday, Warren Nielsen, Larry Pate, Richard Schonberger, Cary Thorp, and William Torrence. I would also like to thank Associate Dean Gary Schwendiman and Dean Ronald Smith of the College of Business Administration of the University of Nebraska for their encouragement and support. I also value my close association over the years with Professors Donald Beard of the University of Washington, Kenneth Bond of Creighton University, Brad Chapman of the University of Nebraska-Omaha, James Francis of Colorado State University, Thomas Kess of Miami (Ohio) University, Edward Knod of Western Illinois University, Robert Kreitner of Arizona State University, Cheedle Millard of the University of Texas-Dallas, Russell Morey of Western Illinois University, Robert Ottemann of the University of Nebraska-Omaha, William Reif of Arizona State University, Peter Van Ness of Western Illinois University, Jerry Wallin of Louisiana State University, Donald White of the University of Arkansas, and Max Wortman of the University of Massachusetts. They have all influenced me in my approach to the management field. I am also very grateful to those professors who used the first edition of the book and gave me valuable feedback for making this revision. In particular, I would like to thank Professors David C. Anderson of California State University at Fresno, William G. Ouchi of Stanford University, and Frank Ziol of Pasadena City College, who read and gave their comments on the manuscript. Finally, as always, I am deeply appreciative of my wife and children, who gave me the time and encouragement to complete this book.

Fred Luthans

Part One

Introductory
Foundation for
Organizational Behavior

Chapter 1

Historical Development

Management in general and the behavioral approach in particular have a rich heritage. Practitioners and students of management sometimes ignore this important history or feel that it is totally removed in time and relevance from today's problems. "Old-timers," who know and have actually experienced firsthand some of this development of the field of management, often chide their younger counterparts for "reinventing the wheel." There is certainly some truth to this accusation. The purpose of this introductory chapter is to trace through some of the important phases in the practice of management over the last hundred years. Particular attention is given to the reasons and research support for the human relations movement that took place in the practice of management. An extension of human relations, a human resource management perspective, is used as the point of departure for the study of organizational behavior.

THE EARLY PRACTICE OF MANAGEMENT

Managers have been in existence for as long as individuals have put others in a position subordinate to them for the purpose of accomplishing predetermined goals. Some of the earliest recovered documents written by Sumerian temple priests about 5000 B.C. offer tangible evidence of managerial practices.[1] Throughout history, managers have played a vital role in their respective societies. Much of the success of the Egyptian and Roman civilizations can be credited to their astounding managerial accomplishments. Nevertheless, practicing managers were not initially recognized in academic circles. For example, in the writings of Adam Smith, the founding father of economics, only land, labor, and capital were viewed as specific agents of production. It was not until the beginning of the nineteenth century that economists such as J. B. Say added the entrepreneurial concept as an ingredient of production. The "undertaker of industry" was defined by Say as one who unites all means of production—the labor of the one, the capital or the land of the others—". . . and who finds in the value of the products which result from them, the reestablishment of the entire capital he employes, and the value of wages, the interest and the rent which he pays, as well as the profits belonging to himself."[2]

Say's requirements for the entrepreneurial role sound like a job description for modern executives. He felt that the necessary qualities were

> . . . judgement, perseverance, and a knowledge of the world as well as of business. He is called upon to estimate, with tolerable accuracy, the importance of the specific product, the probable amount of the demand, and the means of its production: at one time he must employ a great number of hands; at another, buy or order the raw material, collect labourers, find consumers, and give at all times a rigid attention to order and economy; in a word, he must possess the art of superintendence and administration.[3]

Thus, the classical entrepreneurs were risk-bearing proprietors who coordinated labor and capital and practiced the art of management. At first they were termed "merchant princes" or "pretty capitalists," but later, with the advent of the industrial revolultion, the term "captains of industry" became a more appropriate description. The successful captains were a rare combination of power and genius and were primarily responsible for launching modern industrialism.

The "Captain" of General Motors

William C. Durant, the founder of General Motors, is an outstanding example of this initial phase of the practice of management in the twentieth century. In 1908 he laid the building blocks for the company that was to become the largest

---

[1]For a discussion of management practices in ancient civilizations, see Claude S. George, Jr., *The History of Management Thought,* 2d ed., Prentice-Hall, Inc., Englewood Cliffs, N.J., 1972, pp. 1–27, and Daniel A. Wren, *The Evolution of Management Thought,* The Ronald Press Company, New York, 1972, pp. 14–22.

[2]Jean Baptiste Say, *Catechism of Political Economy,* trans. John Richter, Sherwood, Neely and Jones, London, 1816, pp. 28–29.

[3]Jean Baptiste Say, *A Treatise on Political Economy,* New American ed., J. B. Lippincott and Company, Philadelphia, 1867, pp. 330–331. First printed in Paris in 1803.

manufacturing concern in the world. Durant had the necessary managerial skills to build the giant corporation's foundation. The approach was essentially a one-man operation where Durant made all major decisions, and he preferred subordinates who were "yes" men. All pertinent information and records were carried in his head. His day-to-day activities and decision making were based on hunch, experience, and intuition.

Other famous captains of industry were Henry Ford, Cornelius Vanderbilt, Andrew Carnegie, and John D. Rockefeller. All these men were brilliant but sometimes ruthless. They possessed the managerial qualities necessary for the initial stages of industrialization. However, when the industrial revolution began to mature and become stabilized, this approach was no longer appropriate. Although Durant's style was highly effective in the early days of General Motors, after a while "chinks began to appear in the armor."[4] By 1920, General Motors was in serious financial trouble. Within a few weeks' time Durant himself had lost nearly $100 million. In his analysis, Ernest Dale makes it clear that there were many contributing causes to the General Motors crisis. For example, insufficient use of accounting and inventory control was a big problem.[5] However, two major difficulties stood out from all the rest: Durant refused to utilize staff advice; and he failed to come up with an organizational plan that could hold together the tremendous corporate structure he had created.

Some of Durant's behaviorally oriented shortcomings are exemplified by his handling of two brilliant subordinates, Walter Chrysler and Alfred P. Sloan. Chrysler, who at the time headed the Buick Division of General Motors, remembered how he pleaded with Durant to

> . . . please, now say what your policies are for General Motors. I'll work on them; whatever they are, I'll work to make them effective. Leave the operations alone; the building, the buying, the selling and the men—leave them alone, but say what your policies are.[6]

Chrysler also told of an almost unbelievable encounter he had with Durant.

> Once I had gone to New York in obedience to a call from him [Durant]; he wished to see me about some matter. For several days in succession I waited at his office, but he was so busy he could not take the time to talk with me. . . . During a lull I gained his attention for a minute. "Hadn't I better return to Flint and work? I can come back here later." "No, no. Stay right here." I waited four days before I went back to Flint; and to this day I do not know why Billy (Durant) had required my presence in New York.[7]

[4]Ernest Dale, *The Great Organizers*, McGraw-Hill Book Company, New York, 1960, pp. 73–74.

[5]Ibid., p. 74.

[6]Walter P. Chrysler, with Boyden Sparkes, *Life of an American Workman*, Dodd, Mead & Company, Inc., New York, 1950, p. 148. Originally published in 1937.

[7]Ibid., pp. 156–157.

Because of this kind of shabby treatment, Chrysler eventually quit General Motors and founded what was to become one of that company's biggest competitors.

A similar blunder was Durant's treatment of Alfred P. Sloan. In May 1920, when General Motors was in the beginning of its decline, Sloan submitted to Durant an ingenious plan of organization. The plan reflected many insights into the company's problems and contained some logical solutions. Durant apparently ignored the plan completely. Sloan was so distraught over the outright rejection without discussion or consultation that he was about to resign from the company when the du Pont family assumed control of the corporation. In December 1920, Pierre S. du Pont resubmitted Sloan's organizational plan to the board of directors, and this time it was accepted. Sloan was made president of the company and was allowed to implement his plan. Using his new methods of management, he practically single-handedly rescued General Motors from the sure-death management methods used by Durant. Captains of industry, such as Durant, played a necessary initial role, but it was organizational specialists such as Sloan who then perpetuated and strengthened what the captains had founded.

Organizational Specialists

Two pioneering practicing managers, the French engineer and executive head Henri Fayol and General Motors' Alfred P. Sloan, best represent the "Great Organizers." Fayol's career embodied many different phases. He made his initial mark as a practicing mining engineer. Then, as a research geologist, he developed a unique theory on the formation of coal-bearing strata. This experience gave him a keen appreciation of the technical side of enterprise. However, the major portion of his career was spent practicing, and then writing about, the managerial functions and process.

In 1888, Fayol became managing director of Comambault, the well-known French combine. When he assumed the top position, a dividend had not been paid for three years and bankruptcy was approaching. Fayol's ingenious managerial and organizational methods soon paid off. The decline was shortly reversed, and by the time of World War I, the combine was able to make a significant contribution to the French cause. Fayol retired in 1918, but, through writing and speaking engagements, he succeeded in popularizing his theories and techniques of management. He maintained that the successful practicing manager should be able to handle men and should have considerable energy and courage, continuity of tenure, and a great deal of specialized and general experience.[8] He particularly stressed the methods of specialization and organization as necessities for success. In discussing specialization he stated:

> The object of division of work is to produce more and better work with the same effort. The worker always on the same part, the manager concerned always with

[8]Henri Fayol, *General and Industrial Management*, trans. Constance Storrs, Sir Isaac Pitman & Sons, London, 1949, p. 50.

the same matters, acquire an ability, sureness, and accuracy which increase their output.[9]

Devoting most of his attention to the process of organizing, he observed:

> To organize a business is to provide it with everything useful to its functioning: raw materials, tools, capital, personnel. All this may be divided into two main sections, the material organization and the human organization.[10]

Alfred P. Sloan is the other outstanding historical example of a Great Organizer. His basic organizational plan was for General Motors to maintain centralized control over highly decentralized operations. Although the du Ponts undoubtedly influenced Sloan, he is widely recognized as making a tremendous managerial contribution.[11] His plan is largely responsible for the success story of General Motors. Dale states,

> Sloan's organization study—the report on which the G.M. reorganization was based—is a remarkable document. Almost entirely original, it would be a creditable, if not a superior, organization plan for any large corporation today. It is a landmark in the history of administrative thought.[12]

In the first year after the du Ponts installed Sloan as president, the company almost doubled its manufacturing capacity. The reorganization went hand in hand with increased productivity and higher profits.

Scientific Managers

The Great Organizers were primarily concerned with overall managerial organization in order to survive and prosper. On the other hand, the scientific management movement around the turn of the century took a narrower operating perspective. Yet, the two approaches were certainly not contradictory. The managers in both cases applied the scientific method to their problems, and they thought that effective management at all levels was the key to organizational success. The two approaches differed chiefly in that the scientific managers worked from the bottom of the hierarchy upward, whereas the organizationalists worked from the apex downward. In other words, both had essentially the same goals, but they tried to reach them from different directions.

Frederick W. Taylor is the recognized father of scientific management. He had actual shop and engineering experience and therefore was intimately involved with tools, products, and various machining and manufacturing operations. His well-known metal-cutting experiments demonstrate the scientific

[9]Ibid., p. 20.
[10]Ibid., p. 53.
[11]Dale, op. cit., p. 84.
[12]Ibid., p. 86.

management approach. Over a period of twenty-six years, Taylor tested every conceivable variation in speed, feed, depth of cut, and kind of cutting tool. The outcome of this experimentation was high-speed steel, considered one of the most significant contributions to the development of large-scale production.

Besides metal cutting, Taylor dramatically contributed to increased productivity through his scientific management philosophy and principles. In Taylor's words, this approach can be summarized as: (1) science, not rule of thumb; (2) harmony, not discord; (3) cooperation, not individualism; (4) maximum output, in place of restricted output; and (5) the development of each man to his greatest efficiency and prosperity.[13] These concepts represented a total system of management as well as day-to-day operating procedures.[14]

Two of the most famous applications of Taylor's principles were to the pig-iron handling and shoveling operations at Bethlehem Steel Company. In the first situation, a gang of seventy-five workers loaded pigs of iron, each weighing 92 pounds, into box cars. By applying scientific management, the company achieved about a threefold increase in productivity. A similar rise in productivity was attained when the principles were applied to the men who shoveled iron ore and rice coal.[15] At first, these achievements were not widely recognized, but it was not long before scientific management became practically synonymous with management itself. The upsurge in popularity was primarily a result of a 1910 railway rate hearing before the Interstate Commerce Commission. Testimony by Harrington Emerson, a consultant on efficiency engineering, indicated that the railroads could save "a million dollars a day" through the use of scientific management. The newspapers headlined this testimony, and scientific management became renowned throughout American industry and also popular in Europe and Japan.

Taylor was by no means the only noteworthy scientific manager. Others in the movement, such as Frank Gilbreth and Henry L. Gantt, made especially significant contributions. Furthermore, the scientific managers were not the first or only group that recognized the importance of the operating function. A hundred years earlier, Adam Smith had carefully pointed out the advantages of division of labor, and in 1832, Charles Babbage, a British mathematician with some astounding managerial insights, discussed transference of skill in his book *Economy of Machinery and Manufacture.* Although Henry Ford could also be thought of as a captain of industry, the achievement of 10,000 Model T's a day would rival any scientific management accomplishment.

The Emergence of Functional Specialists

The captains of industry were primarily financial specialists. They created most of today's large corporations from a series of combinations, mergers, and financial manipulations. This financial phase was then replaced by an organiza-

---

[13]Frederick W. Taylor, *The Principles of Scientific Management,* Harper & Brothers, New York, 1911, p. 140.

[14]George, op. cit., p. 93.

[15]A detailed account of the Bethlehem experiments may be found in Frederick W. Taylor, op. cit., pp. 41–48 and 57–76.

tional orientation. The Great Organizers established structures which permitted their corporations to survive and meet the challenges of increased production. The scientific managers fed the insatiable consumer appetite for goods and services. These experts achieved phenomenal production results. In fact, like the captains of industry, they did their job almost too well. Inventories began to pile up as a result of the tremendous increases in productivity. The managerial problem shifted from one of not being able to produce enough to one of trying to dispose of the deluge of manufactured goods. At this point marketing specialists entered the picture. The marketing functions, consisting of the promotion, distribution, and sale of goods and services, became an integral part of practicing management. Thus, the functions of finance, production, and marketing each in turn received emphasis in the practice of management. Each of these functional specialties is still very much in evidence today and makes extremely important contributions to modern organizations.

The personnel manager, the other traditionally recognized functional specialist, has not yet been mentioned. This does not imply that the functional specialists ignored the importance of the personnel function. Sloan, in reflecting on his years with General Motors, was careful to point out that as far back as the 1920s the company provided many employee benefits, such as excellent employee facilities, group life insurance, and a savings and investment plan.[16] Furthermore, the now famous General Motors bonus plan provided the necessary managerial incentives to make his decentralized organizational plan effective. In his book, Fayol emphasized the importance that incentive payments, especially profit sharing, played in effective management. He also gave selection and training a great deal of attention.[17] The pioneering scientific managers developed sophisticated differential piece-rate incentive plans and recognized the impact that the group had on the individual.[18] Henry Ford, of course, was almost as famous for paying his workers $5 a day as he was for mass-producing the Model T. These examples offer ample evidence that the personnel function was very much in existence before the 1930s. However, the major change in the practice of management that included the personnel function, with its accompanying concern for the human element, did not occur until the sociopsychological upheavals in the late 1920s and early 1930s. At that time, in addition to the creation of personnel departments, practicing general managers also began to shift from a relatively strict production orientation to a growing awareness and concern for the human aspects of management.

THE HUMAN RELATIONS MOVEMENT

The practice of management which places heavy emphasis on employee cooperation and morale might be classified as human relations. Raymond Miles

---

[16]Alfred P. Sloan, Jr., *My Years with General Motors,* John McDonald and Catharine Stevens (eds.), Doubleday & Company, Garden City, N.Y., 1964, p. 391.

[17]Fayol, op. cit., pp. 26–32 and 78–81.

[18]For some of Taylor's insights into the impact of the group on human behavior, see his *Principles,* op. cit., p. 50.

states that the human relations approach was simply to "treat people as human beings (instead of machines in the productive process), acknowledge their needs to belong and to feel important by listening to and heeding their complaints where possible and by involving them in certain decisions concerning working conditions and other matters, then morale would surely improve and workers would cooperate with management in achieving good production."[19] There are, of course, varied and complex reasons for this human relations position. Historically, three of the most important contributing factors would be the Great Depression, the labor movement, and the results of the now famous Hawthorne studies.

The Great Depression

The economy was operating in high gear just before the thundering financial crash occurred in 1929. The production and organizational specialists had achieved amazing results. What went wrong? With maximized production, would not the "invisible hand" of laissez faire economics take care of the rest? Obviously, it did not. Most economic analyses include one or more of the following as major causes of a depression: (1) piling up of business inventories and accumulation of large stocks of new durables in consumers' hands; (2) consumer resistance to rising prices and increasing business costs; (3) an end of the upward acceleration effect and a resulting decline in investment spending; (4) accumulation of vast amounts of new productive capacity and new technological developments; (5) a growing scarcity of promising large-scale investment outlets and exhaustion of excess bank reserves; and (6) a weakening of confidence and expectations.[20]

Before the Great Depression, production specialists had contributed to some of these causes. After the crash, management began to realize that production could no longer be the only major responsibility of management. Marketing, finance, and personnel were also required in order for a business to survive and profit. The Depression's aftermath of unemployment, discontent, and insecurity brought to the surface human problems that managers were now forced to recognize and cope with. Personnel departments were either created or given more emphasis, and most managers now began to develop a new, awakened view of the human aspects of work. Human relations took on added significance as an indirect, and in some cases a direct, result of the Depression.

The Labor Movement

Another important contributing factor to the human relations movement was the organized labor movement. Although labor unions (for example, the Philadelphia Shoemakers) were in existence in America as early as 1792, it was not until the passage of the Wagner Act in 1935 that organized labor made a substantial impact on management. Why did the movement develop? Perhaps

    [19]Raymond E. Miles, *Theories of Management*, McGraw-Hill Book Company, New York, 1975, p. 40.
    [20]George L. Bach, *Economics*, 8th ed., Prentice-Hall, Inc., Englewood Cliffs, N.J., 1974, p. 173.

the best explanation is simply that practicing managers did not properly recognize the human contribution to the goals of the organization. A "fair wage," decent hours, and adequate working conditions were often sacrificed for more production. Some of the more enlightened pioneers in management, such as Taylor, Ford, and Sloan, openly expressed their sincere desire to give labor its fair share. However, except for these few exceptions and some scattered paternalistic managers, management often exploited labor.

In 1935, when unions became legally entrenched, managers began to wake up and take notice. The general reaction was either to fight the union movement or to realize that it was here to stay and might possibly have something to contribute. Although open conflicts were not uncommon in this era, most managers assumed the latter position and formed personnel departments either to deal with the unions or to keep them out. In either case, primary emphasis was placed on employee relations and secondary attention was given to wages, hours, and conditions of employment. The personnel department's activities carried over into all other management functions.

Unfortunately, the human relations role too often came about for the wrong reasons. In too many cases, it was forced on managers by labor's threatening them with the consequences of noncompliance with union demands. Ideally, it would have been better had human relations developed because of the intrinsic motivation of practicing managers to better understand and provide for the welfare of their employees.

THE HAWTHORNE STUDIES

Although the Depression and the labor movement were at least important indirect causes of the practice of human relations, the Hawthorne studies dominate the academic historical development. Understanding all aspects of these well-known studies is vital to an appreciation of the historical development of organizational behavior.

Before the Hawthorne studies officially started, Elton Mayo headed a research team which was investigating the causes of very high turnover in the mule-spinning department of a Philadelphia textile mill in 1923 and 1924. After interviewing and consulting the workers, they set up a series of rest pauses which resulted in greatly reduced turnover and more positive worker attitudes and morale.

About the same time that Mayo and his group were conducting the Philadelphia study, a typical scientific management study, sponsored by the National Research Council, was being made at Hawthorne. This latter study was attempting to determine experimentally the effects that varying degrees of illumination had on worker productivity.

Illumination Experiments

The light experiments were conducted on female workers, who were divided into two groups. One group was placed in a test room where the intensity of illumination was varied, and the other group worked in a control room with supposedly constant conditions. The results were baffling to the researchers. Productivity increased in both rooms. Furthermore, in the test room no correlation developed. The production of the women continually increased whether the footcandles of light were raised, retained at the original level, or even brought down to moonlight intensity so that the workers could barely see. Obviously, some variables in the experiment were not being held constant or under control. Something besides the level of illumination was causing the change in productivity. This something, of course, was the complex human variable.

It is fortunate that the illumination experiments did not end up in the wastebasket. Those responsible for the Hawthorne studies had enough foresight and spirit to accept the challenge of looking beneath the surface of the apparent failure of the illumination experiment. In a way, the results of the illumination experiments were a serendipitous discovery. In reference to research, *serendipity* means accidental discovery.[21] The classic case is the breakthrough for penicillin which occurred when Sir Alexander Fleming accidentally discovered green mold on the side of a test tube. The reason why the green mold was not washed down the drain or why the results of the illumination experiment were not thrown in the trashcan can be credited to the researchers' not being blinded by the unusual or seemingly worthless results of their experimentation. The serendipitous illumination experiment provided the impetus for the relay room phase of the Hawthorne studies.

Relay Room Experiments

In 1927, the relay room experiments got under way. These experiments represent the actual beginning of the Hawthorne studies attributed to Elton Mayo. In reality, he was only one member of a large research team composed of Harvard colleagues and company representatives.[22] This team of researchers utilized their earlier experience with rest pauses at the Philadelphia textile company. Thirteen variables tested the effects that place of work, place and

---

[21]The term can be traced to Horace Walpole's story *The Three Princes of Serendip.* The princes in the story searched the world but did not find what they were seeking. Instead, they stumbled on many interesting and exciting events that they had not planned to encounter. An expanded discussion of serendipity appears in Arthur J. Bachrach, *Psychological Research,* 2d ed., Random House, Inc., New York, 1965, chap. 1.

[22]In the preface to *Management and the Worker,* Mayo stated, "I cannot name all who have thus participated ... An attempt to name everyone would read, a colleague suggests, like a telephone book." He specifically cited Fritz J. Roethlisberger and William J. Dickson, the authors of *Managemement and the Worker,* the most detailed account of the studies, as having been intimately involved. Roethlisberger was a Harvard colleague and Dickson represented the Western Electric Company. He also stated that Dean Wallace B. Donham and Dr. Lawrence J. Henderson of Harvard's Committee on Industrial Physiology were very active participants. An equally active group of company participants consisted of C. G. Stoll and W. F. Hosford of the New York office and C. L. Rice of the Hawthorne Works in support of G. A. Pennock, G. S. Rutherford, and M. L. Putnam.

length of rest pause, length of working day, length of workweek, method of payment, and a free mid-morning lunch had on productivity.[23]

Taking a cue from the earlier illumination experiment at the plant, the researchers attempted to set up the test room so that there would be more control over the independent variables. Two female assemblers were selected for the experiment. They were permitted to choose four others to join them in the test room, which was segregated from the rest of the plant. During the experiment, the women were often consulted and sometimes allowed to express themselves about the changes that took place in the experiment. This had also been done in the previous studies in Philadelphia. In the relay test room, the female assemblers were insulated from the traditional restrictions of management. In total, they were treated and recognized as individuals with something to contribute.

The results in the relay room were practically identical with those in the illumination experiment. Each test period yielded higher productivity than the previous one had done. Even when the women were subjected to the original conditions of the experiment, productivity increased. The conclusion was that the independent variables (rest pauses and so forth) were not by themselves causing the change in the dependent variable (output). As in the illumination experiment, something was *still* not being controlled.

Second Relay and Mica Splitting Test Room Experiments

The relay room experiment was followed up by a second relay room experiment and the mica splitting test room study. The second relay assembly group was set up to further test the impact of wage incentives on output. A group of five experienced workers was moved to adjacent positions in the regular department. Hence, supervision, general working conditions, and the setting were basically the same as for the workers in the regular department. The difference was that the assemblers in the second relay group were placed on a separate, small-group piece-rate incentive system that duplicated the third test period of the first relay room experiment. This resulted in a 12 percent increase in production by the experimental group.

In the mica splitting study, the segregated test room conditions of the original relay study were reproduced. However, the mica splitting operators worked under their normal individual piece-rate plan instead of the small-group incentive system used with the relay room experimental subjects. Over a fourteen-month period, the mica splitting room showed an average production increase of 15 percent.

The results of these two follow-up studies were judged to be mostly inconclusive. Noting that output increased about 30 percent in the original relay room, Roethlisberger and Dickson concluded:

[23]Unless otherwise noted, references made to the procedures and results of the Hawthorne studies are drawn from Fritz J. Roethlisberger and William J. Dickson, *Management and the Worker,* Harvard University Press, Cambridge, Mass., 1939.

1   There was absolutely no evidence in favor of the hypothesis that the continuous increase in output in the Relay Assembly Test Room during the first two years could be attributed to the wage incentive factor alone.

2   The efficacy of a wage incentive was so dependent on its relation to other factors that it was impossible to consider it as a thing in itself having an independent effect on the individual.[24]

Mass Interviewing Program

The next major phase of the Hawthorne studies consisted of 20,000 interviews conducted from 1928 to 1930. The original purpose was to provide information that would improve supervisory training. To accomplish this purpose, interviewers initially asked employees direct questions about their attitudes toward supervision, working conditions, and the job in general. The direct-questioning technique resulted in standard, stereotyped responses. Therefore, in July 1929 a nondirective approach was substituted. The new technique permitted the interviewees to select the relevant topic that was most important to them. It also allowed the interviewer to get at things that had stayed under the surface during the direct-questioning interview.

The employees' reaction to the nondirective interviewing was very favorable. The cathartic effect (talking things out) had therapeutic value for the workers. From a research standpoint, much valuable information about employee attitudes and group dynamics was obtained. Specifically, the insights into the impact that informal work groups have on restriction of output led to the last major research effort in the Hawthorne studies.

Bank Wiring Room Study

The final phase of the research program was the bank wiring study, which started in November 1931 and lasted until May 1932. The primary purpose was to make an observational analysis of the informal work group. The group chosen for observation consisted of fourteen male operators: nine wiremen, three soldermen, and two inspectors.

The methods used in this study were in some ways similar to the preceding relay room experiments. As in the relay experiments, the bank wirers were placed in a separate test room. The researchers were reluctant to segregate the bank wiring group because they recognized this would alter the realistic factory environment they were attempting to simulate. However, for practical reasons, the research team decided to use a separate room.[25] Unlike the relay room experiments, the bank wiring study involved no experimental changes once the study had started. Instead, an observer and an interviewer gathered objective data for study. The observer gained the confidence of the group and was recognized as a regular member. The interviewer, on the other hand, remained an outsider. The interviewer's major function was to obtain information about

[24]Ibid., p. 160.
[25]Ibid., pp. 387–388.

the workers' attitudes, thoughts, and feelings. With the exceptions of the separate room, the observer, and the interviewer, all the conditions were designed to duplicate those in the bank wiring department itself. Of particular interest was the fact that the department's regular supervisors were used in the bank wiring room. Just as in the department out on the factory floor, their main function was to maintain order and control.

Results of the Bank Wiring Room Study

The results in the bank wiring room were essentially opposite to those in the relay room. In the bank wiring room there were not the continual increases in productivity that occurred in the relay room. Rather, output was actually restricted by the bank wirers. By scientific management analysis, e.g., time and motion study, the industrial engineers had arrived at a standard of 7,312 terminal connections per day. This represented two and one-half equipments. The workers had a different brand of rationality. They decided that two equipments was a "proper" day's work. Thus, two and one-half equipments represented the management norm for production but two equipments was the informal group norm and the actual output.

The researchers determined that the informal group norm of two equipments represented restriction of output rather than a lack of ability to produce at the company standard of two and one-half equipments. The following evidence supports this contention:

1   The observer noted that all the men stopped before quitting time.
2   Most of the men admitted to the interviewer they could easily turn out more work.
3   Tests of dexterity and intelligence indicated no relationship between capacity to perform and actual performance.

The logic for restriction of output revolved around factors such as the following:

1   *Fear of unemployment.* The lump-sum theory of work was supported by reasoning such as, "Don't work yourself out of a job."
2   *Fear of raising the standard.* Most workers were convinced that once they had reached the standard rate of production, management would raise the standard, reasoning that it must be too easy to attain.
3   *Protection of the slower workers.* The workers were friendly off the job as well as on the job. They appreciated the fact that all workers, including the slower ones, had family responsibilities that required them to remain employed. Therefore, the faster workers protected the slower ones by not outproducing them by too much. The group did not want to make the slower workers look bad in the eyes of management.
4   *Satisfaction on the part of management.* Management seemed to accept the lower production rate. No one was being fired or even reprimanded for restricted output.

From a group dynamics standpoint, of particular interest were the social pressures used to gain compliance to the group norms. The incentive system dictated that the more an individual produced, the more money earned. Also, the best producers would be laid off last, and thus they could be more secure by producing more. Yet, in the face of this management rationale, almost all the workers restricted output. Social ostracism, ridicule, and name-calling were the major sanctions utilized by the group to enforce this restriction. In some instances, actual physical pressure in the form of a game called "binging" was applied. In the game, a worker would be hit as hard as possible, with the privilege of returning one "bing" or hit. Forcing rate busters to play the game became an effective sanction. These group pressures had a tremendous impact on all the workers. Social ostracism was more effective in gaining compliance to the informal group norm than money and security were in attaining the scientifically derived management norm.

IMPLICATIONS OF THE HAWTHORNE STUDIES

The Hawthorne studies are unquestionably the single most important historical foundation for the behavioral approach to management. They have been cussed and discussed, revisited, discounted, and lauded throughout the succeeding years. Henry Landsberger, in *Hawthorne Revisited,* observed that

> . . . a most spectacular academic battle has raged since then—or perhaps it would be more accurate to say that a limited number of gunners has kept up a steady barrage, reusing the same ammunition. . . . The beleaguered Mayo garrison, however, has continued its existence behind the solid protection of factory walls.[26]

Admittedly, there is much obvious "ammunition" to which the Hawthorne studies are vulnerable. Sociologist Alex Carey, after a thorough reexamination of the relay room studies, summarizes the major deficiencies as:

> **1** There was no attempt to establish sample groups representative of any larger population than the groups themselves. Therefore, no generalization is legitimate.
> **2** There was no attempt to employ control data from the output records of the women who were *not* put under special experimental conditions.
> **3** Even if both of these points had been met, the experiments would still have been of only minor scientific value since a group of five subjects is too small to yield statistically reliable results.[27]

Despite these methodological limitations, there are some insights from the Hawthorne studies that contribute to the better understanding of human behavior in organizations.

---

[26]Henry A. Landsberger, *Hawthorne Revisited,* Cornell University, Ithaca, N.Y., 1958, pp. 1–2.
[27]Alex Carey, "The Hawthorne Studies: A Radical Criticism," *American Sociological Review,* June 1967, p. 416.

Relay Room versus Bank Wiring Room Studies

One interesting aspect of the Hawthorne studies is the contrasting results found in the relay room and the bank wiring room. In the relay room, production continually increased throughout the test period and the relay assemblers were very positive. The opposite was true in the bank wiring room; blatant restriction of output was practiced by disgruntled workers. Why the difference in these two phases of the studies?

One clue to answering this question may be traced to the results of a questionnaire administered to the women in the relay room. The original intent of the questions was to determine the health and habits of the women. Their answers were generally inconclusive except that *all* the operators indicated they felt "better" in the test room.[28] A follow-up questionnaire then asked about specific items in the test room situation. In discussions of the Hawthorne studies, the follow-up questionnaire results, in their entirety, usually are not mentioned. Most discussions cite the women's unanimous preference for working in the test room instead of the regular department. Often overlooked, however, are the women's explanations for their choice. In order of preference, the women gave the following reasons:

1 Small group
2 Type of supervision
3 Earnings
4 Novelty of the situation
5 Interest in the experiment
6 Attention received in the test room[29]

It is important to note that novelty, interest, and attention were relegated to the fourth, fifth, and sixth positions. These last three areas usually are associated with the famous "Hawthorne effect." Many social scientists imply that the increases in the relay room productivity can be attributed solely to the Hawthorne effect. They ignore, or at least do not emphasize, the seemingly important impact of the small group, the type of supervision, and earnings.

In *Management and the Worker,* Roethlisberger and Dickson recognized the importance that the highly cohesive small group had for the women.

> No longer were the girls isolated individuals, working together only in the sense of an actual physical proximity. They had become participating members of a working group with all the psychological and social implications peculiar to such a group. . . . They had become bound together by common sentiments and feelings of loyalty.[30]

The effect of earnings also was analyzed in the second relay room and mica

[28]Roethlisberger and Dickson, op. cit., p. 66.
[29]C. E. Turner, "Test Room Studies in Employee Effectiveness," *American Journal of Public Health,* June 1933, p. 584.
[30]Roethlisberger and Dickson, op. cit., p. 86.

splitting room experiments. Although earnings were shown to have a definite impact, no firm conclusions were drawn. Probably the most important insights can be gained from a more thorough analysis of the role that supervision played in the work groups studied at Hawthorne.

Supervision in the Relay and Bank Wiring Rooms

The relay and bank wiring rooms had some common variables. Both rooms contained small, highly cohesive groups that worked on an incentive basis and were segregated from the rest of the plant. The major difference was the supervisory climate. In the relay room there were no regular supervisors per se. Yet, the relay women stated that after the small group it was the type of supervision that made them feel so good and produce at a high rate. They consistently mentioned "freedom" and "the nice way we are treated" as explanations for their attitudes and behavior. In other words, the women were perceiving the friendly, attentive, genuinely concerned researchers as their supervisors. The relay test room observers were directed to build a friendly rapport with the female operators. They made a point of constantly interacting with the women. Roethlisberger and Dickson noted, "Sometimes the topics he [the observer] brought up pertained to their work, sometimes to personal matters, and occasionally they took the form of a general inquiry as to the attitude of the operators toward the test."[31]

In the bank wiring room, an entirely different supervisory climate existed. Regular department supervisors were used to maintain order and control in the test room. It was observed that this supervisory arrangement produced an inhibiting atmosphere.[32] The observer played a different role from that performed in the relay room. In the bank wiring room, he was directed to be a disinterested spectator. His general conduct precluded the workers' perceiving him as a supervisor. For instance, he was not allowed to issue orders or answer any questions that implied the assumption of authority. Thus, in the bank wiring room the observer came to be viewed as a member of the group rather than as a supervisor.

The Importance of Supervisory Climate

Elton Mayo's original analysis emphasized the importance of supervision in assessing the output record in the relay room. He noted that while the women in the relay room were ". . . getting closer supervision than ever before, the change is in the quality of the supervision. This—change in quality of supervision—is by no means the whole change, but it is an important part of it."[33] Mayo and others, such as C. E. Turner, a consultant to the Hawthorne studies, played down the importance of the Hawthorne effect as an explanation for the results. Turner stated: "We at first thought that the novelty of test room conditions might be partly responsible for increased output but the continuing

---

[31]Ibid., p. 37.
[32]Ibid., p. 458.
[33]Elton Mayo, *The Human Problems of an Industrial Civilization.* The Viking Press, Inc., New York, p. 75. Original 1933 copyright held by the President and Fellows of Harvard College.

increase in production over a 4-year period suggests that it was not of great importance."[34]

Despite these initial observations, most contemporary discussions of the Hawthorne studies emphasize the novelty aspects and exclude the important implications concerning supervision. Much of the problem lies in the fact that the Hawthorne studies suffer from guilt by association stemming from the general indictment against the Mayo ideological school of thought.[35] If novelty were, in fact, the only explanation for the results of the relay room, one could question why the bank wirers, who were also placed in a separate room, did not react the same way. Were the research methods so much improved that the bank wiring room perfectly simulated the factory floor and that no novelty was present? If the novelty argument is used in the relay room, should it not also apply to the bank wiring room?

To reiterate, the major difference between the two rooms was not necessarily that one situation was novel and the other was not. Rather, the important point seems to be the differing climates of supervision that existed in the two rooms. To be sure, one cannot and should not dismiss other disparities, such as male versus female, mere observation and interviewing versus quasi-experimental techniques, or even the degree of novelty that existed in the two rooms. Another difficulty in the interpretation of most discussions is the semantical problem of whether the novelty and special attention given the women are considered to be the Hawthorne effect, a unique, attentive type of supervision, or both. Regardless of these complications and definite methodological limitations, the analysis of the Hawthorne studies seems to point out the impact that climate of supervision has on human behavior in organizations.

THEORIES X AND Y AND THE HUMAN RESOURCE MODEL

This chapter on the historical development of the behavioral approach can probably best be concluded by examining the contrasting theories of the late Douglas McGregor and the human resource model formulated by Raymond Miles. McGregor's Theory X represents the old-style, authoritarian type of management and is based on three primary assumptions about human beings:

> **1** The average human being has an inherent dislike of work and will avoid it if he can.
> **2** Because of this human characteristic of dislike of work, most people must be coerced, controlled, directed, threatened with punishment to get them to put forth adequate effort toward the achievement of organizational objectives.

[34]C. E. Turner, op. cit., p. 584.

[35]This school of thought is presented in Mayo's books *The Human Problems of an Industrial Civilization*, 2d ed., 1946, *The Social Problems of an Industrial Civilization*, 1945, and *The Political Problems of an Industrial Civilization*, 1947, all published by Harvard University Graduate School of Business Administration, Division of Research, Boston; and in T. North Whitehead's *Leadership in a Free Society*, 1936, and Roethlisberger's book *Management and Morale*, 1955, both published by Harvard University Press, Cambridge, Mass.

3   The average human being prefers to be directed, wishes to avoid responsibility, has relatively little ambition, and wants security above all.[36]

It follows that high degrees of control and threats of punishment are the way to manage such people. If managers appeal to a worker's security motives, provide explicit directions, and do not give any responsibility, they supply what the employee actually prefers.

Theory X was widely accepted and, with few exceptions, universally practiced before the human relations movement. The theory conformed to what Mayo had termed the *Rabble Hypothesis*. The human relations movement, however, slowly began to undermine the assumptions of Theory X. The Hawthorne studies in particular pointed out that the simplistic assumptions about human behavior were at least questionable if not unacceptable. Most theories of management and many practicing managers in the 1940s and 1950s could no longer abide by Theory X assumptions. Human relations theory and research restructured practioners' thinking about the management of people. McGregor summarized this rethinking in his Theory Y. The major parts of this theory are as follows:

1   The expenditure of physical and mental effort in work is as natural as play or rest.

2   External control and the threat of punishment are not the only means for bringing about effort toward organizational objectives. Man will exercise self-direction and self-control in the service of objectives to which he is committed.

3   Commitment to objectives is a function of the rewards associated with their achievement.

4   The average human being learns, under proper conditions, not only to accept but to seek responsibility.[37]

The Theory X approach precedes the human relations theory and practice of management. Theory Y, on the other hand, marks the point of departure for the newer human resource management model. The basic assumptions of the human resource approach are similar to Theory Y, but it goes beyond Theory Y by stating what the actual policy implementation for the practice of management and the expectations of managers and workers will be. The human resources model uses the following policies for the practice of management:

1   The manager's basic task is to make use of his "untapped" human resources.

2   He must create an environment in which all members may contribute to the limits of their ability.

3   He must encourage full participation on important matters, continually broadening subordinate self-direction and control.[38]

[36]Douglas McGregor, *The Human Side of Enterprise*, McGraw-Hill Book Company, New York, 1960, pp. 33–34.
[37]Ibid., pp. 47–48.
[38]Miles, op. cit., p. 35.

The expectations of following these policies would be:

> **1** Expanding subordinate influence, self-direction, and self-control will lead to direct improvement in operating efficiency.
> **2** Work satisfaction may improve as a "by-product" of subordinates making full use of their resources.[39]

The human resources manager is an extension of the traditional (Theory X) and human relations (Theory Y) type of manager. In the human relations approach, the manager was concerned with employee morale but had no real understanding of the complexities of human motivation; had concern for proper orientation and training but no understanding of learning theory and behavior modification; had concern over individual behavior but no understanding of psychological processes and personality theory; had concern over why one employee behaved differently from other employees but no understanding of the dynamics of individual differences; and was concerned with the impact of the informal group without understanding group dynamics or other sociological considerations. These are only a very few examples of the differences between the older human relations and the newer human resource management approach. The human relations approach had many of the proper concerns, but it did not recognize the complexities involved and it lacked the analytical depth, backed by research findings, that characterizes the human resource management approach.

This chapter has pointed out that a solid historical base exists for the study of organizational behavior. Now the time has come to build on this foundation. Too often in the past the behavioral approach was depicted as only this foundation, with Theory X and Theory Y used as the summarizing statements. This book will regard the preceding as only the historical foundation, and it will use the human resource approach to management as the point of departure for the study of organizational behavior.

SUMMARY

The early practice of management evolved through several phases. About a hundred years ago the captains of industry, exemplified by General Motors founder William C. Durant, dominated. Their ruthless, one-person style then gave way to organizational specialists and scientific managers. These latter managers nurtured what the captains had founded. The financial and production function specialists were soon joined by marketing and personnel specialists. The personnel function is directly relevant to the behavioral approach to management, but all managers of people, regardless of functional specialty, are relevant to the study of organizational behavior. The human relations movement evolved from causes such as the Depression and the organized labor movement, but the Hawthorne studies dominate the academic historical

---

[39]Ibid.

development. These celebrated studies, which took place over a time span of several years, were the first attempt to systematically analyze human behavior in an organizational setting. Most modern behavioral scientists are very critical of the research design and discount the results. Admittedly, the design, as in any pioneering effort, was crude by modern standards. However, this should not completely negate the insights concerning the role that group dynamics and supervisory climate play in the workplace. Finally, Theories X and Y and the human resource assumptions and approach were reviewed. The human resource management perspective which extends the traditional and human relations approaches is used as the point of departure for the study of organizational behavior in the remainder of the book.

CASE: TOO NICE TO PEOPLE

John had just graduated from the College of Business Administration at State University and joined his family's small business, which employs 25 semi-skilled workers. The first week on the job his dad called him in and said, "John, I've had a chance to observe your working with the men and women for the past two days and, although I hate to, I feel I must say something. You are just too nice to people. I know they taught you that human relations stuff at the University, but it just doesn't work here. I remember when the Hawthorne studies were first reported and everybody at the University got all excited about them, but, believe me, there is more to managing people than just being nice to them."

   1   How would you react to your father's comments if you were John?
   2   Do you think John's father understood and interpreted the Hawthorne studies correctly?
   3   What phases of management do you think John's father has gone through in this family business?

SELECTED REFERENCES

Albers, Henry H.: *Principles of Management,* 4th ed., John Wiley & Sons, Inc., New York, 1974.
Carey, Alex: "The Hawthorne Studies: A Radical Criticism," *American Sociological Review,* June 1967, pp. 403–416.
Dale, Ernest: *The Great Organizers,* McGraw-Hill Book Company, New York, 1960.
George, Claude S., Jr.: *The History of Management Thought,* 2d ed., Prentice-Hall, Inc., Englewood Cliffs, N.J., 1972.
"Hawthorne Revisited: The Legend and the Legacy," *Organizational Dynamics,* Winter 1975, pp. 66–80.
Kakar, Sudhir: *Frederick Taylor: A Study in Personality and Innovation,* M.I.T. Press, Cambridge, Mass., 1970.
Landsberger, Henry A.: *Hawthorne Revisited,* Cornell University, Ithaca, New York, 1958.

McGregor, Douglas: *The Human Side of Enterprise,* McGraw-Hill Book Company, New York, 1960.

Merrill, Harwood F. (ed.): *Classics in Management*, American Management Association, New York, 1960.

Roethlisberger, Fritz J., and William J. Dickson: *Management and the Workers,* John Wiley & Sons, Inc., New York 1964. Original copyright 1939 by the President and Fellows of Harvard College.

Shapiro, H. Jack, and Mahmoud A. Wahba: "Frederick W. Taylor—62 Years Later," *Personnel Journal,* August 1974, pp. 574–578.

Sloan, Alfred P., Jr.: *My Years with General Motors,* John McDonald and Catharine Stevens (eds.), Doubleday & Company, Inc., Garden City, New York, 1964.

Wrege, Charles D., and Amedeo G. Perroni: "Taylor's Pig-Tale: A Historical Analysis of Frederick W. Taylor's Pig-Iron Experiments," *Academy of Management Journal,* March 1974, pp. 6–27.

Wren, Daniel A.: *The Evolution of Management Thought,* The Ronald Press Company, New York, 1972.

Chapter 2

The Behavioral Sciences

The last chapter gave a historical foundation for the study of organizational behavior. This chapter builds on that foundation by presenting an overview of the behavioral sciences. The first part delineates the scope of behavioral science and gives particular attention to scientific methodology and research designs that are used to accumulate knowledge about human behavior in general and organizational behavior in particular. The remainder of the chapter examines, in turn, the major behavioral science disciplines of anthropology, sociology, psychology, and social psychology. A working knowledge of the behavioral sciences is a necessary prerequisite for the study of organizational behavior.

THE SCOPE OF BEHAVIORAL SCIENCE

Behavioral science is a relatively new academic discipline. Robert Merton probably best summarized its development when, paraphrasing Galileo, he concluded that behavioral science is "a very new science of a very ancient subject."[1] No science can realistically pin a specific date to its origin. As long as humans have inhabited the earth, their behavior has been a matter for

---

[1] Robert K. Merton, "The Mosaic of the Behavior Sciences," in Bernard Berelson (ed.), *The Behavioral Sciences Today*, Basic Books, Inc., Publishers, New York, 1963, p. 249.

concern and attempted understanding. However, compared to the other sciences, the *scientific* study of human behavior is relatively new.

Behavioral science got a start in the late 1800s and early 1900s. The first systematically controlled investigation of human behavior occurred in 1879 at Wilhelm Wundt's famous experimental laboratory in Leipzig, Germany. Prior to this time, there had been many peripheral and speculative attempts to understand behavior. For example, Aristotle stressed the objective observation of human behavior. In 1842, Auguste Comte coined the word *sociology*. In the mid-1800s the German physiologists Müller and Helmholtz provided insights into psychological phenomena. In 1860, a German physicist, Gustav Fechner, published *Elements of Psychophysics*. This book concentrated on techniques for measuring the relationship between physical stimuli and experienced sensations. Also in the 1860s, Sir Francis Galton studied individual differences and attempted to apply Darwin's evolution ideas. Sir Edward Tylor, generally recognized as the father of anthropology, published his book *Primitive Culture* in 1879. However, these earlier contributions were not scientifically based. Wundt's laboratory marks the beginning of the *scientific* study of human behavior, but the behavioral sciences did not really arrive in full force until the twentieth century. This is about two hundred years after the physical sciences and one hundred years after the biological sciences were developed.

The use of the interdisciplinary term *behavioral science* is of very recent vintage. The term can be traced to the World War II era, but it was in the 1950s that the Ford Foundation popularized it. The foundation's multimillion-dollar program, Individual Behavior and Human Relations, became widely known as the Behavioral Sciences Program. Probably the best definition of *behavioral science* is the scientific study of human behavior. This definition differentiates behavioral science from the other biological and physical sciences, the humanities, and even certain disciplines within the social sciences. Figure 2-1 clarifies the exact relationship of behavioral science to other academic disciplines. The figure shows that behavioral science with its three primary

ARTS AND SCIENCES
    Humanities
    Physical sciences
    Biological sciences
    and
SOCIAL SCIENCES
    Economics
    History
    Political science
    and
    BEHAVIORAL SCIENCES
        Anthropology
        Sociology
        Psychology

Figure 2-1 Relationship between academic disciplines.

disciplines is a subclassification in the social sciences. The social sciences, in turn, are a major subpart of the overall arts and sciences. The chief difference between the behavioral sciences and the other social sciences, such as history, economics, and political science, is the methodology used to accumulate knowledge. A behavioral science depends on rigorous scientific methodology in the collection of original data on human behavior. The other social sciences commonly use aggregate or indirect documentary practices in building their body of knowledge.

SCIENTIFIC METHODOLOGY

Behavioral science has followed the lead of the physical and biological sciences in using scientific methodology to build its body of knowledge. This does not deny that there are other ways of gaining insight into behavior. For example, the humanities utilize philosophical and artistic expression. However, Berelson explains why the scientific method seems to be the best alternative: ". . . the scientific approach is another way, and . . . for many purposes, especially those in which establishing the facts is important, it is a particularly good way."[2]

Discovering the truth of why humans behave the way they do is a very delicate and complex process. In fact, the problems are so great that many scholars, chiefly from the physical and applied sciences, argue that there can be no precise science of behavior. They maintain that humans cannot be treated like chemical or physical elements; they cannot be effectively controlled or manipulated. For example, the critics state that, under easily controllable conditions, two parts of hydrogen combined with one part of oxygen will always result in water, and that no analogous situation exists in human behavior. Human variables such as motives, learning, perception, values, and even "hangovers" on the part of both subject and investigator infect the controls that are attempted. For these reasons, behavioral scientists are often on the defensive and must be very careful to comply with accepted methods of science.

Behavioral scientists strive to attain the following hallmarks of any science:

1   The procedures are public.
2   The definitions are precise.
3   The data-collecting is objective.
4   The findings are replicable.
5   The approach is systematic and cumulative.
6   The purposes are explanation, understanding, and prediction.[3]

[2]Bernard Berelson (ed.), *The Behavioral Sciences Today,* Basic Books, Inc., New York, 1963, p. 5.

[3]Bernard Berelson and Gary A. Steiner, *Human Behavior,* Harcourt, Brace and World, Inc., New York, 1964, pp. 16–17.

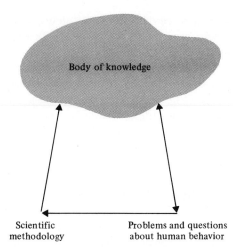

Body of knowledge

Scientific   Problems and questions   **Figure 2-2** Simple relationship between
methodology   about human behavior   problems, methodology, and knowledge.

Figure 2-2 summarizes the relationship between practical behavioral problems and unanswered questions, scientific methodology, and the existing body of knowledge. When a question arises or a problem evolves, the first place to turn for an answer is the existing body of knowledge. It is possible that the question can be immediately answered or the problem solved without going any further. Unfortunately, this usually is not true in the case of human behavior. One reason is that the amount of knowledge directly applicable to human behavior is relatively very small. The small quantity is due primarily to the newness of the field. Merton points out the startling statistic that approximately 90 percent of all behavioral scientists who have ever lived are alive today.[4] The sober fact is that many questions and problems in human behavior cannot be directly answered or solved by existing knowledge. This situation is definitely changing as more research is expanding the body of knowledge.

RESEARCH DESIGNS

The research design is at the very heart of scientific methodology. The three major designs most often used in the behavioral sciences are the experiment, the case, and the survey. All three designs have played important roles in the development of behavioral science. The experimental design has been most closely related with psychology, and the case and survey have played a more important role in sociology. All three designs can be used in the study and accumulation of knowledge of organizational behavior.

Experimental Design

A primary aim of any research design is to establish a cause-and-effect relationship. The experimental method offers the best chance of accomplishing

[4]Robert Merton, "The Mosaic of the Behavioral Sciences," in Berelson, op. cit., p. 249.

this purpose. All other factors being equal, most researchers prefer this method of testing hypotheses. Simply defined, an experiment involves the manipulation of independent variables to measure their effect on, or the change in, dependent variables, holding everything else constant or under control. Sometimes an experimental group and a control group are formed. The experimental group receives the input of the independent variable and the control group does not. Any measured change in the dependent variable in the experimental group is caused by the independent variable, assuming no change has occurred in the control group. The controls employed are the key to the successful use of the experimental design. If all intervening variables are held constant or equal, the experimenter can conclude with a high degree of confidence that the independent variable caused the change in the dependent variable.

Laboratory Experiments   There are three general types of experimental designs—laboratory, natural, and field. The laboratory experiment permits high degrees of control but has a major disadvantage in its limited applicability. Under laboratory conditions, it is relatively easy, for example, to find in a learning experiment using white rats the schedule of reinforcement that leads to the greatest resistance to extinction, or to determine the effects of cooperation versus competition on task efficiency and satisfaction among college sophomores. However, meaningful generalizations from this kind of experimentation are not always possible. In more complex and realistic settings, it is very difficult to isolate and manipulate independent variables, and in some situations it is almost impossible to control all relevant intervening variables.

Natural Experiments   Some of the difficulties inherent in the laboratory experimental method can be eliminated or lessened by natural and field experiments. A natural experiment allows the independent variable to be manipulated or changed by the normal course of events and not by the experimenter. Cartwright and Zander, in pointing out the importance of natural experimentation, stated that ". . . the researcher does not impose disruptive changes in the group under study, that changes of significance can be studied, and that the direction of causality can be inferred with considerable confidence."[5] Although natural experiments are ideal for research in complex settings, the opportunities for utilizing the technique are very limited.

Field Experiments   Perhaps the most useful and adaptable experimental technique for understanding human behavior in organizations is the field experiment. "It differs from the natural experiment primarily in the fact that now changes are introduced in the group with the explicit purpose of testing some hypothesis or evaluating the effectiveness of some innovation in methods of group management."[6] This type of experiment is more applicable to

---

[5]Dorwin Cartwright and Alvin Zander, *Group Dynamics,* 3d ed., Harper & Row, Publishers, New York, 1968, p. 33.
[6]Ibid.

organizational behavior problems than any other research design, but there are still problems and limitations. The introduction and/or manipulation of independent variables into an organizational group (e.g., a work group or management committee) may significantly alter its members' typical behavior patterns. In addition, strict control of all intervening variables is not always possible.

Experimental Design in Perspective If conditions permit, the experimental method (laboratory, natural, or field) is preferable to any other design available for researching organizational behavior. Laboratory experimentation often allows safe generalizations from specific behavioral events. However, the behavior of the white rat or the college sophomore in the psychology laboratory of a university is usually far removed from the reactions of assembly-line workers in a large factory or group managers of a conglomerate. Even though the control problems are greater, natural and field experiments are generally preferable to laboratory experiments with their risks of generalizations. One problem is that the behavioral science body of knowledge is mainly a result of laboratory experimentation and that organizational behavior is highly dependent upon this body of knowledge. Organizational behavior hypotheses and conclusions must often come from experimentation performed under laboratory conditions, but, ideally, the hypotheses should be tested in the field before generalized conclusions are drawn.

Case Method

The case design makes a complete examination and analysis of one or a few behavioral entities (worker, supervisor, executive work group, department, organization) over an extended period. The purpose is to discover and analyze *every* aspect of the particular case under investigation. The case method of research should not be confused with the case-study approach used by social workers and psychotherapists. The case method as used in behavioral science research is much more rigorous and comprehensive.

The actual conduct of case research is most critical to its success. Selltiz et al. pinpoint three key areas in successful case research:

1 *The attitude of the investigator.* In order for the case technique to be successful, the investigator must be alertly receptive and be seeking rather than testing. He should be continuously reformulating and redirecting as he uncovers new information.

2 *The intensity of study.* An effective case analysis should obtain all information unique to the particular unit being studied and also those features that are common to other cases.

3 *The integrative ability of the investigator.* The case approach must rely on the talent of the researcher to successfully pull together many diverse findings into a unified interpretation. The final interpretation should not merely reflect the investigator's predispositions.[7]

---

[7]Claire Selltiz et al., *Research Methods in Social Relations,* rev. ed., one vol., Holt, Rinehart and Winston, Inc., New York, 1959, pp. 60–61.

If careful attention is given to key points such as those just outlined, the case can be a very effective research technique. The depth of analysis attained through the technique is its major advantage. The glaring disadvantage is that it is not usually practical or logical to generalize the results of one case analysis to other cases or to the whole. This limitation drastically reduces the usefulness of the case method for building a meaningful body of knowledge. The case method does not normally provide enough evidence to prove cause and effect. On the other hand, this method usually uncovers some very meaningful insights and hypotheses for further testing.

Survey Technique

The third major design available to the research of human behavior is the survey. This easy-to-use technique depends upon the collection of empirical data. It is extremely useful in solving some questions and problems of organizational behavior. "In general, whenever the investigator is interested in assessing or estimating the present state of affairs with regard to some variable that changes over time for a large group of subjects, a sample survey is the only practical way to get an answer."[8]

The survey overcomes the major disadvantage of the case design. If properly designed, its results can be generalized. Whereas the case is restricted to a single, or very few, units of analysis, the survey has very broad coverage. Another advantage is that the survey collects original data. The major drawback is the lack of depth obtained from the two major data-collection tools, the mailed questionnaire and the personal interview. Because of this limitation some scholars within, and many outside, the behavioral sciences have totally discredited the survey as a legitimate research design. Some of this criticism, especially that relating to some of the early surveying done in the behavioral sciences, is certainly justified. Even today, some surveys concentrate only on empiricism and neglect the necessary planning and design aspects. On the other hand, if there is effective planning and design, most of the problems with the survey method can be overcome.

ANTHROPOLOGY

The first behavioral science discipline that will be examined in the rest of this chapter is *anthropology.* This is literally defined as the science of man. The term combines the Greek stem *anthropo* (man) and the noun ending *logy* (science). The use of the word "anthropology" can be traced back to the ancient Greek and Roman civilizations. For example, Aristotle used the word to refer to a man who "talks about himself."[9] In this Greek sense, anthropology is as old as any academic discipline. However, as a modern discipline incorporating a scientific viewpoint and methodology, it is relatively new. The

---

[8]Berelson and Steiner, op. cit., p. 26.
[9]Alfred C. Haddon, *History of Anthropology,* Watts and Company, London, 1910, p. 6.

body of anthropological knowledge that has been accumulated by scientific methodology is currently relatively small but rapidly expanding.

Delineation of the Field

Anthropology is a very wide-scoped discipline. One noted anthropologist candidly observed that her colleagues ". . . have embraced enthusiastically and immodestly the literal meaning of the word anthropology—the science of man. Not satisfied with the science of man, they honor many in their profession who are avowed humanists."[10] Figure 2-3 summarizes the breakdown of anthropology into its various subfields. Cultural anthropology is particularly relevant to the study of organizational behavior.

Cultural Anthropology

Cultural anthropology deals with people's learned behavior as influenced by their culture. In more definitive terms, "Cultural anthropology studies the origins and history of man's cultures, their evolution and development, and the structure and functioning of human cultures in every place and time."[11] Obviously, the overriding concept is culture.

Definition of Culture There are numerous definitions of culture. After surveying more than a hundred of them, Kroeber and Kluckhohn conclude that the best definition is the following:

Culture consists of patterns, explicit and implicit, of and for behavior acquired and

[10]Cora DuBois, "Anthropology–Its Present Interests," in Berelson (ed.), *The Behavioral Sciences Today*, op. cit., p. 26.
[11]Ralph L. Beals and Harry Hijer, *An Introduction to Anthropology*, 2d ed., The Macmillan Company, New York, 1959, p. 9.

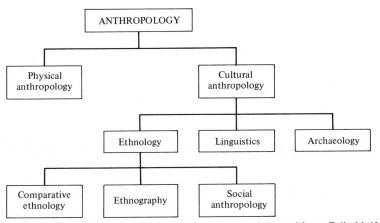

Figure 2-3 Subfields of anthropology. (*Source: Adapted from Felix M. Keesing,* Cultural Anthropology, *Holt, Rinehart and Winston, New York, 1966, p.4.*)

transmitted by symbols, constituting the distinctive achievement of human groups, including their embodiments in artifacts.[12]

To cite the major characteristics of the concept, culture

1 is historical
2 includes ideas, patterns, and values
3 is selective
4 is learned
5 is based upon symbols
6 is an abstraction from behavior, and
7 is a product of behavior[13]

Theories of Culture Cultural anthropologists have developed several theories to explain the impact of culture on human behavior. The three most prominent theories may be summarized by the descriptive "isms" of *evolutionism, historicalism,* and *functionalism.* These three theories have become schools of thought in anthropology. The oldest is evolutionism. This school identifies three general stages of cultural development. The first stage is savagery, which is followed by barbarism and eventually by civilization. The evolutionists point out that at any given time the world contains geographic areas that are in each stage of cultural development. Today, the evolutionism theory is generally discounted by anthropologists. The argument is that the evolutionists' assumptions are too simplistic and that there is too much contradictory evidence to justify their adoption.

The historical theories directly challenge the assumptions of evolutionism and environmental determinism. The aim of the historical approach to cultural anthropology is to accumulate and analyze all the traits, customs, and characteristics of a given culture. The collection of data is accomplished by objective observation and field research which generate a wealth of empirical facts about a culture. The problem then becomes one of applying and generalizing the results.

The functional theories of culture take a systems viewpoint. As will be discussed in the next chapter, the systems approach is playing an increasingly important role in all academic disciplines, and it is probably the approach most widely accepted by today's anthropologists. The functionalists concentrate on the various elements or functions that make up a cultural system. They recognize and emphasize that the cultural elements are interrelated and that they become integrated into a holistic system. Functionalism seems to provide the best framework for understanding the nature and significance of culture.

Significance of Culture The important role that culture plays in human behavior may be one of the most underrated concepts in the behavioral

---

[12]Alfred L. Kroeber and Clyde Kluckhohn, "Culture: A Critical Review of Concepts and Definitions," in *Papers of the Peabody Museum,* vol. 47, no. 1, Harvard University, Cambridge, Mass., 1952, p. 181.
[13]Ibid., p. 157.

sciences. The culture dictates what people learn and how they behave. Ross Webber points out the nature and significance of culture by making an analogy with the sea: "We are immersed in a sea. It is warm, comfortable, supportive, and protecting. Most of us float below the surface; some bob about, catching glimpses of land from time to time; a few emerge from the water entirely. The sea is our culture." [14]

The culture not only tells a person what fork to use when eating a salad; it also indicates what is right and good or wrong and evil. Marston Bates cites the custom of kissing to demonstrate the impact of culture. In America a kiss is considered socially acceptable and sexually stimulating. In certain primitive parts of Micronesia, the idea of placing one person's mouth on another's is unthinkable and repulsive. In a similar comparison, some Micronesians, in addition to many other groups, do not attach sexual significance to the female breast. They view it only as an organ which provides food for the nursing infant.[15] A line waiting to see an X-rated movie or the "topless" fad gives evidence that the American male views this part of the female body quite differently. Although the potential value of culture has not yet been fully realized, its concept and implications will undoubtedly play an expanded role in the future study of human behavior.

Unifying Assumptions

Figure 2-3 points out the almost overwhelming diversity found in anthropology. However, there are two basic assumptions that are held by practically all anthropologists: the holistic assumption, and the comparative approach.

Holistic Assumption   The purpose of anthropology is to study humans as a whole. To accomplish this purpose, the individual, group, institution, society, and culture must be considered as interrelated and interdependent. This view implies a holistic or systems approach. The holistic assumption separates anthropology from the other social and behavioral sciences. For example, economics is primarily concerned with people's production and distribution of goods and services. Political science emphasizes the government of people. The other behavioral sciences of psychology and sociology also take a different approach. Psychology is primarily concerned with individual behavior, and sociology concentrates on social behavior. Obviously, much overlap exists between anthropology and the other social and behavioral disciplines. Yet, the holistic assumption is definitely characteristic of anthropology and may be summarized as follows:

A fundamental proposition of anthropology is that no part can be fully, or even accurately understood apart from the whole. And conversely, the whole—man and

[14]Ross A. Webber, *Culture and Management*, Richard D. Irwin, Inc., Homewood, Ill., 1969, p. 10.

[15]Marston Bates, *Gluttons and Libertines—Human Problems of Being Natural*, Random House, Inc., New York, 1967, p. 23. Originally copyrighted in 1958.

his manifestations—cannot be accurately perceived without acute and specialized knowledge of the parts.[16]

Comparative Approach   The second unifying assumption common to all facets of anthropology is the use of the comparative method of analysis. "An anthropologist refuses to accept any generalization about human nature that emerges from his experience with his own society alone, or even with two or three other societies, especially if these are a part of the same cultural tradition in which he has been brought up."[17]

Anthropologists express the comparative approach by their use of cross-cultural analysis. Ruth Benedict's famous study of the Zuñi Indians of New Mexico, the Kwakiutls of Vancouver Island, and the Dobus of Melanesia is an excellent example of the understanding of humans that can be gained through cross-cultural analysis.[18] Margaret Mead, probably the most widely known anthropologist of the 1970s, stated that the Benedict study ". . . is the best introduction we have to the widening of horizons by a comparative study of different cultures, through which we can see our own socially transmitted customary behavior set beside that of other and strangely different people."[19] Because of the extreme importance attached to comparative analysis, the training of a professional anthropologist usually includes field work in another culture.

At face value, the holistic and comparative assumptions seem contradictory. Holism stresses the integration of the human being into a unified whole, while comparativism assumes the opposite view in analyzing a person from the standpoint of divergent cultures. DuBois resolves the apparent dilemma by explaining that ". . . anthopologists generally agree that societies are to a greater or lesser extent integrated and that the search for such linkages within any society is of equal importance with comparisons between societies." [20] The two unifying assumptions are thus complementary, not conflicting. The goal of anthropology is to understand a person as a whole, and this goal is best accomplished by comparison between, and integration within, cultures. Once again, the dominant theme is culture.

SOCIOLOGY

Sociology is traditionally defined as the *science of society.* To the uninformed, its purposes and goals are often unclear. Many equate sociology with social work and the solving of social problems. Some even relate sociology to the

---

[16]E. Adamson Hoebel, *Anthropology,* 3d ed., McGraw-Hill Book Company, New York, 1966, p. 4.

[17]Ibid.

[18]See Ruth Benedict, *Patterns of Culture,* Mentor Books, New American Library, Inc., New York, 1959. Originally copyrighted in 1934.

[19]Ibid., "A New Preface by Margaret Mead," p. v.

[20]Cora DuBois, op. cit., p. 32.

political philosophy of socialism. In reality, sociology is at the same time more narrow and broader than the areas with which it is often confused. Perhaps sociology can most accurately be described as an academic discipline that utilizes the scientific method in accumulating knowledge about social behavior. The other areas do not have this specific purpose and goal. The overall focus of sociology is on social behavior in societies, institutions, and groups.

Historical Development of Sociology

Similar to the other behavioral sciences, sociology is a relatively young academic field, and the word itself did not come into existence until 1842. Auguste Comte (1798–1857) used the term *sociology* to identify a new science of society based upon systematic methodology rather than philosophical speculation. He used the concepts of statics and dynamics to delineate the field.[21] Through the application of the static concept, Comte wanted to demonstrate how the various parts of society interact and interrelate. In his book *The Positive Philosophy,* he wrote that, "The statical study of sociology consists in the investigation of the laws of action and reaction of the different parts of the social system." In contrast, his concept of social dynamics focused on whole societies. Attention was devoted to the development and change of total societies through time. Both social statics and dynamics have greatly influenced the development of modern sociology.

After Comte, other pioneers in the field also made significant contributions. Émile Durkheim, who, like Comte, was French, Herbert Spencer of England, and Max Weber of Germany are the most widely known early sociologists, and they represent the national centers that substantially affected the development of the field. Herbert Spencer (1820–1903) is credited with writing the first book dealing directly with sociology. His three-volume *Principles of Sociology* was published in 1877. Spencer essentially refined what Comte had said approximately thirty-five years earlier, but it was Durkheim and Weber who really extended the discipline.

Contributions of Durkheim   Émile Durkheim (1858–1917) was a prolific writer on a diversity of sociological topics. His best-known works include *Suicide, On the Division of Labor, Rules of Sociological Method,* and *The Elementary Forms of Religious Life.* One idea in particular illustrates Durkheim's far-reaching thinking. He presented the concept of *anomie* to explain certain sociological phenomena. Anomie can best be defined as a state of isolation or normlessness in which social rules or norms no longer have an effect on individual behavior. In modern times, the breakdown of traditional institutions like the family and the societal disorganization and individual alienation created by industrialization and urbanization reflect Durkheim's anomie.

[21]See Alex Inkeles, *What Is Sociology?,* Prentice-Hall, Inc., Englewood Cliffs, N. J., 1964, pp. 3–4.

Contributions of Weber   Max Weber (1864–1920) is most often associated with the organization concept of bureaucracy. Using Comte's social dynamics as a starting point, he analyzed the development and change of Western society. He noted that the common denominator for social change in the Western world was the cultural value of rationalization. The best example for Weber was the bureaucratic form of organization, which is completely rational. He was the first to utilize this phenomenon as a unit of analysis for society. The characteristics and ramifications of bureaucracy are thoroughly discussed in Chapter 6.

Closely related to the rationalization theme was Weber's institutional analysis of religion. He felt that religion played an important part in the development and change of Western civilization. His purposes ". . . were to examine the effect of religious ideas on economic activities, to analyze the relation between social stratification and religious ideas, and to ascertain and explain the distinguishing characteristics of Western civilization."[22] His analysis, presented in *The Protestant Ethic and the Spirit of Capitalism,* accomplishes these purposes. This book is a classic study of the fundamental comparative relationships between religion and the economic and social life in Western culture.

Modern Perspectives

The above discussion indicates that sociology has a rich heritage. The early sociologists concentrated on immediate, practical social problems and strove for societal betterment. Contemporary sociology is characterized by rigorous methodology with an empirical emphasis and conceptual consciousness.[23] The major thrust common to all areas of sociology is toward the goal of understanding interdependent social behavior. The primary units of analysis studied by modern sociologists, going from largest to smallest, are the society, institution, group, and norms and roles.[24]

Societal Analysis

The oldest and largest unit of analysis in sociology is the society. A very comprehensive definition states, "A society exists to the degree that a territorially bounded population of animals of a single species maintains ties of association and interdependence and enjoys autonomy."[25] More directly, a society is a territorially bounded, interacting group of people who share some common goals and remain autonomous from outside influences.

[22]Reinhard Bendix, *Max Weber: An Intellectual Portrait,* Doubleday & Company, Inc., Garden City, N. Y., 1960, p. 266.

[23]Harry Alpert, "Sociology: Its Present Interests," in Berelson (ed.), *The Behavioral Sciences Today,* op. cit., p. 52.

[24]See Alan P. Bates, *The Sociological Enterprise,* Houghton Mifflin Company, Boston, 1967, pp. 40–45.

[25]Gerhard Lenski, *Human Societies,* McGraw-Hill Book Company, New York, 1970, p. 9.

In studying society, sociologists take either an external or internal approach. The traditional external approach explores such questions as: "Is there any evidence that particular types of society, say the great empires, tend to endure for any specific period of time? Do societies go through definite stages of development?"[26] Such external analysis is closely allied to the theory of social evolution. Originating with Charles Darwin, this theory was developed and popularized by early sociologists such as Spencer. Ideas of social evolution have since been discredited and the external approach has suffered because of guilt by association.

The newer, internal approach to the analysis of society is much more widely accepted and used by today's sociologists. The major interest is the internal structure of a society. Among the questions for analysis are: "What are the internal problems which any society must face? What are the most common components found in most societies? How do societies typically allocate responsibility for various functions?"[27] This approach is interested in the total society but only insofar as it is affected by the internal subsocieties. For example, relationships between institutions in a society would be a legitimate area of inquiry in internal analysis, but the institution per se would not. The following units of analysis are concerned with subunits of the total society.

Institutional Analysis

Institutions evolve from, and are an important part of, society. An institution is formed when a given society focuses its structure on certain values or issues. It is the largest subunit of a society. An institution is comprehensively defined as "a normative order defining and governing patterns of social action deemed by its members as morally and socially crucial to the existence of the society."[28] One example is the society that becomes concerned with the process of mating, conceiving, and caring for its young. From this concern, the society creates an institution called marriage, which determines morally and socially acceptable behavior that is required for its perpetuation. Other obvious societal needs have resulted in political, economic, legal, and religious institutions. As the society matures and grows in size and complexity, scientific, military, welfare, health, educational, recreational, and aesthetic institutions also emerge.

Sociologists study all aspects of institutions. Subspecialties of sociology, such as the sociology of religion or law, examine the institution as a single entity. More often, however, sociology is concerned with the changes that take place in institutions, for example, the shift of welfare responsibility from the family to the state, or the persistence of certain basic institutions like religion. Most important to sociological analysis is the interdependence that exists between the various institutions and the society as a whole.

[26]Inkeles, op. cit., p. 14.
[27]Ibid., p. 14.
[28]James B. McKee, *Introduction to Sociology*, Holt, Rinehart and Winston, Inc., New York, 1969, p. 132.

Group Analysis

The group is the unit of analysis most closely associated with modern sociology. The main reason is that it is such a common social unit. A universal definition of a group does not exist. The definition partially depends on whether a perspective of societies as groups or of groups as societies is taken. Most sociologists have traditionally viewed societies as groups.[29] Such a perspective has led to the sociological connotation of a group to mean a primary group.

Primary Groups   Charles H. Cooley was the first to define and analyze a primary group. In his book *Social Organization,* first published in 1909, he wrote, "By primary groups I mean those characterized by intimate, face-to-face association and cooperation. They are primary in several senses, but chiefly in that they are fundamental in forming the social nature and ideals of the individual."[30] Cooley's primary group concept was further developed and refined by George Homans. In Homans' classic book *The Human Group,* a group is described as "a number of persons who communicate with one another often over a span of time, and who are few enough so that each person is able to communicate with all the others, not at secondhand, through other people, but face-to-face."[31]

Often the terms *small group* and *primary group* are used interchangeably. Technically, there is a difference. A small group has to meet only the criterion of small size. Usually, no attempt is made to assign precise numbers, but the accepted criterion is that the group must be small enough for face-to-face interaction and communication to occur. In addition to being small, a primary group must have a feeling of comradeship, loyalty, and a common sense of values among its members. Thus, all primary groups are small groups but not all small groups are primary.

Two examples of a primary group are the family and the peer group. Initially, the primary group was limited to a socializing group, but then a broader conception was given impetus by the results of the Hawthorne studies. Work groups definitely had primary group qualities. Later, equally renowned studies, described in *Street Corner Society,* by William F. Whyte, and in *The American Soldier,* by Samuel Stouffer et al., further expanded the concept of the primary group.[32] These and many recent studies all point to the tremendous impact that the primary group has on individual behavior, regardless of context

---

[29]Michael S. Olmsted, *The Small Group,* Random House, Inc., New York, 1959, pp. 16–18.
[30]Charles H. Cooley, *Social Organization,* Charles Scribner's Sons, New York, 1911, p. 23. Originally published in 1909.
[31]George C. Homans, *The Human Group,* Harcourt, Brace & World, Inc., New York, 1950, p. 1.
[32]See Fritz J. Roethlisberger and William J. Dickson, *Management and the Worker,* Harvard University Press, Cambridge, Mass., 1947; W. F. Whyte, *Street Corner Society,* The University of Chicago Press, Chicago, 1943 and 1955; and Samuel A. Stouffer et al., *The American Soldier,* Princeton University Press, Princeton, N. J., 1949.

or environmental conditions. The primary group is a basic building block of the total society.

Small-Group Research   Over the past two decades, much research has been conducted on small groups. Traditionally, the study of primary groups relied on the case and field-experiment methods of research. Today, sociologists who conduct small-group research, which includes but is not limited to primary groups, depend upon highly controlled laboratory techniques. Small-group research emphasizes ". . . the *forms* of behavior that emanate from the interaction, rather than the *content* of the interaction. They are more interested in *how* the group interacts than in *what* it interacts about."[33]

Although Georg Simmel was probably the first to advocate a structured type of group study, Robert Bales is most often associated with the beginning of small-group research.[34] Bales and his Harvard colleagues developed the technique of interaction analysis.[35] Under laboratory conditions, they carefully observed a small group of subjects perform assigned tasks. From observations, they analyzed specific variables, such as leadership, participation, and social interaction. From this start, small-group research has primarily concentrated on the impact of the group from the standpoint of the bases of its formation, problem solving, leadership styles, communication networks, and cohesion. Group analysis has probably contributed more to the understanding of organizational behavior than any other single area of sociology. It is covered in more depth in Chapter 15.

Norms and Roles

With the exception of a single social act such as extending a hand upon meeting, the smallest units of analysis in sociology are norms and roles. Many behavioral scientists make a point of distinguishing between the two units, but conceptually they are very similar. *Norms* are the *oughts* of behavior. They are prescriptions for acceptable behavior determined by a group, institution, or society. A *role* consists of a pattern of norms and is directly related to the theatrical use of the term. A role is a position that can be acted out by an individual. The content of a given role is prescribed by the prevailing norms. Probably the best definition of a role is, "a position that has expectations evolving from established norms." Alan Bates further refines the role concept by making this distinction: "As a pattern of *prescribed* behavior a role is a

[33]McKee, op. cit., p. 155.

[34]At the turn of the century, Georg Simmel suggested that changes would occur in social interaction when the number of members of a group was altered. "The Number of Members as Determining the Sociological Form of the Group," *American Journal of Sociology,* vol. 8, 1902–1903, pp. 1–46 and 158–196.

[35]Robert F. Bales, *Interaction Process Analysis: A Method for the Study of Small Groups,* Addison-Wesley Press, Inc., Cambridge, Mass., 1950. Also see Robert F. Bales, *Personality and Interpersonal Behavior,* Holt, Rinehart and Winston, Inc., New York, 1970.

bundle of norms. As a pattern of *actual* behavior a role is one side of a set of social relationships."[36]

Norms can be social, moral, or institutional in nature. Examples of social norms include expectations about dress (wearing a necktie); courtesies (excusing oneself from dinner); or authority relationships (taking orders from the boss). Moral norms relate to personal obligations, rights, and privileges, and they play an important part in societal institutions such as religion, family, and marriage. Norms can also take on institutional properties themselves. Common law is an example of an institutionalized norm. All forms of group norms are very important in analyzing organizational behavior.

There are numerous roles in every society. For example, in modern American society, the family, occupational, and educational areas all contain many roles. Mother, father, and child are three family roles. Doctor, lawyer, manager, and worker are some occupational roles. Dean, professor, and student are roles associated with higher education. Each of these roles has clearly understood and widely accepted expectations of how a person should perform in the given position. Both the person occupying the position and those outside are familiar with the role expectations. Guilt, anxiety, and even psychotic depression and suicide may result when people feel they have not lived up to the expectations of roles such as that of father of a family. Role analysis has potentially great value for understanding much of organizational behavior.

Other Sociological Units of Analysis

Societies, institutions, groups, and norms and roles have been presented as the major units of analysis for sociology. These are not the only units that a sociologist studies, however. Most of the other areas of analysis fall, in size, somewhere between an institution and a group. For instance, some sociologists argue that community, organization, and social class are major areas of study.[37] A community may be thought of as a territorial group and an organization as a group with a specific goal. Thus, both community and organization may be defined in terms of groups. However, neither is necessarily a small, primary group. The social-class unit of analysis is more closely associated with the total society than community and organization. It can be defined as the structure of a society that is based upon ranking by social and/or material attributes.

Sociology in Perspective

The units of analysis just discussed can serve as a brief overall outline of what the field of sociology is all about. There are many specialized subfields. Some of the better-known are:

[36]Alan P. Bates, op. cit., p. 44.
[37]Ibid., pp. 40–45.

1 Urban and rural influences
2 Race and ethnic relations
3 Population or demography
4 Communications research
5 Public opinions and attitudes
6 Collective behavior
7 Occupations
8 Social disorganization and deviant behavior.[38]

The study and research findings coming from these specialties of sociology have led to insights and solutions to many problems facing modern society. Overall, sociology has made, and will continue to make, many significant contributions to the better understanding of human social behavior in general and of organizational behavior in particular.

PSYCHOLOGY

Modern psychology is almost universally defined as the *science of behavior.* This definition is nearly identical with that of behavioral science in general. Although psychology is only one of the disciplines making up the behavioral sciences, it is probably more closely identified with overall behavioral science than is sociology or anthropology.

Psychology generally includes animal as well as human behavior. The inclusion of animal behavior is not without criticism. In many types of psychological experimentation, animals such as rats or monkeys are utilized because of the high degree of control that can be exercised over them. The difficulty comes from trying to generalize the results and conclusions drawn from animal experimentation to human behavior. Despite the differing opinions regarding the place of animal research, all psychologists are united in their belief that individual human behavior should be the principal focus of psychology. The understanding, prediction, and control of human behavior are the goals of modern psychology.

Common Misconceptions

Psychology is a much-misunderstood academic discipline. The problem stems from the fact that everyone from the illiterate to the Ph.D. is intimately involved with, and a student of, human behavior. Everyone has preconceived notions about human nature that are based on one's own experience. These beliefs are staunchly defended. As a result, there are many misconceptions and sometimes ill feelings toward the academic discipline that tries to tell the individual about human behavior.

With regard to human behavior, it is not unusual to find common sense and

[38]See Alpert, op. cit., pp. 58–62, for a brief discussion of these subfields.

science in opposition. The major differences between the two may be summarized as follows:

    1 Common sense is vague compared to scientific knowledge.

    2 Flagrant inconsistencies often appear in common sense knowledge, whereas the demand for logical consistency is a hallmark of science.

    3 Science systematically seeks to explain the events with which it deals; common sense ignores the need for explanation.

    4 The scientific method deliberately exposes claims to the critical evaluation of experimental analysis; the informal methods of common sense fail to test conclusions in any systematic fashion.[39]

These differences are seen in the psychological and the lay approaches to human behavior. The psychologist possesses the scientific viewpoint and utilizes the scientific method in gathering facts about human behavior. The layperson relies on common sense and not science.

In the past and even to some extent today, psychologists are viewed by the general public with a great deal of misunderstanding and, in some cases, suspicion. Kimble and Garmezy have tried to clear up some of the more common misconceptions as follows:

    1 Psychologists cannot "read your mind" simply by looking at you.

    2 Psychologists have no peculiar interest in psychoanalyzing you.

    3 Psychologists are not fortune-tellers.

    4 Neither a psychologist nor anyone else can tell anything about a person from the bumps on his head (phrenology).

    5 Neither psychologists nor anyone else can tell anything about you by the numbers of letters in your name (numerology) or by the lines in your hand (palmistry).

    6 By and large, psychologists are not interested in mystical phenomena such as telepathy or clairvoyance.[40]

In other words, psychology does not deal with mysticism or superstition.

Too often, people seem interested only in the sensational aspects of psychology and prone to accept "facts" without considering the source. Kendler believes that "self-styled psychological experts who offer advice to anyone, anywhere, at any time after seeing two psychiatric movies and reading one book by Freud are all too common."[41] The understanding of human behavior is a very complex and demanding undertaking. Although there are very few simple answers, psychologists always attempt to approach their study from the viewpoint of science.

   [39]Howard H. Kendler, *Basic Psychology*, 3d ed., W. A. Benjamin Inc., Menlo Park, Calif., 1974, pp. 12–13.

   [40]Gregory A. Kimble and Norman Garmezy, *General Psychology*, 2d ed., The Ronald Press Company, New York, 1963, p. 3.

   [41]Kendler, op. cit., 2d ed., 1968, p. xi.

The Founding of Psychology

A common summary statement concerning the development of psychology is that it has a long past but a short history. Similar to the other behavioral sciences, psychology is a relatively new area of study compared with the physical and biological sciences. Also similar to other academic disciplines, it cannot realistically be assigned a specific date for its founding. The generally agreed-upon starting point for the study of psychology as an independent science, and of the behavioral sciences in general, was Wundt's laboratory in 1879, as indicated earlier. There had been many indirect contributions previously, but "before Wundt there had been plenty of psychology but no psychologists."[42]

Development of the Field

There are two ways to explore the trends and development of psychology. One method is to examine the changing concerns of those in the field. Early psychologists were mainly interested in the mind. As recently as fifty to sixty years ago, psychology was commonly defined as the *science of the mind.* As stated previously, the modern definition is the *science of behavior.* The contrasting definitions illustrate the change in emphasis during the past half-century. Early psychologists dwelled on mental processes of consciousness and experience. They concentrated on things like memory and measurement of sensation. Modern psychologists deal with more objective behavior. The measurement and understanding of overt behavior dominate present-day psychological theory and practice. However, as Morgan and King carefully point out, the shift of interest from the mind to behavior is only one of degree; "psychology has not yet lost its mind."[43]

The other way of tracing the development of an academic field is to note the changes in methods used in accumulating knowledge. Behavioral science in general and psychology in particular have moved from philosophical speculation to rigorous empiricism. Modern psychologists utilize the laboratory experiment primarily to analyze behavior. Most of them do not consider that psychology even existed before Wundt's laboratory was established. In the United States, the first psychological laboratory was founded at Johns Hopkins University in 1883. Today, every major university in the country has an extensive laboratory to study behavior.

Schools of Thought

As an academic field develops, there is a natural tendency to structure and logically relate diverse facts into specific schools of thought. In a growing discipline that has not fully matured or stabilized, adherents to a particular theory often become defensive of their position, and a sense of competition

[42]Ibid., p. 33.

[43]Clifford Morgan and Richard King, *Introduction to Psychology,* 3d ed., McGraw-Hill Book Company, New York, 1966, p. 22.

frequently results. The formative years of psychology were characterized by schools of thought which were highly competitive. The most widely known are those relating to structuralism, functionalism, behaviorism, gestalt psychology, and psychoanalysis.

Structuralism   Founded by Wundt, structuralism represents the earliest theoretical school. The theory revolved around conscious experience and attempted to build a science of the mind. Wundt and his followers proceeded by breaking down the mind into various structural units, which led to the label of structuralism.

The structuralists concentrated on mental states such as sensation, memory, imagery, and feelings. Drawing on their heritage in physiology and the physical sciences, they were determined to measure processes. Introspection was the primary tool developed for this purpose. Essentially, it is a self-observation technique where subjects are asked to describe in minute detail their reaction to sensory stimuli such as color, smell, and sound. Unfortunately, this technique did not produce any profound results or implications, and it soon became apparent that the structuralist approach was too narrow. The mind is much more complex than just a group of structural units made up of conscious sensation and experience.

Functionalism   Around the turn of the century, structuralism gave way to functionalism as the dominant school of thought. Functionalism was derived in America, where philosophers William James (1842–1910) and John Dewey (1859–1952) were very critical of the structuralists. They felt the key to understanding the mind was an understanding of how it *functions,* not of how it is structured. Thus emphasis was placed on people's adjustment and adaptation to their environment. Compared with the structuralists, the functionalists were all-encompassing and more pragmatic. Although they did borrow the introspection tool for analyzing mental states, they went one step further by observing and recording total behavior patterns. Besides their sensory experience, people's learning, forgetting, motivation, and general adaptability to a new situation were studied. "So functionalism had two chief characteristics; the study of the total behavior and experience of an individual, and an interest in the adaptive functions served by the things an individual does."[44]

Behaviorism   Behaviorism was a natural outgrowth of functionalism. The theoretical trend had been away from the mind and toward behavior. The structuralists had been concerned only with the mind, but the functionalists emphasized both mind and behavior. Now the behaviorists felt that only observable, objective behavior was of significance to psychology.

Behaviorism was influenced by the work of the Russian physiologist Ivan

[44]Ibid., p. 24.

Pavlov (1849–1936). However, the generally recognized founder of behaviorism (sometimes called the stimulus-response, or S-R, school of thought) was the American John B. Watson (1878–1958). In the early 1900s he questioned whether the use of the introspective technique was within the realm of science. He maintained that only observable, objective behavior qualified for scientific investigation. Therefore, psychology should be concerned only with S-R connections, or the observation, measurement, and analysis of stimuli and the resulting responses.

The results of Pavlovian experimentation convinced most early behaviorists that identifiable S-R conditioned reflexes were the basic elements of all behavior. In this regard, they were ironically similar to the structuralists whom they so vehemently rejected. Behaviorism promoted the learned aspects of behavior. The behaviorists did not attach any importance to unlearned or instinctual behavior. In fact, Watson and his followers believed that humans were solely products of learning, and they boasted that they could condition a person to become almost anything.

The behaviorist school of thought has greatly influenced modern psychology. By dealing only with observable, overt events, behaviorism forced psychology to become more research- and science-oriented. Even the currently used definition of psychology—the science of behavior—is attributable to behaviorism. A great many modern psychologists would probably consider themselves behaviorists. They agree upon the importance of learned behavior and discount instincts as having any value in understanding human behavior; but, of course, modern behaviorism has gone way beyond the mechanistic S-R approach of Watson. Chapters 5, 12, and 20 examine the concepts of modern behaviorism.

Gestalt Psychology   While functionalism and behaviorism were becoming popular in America, the *gestalt* school was replacing structuralism in Germany. The founding is usually attributed to Max Wertheimer and dated around 1912. Whereas the structuralists were noted for their attempt to isolate sensory units of the brain and the behaviorists for their emphasis on specific conditioned reflexes, gestaltists felt that the whole, not the parts, was the important subject matter of psychology.

Gestalt is difficult to define because the word was brought directly into English from German. Loosely, the term means pattern, configuration, form, or organization. A simplified explanation of this school of thought is that its adherents believe the whole to be greater than the sum of its parts. A simple illustration of gestaltism is the classic Müller-Lyer illusion found in Figure 2-4. The lines *X* and *Y* are of exactly equal length. However, they are perceived to be unequal because of their relationship to the whole. In other words, the whole is perceived differently from the way the sum of its parts would be perceived.

Just as German physical scientists had influenced structuralism, they also influenced gestaltism. The gestaltists made an analogy between the "field" of behavior and a magnetic field in physics. Such analysis has resulted in the label

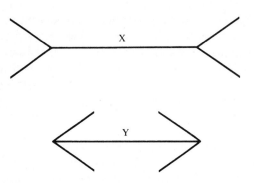

Figure 2-4 The Müller-Lyer illusion.

field theorists for those who adhered to this approach. For example, Kurt Lewin, who used the analogy of magnetic fields in explaining group dynamics, is often called a field theorist.

Like the structuralists, gestaltists used introspection—but with a different emphasis. They were more concerned with the free response of a subject than with the elaboration or interpretation of a trained observer. This different use of introspection dealt with phenomena of experience and perception, and it is commonly known as *phenomenology.* Along with the behaviorists, the gestaltists have had a great impact on modern psychology. They were the forerunners of general systems theory, which is currently playing an important role in all fields of study. Modern cognitive theorists also have roots in gestaltism and phenomenology.

Psychoanalysis   A discussion of the historical development of psychological thought would not be complete without mentioning the works of Sigmund Freud (1856–1939). His ideas about unconscious motivation, the development and structure of personality, and his treatment technique, which he called *psychoanalysis,* have all had a vast influence on the development of modern psychology. Freud and his colleagues, such as Alfred Adler and Carl Jung, both of whom later broke away to formulate their own theories, were active in Europe about the same time functionalism was popular in America.

By itself, psychoanalysis is really not a separate school of psychological thought. More accurately, it is a treatment technique and form of therapy for persons suffering from psychological problems. The method utilizes free association to encourage the patient to cope consciously with underlying or repressed problems or trauma. Psychoanalysis is still a widely used technique for the therapeutic treatment of mental patients and even of normal persons.

Freud was a practitioner—a medical physician and a psychiatrist. He was not an experimental researcher. However, in treating the mentally ill, he keenly observed that their problems were often subject to cause-and-effect relationships that the patients themselves were not consciously aware of. From this observation, Freud concluded that unconscious mental processes (usually sexually linked) motivated much of human behavior. Because these conclusions were based on clinical observation and not on experimental methods, many behavioral scientists have been critical of psychoanalytic theories. Regardless of this criticism, Freudian concepts are widely recognized, and they are used as the starting point for discussions of motivation and the development and structure of personality in Chapters 13 and 14.

Modern Approaches to Psychology

All the historical schools of thought contribute some theoretical understanding and research techniques to the modern approach to psychology. In varying degrees, all are still in evidence today. However, in contrast to the pioneers in the field, modern psychologists do not necessarily identify themselves with any one school of thought. Yet, in their basic theoretical orientation and research methods, they certainly lean toward one or another of the schools. In particular, the behaviorist and gestalt schools have had a tremendous impact on the orientation of modern psychologists. However, on the whole, contemporary psychologists take an eclectic theoretical approach and utilize the laboratory-experiment method of research.

Contemporary psychological theory may be divided into several areas of concentration. There is no universal agreement on the divisions because they greatly depend on how finely one draws the line between the various areas. Three broad classifications would include the biological-physiological aspects; the psychological processes; and the whole-person personality concept.

Biological-Physiological Aspects One major approach taken by modern psychology is to give attention to the biological-physiological aspects of behavior. The behaviorist school generally played down the importance of biological-physiological analysis. However, about twenty-five years ago there was an awakened interest in the role that this type of analysis could play in understanding behavior.

The biological contributions to behavior center on heredity. The impact of heredity is an old but still unsettled issue. The behaviorists almost completely discounted heredity, but most of today's psychologists recognize that it plays at least some role in behavior. One of the most controversial issues in psychology is the heredity-versus-environmental influence on intelligence, which is still being debated. In reality, heredity can never be completely separated from environment or vice versa. From the moment of conception on, the environment interacts with the genetic endowment of the human being.

The most direct physiological impact on behavior comes from the endocrine glands and the central nervous system. There are other physiologically related concepts in psychology, such as the "general adaptation syndrome," which is related to the analysis of stress, and the "reticular formation," which is related to sleep, waking, and energetic action. The endocrine glands secrete hormones directly into the blood stream and have a definite effect on emotion and other psychological states. However, the focus of greatest interest to psychology has been the central nervous system, which consists of the brain and nervous system. The brain was the original concern of psychologists, and certain parts of it, particularly the hypothalamus, have been determined to directly influence psychological states. But many other parts and functions of the brain remain a mystery. Part of the problem stems from the fact that physiologists have not helped much in providing an understanding of the brain's inner workings. Nevertheless, the brain's role in behavior is certainly not a dead issue in psychology. An example of this is the current interest and spectacular preliminary results that are emerging from the study of electrical stimulation of the brain (ESB). (Some of the major findings and implications of ESB are discussed in Chapter 14.) This research, plus the work being done in related areas, points to the almost unlimited potential of biological-physiological analysis as an aid to understanding human behavior.

Psychological Processes   The most common topical breakdown of the discipline of psychology is into its basic processes. Perception, learning, and motivation are the three most generally accepted classifications. These processes operate and interact to produce the psychologically whole person and represent the major units of analysis for modern psychology. They are given the primary attention in psychological theory and research. In this book, Chapter 11 is devoted to perception, Chapters 12 and 20 concentrate on learning, and Chapters 13 and 17 discuss motivation. An understanding of these basic processes is vital to the study of organizational behavior.

Personality   The third major conceptual area in psychology is the study of personality. The separation of psychology into the processes of perception, learning, and motivation, mentioned above, is largely artificial and unrealistic. An individual operates and behaves as a whole, not as a collection of separate parts. Personality is concerned with the whole person. As a major area in psychology, the study of personality is principally concerned with its development and structure. Chapter 14 is specifically focused on personality development and theories of structure. An understanding of personality, as well as of the psychological processes, is extremely relevant to the study of organizational behavior.

Professional Subfields

The number of professional psychologists has been growing at the rate of about 10 percent a year. This remarkable growth has resulted in the proliferation of the basic discipline. Today there are numerous highly specialized subfields. The best all-encompassing breakdown of psychologists would be into two categories: theorists-researchers and practitioners. Most of the theorists-researchers are employed by universities to teach and/or to do research. These academicians have specialties in experimental, physiological, social, educational, industrial, developmental, personality, psychometric, or clinical psychology. Members of the other major branch of psychologists, the practitioners, apply these academic specialties in the real world.

By far the greatest proportion of practicing psychologists are clinical specialists. If school psychologists and counselors are included in the clinical classification, the combination accounts for about half of all practicing psychologists. Along with the psychiatrist (who is medically trained) and the social worker, the clinical psychologist (who is *not* medically trained) is an essential member of the team for treating mental patients.

Next to clinical psychology, the major applied subfield is industrial psychology. Traditionally, industrial psychologists were chiefly used in the screening and training functions of employment. Today, they have a much expanded role. Besides working in selection and training, they are deeply involved with organizational development, human engineering, organizational communcation, and employee relations. Industrial psychology is very closely related to organizational behavior. The major difference is that industrial psychology is an applied field with a narrower perspective. Organizational behavior is a broader academic field which includes all aspects of human behavior in organizations. Pragmatically the industrial psychologist probably comes closest to being a practicing organizational behaviorist, but it should be emphasized that the study of organizational behavior serves as the basis for all managers of human resources.

SOCIAL PSYCHOLOGY

Social psychology is generally not mentioned as a separate discipline in the behavioral sciences. There are two major reasons for this exclusion. First, social psychology is frequently classified as a subfield in both psychology and sociology. This often confuses students and committees concerned with the duplication of courses in universities. The typical university curriculum includes two separate courses called social psychology, one in the psychology department and one in the sociology department. The difference between the two is a matter of emphasis and professional orientation. The second reason that social psychology has not been treated separately is that it can almost be equated with behavioral science itself. Similar to behavioral science, social psychology is academically interdisciplinary. It consists of an eclectic mixture of psychology and sociology. The exclusion of social psychology as a behavioral science, however, in no way deemphasizes its importance. Social psychology, if considered a separate discipline, is more closely aligned with behavioral science as a whole than any other single discipline.

There are many slight variations given to definitions of social psychology. One comprehensive definition is that it is the study of individual behavior in relation to the social environment. The most important part of the social environment is other persons, individually and collectively. More simply, social psychology is the *study of individual behavior within a group*. This definition points out the close ties that social psychology has to psychology (individual emphasis) and sociology (group emphasis). It was only fitting that the first two books on social psychology, simultaneously published in 1908, were written by a psychologist, William McDougall, and a sociologist, Edward Ross.[45]

The logical breakdown for analysis and study in social psychology is the individual, the group, and the interaction between the individual and the group. The last-named provides the key difference between the study of social psychology and the study of psychology and sociology. An example is the approach taken in the study of groups. Social psychology is more concerned with why an individual joins a group (affiliation) and wants to remain a member of the group (cohesion). The social psychologist focuses primarily on group structure and function only to the extent that they affect individual behavior. Besides the study of groups, topics of general interest to the social psychologist include:

1 *Attitudes,* their formation and change
2 *Communication research,* the effect that networks have on individual and group efficiency and satisfaction
3 *Problem solving,* the analysis of cooperation versus competition
4 *Social influences,* the impact of conformity and other social factors on individual behavior
5 *Leadership,* especially the identification and functions of leaders and their effectiveness.

More specialized theories (such as cognitive-dissonance) and analysis (such as approach-avoidance conflict) are also a vital part of social psychology.

As an academic field, social psychology is very closely related to organizational behavior. This is evidenced by the overall orientation and conceptual framework of this book. Parts Three and Four borrow heavily from the theories and research findings of social psychology. Moreover, there seems to be a mutually beneficial relationship that can exist between the disciplines of social psychology and organizational behavior. One of the major purposes of this book is to help develop and refine this relationship.

SUMMARY

The behavioral sciences provide a necessary foundation for the study of organizational behavior. Defined as the scientific study of human behavior, behavioral science is moving in the direction of a truly interdisciplinary field of study. Behavioral science greatly depends on scientific methodology to accumulate knowledge. Experimental, case, and survey designs are used. The academic disciplines of anthropology, sociology, and psychology make up behavioral science. Anthropology, literally defined as *the science of man,* concentrates primarily on the role that culture plays in human behavior.

---

[45]William McDougall, *Introduction to Social Psychology,* Methney, London, 1908; and Edward A. Ross, *Social Psychology: An Outline and Source Book,* The Macmillan Company, New York, 1908.

Sociology is directly concerned with social behavior—in societies, institutions, groups, and roles. Psychology makes the greatest contribution of any of the single behavioral science disciplines to the study of organizational behavior. It gives primary attention to individual behavior from the perspective of the biological-physiological aspects, psychological processes, and personality. In particular, a knowledge of the psychological processes of perception, learning, and motivation are vital to the understanding of organizational behavior. Social psychology is closest to overall behavioral science and organizational behavior.

QUESTIONS FOR DISCUSSION AND REVIEW

1   How does behavioral science differ from social science?
2   What are the strengths and weaknesses of the three major research designs?
3   Why is the study of culture important to organizational behavior?
4   What are the major units of analysis studied by modern sociologists? Which one do you think is most relevant to organizational behavior? Why?
5   Why do you think psychology is such a commonly misunderstood academic discipline?
6   Briefly summarize the various schools of thought in psychology.
7   How does social psychology relate to sociology? To psychology?

CASE: MR. CHEMIST TACKLES
THE PERSONNEL DEPARTMENT

Jerry Bradley brought a unique background with him into his new job in the personnel department of Huge Company. Jerry had majored in chemistry at college and had worked in the company's research and development laboratory on new-product development for the past five years. Jerry had a knack for getting along with people around the lab; so when the job in personnel opened up, his boss suggested that he try for it. Jerry had never thought of going into personnel work but decided it would be a new challenge, and he did like working with people. After getting the standard orientation for new employees, Jerry was appalled at the way in which the personnel department attacked their problems. As far as he could tell, no attempt was made to use accepted scientific methodology in solving personnel problems. For example, they had no idea whether supervisors should tell their subordinates the results of the performance evaluation. When Jerry asked his boss about this situation, the boss tersely replied, "Well, Mr. Chemist, how would you go about solving our problems?"

1   If you were Jerry, how would you answer the boss?
2   Briefly, how would an experiment be set up to answer the question of whether supervisors should communicate the results of the performance evaluation to their subordinates? What would be the independent, dependent, and control variables in such an experiment?
3   What contribution can knowledge of the behavioral sciences make to

solving problems in a personnel department? In a research and development laboratory? Will Jerry be handicapped in his new job by having no knowledge of the behavioral sciences?

SELECTED REFERENCES

Berelson, Bernard (ed.): *The Behavioral Sciences Today,* Basic Books, Inc., Publishers, New York, 1963.

Berelson, Bernard, and Gary A. Steiner: *Human Behavior,* Harcourt, Brace & World, Inc., New York, 1964.

Birnbaum, Norman: "An End to Sociology?" *Social Research,* Autumn 1975, pp. 433–466.

Cherns, A. B.: "Can Behavioral Scientists Help Managers Improve Their Organization?" *Organizational Dynamics,* Winter 1973, pp. 51–67.

Goodwin, Leonard: "The Relation of Social Research to Practical Affairs," *The Journal of Applied Behavioral Science,* January-February-March 1975, pp. 7–12.

Hoebel, E. Adamson: *Anthropology: The Study of Man,* 4th ed., McGraw-Hill Book Company, New York, 1972.

Inkeles, Alex: *What Is Sociology?* Prentice-Hall, Inc., Englewood Cliffs, N. J., 1964.

Rhine, Shirley H.: "The Emergence of the Social Scientist," *The Conference Board Record,* February 1974, pp. 38–46.

Richardson, F. L. W.: "An Anthropological Alternative," *The Conference Board Record,* February 1975, pp. 52–54.

Rush, Harold M. F.: *Behavioral Science: Concepts and Management Application,* National Industrial Conference Board, Inc., New York, 1969.

Sarup, Gian: "Levels of Analysis in Social Psychology and Related Social Sciences," *Human Relations,* October 1975, pp. 755–769.

Schultz, Duane P.: *A History of Modern Psychology,* Academic Press, Inc., New York, 1969.

Chapter 3

Approaches to Management

The last chapter added to the historical foundation by giving an overview of the behavioral sciences. This chapter also adds to the foundation by giving an overview of the field of management. An understanding of both the behavioral sciences and management is necessary to the study of organizational behavior. The behavioral approach to management, of course, is embodied in organizational behavior. However, knowledge of other approaches (process, quantitative, systems, and contingency) helps put the behavioral approach into proper perspective and adds to the better understanding and management of human behavior in organizations. This chapter examines, in turn, the process, quantitative, systems, and contingency approaches. The other major approach, the behavioral approach, is what the rest of this book is about.

THE PROCESS APPROACH

The process approach to management is also variously called the *universal, functional, operational, traditional,* or *classical* approach. The pioneers of this approach first attempted to identify universal management functions and then to establish fundamental principles. Henri Fayol is most closely associated with the classical process. He first presented his views at the International Mining and Metallurgical Congress held in 1900.[1] However, it was not until 1949 that his book *General and Industrial Management* was translated into English and became part of the mainstream of American management theory.[2]

Fayol identified five functions of management: planning, organizing, command, coordination, and control. Other pioneering process theorists offered essentially the same functions but gave them slightly different names. For example, in 1937 Luther Gulick described the management process as POSD-CORB. This acronym stands for *p*lanning, *o*rganizing, *s*taffing, *d*irecting, *co*ordinating, *r*eporting, and *b*udgeting.[3] More recently, managerial processes have served as the conceptual framework for widely used principles of management textbooks. George Terry uses planning, organizing, actuating, and controlling, and Koontz and O'Donnell use planning, organizing, staffing, directing, and controlling.[4]

After determining appropriate names to attach to the various management functions, the process theorists attempted to formulate universal principles. In his *Elements of Administration,* Lyndall Urwick listed twenty-nine such principles.[5] Figure 3-1 summarizes these principles. They include most of the concepts that are included in the classical approach. However, the four principles that emerge as most representative of the classical process approach are: (1) unity of command; (2) equal authority and responsibility; (3) limited span of control; and (4) delegation of routine matters.

Unity of Command

The principle of unity of command states that each participant in the formal organization should be responsible to, and receive orders from, only one superior. Fayol stressed this principle above all others. He felt that if it is violated, "authority is undermined, discipline is in jeopardy, order disturbed and stability threatened."[6] The principle is closely associated with military organization.

An interesting contrast to unity of command is Taylor's concept of functional foremanship. Tyalor proposed that an individual worker be directly responsible to, and take orders from, as many as five different superiors. Each supervisor was a specialized expert in one function of the operation. Taylor

[1]For a discussion of Fayol's early work, see Henry H. Albers, *Principles of Management,* 4th ed., John Wiley & Sons, Inc., New York, 1974, pp. 23–24.

[2]Henri Fayol, trans. Constance Storrs, *General and Industrial Management,* Sir Isaac Pitman & Sons, Ltd., London, 1949.

[3]Luther Gulick, "Notes on the Theory of Organization," in Luther Gulick and Lyndall Urwick (eds.), *Papers on the Science of Administration,* Institute of Public Administration, New York, 1937, p. 13.

[4]George Terry, *Principles of Management,* 6th ed., Richard D. Irwin, Inc., Homewood, Ill., 1972; and Harold Koontz and Cyril O'Donnell, *Management,* 6th ed., McGraw-Hill Book Company, New York, 1976.

[5]Lyndall Urwick, *The Elements of Administration,* Harper & Brothers, New York, 1943.

[6]Fayol, op. cit., p. 24.

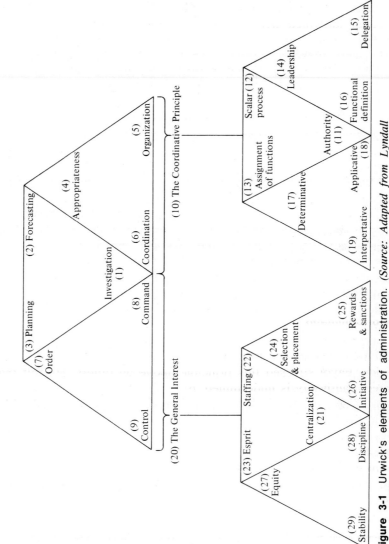

Figure 3-1 Urwick's elements of administration. *(Source: Adapted from Lyndall Urwick, The Elements of Administration, Harper & Row, Publishers, Incorporated, New York, 1943, p. 119.)*

was convinced that this inverted organizational arrangement would lead to maximum productivity. In "Shop Management," he advocated the functional plan as follows:

> Throughout the whole field of management the military type of organization should be abandoned, and what may be called the "functional type" substituted in its place . . . If practicable, the work of each man in the management should be confined to the performance of a single leading function.[7]

Fayol answered Taylor's functional idea of management in these words:

> For myself I do not think that a shop can be well run in flagrant violation of [unity of command]. Nevertheless, Taylor successfully managed large-scale concerns. How, then, can this contradiction be explained? I imagine that in practice Taylor was able to reconcile functionalism with the principle of unity of command . . . I think it dangerous to allow the idea to gain ground that unity of command is unimportant and can be violated with impunity.[8]

Other classical theorists, such as Urwick, have also emphasized the importance of unity of command over functionalization.[9] The solution to the dilemma is usually found in the more modern concept of *staff*, which is discussed in Chapter 6.

Equal Authority and Responsibility

Equal authority and responsibility is a time-honored process principle. It simply means that if managers are charged with the responsibility of accomplishing a given task, they must be given the commensurate authority to carry it out. An example is supervisors who are given the responsibility of keeping within a given budget. According to the principle, they should also have the authority to influence every item in the budget. If they do not have influence, say, over certain overhead items, these items should be divorced from their responsibility. Some of the newer responsibility-accounting techniques discussed in Chapter 10 are a direct reflection of this classical principle.

Urwick emphatically states:

> To hold a group or individual accountable for activities of any kind without assigning to him or them the necessary authority to discharge that responsibility is manifestly both unsatisfactory and inequitable. It is of great importance to smooth working that at all levels authority and responsibility should be coterminous and coequal.[10]

---

[7]Frederick W. Taylor, "Shop Management," in *Scientific Management*, Harper & Brothers, New York, 1947, p. 99. Original copyright held by Taylor in 1911.

[8]Fayol, op. cit., pp. 69–70.

[9]For example, see Lyndall Urwick, *The Load on Top Management—Can It Be Reduced?* Urwick, Orr & Partners, Ltd., London, 1954, p. 28.

[10]Urwick, *The Elements of Administration*, op. cit., p. 46.

The principle is complicated by the staff concept. Moreover, committee management and dual and functional authority structures also severely test the applicability of this classical principle. In Chapter 7 the project and matrix organization structures will be shown to complicate equal authority and responsibility even further.

Limited Span of Control

Span of control is defined as the number of subordinates directly reporting to a superior. Even in antiquity, there was concern over the proper span of control. An interesting passage in the Bible, Book of Exodus, Chapter 18, relates that "Moses sat to judge the people: and the people stood by Moses from the morning unto the evening." Jethro, Moses' father-in-law, viewed this with a critical eye. He noted the span-of-control implications of Moses' methods and warned him, "The thing thou doest is not good. Thou will surely wear away, both thou, and this people that is with thee: for the thing is too heavy for thee; thou are not able to perform it thyself alone." Jethro then proposed an organization with a much more limited span of control. Moses heeded the advice and "chose able men out of all Israel, and made them heads over the people, rulers of thousands, rulers of hundreds, rulers of fifties, and rulers of tens."

Similar to Jethro, the classical process theorists were in general agreement that there should be a limited number of subordinates reporting to a superior. They even made the fatal mistake of attaching precise numbers to the optimum span. A military management expert, Sir Ian Hamilton, a British general in World War I, is given credit for one of the first systematic analyses of span of control. After thoroughly studying military units, he concluded that each span should range between three and six subordinates. He reasoned that the average human brain can effectively handle only three to six other brains, and that "the nearer we approach the supreme head of the whole organisation, the more we ought to work towards groups of three; the closer we get to the foot of the whole organisation (the Infantry of the Line) the more we work towards groups of six."[11]

Hamilton's ideas on limiting the span were perpetuated by other classical theorists such as V. A. Graicunas. A management consultant, Graicunas figured out a mathematical formula that gave the exact number of relationships in a span of control. He emphasized that the number of social relationships was more crucial to analyzing span of control than merely the number of subordinates. For example, the simple organization in Figure 3-2 shows six different relationships but only two subordinates. Graicunas calculated the number of relationships as follows:

1   X to Y and X to Z are two direct-single relationships.

---

[11]Sir Ian Hamilton, *The Soul and Body of an Army*, George H. Doran Company, New York, 1921, p. 230.

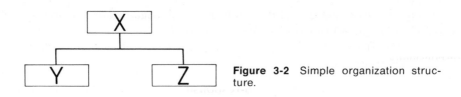

Figure 3-2 Simple organization structure.

    2 X to Y, with Z present, and X to Z, with Y present, are two direct-group relations.

    3 Finally, Z to Y and Y to Z are two cross-relationships.

The total of the direct-single, direct-group, and cross-relationships in Figure 3-2 comes to six.

    Under the formula provided by Graicunas, the number of relationships in a span of control increases at a tremendous rate. For instance, 12 subordinates under a superior yield over 20,000 relationships, and 20 subordinates result in over 10 *million* relationships. The implication that Graicunas was trying to show is obvious. Twenty thousand or ten million relationships would be an impossible burden for effective management. Armed with this type of logic, the classical theorists concluded, "No superior can supervise directly the work of more than five or, at the most, six subordinates whose work interlocks."[12]

Delegation of Routine Matters

The classical principle of delegation states that decisions should be made at as low an organization level as possible. Accordingly, top management should not be making decisions on routine matters that could be effectively handled by first-line supervision. Once again, this principle can be traced to ancient times. The passage from Exodus, cited earlier, also contains a directive for delegation. "And they judged the people at all seasons: the hard cases they brought unto Moses, but every small matter they judged themselves." This, of course, also hints of Frederick Taylor's exception principle, which stated that managers should control by giving attention to the exceptions. All classical theorists advocated delegation but recognized that it was not easily accomplished. Mooney and Reiley noted that "One of the tragedies of business experience is the frequency with which men, always efficient in anything they personally can do, will finally be crushed and fail under the weight of accumulated duties that they do not know and cannot learn how to delegate."[13]

    The major reason it takes courage to delegate is that delegation does not absolve one from responsibility. The fear of being ultimately responsible may prevent delegation. Fayol recognized the existence of this fear but condemned it. He stated,

    [12]Urwick, *The Elements of Administration*, op. cit., pp. 52–53.

    [13]James D. Mooney and Alan C. Reiley, *Onward Industry!*, Harper & Brothers, New York, 1931, p. 39.

. . . responsibility is feared as much as authority is sought after, and fear of responsibility paralyses much initiative and destroys many good qualities. A good leader should possess and infuse into those around him courage to accept responsibility.[14]

One way of solving the delegation-responsibilty question would be as Fayol suggested—with executive courage and leadership. Another approach would be to change the attitude of superiors regarding the capabilities of their subordinates. If one assumes that people are basically lazy, must be closely controlled, and do not want responsibility, i.e., McGregor's Theory X, it is only logical that the superior would be reluctant to delegate. On the other hand, if one believes that people react in the way they are treated, work better under self-control, and will actually thrive under the challenge of responsibility, i.e., McGregor's Theory Y, delegation becomes much easier. The classical theorists never really addressed themselves to this type of behavioral analysis. Nevertheless, from a behavioral standpoint, delegation is the most forward-thinking classical principle.

A Critique of the Classical Process Approach

The traditional process approach has been vehemently attacked by the other schools of management thought. The critics ask the legitimate question of what progress has been made since Fayol's perceptive analysis at the beginning of the century. To be sure, Fayol made a very significant, if not the most significant, contribution to an overall theory of management. However, since Fayol, the process theorists seem excessively concerned with semantical problems of what to call the functions, for example, directing or commanding, budgeting or planning, and reporting or controlling. Furthermore, the sacred principles have generally turned out to have neither empirical validity nor universal applicability.

Universal Truths?   Perhaps the most legitimate criticism of the classical process theorists was that they passed off their ideas as universal truths. Each "principle" has been empirically shown not to be applicable to *all* organizational situations. In fact, in some cases the principles even contradict one another. An example is span of control. Numerous surveys have revealed that highly successful organizations have spans that would cause classical theorists to shudder. Mason Haire, a behaviorally oriented theorist, calls Graicunas's analysis of social relationships "just plain silly." He explains that "Making the superior responsible in any direct sense for all the relationships between and among his subordinates seems to extend unduly the functions of the executive."[15]

---

[14]Fayol, op. cit., p. 22.

[15]Mason Haire, "Biological Models and Empirical Histories of the Growth of Organizations," in Mason Haire (ed.), *Modern Organization Theory: A Symposium of the Foundation for Research on Human Behavior,* John Wiley & Sons, Inc., New York, 1959, p. 295.

Herbert A. Simon, a well-known management theorist, was one of the early critics of the universal, classical principles. A major portion of his book *Administrative Behavior* was devoted to discounting the classical principles of specialization, hierarchy, and limited span of control.[16] He noted that unity of command is often inconsistent with specialization and cited the following cases:

> For example, if an accountant in a school department is subordinate to an educator, and if unity of command is observed, then the finance department cannot issue direct orders to him regarding the technical, accounting aspects of his work. Similarly, the director of motor vehicles in the public works department will be unable to issue direct orders on care of motor equipment to the fire truck driver.[17]

After a detailed analysis, Simon concluded that the classical principles "cannot be more than proverbs."[18] In more recent years the situational or contingency approach to management has evolved to directly counter the universal principles approach. The last section of this chapter spells out what is involved in this new contingency approach.

Lack of Behavioral Sensitivity In addition to the criticism aimed at universality, fault is also found with the classicists' lack of behavioral sensitivity. The classical theorists are accused of making too simple and mechanistic assumptions. Dale summarizes classical assumptions concerning what top management must do to be successful. It need only:

  1 Know what it wants done;
  2 Arrange a structure in which the various tasks are exactly dovetailed;
  3 Provide for coordination through common superiors or some other formal arrangement;
  4 Issue the necessary orders down through the chain of command; and
  5 See that each person is held accountable for his part of the work.[19]

The classicists assumed that if these conditions were met, there would be a smooth-running organization. Any minor obstacles could be overcome by management leadership. In reality, of course, things are not quite this simple. One major reason is the extreme complexity of the human being. For instance, there are motivation and behavior problems that may be compounded, instead of solved, by the classical principles. For example, one of the best-known behavioral theorists, Chris Argyris, notes that "the formal organizational principles make demands of relatively healthy individuals that are incongruent

---

[16]Herbert A. Simon, *Administrative Behavior*, 2d ed., The Macmillan Company, New York, 1957, pp. 20–36.

[17]Ibid., p. 24. Also see Herbert A. Simon, "Decision Making and Administrative Organization," *Public Administration Review*, Winter 1944, pp. 16–30.

[18]Ibid., p. 44.

[19]Ernest Dale, *Management: Theory and Practice*, 3d ed., McGraw-Hill Book Company, New York, 1973, p. 176.

with their needs. Frustration, conflict, failure, and short time perspective are predicted as resultants of this basic incongruency."[20]

Defense of the Classical Principles   Defenders of the classical principles accuse their critics of not fully understanding their content or intent. For example, Koontz claims that the Argyris analysis is a classic case of misunderstanding and misapplication. He states, "Argyris has simply proved that wrong principles badly applied will lead to frustration; and every management practitioner knows this to be true!"[21] There is no doubt that those who argue against the classical theories carefully select the principles they use to demonstrate their points. This is especially true of unity of command and limited span of control. Equal authority and responsibility and delegation are often conveniently overlooked when condemning classical ideas.

The classical process approach is still widely used and staunchly defended by practitioners and academicians. For example, in a survey conducted by the American Management Association, medium- and large-sized companies were asked what management concepts were particularly useful to them. A great majority responded with one or more of the classical principles. Almost half the large companies stated that they had found the principle of equal authority and responsibility of value, and more than two-thirds mentioned one or more of the classical principles.[22] Harold Koontz, among others, has defended these principles. In his noted article "The Management Theory Jungle" he wrote:

> Those who feel that they gain caste or a clean slate for advancing a particular notion or approach often delight in casting away anything which smacks of management principles. Some have referred to them as platitudes, forgetting that a platitude is still a truism and a truth does not become worthless because it is familiar.[23]

Some of the defense of the classical approach seems completely justified. However, part of the problem is delineating what is to be included as classical and what is not. A blanket criticism of all classical principles merely because they are old and familiar is neither logical nor desirable. On the other hand, the defenders must face up to the question of whether the classical principles are still relevant and applicable to organizations in the 1970s and beyond. One necessary modification is to make the management process dynamic. The following section presents such a dynamic approach.

A Dynamic Process

To argue over the naming or the number of functions and to search for universal principles is certainly of limited value in a field like management.

---

[20]Chris Argyris, *Personality and Organization,* Harper & Brothers, New York, 1957, p. 74.
[21]Harold Koontz, "The Management Theory Jungle," *Academy of Management Journal,* December 1961, p. 185.
[22]Ernest Dale, *Organization,* American Management Association, New York, 1967, p. 41.
[23]Koontz, op. cit., p. 184.

However, the management process, whatever the exact names of the functions or the nature of the principles, can serve a useful purpose in management theory if the static classical approach is made dynamic. The basic purpose of any theory is to better understand the given phenomenon or concept. Truly to understand management, dynamism must replace the static nature of the traditional process approach. One step toward making the process framework more dynamic is to incorporate feedforward and feedback communication. Henry Albers suggests such a dynamic process, which consists of decision making, communication, and control.[24] Figure 3-3 summarizes this approach.

A manager occupying a position involving a superior-subordinate relationship makes various kinds of decisions. Planning, organizing, and coordination are some general examples. If the process stopped at this stage, it would be only a static approach. It would not differ from the earlier process approach except for its combining of the functions under the general classification of decision making. To make the static model dynamic, there must be a systems integration of feedforward and feedback communication. Once managers make planning decisions or other kinds of decisions, they must communicate them forward to subordinates. Types of feedforward communication range from the lifting of an eyebrow to a sophisticated, computerized information system monitoring inputs. After receiving the communication, the subordinate performs. To complete the dynamic process, feedback communication about subordinate performance must be obtained by the manager. Types of feedback vary from simple observation to the profit and loss statement. Using feedback communication, the manager makes a control decision. If feedback indicates that planning or organizing decisions are not being carried out in actual

[24]Albers, op. cit., pp. 43–45.

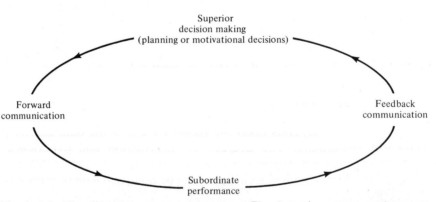

Figure 3-3   The dynamic management process. The dynamic management process begins with planning decisions setting forth previously nonexistent behavioral norms. These norms are then communicated to subordinate personnel. Performance information is relayed back to the superior, who may make motivational or control decisions if behavior is not in accord with the norms of the planning decisions. *(Source: Henry H. Albers,* Principles of Management, *3d ed., John Wiley & Sons, Inc., New York, 1969, p. 90. Used with permission.)*

practice, the decision to alter the original plan or organization may be made. Another decision may be to motivate or reinforce subordinates by involving them through more participation in the decision-making process or providing them feedback about individual performance. Such control decisions are then communicated forward, and the entire process continually repeats itself. Normally, the dynamic process occurs in the sequence described. However, Albers carefully points out that there are exceptions. For example, "Decisions involving motivation are often made without regard to particular plans. Some plans are not activated by the communication function because they may not now be pertinent."[25]

The dynamic process approach described above seems to lead to effective understanding of what management is all about. Presenting the processes of decision making, communication, and control in a dynamic systems framework provides insights into the quantitative, the behavioral, and, most directly, the systems approaches to management. Such a dynamic process can also be incorporated into the contingency approach.

THE QUANTITATIVE APPROACH

The quantitative approach is often referred to as *management science.* It focuses primarily on management from the perspective of mathematical models and quantitative processes. Frederick Taylor's scientific management was a forerunner, but mathematical techniques and operations research (OR) best represent the modern quantitative approach.

Mathematical Techniques

It is probably true that the single most important contribution to the practice of management in the last several years has come from mathematics. Most of the math techniques take the form of models, which fall more appropriately under the heading of operations research, which is covered in the next section. This section is more directly concerned with general mathematical techniques.

Applied rather than pure mathematics is most relevant to management decision making. Statistical probability can be particularly effective when applied to the risk type of decision. Many managers have only a limited amount of empirical information or experience with which to make a choice. The exact amount of information depends upon the thoroughness of the data gathering and real-world constraints. The degrees of information and experiences available to managers can be represented by the certainty, risk, and uncertainty types of decisions. Mathematical techniques can be analyzed with reference to these three categories.

Certainty Under certainty, decisions are very simple because for each alternative there is a certain outcome. Although certainty decisions are fairly

[25]Ibid., p. 44.

common for lower-level managers, mathematics does not help much in making them. The traditional techniques of habit, standard operating procedures, and classical structure are just as effective. In some certainty decisions where there are numerous alternatives to choose from, however, calculus and certain mathematical programming techniques can be of assistance.

Risk   Under risk, decisions are more difficult to make than certainty decisions. There is only limited information and experience, and there are many possible outcomes for each alternative. Most important management decisions at middle and upper levels are risk decisions. The traditional methods break down when applied to these decisions. It is with risk decisions that the mathematical technique of probability makes its biggest contribution.

Two types of probability can be applied to risk decisions, objective statistical probability and subjective probability. Objective statistical probability is a precise mathematical technique that permits the decision maker to calculate possible outcomes and make inferences. The probability calculation is based upon past experience. Tossing a coin provides a simple example of the method and has implications for statistical probability.

> A person tosses an unbiased, balanced coin 100 times. The outcome of the 100 tosses is 50 heads and 50 tails. With this experience, the decision maker will assign a probability of .5 that, on the 101st toss, the coin will show a head (or a tail).

The coin-tossing example represents an ideal situation for the manager. Unfortunately, most management decision makers in a modern organization do not have so much or such relevant experience as does the coin tosser. Furthermore, the coin tosser can be pretty sure that half the time the 101st toss will be heads. Yet, if he gets several tails in a row, it will take little time and effort on his part to toss the coin 100 more times and to end up with 50 heads. In other words, it may take a great number of outcomes in order for the probability to work itself out. Typically, management decision makers must place all their eggs in one basket, the next outcome. They do not have the time or resources to let the probability work itself out. In short, objective statistical probability has certain realistic constraints which cannot and should not be overlooked. Yet, despite the limitations, statistical probability, when properly applied and interpreted, has proved to be a very effective tool in helping managers make risk decisions.

Besides utilizing the calculation of objective statistical probability, many decision makers rely on subjective probability assignment. This represents more of an educated guess than a mathematical computation as to what the outcome of a decision will be. Basing their judgment on some type of experience, managers will formally or informally guess what the probable outcome of choosing a given alternative will be. Obviously, relying too heavily on subjective probability assignments can become very risky. Many social factors can also enter into subjective probability. Nevertheless, subjective probability is more effective than reliance on chance alone.

Uncertainty Uncertainty decisions are the most complex type of decision. No meaningful experience or probability of outcomes can be assigned for extreme cases of uncertainty. It follows that mathematical techniques are useless in true cases of uncertainty. However, when decisions lie between risk and uncertainty, certain mathematical techniques can be applied. Two of the more common are minimax analysis and Bayes' procedure. Under minimax, the decision maker attempts to calculate the worst outcome that can possibly occur for each alternative. In Bayes' procedure the decision maker utilizes the concept of expected value and assumes that each possible outcome has an equal chance of occurring. These techniques show some potential promise, but by and large, mathematics is most useful when applied to risk, not certainty or uncertainty, decisions.

Operations Research Techniques

Operations research (OR) has become almost synonymous with the quantitative approach to management, but it is practically as broad in scope as mathematics. Frederick Taylor's scientific management was the forerunner of OR, but its recognized beginning was during World War II. OR differs from scientific management by taking a broader perspective and by making more extensive use of mathematically based models. Iconic (scaled reproductions) or analogue (one set of properties to represent another set) models can be used, but generally OR models are symbolic or mathematical in nature.

Applications of OR Specific applications of OR include inventory, resource allocation, and waiting-line problems. In the certainty type of inventory situations, Economic Order Quantity (EOQ) models are very precise and lead to optimum results. On the other hand, where the inventory variables are less certain (risk and uncertainty), only a satisficing, rather than a maximizing, solution can be obtained through operations research.

Resource-allocation problems are especially adaptable to the more sophisticated mathematical models. Every organization operates with limited resources. The management problem is one of allocating the given resources properly so as to attain the desired objectives. Linear programming is widely used for this purpose. It utilizes simultaneous algebraic equations to represent allocation variables. Some of the more common variables include machine capacities, storage space, and transportation routes. Solutions to the equations give the optimum allocations according to the algebraic statement of the payoff criterion. The effectiveness of linear programming depends on the degree to which the decisional problem is linear. Recently, effective nonlinear models have also been developed.

Queuing models are used to help solve waiting-line problems. A service type of operation that faces an irregular demand will produce situations where there are lax periods and periods when there is overcrowding and waiting in line. Examples include maintenance on machinery, trucks at a loading dock, customers at a supermarket, students at registration, and patients in a hospital emergency room. Waiting time is costly to the organization. Costs are incurred from the time wasted by those standing in line and by personnel who have nothing to do during slack periods. Queuing models which incorporate mathematical techniques allocate time, personnel, and equipment. The model will also determine priorities and assign probabilities to minimize the costs of waiting. The more complex waiting problems have turned to simulation techniques for more satisfactory results.

Other OR Models Other specific OR models include game models, decision-tree diagrams, and PERT, an acronym for Program Evaluation Review Technique. Game models are used to work out competitive strategies. Originally developed by mathematicians and economists, game theory tries to account for the strategy of others. For example, if one organization raises its price, how will its competitors react? Game models have also been effectively adapted to management training.

The decision tree is a graphic representation of a decision. The alternatives of the decision may be thought of as the branches of a tree. Each branch is traced out to show how the various outcomes are achieved. This technique forces the decision maker to attempt to determine the outcome of each course of action.

PERT is used primarily as a planning and control technique. Similar techniques are CPM (Critical Path Method), MCP (Milestone Control Procedure), and PEP (Program Evaluation Procedure). PERT is a type of flow diagram or network which reflects events and activities used in management planning, scheduling, controlling, and evaluating progress on a program. Since PERT's inception at the U. S. Navy's Special Projects Office in 1958, it has been applied to a wide variety of management problems. For example, PERT has been utilized for atomic, military, and space projects, inventory, advertising, recruiting, maintenance, construction, publishing, and even matrimony.

Quantitative Approach in Perspective

Operations research and the quantitative approach as a whole should not be thought of as a panacea for all the problems of management. As Henry H. Albers cautions: "Operations research like other innovations in human history, has had its share of zealots proclaiming the dawn of a new management order. Executives should be wary of attempts to make operations research sound as though miracles were somehow possible through the magic of higher mathematics."[26] But despite the potential oversell of the quantitative approach, there is little question that it has made a substantial contribution to more effective certainty and risk types of decisions, especially in the areas of planning and control. The quantitative approach does provide more and better alternatives for management decision making. When constructing a model of the decisional problem under consideration, management is forced to make a logical analysis

[26]Ibid., p. 388.

which stresses goals and measures of effectiveness. However, it must be remembered that these techniques only aid the decision maker. The quantitative approach is not the whole of management but, instead, provides very effective techniques for certain management problems.

THE SYSTEMS APPROACH

The systems approach to management, currently very popular, often gives the impression of being extremely new and different. The truth is that systems theory is not new at all. A systems viewpoint has been developed and used in the natural and physical sciences for years.[27] Moreover, systems concepts were indirectly utilized, to varying degrees, by management pioneers such as Frederick W. Taylor. His analysis of human-machine interactions is one example. Operations research and information theory, initiated in the late 1940s, also incorporated a systems viewpoint. However, the emphasis given today to the direct study, analysis, and operation of management as a system is relatively new.[28]

In 1956, Kenneth Boulding wrote a now famous article titled "General Systems Theory: The Skeleton of Science."[29] It described the general nature and purpose of and needs for a systems approach to all scientific phenomena. Boulding felt there was a need for a systematic, theoretical framework which would describe general relationships of the empirical world. He carefully pointed out that the purpose of "General Systems Theory" (GST) is not "to establish a single, self-contained 'general theory of practically everything' which will replace all the special theories of particular disciplines."[30] Rather, the goal is to reach a happy medium between the "specific that has no meaning and the general that has no content . . . It is the contention of the General Systems Theorists that this optimum degree of generality in theory is not always reached by the particular sciences."[31] This viewpoint has been adopted by the systems approach to management.

Levels of Systems

Under a GST approach there are recognized levels of systems complexity. Boulding classified nine such levels:[32]

[27]A classic article specifically using the term *systems theory* appeared over two decades ago in Ludwig von Bertalanffy, "General Systems Theory: A New Approach to the Unity of Science," *Human Biology,* December 1951, pp. 302–312. The paper was originally presented at the 47th Annual Meeting of the American Philosophical Association, Eastern Division, Dec. 29, 1950.

[28]Albers, op. cit., 1st ed., 1961, presented the management process from a systems viewpoint, but the 1963 book by Richard A. Johnson, Fremont E. Kast, and James E. Rosenzweig, *The Theory and Management of Systems,* McGraw-Hill Book Company, New York, is probably the most widely known approach which specifically analyzed management from a systems viewpoint.

[29]Kenneth Boulding, "General Systems Theory: The Skeleton of Science," *Management Science,* April 1956, pp. 197–208.

[30]Ibid., p. 197.

[31]Ibid.

[32]Ibid., pp. 202–205.

1   The most basic level is the static structure. It could be termed the level of *frameworks*. An example would be the anatomy of the universe.

2   The second level is the simple dynamic system. It incorporates necessary predetermined motions. This could be termed the level of *clockworks*.

3   The next level would be a cybernetic system characterized by automatic feedback control mechanisms. This could be thought of as the level of the *thermostat*.

4   The fourth level is called the "open system." It is a self-maintaining structure and is the level where life begins to differentiate from nonlife. This is the level of the *cell*.

5   The fifth level can be termed the genetic-societal level. It is typified by the *plant* and preoccupies the empirical world of the botanist.

6   The next is the *animal* system level which is characterized by increased mobility, teleological behavior, and self-awareness.

7   The seventh level is the *human* level. The major difference between the human level and the animal level is a person's possession of self-consciousness.

8   The next level is that of *social organizations.* The important unit in social organization is not the human per se but rather the organizational role that the person assumes.

9   The nineth and last level is reserved for *transcendental systems.* This allows for ultimates, absolutes and the inescapable unknowables.

At present, varying degrees of knowledge exist at each of these levels. Each level is more developed than the one preceding it. For example, much knowledge exists at the static level; most disciplines have very good descriptive static models. However, even this first level is not completely developed (e.g., the theory of cataloging and indexing is still not complete). In each succeeding level in the hierarchy, there is more and more incompleteness. In fact, beyond the second level, comprehensive theoretical models are very rare. At the very complex human and social organization levels, Boulding felt twenty years ago that there are not even the rudiments of meaningful theoretical systems. Desirably this is changing with the development of the modern theories of management.

Application of Systems Analysis

As a fundamental principle, the systems approach is quite basic. It simply means that everything is interrelated and interdependent. A system is composed of elements that are related and dependent upon one another but that, when in interaction, form a unitary whole. Thus, by definition, almost any phenomenon can be analyzed or presented from a systems viewpoint. Biological, physical, economic, and cultural-social systems are examples.

As an approach to management, "systems" encompasses both general and specialized systems and closed and open analysis. A general systems approach to management can be concerned with formal organization and technical, sociopsychological, and philosophical concepts. Specific management systems analysis includes areas such as organization structure, job design, accounting, computerized information, and planning and control mechanisms. Actual occupational positions called systems analysts are in great demand by all types of up-to-date organizations.

In theorizing, observing, and analyzing, either a closed- or open-systems approach can be taken. A closed-systems perspective is closed-loop. No external input is recognized. Such a closed-systems approach is relatively easy to accomplish with the proper assumptions and a common-sense philosophy. Katz and Kahn write that the use of this approach requires two major assumptions, namely:

> . . . that the location and nature of an organization are given by its name; and that an organization is possessed of built-in goals—because such goals were implanted by its founders, decreed by its present leaders, or because they emerged mysteriously as the purposes of the organization system itself.[33]

The second approach is to apply an open-systems concept in the development of an original theory and design and then to implement it in practice. Katz and Kahn depict the organization as an energetic input-output system which is flagrantly open in its interaction with the environment. The common characteristics of all open systems are the following:[34]

1 The *input of energy* from the environment.
2 The *through-put* or transformation of the imported energy into some product form.
3 The *exporting of the product* back into the environment.
4 A *re-energizing of the system* from sources in the environment.
5 *Negative entropy*, which helps the system survive by importing more energy from the environment than is expended.
6 The *feedback* of information which helps the system maintain a steady state or homeostasis.
7 The tendency for *differentiation* and elaboration because of sub-system dynamics and the relationship between growth and survival.
8 The existence of *equifinality* whereby the system can reach the same final state from different initial conditions and by different paths of development.

In modern management analysis, both closed- and open-systems approaches are taken. However, the classical theorists recognized only a closed-systems viewpoint; they did not design and implement from an open-systems standpoint. Only the closed-systems aspects of existing organizations were sometimes emphasized by the classical theories. This closed-systems approach concentrated on internal relationships and consistency, which were represented by principles such as unity of command, span of control, and equal authority and responsibility. The closed-systems approach ignores effects of the environment. The more recent open-systems approach recognizes the input of the

---

[33]Daniel Katz and Robert L. Kahn, *The Social Psychology of Organizations,* John Wiley & Sons, Inc., New York, 1966, p. 14.
    [34]Ibid., pp. 19–29.

environment but does not functionally relate it to management concepts and techniques that lead to goal attainment. The contingency approach to management attempts to do the latter and takes up where the open-systems approach leaves off.

THE CONTINGENCY APPROACH

Theorists of the process, quantitative, behavioral, and systems approaches to management have not integrated the environment and often assume that their concepts and techniques have universal applicability. For example, the process theorist often assumes that strategic planning applies to all situations; the quantitative expert generally feels that linear programming can be used under all conditions; the behavioral theorist usually advocates participative goal setting for all superior-subordinate pairs; and the systems advocate tends to emphasize the need for computerized information flows in all situations. On the other hand, practicing managers are finding out that a particular concept or technique from the various approaches just does not work effectively in their situation. The theorists accuse practitioners of not applying the concept or technique properly and the practitioners accuse the theorists of being unrealistic. The contingency approach does incorporate the environment and attempts to bridge this existing theory-practice gap.[35]

The "If-Then" Management Contingency

A contingent relationship can be simply thought of as an "if-then" functional relationship. The "if" is the independent variable and the "then" is the dependent variable. In contingency management the environment serves as an independent variable. For example, *if* prevailing social values are oriented toward nonmaterialistic, free expression and the organization employs professional personnel in a high technology operation, *then* a participative, open leadership style would be most effective for goal attainment. On the other hand, *if* prevailing social values are oriented toward materialism and obedience to authority and the organization employs unskilled personnel working on routine tasks, *then* a strict, authoritarian leadership style would be most effective for goal attainment. In order for such contingency relationships to be part of contingency management and serve as effective guidelines for practitioners, they must be empirically validated. In addition, although the environment variables are usually independent and the management concepts and techniques are usually dependent, the reverse can also occur. In some cases management variables are independent and the environment variables are dependent. For example, *if* a very participative, open leadership style is instituted by top management, *then* personnel will respond by exhibiting

[35]See Fred Luthans, *Introduction to Management: A Contingency Approach,* McGraw-Hill Book Company, 1976. This book, especially Chap. 2, contains an expanded discussion of all aspects of contingency management.

self-control and responsible social values. Although it is recognized that it is possible for management concepts and techniques to affect the environment in the systems interaction sense, contingency management generally treats the environment as independent (the "if's") and the management concepts and techniques as dependent (the "then's").

An Overall Conceptual Framework for Contingency Management

There are three major parts to the overall conceptual framework for contingency management: the environment, management concepts and techniques, and the contingent relationship between them. Figure 3-4 depicts a general framework for contingency management. It is very broad and abstract because at this point contingency management can provide only a conceptual framework for theory and practice. The independent "if's" are along the horizontal axis of the matrix and the dependent "then's" are along the vertical axis. The future goal of contingency management is to fill in as many cells of the matrix as possible. For example, in the bottom left-hand cell of the matrix a relevant environmen-

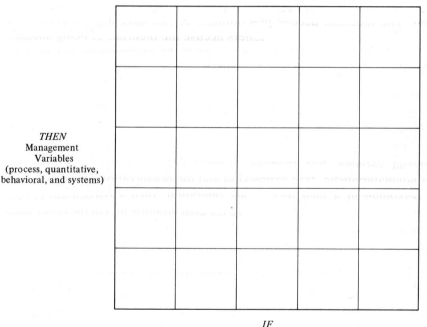

THEN
Management
Variables
(process, quantitative,
behavioral, and systems)

IF
Environment
Variables
(external—social, technical, economic, political/legal)
(internal—structure, processes, technology)

Figure 3-4 A conceptual framework for contingency management. *(Source: Fred Luthans, Introduction to Management: A Contingency Approach, McGraw-Hill Book Company, New York, 1976, p. 48. Used with permission.)*

tal condition would be identified (one or a combination of the "if's") and then be contingently related to an appropriate management variable (one or more of the "then's") for the most effective goal attainment possible.

A contingency approach seems to hold a great deal of promise for the future development of management theory and practice. The other approaches to management can all be incorporated into the contingency framework. In the past the unrealistic assumption of universality was often made by the other approaches, and the environment did not play an integral role. This is as true of the behavioral approach as it is of the other approaches to management. The next chapter is specifically devoted to the relevant environment, and in Part Five of the book, on applications, especially, a contingency perspective is taken.

SUMMARY

The process approach initiated the search for a theoretical base for management. The classical process approach identified certain functions of management and universal principles such as unity of command, equal authority and responsibility, limited span of control, and delegation of routine matters. The breakdown of the universality assumption and a lack of behavioral sensitivity have led to much criticism of the classical approach. A more dynamic approach incorporating decision making, feedforward and feedback communication, and control leads to better understanding of the management process. The quantitative approach uses mathematical and operations research techniques to solve decisional problems. This approach forces logical analysis and generates decision alternatives but is not the whole of management. Systems is the most recent established approach to management and can be viewed from a general systems theory standpoint or systems analysis. A systems approach stresses the interrelatedness and interdependency of the parts to the whole. The open-systems perspective recognizes the input of the external environment and serves as a point of departure for contingency management. The contingency approach has emerged out of the dissatisfaction with the universality assumption and the need to incorporate the environment into management theory and practice. The contingency approach uses "if-then" functional relationships where the independent "if's" represent environmental variables and the "then's" consist of management concepts and techniques that lead to goal attainment. The empirical validation of such contingency relationships can serve as a unifying force in the development of management knowledge and supply guidelines for the more effective practice of management.

QUESTIONS FOR DISCUSSION AND REVIEW

1   Which theoretical approach to management do you believe is the best? Defend your choice.
2   Is the classical process approach and the accompanying principles of any value to management today? Why or why not?

3 Explain the systems approach in your own words.

4 What is contingency management? How can it contribute to the theory and practice of management?

CASE: KNOW IT FOR THE TEST, BUT DO IT THE OLD WAY

Henry James, the manager of a large supermarket, was taking a management course in the evening program at the local college. The professor had given an interesting but disturbing lecture the previous night on the various approaches to management. Henry had always thought that management involved just planning, organizing, and controlling. Now this professor was saying that management could also be thought of as quantitative models, systems theory and analysis, and even something called *contingency relationships.* Henry had always considered himself a good manager, and his record with the supermarket chain had proved it. He thought to himself, "I have never used operations research models, thought of my store as an open system, or developed or utilized any contingency relationships. By doing a little planning ahead, organizing the store, and making sure things got done, I have been a successful manager. That other stuff just does not make sense. All that professor was trying to do was complicate things. I guess I'll have to know it for the test, but I'm sticking with my old plan-organize-and-control approach to managing my store."

1 Critically analyze Henry's reasoning.

2 If you were the professor and you knew what was going through Henry's mind, what would you say to Henry?

3 Explain, if possible, how each of the approaches discussed in the chapter could apply to the management of a supermarket.

SELECTED REFERENCES

Barnard, Chester I.: *The Functions of the Executive,* Harvard University Press, Cambridge, Mass., 1962. Original copyright 1938 by the President and Fellows of Harvard College.

Burack, Elmer H., Robert Bom, and D. Batlivala: "Operations Research: Recent Changes and Future Expectations in Business Organizations," *Business Perspectives,* Fall 1972, pp. 15–22.

Carlisle, Howard M.: *Situational Management,* AMACOM, American Management Association, New York, 1973.

Greenwood, Royston, C. R. Hinings, and Stewart Ranson: "Contingency Theory and the Organization of Local Authorities; Part I: Differentiation and Integration," *Public Administration,* Spring 1975, pp. 1–23.

Kast, Fremont E., and James E. Rosenzweig (eds.): *Contingency Views of Organization and Management,* Science Research, Chicago, 1973.

Kast, Fremont E., and James E. Rosenzweig: "General Systems Theory: Applications for Organization and Management," *Academy of Management Journal,* December 1972, pp. 447–465.

Koontz, Harold (ed.): *Toward a Unified Theory of Management,* McGraw-Hill Book Company, New York, 1964.

Levin, Richard I., and Charles A. Kirkpatrick: *Quantitative Approaches to Management,* McGraw-Hill, New York, 1971.

Lilienfeld, Robert: "Systems Theory as an Ideology," *Social Research,* Winter 1975, pp. 637–660.

Luthans, Fred: "Contingency Theory of Management: A Path Out of the Jungle," *Business Horizons,* June 1973, pp. 67–72.

Luthans, Fred: *Introduction to Management: A Contingency Approach,* McGraw-Hill Book Company, New York, 1976.

McGuire, Joseph W. (ed.): *Contemporary Management Issues and Viewpoints,* Prentice-Hall, Englewood Cliffs, N. J., 1974.

Miles, Raymond E.: *Theories of Management,* McGraw-Hill Book Company, 1975.

Mockler, Robert J.: "Situational Theory of Management," *Harvard Business Review,* May-June 1971, pp. 146–151, 154–155.

Van Gigch, John P.: *Applied General Systems Theory,* Harper & Row, Publishers, Incorporated, New York, 1974.

Whitsett, David A.: "Making Sense of Management Theories," *Personnel,* May–June 1975, pp. 44–52.

Wortman, Max, and Fred Luthans: *Emerging Concepts in Management,* 2d ed., Macmillan Company, New York, 1975.

Chapter 4

The Relevant Environment

The discussion of contingency management in the last chapter pointed out the important role that the environment plays in modern management. Although this is true in all the approaches, the environmental impact on the behavioral approach is especially dramatic. To give detailed discussion of all the environmental variables that impact on human behavior in organizations would be an impossible task. Therefore, this chapter is limited to a general discussion of three very important environmental impacts on behavior in general and organizational behavior in particular. The physical, sociocultural, and, mainly, technological enivronments are given attention. This chapter completes the necessary introductory foundation (historical, behavioral science, managerial, and environmental) for the development of an overall conceptual framework for organizational behavior.

THE PHYSICAL ENVIRONMENT

Climate, terrain, resources, and population density are some of the variables in the physical environment which affect human behavior and even, in some cases, physical makeup.[1] Examples of environmental impact on physical

---

[1] James C. Coleman, *Psychology and Effective Behavior,* Scott, Foresman and Company, Glenview, Ill., 1969, pp. 50–52.

makeup include the Eskimo, whose circulatory system is contained within a fatty layer of tissue to conserve body heat, and the Bolivian Indian, who works at very high altitudes and has relatively more red corpuscles and a greater lung capacity than people living closer to sea level.[2]

There is some evidence that behavior may be affected by climate and terrain. An example is David McClelland's finding that the average level of achievement motivation is highest in societies that live in temperatures with a mean between 40 and 60°F. Although this type of research is very interesting and seems to have a great deal of potential, much more needs to be done before any meaningful generalizations can be drawn. Nevertheless, a safe conclusion probably is that weather and terrain, at least when extreme, have a definite but not precisely known effect on human behavior.

The Impact of Limited Resources

Resources, both natural and human-made, can have an effect on behavior. Food, water, housing, and medical care obviously influence a person's well-being. These resources, along with many others, are needed to sustain physical activity and life itself. Although it is not quite so obvious, resources also have an enormous impact on a person's behavior.

Frustrated behavior is directly related to the deprivation of resources. People may exhibit aggressive or withdrawn behavior if they are denied food, water, or housing. A better understanding of the behavior patterns of people in underdeveloped countries and in the American poverty pockets is desperately needed but, as yet, these are practically unexplored. An example is the housing resource. It certainly seems to make a difference in human behavior whether a person lives in a mud hut, a single-room shack, a large tenement, a split-level suburban house, or a palatial mansion. Not only the structural aspects of the dwelling are important, but also the number of people living within it. Dewey and Humber note that "nearly thirty-five million American households hold an average of .75 persons per room. Interpersonal relationships under these conditions can be very different from those surrounding the approximately two million households wherein there are 1–5 persons per room."[3] One implication that this housing analysis uncovers is perhaps the most profound physical environmental factor facing modern society—population density.

The Population Explosion

The world population has been growing at an alarming rate. In 6000 B.C. the total population was about 5 million people. It took almost 8,000 years for the population to reach 500 million about A.D. 1650. After that, only 200 years were required for the population to double to a billion people in 1850. Today, there

[2]See Marshall T. Newman, "Biological Adaptation of Man to His Environment: Heat, Cold, Altitude, and Nutrition," *Annals of the New York Academy of Sciences,* vol. 91, art. 3, 1961, pp. 617–633.

[3]Richard Dewey and W. J. Humber, *An Introduction to Social Psychology,* The Macmillan Company, New York, 1966, p. 92.

are about 3.5 billion people and the doubling time is down to approximately thirty-five years. Paul Ehrlich has made a very dramatic prediction of what may happen if this growth rate continues:

> If growth continued at that rate for about 900 years, there would be some 60,000,000,000,000,000 people on the face of the earth. Sixty-million-billion people. This is about 100 persons for each square yard of the Earth's surface, land and sea.[4]

The impact of a tremendously dense population on biological ecosystems (the relationship of plants and animals with their environment) has become one of the most important current issues. Humans are dependent upon their biological ecosystems for their survival. If these ecosystems are poisoned or destroyed by the "population bomb," people will be deprived of food, water, and oxygen, and they will die. Biological ecologists, such as Ehrlich and Barry Commoner, have led the popular cause to save people's physical environment from themselves.

Human Ecology   Not so popular nor so well researched as biological ecology is the area of *human ecology*. Although the term is commonly used interchangeably with *biological ecology,* human ecology is more concerned with constellations of persons and institutions.[5] R. D. McKenzie, one of the pioneers in human ecology, stated that its goal is "to discover the principles and factors involved in the changing patterns of spatial arrangement of population and institutions resulting from the interplay of living beings in a continuously changing culture."[6] Today, the most important issue facing human ecology is the impact of dense population on the psychological aspects of humans. As Megginson and Chung have pointed out, people must not only adapt to their physical environment; they "must also adjust to the psychological, philosophical, and spiritual environments as well."[7]

Effects of Overpopulation   Today's ecologists, human and biological, have not yet provided much insight into the psychological effects of overpopulation. Ehrlich has implied that deteriorating biological ecosystems will lead to a deprived "psychic environment." He cites an unpublished manuscript by three biologists whose thesis is that the human genetic heritage has been shaped by evolutions to require "natural surroundings for optimum mental health."[8] Population density is certainly a factor. In an interview Ehrlich indicated that he was attempting to research the effects of crowding on human beings, but

[4]Paul R. Ehrlich, *The Population Bomb*, Ballantine Books, Inc., New York, 1968, p. 18.
[5]Robert E. Park, *Human Communities*, The Free Press, Glencoe, Ill., 1952, p. 14.
[6]R. D. McKenzie, "Human Ecology," *Encyclopaedia of the Social Sciences,* vol. 5, The Macmillan Company, New York, 1931, p. 314.
[7]Leon C. Megginson and Kae H. Chung, "Human Ecology in the Twenty-first Century," *Personnel Administration*, May–June 1970, p. 47.
[8]Ehrlich, op. cit., p. 64.

confessed that it is a very complex and difficult area in which to determine cause and effect. He summarized his work so far as follows:

> There are indications that crowding increases aggression, etc., but there is no way to correlate population density with events and conditions in various areas of the country and to be certain that crowding is the critical factor. In addition to too many people, crowded areas also have a different racial composition, educational level, and so on, from noncrowded areas.[9]

Basic research on the psychological effects of crowding is very sparse. In a study that allowed a population of white rats to expand within a confined space, it was found that a high degree of behavior pathology developed in both males and females. The researcher, John B. Calhoun, highlighted his findings in these words:

> The consequences of the behavioral pathology we observed were most apparent among the females . . . [They] fell short in their maternal functions. Among the males the behavior disturbances ranged from sexual deviation to cannibalism and from frenetic overactivity to a pathological withdrawal . . . The social organization of the animals showed equal disruption.[10]

This pathological behavior occurred although the rats were given plenty of food and nesting materials. In other words, even though the biological ecosystems were compatible with the rats' needs (adequate food and housing), the mere presence of too many other rats had a deteriorating effect on the individual rat's psychological makeup.

Obviously, humans cannot be submitted to the kind of highly controlled experimentation conducted by Calhoun. In fact, at least one psychologist believes that the animal research on population should not be generalized to human beings. Basing his thinking on the few studies of the effects of population density on human behavior, plus some work on his own done in collaboration with ecologist Paul Ehrlich, Jonathan Freedman has guessed (and emphasized that it was only a guess at that point) that

> Density per se is not particularly detrimental to human beings . . . overpopulation should be worried about primarily in terms of its effect on the environment and the difficulties it causes in terms of supplying needs, rather than in terms of its psychological effects on human beings.[11]

Freedman's interpretations and research findings represent the exception, however. Most behavioral scientists would agree that unless the population

---

[9]Paul R. Ehrlich, "Playboy Interview," *Playboy,* August 1970, p. 58.

[10]John B. Calhoun, "Population Density and Social Pathology," *Scientific American,* February 1962, p. 139.

[11]Jonathan L. Freedman, "A Positive View of Population Density," *Psychology Today,* September 1971, p. 86.

rate decreases or at least stabilizes, the most serious problems for the near future will be psychological as well as biological in nature. The shortages of food and energy will definitely affect the physical well-being *and* the behavior of people in the future.

THE SOCIOCULTURAL ENVIRONMENT

Chapter 2 discussed the nature and significance of culture and depicted humans as being suspended in a "sea of culture" which completely surrounds them. As Margaret Mead has succinctly stated:

> . . . the functioning of every part of the human body is moulded by the culture within which the individual has been reared—not only in terms of diet, sunlight, exposure to contagious and infectious diseases, overstrain, occupational disease, hazards, catastrophes, and traumatic experiences, but also by the way he, born into society with a definite culture, has been fed and disciplined, fondled and put to sleep, punished and rewarded . . . [12]

In short, the culture prescribes and teaches what an individual learns and accepts. All language, customs, habits, values, and attitudes are culturally derived. In some ways, the culture overwhelms the individual. This is explained by Dewey and Humber as follows:

> The happenstance of birth, the inadvertent consequences of one's unique experience, and the attending circumstances over which the individual may have little or no control, often operate to assign a person to a particular group or status . . . [and are maintained] by personal preference, society's rules and laws, tradition's "heavy hand," and an array of cultural influences.[13]

In any event, the importance of understanding the role that the sociocultural environment plays in behavior can never be underestimated.

Every society depends on its culture to instill normative behavior into the populace so that it can be maintained and survive. Parents and siblings (brothers and sisters) are the most important distributors of culture. This is so because they play such dominant roles in the critical early-developmental years. Later, as a child enters adolescence, the peer-group influence becomes more significant. Finally, as a person matures into an adult, marriage and family, religion, politics, the organization that provides the person's livelihood, and other institutions have an increasing cultural influence on the person's values.

In recent years, it is generally recognized that societal values are undergoing drastic change. Social change has occurred throughout human history, but

[12]Margaret Mead, "The Concept of Culture and the Psychosomatic Approach," in Arthur Weider (ed.), *Contributions toward Medical Psychology,* vol. 1, The Ronald Press Company, New York, 1953, p. 377.
[13]Dewey and Humber, op. cit., pp. 121–122.

not at its current rate. A person growing up in the 1920s (who is in his or her sixties today) had a vastly different sociocultural environment contributing to value development from that of the person growing up in the 1960s (who is in his or her twenties today) or today. An interesting contrast between these two sociocultural environments would be the young man growing up in the 1920s who got his thrills by getting into an older friend's "tin lizzie" (Model *T* Ford) and racing down a cow path at 18 mph guzzling "bootleg" gin. This contrasts with the young man in the 1960s who got his thrills by getting into his older friend's "vet" (Chevrolet *Corvette*) and racing down an interstate highway at 118 mph smoking a "joint" (marijuana cigarette).[14] The contrasting situations of the 1920s versus those of the 1960s are "tin lizzies" versus "vets," cow paths versus interstate highways, 18 mph versus 118 mph, and alcohol versus drugs. The 1920s situations were probably just as thrilling and daring as the 1960s situations, but the speed was different. The 1960s and today are a fast-paced, 118-mph type of technical and sociocultural environment.

One result of this contrast between "then" and "now" sociocultural environments is a differing set of values for the people growing up during these times. In other words, people in their sixties will tend to have a different set of values from people in their twenties. Douglas T. Hall labels this a "value gap" and pinpoints six value areas that are especially relevant to managing people in modern organizations.

1 There is now more concern about values per se, not just different values.

2 Action is more important. Merely talking about values is not enough. One's values must be backed by action.

3 Values such as integrity, honesty, openness, and realness are more important.

4 In general, values are more humanistic. There are different motivating factors.

5 There is increased concern for the ultimate social value of one's work.

6 Authority based on expertise, personal style, and convictions or accomplishments is more legitimate than authority based on age or position.[15]

THE TECHNOLOGICAL ENVIRONMENT

An understanding of technology and its impact is vital to the study of organizational behavior. First of all, the question of what is technology, which accomplishes the incredible and makes tomorrow today, must be answered. Is it like Superman, who was faster than a speeding bullet, stronger than a locomotive, and able to leap tall buildings with a single bound? Is it a machine, an idea, or a concept? Is it an invention, a science, or a philosophy? Probably

---

[14]This example was used by Professor Morris Massey, University of Colorado, in a lecture heard by the author.

[15]Douglas T. Hall, "Potential for Career Growth," *Personnel Administration,* May–June 1971, pp. 18–19.

the best answer is that technology is all of these but, at the same time, none of them.

In a very narrow sense, technology can be equated with simple mechanical techniques, and, in a very broad sense, it can be thought of as the total body of knowledge possessed by society. For the purposes of this book, the technological environment is conceptually limited to that which impacts on management and organizations. Accordingly, technology is defined here as the mechanical techniques and abstract knowledge that are employed by humans to help attain organizational objectives.

In the literature, there are many classification schemes of technology. One of the best-known and accepted is the three-way classification by James D. Thompson.[16] His scheme is applicable to the wide range of technologies found in all complex organizations. The first classification is what he calls *long-linked technology*. This type of technology is characterized by serial interdependence between organizational units, the best example being the mass-production assembly line. The second category he labels *mediating technology,* in which there is a joining together of independent persons, such as clients or customers. Examples of organizations that operate on a mediating technology include financial institutions, utilities, and the post office. Thompson's third and last category he calls *intensive technology.* Under this type, many diverse technologies are brought together to solve a problem or achieve a change in some object. The modern general hospital and research and development laboratories are a couple of examples.

Attempts to classify concepts such as technology usually turn out to be largely artificial. It is difficult to determine precisely where one category of technology ends and another begins. Thus, the most realistic way to present a classification scheme for technology seems to be in the form of a continuum. Kast and Rosenzweig present a continuum that ranges from a very simple, stable, and uniform technology to a very complex, dynamic, and nonuniform technology. Their technological stages on the continuum start with craft and then move, in order, to machine-tending, mass-production-assembly-line, continuous-process, and, finally, advanced technology. They stress that their classification scheme contains two separate dimensions—degrees of complexity and uniformity—and therefore results in many possible combinations which can be found in different types of organizations as well as within the same organization.[17] The classification used in this chapter is primarily industry-oriented, but it can be loosely applied to other types of organizations.

Stages of Technological Development

The tremendously complex state of modern technology did not just appear overnight or even A.S. (After Sputnik). As Davis and Blomstrom dramatically

[16]James D. Thompson, *Organizations in Action,* McGraw-Hill Book Company, New York, 1967, pp. 15–18.

[17]Fremont E. Kast and James E. Rosenzweig, *Organization and Management,* 2d ed., McGraw-Hill Book Company, New York, 1974, pp. 186–187.

observe, "Throughout history technology has pressed onward like a glacier, overturning everything in its way and grinding all opposition into dust."[18]

The industrial revolution is usually recognized as marking the beginning of modern technology. Today, many scholars and practitioners contend that organizations are in the midst of a second industrial revolution or even a post-industrial stage. Yet, despite the common use of the term *revolution,* on the whole technology has progressed more in an evolutionary than in a revolutionary fashion. This type of development does not deny that there are certain technological milestones which can be pinpointed as having had an enormous impact on the state of technology. The invention of the steam engine, the practical application of computers, the launching of Sputnik, and humans' walking and riding on the moon are a few specific examples that come quickly to mind. Yet, overall, there has been an evolutionary progression of technology between such landmark achievements.

What is changing dramatically in the development of modern technology is the shortened time period between one technological breakthrough and the next. Cameron Hall has noted that "because of technology it is taking *less time* to do some things; hence, we have *more time* to do other things. These two results of technology—it takes less time; it gives more time—are basic to an understanding of technology's time-table."[19] The speedup of technology can be seen from the timing of the following events in history:

1 There was a 250-year spread between the early experiments on magnetism by Gilbert and others and the theory of electricity and magnetism by James Clerk Maxwell in the 1870s.

2 There was a 50-year period between Faraday's work on a wire carrying current and its commercial use in electric dynamos and motors.

3 There was a 25-year lapse between Becquerel's discovery of x-rays and practice.

4 There were eleven years between the discovery of nuclear fission and the self-sustained nuclear pile.

5 There were seven years between the theoretical possibility of the atomic bomb and the dropping of the first two in Japan.[20]

Today, of course, the gap between discovery and application is even narrower. The *total* accumulation of scientific knowledge is presently doubling about every ten years. Hall compares the rapidly developing technology with an automobile ". . . whose driver is steadily pressing down on the accelerator of an increasingly powerful engine. The view behind recedes more quickly, the surrounding scenery becomes more quickly unfamiliar, and the speed of the movement gives one a feeling of strangeness and insecurity."[21] Davis and

[18]Keith Davis and Robert L. Blomstrom, *Business and Society,* 3d ed., McGraw-Hill Book Company, New York, 1975, p. 115.

[19]Cameron P. Hall, *Technology and People,* Judson Press, Valley Forge, Pa., 1969, p. 34.

[20]C. A. Coulson, *Science, Technology and the Christian,* Abingdon Press, Nashville, Tenn., 1960, pp. 25–26.

[21]Hall, op. cit., p. 35.

Blomstrom, when describing the situation facing modern managers in their attempt to deal with the rapidly changing technological environment, paraphrased an appropriate passage from *Alice in Wonderland:* "You have to run as fast as you can to stay where you are."[22]

Despite the rapidly accelerating evolution of modern technology, for purposes of study and analysis it is useful to delineate certain stages of development. Figure 4-1 presents a continuum of certain definable stages of technological development. However, once again the reader should be reminded that there are no clear-cut lines of demarcation between these various stages. All are still very much in evidence today and parts of one are contained in the others.

Handicraft Technology   Although there are earlier forms of technology, the handicraft system marks the beginning of technology that is relevant to an organizationally oriented society. Handicraft technology is closely associated with the craftspeople who use certain tools in their work but rely primarily on their skilled hands. Initially, the typical craftsperson made a product, for example, a pair of shoes, a suit of clothes, or a piece of furniture, from beginning to end within the home. However, toward the end of the Middle Ages, many of the highly skilled craftspeople accumulated a great deal of capital and many apprentices. They began "putting out" some of their work to other craftspeople in the community. This putting out, or cottage system, of production eventually led to the factory system. In a factory, a large group of workers under the direction of a manager manufactured products from start to finish under one roof. Mechanization made the factory system become a reality.

Mechanized Technology   Mechanization is the second stage on the continuum of technological development. As stated earlier, there are no clear-cut distinctions between the end of one stage of technology and the beginning of the next. Nevertheless, the mechanistic stage generally marks the end of a dominating handicraft form of technology and the beginning of a mechanistically oriented technology. The emphasis changes from the craftsperson's skilled hands to a machine that does most of the production of goods. Yet, even though the emphasis shifts from left to right on the continuum, all stages, including the handicaft form of technology, are still practiced today.

The dominant characteristic of mechanistic technology is the power-driven machine. The advent of this stage of technology, which accompanied the factory system, is commonly referred to in history as the *industrial*

[22]Davis and Blomstrom, op. cit., p. 115.

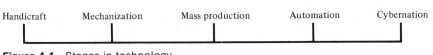

Handicraft   Mechanization   Mass production   Automation   Cybernation

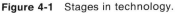

Figure 4-1   Stages in technology.

revolution. The following specific inventions, in chronological order, made the greatest contributions to mechanistic technology:

1733   Flying shuttle
1767   Spinning jenny
1769   Water frame
1769   Steam engine
1779   Spinning mule
1787   Power loom
1792   Cotton gin

In other words, more efficient textile looms, which became power-driven after Watt's invention of the steam engine in 1769, marked the beginning of the mechanistic form of technology. Many scholars believe that mechanization was one of the greatest single influences on human societies in all of history. It started in the textile mills of England but soon spread, in varying degrees, to all types of industry around the entire world.

Mass-Production Technology   The mechanistic technology as a dominant form gave way to the mass-production or continuous-process form around the beginning of this century. While mechanistic technology is characterized by power-drive machines, mass-production technology represents a new way of organizing and implementing mechanization. The assembly line is the best example of this stage of technological development. Using standardized parts, the worker on an assembly line stands in one spot while performing in a highly specialized manner. The task continuously moves past the worker on a conveyor belt.

The introduction of mass-production technology is usually attributed to Henry Ford. Between 1905 and 1910 he built an innovative plant in Detroit that mass-produced his famous Model T. As many writers have pointed out, Ford's mass production was not entirely new. A well-developed mass-production operation had existed at the Arsenal of Venice almost 500 years earlier, and Eli Whitney had been using interchangeable machine parts a century before Ford. Even the conveyor-belt method of moving materials had been in use for more than thirty years in the Chicago meatpacking industry. Ford's major technological contribution was the provision of "a technical solution to the economic problem of producing the largest number of finished products with the greatest reliability of quality at the lowest possible cost."[23]

Ford's techniques led to phenomenal increases in productivity. Mass production was soon implemented by other auto makers and quickly spread to other types of industries. By World War II, it had developed to the point where it no longer required human hands to operate the process. Machines on the assembly line could "handle a piece of work, put it in proper position, fasten it

[23]Peter F. Drucker, *Technology, Management and Society,* Harper & Row, Publishers, Incorporated, New York, 1970, p. 69.

in place, perform some operation on it, release it, move it on to the next stage, and receive the next piece."[24] This peak of development in mass production marked the beginning of automation.

Automated Technology   A management consultant, John Diebold, is generally given credit for coining the term *automation.* However, Diebold himself recognized that a vice president of Ford, Delmar Harder, probably first used the term in 1946 when his company was building a push-button type of plant in Cleveland. In 1952, Diebold explained his use of the word in the following manner:

> Automation is a new word denoting both automatic operation and the process of making things automatic. In the latter sense it includes several areas of industrial activity such as product and process redesign, the theory of communication and control, and design of machinery.[25]

Automated technology is what is commonly referred to as the second industrial revolution. Under mechanization, machines perform much of the work that was formerly done by skilled craftspeople, but a human being is still required to operate the machine. The individual is also a vital cog in mass-production technology. Workers perform highly specialized operations on the product as it moves past them on the assembly line. Under automation the human operator is entirely eliminated. A man or woman is no longer required to run the machine because it is run automatically. Humans play only a control role in automated technology. They push buttons and watch dials.

Cybernated Technology   At the close of the 1960s a new form of technology, commonly known as *cybernetics,* came on the scene. As in the transition between the stages of mechanization, mass production, and automation, there is no clear-cut distinction between automation and cybernation. Some writers argue that cybernation is only a part of the more general automated technology. For example, Julius Rezler states that "cybernation is a type of automation and particularly refers to the application of computers to the production process in both the office and the factory."[26] The more restricted conceptualization of cybernetics is particularly evident in the United States, where "there has been a tendency to institutionalize fairly narrow disciplines concerned with limited formal or material applications of these concepts, such as computer engineering, bionics, and control systems engineering."[27] On the other hand, the term *cybernetics* is used in Russia, for example, in a very broad sense to incorporate

[24]Walter Buckingham, *Automation,* Mentor Books, New American Library, New York, 1961, p. 18.

[25]John Diebold, *Automation,* D. Van Nostrand Company, Inc., New York, 1952, p. ix.

[26]Julius Rezler, *Automation and Industrial Labor,* Random House, Inc., New York, 1969, p. 6.

[27]Charles R. Dechert, "The Development of Cybernetics," *American Behavioral Scientist,* June 1965, p. 16.

the general science of control over complex systems, information, and communication.

The wide-ranging use of the term reflects a great deal of misunderstanding. As Stafford Beer points out, "Some people think that cybernetics is another word for automation; some that it concerns experiments with rats; some that it is a branch of mathematics; others that it wants to build a computer capable of running the country."[28] As used in this discussion, *cybernetics* means an automatic-feedback control type of technology. Under cybernated technology, humans are not needed even to push buttons and watch dials as they are under automation. Cybernation is a technological stage beyond automation where machines run and control other machines. Computers, not humans, play the most important role in cybernated technology.

Development of the Computer

The computer dominates the modern technological environment. It has been commercially available only for the past two decades. However, its origin can be traced as far back as the early 1800s, when Charles Babbage, a British mathematician, labored some forty years to build an analytical engine. Although the engine was never successfully completed, the drawings and notes from Babbage's work are usually recognized as the starting point for the modern computer. The next major landmark in computer development was Herman Hollerith's tabulation device that was used in the 1890 United States census. Utilizing a primitive, punched-card, data-processing device proved to be easier and faster than manual methods. However, it was not until 1945 that the first electronic computer was developed. This Electronic Numerical Integrator and Calculator, called ENIAC, was designed by J. P. Eckert and J. W. Mauchly at the University of Pennsylvania. It was closely followed by UNIVAC, the first commercial electronic computer, which was installed for use in the Census Bureau in 1951.

Since UNIVAC there have been three recognized generations of computers.[29] The first generation came to life in the 1950s. These early computers depended upon punch cards and paper tapes. Memories were limited and their design was dominated by the vacuum tube. There were many growing pains during this first generation. Errors were relatively common, there was much downtime, and programming was very tedious. The breakthrough which provided the impetus for the second generation of computers was made possible by the transistor. Starting in about 1960, solid-state, transistorized components were more accurate than the vacuum tubes and reduced the size of computers, thus facilitating greater speed. There was increased use of magnetic tapes with the second-generation machines. New languages, such as FOR-

[28]Stafford Beer, *Cybernetics and Management,* John Wiley & Sons, Inc., Science editions, New York, 1959, p. xii.
[29]See Richard J. Hopeman, *Production,* 2d ed., Charles E. Merrill Books, Inc., Columbus, Ohio, 1971, pp. 300–301.

TRAN and COBOL, simplified programming and led to many diverse applications. About 1965, third-generation computers, characterized by miniature, integrated circuits, came on the market. These components further reduced the size of the computer and greatly increased the operating speed. Computer speeds are now measured in billionths of a second and even in picoseconds, which hold the same relationship to a billionth of a second as a second holds to thirty years.[30] The memory capacity of the newest machines, which the computer manufacturers, at least, state are the beginning of the fourth generation, is much greater, and there is more flexibility possible in programming and in expansion and conversion. Perhaps the most important capability of the newest computers is time sharing from remote terminals in real time. As noted by Hopeman, "Both card I/O (Input-Output) and magnetic tape I/O became unnecessary where these terminals were remote typewriters tied into the CPU (Central Processing Unit). In such cases programs could be loaded on discs and recalled for use at any time by typing in the program name."[31]

The Current and Future Use of Computers

The fourth generation of computers emphasize the software (programming), rather than the hardware, aspects. Through new software techniques such as heuristic programming, the electronic computer is starting to take over activities formerly reserved for the human brain. Hall observes that "whereas up to now technology has extended or even taken over what men do with their physical equipment—their hands and eyes and legs—with our generation for the first time the computer is providing brain power."[32]

There are many pro and con arguments about the computer's capability to think. Albers, after reviewing both sides, concluded:

> Present-day computers can "think" in the sense that they have the capacity to make such logical choices. The programmer provides the instructions as to when and how a choice is to be made; the computer then automatically makes these choices as information is processed . . . There would appear to be no absolute barrier to the development of computers that simulate the human thinking apparatus.[33]

Although many people fear that a "thinking" computer may take over the world, this idea seems more science fiction than reality. Computers like HAL 9000 in Stanley Kubrick's movie *2001—A Space Odyssey* are possible but not probable. The catch is that computers will never be able to make a value decision (to determine what is ethically right or wrong) unless humans choose

---

[30]Ralph Lazarus, "Automation's Perplexing Boon: Years of Time to Spare," *Personnel,* March–April 1964, p. 9.

[31]Hopeman, op. cit., p. 301.

[32]Hall, op. cit., p. 27.

[33]Henry H. Albers, *Principles of Management,* 4th ed., John Wiley & Sons, Inc., New York, 1974, pp. 283–284 and 286.

to live in a computer culture. It is hoped that modern society will make the decision to live in a human rather than a computer culture. This choice is up to humans, not computers.

THE IMPACT OF TECHNOLOGY ON BEHAVIOR

The discussion of the environment so far has implied that physical, sociocultural, and technological variables have an impact on human behavior. Little systematic evidence exists on the impact of the physical and sociocultural environments, but relatively greater attention has been given to the technological impact on behavior. This final section of the chapter will analyze this impact.

Views of the Impact of Technology on Humans

Discussions of the impact of technology on human beings, individually or as a total society, cover the entire spectrum. On the one extreme are those who say that technology has had a very positive and good effect on people. Typical of this line of reasoning is the following:

> Technology is seen as the motor of all progress, as holding solutions for most of our social problems, as helping to liberate the individual from the clutches of a complex and highly organized society, and as the source of permanent prosperity—in short, as the promise of utopia in our time.[34]

The opposite view is that technology has affected people very negatively and badly. This view is typically stated in these words:

> . . . the emergence of vast dense urban agglomerations with the loss of individual privacy, the crush of crowds, and the standardization of goods and services . . . The increasing environmental pollution in the wake of industrialization and urbanization has brought cries of despair. The social upheavals attendant on automation have placed the concepts of alienation and anomie to the forefront of social concern.[35]

There is even the view, although seldom heard, that technology has had no noticeable effect on people. The reasoning goes as follows:

> Technology is not new, and it has moreover been recognized as a factor in social change at least since the Industrial Revolution . . . research has shown that technology has done little to accelerate the rate of economic productivity since the 1880's . . . If anything, therefore, technological change is likely to be less upsetting

---

[34]Emmanuel G. Mesthene, *Technological Change,* Harvard University Press, Cambridge, Mass., 1970, p. 16.

[35]Simon Marcson (ed.), *Automation, Alienation, and Anomie,* Harper & Row, Publishers, New York, 1970, p. 1.

than in the past, because its scope and rate are roughly in equilibrium with man's social and psychological development.[36]

Although there is some empirical evidence to support the "no effect" view, in general it ignores too many overwhelming variables. Sheer physical power, computerization, speed of communication, population density, and space exploration are but a few of the variables that make modern technology, positive or negative, have a tremendous influence on the human being.

On balance, most behaviorally oriented scholars lean toward the negative view of the effect of technology on humans. For example, one sociologist notes,

> Because technology increasingly shapes almost every realm of our everyday lives, and through formal education has increasingly become the dominant form of modern thought, it could transform or destroy the social foundations of our most cherished human values.[37]

This view has become very prevalent in recent years. The American public in general is seriously questioning the real value and meaning of technology. People are wondering if they have created a Frankenstein. Many of the serious problems plaguing modern society—poverty, war, ecological imbalance, and drug abuse—are being blamed on technology; it has become a convenient scapegoat. The landing of the first astronaut on the moon on July 20, 1969, probably started much of the soul searching and served as an impetus to marshal the voices calling for a reordering of priorities. People are asking not what *can* technology do, but instead what *should* technology be allowed to do. These voices are demanding that technology be aimed at the human, and not merely the physical, problems of the world. Today, few would question that human priorities have surged ahead.

Besides its societal implications, technology has been shown to have an enormous influence on individual behavior. It directly affects behavior in organizations as well as having a pervasive effect on the entire human society. A realistic example of technology's impact on organizational behavior is provided by the electronic and space industries. The technology inherent in these industries creates a situation of rapid obsolescence, frequent changes in work volume, continual transfer of personnel, and constant retraining. As a result, the participants who work in electronic and aerospace organizations tend to exhibit the following specific behaviors:

1   They form weak social relationships.
2   They do not develop loyalty to the employing organization.

---

[36]Mesthene, op. cit., pp. 18–19. Mesthene does not subscribe to the view quoted but is merely giving the "no effect" argument.

[37]Jack D. Douglas, *The Technological Threat*, Prentice-Hall, Inc., Englewood Cliffs, N.J., 1971, p. 2.

3   They work to build reputations that can be easily communicated to strangers.[38]

More generally, technology can directly affect organizational behavior when it is so implemented that it will

1   Place limits on how a job is divided among people and groups;
2   Determine status relations among people and groups according to educational requirements or positions in the flow of work;
3   Position people, for example, so they can be close enough to talk to one another; and,
4   Affect the conditions of work, for example, noise level and temperature.[39]

These are just some of technology's very practical and obvious effects on human behavior in organizations. It may also have a more complex and profound impact through the alienation of participants in the modern organization.

Alienation Resulting from Technology

The behavioral implications of technology usually focus on the concept of alienation. Alienation has diverse meanings,[40] but usually the concept incorporates one or more of the following:

1   *Powerlessness.*   Probably the most frequently used connotation of alienation, this view was originally espoused by the spiritual father of communism, Karl Marx. He argued that the capitalistic, technological system usurped all the prerogatives and means of decision making from the workers. Capitalism stripped workers of their power and left them alienated. This strict Marxian view of alienation was later modified and expanded by sociologists such as Max Weber and C. Wright Mills.
2   *Meaninglessness.*   In this view, people cannot grasp the overall meaning of the technology with which they are faced. They are unclear as to what they ought to believe about technology and end up searching for meaning, but they have a "low expectancy that satisfactory predictions about future outcomes of behavior can be made."[41]
3   *Normlessness.*   This view is most closely related to the concept of anomie. Chapter 2 mentioned anomie as a major contribution of Emile Durkheim to modern sociological thought. Technology is seen as the cause of a person's losing sight of, and adherence to, social rules or norms. Human behavior is no longer guided by the norms of society.

[38]John Seiler, "Sociotechnical Systems," in John Seiler (ed.), *Systems Analysis in Organizational Behavior,* Richard D. Irwin, Inc., Homewood, Ill., 1967, p. 26.
[39]Ibid.
[40]Melvin Seeman, "On the Meaning of Alienation," *American Sociological Review,* December 1959, pp. 784–790.
[41]Ibid., p. 786.

4 *Isolation.* When alienation is viewed as isolation, technology is said to cause the individual to become detached or isolated from society. The individual assigns a low value to beliefs or goals that are held in high esteem by others in the society. The person becomes isolated from the popular or prevailing culture.

5 *Self-Estrangement.* This last view of alienation states that technology has created a situation where the individual can no longer find intrinsically satisfying activities. An example is the worker who gets no self-satisfaction from the job but merely puts in time in order to earn wages.

The impact that technology has had on the alienation of people, in one or more of the forms just mentioned, has been of great concern to industrial sociologists. However, psychologists, anthropologists, philosophers, political scientists, and historians have also either directly or indirectly been involved with alienation. The general consensus is that technological advance has been a primary cause of the alienation. This thesis is expressed in well-known books, such as David Riesman's *The Lonely Crowd,* Robert Nisbet's *Quest for Community,* Erich Fromm's *Escape from Freedom,* and Karl Menninger's *Man Against Himself.* Faunce summarizes the prevailing opinion in these words:

> The most persistent indictment of industrial society is that it has resulted in the alienation of industrial man. Loneliness in the midst of urban agglomeration; loss of social anchorage in mass society; the absence of a predictable life trajectory in an era of unprecedented social change; and the powerlessness of man within the complex social, economic, and political systems he has created are common themes in the social criticism of the industrial way of life.[42]

Research on Technological Alienation

At first, research findings seemed to support the position that all forms of advanced technology cause alienation.[43] However, as automation became more sophisticated, later findings by Blauner and by Mann and Hoffman indicated the reverse.[44] It can be argued that certain types of technology can actually reduce alienation.

✳ Blauner studied four diverse technological situations—a print shop, a textile mill, an automobile assembly line, and a highly automated chemical plant. He found that alienation was a direct function of the type of technology in operation. For example, in the automobile assembly line, alienation of the workers was widespread. On the other hand, in the chemical plant, which operated on a continuous-process form of technology, alienation was noticea-

[42]William A. Faunce, *Problems of an Industrial Society,* McGraw-Hill Book Company, New York, 1968, p. 84.

[43]See Charles R. Walker, *Toward the Automatic Factory,* Yale University Press, New Haven, Conn., 1957.

[44]See Robert Blauner, *Alienation and Freedom,* The University of Chicago Press, Chicago, 1964; and Floyd C. Mann and L. Richard Hoffman, *Automation and the Worker,* Henry Holt and Company, Inc., New York, 1960.

bly absent.[45] The reasons given were that on the assembly line the workers were powerless and suffered from self-estrangement, whereas in the chemical plant the workers had meaningful jobs in which they had a great deal of responsibility and control. Thus, there is little doubt that technology has an effect on the alienation of workers, but it appears to be highly selective in nature. Different types of technology have different impacts. People themselves hold the key to their own destiny. If management chooses to install a type of technology that results in powerlessness, meaninglessness, isolation, and self-estrangement, the workers will undoubtedly suffer the consequences of alienation. But if management chooses a state of technology which has the opposite effects, it follows that the workers will not become alienated.

SUMMARY

An introductory foundation for organizational behavior would not be complete without a discussion of the environment. The physical environment consists of climate, terrain, limited resources, and population density. Limited resources, especially food and energy, and the population explosion, which contribute to the limited resources problem, are particularly relevant to the study of organizational behavior. The sociocultural environment has a more direct impact. Changing social values, often resulting in a "value gap," are especially relevant. The biggest and most direct impact on organizational behavior, however, comes from the technological environment. Technology includes both mechanical techniques and abstract knowledge. Certain stages of technological development can be identified. Modern technological processes started with the handicraft system, then moved to mechanization, mass production, automation, and, finally, cybernation. Each of these types of technology exists in today's organizations, but the rate of technological advance is accelerating very rapidly. Computer technology, in particular, has recently had, and will continue to have, an almost revolutionary influence on all aspects of management and organizational behavior.

QUESTIONS FOR DISCUSSION AND REVIEW

1 How can limited resources affect human behavior?
2 What impact can population have on the environment which affects behavior?
3 What is the explanation for a "value gap"?
4 How does automation differ from cybernation?
5 Computers have gone through three generations and are currently entering into a fourth. What are the characteristics of each generation?
6 What is alienation? How is it affected by technology?

CASE: GENERATION GAP

Harry Aims is sixty-one years old. After graduating from high school he had worked on the family farm until he was called into the armed services at the

---

[45]Blauner, op. cit., p. 178.

outbreak of World War II. When the war was over, Harry settled down with his wife and young child and went to work as a clerk in one of the branch offices of a small electric utility. By hard work and loyalty to the company, Harry became office manager, a position he has now held for seventeen years. One of his employees in the billing section, Jerry Rees, was really at odds with Harry. Jerry, who was twenty-one, had attended technical school, where he had learned computer programming. Every time Harry gave Jerry an order or some assignment, Jerry would question the logic, especially why Harry did not try to computerize more of the work around the office, and only after much heated discussion would he reluctantly comply. After a few months of this, Harry could no longer take it. He called Jerry into his office, told him to close the door, and said, "Jerry, I've had it with you. You young long-haired guys are all alike. You think the world owes you a living. Well, I'll tell you, I had to work darn hard for everything I have, and I don't see why it should be any different for you. On the other hand, I am willing to listen to your side of the situation. What do you have to say about this impasse we have apparently reached?"

1 If you were Jerry, how would you respond to the boss? If you were Harry, how would you then respond to this answer just given by Jerry?
2 In terms of the sociocultural environment, how would you explain the conflict between Harry and Jerry?
3 The case points out that the office manager did not try to computerize much of the work. What impact do you think computerized technology (or the lack of it) can have on the behavior of employees like Jerry? What impact would the computerized technology have on the behavior of people like the boss, Harry?

SELECTED REFERENCES

Bearinger, Van W.: "Emerging Technologies and Their Impacts," *S. A. M. Advanced Management Journal,* January 1974, pp. 25–28.

Bell, Daniel: "The Coming of Post-Industrial Society," *Business and Society Review/ Innovation,* Spring 1973, pp. 5–23.

Debutts, Thomas C.: "The Work Ethic Is Alive and Well," *Personnel,* September–October 1975, pp. 22–31.

Hall, Cameron P.: *Technology and People,* Judson Press, Valley Forge, Pa., 1969.

Juricovich, Ray: "A Core Typology of Organizational Environments," *Administrative Science Quarterly,* September 1974, pp. 380–394.

Luthans, Fred, and Richard M. Hodgetts: *Social Issues in Business,* 2d ed., The Macmillan Company, New York, 1976.

Marcson, Simon (ed.): *Automation, Alienation, and Anomie,* Harper & Row, Publishers, Incorporated, New York, 1970.

Mesthene, Emmanuel G.: *Technological Change,* Harvard University Press, Cambridge, Mass., 1970.

Miles, Raymond E., Charles C. Snow, and Jeffrey Pfeffer: "Organization-Environment: Concepts and Issues," *Industrial Relations,* October 1974, pp. 244–264.

Myers, M. Scott, and Susan S. Myers: "Toward Understanding the Changing Work Ethic," *California Management Review,* Spring 1974, pp. 7–19.

Osborn, Richard N., and James G. Hunt: "Environment and Organizational Effectiveness," *Administrative Science Quarterly,* June 1974, pp. 231–246.

Ouchi, William G., and Reuben T. Harris: "Structure, Technology, and Environment," in George Strauss, et al. (eds.), *Organizational Behavior Research and Issues,* Industrial Relations Research Association, University of Wisconsin, Madison, Wisconsin, 1974, pp. 107–140.

Ramo, Simon: "The Computer in Management," *The Conference Board Record,* February 1974, pp. 14–16.

Roeber, Richard J. C.: *The Organization in a Changing Environment,* Addison-Wesley Publishing Company, Inc., Reading, Mass., 1973.

Schrank, Robert: "Work in America: What Do Workers Really Want?" *Industrial Relations,* May 1974, pp. 124–129.

Simon, Herbert, "Technology and Environment," *Management Science,* June 1973, pp. 1110–1121.

Terkel, Studs: "Work Without Meaning," *Business and Society Review/ Innovation,* Spring 1974, pp. 15–22.

Thompson, James D.: *Organizations in Action,* McGraw-Hill Book Company, New York, 1967.

Withington, Frederic G.: "Five Generations of Computers," *Harvard Business Review,* July-August 1974, pp. 99–108.

Woodward, Joan: *Industrial Organization,* Oxford University Press, London, 1965.

Chapter 5

A Conceptual Model for Organizational Behavior

The purpose of this chapter is to review the various models of human behavior and develop a model for organizational behavior. Particular attention is given to the psychoanalytic, existentialistic, cognitive, and behavioristic models. These serve as the point of departure for developing an eclectic model (mainly taken from the cognitive and behavioristic approaches) for understanding, predicting, and controlling organizational behavior. A model labeled $S \longleftrightarrow O \longrightarrow B \longrightarrow C$ is presented for this purpose. When the variables of organizational behavior are put into the $S \longleftrightarrow O \longrightarrow B \longrightarrow C$ model, the result is a conceptual framework for the study of organizational behavior.

MODELS OF HUMAN BEHAVIOR

What separates humans from animals or other objects in the universe? What are people really like? What is their real nature? These questions have been debated since the beginning of civilization. Philosophers, theologians, politicians, scientists, managers, and the person on the street have been and still are preoccupied with these questions. Are people good or evil, rational or irrational, free or determined? Most often, scholars and lay persons have ready answers to these questions and staunchly defend their positions. To date, however, the true nature of human behavior is largely undefined and still open for discussion and research.

Floyd Allport describes an intriguing situation that may be analogous to the current status of understanding human behavior.

> Suppose the ill-fated occurrence of an atomic holocaust had come to pass on earth, and after the debris had cleared the only two remaining objects to be seen were an ultraprimitive man and a watch, still going, which he had picked up in the desert. Since the man might be presumed to be in a state of almost complete ignorance, all realization of the purpose of the watch had now been obliterated from the earth. . . . That this structure would present the primitive man with a puzzle if he were to try accurately to describe it, to say nothing of explaining its origin, seems evident. We, too, are like watches—lost in the desert of time. And similarly, we are at a loss to understand either our origin or our essential nature.[1]

Is the picture really as bleak as Allport describes? Is nothing known about human behavior? Whether scholar or layperson, everyone has had abundant experience in living and dealing with, reading about, and observing fellow human beings. A normal outgrowth of this lifetime of experience is that everyone has a definite opinion about human behavior. Unfortunately, when common-sense approaches to human behavior are put to the test of science, they are often proved wrong. Yet, it is through the applications of science that human behavior can best be understood. This, of course, is the approach of behavioral science that was outlined in Chapter 2.

The behavioral scientist analyzes human behavior on the basis of scientific methodology. The major goal of behavioral science is to understand behavior. On the other hand, philosophers, theologians, and managers are interested primarily in evaluating behavior. The emphasis on understanding versus evaluation is the major difference between the behavioral sciences and the other approaches used in analyzing human behavior.

The objective of any science is to discover truth and develop understanding. Scientists always attempt to divorce their own value judgments from this quest. The following models take an understanding, not an evaluating, approach to the overall nature of human behavior. These models serve as important background information for developing a specific model for organizational behavior.

Freudian Psychoanalytic Model

The Freudian approach relies on a psychoanalytic or conflict model of humans. At least in Western culture, the conception of people being in constant inner conflict is one of the oldest explanations. The conflict model portrayed primitive humans' constant inner struggle between good and evil. Good (angels) and evil (devils) were believed to be competing for the domination of the body and soul. Common sayings, such as "He is possessed by the devil" or "She is a little angel," reflect this view. Under this model, individuals are merely innocent bystanders and the situation completely overwhelms them. This

[1]Floyd H. Allport, "A Theory of Enestruence (Event-Structure Theory): Report of Progress," *American Psychologist*, January 1967, p. 1.

primitive view of conflict still exists in many parts of the world, even within subcultures of highly developed countries. Obviously, the primitive good-evil conflict model cannot be substantiated by scientific methodology. It is based on magic and the supernatural, which are outside the realm of science.

A more meaningful, comprehensive, and systematically based conflict model stems from the theories of Sigmund Freud. These theories can be summarized into what can be called the *psychoanalytic model.* Although Freud is most closely associated with the model, others, such as Carl Jung, Alfred Adler, Karen Horney, and Eric Fromm, who all broke away from Freud, made additional contributions and extended the model.

Clinical techniques were used primarily to develop the psychoanalytic model. Through the clinical techniques of free association and psychotherapy, Freud noted that his patients' behavior could not always be consciously explained. This clinical finding led him to conclude that the major motivating force in humans is unconscious in nature. The personality structure can be explained within the unconscious framework, Freud believed, by three interrelated, but often conflicting, psychoanalytic concepts: the *id,* the *ego,* and the *superego.*

The Id The id is the core of the unconscious. It is the unleashed, raw, primitive, instinctual drive of the Freudian model. The id, constantly struggling for gratification and pleasure, is manifested mainly through the libido (sexual urges) or aggression. The libido strives for sexual relations and pleasure, but also for warmth, food, and comfort. Aggressive impulses of the id are destructive and include the urges to fight, dominate, and generally destroy. In a conflict sense, the id incorporates life instincts that compete with its death instincts. As individuals develop and mature, they learn to control the id. But even then it remains a driving force throughout life and an important source of thinking and behaving.

The Ego Whereas the id represents the unconscious, the ego is the conscious. It is the logical part of the Freudian model and is associated with the reality principle. The ego keeps the id in check through the realities of the external environment. The ego is constituted so that it can interpret reality for the id through intellect and reason. Instrumental behavior, such as dating or looking for food, is developed by the ego to satisfy the needs of the id. However, many conflict situations arise between the id and the ego because the id demands immediate pleasure while the ego dictates denial or postponement to a more appropriate time and place. In order to resolve the conflicts, the ego gets support from the superego.

The Superego The superego is the third element of the Freudian model. It can best be depicted as the conscience. The superego provides the norms that enable the ego to determine what is right or wrong. The superego conscience should not be confused with the conscious aspects of the ego. In fact, according to Freud, the superego is mostly unconscious.

The person is not aware of the workings of the superego. The conscience is developed by absorption of the cultural values and morals of a society. Accordingly, the parents have the most influence on the development of the superego. After resolving the Oedipus complex (love of parent), the child will unconsciously identify with the parents' values and morals.

The superego aids the person by assisting the ego to combat the impulses of the id. However, in some situations the superego can also be in conflict with the ego. An example is the situation where the reality-seeking ego violates the conscience. The conflict between ego and conscience provokes the wrath and vengeance of the largely unconscious superego. The inevitable struggles between the id, ego, and superego cause this to be considered a conflict model of behavior.

The Freudian Model in Perspective

Freud's model is characterized by the conflicting personality constructs (id, ego, and superego) and unconscious motivation. Psychological adjustment occurs only when the ego properly develops to resolve the conflicts stemming from the id and superego. The ego concept implies that humans are rational, but the id, the superego, and unconscious motivation give the impression that humans are very irrational. In the Freudian model, behavior is based on emotion. If the ego cannot control the id, the person is an aggressive, pleasure-seeking menace to society. If the id is too severely checked by the ego, the person is equally maladjusted. The person may have an abnormal sex life and be extremely passive. Moreover, if the superego is very strong, the result may be acute anxiety and guilt.

Freud has had a great impact in many areas of twentieth-century thought. He had a great influence on treatment techniques for the mentally ill, and he did make some contribution to the understanding of human behavior. His ideas have proved to be very far-reaching and long-lasting. Yet, today he is criticized as much as he is praised. Most of the criticism centers on the overemphasis given to sexual motivation.

From a behavioral science viewpoint, however, the most valid criticism of the Freudian model is that it is not based on empirically verifiable facts. The psychoanalytic elements are largely hypothetical constructs and not measurable, observable items for scientific analysis and verification. The id, ego, and superego are primarily a "black box" explanation of humans. This is why most modern behavioral scientists reject the psychoanalytic model as the total explanation of human personality and behavior. Nevertheless, important insights into personality structure and the idea of unconscious motivation are significant contributions, and they will be expanded upon in the chapters in Part Three of this book.

Existentialistic Model

Existentialism, broadly defined as the search for meaning, is based on the analysis of existence and being. The existentialistic model is not a behavioral science model. Its roots lie more in the realm of philosophy and literature and are not scientifically based.

Existentialism is European in origin and can be traced to the writings of the philosophers Kierkegaard, Nietzsche, and Schopenhauer. Among the philosophers with an existentialist orientation are Martin Heidegger, Martin Buber, and Jean-Paul Sartre. The best-known American spokesman has been Rollo May. May and Sartre, in particular, have been critical of the usual scientific approaches that are employed to gain an understanding of humans. They are afraid that a scientific behavioral analysis may destroy or lose sight of the person's true nature or "being."

Existentialism is conceptually similar to Durkheim's sociological concept of anomie, which was discussed in Chapter 2. Similar to Durkheim, existentialists see a breakdown of traditional norms and the ties that individuals have traditionally had with society. For example, Rollo May views people as suffering from unconstructive anxiety. He defines "unconstructive" or "neurotic" anxiety as the "shrinking of consciousness, the blocking off of awareness; and when it is prolonged it leads to a feeling of depersonalization and apathy" which is "the state, to a greater or lesser degree, of those who have lost, or never achieved, the experience of their own identity in the world."[2] This feeling of "depersonalization and apathy" is what Durkheim referred to as *anomie.*

In modern times the individual is faced with a very large, urbanized environment. The existentialists believe that the depersonalizing effects of this environment force individuals to determine their own destiny. People shape their own identity and make their "existence" meaningful and worthwhile to themselves. This process is accomplished through the individual's experience of being. Coleman views this being as "a matter of commitment to increased self-awareness and self-direction, to true communication with others, to concern with values and evaluation, and to acceptance of the responsibility for making choices and directing his own destiny."[3]

The emphasis attached to self-awareness and action in the existential scheme is different from that in the psychoanalytic model. Existential people seek self-awareness, direction, and control. Their existence in a depersonalized environment is a given. What they make of this existence is entirely up to them. The existentialist approach maintains that people have free will to chart their existence and being.

The Impact of the Existential Model

The existentialist approach becomes very relevant in a society suffering from environmental and moral decay. In a world that is overpopulated, undernourished, polluted, ravaged by war and crime, with racial injustice and poverty

[2]Rollo May, *Psychology and the Human Dilemma,* D. Van Nostrand Company, Inc., Princeton, N. J., 1967, p. 41.
[3]See James C. Coleman, *Psychology and Effective Behavior,* Scott, Foresman and Company, Glenview, Ill., 1969, p. 33.

rampant amidst affluence and material excess, it is extremely difficult for an individual to carve out a meaningful existence. The problem is compounded if the old, tradition-bound values of the past linger on as norms for the present although they are irrelevant and incapable of practical application under current conditions or in the foreseeable future.

Certainly some aspects of the modern American scene seem directly relevant to an existentialist approach. Similarly, on a micro level, human behavior in organizations seems appropriate for existentialist study and analysis. Determining a meaningful occupational existence may be a severe challenge for an individual faced with the characteristics of the modern formal organization. Although not scientifically based and not conceptually integrated into this book, existentialism provides some very useful insights. It can be effectively used to set a tone and to supplement more scientifically based discussions of human behavior.

Cognitive Model

The psychoanalytic and existentialistic models are on the fringe of the study of human behavior. Two more scientifically based models can also be used to explain human behavior. Although other names are sometimes applied and there are many other distinct models contained within each, these two important models of human behavior are the cognitive and the behavioristic.

The cognitive model of human behavior has many sources of input. The gestalt and phenomenological schools of thought in psychology, which were discussed in Chapter 2, provide a historical base for the cognitive approach. In general, the cognitive model came about as a reaction to the other models of human behavior. In particular, pioneering psychologists such as Edward Tolman became disenchanted with the psychoanalytic and early behavioristic models. They felt that the Freudian conception placed too much emphasis on negative, irrational, and sexually motivated behavior and that the behavioristic model was too deterministic and mechanistic. The alternative that was proposed gave humans much more "credit" than the other models. The cognitive model emphasizes the positive and free-will aspects of humans and utilizes concepts such as expectancy, demand, and incentive.

The work of Tolman, in particular, can best demonstrate the cognitive approach. He felt that behavior was purposive; it was directed toward a goal. In his laboratory experiments, he found that animals learned to expect that certain events will follow one another. For example, rats learned to behave as if they expected food when a certain cue appeared. Thus, to Tolman learning consisted of the *expectancy* that a particular event will lead to a particular consequence. This expectancy concept, of course, implies mentalistic phenomena. In other words, the cognitive explanation implies that the organism is thinking about or is conscious or aware of the goal. Behavior is based on these cognitions.

Contemporary psychologists, such as Robert Bolles, carefully point out that a cognitive concept such as expectancy "does not reflect a guess about what is going on in the animal's mind; it is a term that describes the animal's behavior."[4] For example, even though Tolman used concepts such as expectancy, he considered himself a behaviorist. In other words, the cognitive and behavioristic models are not as opposite as they appear on the surface and sometimes are made out to be. Yet, despite some conceptual similarities, there has been a controversy through the years in the behavioral sciences on the relative contributions of the cognitive versus the behavioristic model. Although the sequence is reversed (only recently have behavioristic models been proposed in organizational behavior because of the dissatisfaction with the cognitive approach[5]) the controversy has carried over into the field of organizational behavior. Before discussing the input that the cognitive model can make to organizational behavior, it is necessary to understand fully the behavioristic model.

Behavioristic Model

Chapter 2 discussed the behavioristic school of thought in psychology. Its roots can be traced to the work of Pavlov and Watson. These pioneering behaviorists stressed the importance of dealing with observable behaviors instead of the elusive mind that had preoccupied the earlier structuralists and functionalists. They used classical conditioning experiments to formulate the stimulus-response (S-R) explanation of human behavior. Both Pavlov and Watson felt that behavior could be best understood in terms of S-R. A stimulus elicits a response. They concentrated mainly on the impact of the stimulus and felt that learning occurred when the S-R connection was made.

Modern behaviorism marks its beginning with the work of B. F. Skinner. Skinner is generally recognized as the most influential living psychologist. He felt that the early behaviorists helped to explain respondent behaviors but not the more complex operant behaviors. In other words, the S-R approach helped explain physical reflexes [e.g., when stuck by a pin (S), the person will flinch (R); or when tapped below the kneecap (S), the person will extend the lower leg (R)] and certain emotional reactions [e.g., a loud noise (S) will lead the person to cry out (R)]. On the other hand, Skinner found through his operant conditioning experiments that the consequences of a response could better explain most behaviors than could eliciting stimuli. He emphasized the importance of the R-S relationship. The organism has to operate on the environment in order to receive the desirable consequence. The preceding stimulus does not cause the behavior in operant conditioning; it serves as a cue to emit the behavior. For Skinner, behavior is a function of its consequences.

Both classical and operant conditioning are given more detailed attention in Chapter 12. For now, however, it is important to understand that the behavioristic model is environmentally based. It implies that cognitive processes such as thinking, expectancies, and perception do not play a role in behavior. However, as in the case of the cognitive having behavioristic concepts, some

---

[4]Robert C. Bolles, *Learning Theory*, Holt, Rinehart and Winston, Inc., New York, 1975, p. 84.

[5]For example, see Fred Luthans and Robert Ottemann, "Motivation versus Learning Approaches to Organizational Behavior," *Business Horizons*, December 1973, pp. 55–62.

psychologists feel that there is room for cognitive variables in the behavioristic model.[6] Nevertheless, as the cognitive model has been accused of being mentalistic, the behavioristic model has been accused of being deterministic. Cognitive theorists argue that the S-R model, and to a lesser degree the R-S model, are much too mechanistic an explanation of human behavior. A strict S-R interpretation of behavior seems justifiably open to the criticism of being too mechanistic, but because of the scientific approach that has been meticulously employed by behaviorists, the operant model in particular has made a tremendous contribution to the study of human behavior.

AN ECLECTIC MODEL FOR ORGANIZATIONAL BEHAVIOR

Organizational behavior has the advantage of being a relatively young and growing field of study. It can legitimately borrow, in an eclectic manner, the best from the various established models of human behavior. At one point in its early development, the field of organizational behavior seemed to be in a dilemma in searching for a theoretical orientation. Over the past couple of decades, most writers in organizational behavior have taken a humanistic, cognitive approach. For example, Douglas McGregor and Rensis Likert depended mainly on a cognitive approach in their writings on organizational behavior. In the last couple of years, the behavioristic model has begun to be utilized in the theorizing and research on organizational behavior.[7] In many ways, what the field of organizational behavior has been going through in recent years is a replay of the behavioristic-versus-cognitive controversy that has been and, in many respects, still is going on in psychology. Now, in organizational behavior, the time seems to have come to recognize the contributions of both models and to begin to synthesize and integrate both approaches into a meaningful model of organizational behavior.

The Goals of the Organizational Behavior Model

As stated earlier, the goal of the models presented so far is to better understand, not evaluate, the complex phenomena called *human behavior.* Understanding human behavior in organizations is also a vital goal for a model of organizational behavior. In addition, however, because organizational behavior is more of an applied field than is psychology, other desirable goals besides understanding are prediction and control. The study of organizational behavior serves as the basis for modern human resource management. Predicting and controlling human resources are critical to the goals of modern management. Thus, the goals of a model of organizational behavior are to understand, predict, and control human behavior in organizations.

The cognitive approach seems essential to the understanding of organiza-

---

[6]For example, see Donald Meichenbaum, "Cognitive Behavior Modification," in *University Programs Modular Studies,* General Learning Press, Morristown, N. J., 1974.

[7]For a summary of the literature on the operant model in organizational behavior, see Fred Luthans and Robert Kreitner, *Organizational Behavior Modification,* Scott, Foresman and Company, Glenview, Ill., 1975.

tional behavior. The behavioristic approach can also lead to understanding, but perhaps even more important is the contribution it can make to prediction and control. On the basis of Edward Thorndike's classic law of effect, the behavioristic model would say that organizational behavior followed by a positive or reinforcing consequence will be strengthened and increase in subsequent frequency, and organizational behavior followed by an unpleasant or punishing consequence will be weakened and decrease in subsequent frequency. In other words, organizational behavior can be predicted and controlled on the basis of managing the contingent environment. In any event, if the threefold goals of understanding, prediction, and control are to be met by a model of organizational behavior, both the cognitive and the behavioristic approaches become vitally important. Both the internal causal factors which are cognitively oriented and the external environmental factors which are behavioristically oriented are important to the understanding, prediction, and control of organizational behavior.

The S ←→ O —→ B —→ C Model

An S←→O—→B—→C model can be formulated to incorporate both cognitive and behavioristic approaches. The S←→O—→B portion is largely an extension of the widely recognized S-O-R model of psychology. The addition of the consequence (C) is given recognition by the industrial psychologist Norman Maier in his S←→O—→B—→A model.[8] The S-O-R model incorporates both cognitive and behavioristic thinking. The human organism (O) plays an active mediating or intervening role between stimulus and response. The O is inserted into the classic behavioristic S-R model, thus producing the S-O-R version. This O is not passive and immobile, as is assumed in S-R. Instead, in S-O-R the O is viewed as a mediating, maintenance, and adjustment function between stimulus (S) and response (R). Floyd Ruch states that the O is "constantly active, scanning its own actions, seeking certain conditions and avoiding others."[9]

As a maintenance function, the organs of the O are responsible for its health and growth. The three primary categories of maintenance organs are the receptors, connectors, and effectors, which are shown in Figure 5-1. As shown in the diagram, the nervous system plays a central role. Behavior is mediated by neural activity. The nervous system serves as connectors for the receptors of stimuli (sense organs) and the effectors of behavior (muscles and glands). Significant breakthroughs have already occurred, and many scholars and students of behavior feel that the key area for future understanding of behavior lies in this mediating structure of the human being. The adjustment function of the O monitors people's activities in the environment so that they can overcome obstacles and thus satisfy their needs.

Even though the insertion of O in the S-R model gives some recognition to

[8]Norman R. F. Maier, *Psychology in Industry,* 3d ed., Houghton Mifflin Company, Boston, 1965.

[9]Floyd L. Ruch, *Psychology and Life,* 6th ed., Scott, Foresman and Company, Chicago, 1963, p. 14.

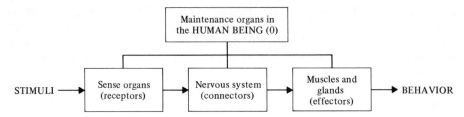

Figure 5-1 The maintenance organs which intervene between stimulus and response.

the importance of cognitive variables and the complexity of behavior, it still does not give recognition to the important role that consequences play in behavior. This is why the C is added to the model presented here. Figure 5-2 shows the S$\longleftrightarrow$O$\longrightarrow$B$\longrightarrow$C model, which is an expanded and modified version of the S-O-R and Maier's S$\longleftrightarrow$O$\longrightarrow$B$\longrightarrow$A models. The vital elements of the S$\longleftrightarrow$O$\longrightarrow$B$\longrightarrow$C model are the interactive effect between the situation and the human organism, the important role of consequences, and the feedback of the consequences to the situation and the human organism. In addition, of course, the S$\longleftrightarrow$O$\longrightarrow$B$\longrightarrow$C model has variables that are much more comprehensive than the classic S-O-R and S$\longleftrightarrow$O$\longrightarrow$B$\longrightarrow$A models.

The Variables in the Model

An underlying theme throughout the various models of human behavior is the relative importance of heredity versus environment. Although different terms are sometimes used and there are differing degrees of emphasis, the psychoanalytic, existentialistic, cognitive, and behavioristic models have all entered the controversy. Almost all psychologists agree that both heredity and environment play a role in behavior, but a disagreement revolves around the comparative importance of each. In reality, the argument is self-defeating. It is impossible to separate heredity completely from environment for scientific analysis. From the moment of conception, the environment begins to interact with the genetically determined physical human being.

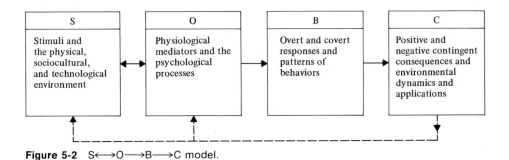

Figure 5-2 S$\longleftrightarrow$O$\longrightarrow$B$\longrightarrow$C model.

Because of the impact that the behavioristic model has had, most contemporary psychologists favor the greater importance of the environment over heredity in analyzing behavior. However, the modern viewpoint in general can perhaps best be summarized by Kurt Lewin's celebrated formula for behavior:

$$B = f(P, E)$$

Translated into words, the formula says that behavior (B) is a function (f) of person (P) and environment (E). Leo Meltzer states that "few would deny that to understand a person's behavior at a given point in time, it is necessary to have knowledge both of the person and of his environment at that time."[10]

The Person Variable The $S \longleftrightarrow O \longrightarrow B \longrightarrow C$ model incorporates both the person (O) and the environment (S and C); it follows the Lewin formula. The O variable in the model in Figure 5-2 incorporates both the physiological and psychological (or cognitive) mediators, which are vital to human behavior. As explained by Dewey and Humber:

> Man acts like man because he cannot do otherwise. Any member of a given biological order is restricted in the things that it can do and cannot do, in what it wants to do and does not want to do, and in the way it can and does feel about life, by the very nature of its biological structure.[11]

In other words, humans' genetically determined physical and biological structure makes them behave differently from ants or trees. Yet, humans are much more complex than merely a conglomeration of organs, senses, glands, nerves, bones, muscles, and brains. These mechanisms are essential to their maintenance and adjustment but cannot be equated with their behavior.

Human behavior is more a function of the psychological processes than of the physiological ones. From the moment of birth, learning, perception, and motivation are an integral part of the person. Naturally, these processes do not operate as isolated, separate entities any more than do the physiological mechanisms of the body. The human functions as a whole, not as a series of parts. The psychological processes, taken as a whole, are included in the concept of personality. The latter concept plays a very major role in understanding behavior.

The recognition of the psychological processes and personality as essential parts of the human being marks a major departure from a strict hereditary or physiological interpretation. For the purpose of developing a model of organizational behavior, the person is considered to be made up of both the

[10]Leo Meltzer, "The Need for a Dual Orientation in Social Psychology," *Journal of Social Psychology,* October 1961, p. 43.

[11]Richard Dewey and W. J. Humber, *An Introduction to Social Psychology,* The Macmillan Company, New York, 1966, p. 29.

physiological and psychological processes. Both are important variables of human behavior, although the psychological variables are considered here to have relatively much more influence on organizational behavior.

The Environment Variable   The environment is the other variable recognized in the Lewin equation for behavior. In the most basic and narrow sense, the environment consists of a stimulus. Common stimuli include lights, sounds, odors, pinpricks, and persons. In a strict S-R behavioristic interpretation, such stimuli (S) play the crucial role in eliciting behavior. Stimuli goad humans into action, interrupt what they are doing, and direct their choices. In this classical behavioristic view, the immediate stimulus object is the primary causal factor in behavior. In the more modern operant view, the stimulus serves as the antecedent cue which emits (*not* causes) the behavior. However, it must also be remembered that the contingent consequence is also a stimulus (R-S), and in the operant approach, behavior is a function of its consequences.

The immediate stimulus is a basic element in the $S \longleftrightarrow O \longrightarrow B \longrightarrow C$ model, but it is not equated with the total environment. The more comprehensive environment is represented in the $S \longleftrightarrow O \longrightarrow B \longrightarrow C$ model in both the S and the C. The S includes the immediate stimulus but also the broader physical, sociocultural, and technological environment as discussed in Chapter 4. The C in the model is also an environmental variable. As in the operant behavioristic model, the person must operate on the environment in order to obtain a certain consequence. This is the contingent-consequence emphasis from modern behaviorism, but the C also includes broader-based dynamics (e.g., conflict) and applications (e.g., appraisal) as part of the environmental consequences of organizational behavior.

The Behavior Variable   Perhaps the best way to describe the behavior variable is to state what it is and what it is not. Behavior is anything that the human does: it is not something that is done to the person. The nature of behavior can be clarified by analyzing two sets of examples of behavior. In the first set are five possible behaviors of an assembly-line worker in a widget factory:

1   The worker started the machine.
2   The worker produced many widgets.
3   The worker did not produce many widgets.
4   The worker came to work late.
5   The worker came to work on time.

In these five instances the worker did something. Thus, according to the simple definition, these examples are forms of behavior. However, before jumping to this conclusion, a refinement is necessary. Each of the five examples implies an outcome of the worker's behavior rather than the actual overt (outward) or covert (inward) behavior. In understanding the behavioral variable, it is extremely important to separate the actual behavioral events from the out-comes of these events. The same five examples can be translated into more precise behavioral events in the following manner:

1 The worker pushed the button.
2 The worker moved his or her arms and hands very fast.
3 The worker moved his or her arms and hands very slowly.
4 The worker walked very slowly from the parking lot.
5 The worker walked very fast from the parking lot.

This second set of examples describes the specific, overt behavior, not outcomes of the behavior.

Specific behavioral events and the patterns of these specific behaviors are what are included in the S$\longleftrightarrow$O$\longrightarrow$B$\longrightarrow$C model. There may be many reasons for the outcomes of behavior. In the first set of examples, there are a number of possible reasons why the machine started, why productivity was high or low, and why the worker did or did not get to work on time. Because of these many possibilities, plus the chance factor, it is extremely difficult to make an analysis of the outcomes of behavior. On the other hand, specific, observable behavioral events and their patterns provide useful data in order to analyze the S$\longleftrightarrow$O interaction which precedes the behavior and the conse-quences that follow the behavior. Such an analysis of the S$\longleftrightarrow$O antecedent and the consequences is crucial to the understanding, prediction, and control of the behavior.

The Interactive Connections and Feedback Loops The final explanation of the S$\longleftrightarrow$O$\longrightarrow$B$\longrightarrow$C model lies in the directionality of the connections and feedback loops shown in Figure 5-2. First is the interactive connection between S and O. This interactive process must occur between the situation and the person before behavior results. Merely placing the S and O together is not enough. The interaction usually takes the form of the O's cognitive interpreta-tion of the immediate S. This type of interaction can be thought of as the process of perception. However, this is only one simple form of interaction. In the S$\longleftrightarrow$O$\longrightarrow$B$\longrightarrow$C model the perceptual process is part of the O, along with the other psychological processes of learning and motivation. When the influence of the physiological being and personality and the greatly expanded conception of S are added, the complexity of the interaction between the S and O becomes clear. Yet, in abstract, simplistic terms, the S$\longleftrightarrow$O can be thought of as the antecedent of behavior. This S$\longleftrightarrow$O interaction should not be thought of as causing the behavior in the S-R sense. Instead, S$\longleftrightarrow$O should be thought of as preceding the behavior, with the S serving as an emitting cue for the behavior, the O as the mediating physiological and cognitive processes, and the $\longleftrightarrow$ as the complex interactive effect between the S and the O that leads to (*not* causes) the behavior.

The second important connection in the S$\longleftrightarrow$O$\longrightarrow$B$\longrightarrow$C model is the

B⟶C relationship. This is an outgrowth of the R-S relationship of the operant model in behavioristic psychology. One key to the connection between behavior and its consequence is the contingency concept. A contingent relationship, as was explained and used in the discussion of contingency management in Chapter 3, is an "if-then" relationship. As used here, this simply means that the person's behavior is affected by its contingent consequences. *If* the person behaves a certain way, *then* a particular consequence will follow. Such contingent consequences can be used to predict and control behavior.

The feedback loops from the consequence to the person and the situation are also important to the model. These feedback loops, shown as the dashed lines in Figure 5-2, show that the consequences affect the person's cognitions and the situational cues. In the simplest sense, these feedback loops can be thought of as learning. Based on the consequences of behavior, the person's (O) perceptions and motives will be affected and situational cues (S) will become associated with or even change on the basis of certain consequences. However, just as the interaction between S and O involves more than perception, the feedback loops from C to O and S involve more than learning. Furthermore, just as perception is placed in the O portion of the model, so is learning. The S⟷O⟶B⟶C model is much more comprehensive than and not as rigorous as the behavioristic and cognitive models upon which it is based.

A CONCEPTUAL FRAMEWORK FOR THE STUDY OF ORGANIZATIONAL BEHAVIOR

The S⟷O⟶B⟶C model can serve as the conceptual framework for the study of organizational behavior. The model attempts to synthesize the cognitive and behavioristic explanations of human behavior. In a very simplified summary, the S⟷O represents the causal, mainly cognitive factors in behavior, and the B⟶C represents the modern behavioristic emphasis on the role that consequences play in behavior. The addition of the S in the antecedent to the behavior and the feedback loops from the C to the O and the S represent the attempt to integrate both cognitive and behavioristic variables. The S⟷O portion of the model primarily contributes to the goal of understanding organizational behavior, and the B⟶C primarily contributes to the goals of prediction and control of organizational behavior.

Obviously, the S⟷O⟶B⟶C model as presented in this chapter and briefly summarized above is only a "barebones" sketch of the complexities of human behavior. Desirably, as the remaining chapters of the book unfold, some of the fine points of the model will become clearer and some of the seemingly simplistic assumptions and unsupported statements will begin to make more sense. The purpose of the model, as with any model, is to identify the important variables and show how they relate to one another. Particularly with the field of organizational behavior, which is still developing and searching for a theoretical base, such a model is extremely important for structuring study and further development. Figure 5-3 places the major variables of organizational behavior (human behavior in organizations) into the $S \longleftrightarrow O \longrightarrow B \longrightarrow C$ model.

The Formal Organization

The framework shown in Figure 5-3 plugs the formal organization into S. The formal organization, of course, is the most important situational environment for the study of organizational behavior. Viewing the organization as a system, there are three subsystems that are especially important to the study of organizational behavior. The first, the structure, serves as the skeleton for the formal organization system. Structure allows the other subsystems, management processes and technology, to operate. The bureaucratic model best represents the classical organization structure. Extensions and modifications of the bureaucratic model, such as centralization-decentralization, flat-tall, departmentation, and line-staff, also have an important role in classical organization structures. The modern structures of organization are based on behavioral, systems, and contingency theories and are designed to meet the challenges of growth, complexity, conflict, and change. Project, matrix, and free-form designs are examples of modern structural forms.

Interacting and interdependent with the organization structure are the management processes. As brought out in the discussion of the management theories in Chapter 3, numerous names are attached to the various processes. Fayol's static processes of planning, organizing, commanding, coordinating, and controlling are still relevant to today's formal organization. However, of even more pertinence and meaning is the dynamic process, which includes

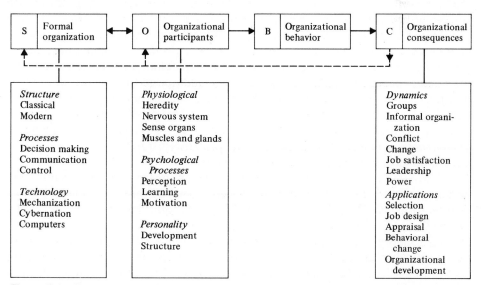

Figure 5-3 The conceptual framework for the study of organizational behavior.

decision making, communication, and control. These management processes are an integral subsystem of the formal organization system.

Although presented as part of the external environment, technology is also a vital subsystem of the formal organizational system. Used in this organizational context, "technology" means the internal technological environment that is used to attain the objectives of an organization. It includes productive operations technologies such as mechanization and cybernation and, of course, computers. The technological subsystem affects and is affected by the organization structure and management processes.

Organizational Participants

Organizational participants or employees are plugged into the O portion of the model. Analogous to the formal organization, these participants can be conceptualized as a system, consisting of three primary subsystems: physiological structure, psychological processes, and personality. For discussion purposes, these subsystems can be made analogous to the three subsystems of the formal organization. For instance, the physiological structure relates to and serves the human as the structure relates to and serves the formal organization. The physiological structure consists of basic units of heredity and includes the nervous system, sense organs, muscles, and glands.

Analogous to the management processes of the formal organization are the participant's psychological processes of perception, learning, and motivation. These processes are at the very heart of the study of organizational behavior. They are probably more vital than any other single part of the overall framework to the understanding of organizational behavior. However, just as separating the processes from the formal organization is largely artificial, so is abstracting the psychological processes from the total human being. Organizational participants behave as a whole, not as a collection of separate parts or processes. When the individual is viewed as this whole, the study of behavior becomes involved with personality. Personality is to the organizational participant as technology is to the formal organization. Both personality and technology pervade their respective entities and are vitally responsible for the outputs. The study of the development and structure of personality is therefore very important to the understanding of organizational behavior.

Just as the systems concept was shown to be relevant to the formal organization, the same concept seems applicable in relating the parts of the human being. The biological-physiological structure, psychological processes, and personality are related to one another and, analogously, to the formal organization subsystems in the manner shown in Figure 5-4. As the triangular presentation shows, the primary base for the organizational participant (formal organization) is the personality (technology). Interacting with and supporting the personality (technology) are the physiological structure (organization structure) and the psychological processes (management processes). It must be realized that the triangular model represents only a very highly simplified

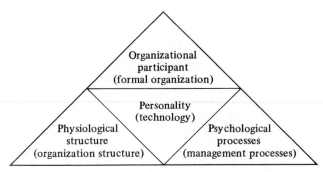

Figure 5-4 Foundation for the human and organizational systems.

abstraction, but it does serve as a starting point for the elementary understanding of the very complex organizational and human variables that make an input into understanding organizational behavior.

Organizational Consequences

The study of the formal organization and the organizational participant lead to the better understanding of organizational behavior. The study of the organizational consequences, on the other hand, can help better predict and control organizational behavior. Again the reader should be reminded that this is a highly simplified generalization. Cognitive theorists are beginning to provide ways to predict and control behavior,[12] and behavioristically oriented theorists are certainly contributing to the better understanding of behavior. Nevertheless, the *emphasis* in the S$\longleftrightarrow$O is for understanding and in the B$\longrightarrow$C is for prediction and control.

Figure 5-3 indicates that certain dynamics and human resource management applications are especially relevant environmental consequences. The dynamics of groups, informal organization, conflict, change, job satisfaction, leadership, and power are particularly important consequences in the study of organizational behavior. The application of managerial techniques in the areas of selection, job design, appraisal, applied behavioral analysis, and organization development can be fed back and change the formal organizational situation and, through learning, the organizational participant. In other words, these managerial applications can lead to the goals of prediction and control of organizational behavior.

A PROLOGUE

Thus far this book has attmpted to provide a solid historical (Chapter 1), behavioral science (Chapter 2), managerial (Chapter 3), and environmental (Chapter 4) foundation for the study and analysis of human behavior in

---

[12]For example, the expectancy models of motivation discussed in Chapter 17 offer some insights and actual methodologies for predicting and controlling behavior.

organizations or organizational behavior. The rest of the book closely follows the conceptual framework shown in Figure 5-3. In Part Two, the structure and processes of organizations are examined. Part Three gives a detailed understanding of human behavior through the psychological processes of perception, learning, and motivation, and the development and theory of personality. In Part Four, some of the dynamic consequences of organizational behavior are analyzed. Particular attention is given to groups, informal organization, conflict, change, job satisfaction, leadership and power. In Part Five, the final part, some specific applications for the management of organizational behavior are presented. Attention is given to techniques and approaches for selection, job design, appraisal, behavioral change, and organization development. Even though this last part is the only one dealing directly with techniques for application, the small cases at the end of each chapter always brings the discussion in the text back to a very realistic, practical application.

SUMMARY

Everyone is concerned with human behavior. Yet philosophers, theologians, behavioral scientists, and the person on the street have still not completely uncovered the true understanding of human behavior. All people think they are experts and are defensive about their views. The difference between the behavioral science approach and the other approaches is that behavioral scientists use the methods of science and take an understanding, rather than an evaluating, approach. Some widely recognized approaches include Sigmund Freud's psychoanalytic model, the more philosophically based existentialistic model, and the two major models from the behavioral sciences, the cognitive and behavioristic. The cognitive model gives the human more "credit" and assumes that behavior is purposive and goal-oriented. Cognitive processes such as expectancy and perception help explain behavior. The behavioristic model deals with observable behaviors and the environmental contingencies of the behavior. Classical behaviorism explained behavior in terms of S-R while more modern behaviorism gives more emphasis to contingent consequences or R-S.

The field of organizational behavior has the goals of understanding, prediction, and control. An eclectic model taken from the cognitive and behavioristic approaches is portrayed by $S \longleftrightarrow O \longrightarrow B \longrightarrow C$. This model can perhaps best meet the goals of organizational behavior. The $S \longleftrightarrow O$ portion deals mainly with understanding and the $B \longrightarrow C$ portion with prediction and control. If the formal organization is substituted for S, the organizational participant for O, and the dynamics and applications are put into C, the model can serve as a conceptual framework for the study of organizational behavior. The parts of this framework are used to structure the remaining chapters of the book.

QUESTIONS FOR DISCUSSION AND REVIEW

1 In your own words, identify and summarize the models of human behavior.
2 Identify and explain the various parts of the S$\longleftrightarrow$O$\longrightarrow$B$\longrightarrow$C model. What role do the feedback loops play?
3 What parts of the S$\longleftrightarrow$O$\longrightarrow$B$\longrightarrow$C model are cognitively oriented and what parts are behavioristically oriented? What parts can be more identified with understanding and what parts with prediction and control?
4 Briefly summarize the conceptual framework for organizational behavior.
5 Justify the analogy made between the formal organization and the organizational participant and their corresponding elements (as in Figure 5-4).

CASE: CONCEPTUAL MODEL: DREAM OR REALITY?

Hank James has been section head for the accounting group at Yake Company for fourteen years. His boss, Mary Stein, felt that Hank was about ready to be moved up to the corporate finance staff. However, it was company policy to send people like Hank to the University Executive Development Program before such a promotion was made. Hank became enrolled in the program and found that one of the first parts dealt with organizational behavior. Hank felt that with fourteen years of managing people, this would be a snap. However, during the lecture on organizational behavior the professor made some comments that really bothered Hank. The professor said,

> "Most managers know their technical job but do a lousy job of managing their people. One of the problems is that just because supervisors have a lot of experience with people, they think they are experts. The fact is that psychologists are just beginning to scratch the surface of understanding human behavior. In addition, to effectively manage people we also have to somehow be able to better predict and control organizational behavior. There are some models that are just beginning to be developed that will hopefully help the manager better understand, predict, and control organizational behavior."

Hank was upset by the fact that this professor was apparently discounting the value of experience in managing people, and he could not see how a conceptual model that some professor dreamed up could help him manage people better.

1 Do you think Hank is justified in his concerns after hearing the professor? What role can experience play in managing people?
2 What is the purpose of conceptual models such as those presented in this chapter? How would you weigh the relative value of studying theories and research findings versus the "school of hard knocks" experience for the effective management of people?
3 Using the S$\longleftrightarrow$O$\longrightarrow$B$\longrightarrow$C model presented in the chapter how would you explain to Hank that this could help him better manage people in his organization?

SELECTED REFERENCES

"An Overview of the Field," in George Strauss, et al. (eds.), *Organizational Behavior Research and Issues,* Industrial Relations Research Association, University of Wisconsin, Madison, Wisconsin, 1974, pp. 1–17.

Davis, Keith: "A Law of Diminishing Returns in Organizational Behavior?" *Personnel Journal,* December 1975, pp. 616–619.

Heilbroner, Robert L.: "Marxism, Psychoanalysis, and the Problem of a Unified Theory of Behavior," *Social Research,* Autumn 1975, pp. 414–432.

Hughes, Charles L., and Vincent S. Flowers: "Toward Existentialism in Management," *The Conference Board Record,* September 1975, pp. 60–64.

Meltzer, H., and Walter Nord: "The Present Status of Industrial and Organizational Psychology," *Personnel Psychology,* Spring 1973, pp. 11–29.

Nichols, Theo: "The 'Socialism' of Management: Some Comments on the New 'Human Relations,'" *The Sociological Review,* May 1975, pp. 245–265.

Rogers, Carl R., and B. F. Skinner: "Some Issues Concerning the Control of Human Behavior: A Symposium," *Science,* November 30, 1956, pp. 1057–1066.

Part Two

The Structure
and Processes
of Organizations

Chapter 6

Classical Organization Theory and Structure

Structure, while it represents only the skeletal framework, is an important subsystem of the formal organization system. The usual starting point in analyzing organization structure is the bureaucratic model. After presenting and discussing this model, the chapter gives an overview and analysis of some of the extensions and modifications represented by the concepts of centralization-decentralization, flat-tall, departmentation, and line-staff. Behavioral implications are given attention throughout the chapter.

THE BUREAUCRATIC MODEL

A logical starting point in the analysis of any theory would be the ideal. Max Weber, who was presented in Chapter 2 as one of the pioneers of modern sociology, was concerned with an ideal organization structure called a *bureaucracy.* His concern was a natural extension of his interest in the development and change of Western society. He believed that rationalization was the most persistent cultural value of Western society. On a micro level, the bureaucracy represented a completely rational form of organization.

The Characteristics of Bureaucracy

Weber specified several characteristics of an ideal bureaucracy. The four major ones are the following:

117

1 *Specialization and division of labor.*   Weber's bureaucracy contained: "A specified sphere of competence. This involves (*a*) a sphere of obligations to perform functions which has been marked off as part of a systematic division of labour (*b*) The provision of the incumbent with the necessary authority . . . (*c*) That the necessary means of compulsion are clearly defined and their use is subject to definite conditions."[1] This statement implies that Weber recognized the importance of having the authority and power to carry out assigned duties. In addition, the bureaucrat must know the precise limits of his sphere of competence so as not to infringe upon that of others.

2 *Positions arranged in a hierarchy.*   Weber stated, "The organization of offices follows the principle of hierarchy; that is, each lower office is under the control and supervision of a higher one."[2] This bureaucratic characteristic forces control over every member in the structure. Some organization theorists, such as Herbert Simon, have pointed out that hierarchy is in the natural order of things. An example lies in the biological subsystems, such as the digestive and circulatory, which are composed of organs, the organs composed of tissues, and the tissues composed of cells. Each cell is in turn hierarchically organized into a nucleus, cell wall, and cytoplasm. The same is true of physical phenomena such as molecules, which are composed of electrons, neutrons, and protons.[3] In a manner analogous to the biological and physical structures, hierarchy is a basic characteristic of complex organizational structures.

3 *A system of abstract rules.*   Weber felt a need for "a continuous organization of official functions bound by rules."[4] A rational approach to organization requires a set of formal rules to ensure uniformity and coordination of effort. A well-understood system of regulations also provides the continuity and stability that Weber thought were so important. Rules persist, whereas personnel may frequently change. They may range from no smoking in certain areas to the need for board approval for multithousand-dollar capital expenditures.

4 *Impersonal relationships.*   It was Weber's belief that the ideal official should be dominated by "a spirit of formalistic impersonality, without hatred or passion, and hence without affection or enthusiasm."[5] Once again Weber was speaking from the viewpoint of ideal rationality and not of realistic implementation. He felt that in order for bureaucrats to make completely rational decisions, they must avoid emotional attachment to subordinates and clients.

The four characteristics just described are not the only ones recognized and discussed by Weber. Another important aspect of ideal bureaucracy is that employment is based on technical qualifications. The bureaucrat is protected against arbitrary dismissal, and promotions are made according to seniority

---

[1]A. M. Henderson and Talcott Parsons (trans. and ed.), *Max Weber: The Theory of Social and Economic Organization,* The Free Press, New York, © 1947 by Oxford University Press, New York, p. 330.

[2]Ibid., p. 331.

[3]Herbert A. Simon, *The New Science of Management Decision,* Harper & Row, Publishers, Incorporated, New York, 1960, pp. 40–41.

[4]Henderson and Parsons, op. cit., p. 330.

[5]Ibid., p. 340.

and/or achievement. In total, it must be remembered that Weber's bureaucracy was intended to be an ideal construct: no real-world organization exactly follows the Weber model. Peter M. Blau summarizes Weber's thinking as follows:

> Weber dealt with bureaucracy as what he termed an ideal type. This methodological concept does not represent an average of the attributes of all existing bureaucracies (or other social structures), but a pure type, derived by abstracting the most characteristic bureaucratic aspects of all known organizations.[6]

The ideal is only the starting point, not the end, of formal organizational analysis.

Historical Conditions for Bureaucracy

Blau outlined four historical conditions which help promote the development of a bureaucratic form of organization.[7] They are:

1 Money economy
2 Capitalistic system
3 Protestant Ethic
4 Large size

Blau carefully points out that all four conditions are *not* necessary in order for bureaucracy to exist. For example, the bureaucratic organizations of ancient civilizations, plus the widespread existence of bureaucratic organizations in contemporary noncapitalistic and non-Protestant countries such as Russia, give ample evidence that especially points 2 and 3 above are not prerequisites. Nevertheless, each of Blau's conditions, including capitalism and Protestantism, may help create an atmosphere that is conducive to a bureaucratic form of organization structure. A better understanding of bureaucracy can be gained by analyzing the four conditions outlined by Blau.

Money Economy   A monetary economy can promote the development of a bureaucratic organization. The major reason is that the payment of money for services rendered creates the proper degree of commitment in organizational participants. A slave or volunteer economy does not foster bureaucratic development. In a slave economy, there is too much dependence between slave and master. The slave generally refuses to assume any responsibility and will not exercise personal initiative. A bureaucracy or any other kind of organization cannot survive in the long run with this kind of commitment from its personnel. Unpaid volunteers have essentially an opposite effect. Volunteers are too independent and refuse to follow bureaucratic rules. No discipline is maintained. The monetary economy does not have the problems inherent in

[6]Peter M. Blau, *Bureaucracy in Modern Society,* Random House, Inc., New York, 1956, p. 34.
[7]Ibid., pp. 36–40.

slavery or an all-volunteer arrangement. "The economic dependence of the salaried employee on his job and his freedom to advance himself in his career engender the orientation toward work required for disciplined *and* responsible conduct."[8]

Capitalism   It is conceptually difficult to separate a money economy from capitalism. Both go hand in hand in promoting bureaucracy. A capitalistic or free enterprise system is characterized by competition with market determination of wages and prices. In theory, free competition would seem to create a large number of small organizations. In reality, private enterprise tends to spawn large organizations which must bureaucratize in order to become efficient. History has shown that under capitalism giant corporations are formed, and in order to preserve competition, large governmental operations also become necessary. To countervail large business and government, giant labor unions evolve. Thus, at least indirectly, the free enterprise system seems to contribute to the bureaucratization of business, government, and unions.

Protestant Ethic   Weber is as well known for his study of the impact of religion on Western culture as he is for his analysis of the bureaucratic model. It was only natural that he was especially cognizant of the role of religious values in his study of bureaucracy. In analyzing Weber's classic book *The Protestant Ethic and the Spirit of Capitalism,* Blau points out that

> . . . the Reformation—especially Calvinism, the religious doctrine of the Puritans—apart from its spiritual significance, had the social consequence of giving rise to this-worldly asceticism, a disciplined devotion to hard work in the pursuit of one's vocation.[9]

The thesis of Weber's book is that the hard-working, individualistic values described above, i.e., the Protestant Ethic, gave rise to capitalism and capitalism in turn fostered the development of bureaucracy. This analysis points out the holistic or systems aspects of society: one part affects, and is affected by, the others.

Large Size   The large size of organizations is undoubtedly the single most important condition that leads to bureaucratization and that can overcome the other conditions of a money economy, capitalism, and Protestantism. All characteristics of a bureaucracy are built around the framework of large-scale administrative tasks. Bureaucratic adaptability to large size is well documented in history. The administration of the large system of waterways in ancient Egypt; the maintenance of a far-reaching system of roads in the Roman Empire; and the control over millions of people's religious lives by the Roman Catholic Church could probably not have been accomplished without the

[8]Ibid., p. 37.
[9]Ibid., p. 39.

bureaucratic form of organization. To varying degrees all large organizations of modern society, regardless of economic or religious orientation, are also bureaucracies. Large business, industrial, governmental, church, military, hospital, union, and educational organizations throughout the contemporary world are bureaucratic in nature. In order to survive and maintain some degree of efficiency in accomplishing their goals, most of these large organizations have greatly depended upon hierarchy, specialization, rules, and impersonality.

The relevant question is not whether today's organizations are using the bureaucratic principles because, to a large degree, they all are. Rather, the critical question for contemporary analysis of classical organization theory is whether the functions of bureaucracy outweigh some of the very serious dysfunctions. Weber can be legitimately accused of ignoring this question. He almost completely disregarded or, at least, deemphasized the dysfunctional consequences of the bureaucratic model. A very close reading of Weber's work does indicate that he recognized certain conflicts or dilemmas inherent in bureaucracy. However, he so greatly stressed the functional attributes, either explicitly or implicitly, that the significant dysfunctions were never properly considered in his classic organizational analysis.

BUREAUCRATIC DYSFUNCTIONS

With the exception of Weber, other sociologists and philosophers have been very critical of bureaucracies. For example, Karl Marx believed that bureaucracies were used by the dominant capitalist class to control the other, lower social classes. Marxist bureaucracies were characterized by strict hierarchy and discipline, veneration of authority, incompetent officials, lack of initiative or imagination, fear of responsibility, and a process of self-aggrandizement.[10] This interpretation of bureaucracy is basically listing the opposite of the functions that Weber proposed.

The Weber model can serve equally well in analyzing either the functional or the dysfunctional ramifications of classical organization structure. The characteristic of specialization is a good illustration. The Weber bureaucratic model emphasizes that specialization serves as a function for efficiency. The model ignores, but can be used to point out, the dysfunctional qualities of specialization. Empirical investigation has uncovered both functional and dysfunctional consequences. In other words, specialization has been shown to lead to increased productivity and efficiency but also to create conflict between specialized units to the detriment of the overall goal of the organization. For example, specialization may impede communication between units. The management team of a highly specialized unit has its own terminology, similar interests, attitudes, and personal goals. Because "outsiders are different," the specialized unit tends to withdraw into itself and not fully communicate with units above, below, or horizontal to it.

What was said of specialization also holds true for the other characteristics

[10]Rolf E. Rogers, *Organizational Theory*, Allyn and Bacon, Inc., Boston, 1975, p. 4.

of bureaucracy. The functional attributes of hierarchy are that it maintains unity of command, coordinates activities and personnel, reinforces authority, and serves as the formal system of communication. In theory, the hierarchy has both a downward and an upward orientation, but in practice it has often turned out to have only a downward emphasis. Thus, individual initiative and participation are often blocked, upward communication is impeded, and there is no formal recognition of horizontal communication. Personnel who only follow the formal hierarchy may waste a great deal of time and energy.

Bureaucratic rules probably have the most obvious dysfunctional qualities. Contributing to the bureaucratic image of red tape, rules often become the ends for behavior rather than the means for more effective goal attainment. Drucker cites the following common misuses of rules that require reports and procedures:

> **1** First is the mistaken belief that procedural rules are instruments of morality. They should only be used to indicate how something can be done expeditiously, not determine what is right or wrong conduct.
>
> **2** Secondly, procedural rules are sometimes mistakenly substituted for judgment. Bureaucrats should not be mesmerized by printed forms; they should only be used in cases where judgment is not required.
>
> **3** The third and most common misuse of procedural rules is as a punitive control device from above. A bureaucrat is often required to comply to rules that have nothing to do with his job. An example would be the plant manager who has to accurately fill out numerous forms for staff personnel and corporate management which he cannot use in obtaining his own objectives.[11]

Drucker would like to see every procedural rule put on trial for its life at least every five years. He cites one case where all the reports and forms of an organization were totally done away with for two months. At the end of the suspension, three-fourths of the reports and forms were deemed unnecessary and were eliminated.[12]

The impersonality characteristic of the bureaucracy has even more dysfunctional consequences than specialization, hierarchy, and rules. Behaviorally oriented theorists and researchers, including Robert K. Merton and Philip Selznick, two widely known scholars, have given a great deal of attention to the behavioral dysfunctions of bureaucratic structures. Merton concluded that one major behavioral consequence of bureaucratic structuring is the disruption of overall goal attainment. He felt that exaggerated adherence to bureaucratic rules and discipline affects participants' personalities to the point where the rules and discipline become ends in themselves.[13] Selznick made

---

[11]Peter Drucker, *The Practice of Management*, Harper & Row, Publishers, Incorporated, New York, 1954, pp. 133–134.

[12]Ibid., p. 135.

[13]Robert K. Merton, *Social Theory and Social Structure*, The Free Press, Glencoe, Ill., 1949, pp. 153–157.

specific recommendations to overcome some of the behavioral dysfunctions of bureaucracy. Most of his insights were gained from his noted study of the Tennessee Valley Authority. He was convinced that more enlightened organizational concepts, such as delegation of authority, must be incorporated into bureaucratic structures for them to become workable, cooperative systems.[14]

THE GOULDNER RESEARCH ON BUREAUCRACIES

Besides the work by Merton and Selznick, the research on bureaucracy conducted by Alvin Gouldner has important insights for the study of organizational behavior.[15] An intensive, three-year case analysis was made of the bureaucratization of a gypsum plant. This organization employed 225 workers, 75 in the mining operation and 150 in the various departments in the surface plant. The critical variables studied were the change of leadership and the mining-surface situational distinction.

Change in Leadership

The old management in the plant studied was classified by Gouldner as an indulgency pattern. This leadership pattern operated in a very informal and lenient manner under "Old Doug," the plant manager. He ran a pretty loose ship, as is evident in the following comment of a surface worker. "I really like to work in this place . . . There is nobody coming around pushing you all the time. The boys at the top are certainly lax in their treatment. There is none of this constant checking up on the job . . . Your free time is your own."[16]

When Old Doug died, a new manager, given the pseudonym of Vincent Peele, took over the plant. The indulgency pattern died along with Old Doug. Mr. Peele was anxious to integrate himself into the existing organization but found he was unable to cope with the informal methods and relationships that were part of the indulgency pattern. One worker noted that Peele was the opposite of Old Doug and that he failed to adapt to Doug's style of management. The worker observed that Peele ". . . always came around checking on the men and standing over them. As long as production was going out Doug didn't stand over them. Peele is always around as though he doesn't have faith in the men like Doug."[17]

Soon after Peele assumed command, he replaced the indulgency pattern with a very formal bureaucratic style of leadership, including strict rules and discipline. The method of handling absenteeism typified the contrast between the old and the new. "Among other things, Vincent is cracking down on absenteeism . . . Doug used to go right out and get the men . . . He would hop

[14]Philip Selznick, *TVA and the Grass Roots,* University of California Press, Berkeley, Calif., 1949, especially part three, pp. 217–266.

[15]Alvin W. Gouldner, *Patterns of Industrial Bureaucracy,* The Free Press, Glencoe, Ill., 1954.

[16]Ibid., p. 46.

[17]Ibid., p. 81.

into his car, drive down to their house and tell the men that he needed them . . . Vincent doesn't stand for it, and he has let it be known that any flagrant violations will mean that the man gets his notice."[18]

One of Peele's strategies was to fire subordinates who were not able to give him complete loyalty and adapt to his new bureaucratic methods. The replacements were loyal outsiders who were sympathetic to his cause. The disciplinary moves self-perpetuated the bureaucracy, but the firing of Old Doug's management team and their replacement by outsiders further alienated the workers from Peele. Their reaction only caused Peele to institute more and stricter rules and discipline.

The Situational Impact of Bureaucratization

The second important aspect of the study was the effect that Peele's bureaucratization had on two distinct situational variables. The study has some interesting implications for contingency management. Two clearly separate impacts were caused by the bureaucracy on the surface plant and on the mine. In the surface operation, bureaucratization worked out quite well and was even reluctantly accepted by the workers. In the mine, workers literally refused to adapt to the bureaucratic form of organization. Their informal group norms and differing belief system were strong enough to resist the formal bureaucratic methods. The very inherent dangers of mining resulted in a completely different set of attitudes toward work and authority. Often the miner's life itself depended on the procedures and rules that existed. Therefore, a miner felt justified in refusing orders from the top because "down here we are our own bosses." Furthermore, to escape the pressures of the dangerous work, an occasional drinking spree that resulted in not showing up for work the next morning was acceptable to the miners. The head of the mine, "Old Bull," scoffed at Peele's no-absenteeism rule as "red tape." He complained that "If we laid off a man for absenteeism, we'd have to lay off four or five all the time."[19] Peele forced his form of bureaucracy on the mine unsuccessfully. If he had used a contingency approach, this could have been avoided.

Implications of Gouldner's Research

Gouldner's study clearly pointed out that certain physical and psychological conditions must exist in order for bureaucracy to be functional. However, before broad generalizations are made, it must be remembered that this was a case study. Gouldner himself stated, "As a case history of only one factory, this study can offer no conclusions about the 'state' of American industry at large, or about the forces that make for bureaucratization in general."[20] Nevertheless, the study pointed out the importance of situational variables in organizational structure. It represents a landmark case for contingency man-

[18]Ibid., p. 80.
[19]Ibid., p. 151.
[20]Ibid., p. 231.

agement. The study also documented the importance and power of the informal organization in a bureaucracy.

Gouldner definitely refined and extended Weber's classic model. Through his research, he was able to determine the aspects of bureaucracy that created tensions. He identified three bureaucratic patterns: *mock, representative,* and *punishment-centered.* The characteristics of these three types of bureaucracy are summarized in Figure 6-1. Both the representative and the punishment-centered forms have certain parallels with the Weber model. The key difference between Gouldner's three types is the extent to which rules are enforced. Evidence from his research indicated that a punishment-centered bureaucracy creates the most tension and generates the most complaints about dysfunctions such as red tape and impersonality.

THE FATE OF BUREAUCRACY

Many modern organization theorists are predicting the complete disappearance, or at least a drastic modification, of the classical bureaucratic structure. Warren Bennis has probably been the most vocal prophet of its death. He contends that "the bureaucratic form of organization is becoming less and less effective; that it is hopelessly out of joint with contemporary realities; that new shapes, patterns, and models are emerging which promise drastic changes in the conduct of the corporation and of managerial practices in general."[21] Most people can testify to the following types of experiences from their own observations of a bureaucracy:

[21]Warren Bennis, "Beyond Bureaucracy," *Trans-Action,* July-August 1965, p. 31.

Figure 6-1 Summary of Characteristics of Gouldner's Three Patterns of Bureaucracy

Mock	Representative	Punishment-centered
1. Rules are neither enforced by management nor obeyed by workers.	1. Rules are both enforced by management and obeyed by workers.	1. Rules are enforced by either workers or management and evaded by the other group.
2. Usually, little conflict occurs between the two groups.	2. A few tensions but little overt conflict are generated.	2. Relatively great tension and conflict are entailed.
3. Joint violation and evasion of rules are buttressed by the informal sentiments of the participants.	3. Joint support for rules is buttressed by informal sentiments, mutual participation, initiation, and education of workers and management.	3. Rules are enforced by punishment and supported by the informal sentiments of *either* workers or management.

Source.: Adapted from Alvin W. Gouldner's *Patterns of Industrial Bureaucracy,* The Free Press, Glencoe, Ill., 1954, p. 217. Used with permission.

    1   Bosses without (and underlings with) technical competence

    2   Arbitrary and zany rules

    3   An underworld (or informal) organization which subverts or even replaces the formal apparatus

    4   Confusion and conflict among roles

    5   Cruel treatment of subordinates based not on rational or legal grounds but upon inhumanity.[22]

The above observations support the red-tape, bureaupathic image of the bureaucratic form of organization. Victor Thompson describes the often-existing "bureaupathology" thus:

> Everyone has met the pompous, self-important official at some time in his life, and many have served under autocratic, authoritarian superiors. Employees who seem to be interested in nothing but a minimal performance of their own little office routines are numerous enough, and impersonal treatment of clients and associates that approaches the coldness of absolute zero is not, sadly, uncommon.[23]

Observations such as the above have led to the tremendously popular "Parkinson's Laws" (for example, bureaucratic staffs increase in inverse proportion to the amount of work done[24]) and the more recent "Peter Principle" (managers rise to their level of incompetence in bureaucracies[25]). These "laws" and "principles" have received wide public acceptance because everyone has observed and experienced what Parkinson and Peter wrote about. But as one organizational scholar has noted,

> These two writers have primarily capitalized on the frustrations toward government and business administration felt by the general public, which is not familiar with the processes necessitated by large-scale organization. Parkinson and Peter made a profit on their best sellers; they added little to the scientific study of organizations.[26]

In addition to the popularized criticisms of bureaucracy, a more academic analysis also uncovers many deficiencies. Bennis summarized some of them as follows:

    1   Bureaucracy does not adequately allow for personal growth and the development of mature personalities.

    2   It develops conformity and "group-think."

---

[22]Ibid., p. 32.

[23]Victor A. Thompson, *Modern Organization,* Alfred A. Knopf, Inc., New York, 1961, p. 23.

[24]Northcote Parkinson, *Parkinson's Law and Other Studies in Administration,* Houghton Mifflin Company, Boston, 1957.

[25]Laurence J. Peter, *The Peter Principle,* William Morrow & Company, Inc., New York, 1969.

[26]Rogers, op. cit., p. 4.

3 It does not take into account the "informal organization" and the emergent and unanticipated problems.

4 Its systems of control and uathority are hopelessly outdated.

5 It has no juridical process.

6 It does not possess adequate means for resolving differences and conflicts between ranks, and most particularly, between functional groups.

7 Communication (and innovative ideas) are thwarted or distorted due to hierarchical divisions.

8 The full human resources of bureaucracy are not being utilized due to mistrust, fear of reprisals, etc.

9 It cannot assimilate the influx of new technology or scientists entering the organization.

10 It modifies personality structure so that people become and reflect the dull, gray, conditioned "organization man."[27]

Also from an academic viewpoint, Thompson states that bureaupathology occurs because "the growing imbalance between the rights of authority positions, on the one hand, and the abilities and skills needed in a technological age, on the other, generates tensions and insecurities in the system of authority."[28] Thompson regards this growing imbalance between ability and authority as the most symptomatic characteristic of modern bureaucracy.

Parkinson, Peter, Bennis, and Thompson represent the extreme critics of bureaucratic organization. Nevertheless, during the past few years popular writers, scholars, practitioners, and the general public have felt increasing dissatisfaction with classical bureaucratic concepts. In the case of the public, the recent consumerism movement is largely a result of dissatisfaction with bureaucracies. The argument is not that the classical bureaucratic theorists were necessarily wrong but, rather, that the times have rendered their concepts and principles no longer relevant. Bureaucratic organization is thought to be too inflexible to adapt readily to the dynamic nature and purpose of many of today's organizations and public needs. Flexibility and adaptability are necessary requirements for modern organization structures. The increasing size of organizations, in terms of both mergers and internal growth, the advent of the computer, and the tremendous strides made in all types of technology are but a few of the things which have contributed to a new organizational environment. Sociologist Charles Perrow probably best summarizes the current situation facing many bureaucracies thus: ". . . the rate of change is so rapid, the new techniques so unproven and so uncertain, the number of contingencies so enormous, that the bureaucratic model is only partly applicable . . . Something else is needed."[29] The rest of this chapter and the next discuss this "something else."

---

[27]Bennis, op. cit., p. 33.

[28]Thompson, op. cit., p. 23.

[29]Charles Perrow, *Organizational Analysis: A Sociological View,* Wadsworth Publishing Company, Inc., Belmont, Calif., 1970, p. 60.

EXTENSIONS OF CLASSICAL CONCEPTS

Besides the bureaucratic and classical aspects of organization, the concern over vertical and horizontal structural arrangements emerged in the 1950s and 1960s. Vertical analysis of structure concentrates on centralization versus decentralization and flat versus tall. These concerns are modifications of the classical principles of delegation and span of control. Decentralization expands the principle of delegation to the point of an overall philosophy of organization and management. A *tall* organization structure simply means a series of narrow spans of control, and a *flat* structure incorporates wide spans. The bureaucratic principle of hierarchy is also closely related to the vertical concepts.

Horizontal structural analysis is concerned with organizing one level of hierarchy. The concepts of departmentation and line-staff represent this approach. They are derived chiefly from the bureaucratic doctrine of specialization. Departmentation concentrates on organizing each level to attain maximum benefit from high degrees of specialization. The staff concept attempts to resolve the vertical and horizontal conflicts that appeared in the classical scheme. In general, the concepts discussed in the rest of this chapter carry the classical concepts one step further. They give greater weight to the importance of the human element and recognize that simple, mechanistic structural arrangements are not satisfactory for complex organizations.

Centralization and Decentralization

The terms *centralization* and *decentralization* are freely tossed about in both management literature and practice. Most often, both the scholar and the practitioner neglect to define what they mean by the concept. There are three basic types of centralization-decentralization. One is the geographical or territorial concentration (centralized) or dispersion (decentralized) of operations. For example, the term *centralized* can be used to refer to an organization that has all its operations under one roof or in one region. On the other hand, the dispersion of an organization's operations throughout the country or the world is a form of decentralization. The word *geographical* is often not prefixed, thereby adding to the confusion. A second type is functional centralization and decentralization. A good example is the personnel function of an organization. A separate personnel department that performs personnel functions for the other departments is said to be centralized. However, if the various functional departments, e.g., marketing, production, and finance, handle their own personnel functions, then personnel is considered to be decentralized. Figure 6-2 shows how functional centralization-decentralization would appear on a simplified organization chart. Both geographical and functional centralization and decentralization are descriptive rather than analytical in nature.

The third type is the only analytical use of the concept. This is where the terms *centralization* and *decentralization* refer to the retention or delegation of decision-making prerogatives or command. From an organization theory and

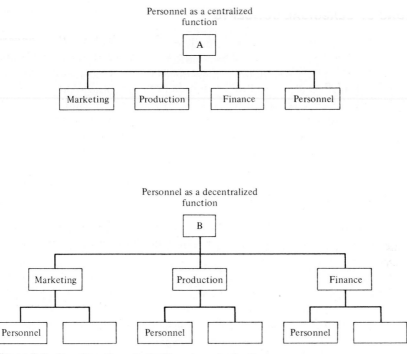

Figure 6-2 Functional centralization-decentralization.

analysis standpoint, this third type is the most relevant use of centralization and decentralization. They are relative concepts because every organization structure contains both features, and they differ only in degree.

Contrary to common belief, it is not possible to determine whether an organization is centralized or decentralized by merely looking at the organization chart. The determining factor is how much of the decision making is retained at the top and how much is delegated to the lower levels. This retention or delegation is not reflected on the organization chart.

Determining Decentralization Both management writers and practitioners generally favor decentralization. It represents one of the "in" concepts and identifies the advocate as a modern-thinking theorist or practitioner. On the other hand, centralization has taken on the connotation of being traditional and even authoritarian. Albers observed that,

> In recent years, decentralization has become the golden calf of management philosophy. It has been lauded by such terms as "more democratic," "a step toward world peace," "greater freedom of spirit," and "less authoritarian." The implicit assumption is that centralization reflects the opposite of these worthy qualities.[30]

[30]Henry H. Albers, *Principles of Management,* 3d ed., John Wiley & Sons, Inc., New York, 1969, p. 186.

Although most contemporary managers proselytize the values of decentralization, in reality their use of the concept turns out to be more fiction than fact. A typical case is the executive who gives a speech at the Rotary Club luncheon praising the values of decentralization. More often than not, these individuals are likely to be practicing a high degree of centralization although they may truly think they are running a thoroughly decentralized operation. Obviously, the mere verbalization of decentralization by top management is not sufficient to determine the extent of decentralization. Ernest Dale has formulated some objective criteria that can be very helpful in measuring the extent of decentralization. He states that decentralization is greater:

1   The greater the number of decisions made lower down the management hierarchy.
2   The more important the decisions made lower down the management hierarchy. For example, the greater the sum of capital expenditure that can be approved by the plant manager without consulting anyone else, the greater the degree of decentralization in this field.
3   The more functions affected by decisions made at lower levels. Thus companies which permit only operational decisions to be made at separate branch plants are less decentralized than those which also permit financial and personnel decisions at branch plants.
4   The less checking required on the decision. Decentralization is greatest when no check at all must be made; less when superiors have to be informed of the decision after it has been made; still less if superiors have to be consulted before the decision is made. The fewer people to be consulted, and the lower they are on the management hierarchy, the greater the degree of decentralization.[31]

Optimum Degree of Decentralization   So far, the discussion has probably implied that decentralization is somehow better than centralization. In truth, neither concept is an ideal or intrinsically good or bad. Generally speaking, decentralization is much more compatible with the behavioral aspects of management. This relevancy is due in part to the lower-level participation in decision making that results from decentralization. Increased motivation is an extremely important by-product. Besides the behavioral benefits, more effective decisions are possible because of the speed and first-hand knowledge that decentralization provides. Decentralization also affords invaluble experience in decision making for lower-level executives. Finally, it allows more time for top management to concentrate on policy making and creative innovation. On the other side of the ledger, centralization "produces uniformity of policy and action, lessens risks of error by subordinates who lack either information or skill, utilizes the skills of central and specialized experts, and enables closer control of operations."[32]

[31]Ernest Dale, *Planning and Developing the Company Organization Structure*, Research Report 20, American Management Association, New York, 1952, p. 118.
[32]Edwin B. Flippo and Gary Hunsinger, *Management,* 3d ed., Allyn and Bacon, Inc., Boston, 1975, p. 183.

On balance, the answer to the problem of what is the optimum degree of decentralization is that it depends on the situation. Newman, Summer, and Warren suggest seven questions that should be considered in determining the degree of decentralization:

    1 Who knows the facts on which the decision will be based, or who can get them together most readily?

    2 Who has the capacity to make sound decisions?

    3 Must speedy, on-the-spot decisions be made to meet local conditions?

    4 Must the local activity be carefully coordinated with other activities?

    5 How significant is the decision?

    6 How busy are the executives who might be assigned planning tasks?

    7 Will initiative and morale be significantly improved by decentralization?[33]

An analysis and weighing of these seven factors can provide the needed insight into determining the proper degree of centralization-decentralization.

A Model of Decentralization   Traditionally, the most widely cited model of decentralization has been the General Motors Corporation. Alfred P. Sloan, the "Great Organizer," was primarily responsible for the formulation of the original model. Contrary to common belief, centralization, as well as decentralization, played a vital role in his scheme. His model was based on two important premises:

    1 The responsibility attached to the chief executive of each operation shall in no way be limited. Each such organization headed by its chief executive shall be complete in every necessary function and enabled to exercise its full initiative and logical development. (Decentralization of operations.)

    2 Certain central organization functions are absolutely essential to the logical development and proper coordination of the Corporation's activities. (Centralized staff services to advise the line on specialized phases of the work, and central measurement of results to check the exercise of delegated responsibility).[34]

Simply stated, Sloan's General Motors model utilizes centralized control of decentralized operations.

Many large industrial organizations have patterned themselves after the Sloan model. This is undoubtedly a major reason why American industry has been able to overcome the economic concept of decreasing returns to scale. This concept states that when a firm gets very large, further growth will result in a proportionately lower amount of output. The chief reasons given for decreasing returns to scale are that a breakdown in communication occurs, there is a loss of control, and a general decline in organization and management

---

[33]William H. Newman, Charles E. Summer, and E. Kirby Warren, *The Process of Management,* 3d ed., Prentice-Hall, Inc., Englewood Cliffs, N. J., 1972, pp. 54–55.

[34]Ernest Dale, "Contributions to Administration by Alfred P. Sloan, Jr., and GM," *Administrative Science Quarterly,* June 1956, p. 41.

efficiency develops. To date in American industry, this point of decreasing returns has not really occurred. The industrial corporations keep growing larger and larger. For example, there are about twenty United States corporations with over $3.5 billion worth of assets. There are tremendously large organizations with worldwide operations that employ hundreds of thousands of employees. One important way they have overcome breakdowns in communication, control, and managerial effectiveness is through centralized control of decentralized operations.

Besides the overall planning, organizing, and controlling advantages of the Sloan type of decentralization, there are also some very practical day-to-day benefits. These advantages were summarized in the following manner by Peter Drucker on the basis of interviews with several GM executives who had worked under the Sloan type of structure:

1 The speed and lack of confusion with which a decision can be made.

2 The absence of conflict of interest between corporate management and the divisions.

3 The sense of fairness, appreciation, confidence, and security that comes when organizational "politics" are kept under control.

4 The democracy and informality in management where everyone is free to criticize but no one tries to sabotage.

5 The absence of a gap between the "privileged few" top managers and the "great many" subordinate managers in the organization.

6 The availability of a large supply of good, experienced leaders capable of taking top responsibility.

7 The inability of weak divisions and managers to ride on the coat tails of successful divisions or trade on past performance.

8 The absence of "edict management" and the presence of public policies which are a product of the experiences of all the people concerned.[35]

Strategy and Structure   The Sloan model is the most widely recognized, but not the only, influence on decentralized organization. Alfred D. Chandler, Jr., a professor of history, made a significant contribution to the understanding of the reasons why organization structure evolves. He proposed a thesis that structure follows managerial strategy.[36] To test this thesis, he made an in-depth study of the structural changes that occurred in four companies. Data were obtained from internal company records, correspondence, reports, minutes, and interviews with company executives who had participated in the changes. He discovered that each company eventually evolved into a decentralized structure, but for different reasons. The decentralization of the four companies, very briefly, developed as follows:

[35]Peter F. Drucker, *Concept of the Corporation*, The John Day Company, Inc., New York, 1946, pp. 47–48.

[36]Alfred D. Chandler, Jr., *Strategy and Structure*, Doubleday & Company, Inc., Anchor Books, Garden City, N.Y., 1966. The book was originally published by the MIT Press in 1962.

1   *Du Pont* went from a centralized to a decentralized structure. Decentralization was needed to accommodate a management strategy of product diversification.

2   *General Motors* was a different situation. As was pointed out in Chapter 1, in the early years of GM there was a lack of centralized control over diverse products and functions. This precarious situation can be attributed to the one-man, authoritative management style practiced by the founder, William C. Durant. In 1920, GM switched to Sloan's model of decentralization. Sloan's strategy of centralized control over decentralized operations put GM back on its feet and was a major contributing factor to its tremendous success.

3   *Standard Oil (New Jersey)* had a different experience. The company had many of the same problems as Du Pont and GM but moved toward decentralization on a piecemeal, unsystematic basis. It differed from the other companies studied by Chandler in that its eventual decentralized structure was not the result of a one-shot, overall policy change. Nevertheless, once more management strategy played a crucial role in instituting the changes to decentralization.

4   *Sears, Roebuck* experienced still another pattern. The company started off with a decentralized organization which proved to be unsuccessful because of unclear channels of authority and communication and lack of overall planning. Next the company moved to a highly centralized structure which also proved to be unworkable, but it gradually evolved into a very successful decentralized structure. Once again managerial strategy preceded the eventual decentralized structure.

After completing these comprehensive case studies, Chandler concluded that decentralized structure was a result of management strategy. This was not necessarily a strategy of decentralization per se but, rather, was a strategy designed to accommodate growth. At least in the companies he studied, the strategies developed for different reasons. Wide territorial expansion, combinations, and, to a greater extent, product diversification, all played a role. However, overall growth seemed to be the most common denominator of the histories of the decentralized companies Chandler studied.[37]

The Recentralization Issue   Although decentralization has been the "golden calf" for the past couple of decades, many scholars and practitioners are now forecasting a recentralization of organization structure. Even General Motors, the classic textbook example of decentralization, is moving away from the Sloan model toward a more centralized operating structure. One news report noted:

> Carried through, the centralization will find GM operating with a single engine division, for example, supplying engines for all car lines, a single assembly division building the cars and supplying the finished product to the sales divisions. Consolidation of other operations, now spread among various divisions, could

[37]Ibid., pp. 50–60.

result in single divisions for forgings, chassis, transmissions, suspension and so on.[38]

Although this development at GM is primarily concerned with the functional, as opposed to decision-making, aspects of centralization-decentralization, it is still of great significance to organizational analysis. Of even greater interest is the reason for the movement toward centralization. Besides taking advantage of some of the managerial-efficiency benefits of centralization, GM may have adopted this strategy in order to avoid antitrust action.[39] Under the Sloan plan, the comparatively autonomous product divisions could be easily separated by the government from the parent corporation, but not under a centralized plan. This, of course, is only speculation, but it is interesting from the standpoint that environmental factors (antitrust suits) can affect organization structure and vice versa. In addition to antitrust, most organizations today are also responding to external environmental pressures such as equal opportunity, environmental protection, and OSHA (Occupational Safety and Health Act) by centralizing. These very real examples point out the open-systems nature of modern organizations. The next chapter will explore these open-systems implications further.

Behavioral Implications of Decentralization   Although delegation was probably the most behaviorally oriented classical principle, decentralization is an even more concerted attempt to incorporate behavioral ideas into organization structure. Decentralization recognizes and actually capitalizes on the importance of the human element. Most importantly, decentralization gives an opportunity for individual responsibility and initiative at the lower levels. Because of the popularity of decentralization, many organizations have been stimulated to incorporate the accompanying behavioral ideas. Yet, as has been pointed out, decentralization may be more fiction than fact, in actual practice. Moreover, as mentioned earlier, there is a distinct possibility that recentralization may be occurring. Such a turn of events may wipe out the human advances in organization that have been stimulated by decentralization.

From another viewpoint, there is a convincing argument that decentralization, as practiced, never did have a behavioral impact. Simon gives two reasons for this view:

> *First,* we should observe that the principle of decentralized profit-and-loss accounting has never been carried much below the level of product-group departments and cannot, in fact, be applied successfully to fragmented segments of highly interdependent activities. *Second,* we may question whether the conditions under which middle management has in the past exercised its decision-making prerogatives were actually good conditions from a motivational standpoint.[40]

---

[38] *Automotive News,* Sept. 20, 1971, p. 1.
[39] Ibid.
[40] Herbert A. Simon, *The New Science of Management Decision,* op. cit., pp. 46–47.

It is fair to say that, overall, decentralization has supported, and in some cases has stimulated, the behavioral approach to management. At the same time, there is little doubt that a wide discrepancy exists between the theory of decentralization and its practice. Yet, because of its wide adoption, decentralization has had a definite impact on developing a mangerial attitude toward acceptance and implementation of behavioral concepts in organization. However, in the future, this may all change because of the movement to recentralize.

Flat and Tall Structures

In organizational analysis, the terms *flat* and *tall* are used to describe the total pattern of spans of control and levels of management. Whereas the classical principle of span is concerned with the number of subordinates one superior can effectively manage, the concept of flat and tall is more concerned with the vertical structural arrangements for the entire organization. The nature and scope are analogous to the relationship between delegation and decentralization. In other words, span of control is to flat-tall structures as delegation is to decentralization.

The difference between flat and tall structures may be easily seen in the two simplified organization charts in Figure 6-3. The tall structure has very small or narrow spans of control, whereas the flat structure has large or wide spans. In tall structures, the small number of subordinates assigned to each superior allows for tight controls and strict discipline. Classical bureaucratic structures are typically very tall.

The most noteworthy departure from the tall structural concept of organization is attributed to the pioneering work of James C. Worthy, a former vice president of Sears, Roebuck and Company. About twenty-five years ago he was involved with a comprehensive organizational study of Sears.[41] The results obtained from surveys of several hundred company units contradicted the classical assumptions about span of control. He found that stores that were organized into flat structures had better sales, profit, morale, and management competence than stores that were formed into tall structures. These results gave empirical evidence to challenge the classical tall structures. Worthy summarized his reasoning as follows: ". . . the emphasis is constantly on *shortening* the span, without giving much more than lip service to the fact that circumstances often differ and that under certain conditions there may be positive advantages in *lengthening* the span."[42]

Advantages and Disadvantages   Tall structures assume a role in assessing the value of flat structures similar to that of centralization in assessing the relative merits of decentralization. Tall structures are often negatively viewed

---

[41]James C. Worthy, "Organization Structure and Employee Morale," *American Sociological Review,* April 1950, pp. 169–179; and "Factors Influencing Employee Morale," *Harvard Business Review,* January 1950, pp. 61–73.

[42]James C. Worthy, *Big Business and Free Men,* Harper & Brothers, New York, 1959, pp. 101–102.

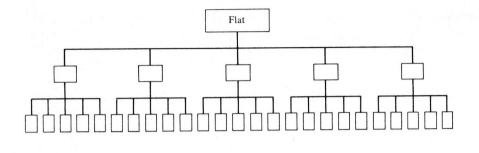

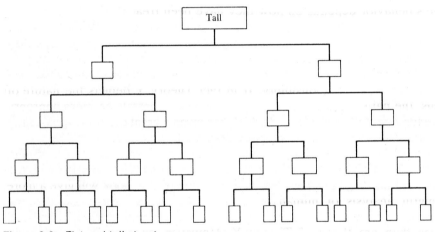

Figure 6-3 Flat and tall structures.

in modern organizational analysis. More accurately, there are advantages and disadvantages to both flat and tall structures. Furthermore, flat and tall are only relative concepts; there are no ideal absolutes.

Both charts shown in Figure 6-3 have the same number of personnel. However, the tall structure has four levels of management and the flat one has only two levels. The tall structure has the definite advantage of facilitating closer control over subordinates. Notice that the term *closer* and not *better* control was used. The classicists, of course, equated "closer" with "better"; the more behaviorally oriented theorists do not. The very nature of flat structures implies that superiors cannot possibly keep close control over many subordinates. Therefore, they are almost forced to delegate a certain amount of the work. Thus, wide spans structurally encourage decentralization. The behavioral theorists would say that this opens up the opportunities for individual initiative and self-control.

From a behavioral viewpoint, self-control is much more effective than control imposed from above. This behavioral advantage of flat organizations hinges on the assumption that there are capable people who can produce under conditions of relative independence. In other words, the analysis of flat and tall structures depends a great deal on what hypotheses are made about the basic nature of people. For discussion purposes, McGregor's Theories X and Y assumptions may be used to assess the merits of flat versus tall structures.

Relationship to Theories X and Y   As covered in Chapter 1, the traditional Theory X sees humans as innately lazy and in need of close control. In this view, the individual prefers to be told what to do and shuns responsibility. If this is correct, tall structures which encourage close controls would be the most appropriate form of structure. Theory Y takes an essentially opposite view of people, holding that they are not inherently lazy or inherently productive. People's behavior depends on how they have been treated. If they have been held under close controls and given no responsibilities, they will react by being stubborn, uncooperative, or just plain lazy. On the other side of the coin, if they are not given close controls but are assigned responsibility, according to Theory Y they will react by being highly motivated and self-controlled, and they will seek more responsibility. If in fact Theory Y depicts the nature of humans, the flat structure which has built-in loose controls or, more appropriately, ends-oriented controls, and which has given a great deal of responsibility to subordinates, will be more effective than a tall structure.

As to which view is correct, there are no ready answers. There is no doubt, however, that a simple X or Y interpretation of human behavior is much too abstract and limiting. The chapters in Part Three of this book will give a more meaningful analysis of human behavior. For now, let it be said that the assumptions of Theory Y are generally more compatible with the behavioral sciences than are those of Theory X. However, once again, it should be remembered that the nature of behavior is much more complex and varied than is implied by McGregor's theories.

Behavioral Implications of Flat versus Tall   One behavioral implication that is often overlooked in analyzing flat versus tall structures is the opportunity that tall structures offer for more personal contact between superior and subordinate. This contact is generally assumed to be negative and conflicting, but it need not be. In a tall structure, the superior may create a positive rapport with his subordinate that may not be possible in a flat structure.

Another consideration besides personal contact is the levels of communication in the two structures. In the flat structure there are fewer levels, which means that both downward and upward communication is simplified. There should be less distortion and inaccuracy. The red tape and endless communication channels associated with bureaucratic tall structures are not present in a flat structure. On the other hand, the increased equality that exists between subordinates in a flat structure may lead to communication problems. If no status or authority differentials are structurally created, a heavy burden is placed upon horizontal communications. As Chapter 9 will bring out, the horizontal communication system is notably deficient in most organizations.

The problem may be compounded in flat organizations where more dependence is placed on this type of communication, but it is not structurally facilitated. Also, coordination may be seriously impaired by a flat structure for the same reason.

Overall, the flat structure, at least from a behavioral standpoint, is generally preferable to the tall. It can take advantage of the positive attributes of decentralization and personal satisfaction and growth. Although managers who have wide spans will have to give a great deal of attention to selecting and training subordinates, a flat structure has the advantage of providing a wealth of experience in decision making. Perhaps Worthy best summarizes the behavioral advantages of flat structures in these words: "Flatter, less complex structures, with a maximum of administrative decentralization, tend to create a potential for improved attitudes, more effective supervision, and greater individual responsibility and initative among employees."[43]

Together with these advantages, however, it must be remembered that flat structures only *encourage* decentralization and individual responsibility and initiative. The supervisor of a small span does not always keep close control and never decentralize, nor does the supervisor of a large span always create an atmosphere of self-control and decentralization. The degree of centralization or its reverse depends on the overall management and organization philosophy and policies and on individual leadership style and personality. All a flat or tall arrangement does is structurally promote, not determine, centralization or decentralization and the approach taken toward the behavioral aspects of managing.

Departmentation

Departmentation is concerned with horizontal organization on any one level of the hierarchy, and it is closely related to the classical bureaucratic principle of specialization. There are several types of departmentation. Traditionally, purpose, process, persons or things, and place were the recognized bases for departmentation.[44] In more recent terminology, "product" is substituted for "purpose," "functional" has replaced "process," and "territorial" or "geographical" is used instead of "place." In addition, time, service, customer, equipment, and alpha-numerical have also become recognized types of departmentation. Each of these latter types of departmentation is fairly self-explanatory. Specific examples of each follow.

1   *Time* may be divided into first shift, second shift, and third shift.
2   *Service* may reflect first class, second class, and tourist class on a passenger ship.
3   *Customer* organization may exist in a large commercial loan department that lends to farmers, small businesses, and large industries.

[43]Worthy, "Organization Structure and Employee Morale," op. cit., p. 179.
[44]Luther Gulick, "Notes on the Theory of Organization," in Luther Gulick and Lyndall Urwick (eds.), *Papers on the Science of Administration*, Institute of Public Administration, New York, 1937, p. 15.

   4 *Equipment* may be broken down in a production unit into drill-press, punch-press, and polishing departments.

   5 *Alpha-numerical* may be utilized in telephone servicing where numbers 0000-5000 are placed in one department and 5001-9999 in another.

   Because organizations of any size will contain more than one hierarchical level, there will always be different types of departmentation represented. A typical large industrial corporation may be territorially organized on the first major horizontal level, and each succeeding level may be organized by product, function, time, and equipment. Confusion is often created when a given organization is identified as one type of departmentation, e.g., General Motors has traditionally been product-departmentalized. The confusion can be cleared up if it is remembered that an organization is identified as one particular type of departmentation because at the primary level, i.e., the first major organizational breakdown, it is organized and identified in this way. General Motors has been known as a product-departmentalized company because the primary level was organized into automotive and nonautomotive product divisions. However, it must be noted that many other types of departmentation are found in the lower levels of GM or any other organization that is designated by only one particular type of departmentation.

   Functional Departmentation   By far the most widely used and recognized type of departmentation is functional in nature. Koontz and O'Donnell explain the importance that functions play in all organized endeavor:

> Since all undertakings involve the creation of utility and since this occurs in an exchange economy, the basic enterprise functions consist of production (creating utility or adding utility to a good or service), selling (finding customers, patients, clients, students, or communicants who will agree to accept the good or service at a price), and financing (raising and collecting, safe-guarding, and expending the funds of the enterprise).[45]

It logically follows that functional departmentation may be found in all types of organizations. For example, in a manufacturing organization the major functions usually are production, marketing, and finance, the vital functions that enable a manufacturing concern to operate and survive. On the other hand, in a railroad organization the major functions are called *operations, traffic,* and *finance,* and in a general hospital they are *medical service, housekeeping, dietetics,* and *business.* Although the titles are different, the railroad and hospital functions are nevertheless analogous to the manufacturing functions in terms of importance and purpose. The titles of various functional departments may differ among industries and even between organizations within the same industry. All businesses, hospitals, universities, governmental agencies, reli-

---

[45]Harold Koontz and Cyril O'Donnell, *Principles of Management,* 5th ed., McGraw-Hill Book Company, New York, 1972, p. 265.

gious organizations, and the military contain vital functions and can be functionally departmentalized.

The greatest single advantage of functional departmentation is that it incorporates the positive aspects of specialization. Theoretically, functionalism should lead to the greatest efficiency and the most economical utilization of employees. In practice, however, certain dysfunctions that were discussed with regard to specialization may also negate the advantages of functional departmentation. For example, functional empires may be created that conflict to the point of detracting from overall goal attainment. A typical case is the salesperson who is guided by the sales department goal of maximizing the number of units sold. In order to sell 2,000 units to a customer, this salesperson may have to promise delivery by the end of the week and to require no money down. The production department, on the other hand, has a goal of keeping costs as low as possible and therefore does not carry a very large inventory. It cannot possibly supply the customer with 2,000 units by the end of the week. Finance has still another goal. It must keep bad-debt expense at a minimum and therefore must require substantial down payments and thorough credit checks on every customer. In this situation, the sales department is in conflict with production and finance. If the salesperson goes ahead and makes the sale under the conditions in the example, the customer will not receive the order on time, and if and when it is received, may not be able to pay the bill. In either or both outcomes, the company goals of customer goodwill and bad-debt expense minimization will suffer because of the salesperson's action.

It is easy to place the blame in the above example on the individual salesperson or on the lack of management coordination and communication. They are both definitely contributing factors. However, an equal, if not overriding, difficulty is the subgoal loyalties that are fostered by functionalization. A true story told by Peter Drucker reinforces this reasoning.

> A railroad company reported a $20,000 per year cost item for broken glass doors in their passenger stations. Upon investigation it was found that a young accountant had "saved" the company $200 by limiting each station to one key for the rest room. Naturally, the key was always lost and the replacement cost only 20 cents. The catch, however, was that the key cost was set up by financial control to be a capital expenditure which required approval from the home office. This home office approval accompanied by the appropriate paperwork took months to accomplish. On the other hand, emergency repairs could be paid immediately out of the station's cash account. What bigger emergency than not being able to get into the bathroom? Each station had an axe and the result was $20,000 for broken bathroom glass doors.[46]

The presentation of such examples does not imply that conflict is always bad for the organization. In fact, as will be discussed in Chapter 16, many modern organization theorists think that conflict has a good effect on the organization which, in fact, outweighs the bad. Yet, as in the cases cited above,

[46]Peter Drucker, *The Practice of Management,* Harper & Brothers, New York, 1954, p. 125.

where functionalization creates conflict that hinders overall goal attainment, conflict is detrimental. A discussion of the positive aspects of conflict will be deferred to Chapter 16.

Product Departmentation At the primary level, many organizations have chosen to organize along product or unit lines rather than functionally. The product form of departmentation is particularly adaptable to the tremendously large and complex modern organizations. It goes hand in hand with profit-centered decentralization. It allows the giant corporations, such as General Motors, General Electric, and Du Pont, to be broken down into groups of self-contained, smaller product organizations. Thus, the advantages of both large and small size can occur in one large organization.

The classical principle of specialization was earlier said to be the greatest benefit derived from functional departmentation. Although often ignored, specialization can also be applied to product departmentation. This was brought out by Albers as follows: "The executive who heads a battery manufacturing department generally knows more about production than other functional executives, but he also knows more about batteries than other production executives."[47] However, a greater advantage of organizing on a product basis is the matter of control. Because of their self-contained nature, product departments are very adaptable to accounting-control techniques and management appraisal. Product department performance, measured according to several different criteria, can usually be objectively determined. Another advantage is that product departments can be readily added or dropped with minimum disruption to the rest of the organization.

As a structural form, product departmentation is very compatible with the behavioral approach. Many of the conflicts that exist in the upper level under functional departmentation are generally resolved by product departmentation. Under product organization, however, the functional conflicts may disappear at the upper levels but reappear in the lower levels that are functionalized. Yet, from the standpoint of overall organization goals, functional conflict at lower levels may be preferable. Besides reducing the potential for conflict, product division lends itself to many of the same behavioral advantages found in decentralization and flat structures. They include more opportunity for personal development, growth, and self-control. Once again, this does not imply a universal truth, because the advantages still depend on many other personal and organizational variables. All in all, however, product organization, through its self-contained characteristics, is potentially more structurally adaptable to the behavioral aspects of organization than is functional departmentation.

The Staff Concept of Organization

The staff organization has been in existence for many, many years. The military is given credit for its modern development. As early as the seventeenth century, Gustavus Adolphus of Sweden used a military general staff. The

[47]Albers, op. cit., 4th ed., 1974, p. 95.

Prussians, with some influence from the French, refined the theory and practice of this concept. At the beginning of the twentieth century, the European version of military staff was installed in the United States armed forces. However, it was not until after the Great Depression that the staff concept was widely adapted to American business and industry.

Staff is not a clear-cut organizational concept. It often creates confusion and problems for the organization. In assessing the staff concept, Koontz and O'Donnell state that "there is probably no area of management which causes more difficulties, more friction, and more loss of time and effectiveness."[48] Many of the problems stem from conflicting definitions regarding line and staff and the hybrid forms of staff used by many organizations. The military have escaped some of these problems because they have precisely defined and successfully implemented a pure staff system. The difference between the pure forms of line and staff is that line carries command responsibilities whereas staff gives advice.

The Military Staff Concept   Figure 6-4 summarizes the function, authority, and responsibility for the line and for the three types of military staff: personal, special, and general. The key to the success of military staff is that unity of command is maintained while simultaneously advantage is taken of high degrees of specialization. The line commander has several "heads" but gives orders from only one mouth. Traditionally, the specialized back-up provides the line commander with what is termed "completed staff action." All the commander must do is approve or disapprove a decision and issue the covering order under his or her name.

In reality, military staff officers have a great deal of implied authority even though, technically, their role is limited to advice. The informal organization knows that staff officers are close to the "old man" and can always revert to formal channels in the name of the commander. The actual amount of implied authority of staff officers depends on the leadership style and personality of the line commander. Some line commanders insist on approving all staff reports and activities and on issuing the orders themselves; others do not want to be bothered with details and allow their staff officers to exercise authority in

[48]Koontz and O'Donnell, op. cit., p. 302.

Figure 6-4   Summary of the Characteristics of Military Staffs

Position	Function	Authority	Responsibility
Line	Executive	Direct	General
Personal staff	Personal aid	None	Personal
Special staff	Specialized	Indirect	Functional
General staff	Functional aid	Representative	Coordinative

Source: Ernest Dale and Lyndall F. Urwick, *Staff in Organization,* McGraw-Hill Book Company, New York, 1960, p. 102. Used with permission.

implementing as well as designing plans and activities. However, even in the latter case commanders must still maintain some degree of control, but they will usually manage by exception. On the whole, the military staff has proved to be one of the most effective concepts applied to large-scale organization structure.

The Modified Staff Concept   Almost every type of modern organization has attempted to adopt to some degree the military staff concept. In contrast to the military, however, the business, hospital, educational, and government organizations have not given proper attention to defining operationally the difference between line and staff. In the military, there definitely exists an informal, implied staff authority, but everyone understands the system and realizes that conflicts can be resolved by reverting to pure line-staff relationships. Unfortunately, this is generally not the case in other types of organizations. What usually develops is a lack of understanding of the line-staff roles and relationships which often results in a breakdown of communication and open conflict. A typical example is the business corporation which has a myriad of line-staff roles and relationships. It is not unusual to find many lower and middle managers who do not really know if and when they are line or staff. One reason is that they generally wear more than one hat. Normally, managers are line within their own departments and become line or staff when dealing with outside departments. The manager's functional authority is often not spelled out in the policies of the organization. As a result, personal conflicts and dual-authority situations run rampant.

Although these weaknesses exist in a hybrid staff concept, benefits have also been derived. The larger, more technologically complex organizations have been almost forced to depend greatly on an executive staff organization. In general, these staff organizations have accomplished their purpose. Yet, from a behavioral viewpoint, one of the dominant themes associated with the staff concept is the great amount of conflict that is generated.

Line-Staff Conflicts   Line-staff conflicts have been one of the most commonly identifiable problem areas associated with the behavioral approach to management. The following excerpts of a humerously written "Ode to Line vs. Staff" point to some of the animosity toward staff from the perspective of a line manager:

Oh, Corporate Staff
How wise you look
When you first open your Policy Book.
How clear your thought, how wide your vision.
While you attempt to make me your pigeon.

But I am Line
And you are not,
And the real hard authority I have got.

You diplomatically ask that I review
Your argument, your point of view.

I listen attentively with brittle smile
While in me churns a hostile bile.
For I am Line
And you are Staff,
And I'll shove it up your epitaph.

I make things hard for you, you see,
For you are you and I am me.
My commission permits me to decide
And tramp my feet upon your hide.

Now we don't want Staff to get the notion
That Line would like to be separated by an ocean.
But maybe, retrospectively,
If we were separated by the sea,
Things would run smoother done our way
With no Staff man around to say "nay."
So let us do Line's thing our way:
Take your policy Manuals somewhere else to play.[49]

The classic case of conflict is that of the old line supervisor versus the young staff engineer. The supervisor typically has been with the organization for years and has had a wealth of experience in the present job. The supervisor does not have much formal education but is very confident and even bullheaded about the way he is conducting his operation. The other combatant in the classic battle is the staff engineer. With one exception, he has essentially the opposite background and characteristics of the supervisor. He is fresh out of college and has little or no organization or job experience. The only things he has in common with the line supervisor are his high degree of confidence and bullheadedness. The opposing and same characteristics of these two individuals chart an obvious collision course. When the staff engineer ventures down to the factory floor to *tell* the line supervisor that he has discovered on his drawing board a much better way to conduct some aspect of the supervisor's job, the result leaves little to the imagination. The situation brings to mind a much-quoted line spoken by the hard-nosed warden in the movie *Cool Hand Luke.* The warden, referring to the constant rebuffs and difficulties with the problem-prisoner Luke (played by Paul Newman), says, "What we have here is a failure to communicate." This statement accurately describes the line-staff conflict situation outlined above. Naturally, there are many exceptions. Not all supervisors are old and bullheaded, nor are all staff engineers fresh college graduates who think they know it all. Yet, to varying degrees, the hypothetical supervisor-engineer example represents the state of line-staff relations in many organizations.

---

[49]Jack J. Gilbert, "Ode to Line vs. Staff—A Perspective," *Dun's Review,* October 1971, p. 79.

Line-staff conflict has been thoroughly researched by Melville Dalton.[50] His case study of Milo (a pseudonym), a factory of 8,000 employees, has become a classic. Through detailed observations, he was able to record actual conflicts that occurred between line and staff personnel at Milo. One of his major conclusions was that line managers often view staff advice as a threat. An example was the case of R. Jefferson, a staff engineer who devised a new plan for toolroom operations. At least two line supervisors admitted privately to Dalton that the plan had merit, but they nevertheless rejected it. One of them, H. Clause, explained why.

> Jefferson's idea was pretty good. But his damned overbearing manner queered him with me. He came out here and tried to ram the scheme down our throats. He made me so damn mad I couldn't see. The thing about him and the whole white-collar bunch that burns me up is the way they expect you to jump when they come around. Jesus Christ! I been in this plant twenty-two years. I've worked in tool rooms, too. I've forgot more than most of these college punks'll ever know. I've worked with all kinds of schemes and all kinds of people. You see what I mean—I've been around, and I don't need a punk like Jefferson telling me where to head in. I wouldn't take that kind of stuff from my own kid—and he's an engineer too. No, his [Jefferson's] scheme may have some good points, but not good enough to have an ass like him lording it over you. He acted like we *had* to use his scheme. Damn that noise! Him and the whole white-collar bunch—I don't mean any offense to you—can go to hell. We've got too damn many bosses already.[51]

In support of the classic conflict situation. Dalton documented that at Milo the staff personnel were substantially younger and had more formal education than the line supervisors. Combined with social factors, these personal characteristics were given as the major factors explaining the conflicts which existed at Milo. However, in a later study, Dalton found some indication that the traditional line-staff conflict model may be changing, at least in some industries. His study of Transode Corporation, a fictitious name given to an electronics firm that employed a highly technical engineering staff who had no official hierarchy and a group of line officers who were formed into a strict hierarchy, provided insights into how conflict can be reduced. In this situation, friction was decreased by "assigning each individual a specific authority, by obscuring status symbols and by stressing symbols of science, quality, and service that allowed all officers to share the luster of association with a vital product."[52]

A very simple solution to help alleviate line-staff conflict and improve communications would be for all staff personnel to use the approach of "sell before tell" when dealing with line personnel. Taken philosophically and literally, this approach has great merit for improving line-staff relationships in any organization.

---

[50]Melville Dalton, *Men Who Manage,* John Wiley & Sons, Inc., New York, 1959; "Conflicts between Staff and Line Managerial Officers," *American Sociological Review,* June 1950, pp. 342–350; and "Changing Staff-Line Relationships," *Personnel Administration,* March-April 1966, pp. 3–5 and 40–48.

[51]Dalton, *Men Who Manage,* op. cit., p. 75.

[52]Dalton, "Changing Staff-Line Relationships," op. cit., p. 45.

SUMMARY

Bureaucracy dominates classical organization theory and structure. Weber's bureaucratic model consists of specialization, hierarchy, rules, and impersonal relationships. Weber believed that this model was an ideal organization structure that would lead to maximum efficiency. Unfortunately, it does not always turn out this way in practice. In fact, there are probably as many dysfunctions as there are functions of a bureaucracy. Specialization or hierarchy can lead to organizational efficiencies, but either can also provoke detrimental conflict and impede the communication process. Rules often become ends in themselves rather than means to assist goal attainment, and everyone can attest to the dysfunctional consequences of the impersonal characteristic. Because of these and a number of other dysfunctions, many of today's theorists are predicting the decline and fall of the classical bureaucratic form of organization. Decentralization, flat structures, departmentation, and staff organization have developed to extend and modify the pure bureaucratic and classical principles of organization. In general, the behavioral approach is more compatible with the modified concepts.

QUESTIONS FOR DISCUSSION AND REVIEW

1 What are the major characteristics of the Weber bureaucratic model? Discuss the functions and dysfunctions of each.
2 What are some conditions which promote a bureaucratic form of organization? Which one do you believe is most conducive to bureaucratization? Why?
3 Do you agree or disagree with those who are predicting the fall of bureaucracy? Defend your answer.
4 What are the various kinds of centralization and decentralization? Which one is most relevant to organizational analysis? Why?
5 Defend centralization as an important organizational concept. Do the same for decentralization.
6 Critically analyze functional versus product (unit) departmentation.
7 How does the military line-staff concept differ from most other organizations' line-staff structure?
8 Why does conflict develop between line and staff? How can it be resolved?

CASE: THE GRASS IS GREENER—OR IS IT?

Alice Jenkins had been a supervisor of case workers in the county welfare department for nine years. The bureaucratic procedures and regulations were becoming so frustrating that she finally decided to look for another job in private industry. She had an excellent educational and employment record and soon landed a supervisory position in the clerical end of a large insurance firm. After a few weeks on her new job she was having coffee with one of the supervisors of another department. She said, "I just can't win for losing. I quit my job at county weflare because I was being strangled by red tape. I thought I could escape that by coming to work in private industry. Now I find out that it is even worse. I was under the illusion that private industry did not have the bureaucratic problems that we had in welfare. Where can I go to escape these insane rules and impersonal treatment?"

    1 Is Alice just a chronic complainer, or do you think it was as intolerable at her former and present job as she indicates? Do you think Alice is typical of most employees in similar types of positions?
    2 How would you answer Alice's last question? Can you give an example of a large organization that you are familiar with that is *not* highly bureaucratized? Does the county welfare department or the insurance company have to be bureaucratized?
    3 Can the concepts of decentralization, flat structures, departmentation, and staff be used in a welfare department or in the clerical area of a large insurance company? Give some examples if possible.

SELECTED REFERENCES

Blau, Peter M., and W. Richard Scott: *Formal Organizations: A Comparative Approach,* Chandler Publishing Company, San Francisco, 1962.

Browne, Philip J., and Robert T. Golembiewski: "The Line-Staff Concept Revisited: An Empirical Study of Organizational Images," *Academy of Management Journal,* September 1974, pp. 406–417.

Carlisle, Howard M.: "A Contingency Approach to Decentralization," *S. A. M. Advanced Management Journal,* July 1974, pp. 9–18.

Coleman, Charles, and Joseph Rich: "Line, Staff and the Systems Perspective," *Human Resource Management,* Fall 1973, pp. 20–27.

Hall, Richard H.: *Organizations: Structure and Process,* Prentice-Hall, Inc., Englewood Cliffs, N. J., 1972.

Henderson, A. M., and Talcott Parsons (trans. and ed.): *Max Weber: The Theory of Social and Economic Organization,* The Free Press, New York, © 1947 by Oxford University Press, New York.

Henry, Nicholas: "Bureaucracy, Technology and Knowledge Management," *Public Administration Review,* November-December 1975, pp. 572–577.

Kochen, Manfred, and Karl W. Deutsch: "A Note on Hierarchy and Coordination: An Aspect of Decentralization," *Management Science,* September 1974, pp. 106–113.

Mansfield, Roger: "Bureaucracy and Centralization of Organizational Structure," *Administrative Science Quarterly,* December 1973, pp. 477–488.

March, James G., and Herbert A. Simon: *Organizations,* John Wiley & Sons, Inc., New York, 1958.

Miewald, Robert D.: "The Greatly Exaggerated Death of Bureaucracy," *California Management Review,* Winter 1970, pp. 65–69.

Perrow, Charles: *Organizational Analysis: A Sociological View,* Wadsworth Publishing Company, Inc., Belmont, Calif., 1970.

Perrow, Charles: "The Short and Glorious History of Organizational Theory," *Organizational Dynamics,* Summer 1973, pp. 3–14.

Reimann, Bernard C.: "On the Dimensions of Bureaucratic Structure: An Empirical Reappraisal," *Administrative Science Quarterly,* December 1973, pp. 462–476.

Rogers, Rolf E.: *Organizational Theory*, Allyn and Bacon, Inc., Boston, 1975.

Scott, William G.: "Organization Theory: A Reassessment," *Academy of Management Journal*, June 1974, pp. 242–254.

Shetty, Y. K., and Howard M. Carlisle: "A Contingency Model of Organization Design," *California Management Review*, Fall 1972, pp. 38–45.

Simonds, Rollin H.: "Are Organizational Principles a Thing of the Past?" *Personnel*, January-February 1970, pp. 3–17.

Thompson, Victor A.: *Modern Organization*, Alfred A. Knopf, Inc., New York, 1961.

Vidich, Arthur J.: "Political Legitimacy in Bureaucratic Society: An Analysis of Watergate," *Social Research*, Winter 1975, pp. 778–811.

Chapter 7

Modern Organization Theory and Structure

The last chapter was concerned with the traditional theories and ways of structuring organizations. As indicated, these classical approaches are still very much in evidence today, but all areas of modern society are undergoing a process of dramatic change. This is especially true of formal organizations. Traditional ways of structuring are no longer always relevant to the modern organization. New theories and structural forms are emerging to meet the demands of growth, complexity, and change. This chapter is devoted to the modern organization theories and presents some specific, newer structural models. The introductory section discusses the behavioral, systems, and contingency theories of organization. This is followed by a description and an analysis of project, matrix, and free-form structural models of organization.

THE MODERN THEORIES OF ORGANIZATION

Chester Barnard had an early influence on the break from classical thinking on organizing. In his tremendous contribution, *The Functions of the Executive,* he defined a formal organization as a system of consciously coordinated activities of two or more persons.[1] It is interesting to note that in this often cited

---

[1]Chester I. Barnard, *The Functions of the Executive,* Harvard University Press, Cambridge, Mass., 1938, p. 73.

definition, the words *system* and *persons* are given major emphasis. People, not boxes on an organization chart, make up a formal organization. Barnard was critical of the existing classical organization theory because it was too descriptive and superficial.[2] He was especially dissatisfied with the classical view that authority came from the top down. Barnard, utilizing a more analytical approach, took an opposite viewpoint. He maintained that authority came from the bottom up. Furthermore, he cited four conditions that must be met before a person will decide to accept a communication as being authoritative:

1 He can and does understand the communication.
2 At the time of his decision he believes that it is not inconsistent with the purpose of the organization.
3 At the time of his decision he believes it to be compatible with his personal interest as a whole.
4 He is able mentally and physically to comply with it.[3]

This analysis has become known as the *acceptance* theory of authority. Barnard recognized that not every executive order can be consciously analyzed, judged, and either accepted or rejected. Rather, most types of orders fall within a person's "zone of indifference." If an order falls within the zone, the person will respond without question, but if it falls outside the zone, he or she will question and accept or reject it. The width of the zone depends upon the degree to which the inducements exceed the burdens and sacrifices.[4]

Besides authority, Barnard stressed the cooperative aspects of organization. This concern reflects the importance which he believed the human element has in organization structure and analysis. It was Barnard's contention that the existence of a cooperative system was contingent upon the human participants' ability to communicate and their willingness to serve and strive toward a common purpose.[5] Under such a premise, the human being plays the most important role in the creation and perpetuation of formal organization.

From this auspicious beginning, modern organization theory has evolved in three major directions. First are the behaviorally oriented theories. These theories took up where Barnard left off; they stress the important role that humans play in organization. The next major development in organization theory was to view the organization as a system made up of interacting parts. Especially the open-system concept, which stresses the input of the external environment, has had a tremendous impact on modern organization theory. Finally, the most recent development in organization theory has been the contingency approach. The premise of the contingency approach is that there is no one best way to organize. The organizational design must be fitted to the

[2]Ibid., p. vii.
[3]Ibid., p. 165.
[4]Ibid., pp. 168–169.
[5]Ibid., p. 82.

existing environmental conditions. The following sections discuss these three modern theoretical approaches to organization in more detail. They serve as the foundation for the actual design of practicing organizations, which is covered in the last part of the chapter.

Behavioral Organization Theories

There are many behaviorally oriented organization theories which, of course, are very relevant and closely related to organizational behavior. The major behavioral organization theories deal with balance, fusion, roles, and groups.

The Balance Theory of Organizations   Barnard originally stressed and Herbert Simon later refined the theory of organizational equilibrium or balance. Both Barnard and Simon brought out the importance of the human decision to participate in an organization. This concern takes two areas into consideration: the behavior of participants in joining, remaining in, or withdrawing from organizations; and the balance of inducements and contributions for each participant, measured in terms of his "utilities."[6] Essentially, this analysis becomes almost a theory of motivation. March and Simon conclude:

> Decisions to participate in the organization—either to enter or to withdraw— . . . focus attention on the motivational problems involved in using human beings to perform organizational tasks . . . participation decisions are both more complex and more important to the organization than their position in classical theory would suggest.[7]

In structural terms, Simon depicts the organization as a three-layered cake. On the bottom layer are the basic work processes. The middle layer consists of the routine, programmed decisions, and the top layer is made up of unprogrammed decisions of a policy and control nature.[8] Despite the three-layered concept, he emphasizes the importance and inevitability of the hierarchical nature of organizations. Yet, he admits that the basis for drawing departmental lines may change. "Product divisions may become even more important than they are today, while the sharp lines of demarcation among purchasing, manufacturing, engineering, and sales are likely to fade."[9]

The Fusion Process   A couple of decades ago, E. Wight Bakke analyzed organizations from the viewpoint of a fusion process. His theory is based on a give-and-take arrangement between the individual and the formal organization. In Bakke's words, "The organization to some degree remakes the individual and the individual to some degree remakes the organization." Role expecta-

---

[6]James G. March and Herbert A. Simon, *Organizations,* John Wiley and Sons, Inc., New York, 1958, p. 84.

[7]Ibid., p. 110.

[8]Herbert A. Simon, *The New Science of Management Decision,* Harper & Row, Publishers, Incorporated, New York, 1960, p. 40.

[9]Ibid., p. 50.

tions are changed relative to the demands made by the formal organization and by the role perceptions of the individual participant. Organizational role expectations and individual perceptions of these expectations affect each other. The result is a fusion between the personalizing process and the socializing process. The function of the fusion process, as stated by Bakke, is ". . . to maintain the integrity of the organization in the face of divergent interests of individuals, groups, other organizations, and the organization itself, which each hopes to realize through its contact with the other."[10] The fusion between the personalizing and socializing processes is accompanied by what Bakke calls the "bonds of organization." The primary bonds are functional specifications, the status system, the communication system, the reward-and-penalty system, and the organizational charter.[11]

An expansion and refinement of Bakke's work came from his colleague Chris Argyris. Argyris presented his ideas in the classic book *Personality and Organization.* His basic thesis is that an incongruency exists between the needs of the mature employee and the requirements of the formal organization. The book presents empirical evidence to help support this thesis and cites specific modes of behavior that result from the incongruency. Argyris says that employees who experience frustration, conflict, failure, and short-time perspective may leave the organization, climb the employment ladder, or defend their self-concept and adapt through the use of defense mechanisms; they may pressure themselves to stay by lowering their work standards and becoming apathetic and uninterested, placing more value on material rewards, or teaching their children not to expect satisfaction on the job.[12] This incongruency dramatically points out that human adaptation to formal structures cannot be automatically assumed.

Role Theories of Organizations   The fusion process and the incongruency thesis are more descriptive than normative. Yet, implicit in the theory are certain role prescriptions for management personnel and insights for more effective organization structure. An example is the emphasis Bakke placed on the reciprocal nature of each participant. He states:

> For one man to play the role of "benevolent supervisor," another has to play the role of "grateful subordinate.". . . One is led to wonder whether this situation doesn't throw some light on why industrial paternalism fails to produce desirable results in many cases. No man can play the role of "paternalistic employer" successfully unless others will play the reciprocal roles of "child-like employees."[13]

[10]E. Wight Bakke, "Concept of the Social Organization," in Mason Haire (ed.), *Modern Organization Theory,* John Wiley and Sons, Inc., New York, 1959, p. 60.

[11]E. Wight Bakke, *Bonds of Organization,* Harper & Brothers, New York, 1950, p. 8.

[12]Chris Argyris, *Personality and Organization,* Harper & Brothers, New York, 1957, pp. 78–94.

[13]E. Wight Bakke, *The Fusion Process,* Yale University, Labor and Management Center, New Haven, Conn., 1955, p. 21.

The role concept that Bakke mentions is in and of itself a theoretical basis for organization. A role can be simply defined as the expectations one has of a position and is one of the smallest but most widely used units of analysis in sociology. Applied to organizations, each participant who occupies a position would have certain expectations from others and self as to what would be involved in this role. The organization could be thought of as a system of roles, and when these roles interact with one another, the organization could more realistically be pictured as a system of overlapping role sets.

Robert L. Kahn is most closely associated with the role set theory of organization. In Kahn's view the organization is made up of overlapping and interlocking role sets. These role sets would normally transcend the boundaries of the classical conception of organizations. Figure 7-1 gives an example of the role concept of organization. The figure shows only three possible role sets from a large manufacturing organization. The purchasing agent, executive vice president, and design engineer are called the focal persons of the sets shown. The supplier's and consultant's are vital roles in their respective sets but would not be included within traditional organizational boundaries. They are external to the classical organization. The design engineer is a member of the purchasing

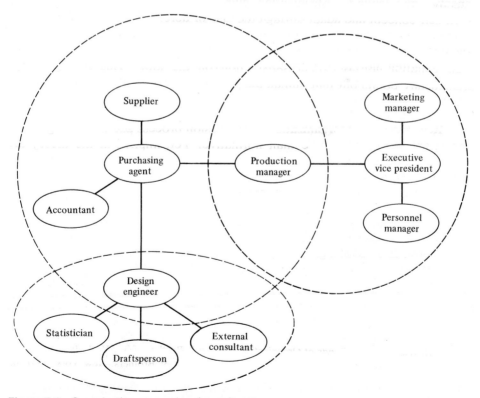

Figure 7-1 Organization as overlapping role sets.

agent's role set but is also a focal person for another role set. The production manager is shown as a member of two role sets.

The overlaps can result in role conflicts and ambiguities. Such dynamics become important in organizational analysis. For example, Kahn and his colleagues found that role conflict will be greater if the role set includes insiders as well as those outside the organizational boundaries. They also found that role conflict and ambiguity tend to be greater the higher the rank of the focal person in the role set.[14] In any case, the overlapping role set conception differs greatly from the classical bureaucratic approach. However, it must be remembered that the role sets mainly describe for theoretical purposes what really goes on in an organization. The role theory approach is not necessarily suggesting that this is how organizations should (normatively) be structured in actual practice. On the other hand, similar to the fusion process and the group approach which follows, the role set idea has definite implications for practice and organization design.

Group Theory of Organization   After a role, the group is the next larger unit of sociological analysis. Rensis Likert has the most widely recognized group theory of organization. He felt that instead of the traditional individual-to-individual relationships in organizations, a more accurate depiction is a group-to-group relationship, with each individual serving as a linking pin. This linking-pin idea, although conceptually very simple, represents an actual model for organization structure. Figure 7-2 depicts the model. It is based on the concept of every individual functioning as a linking pin for the organization units above and below one's own unit. Under this arrangement, every individual is a vital member of two groups. Each participant is the group leader of the lower unit and a group member of the upper unit. Thus, in the linking-pin structure, there is a group-to-group conceptualization of organization.

The linking-pin structure gives the organization an upward orientation. Communication, supervisory influence, and goal attainment are all focused

---

[14]R. L. Kahn, D. M. Wolfe, R. P. Quinn, J. D. Snowe, and R. A. Rosenthal, *Organizational Stress: Studies in Role Conflict and Ambiguity,* John Wiley & Sons, Inc., New York, 1964.

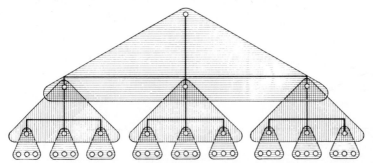

Figure 7-2   Likert's linking-pin model. *(Source: Rensis Likert,* New Patterns of Management, *McGraw-Hill Book Company, New York, 1961, p. 105. Used by permission.)*

upward. This is in contrast to the classical hierarchical structure, which fosters a downward orientation. In later work, Likert added horizontal (lateral) linkages to the model. Figure 7-3 recognizes the need for formalizing lateral linkages for communication, influence, motivation, and coordination purposes. He states his reason for the horizontal dimension as follows:

> Lateral communication and interaction may occur through an informal organization. Since such activity is in violation of the formal system, it is less effective, however, than when done as a legitimate part of the formal system. This is equally true with regard to the exercise of influence and the creation of the motivational forces required for cooperative coordination.[15]

Likert is very careful to point out the important role that group processes play in the linking-pin structure. All groups must be equally effective because the failure of any one group will have adverse consequences for the entire organization. In other words, the linking-pin chain is only as strong as its weakest link. To protect the group chain from breaking, Likert recommends additional staff groups and ad hoc committees. These adjuncts provide multiple overlapping groups through which linking functions are performed and the organization is bound together.[16]

Advantages and Disadvantages of the Linking-Pin Model   The linking-pin idea is often accused of doing nothing more than drawing triangles around the traditional hierarchical arrangements. Other criticisms are that it encumbers and slows down the decision-making process and generally has the same disadvantages as committees. These criticisms, for the most part, seem legitimate. The overlapping-group form of organization structure has definite limitations and disadvantages. However, the key question for organizational

[15]Rensis Likert, *The Human Organization,* McGraw-Hill Book Company, New York, 1967, p. 170.

[16]Rensis Likert, *New Patterns of Management,* McGraw-Hill Book Company, New York, 1961, p. 115.

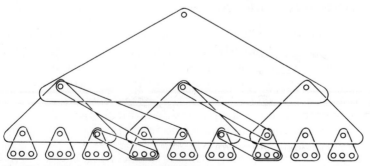

Figure 7-3 Vertical and horizontal linking pins. *(Source: Adapted from Rensis Likert, The Human Organization, McGraw-Hill Book Company, New York, 1967, pp. 168–169. Used by permission.)*

analysis is whether the advantages outweigh the admitted disadvantages. Bernard Bass has noted that groups, as found in the linking-pin structure, provide opportunities for participation, contributions to planning, open communication, and commitments that produce binding decisions.[17] It is only logical that if people feel that they are a vital part of two groups (the one in which they are a subordinate member and the one in which they are the head), they will be more loyal to both groups and will exchange information freely and accept decisions more readily in both groups. Individuals will also exert more real upward influence under this arrangement. The latter point is stressed by Likert. Research findings support his conclusion that the ability to exert an upward influence affects not only morale and motivation, but also productivity and performance.[18]

In summary, it is probably true that the linking-pin idea only emphasizes and facilitates what is theoretically supposed to occur under the classical hierarchical structure. In reality, however, the hierarchy too often ends up having only a downward orientation, while upward and lateral communications are inhibited by the individual-to-individual authority structure. The general disadvantages of group action—the slowness in particular—must be weighed against the advantages. From a behavioral standpoint, the linking-pin arrangement, with the positive additions that are derived from lateral linkages, seems preferable to the traditional hierarchy.

Systems Theory Applied to Organizations

The systems approach recognizes and, in most cases, fills modern organizational requirements which were either ignored or only partially solved by the classical approach. In particular, the following questions, which focus on necessary requirements for the survival of modern organizations, are compatible with a systems approach.

    1 What are the strategic parts of the system?
    2 What is the nature of their mutual dependency?
    3 What are the main processes in the system which link the parts together and facilitate their adjustment to each other?
    4 What are the goals sought by systems?[19]

The systems approach to management, which was introduced in Chapter 3, stresses the interrelatedness and interdependency among the elements of a specified whole. With regard to organization theory, the whole is the formal organization, and the interrelated-interdependent parts are conceived in this book to be organizational structure, processes, and technology. As with any systems approach, each of the major parts of the formal organization may be broken down into interrelated-interdependent subparts. For example, in this

[17]Bernard M. Bass, *Organizational Psychology*, Allyn and Bacon, Inc., Boston, 1965, p. 272.
[18]Likert, *New Patterns of Management*, op. cit., p. 114.
[19]William G. Scott, "Organization Theory: An Overview and an Appraisal," *Academy of Management Journal*, April 1961, p. 16.

book structure is divided into classical and modern structural elements; management processes are considered to consist of decision making, communication, and control; and technology is viewed as the mechanical techniques and total human knowledge used to obtain organization objectives. Each major subsystem in turn can be broken down further and further.

The formal organization model used in this book represents only one conceptualization. Modern organization theory is far from unified. Each writer and researcher in organization and management give a different emphasis and breakdown of the elements. Yet, the systems approach, more than any other conceptual approach, has unified organization theorists to view the organization as a whole made up of interrelated and interdependent parts. This view of organizations reflects the concept of synergism. The *synergistic effect* simply means that the whole organization is greater than the sum of its parts. This is an outgrowth of and closely related to the gestalt school of psychological thought covered in Chapter 2. It encourages theorists and practitioners to view the organization as a whole rather than a series of unrelated parts.

The Organization as an Open System

Both the closed- and open-systems approaches discussed in Chapter 3 are utilized in modern organization theory and practice. However, in today's dramatically changing environment an open-systems approach is becoming much more relevant and meaningful. Last chapter's discussion of how General Motors is moving toward a more centralized structure for antitrust reasons clearly illustrates the point. "The open system is in continual interaction with its environment and achieves a 'steady state' or dynamic equilibrium while still retaining the capacity for work or energy transformation."[20]

The simplest open system consists of an input, a transformation process, and an output. This is graphically depicted thus:

$$\text{Inputs} \longrightarrow \text{Transformation} \longrightarrow \text{Outputs}$$
$$\text{Processes}$$

A system cannot survive without continuous input, the transformation, and output.

There are many types of inputs, transformation processes, and outputs.[21] For example, one kind of input actually enters the open system in the "closed" sense. In other words, this type of input has a direct effect on the internal system rather than an outside effect—in systems jargon, it loads the system. Another type of input affects the system in an "open" sense. Generally, this input would consist of the entire environmental influence on the system, as

---

[20]Fremont E. Kast and James E. Rosenzweig, *Organization and Management,* 2d ed., McGraw-Hill Book Company, New York, 1974, p. 110.

[21]Stanley D. Young, *Management: A Systems Analysis,* Scott, Foresman and Company, Glenview, Ill., 1966, pp. 16–18; and John B. Miner, *Management Theory,* The Macmillan Company, New York, 1971, pp. 26–38.

shown in the GM example discussed in Chapter 6. Still another kind of input takes the form of replacement or recycling. When a component of the system is ejected or leaves, the replacement becomes an input. This recycling process perpetuates the system. Specific examples of inputs into a business organization include monetary, material, and human resources.

At the heart of the open system are the processes, operations, or channels which transform the inputs into outputs. Here is where the internal organizational design plays the important role. The transformation process consists of a logical network of subsystems which lead to the output. The subsystems are translated into a complex systems network that transforms the inputs into the desired outputs.

The third and final major component of any simple open system is the output. This is represented by the product, result, outcome, or accomplishment of the system. Stanley Young mentions stability and reliability as the two major criteria that can be used to judge the output performance of the system. *Stability* refers to the continuity of the output of the system, and *reliability,* as in the testing sense, judges the consistency and the error rate of the output.[22] Specific examples of the outputs of a business organization system that correspond to the inputs of monetary, material, and human resources are profit or loss, product sales, and role behaviors.

The simple open-system concept has universal applicability. Any biological, human, social, economic, or technical phenomenon can be conceptualized in open-systems terms. As has been shown, an economic institution receives inputs of people, raw materials, money, laws, and values. The system then transforms these inputs via complex organizational subsystems into outputs, such as products, services, taxes, dividends, and pollution. From an organization structure standpoint, the critical factor is the design of the transformation process. Oddly, this transformation design involves a closed-system analysis. In other words, the closed system is a subsystem of the open system. The closed-system aspects of the transformation process are concerned with the interrelated and interdependent organizational subsystems of structure, processes, and technology. These subsystems must be organized in such a way that they will lead to maximum goal attainment or output.

Contingency Organization Theory

Analogous to the development of management as a whole has been the recent emphasis given to contingency views of organization theory and design. Open-systems analysis recognizes the environmental input, but the contingency approach goes one step further and relates this environment to specific organization structures. The starting point for contingency organization theory is generally recognized to be the significant research conducted by Joan Woodward. This pioneering effort has since been refined by Paul Lawrence and

---

[22]Young, *Management: A Systems Analysis,* op. cit., pp. 17–18.

Jay Lorsch and others. A detailed understanding of this work is vital to modern organization theory.

The Woodward Study   Up to the Woodward studies in the 1950s, most theorists had viewed the organization as rather narrow and had given little if any attention to environmental variables such as technology. Woodward openly challenged this narrow perspective. She felt that technology plays a role equal to, if not more important than, the roles of structure and processes. Her research findings tended to support a contingency view of organizations.

The major study encompassed about a hundred British (South Essex) firms. They were classified under one of the three following distinct types of productive technological environments:

1   *Unit and small batch.* This type of technology depends upon self-contained units that make products according to customer specifications, prototypes, and fabrication of large equipment in stages.

2   *Large batch and mass.* This technology is characterized by mass production of large batches of goods. A moving assembly line is typically employed.

3   *Process.* This type of technology facilitates the intermittent production of chemicals or continuous-flow production of such substances as liquids, gases, or crystals.

After classifying the firms according to the type of technology they employed, Woodward examined the internal organizational variables of structure, human relations, and status. The results of this analysis are summarized in Figure 7-4. In Woodward's own words:

> Among the organizational characteristics showing a direct relationship with technical advance were: the length of the line of command; the span of control of the chief executive; the percentage of total turnover allocated to the payment of wages and salaries; and the ratios of managers to total personnel, of clerical and administrative staff to manual workers, of direct to indirect labour, and of graduate to non-graduate supervisory in production departments.[23]

As Leonard Sayles notes, "The structural differences could hardly have been accounted for by difference in management philosophy, the advice of consultants, or trial and error. . . . Not only the form but the substance follows from technology."[24] Yet, Woodward herself backs off from an extreme position on the role of technology in formal organization structure by concluding:

> It is not suggested that the research proved technology to be the only important variable in determining organizational structure. . . . Technology, although not the

---

[23]Joan Woodward, *Industrial Organization*, Oxford University Press, London, 1965, p. 51.
[24]Leonard R. Sayles, "Managing Organizations: Old Textbooks Do Die!" *Columbia Journal of World Business*, Fall 1966, p. 84.

Figure 7-4　Summary of Woodward's Findings

Type of technology	Organization structure *KNOW*	Human relationships	High status functions
Unit	Avg. span of control for 1st-line super., 21–30; median number reporting to top exec., 4; median levels of management, 3; and top management committees instead of single head, 12%	Small intimate groups, much participation, permissiveness, and flexibility in job interrelationships	Development personnel Skilled workers Draughtsmen Experienced managers
Mass or batch	Span for 1st-line super., 41–50; reporting to top exec., 7; levels of mgt., 4; and mgt. committees, 32%	Clear-cut duties, line-staff conflict, and generally bad industrial relations	Production personnel (line and staff)
Process	Span for 1st-line super., 11–20; reporting to top exec., 10; levels of mgt., 6; and mgt. committees, 80%	Good interpersonal relations like the unit technology and little conflict or stress.	Maintenance personnel Young, technically competent managers

Source: Adapted from Joan Woodward, *Industrial Organization*, Oxford University Press, London, 1965, pp. 50–67.

only variable affecting organization, was one that could be isolated for study without too much difficulty. The patterns which emerged in the analysis of the data indicated that there are prescribed and functional relationships between structure and technical demands.[25]

It is these "functional relationships" between environment variables (technology) and management variables (organization structure) which have contingency implications.

A Follow-up to the Woodward Study　About a decade after the Woodward research, William L. Zwerman conducted a significant follow-up study.[26] Although the composition of his sample was slightly different and the study was made in Minneapolis instead of South Essex, England, in every other respect Zwerman deliberately tried to replicate the Woodward study. Figure 7-5 summarizes the major findings of the Zwerman study in relation to those of Woodward. As indicated in the figure, the Woodward findings were generally confirmed by the follow-up. Zwerman, as Woodward before him, concluded that the "type of production technology was most closely and consistently related to variations in the organizational characteristics of the firms."[27]

[25]Woodward, op. cit., pp. 50–51.
[26]William L. Zwerman, *New Perspectives on Organization Theory*, Greenwood Publishing Corporation, Westport, Conn., 1970.
[27]Ibid., p. 148.

Figure 7-5   Zwerman's Findings in Relation to the Woodward Study

Findings by Zwerman that support the Woodward study
1   No organizational correlates of operating success existed.
2   The classical prescriptions on organizational structure were found in firms with large batch or mass-production technology.
3   The size of the firm's labor force did not correlate with the organizational variables considered.
4   The type of production technology was correlated with organizational characteristics.
5   There were optimum forms of organization specific to each type of production technology instead of a single form of optimum industrial organization.

Finding by Zwerman that does not support the Woodward study
1   The type of production technology was very strongly related to the span of control of first-line supervisors in the Woodward, but not in the Zwerman study.

Zwerman's extension of the Woodward study
1   Firms with separated ownership and management were more likely to have more levels of management, a broader span of control at the top of the hierarchy, and proportionately lower labor costs than were firms with combined ownership and management.
2   The ratio of nonmanagerial supervisors to managers was correlated with the type of technology.
3   Dependence on local markets was related to both technology and size of the labor force.

Source: Adapted from William L. Zwerman, *New Perspectives on Organization Theory*, Greenwood Publishing Corporation, Westport, Conn., 1970, pp. 144–147.

Lawrence and Lorsch Contingency Study   Besides the Woodward study, the more recent source of support for contingency organization theory has come from a study by Lawrence and Lorsch. For their study, they selected ten firms from three industries (plastics, foods, and containers) on the basis of differing rates of technological change and impacts from different sectors of the environment.[28] They analyzed the internal environment of these organizations according to the dimensions of *differentiation* (differences among managers in various functional departments according to goals, time, interpersonal orientation, and formality of structure) and *integration* (the status of interdepartmental relations, coordination, or collaboration). Then taking a contingency approach, they examined how differences in external environments were related to differences in internal environments.

The results of the Lawrence and Lorsch study indicated that the internal organization variables have a complex relationship with each other and with external environment variables. Put into the "if-then" contingency framework suggested in Chapter 3, the Lawrence and Lorsch findings can be summarized as follows:

1   *If* the environment is uncertain and heterogeneous, *then* the organiza-

[28]Paul L. Lawrence and Jay W. Lorsch, *Organization and Environment*, Division of Research, Graduate School of Business Administration, Harvard University, Boston, Mass., 1967.

tion should be relatively unstructured and have widely shared influence among the management staff.

2   *If* the environment is stable and homogeneous, *then* a rigid organization structure is appropriate.

3   *If* the external environment is very diverse and the internal environment is highly differentiated, *then* there must be very elaborate integrating mechanisms in the organization structure.

Contingency Studies in Perspective   The Lawrence and Lorsch study is not without criticism.[29] And there are other important studies, such as the one conducted by Tom Burns and G. M. Stalker. They studied twenty British firms and found that *mechanistic* organizations (highly specialized and centralized firms which encourage loyalty and obedience) were effective in stable environments while *organic* organizations (firms that were vertically coordinated, had unstructured job definitions, and utilized communication based on advice rather than commands) were effective in dynamic environments.[30] But the important point that the Woodward, Lawrence and Lorsch, and Burns and Stalker studies make is that if the organization's internal environment is compatible with the external environment, the organization will tend to be effective. This empirically derived contingency conclusion has significant implications for the future development of organization theory and design.

MODERN STRUCTURAL DESIGNS

Along with organization theorists, many practicing managers are also becoming disenchanted with traditional ways of organizing. Up to the last few years, most managers attempted only timid modifications of classical structures and balked at daring experimentation and innovation. Jay Forrester offers three possible explanations for the resistance to change: (1) preoccupation with scientific, technological innovation; (2) compartmentalization of knowledge so that no one person sees at the same time the evidence of need, the possibility of improvement, and the route of advance; and (3) reluctance to permit changes in the framework of an individual's existence.[31] Many of today's managers have finally overcome this resistance to making drastic organizational changes. They realize that the simple solutions offered by the classical theories are no longer adequate for many of their complex problems. In particular, the need for flexibility and adaptability to change is among the biggest challenges facing a growing number of modern organizations. The following sections describe and analyze some of the newer structural models that have been designed and implemented to meet these challenges.

[29]Henry Tosi, Ramon Aldag, and Ronald Storey, "On Measurement of the Environment: An Assessment of the Lawrence and Lorsch Environmental Uncertainty Scale," *Administrative Science Quarterly*, March 1973, pp. 27–36.

[30]Tom Burns and G. M. Stalker, *The Management of Innovation*, Tavistock Publications, London, 1961.

[31]Jay W. Forrester, "A New Corporate Design," *Industrial Management Review*, Fall 1965, p. 5.

Project Organization

Lockheed Aircraft Corporation uses project management at its Puget Sound shipbuilding facility for new ship contracts.

General Dynamics Corporation establishes a project organization at the Fort Worth Division for accomplishing the F-111A and F-111B aircraft programs.

Three companies—The Boeing Company, Douglas Aircraft Company, and Lockheed—set up extensive project organizations for their competition for the C-5A transport aircraft program.[32]

The above examples point out the increasing use of project organizations by highly technical industries that require a great deal of planning, research, and coordination. This form of organization is currently commonplace in the aerospace industry and is also becoming widely used in other business, military, and governmental organizations that do contract work or operate on a unit basis. The most salient characteristic of project organization, and the most radical departure from classical organization structures, are the existence of horizontal and diagonal relationships. Cleland and King state that these horizontal and diagonal arrangements have sufficient strength and permanency to become in reality the modus operandi of the project organization.[33]

Projects of various degrees of importance and magnitude are always under way in an organization. The project structure is created when management decides to focus a great amount of talent and resources for a given period on a specific project goal. There are several criteria that should be explored before an organization moves to a project structure. One writer feels that the character of a project should be

1 definable in terms of a specific end result;
2 a unique or infrequent effort to the existing management group;
3 complex with respect to the degree of interdependence among tasks; and
4 [such that its] stake in the outcome is extremely critical to the organization.[34]

These criteria are effective guidelines for assessing the desirability of project structures.

Types of Project Structures

There are several variations of project structures. One is the *individual* project organization. This consists of only the project manager. Such project managers have no activities or personnel reporting directly to them. A second

[32] C. J. Middleton, "How to Set Up a Project Organization," *Harvard Business Review*, March–April 1967, p. 73.

[33] David I. Cleland and William R. King, *Systems Analysis and Project Management*, McGraw-Hill Book Company, New York, 1968, p. 151.

[34] John M . Stewart, "Making Project Management Work," *Business Horizons*, Fall 1965, pp. 57–59.

type is the *staff* project organization. Under this arrangement, the project manager is provided staff back-up for project activities, but the primary functional tasks of the organization are performed by the traditional line departments. A third variation is the *intermix* project organization, wherein project managers have staff personnel and selected primary functional heads reporting directly to them. The fourth type is termed *aggregate* project organization. Here, project managers have all the personnel necessary for the project, staff, and functional line reporting directly to them.[35]

Figure 7-6 represents an individual project organization. The project manager, along with the heads of quality control, research and development, contract administration, and scheduling, acts in a staff capacity to the general manager. The project manager must rely on influence and persuasion in performing a monitoring role with direct line authority exercised only by the general manager. Richard Hodgetts discovered four leadership techniques that were successfully used by project managers who suffered from such an "authority gap": negotiation, personality and/or persuasive ability, competence, and reciprocal favors.[36]

Project managers in Figure 7-7 have authority and control over the staff back-up for their project. However, under this staff project organization, they must still rely on leadership techniques rather than on line authority over the primary functional areas. The same is true, only to a lesser degree, in the intermix form of project organization shown in Figure 7-8. Only in the aggregate form, shown in Figure 7-9, does the project manager have full authority over the entire project. In reality, the aggregate project organization is very similar to the traditional product or unit form of departmentation.

Figures 7-6 through 7-9 are only simplified prototype examples of project

[35]C. J. Middleton, op. cit., p. 78.
[36]Richard M. Hodgetts, "Leadership Techniques in the Project Organization," *Academy of Management Journal,* June 1968, p. 219.

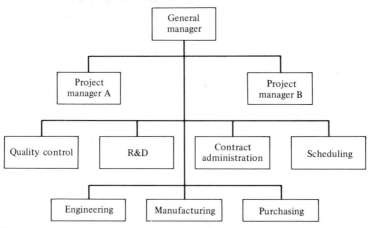

Figure 7-6   Individual project organization.

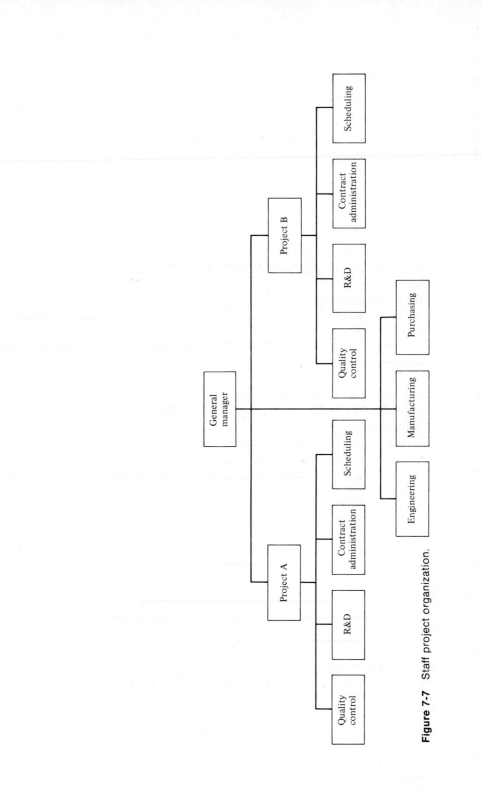

Figure 7-7 Staff project organization.

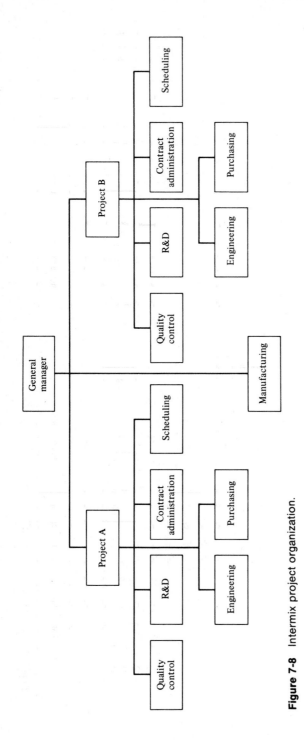

Figure 7-8 Intermix project organization.

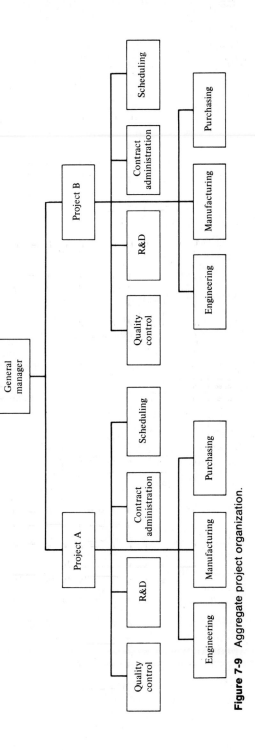

Figure 7-9 Aggregate project organization.

organizations. There are many other possible variations, and the project organization almost always coexists with the more traditional functional structure. Yet, Cleland and King stress that even though there are many similarities between project and functional organization, project managers must take a new approach to their job.

1 He must become reoriented away from the purely functional approach to the management of human and nonhuman resources.

2 He must understand that purposeful conflict may very well be a necessary way of life as he manages his project across many vertical, organizational lines.

3 He must recognize that project management is a dynamic activity where major changes are almost the order of the day.[37]

These three statements make it clear that the project concept is a philosophy of management as well as a form of structural organization. The project viewpoint is quite different from the functional. Figure 7-10 summarizes some of the major differences.

Matrix Organization

When a project structure is superimposed on a functional structure, the result is a matrix. Sometimes the matrix organization is considered to be a form of project organization plus a functional organization and the terms are used interchangeably. However, a more accurate portrayal would show that the matrix organization is a project organization *plus* a functional organization rather than a variation of a project organization. The project overlay provides a horizontal, lateral dimension to the traditional vertical orientation of the functional organization. Figure 7-11 represents a very simplified matrix organization. Here, the functional department heads have line authority over the specialists in their departments (vertical structure). The functional specialists are then assigned to given projects (horizontal structure). These assignments are usually made at the beginning of each project by a collaboration between the appropriate functional and project managers.

Matrix organizations seem to flout the traditional organizational principles. The hierarchy principle and unity of command are flagrantly violated. Furthermore, the matrix concept does not coincide with the usual line-staff arrangements. Obviously, a great deal of conflict is generated in matrix organization. An organizational specialist with IBM has observed that, besides fostering conflict, the matrix structure discourages informal groups and the nurturing of supervisor-subordinate relations. After ten years' experience with the transition from traditional hierarchical to matrix organizations, he concluded that the matrix structure "has seemingly reduced participant motivation for all but the most aggressive personalities and has reduced corporate loyalty and identification with the organization."[38] These disadvantages are countered by many positive aspects of matrix organization.

---

[37]Cleland and King, op. cit., p. 152.

[38]Michael V. Fiore, "Out of the Frying Pan into the Matrix," *Personnel Administration*, July–August 1970, p. 6.

Figure 7-10   A Comparison of the Project versus the Functional Organization

Phenomenon	Project viewpoint	Functional viewpoint
Line-staff organizational dichotomy	Vestiges of the hierarchal model remain, but line functions are placed in a support position. A web of authority and responsibility relationships exists.	Line functions have direct responsibility for accomplishing the objectives; the line commands, staff advises.
Scalar principle	Elements of the vertical chain exist, but prime emphasis is placed on horizontal and diagonal work flow. Important business is conducted as the legitimacy of the task requires.	The chain of authority relationships is from superior to subordinate throughout the organization. Central, crucial, and important business is conducted up and down the vertical hierarchy.
Superior-subordinate relationship	Peer to peer, manager to technical expert, associate to associate relationships are used to conduct much of the salient business.	This is the most important relationship; if kept healthy, success will follow. All important business is conducted through a pyramiding structure of superiors-subordinates.
Organizational objectives	Management of a project becomes a joint venture of many relatively independent organizations. Thus, the objective becomes multilateral.	Organizational objectives are sought by the parent unit (an assembly of suborganizations) working within its environment. The objective is unilateral.
Unity of direction	The project manager manages across functional and organizational lines to accomplish a common interorganizational objective.	The general manager acts as the head for a group of activities having the same plan.
Parity of authority and responsibility	Considerable opportunity exists for the project manager's responsibility to exceed his authority. Support people are often responsible to other managers (functional) for pay, performance reports, promotions, and so forth.	Consistent with functional management; the integrity of the superior-subordinate relationship is maintained through functional authority and advisory staff services.
Time duration	The project (and hence the organization) is finite in duration.	Tends to perpetuate itself to provide continuing facilitative support.

Source: David I. Cleland, "Understanding Project Authority," *Business Horizons*, Spring 1967, p. 66. Used with permission.

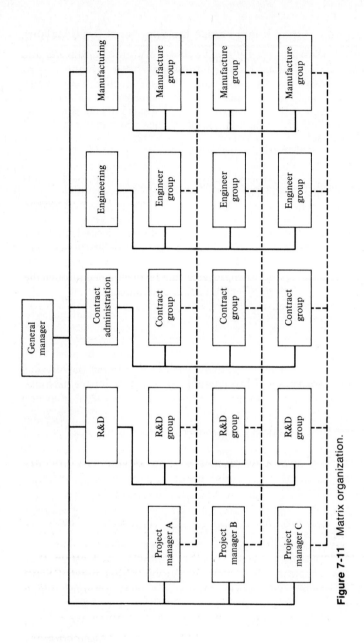

Figure 7-11 Matrix organization.

The matrix organization attempts to incorporate the best of both worlds. In an eclectic manner, it includes the positive aspects of both the functional and project organizations. Cleland and King summarize these advantages as follows:

> **1** The project is emphasized by designating one individual as the focal point for all matters pertaining to it.
>
> **2** Utilization of manpower can be flexible because a reservoir of specialists is maintained in functional organizations.
>
> **3** Specialized knowledge is available to all programs on an equal basis; knowledge and experience can be transferred from one project to another.
>
> **4** Project people have a functional home when they are no longer needed on a given project.
>
> **5** Responsiveness to project needs and customer desires is generally faster because lines of communication are established and decision points are centralized.
>
> **6** Management consistency between projects can be maintained through the deliberate conflict operating in the project-functional environment.
>
> **7** A better balance between time, cost, and performance can be obtained through the built-in checks and balances (the deliberate conflict) and the continuous negotiations carried on between the project and the functional organizations.[39]

Theorists who advocate a matrix structure maintain that these advantages overcome the inherent disadvantages. Many modern organizations which are facing tremendous structural and technical complexity have no choice but to move to such an arrangement. The critical need for coordination and functional interrelationships can be met by adding a horizontal dimension to the formal structure.

In many modern organizations a lateral interface has developed. It occurs when people, departments, or systems must meet to support one another. Interface, more precisely, is "the contact point between relatively autonomous organizations which are nevertheless interdependent and interacting as they seek to cooperate to achieve some larger system objective."[40] Such an interface can result in either conflict or cooperation. The matrix organization depends on effective leadership to overcome the obstacles and attain the positive attributes of coordination and communication. In this regard, Scott and Mitchell offer the following conclusion: "the scalar indeterminacy which exists between project managers and department managers gives rise to a number of transactions that can be only described as political."[41] Cleland and King maintain that only significant conflicts should be presented to a common superior for resolution. In other words, they recommend that management by

[39]Cleland and King, op. cit., p. 172.

[40]Daniel A. Wren, "Interface and Interorganizational Coordination," *Academy of Management Journal,* March 1967, p. 71.

[41]William G. Scott and Terence R. Mitchell, *Organization Theory,* Richard D. Irwin, Inc., Homewood, Ill., 1972, p. 64.

exception become the rule in a matrix organization. The right of appeal should not be exercised unless the following two criteria are met:

1   The issue is clearly drawn, with alternatives and costs described.
2   It is a salient project-functional issue.[42]

This type of systematic approach helps to overcome some of the difficulties of matrix organizations. This form of organization will undoubtedly become more widely used in the future to meet the demands of increased complexity. It should always be measured against the same high standards that are applied to the classical structures.

Free-Form Organizations

Closely related to the project and matrix models are the free-form, sometimes called the *naturalistic* or *organic,* structures of modern organization. The free-form model is based on the premise that the purpose of an organization is to facilitate the management of change. To accomplish this objective, the structural arrangements are highly adaptable and flexible. There are no pre-scribed or rigid roles and the internal structure is not allowed to solidify.[43]

Under the free-form concept, there is no one way of organizing. Organizations that operate under the free-form concept tailor-make the structure to fit their particular needs at a particular time. Usually, the traditional, departmentalized functional structure is replaced by self-contained profit centers. These organizational units are results-oriented and their members are managed as a team. Individual action within a team attempts to incorporate the behavioral approach to management. Participation, self-control, individual initiative, independent judgment, open communication, and sensitivity are some of the human factors that are encouraged and facilitated by free-form organization.

In a sense, the free-form organization is merely an extension of the "Great Organizer" Alfred Sloan's model of decentralization. An executive group at the top of the organization maintains centralized control over highly decentralized profit centers. Keeping the profit centers autonomous facilitates the management of change because whole units can be dropped or added with little disruption to the rest of the organization.

Besides the decentralized pattern, there are two major characteristics common to all free-form organizations. First, they make extensive use of computerized information systems, especially to evaluate the performance of various organizational units. Second, they are populated by young, dynamic managers who are willing to accept calculated risks. These executives usually

---

[42]Cleland and King, op. cit., p. 178.

[43]For discussions of free-form organizations, see Dalton E. McFarland, *Management: Principles and Practices,* 4th ed., The Macmillan Company, New York, 1974, pp. 161–163; and John J. Pascucci, "The Emergence of Free-form Management," *Personnel Administration,* September–October 1968, pp. 33–41.

have had previous experience in one of the firms which pioneered the free-form concept. The firms include Litton Industries, Xerox Corporation, and Textron, Inc.[44]

Companies that have come to depend on a free-form structure are those which must be highly adaptive to products or services that are on the frontiers of public consumption (for example, pollution control devices) or high-demand industrial, consumer, or military products (for example, electronic devices, lenses and frames, and space-age hardware).[45] The free-form structure provides the opportunity for technological and operational leverage. Technologically, it can take advantage of external changes and the transfer of new knowledge. Operationally, it can easily spread, reduce, or prune to meet economic, technological, or social contingencies, even in the short run.[46] Many types of organizations, including conglomerates[47] and highly technical firms, have found the free-form structure to fit their needs.

SUMMARY

Modern organization theory was presented from the perspective of the behavioral, systems, and contingency approaches. The behaviorally oriented approaches include the balance theory of inducements and contributions, the fusion process between the personalizing process and the socializing process, the overlapping-role sets description of organizations from role theory, and the group theory represented by linking pins on a group-to-group basis. Systems theory emphasizes the synergistic effect of organizations (the whole is greater than the sum of the parts) and the impact of the external environment, which is expressed through open-systems analysis. Contingency theory gives specific attention to the environment by relating it to organization structure and design. The Woodward and Lawrence and Lorsch studies give empirical support to the contingency approach.

The new organizational models that have recently come on the scene have been designed by practitioners primarily to meet their dramatically changing needs. The project, matrix, and free-form structures represent a significant departure from the classical, bureaucratic model. The new structures flagrantly violate classical principles, such as unity of command and equal authority and responsibility. Yet, organizations having technologies which require flexibility and adaptability to change are willing to sacrifice the classical concepts. Only time will tell whether the new structural forms are suitable replacements for

---

[44]Pascucci, op. cit., p. 38.

[45]Ibid., pp. 37–38.

[46]Ibid., p. 38.

[47]In a *Fortune* list of forty-six conglomerates (companies with eight or more categories of business), twelve are considered to use free-form structures. See Thomas O'Hanlon, "The Odd News about Conglomerates," *Fortune,* June 15, 1967, pp. 175–177, for a discussion of conglomerates.

bureaucracy. On the other hand, there seems little doubt that the new designs in general and the systems and contingency concepts in particular have already proved themselves valuable enough to become a significant part of organization theory and practice.

QUESTIONS FOR DISCUSSION AND REVIEW

1 What was Chester Barnard's contribution to organization theory?
2 How does Likert's linking-pin model differ from the traditional hierarchical structure?
3 What are two ways that the systems concept can be applied to organizations? Discuss each.
4 How does the open-system theory differ from the contingency idea? How does the open-system concept apply to organizations? How does the contingency concept apply to organizations?
5 What are some different types of project structures? How does the project manager differ from the traditional functional manager?
6 The matrix design of organization is variously said to be based on classical, behavioral, systems, and contingency theoretical bases. Explain how each of these approaches could serve as the basis for the matrix design.

CASE: THE OUTDATED STRUCTURE

Jake Harvey had a position on the corporate planning staff of a large company in a high-technology industry. Although he had spent most of his time on long-range, strategic planning for the company, he was appointed to a task force to reorganize the company. The president and board of directors were concerned that they were losing their competitive position in the industry because of an outdated organization structure. Being a planning expert, Jake convinced the task force that they should proceed by first determining exactly what type of structure they have now, then determine what type of situation the company faces now and in the future, and then design the organization structure accordingly. In the first phase they discovered that the organization was currently structured along classical bureaucratic lines. In the second phase they felt that they were competing in a highly dynamic, rapidly growing industry that required a great deal of flexibility and response to change.

1 What type(s) of organization design do you feel this task force should recommend in the third and final phase of the approach to their assignment?
2 Explain, in turn, how the behavioral, systems, and contingency theories of organization are inherent in this case.
3 Do you think Jake was correct in his suggestion of how the task force should proceed? What types of problems might develop as the by-product of the recommendation you made in question 1?

SELECTED REFERENCES

Avots, Ivars: "Making Project Management Work: The Right Tools for the Wrong Project Manager," *S. A. M. Advanced Management Journal,* Autumn 1975, pp. 20–26.

Cleland, David I., and William R. King: *Systems Analysis and Project Management,* 2d ed., McGraw-Hill Book Company, New York, 1975.

Davis, Keith, "Trends in Organizational Design," *Arizona Business,* November 1973, pp. 3–7.

Delbecq, André, and Alan Filley: *Program and Project Management in a Matrix Organization: A Case Study,* Bureau of Business Research and Service, Graduate School of Business, University of Wisconsin, Madison, Wisconsin, January 1974.

Drucker, Peter F.: "New Templates for Today's Organizations," *Harvard Business Review,* January-February 1974, pp. 45–53.

Galbraith, Jay R.: "Matrix Organization Designs: How to Combine Functional and Project Forms," *Business Horizons,* February 1971, pp. 29–40.

Hellriegel, Don, and John W. Slocum, Jr.: "Organizational Design: A Contingency Approach," *Business Horizons,* April 1973, pp. 59–68.

Hinings, C. R., Royston Greenwood, and Steward Ranson: "Contingency Theory and the Organization of Local Authorities: Part II. Contingencies and Structure," *Public Administration,* Summer 1975, pp. 169–190.

Hinrichs, John R.: "Restructuring the Organization for Tomorrow's Needs," *Personnel,* March–April 1974, pp. 8–19.

Lawrence, Paul L., and Jay W. Lorsch: *Organization and Environment,* Division of Research, Graduate School of Business Administration, Harvard University, Boston, Mass., 1967.

Newman, William H.: "Strategy and Management Structure," *Journal of Business Policy,* Winter 1971–1972, pp. 56–66.

Pugh, D. S.: "The Measurement of Organization Structures: Does Context Determine Form?" *Organizational Dynamics,* Spring 1973, pp. 19–34.

Reimann, Bernard C.: "Dimensions of Structure in Effective Organizations: Some Empirical Evidence," *Academy of Management Journal,* December 1974, pp. 693–708.

Ross, Joel E., and Robert G. Murdick: "People, Productivity, and Organizational Structure," *Personnel,* September–October 1973, pp. 8–18.

Weick, Karl E.: "Amendments to Organizational Theorizing," *Academy of Management Journal,* September 1974, pp. 487–502.

Chapter 8

The Decision Process

A process is any action which is performed by management to achieve organizational objectives. Thus, decision making, communication, and control are managerial processes because they are actually performed by managers. They are also organizational processes because they transcend the individual manager to have an effect on organizational goals. These three management and organization processes are a vital part of the formal organization system and have extremely important behavioral implications.

The purpose of this chapter is to explore the overall nature of the decision process. The first section of the chapter gives the definition and outlines the steps of the decision process. Next the various types of decisions are identified. This is followed by a discussion of the behavioral implications of decision making. Finally, some behaviorally based decision techniques are examined with an eye toward the future.

THE NATURE OF DECISION MAKING

Decision making is almost universally defined as *choosing between alternatives*. It is closely related to all the traditional management functions. For example, when a manager plans, organizes, and controls, he or she is making decisions. Yet, the classical theorists did not generally present decision making this way.

Fayol and Urwick were concerned only with the process to the extent that it affects delegation and authority, while Frederick W. Taylor alluded to the scientific method only as an ideal approach to making decisions. Similar to most other aspects of modern organization and management theory, the beginning of a meaningful analysis of the decision-making process can be traced to Chester Barnard. In *The Functions of the Executive*, Barnard gave a comprehensive analytical treatment of decision making and noted, "The processes of decision . . . are largely techniques for narrowing choice."[1]

Steps in the Decision Process

Most discussions of the decision process break it down into a series of sequential steps. For the most part, the logic can be traced to the stages of thinking developed by John Dewey early in the twentieth century. Dewey outlined three stages of judgment which are analogous to the decision process:

> First, there must be a controversy consisting of opposite claims regarding the same objective situation. Second, there must be a process of defining and elaborating these claims. Finally, a decision is made which closes the matter in dispute and serves as a rule or principle for the future.[2]

Herbert A. Simon, probably the best-known and most widely quoted decision theorist, conceptualizes three major phases in the decision-making process. These are:

> **1** *Intelligence activity.* Borrowing from the military meaning of intelligence, this initial phase consists of searching the environment for conditions calling for decision.
> **2** *Design activity.* In this second phase, inventing, developing, and analyzing possible courses of action take place.
> **3** *Choice activity.* The third and final phase is the actual choice, selecting a particular course of action from those available.[3]

Other presentations of the steps of the decision process are only slightly different from those suggested by Simon. Representative are Newman, Summer, and Warren, who break the design phase into a little more detail and identify four phases: (1) making a diagnosis, (2) finding alternative solutions, (3) analyzing and comparing alternatives, and (4) selecting the plan to follow.[4] Another comprehensive approach is to use systems analysis. Figure 8-1 shows the five steps which Elbing feels the management decision maker is affected by:

[1]Chester I. Barnard, *The Functions of the Executive*, Harvard University Press, Cambridge, Mass, 1938, p. 14.

[2]John Dewey, *How We Think*, D. C. Heath and Company, Boston, 1933, p. 120.

[3]Herbert A. Simon, *The New Science of Management Decision*, Harper & Row, Publishers, Incorporated, New York, 1960, p. 2.

[4]William H. Newman, Charles E. Summer, and E. Kirby Warren, *The Process of Management*, 3d ed., Prentice-Hall, Inc., Englewood Cliffs, N. J., 1972, pp. 247–248.

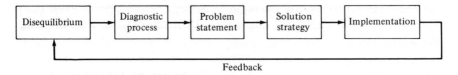

Feedback

Figure 8-1 Elbing's decision-making process. (*Source: Alvar O. Elbing,* Behavioral Decisions in Organizations, *Scott, Foresman and Company, Glenview, Ill., 1970, p. 13.*)

1 A manager inevitably experiences feelings of disequilibrium and regards some situations as problem situations, whether or not he has a clear, rational basis for his identification.

2 His response to the disequilibrium necessarily involves an assumption about the underlying cause, or a diagnosis of the situation, whether or not his diagnosis is rational, systematic, and explicit.

3 His response to the disequilibrium necessarily includes a definition of the problem to be solved, whether his definition of the problem is ambiguous or clear, sound or unsound, explicit or implicit.

4 His response constitutes a selection of method and solution, whether by conscious design or not.

5 Finally, his response also constitutes his implementation of his choice, whether or not it actually leads to the solution of the problem.[5]

Whether expressed in the very simple terms used by Dewey or in more complex systems terms such as those of Elbing, there seem to be identifiable, preliminary steps leading to the choice activity in decision making. The steps become more realistic when they are put into a time framework: "(1) *the past,* in which problems develop, information accumulates, and the need for a decision is perceived; (2) *the present,* in which alternatives are found and the choice is made; and (3) *the future,* in which decisions are carried out and evaluated."[6] Thus, decision making is a dynamic process and what the steps are called is not really important. The essential point is that decision making is composed of a series of dynamically related steps.

The Scope of the Decision Process

Decision making incorporates most of the traditional management functions. Newman, Summer, and Warren equate the process with planning,[7] and Albers classifies planning, motivating, and controlling under decision making.[8] Simon goes all the way and treats decision making as being the same as management. He states that "In treating decision making as synonymous with managing, I shall be referring not merely to the final act of choice among alternatives, but

[5]Alvar O. Elbing, *Behavioral Decisions in Organizations,* Scott, Foresman and Company, Glenview, Ill., 1970, p. 13.

[6]Dalton E. McFarland, *Management Principles and Practices,* 4th ed., The Macmillan Company, New York, 1974, p. 262.

[7]Newman et al., op. cit., p. 243.

[8]Henry H. Albers, *Principles of Management,* 4th ed., John Wiley & Sons, Inc., 1974, pp. 43–44.

rather to the whole process of decision."[9] Some theorists have even gone beyond the realm of management and equate decision making with thinking. This idea is implied in Donald W. Taylor's statement that "decision making is that thinking which results in the choice among alternative courses of action."[10]

In this chapter, decision making is interpreted as encompassing the traditional management function of planning and as somewhat similar to problem solving. Problem solving is any goal-directed activity that must overcome some type of barrier to accomplish the goal. Thus defined, problem solving is somewhat broader than decision making, but conceptually it is not so important for the purposes of this chapter. McFarland explains that while the problem-solving process is a significant generator of decision-making behavior, its importance can be overstressed. "For example, overemphasis on problem solving leads to exaggerating the need for getting answers, whereas it may often be more important to find the right question than the right answer."[11] Although these differences do exist between problem solving and decision making, the terms can generally be used interchangeably.

TYPES OF MANAGEMENT DECISIONS

There are many types of organization and management decisions. The two most widely recognized classifications include personal and organizational decisions and basic and routine decisions.

Personal and Organizational Decisions

Once again, Chester Barnard was in the vanguard of analyzing, or at least making a point about, the difference between personal and organizational decisions. In his opinion, the basic difference is that "personal decisions cannot ordinarily be delegated to others, whereas organization decisions can often if not always be delegated."[12] Thus, the manager makes organizational decisions that are aimed at organizational goals and personal decisions that attempt to achieve personal goals. In reality, it is often difficult or even impossible to separate these two aspects of a management decision. Sometimes personal and organizational decisions are compatible and will facilitate the respective goal attainments of each, and sometimes they are incompatible and impede each other's goal attainment. The following case illustrates the differences and relationships between personal and organizational decisions and goals.

THE HILLTOPPER CASE
The Hilltopper is the name of an exotic night club located at the top of a very steep hill. To lend authenticity to the name, patrons must park their cars at the foot of the hill and walk up a short, but very narrow, path to reach the top.

[9]Simon, op. cit., p.1.
[10]Donald W. Taylor, "Decision Making and Problem Solving," in James G. March (ed.), *Handbook of Organizations*, Rand McNally & Company, Chicago, 1965, p. 48.
[11]McFarland, op. cit., p. 286.
[12]Barnard, op. cit., p. 188.

John was married and his wife was expecting a child any time. One night he was sitting at the Hilltopper bar with a business associate, sipping a drink and watching the "Go Go" girls. Peter, who was still a bachelor, had never been to the Hilltopper. He had just parked his car and was briskly walking up the path. He was very anxious to get to the top because his friends had told him about the superb drinks and beautiful "Go Go" girls at the Hilltopper.

As Peter was proceeding up the path, a large boulder dislodged itself, tumbled down, and came to rest in a precarious bottleneck in the path ahead of him. The boulder spread across the entire path, and there was a steep cliff on the inside and a sharp drop-off on the outside. Peter was baffled. At first he tried pushing the rock, then kicking and swearing at it. These actions were to no avail. The boulder was too big for him to move by himself. Finally, he sat down in exhaustion.

Meanwhile, up at the Hilltopper, John's merriment was interrupted by a phone call from his wife. She told him she was starting to have pains and wanted him to pick her up right away to take her to the hospital. John quickly paid his bill and started to run down the path to his car. His flight came to a halt when he reached the boulder. As Peter had done a few minutes earlier, John pushed, kicked, and swore at the rock, but again to no avail.

As John sat down in despair, he caught a glimpse of Peter through a slight crack between the boulder and the cliff. John yelled, "Hey, buddy, let's get together and shove this darn thing over the edge out of the way. You put your shoulder into it on that side next to the cliff, and I'll put mine into it on my side, and on the count of three we'll push it toward the rim with all our might. Do you understand?" Peter responded, "Yes, I understand."

On the count of three, John and Peter pushed as hard as they could. The boulder moved off the path and rolled over the drop-off. After patting each other on the back, Peter went on up the path to the bar and the "Go Go" girls, and John went on down the path to his car, picked up his wife, and took her to the hospital where she had a beautiful baby girl.

Analysis of the Hilltopper Case   In this fictitious case, Peter and John had two completely different personal goals. Peter's personal goal was to get to a bar, have a drink, and watch "Go Go" girls. John's personal goal was to pick up his expectant wife and get her to the hospital. The organization goal in this case was to move a boulder from a path. Through good organizational decision making (planning, organizing, and coordinating decisions on John's part), communicating, and controlling, the organizational objective was accomplished. Technology, e.g., a stick used as a lever, was another dimension that might have been added to the story. However, leaving technology out of the case has many realistic implications because, even though the use of technology (leverage) was feasible, either it was not readily available (no stick was lying around) or it was conveniently ignored by the participants. Another noteworthy aspect was that the organization dissolved once the organizational goal was accomplished. This is an interesting, but often overlooked, fact of organizational life.[13]

[13]A living example of this factor is seen in the March of Dimes organization. When the National Polio Foundation saw the accomplishment of its goal of conquering the dread disease of polio, it had the choice of either dissolving or changing its goal. The foundation chose to shift its goal to the prevention of birth defects, with an appropriate change in its name.

Although the personal goals of John and Peter were completely different from each other and from the organizational goals there was nevertheless compatibility between the two personal goals and the organizational goal. By making decisions that would accomplish their personal goals, John and Peter at the same time attained the organizational goal. The reverse is also true. By making decisions that would accomplish the organizational goal, they also attained their personal goals. From an organizational standpoint, their situation could not have been better. Unfortunately, this is usually not the case. Personal and organizational goals are often in conflict. Even in the Hilltopper case, accomplishing the organizational goal might have damaged (both literally and figuratively) John's chances for personal goal attainment. When the boulder was removed from the path, it could have landed on top of John's car and demolished it. Thus, at least in this eventuality, the organizational decision made by John would have prevented him from attaining his personal goal. In a similar manner, personal decisions may impede organizational goal attainment. In the Hilltopper case, John might have made a personal decision that he couldn't make it home in time anyway. Therefore, he might have decided to go back to the bar, call his wife to tell her to take a taxi to the hospital, and have another drink. This type of personal decision would obviously have a detrimental effect on the organizational goal of moving the rock. John might have withdrawn from the organization or have made only a half-hearted effort. Peter could pay or threaten John to help attain the organizational goal, but he could still give less than maximum effort because of his personal decision.

Many other interesting implications, variations, and consequences can be uncovered in the Hilltopper case. For the purposes of this discussion, however, it must be remembered that the case represents only a very simplified situation. In more realistic, complex organizational situations, there are not such clear-cut distinctions and outcomes of the personal and organizational decisions. Yet, the case is valuable because it does point out that there is a difference between the two and that many management decisions consist of either or both types.

Basic and Routine Decisions

Another common way to classify types of decisions is into basic and routine categories. McFarland states that "Basic decisions are those which are unique, one-time decisions involving long-range commitments of relative permanence or duration, large investments, and a degree of importance such that a mistake would seriously injure the organization."[14] Examples of basic decisions in a business firm include decisions which deal with things like plant location, organization structure, wage negotiations, product line, and vertical integration. In other words, most top-management policy decisions can be considered basic decisions.

Routine decisions are at the opposite extreme to the basic decisions. They are the everyday, highly repetitive management decisions which by themselves have little impact on the overall organization. However, added together, the

[14]McFarland, op. cit., p. 268.

routine decisions play a tremendously important role in the success of an organization. Among examples of routine decisions are an accountant making a decision on a new entry, a production supervisor deciding what the new tool room procedures will be, a personnel manager hiring a new worker, and a salesperson deciding on what territory to cover. Obviously, a very large proportion (most experts estimate about 90 percent) of the decisions made in an organization are of the routine variety. However, the exact proportion between the basic and routine types depends on the level of the organization at which the decision is made. For example, a first-line supervisor makes practically all routine decisions, whereas the chairperson of the board makes very few routine decisions but many basic decisions.

Classifying decisions into basic and routine categories does not imply that there is a clear distinction between the two. Rather, the difference is only a matter of degree. Basic and routine should be thought of as the two extremes on a continuum. Besides the many organization factors, there are also many personal factors that will determine whether a decision is basic or routine. Experience, motivation, and personality may have a bearing on which type of decision will be made. A lower-level manager faced with a normally routine decision may turn it into a basic decision which has a long-lasting impact on the entire organization.

BEHAVIORAL IMPLICATIONS OF DECISION MAKING

Why does a decision maker choose one alternative over another? The answer to this question involves decision rationality and behavioral decision models. These are given attention in the following sections.

Decision Rationality

Means-ends is the most often used definition of rationality in decision making. If appropriate means are chosen to reach desired ends, the decision is said to be rational. However, there are many complications to this simple test of rationality. To begin with, it is very difficult to separate means from ends because an apparent end may be only a means for some future end. This idea is commonly referred to as the *means-ends chain* or *hierarchy*. Simon points out that "the means-end hierarchy is seldom an integrated, completely connected chain. Often the connection between organization activities and ultimate objectives is obscure, or these ultimate objectives are incompletely formulated or there are internal conflicts and contradictions among the ultimate objectives, or among the means selected to attain them."[15]

Besides the complications associated with the means-ends chain, it may be that the concept is even obsolete. For example, using open-systems analysis, Miller and Starr concede that disturbances in an equilibrium may actually set

---

[15]Herbert A. Simon, *Administrative Behavior,* 2d ed., The Macmillan Company, New York, 1957, p. 64.

up nonrational, goal-seeking behavior.[16] Decision making relevant to the national economy supports their position. Decision makers who seek to make seemingly rational adjustments in the economic system may in fact produce undesirable, or at least unanticipated, end results. Simon also warns that a simple means-ends analysis may have inaccurate conclusions. The following three points should help in avoiding the inherent problems of means-ends analysis:

> *First,* the ends to be attained by the choice of a particular behavior alternative are often incompletely or incorrectly stated through failure to consider the alternative ends that could be reached by selection of another behavior.
> *Second,* in actual situations a complete separation of means from ends is usually impossible.
> *Third,* the means-end terminology tends to obscure the role of the time element in decision making.[17]

One way to clarify means-ends rationality is to attach appropriate qualifying adverbs to the various types of rationality. Thus, *objectively* rational can be applied to decisions that maximize given values in a given situation. *Subjectively* rational might be used if the decision maximizes attainment relative to knowledge of the given subject. *Consciously* rational might be applied to decisions where adjustment of means to ends is a conscious process. A decision is *deliberately* rational to the degree that the adjustment of means to ends has been deliberately sought by the individual or organization. A decision is *organizationally* rational to the extent that it is aimed at the organization's goals, and *personally* rational if the decision is directed to the individual's goals.[18]

Models of Decision-making Behavior

There are many descriptive models of rationality-of-choice behavior. In effect, these have become models for much of management behavior. The models attempt to describe theoretically and realistically how practicing managers make decisions. In particular, the models strive to determine to what degree management decision makers are rational. The models range from complete rationality, as in the case of the *economic* model, to complete irrationality, as in the case of the *social* model. Figure 8-2 summarizes on a continuum the two

[16]David W. Miller and Martin K. Starr, *The Structure of Human Decisions,* Prentice-Hall, Inc., Englewood Cliffs, N. J., 1967, pp. 43–44.
[17]Simon, *Administrative Behavior,* op. cit., p. 65.
[18]Ibid., pp. 76–77.

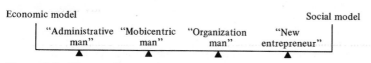

Figure 8-2   The continuum of management decision-making behavior.

major extremes, with other less-known representative models in between. The models shown on the continuum are limited to specific models of management-decision behavior, whereas the various models discussed in Chapter 5 were more concerned with the overall nature of human behavior.

Economic Model   The classical economic model or the entrepreneur of classical economics is perfectly and completely rational in every way. Regarding the entrepreneur's decision-making activities, the following conditions are assumed:

    1   The decision will be completely rational in the means-ends sense.
    2   There is a complete and consistent system of preferences which allow a choice among the alternatives.
    3   There is complete awareness of all the possible alternatives.
    4   There are no limits to the complexity of computations that can be performed to determine the best alternatives.
    5   Probability calculations are neither frightening nor mysterious.[19]

With this almost infallible ability, the economic person always strives to maximize decisions. In the business firm, decisions will be directed to the point of maximum profit where marginal cost equals marginal revenue (MC = MR).

Most economists do not claim that this depiction is a realistic descriptive model of modern management decision-making behavior. They use this economic model primarily for certain theoretical analyses. For example, Fritz Machlup points out that the model is "not, as so many writers believe, designed to explain and predict the behavior of real firms; instead it is designed to explain and predict changes in observed prices as effects of particular changes in conditions."[20] On the other hand, some aspects of the model can be useful in describing actual decision-making behavior. For example, a survey of "excellently managed" firms by James Earley found that short views, innovative sensitivity, marginal costing, and marginal pricing were all preponderant among the respondents.[21] Yet, except for the few indirect exceptions, the economic model is not realistically descriptive of management decision-making behavior. The major criticism has been summarized as follows:

> The theory of the choosing mechanism in economics is completely uninformative on internal structure. The postulates of rationality and goal are given, and behavior is contingent upon environmental or external factors. Economic man, therefore, is an automaton, stripped bare of any of the human characteristics that all real men possess.[22]

    [19]Ibid., p. xxiii.
    [20]Fritz Machlup, "Theories of the Firm: Marginalist, Behavioral, Managerial," *American Economic Review,* March 1957, p. 9.
    [21]James S. Earley, "Marginal Policies of 'Excellently Managed' Companies," *American Economic Review,* March 1956, p. 66.
    [22]Joseph W. McGuire, *Theories of Business Behavior,* Prentice-Hall, Inc., Englewood Cliffs, N.J., 1964, p. 181.

Social Model   At the opposite extreme from the economic model is the completely irrational social model of Freudian psychology. Sigmund Freud presented humans as bundles of feelings, emotions, and instincts, with their behavior guided largely by their unconscious desires. Obviously, such a person would not be capable of making rational management decisons.

Although most contemporary behavioral scientists would take issue with this description of people, almost all would agree that social influences have a significant impact on decision-making behavior. Furthermore, social pressures and influences may cause managers to make irrational decisions. The well-known conformity experiment by Solomon Asch demonstrates a person's irrationality.[23] His study utilized several groups of seven to nine subjects each. They were told that their task was to compare the length of lines. All except one of the subjects in each group had prearranged with the experimenter to give clearly wrong answers on twelve of the eighteen line-judgment trials. About 37 percent of the 123 naïve subjects yielded to the group pressures and gave incorrect answers to the twelve test questions. In other words, more than a third of the experimental subjects conformed to a decision they knew was wrong.

If over one-third of Asch's subjects conformed under "right and wrong," "black and white" conditions, a logical conclusion would be that the real, "gray" world is full of irrational conformists. It takes little imagination to equate Asch's lines with the alternatives of a management decision. There seems to be little doubt of the importance of social influence in decision behavior.

There is still much to be learned of the impact the social model has on decision-making behavior. Certainly, the completely irrational person depicted by Freud is too extreme to be useful. On the other hand, as the chapters in this book unfold, there should be an increasing appreciation and recognition of the role that human behavior does play in management decision making. Some management behavior is irrational but still very realistic. For example, the author and a colleague recently completed a study that showed that subjects without computer experience were more influenced in their choice activities by information presented on computer printout paper than they were by information presented on regular stenographic paper.[24] On the other hand, for those subjects with computer experience, the reverse was true. In other words, decision makers are influenced in their choice activities even by what type of format the information is presented to them in. Managers without computer experience may be in awe of the computer and place more validity on computer-generated information than is justified, while those with computer experience may be highly skeptical and may underrate the importance of computer-generated information.

[23]Solomon E. Asch, "Opinions and Social Pressure," *Scientific American*, November 1955, pp. 31–35.
[24]Fred Luthans and Robert Koester, "The Impact of Computer Generated Information on the Choice Activity of Decision Makers," *Academy of Management Journal*, June 1976, pp. 328–332.

Although the social model is largely a product of psychologists, many social critics and commentators on organizational life have also indirectly developed social models of decision-making behavior. Veblen stressed the impact of the group on individual decision behavior, but most of his work was directed toward consumer rather than management behavior. He challenged the traditional assumptions of consumer rationality in his first and best-known book, *The Theory of the Leisure Class,* published in 1899. The thesis of the book is that consumer decisions are not always based on rational material and economic criteria, but rather on the irrational bases of showing off and gaining prestige. He called this phenomenon the *theory of conspicuous consumption.* The transition to management decisions is obvious; many managers make conspicuous, rather than rational, decisions.

More recent contributions from social critics and commentators come in the form of three interestingly named "men": the *new entrepreneur,* the *organization man,* and the *mobicentric man.* These models, though not directly concerned with decision making per se, do provide stimulating implications and insights into the decision-making process. The exact placement of the models on the rationality continuum is somewhat arbitrary, but the new entrepreneur is probably more irrational than the other two.

New Entrepreneur   The *new entrepreneur* is the subject of one of C. Wright Mills's essays in his book *Power, Politics and People.*[25] His model is an interesting representative of the opposite view of the classical economic model. Mills's spectacular, but somewhat stormy, career embraced three major phases: First, he was a social philosopher; second, he went through an intensive period of empirical research in the middle 1940s; and finally, he combined these interests into a workable style of sociological reflection.[26] It was in this last role that his knowledge and insight were brought to bear on what he called the *new entrepreneur.*

Mills believed that the old economic concept of competitive rationality was dead by the fifties. It was replaced by a competitive spirit and brand of rationality that are personified in what he called the new entrepreneur. The following summarizes the characteristics of this new entrepreneur and the situation in which this person operates.

1   New entrepreneurs must operate in a world in which all the pearls have already been grabbed up and are carefully guarded.
2   The only way they can express their initiative is to service the powers that be and hope to get their cut.
3   They serve the powers by "fixing things" between one big business and another, big business and government, and business as a whole and the public.
4   They get ahead because:

[25]C. Wright Mills, *Power, Politics and People,* Ballantine Books, Inc., New York, 1963. Mills discusses the new entrepreneur in the first essay, "The Competitive Personality," pp. 263–273, in Part III, "People."
[26]Ibid., p. 3.

    a.   people in power do not expect that things can be done honestly;

    b.   people in power experience fear;

    c.   the areas of operation of people in power are greater than their capacities to observe; and

    d.   people in power are not very bright.

    5 Their power rests on personality and skill in manipulating the anxieties of the chieftain.[27]

This caustic description of the "fixer" betweeen countervailing powers is a far cry from the rational, all-knowing economic model portrayed by classical economists. "The supply and demand of the impersonal market does not decide the success or failure of the new entrepreneur; his success is decided by the personal decisions of intimately known chieftains of monopoly."[28]

Mills was not trying to equate the new entrepreneur with all management decision makers. Rather, he is describing a new competitive personality type. New entrepreneurs are envisioned by Mills to be the managers who gravitate into business and industrial staff positions, which include those in public relations, labor relations, and advertising. It is in these positions that the new entrepreneur takes on meaning as a descriptive model for management decision-making behavior.

Organization Man In 1956, William H. Whyte, Jr., an editor of *Fortune* magazine, unveiled the *organization man.*[29] The formal organization had a dominating influence on post-World War II management behavior. The values of loyalty to the organization and cooperation with fellow managers replaced the values of the individual, maximizing, risk-taking entrepreneur of the preceding generation. Whyte called the manager of this era the organization man. This person was a direct reflection of the cultural values of American society in the fifties and early sixties. "Be loyal to the organization and the organization will be loyal to you." "Sacrifice individuality for the sake of the group and the organization." These are the mottoes which guide the organization man's decision-making behavior.

Whyte depicts the organization man as the direct opposite of the old entrepreneur driven by the Protestant Ethic. The guiding credo of individual salvation through hard work, thrift, and competitive struggle is replaced, Whyte says, by the "social ethic" which guides "organization man." This ethic is based upon three major propositions:

    1 The group is the source of creativity. The individual by himself is isolated and meaningless; only when he collaborates with others does he create. The individual helps produce a whole that is greater than the sum of its parts.

    2 Belongingness is the ultimate need of the individual. There should be no

[27]Ibid., pp. 268–270.
[28]Ibid., p. 270.
[29]William H. Whyte, Jr., *The Organization Man,* Doubleday Anchor Books, Garden City, N. Y., 1956.

conflicts between man and society because what is normally considered conflict is merely misunderstanding and breakdown in communication.

    3   The application of science achieves the goal of belongingness. By applying the methods of science, the obstacles to consensus can be eliminated and an equilibrium can be created where society's needs and the needs of the individual are one and the same.[30]

According to the economic concept of rationality, a management decision maker guided by the social ethic would tend to be irrational. In contrast to the economic model, the organization man selects the group and management skill (not knowledge) as the means to accomplish personal and organizational ends. Whyte cites a Youth Institute survey of the 1950s to demonstrate the attitude of the organization man. Four out of five young men in the survey felt they could achieve all their economic desires by working for someone else. This is contrasted to the maximizing, risk-taking attitude of the classical entrepreneur.

    Are organizational loyalty, conformity, and belongingness at any cost qualities of the modern decision maker? Recent surveys, such as one of 2,821 executives conducted by the American Management Association, do indicate that a majority of managers feel that organizational pressures to conform are growing, or at least not decreasing.[31] In other words, the organization man may still be alive and well, but the survey indicates that this situation is very frustrating to most managers. About half of the managers surveyed have changed, or have considered changing, their jobs in the past five years. Loyalty to the organization is changing and movement is increasing. Professor Eugene Jennings has labeled this breed of manager, especially in the 1960s, the "mobicentric man."

    Mobicentric Man   Similar to the new entrepreneur and the organization man, the *mobicentric man* is not a management decision-making model per se. Yet, also like the other two models, the mobicentric man concept provides many insights and has many implications for understanding the rationality of decision-making behavior. Whereas the term *new entrepreneur* was applied to only a small segment of management decision makers (public and labor relations experts and advertisers), and the term *organization man* was more descriptive of managers of the 1950's, the term *mobicentric man* is more descriptive of successful managers in the 1960s. Jennings developed his model from the study of over 1,500 practicing executives and 230 presidents from 500 large industrial firms.

    Jennings claims that mobicentric executives have a different set of values from those of the economic or organization managers of an earlier era. He found that successful managers of a decade or so ago were extremely mobile and that they valued movement not so much as a way to get somewhere or as a

---

[30]Ibid., pp. 7–8.
    [31]Reported in John Cunniff, "Success Image Tarnishing," *McCook Daily Gazette*, May 23, 1973, p. 2.

rational means to an end but as the end itself. Some specific values and characteristics of mobicentric managers are the following:

1 They value motion and action not because they lead to change but because they are change. In other words, change is the ultimate value.

2 Their most dominant characteristic is that they are always in motion. They travel and move frequently for recreation and because changing jobs requires it.

3 They interpret freedom as a form of movement and express this freedom by changing jobs.

4 Their faith is not in institutions but in themselves and perhaps in their wives. They are interested in their capacity to grow and become more useful and not become hung up.

5 They measure success by moving and movement more than by position, title, salary, or performance.[32]

Jennings's studies of corporate presidents support his contention that the above values and characteristics are found in the successful managers of the 1960s. A summary of his findings on presidents follows:

1 Fewer and fewer of the managers emerging at the top have gray hair and stooped shoulders. From 1948 to 1953 the average age of board chairpersons was sixty-three; of corporation presidents, fifty-nine; and of new officers, fifty. Fifteen years later, from 1965 to 1968, the average ages of the individuals in these positions had dropped to fifty-nine, and forty-one.

2 More and more people who become presidents do so after joining the corporation at a high level rather than after working their way up through the ranks at one company.

3 Fewer and fewer of the people who follow an inside route to the presidency do so by plodding along the straight, upward path of traditional insiders. Instead of boring their way through the center, they whirl around the edges of the middle management spiral.[33]

In recent years, managers are probably not quite as mobile as they were during the 1960s when Jennings's study was being done. Quality of life and the declining economy have curtailed some of this mobility among managerial ranks. Nevertheless, executives still move relatively frequently, and this mobility has to have an impact, both positively and negatively, on their decision-making behavior. The values and characteristics of such mobicentric managers have an indirect, and in many cases a direct, influence on their decision-making behavior. Most often, mobility values are rational from a personal, but not necessarily an organizational, viewpoint. For example, the mobicentric managers never expect to complete a job, and they start preparing themselves for departure as soon as they arrive. This behavior may be rational from the personal, but not the organizational, standpoint.

---

[32]Eugene Jennings, "Mobicentric Man," *Psychology Today,* July 1970, p. 35.
[33]Ibid., p. 70.

Administrative Man   As mentioned earlier, the new entrepreneur, the organization man, and the mobicentric man are only indirectly concerned with decision making and are really just refinements of the social model. On the other hand, the *administrative man* is specifically designed by Herbert Simon as a descriptive model of decision-making behavior. Simon's purpose is to present a more realistic sequel to the classical economic model. Administrative man's decision-making behavior may be summarized as follows:

> **1**   In choosing between alternatives, managers attempt to satisfice or look for the one which is satisfactory or "good enough." Examples of satisficing criteria would be share of the market, adequate profit, and fair price.
> **2**   They recognize that the world they perceive is a drastically simplified model of the real world. They are content with this simplification because they believe the real world is mostly empty anyway.
> **3**   Because they satisfice rather than maximize, they can make their choices without first determining all possible behavior alternatives and without ascertaining that these are in fact all the alternatives.
> **4**   Because they treat the world as rather empty, they are able to make decisions with relatively simple rules of thumb or tricks of the trade, or from force of habit. These techniques do not make impossible demands upon their capacity for thought.[34]

In short, those following the administrative man approach try to be rational and maximizing, but they end up satisficing because they do not have the ability to maximize. E. Frank Harrison has summarized the case against maximizing behavior by noting that objectives are dynamic rather than static; information is seldom perfect; there are obvious time and cost constraints; alternatives seldom lend themselves to quantified preference ordering; and the effect of environmental forces cannot be disregarded.[35] The administrative man model recognizes these limitations. The economic model assumptions are viewed as unrealistic. Yet, in the final analysis, the difference between the economic model and administrative man is one of relative degree because, under some conditions, satisficing approaches maximizing, whereas in other conditions satisficing and maximizing are very far apart.

There are many economic, social, and organizational variables which influence the degree to which satisficing becomes maximizing. An example of an economic variable is market structure. The more competitive the market, the more satisficing may approach maximizing. In an agricultural-products market situation, satisficing will by necessity become maximizing. A generalization made by economists is that "In perfectly competitive conditions the more nearly a firm approaches the profit maximum the greater are its chances of survival."[36] Thus, it appears that in order to survive in a competitive market

[34]Simon, *Administrative Behavior,* op. cit., pp. xxv–xxvi.

[35]E. Frank Harrison, *The Managerial Decision-making Process,* Houghton Mifflin Company, Boston, 1975, p. 69.

[36]J. H. Davies, "Entrepreneurial Behaviour and Market Environment," *Review of Economic Studies,* February 1958, p. 131.

situation the decision maker must make maximizing decisions. In an oligopolistic market situation, e.g., the auto and steel industries, satisficing is quite different from maximizing. Oligopolistic firms can still survive on the basis of adequate profit or share of the market. They do not have to operate at the point where marginal cost equals marginal revenue, and, in fact, they may be unavoidably prevented from maximizing.

Besides the economic market constraints, there are many socially based obstacles which prevent maximization in practice. Some of these social barriers are not consciously recognized by the management decision maker. Examples are resistance to change, desire for status, concern for image, and just plain stupidity. On the other hand, the decision maker may in some cases consciously avoid maximizing. Examples of the latter behavior include decisions which discourage competitive entry or antitrust investigation, restrain union demands, or maintain consumer goodwill.

From an organizational standpoint, there are also formal structural barriers to maximization. The last two chapters pointed out both the functional *and* dysfunctional aspects of organization structure. For instance, dysfunctional conflict caused by specialization may impede maximizing decisions. The formal structure is separate from the decision behavior of individual participants. Cyert and March point out that "even if individuals maximize pleasure or expected utility, it does not necessarily follow that organizations maximize profits. Likewise, even if individuals do not maximize, it does not necessarily follow that organizations do not."[37]

Simon claims that the administrative man model is based on common sense, introspective knowledge, and research of judgmental processes from the behavioral sciences. Many scholars besides Simon have utilized the concept of satisficing in their analyses. Among the examples are Cyert and March's substitution of acceptable level of profit norm for profit maximization,[38] Chamberlin's use of the concept of ordinary rather than maximum profit,[39] Joel Dean's criteria that are used to determine a reasonable profit,[40] and R. A. Gordon's explicit use of satisfactory profits.[41] Yet, Simon was the first to put these ideas together into a descriptive model of management decision making.

Of all the models discussed in this section, administrative man seems most descriptive of realistic management decision-making behavior. The economic model is primarily a hypothetical construct to assist in the analysis of economic theory. The social model, at the opposite extreme, holds much potential for future analytical understanding of decision-making behavior. The new entrepreneur, organization man, and mobicentric man were presented only as

[37]R. M. Cyert and James G. March, "Organization Factors in the Theory of Oligopoly," *Quarterly Journal of Economics*, February 1956, p. 47.

[38]Ibid.

[39]Edward H. Chamberlin, *The Theory of Monopolistic Competition*, Harvard University Press, Cambridge, Mass., 1942, p. 105.

[40]Joel Dean, *Managerial Economics*, Prentice-Hall, Inc., New York, 1951, pp. 33–39.

[41]R. A. Gordon, "Short-Period Price Determination in Theory and Practice," *American Economic Review*, June 1948, p. 271.

representative special cases of the social model. The rest of this chapter is devoted to specific techniques of decision making.

DECISION TECHNIQUES

The discussion of the quantitative approach to management in Chapter 3 briefly covered some of the most important mathematically based decision techniques. These quantitative techniques have contributed to a science of decision making. However, managers' decision techniques, such as those that trigger creativity and motivation and acceptance, are lagging far behind the quantitative techniques. But it is creativity and acceptance which are desperately needed to solve the important basic, risk-uncertainty types of decisional problems in modern organizations. Because of this default, many managers have turned to the quantitative techniques to use on decisions requiring creativity. Although these techniques may give a certain degree of comfort and rationalization to the decision maker, they often lead to ineffective and/or misleading results.

At present, there are very few formalized techniques to assist in creative decisions and gain acceptance of employees, and they have been around a long time. What is even more serious, no new significant research and development on these techniques seem to be in the making. Similar to the weather, creativity and acceptance are discussed by everyone, but nothing much is done about them. The following sections present the few creative techniques available and explore participative techniques for gaining acceptance of a decision. Finally, some new techniques for the future are presented and analyzed.

Creative Techniques

A few attempts have been made to provide general guidelines to stimulate individual creativity. Representative are the four general aids to creativity suggested by Newman, Summer, and Warren:

> **1** Recognize psychological barriers, primarily cultural and perceptual blocks;
> **2** Try changing attributes by concentrating on one attribute of the problem at a time—preferably the key attribute; and
> **3** Be alert for serendipity [discussed in Chapter 1 in relation to the Hawthorne studies];
> **4** Recognize that computers have the potential to supplement the human mind in particular stages of the creative process.[42]

This type of approach is about all that is available to assist the individual to make creative decisions. However, in the area of group creativity, two widely known and much-used techniques are available. They are given the exotic-sounding names of *brainstorming* and *synectics*.

[42]Newman et al., op. cit., pp. 274–280.

Brainstorming *Brainstorming* was developed by Alex F. Osborn to help trigger creative ideas in the field of advertising. He explained the term as meaning the use of the brain to storm a creative problem—"and to do so in commando fashion, with each stormer audaciously attacking the same objective."[43] In order to obtain the maximum creativity from the group under the brainstorming technique, four basic rules must be fully understood and faithfully followed:

> **1** Judicial judgment is ruled out. Criticism of ideas must be withheld until later.
> **2** "Free-wheeling" is welcomed. The wilder the idea, the better; it is easier to tame down ideas than to think them up.
> **3** Quantity is wanted. The greater the number of ideas, the more the likelihood of winners.
> **4** Combination and improvement are sought. In addition to contributing ideas of their own, participants should suggest how ideas of others can be turned into better ideas; or how two or more ideas can be joined into still another idea.[44]

Besides these four rules, there are many other specific procedures that will lead to optimum effectiveness:

> **1** The sessions should last 40 minutes to an hour, although brief 10- to 15-minute sessions can be effective if time is limited.
> **2** Generally, the problem to be discussed should not be revealed before the session.
> **3** The problem should be clearly stated and not be too broad.
> **4** A small conference table which allows people to communicate easily should be used.
> **5** If a product is being discussed, actual samples are useful as a point of reference.[45]

Although originally conceived for use on advertising problems, brainstorming has been applied to all types of decisional problems. Examples where brainstorming could be, and often has been, applied include ways to reduce wasted time and absenteeism, new uses for plastic in automobiles, new ways to toast a piece of bread, new methods for making basketballs, and improvement in the performance of secretaries. The ideas may be wild and impractical, but they have also led to creative solutions to decisional problems.

There are several criticisms of brainstorming. The three biggest drawbacks seem to be: (1) Only very simple decisional problems are applicable; (2) it is very time-consuming and thus costly; and (3) only superficial ideas are brought

---

[43]Alex F. Osborn, *Applied Imagination*, Charles Scribner's Sons, New York, 1953, p. 297.
[44]Ibid., pp. 300–301.
[45]Charles S. Whiting, "Operational Techniques of Creative Thinking," *Advanced Management*, October 1955, p. 28.

out. On the other hand, brainstorming can be very helpful for certain kinds of decisions, e.g., to come up with a name for a new product or just to encourage an environment of creativity. Unfortunately, as a technique for assisting decision makers to reach basic, risk-uncertainty decisions, it is too superficial and limiting.

Synectics   Not so well known as brainstorming but of potentially greater value to decision making may be a creative technique developed by William J. J. Gordon.[46] He termed the technique *synectics,* a word of Greek derivation which means fitting together different and irrelevant elements. Synectics is based on the assumption that the creative process can be both described and taught, and its purpose is to increase the creative output of individuals and groups.

The synectics technique involves two basic steps: one, making the strange familiar, and two, making the familiar strange. The strange-familiar phase is primarily analytical in nature, and usually no solutions are accomplished. During the second phase, making the familiar strange, a conscious effort is made to look at the problem from a completely different viewpoint.

Four general types of analogy are used to stimulate creativity on making the familiar strange. Called *personal, direct, symbolic,* and *fantasy* analogies, they are considered by Gordon to be operational mechanisms that are "specific and reproducible mental processes, tools to initiate the motion of creative process and to sustain and renew that motion."[47] An example of the use of *personal analogy* deals with a problem of developing a new and practical constant-speed mechanism. A box with a shaft passing through it was drawn on the blackboard. Using personal analogy, members of the synectics group metaphorically entered the box and tried without tools to effect, with their own bodies, the speed constancy required. From this technique a model eventually evolved which proved to be efficient and economical.[48] The classical example of *direct analogy* was Sir March Isumbard Brunel's solution to underwater construction. Brunel observed that a shipworm tunneled into a timber and then constructed a watertight tube for itself. By direct analogy, Brunel transferred the worm's tube-making activity to the idea of watertight caissons which could be effectively used during underwater construction. *Symbolic analogy* uses objective and impersonal images to describe a problem. In one instance, it was utilized to create a new, self-contained jacking mechanism for use in moving large objects, such as houses and loads of freight. During the synectics group session, someone made the symbolic analogy with the Indian rope trick, which proved to be the breakthrough for the innovative jacking mechanism.[49] *Fantasy analogy* was applied to a problem of inventing a vapor-proof closure for space suits. Here the synectics group asked themselves the question, "How do we in

[46]William J. J. Gordon, *Synectics,* Collier Books, Collier-Macmillan Ltd., London, 1961.
[47]Ibid., pp. 37–38.
[48]Ibid., pp. 39–41.
[49]Ibid., pp. 46–48.

our wildest fantasies want the closure to operate?" A fantasy analogy of little insects closing the opening on command led to a complex, overlapping spring mechanism for closure.[50] These four analogies at first glance seem very simpleminded and easy, but Gordon notes:

> Although the mechanisms are simple in concept, their application requires great energy output. In fact, Synectics does not in any way make creative activity easier. . . . The mere stringing together of metaphors is non-productive. Synectics participants must keep in the back of their minds the problem as understood so that they can identify those mechanisms which illuminate the problem.[51]

Not all managers should automatically assume that they can use synectics to aid them in making creative decisions. To implement synectics properly requires careful selection of talented personnel, complete training in the precise philosophy and methods of the technique, and careful integration back into the decision-making environment.

Synectics differs from brainstorming in several important respects.[52] It is much more adaptable to complex decisional problems. Yet, similar to brainstorming, synectics is very time-consuming and expensive. Overall, synectics seems to have potentially a great deal to offer and might be able to help in making basic or risk-uncertainty decisions that require creative solutions.

Participative Techniques

The decision techniques discussed thus far have definite behavioral implications. However, there are also specific behavioral techniques available that aid the manager gain acceptance of decisions. Most of these techniques, at least traditionally, have revolved around the concept of participation.

Participation as a technique means that individuals or groups are involved in the decision-making process. It can be formal or informal, and it entails intellectual and emotional as well as physical involvement. The actual amount of participation in making decisions ranges from the one extreme of no participation, wherein the superior makes the decision and asks for no help or ideas from anyone, to the other extreme of full participation, where everyone connected with or affected by the decision is completely involved. In practice, the degree of participation will be determined by several factors. Newman, Summer, and Warren suggest three: "(1) who initiates ideas; (2) how completely a subordinate carries out each phase of decision making—diagnosing, finding alternatives, estimating consequences, and making the choice; and (3) how much weight an executive attaches to the ideas he receives."[53] The more there is of each of these factors, the higher will be the amount of participation.

In today's organizations there is much pseudoparticipation. Because of

[50]Ibid., pp. 49–51.
[51]Ibid., p. 56.
[52]Newman et al., op. cit., p. 282.
[53]Newman et al., op. cit., 2d ed., 1967, p. 534.

participation's popularity in the early human relations movement, many managers have attempted to incorporate it into their decision-making processes. However, similar to the organizational concept of decentralization, the participative technique ends up being more fiction than fact. As Dale Beach notes:

> Some managers speak of developing a "sense" of participation in their employees. They exhort them to get their "shoulders to the wheel and all push together." They try to persuade their people to work more enthusiastically to perform jobs and activities designed and regulated exclusively by management.[54]

These are examples of pseudoparticipation. The managers are trying to get their subordinates involved in the task but not in the decision-making process.

Individual, Group, and Program Participation Techniques Participative techniques can be applied informally on an individual or group basis or on a formal program basis.[55] Individual participation techniques are those in which a subordinate somehow affects the decision making of a superior. Group participation utilizes consultative and democratic techniques. Under consultative participation, the superiors ask for and receive involvement from subordinates, but they maintain the right to make the decision. In the democratic form, there is total participation and the group, not the individual head, makes the final decision by consensus or majority vote.

Examples of formal programs of participation include junior boards of executives, collective bargaining between union and management, union-management cooperation committees, Scanlon Plan committees, and suggestion plans. The junior board, first used at McCormick & Company, enables junior executives to participate in top-management decision making. Normally, they are limited to an advisory role. Collective bargaining, defined as the negotiation and administration of an agreement between labor and management over wages, hours, and employment conditions, is generally not associated with participative techniques of decision making. Yet, technically, if the union is a legally elected bargaining agent for the employees, the union participates through collective bargaining in the decisions affecting them. Union-management cooperation committees are formally established to encourage participation of union members in practically all areas of management decision making. Such a committee is usually set up as a last resort to save an organization from closing down. The Scanlon Plan is a special form of labor-management cooperation. The plan, originated by Joseph Scanlon of MIT in the late 1930s, consists of a system of committees which encourages labor to participate in management decisions. The unique feature of the Scanlon Plan is that the rewards for an individual's successful suggestion are equally divided among all members of the group. The commonly used suggestion plans or

---

[54]Dale S. Beach, *Personnel*, 2d ed., The Macmillan Company, New York, 1970, p. 55.
[55]See ibid., pp. 567–578, for an expanded discussion of the various types of participation.

boxes are also a formal type of participation program. If employee responses are properly handled and adequately rewarded, the suggestion box can be a very effective method of obtaining participation in the decision-making process from anyone in the organization.

Positive and Negative Aspects of the Participative Techniques   There are many positive and negative attributes of the participative techniques of decision making. One problem, already mentioned, is the tendency toward pseudoparticipation. This can lead to a boomerang effect on employee satisfaction. If the superior claims to want participation from subordinates but never lets them become intellectually and emotionally involved and never utilizes their suggestions, the results may be disastrous. Participation can be very time-consuming, and it has the same general disadvantages that are attributed to committees in Chapter 15. From a behavioral standpoint, however, the advantages far outweigh the disadvantages. Most of the benefits are touched upon throughout this book. Perhaps the biggest advantage is that the participation techniques recognize that each person can make a meaningful contribution to the attainment of organizational objectives.

New Decision Techniques for the Future

Practically all the advances that have been made in decision-making techniques over the past several years have been quantitative in nature and are applied to the routine and sometimes risk types of decisions. To date, only the techniques discussed so far have been available to managers, and there have been only scattered attempts to develop new techniques for helping make the basic and risk-uncertainty types of decisions. Yet, it is these latter decisions which provide the major challenge facing modern management. Recently, Delphi, nominal grouping, and heuristics have emerged to offer some hope for future help in making basic and risk-uncertainty decisions.

The Delphi Technique   Although Delphi was first developed by N. C. Dalkey and his associates in 1950 at the Rand Corporation's Think Tank, it has only recently become popularized as a technique to assist in making risk-uncertainty decisions, e.g., long-range forecasting. Today, numerous organizations in business, education, government, health, and the military are using Delphi. No decision technique will ever be able to predict the future completely but the Delphi technique seems to be as good a crystal ball as is currently available.

The technique, named after the oracle at Delphi in ancient Greece, has many variations, but generally it works as follows:

1   A panel of experts on the particular problem at hand is drawn from both inside and outside the organization.
2   Each expert is asked to make *anonymous* predictions. For example, the panelists in one Rand session were asked to estimate the year when 20 percent of the world's food supply would come from ocean farming. Half

thought it would occur before the year 2000, the other half thought it would be later.

    3 Each panelist then gets a composite feedback of the way the other experts answered the questions.

    4 Based upon the feedback, new estimates are made and the process is repeated several times.[56]

A major key to the success of the technique lies in its anonymity. Keeping the responses of panel members anonymous eliminates the problem of "saving face" and encourages the panel experts to be more flexible and thus to benefit from the estimates of others. In the traditional interacting group-decision technique, the experts may be more concerned with defending their vested positions than they are with making a good decision. The major objectives of the Delphi process have been summarized by Delbecq, Van deVen, and Gustafson as:

    1 To determine or develop a range of possible program alternatives

    2 To explore or expose underlying assumptions or information leading to different judgments

    3 To seek out information which may generate a consensus on the part of the respondent group

    4 To correlate informed judgments on a topic spanning a wide range of disciplines

    5 To educate the respondent group as to the diverse and interrelated aspects of the topic[57]

Merits

Many organizations testify to the success they have had so far with the Delphi technique. McDonnell, Douglas Aircraft uses the technique to forecast the future uncertainties of commercial air transportation. Weyerhaeuser, a building-supply company, uses it to predict what will happen in the construction business, and Smith, Kline, and French, a drug manufacturer, uses it to study the uncertainties of medicine. TRW, a highly diversified, technically oriented company, has fourteen Delphi panels which average seventeen members each. The panels suggest products and services which have future marketing potential and predict technological developments and significant political, economic, social, and cultural events. Besides business applications, the technique has been used successfully on various problems in government, education, health, and the military. For example, Delphi was used to obtain predictions concerning the impact of a new land-use policy upon population growth, pollution, agriculture, taxes, etc.,[58] and to help set priorities and

---

[56]"Forecasters Turn to Group Guesswork," *Business Week,* Mar. 14, 1970, p. 130.

[57]André L. Delbecq, Andrew H. Van deVen, and David H. Gustafson, *Group Techniques for Program Planning,* Scott, Foresman and Company, Glenview, Ill., 1975, pp. 10–11.

[58]Jerome Kaufman and David H. Gustafson, *Multi-County Land Use Policy Formation: A Delphi Analysis,* Technical Report of the Department of Industrial Engineering, University of Wisconsin, Madison, 1973.

objectives for a large professional association.[59] In other words, Delphi can be applied to a wide variety of program-planning and decision problems in any type of organization.

The major criticisms of the Delphi technique center on its time consumption, cost, and Ouija-board effect. The third criticism implies that, similar to the parlor game, Delphi can claim no scientific approach or support. To counter this criticism, Rand has attempted to validate Delphi through controlled experimentation. The corporation set up panels of nonexperts who use the Delphi technique to answer questions such as "How many popular votes were cast for Lincoln when he first ran for President?" and "What was the average price a farmer received for a bushel of apples in 1940?" These particular questions were used because the average person does not know the exact answers but knows something about the subjects. The result of these studies showed that the original estimates by the panel of nonexperts were reasonably close to being correct, but with the Delphi technique of anonymous feedback, the estimates greatly improved. Rand Corporation's N. C. Dalkey offers the following conclusion: "We have proved Delphi works, but we must convince the scientific and technical experts that they are doing something significant."[60]

Nominal Group Technique   Closely related to Delphi is the nominal group technique or NGT process of group decision making. Nominal grouping has been used by social psychologists for a couple of decades. A nominal group is simply a "paper group." It is a group in name only because no verbal exchange is allowed between the members. In group dynamics research, social psychologists would pit a fully interacting group against a nominal group (a group of individuals added together on paper but not verbally interacting). In terms of number of ideas, uniqueness of ideas, and quality of ideas, research has found nominal groups to be superior to real groups.[61] The general conclusion is that interacting groups inhibit creativity. This, of course, applies only to idea generation because the interactive effects of group members is known to have a significant effect on other variables. The latter effects are given attention in Chapter 15, on group dynamics.

When the nominal grouping approach is used as a specific technique for decision making in organizations, it has been labeled *NGT* by Delbecq and Van deVen. NGT consists of the following specific steps:

    1   Silent generation of ideas in writing.
    2   Round-robin feedback from group members to record each idea in a terse phrase on a flip chart.
    3   Discussion of each recorded idea for clarification and evaluation.

[59]Fred Luthans and Thomas E. Balke, "Delphi Technique Helps Set ASFSA Goals," *School Foodservice Journal,* June 1974, pp. 40–41.
    [60]"Forecasters Turn to Group Guesswork," op. cit., p. 134.
    [61]The classic study is Donald W. Taylor, P. L. Berry, and C. H. Block, "Does Group Participation When Using Brainstorming Facilitate or Inhibit Creative Thinking," *Administrative Science Quarterly,* vol. 3, 1958, pp. 23–47. Follow-up studies support their findings.

   4   Individual voting on priority ideas with the group decision being mathematically derived through rank-ordering or rating.[62]

The difference between this approach and Delphi is that the NGT members are
usually acquainted with one another, have face-to-face contact, and communicate directly with each other. Although research is just starting to emerge on
NGT, there is some evidence that the technique leads to many more ideas than
traditional interacting groups and may do as well as or slightly better than
Delphi groups.[63] This type of technique certainly holds a great deal of promise
for improving basic, creative management decisions.

   The Heuristic Technique   Similar to Delphi and nominal grouping, the
heuristic technique has been around a relatively long time but has only recently
come into its own as a decision-making technique. The classic definition of
heuristic was given by Polya as follows:

> Heuristic, or heuretic, or "ars inveniendi" was the name of a certain branch of
> study, not very clearly circumscribed, belonging to logic, or to philosophy, or to
> psychology, often outlined, seldom presented in detail, and as good as forgotten
> today. The aim of heuristic is to study the methods and rules of discovery and
> inventing. . . . Heuristic, as an adjective, means "serving to discover."[64]

In short, heuristics can be considered as a sophisticated technique of controlled
trial and error.
   When applied to decision making, heuristics, John Hutchinson feels, is a
wedding of the systems and behavioral approaches because it considers both
major variables and the reactions and feelings of people in the system. "In
other words, heuristics allows the decision maker to consider less-than-rational
paths and thus preclude frustration when more preferable alternatives are
somehow available."[65]
   The major cause of the recent widespread use of heuristics as a decision-
making technique is its adaptability to computer programming. Strange as it
may seem, the biggest breakthrough for assistance in making *nonprogrammed*
basic decisions may be through heuristic programming of the computer.
   The traditional algorithmic method of computer programming consists of
tracing through each step to a guaranteed solution. The solution is based on
input variables. At the other extreme is stochastic programming, which uses
trial and error. The stochastic solution is based on intuitive conjecture or
speculation and is tested against known evidence or measurements. Such an
approach has potential for solving long-range, strategy decisions for manage-

   [62]Delbecq et al., op. cit., p. 8.
   [63]A. H. Van deVen, *Group Decision-Making Effectiveness*, Kent State University Center for
Business and Economic Research Press, Kent, Ohio, 1974.
   [64]G. Polya, *How to Solve It*, Princeton University Press, Princeton, N. J., 1945, p. 102.
   [65]John G. Hutchinson, *Management Strategy and Tactics*, Holt, Rinehart and Winston, Inc.,
New York, 1971, p. 126.

ment. The heuristic approach is in between the algorithmic and stochastic approaches. Heuristic programming uses an exploratory method of solving a problem. It continually evaluates progress and through analysis of results permits determination of the next step leading to solution. This is similar to the way a human thinks and makes a judgment. For example, a person playing chess does not attempt to calculate all future moves every time a piece is moved. This would be virtually impossible. Instead the human chess player uses judgment, memory, and trial and error to plan the next move.[66] This is how heuristic programming works.

Heuristic programming closely resembles what is known about human thinking processes. It is this almost-human capacity that gives heuristic programming nearly unlimited potential applicability and has led Herbert Simon to state: "I think you can say that the computer is now showing intuition and the ability to think for itself. Some of us don't see any principles or reason that would prevent machines from becoming more intelligent than man."[67] At present, heuristic programming and artificial intelligence are still in their formative stages of development. They have been successfully applied to the development of strategies and countermoves in games like checkers and chess. The fact that it is theoretically possible to develop decision strategies and learn from experience opens up new vistas for application to nonprogrammed basic and risk-uncertainty decisions. Simon has predicted, "There is now good reason to believe that the processes of nonprogrammed decision making will soon undergo as fundamental a revolution as the one which is currently transforming programmed decision making in business organizations."[68] A major factor in this decision-making revolution will undoubtedly be heuristic programming of the computer. Much of the future handling of all types of decisions promises to be largely dependent upon the computer.

SUMMARY

The decision-making process is a major function of management and plays a key role in the formal organization system. Decision making is simply defined as choosing between two or more alternatives. However, viewed as a process, the actual choice activity is preceded by gathering information and developing alternatives. The types of management decisions include personal decisions and basic and routine organizational decisions. The relevant behavioral models for analyzing decision-making rationality include the completely rational classical economic models; Herbert Simon's intendedly rational, satisficing *administrative man;* Eugene Jennings's *mobicentric man,* interested only in change; William H. Whyte's *organization man,* possessing the social ethic; C. Wright Mills's *new entrepreneur,* who "wheels and deals" and depends on personality; and the completely irrational, emotional social model of Freudian

[66]See Wall Street Journal, June 28, 1973, p.1.
[67]Ibid.
[68]Simon, *The New Science of Management Decision,* op. cit., p. 21.

psychology. Each of these models gives insights into decision-making rationality, but Simon's administrative man is probably most descriptive of its actual practice. The techniques for decision making have been dominated mainly by quantitative models. New, effective techniques applicable to the more basic decisions have not kept pace with the management science techniques. There are only a few creative techniques (brainstorming and synectics), and participative techniques do not begin to approach the sophistication of the quantitative models. Yet, it is the basic, uncertain management decisions which are crucial for organizational success. Techniques such as Delphi, nominal grouping, and heuristics offer some hope, but much more needs to be done in this important but neglected area of management decision making.

QUESTIONS FOR DISCUSSION AND REVIEW

1 What are the three steps in Simon's decision-making process? Relate these steps to an actual decision.
2 Describe the essential differences between personal and organizational decisions and between basic and routine decisions.
3 What is a rational decision?
4 Compare and contrast the economic model with the social model.
5 Describe the major characteristics of Simon's "administrative man." Do you think this model is descriptive of practicing executives? Defend your answer.
6 What are synectics and brainstorming? In what types of management decisions can these techniques be of help?
7 What are Delphi, nominal group techniques, and heuristics? What are the similarities and differences among these three decision techniques?

CASE: HARRY SMART—OR IS HE?

Harry Smart, a very bright and ambitious young executive, was born and raised in Boston and graduated from a small New England college. He met his future wife, who was also from Boston, in college. They were married the day after they both graduated cum laude. Harry then went on to Harvard, where he received an MBA. He was now in his seventh year with Brand Corporation, which was located in Boston.

As part of an expansion program, the president of Brand decided to build a new branch plant. He personally selected Harry to be the manager at the new plant and informed him that a job well done would guarantee him a vice-presidency in the corporation. Harry was appointed chairman, with final decision-making privileges, of an ad hoc committee to determine the location of the new plant. In the initial meeting, Harry explained the ideal requirements for the new plant. The members of the committee were experts in transportation, marketing, distribution, labor economics, and public relations. He gave them one month to come up with three choice locations for the new plant.

A month passed and the committee reconvened. After weighing all the variables, the experts recommended the following cities in order of preference: Kansas City, Los Angeles, and New York. Harry could easily see that the committee members had put a great deal of time and effort into their report and recommendations. A spokesperson for the group emphasized that there was a definite consensus that Kansas City was the best location for the new plant. Harry thanked them for their fine job and told them he would like to study the report in more depth before he made his final decision.

After dinner that evening he asked his wife, "Honey, how would you like to move to Kansas City?" Her answer was quick and sharp. "Heavens, no!" she said. "I've lived in the East all my life, and I'm not about to move out into the hinterlands. I've heard the biggest attraction in Kansas City is the stockyards. That kind of life is not for me." Harry weakly protested, "But, honey, my committee strongly recommends Kansas City as the best location for my plant. Their second choice was Los Angeles and the third was New York. What am I going to do?" His wife thought a moment, then replied, "Well, I would consider moving to New York, but if you insist on Kansas City, you'll have to go by yourself!"

The next day Harry called his committee together and said, "Gentlemen, you should all be commended for doing an excellent job on this report. However, after detailed study, I am convinced that New York will meet the needs of our new plant better than Kansas City or Los Angeles. Therefore, the decision will be to locate the new plant in New York. Thank you all once again for a job well done."

1 Did Harry make a rational decision?
2 What model of decision rationality does this incident support?
3 What decision techniques that were discussed in the chapter could be used by the committee to select the new plant site?

SELECTED REFERENCES

Argyris, Chris: "Some Limits of Rational Man Organization Theory," *Public Administration Review*, May–June 1973, pp. 253–267.

Bacharach, Michael: "Group Decisions in the Face of Differences of Opinion," *Management Science*, October 1975, pp. 182–191.

Carlson, Robert O.: "Is Business Really Facing a Communications Crisis?" *Organizational Dynamics*, Spring 1973, pp. 35–52.

Delbecq, André L., Andrew H. Van deVen, and David H. Gustafson: *Group Techniques for Program Planning*, Scott, Foresman, Glenview, Ill., 1975.

Glueck, William F.: "Decision Making: Organization Choice," *Personnel Psychology*, Spring 1974, pp. 77–93.

Gordon, William J. J.: *Synectics*, Collier Books, Collier-Macmillan Ltd., London, 1961.

Green, Thad: "An Empirical Analysis of Nominal and Interacting Groups," *Academy of Management Journal*, March 1975, pp. 63–73.

Luthans, Fred, and Robert Koester: "The Impact of Computer Generated Information on the Choice Activity of Decision Makers," *Academy of Management Journal*, June 1976, pp. 328–332.

Shull, Fremont A., André L. Delbecq, and L. L. Cummings: *Organizational Decision Making*, McGraw-Hill Book Company, New York, 1970.

Silverman, Robert Stephen, and D. A. Heming: "Exit the Organization Man: Enter the Professional Person," *Personnel Journal,* March 1975, pp. 146–148.

Simon, Herbert A.: *Administrative Behavior,* 2d ed., The Macmillan Company, New York, 1957.

Simon, Herbert A.: *The New Science of Management Decision,* Harper & Row, Publishers, Incorporated, New York, 1960.

Van deVen, Andrew H.: *Group Decision-Making Effectiveness,* Kent State University Center for Business and Economic Research Press, Kent, Ohio, 1974.

Van deVen, Andrew H., and André L. Delbecq: "The Effectiveness of Nominal, Delphi, and Interacting Group Decision Making Processes," *Academy of Management Journal,* December 1974, pp. 605–621.

Vroom, Victor H.: "A New Look at Managerial Decision Making," *Organizational Dynamics,* Spring 1973, pp. 66–80.

Chapter 9

The Communication Process

Communication is one of the most frequently discussed concepts in the entire field of organization and management, but it is seldom clearly understood. In practice, effective communication is a basic prerequisite for the attainment of organizational goals, but it has remained one of the biggest problems facing modern management. Communication is an extremely broad topic and of course is not restricted to the management field. Some estimates of the extent of its use go up to about three-fourths of an active human being's life, and even higher proportions of a typical manager's time.

The communication process is often cited as being at the root of practically all the problems of the world. For example, Hicks and Gullett write, "Perhaps it is true, as someone has suggested, that the heart of all the world's problems—at least of men with each other— is man's inability to communicate as well as he thinks he is communicating."[1] It is given as the explanation for lovers' quarrels, ethnic prejudice, war between nations, the generation gap, industrial disputes, and organizational conflict. These are only representative of the numerous problems which are attributed to ineffective communication. Obviously, this reasoning can go too far. For example, Flippo and Munsinger warn, "However important accurate communication may be, it is no panacea

[1]Herbert G. Hicks and C. Ray Gullett: *The Management of Organizations,* 3d ed., McGraw-Hill Book Company, New York, 1976, p. 467.

for all problems of conflict and lack of motivation."[2] Yet, while communication is recognized as a convenient scapegoat or crutch, the fact remains that the communication process is a very big problem for most human and organizational activities.

Communication has been mentioned in earlier chapters as a vital process in the formal organization system. It interacts and is interdependent with structure and decision making, which were presented in the three preceding chapters, and with control, which will be covered in the immediately following chapter. Johnson, Kast, and Rosenzweig comment on the interrelationship between structure and communication as follows:

> Organization structure is definitely tied to communications systems. The relationship is apparent when formal structures, channels, and media are involved; for informal alignments and irregular information flow, the relationship is not as evident.[3]

Pfiffner and Sherwood make a similar pitch for the closeness of decision making and communication. They state, "If decision making and communication processes are not identical, they are so interdependent they become inseparable in practice."[4] The next chapter will point out the almost inseparable relationship that exists between communication and control.

After a brief discussion of the historical treatment of communication in organization and management, a precise definition of communication is given. Next a brief discussion of information theory and interpersonal communication precedes a discussion of the organizational communication process. The Shannon-Weaver, Berlo, and transactional models are given particular attention. The last part of the chapter examines the three major parts of organizational communication: superior-subordinate, subordinate-initiated, and interactive communication. A personal as opposed to linear information flow perspective is used throughout.

HISTORICAL BACKGROUND
ON THE ROLE OF COMMUNICATION

Classical organization theorists gave very little emphasis to the communication process. Although communication was implicit in their management function of command and their structural principle of hierarchy, they never fully developed or integrated it into organization and management theory. At the same time, they did generally recognize the role of communication in relation to the problem of supplementing the formal, hierarchical channels. But Fayol was about the only one who gave a detailed analysis and meaningful solution.

    [2]Edwin B. Flippo and Gary Munsinger, *Management,* 2d ed., Allyn and Bacon, Inc., Boston, 1975, p. 381.
    [3]Richard A. Johnson, Fremont E. Kast, and James E. Rosenzweig, *The Theory and Management of Systems,* 3d ed., McGraw-Hill Book Company, New York, 1973, p. 103.
    [4]John M. Pfiffner and Frank P. Sherwood, *Administrative Organization,* Prentice-Hall, Inc., Englewood Cliffs, N. J., 1960, p. 308.

Figure 9-1 shows how Fayol presented a simplified version of the formal organization. If the formal channels in this organization were strictly followed and F wanted to communicate with P, he or she would have to go through E—D—C—B—A—L—M—N—O—P and back again. In other words, F would have to go through a total of twenty positions. On the other hand, if F could lay a "gangplank" to P, it would, in the words of Fayol, "allow the two employees F and P to deal at one sitting, and in a few hours, with some question or other which via the scalar chain would pass through twenty transmissions, inconvenience many people, involve masses of paper, lose weeks or months to get to a conclusion less satisfactory generally than the one which could have been obtained via direct contact as between F and P."[5] This gangplank concept has direct implications for horizontal communication systems in modern formal organizations. Unfortunately, such classical insights were few and far between.

It was largely Chester Barnard in the late 1930s who meaningfully developed communication as a vital part of organization and management theory. He was convinced that communication is the major shaping force in the organization. He ranked it with common purpose and willingness to serve as the three primary elements of the formal organization. To him, communication both makes the organization cooperative system dynamic and links the organization purpose to the human participants. Communication techniques, which he considered to be written and oral language, were deemed not only necessary to attain organization purpose but also a potential problem area for the organization. In Barnard's words, "The absence of a suitable technique of communication would eliminate the possibility of adopting some purposes as a basis of organization. Communication technique shapes the form and the internal economy of organization."[6]

[5]Henri Fayol, *General and Industrial Management,* translated by Constance Storrs, Sir Isaac Pitman & Sons, London, 1949, p. 35.
[6]Chester I. Barnard, *The Functions of the Executive,* Harvard University Press, Cambridge, Mass., 1938, p. 90.

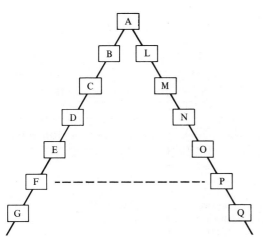

Figure 9-1 Fayol's gangplank concept. (*Source: Henri Fayol,* General and Industrial Management, *translated by Constance Storrs, Sir Isaac Pitman & Sons, London, 1949, p. 34.*)

Barnard also interwove communication into his theory of authority. He emphasized that meaning and understanding must occur before authority can be communicated from superior to subordinate. He listed seven specific communication factors which are especially important in establishing and maintaining objective authority in an organization. He believed them to be, in brief, the following:

    1 The channels of communication should be definitely known.
    2 There should be a definite formal channel of communication to every member of an organization.
    3 The line of communication should be as direct and short as possible.
    4 The complete formal line of communication should normally be used.
    5 The persons serving as communication centers should be competent.
    6 The line of communication should not be interrupted while the organization is functioning.
    7 Every communication should be authenticated.[7]

Since the original contributions by Fayol and Barnard, the organizational communication process has been one, if not *the,* central concern of organization and management theorists. Except in the principles of management textbooks which still rely heavily on a classical process framework, communication is given major attention. In addition, there has been a deluge of books and articles which deal specifically with organizational communication. Unfortunately, practically all of this vast literature gives only a surface treatment of the subject and is seldom based upon systematic research findings. Gellerman sums up the literature on communication as being a bunch of "twaddle."[8] Only recently have some insights begun to emerge on the true meaning of the communication process and especially on how it affects organization and management.

THE DEFINITION OF COMMUNICATION

The term *communication* is freely used by everyone in modern society, including members of the general public and management scholars and practitioners. In addition, as noted earlier, the term is employed to explain a multitude of sins both in the society as a whole and in formal organizations. Despite this widespread usage, very few members of the general public and not a great many more management people can precisely define the term. Part of the problem is that communication experts have not agreed upon a definition themselves.

Most definitions of communication which are used in management litera-

[7]Ibid., pp. 175–181.
[8]Saul W. Gellerman, *Management by Motivation,* American Management Association, New York, 1968, p. 41.

ture stress the use of symbols to transfer meaning or information.[9] Of seemingly more importance, however, is the fact that communication is a personal process that involves the exchange of behaviors. The personal aspects have been noted in no uncertain terms by Schramm in the following observation:

> Let us understand clearly one thing about it: communication (*human* communication, at least) is *something people do.* It has no life of its own. There is no magic about it except what people in the communication relationship put into it. There is no meaning in a message except what people put into it. . . . To understand the human communication process one must understand how people relate to each other.[10]

In addition to its being a human process, Aubrey Fisher emphasizes the behavioral implications of communication by pointing out that "the only means by which one person can influence another is by the behaviors he performs— that is, the communicative exchanges between people provide the sole method by which influence or effects can be achieved."[11] In other words, the behaviors that occur in an organization are vital to the communication process. This personal and behavioral exchange view of communication takes many forms. The following definition by Vardaman and Halterman points out the very comprehensive nature of communication in today's organizations.

> By communication we mean the flow of material, information, perception, and understandings between various parts and members of an organization . . . all the methods, means, and media of communication (communication technology), all the channels, networks, and systems of communication (organizational structure), all the person-to-person interchange (interpersonal communication). . . . It includes all aspects of communication: up, down, lateral; speaking, writing, listening, reading; methods, media, modes, channels, networks, flow; interpersonnel, intraorganizational, interorganizational.[12]

Covering all these aspects of the communication process is beyond the scope of this chapter.

The following continuum can be used to identify the major categories of communication that are especially relevant to the formal organization system. On the one extreme is the technically very sophisticated information theory

[9]For example, see: Joe Kelly, *Organizational Behaviour,* rev. ed., Richard D. Irwin, Inc., and the Dorsey Press, Homewood, Ill., 1974, p. 587, and Daniel K. Stewart, *The Psychology of Communication,* Funk & Wagnalls Company, New York, 1968, pp. 13–14.

[10]W. Schramm, "The Nature of Communications between Humans," in *The Process and Effects of Mass Communication,* W. Schramm and D. Roberts (eds.), University of Illinois Press, Chicago, 1971, p. 17.

[11]B. Aubrey Fisher, *Small Group Decision Making,* McGraw-Hill Book Company, New York, 1974, p. 23.

[12]George T. Vardaman and Carroll C. Halterman, *Managerial Control through Communication,* John Wiley & Sons, Inc., New York, 1968, pp. 3–4.

Information theory	The organizational communication process	Interpersonal communication

approach, and on the other extreme is the behaviorally oriented two-person or interpersonal communication approach. The middle ground is occupied by an organizational process approach, the one taken by this chapter. A very brief overview of the information theory and interpersonal approaches is necessary to put the discussion of the organizational communication process into proper perspective.

Information Theory

Information theory is a strict, scientific approach to the study of communication. Deeply involved with the probability theory of mathematics, it is concerned primarily with the transmission aspects of the communication process. Specifically, the transmission concepts of encoder (sending) and decoder (receiving), in terms of both their functional roles and their contribution to the achievement of a given level of performance, are the distinguishing characteristics of information theory.[13]

The goal of information theory is to encode messages by taking advantage of their statistical nature and to use electrical signals to transmit messages over a given channel with minimum error.[14] Entropy, a statistical law of thermodynamics, further illustrates the information theory approach. This law states that there is a degree of randomness or error in any system; it will become disorganized over time. An example of trying to cope with entropy is given by the physicist who attempts to counteract it by developing control devices for heat machines. In a similar manner, information theorists recognize entropy in their analysis of a communication system; for example, they try to measure and control noise entropy that may arise from distractions, distortions, or the electrical static occurring when a message is transmitted over a communication system.

Information theory has an unusual joint origin. The two founding fathers are usually considered to be Norbert Wiener and Claude Shannon. Separately, they outlined the basic concepts of information theory and cybernetics in 1948.[15] "To MIT's eminent mathematician, Norbert Wiener, goes the major credit for discovering the new continent and grasping its dimensions; to Claude Shannon of Bell Laboratories goes the credit for mapping the new territory in detail and charting some breathtaking peaks."[16] Thus, Wiener and Shannon

---

[13]Robert G. Gallager, *Information Theory and Reliable Communication,* John Wiley & Sons, Inc., New York, 1968, p. 1.

[14]See J. R. Pierce, *Symbols, Signals and Noise: The Nature and Process of Communication,* Harper & Brothers, New York, 1961, p. 44.

[15]See Norbert Wiener, *Cybernetics, or Control and Communication in the Animal and the Machine,* John Wiley & Sons, Inc., New York, 1948; and Claude E. Shannon, "The Mathematical Theory of Communication," *Bell System Technical Journal,* July and October 1948, reprinted in book form with a follow-up article by Warren Weaver, University of Illinois Press, Urbana, 1949.

[16]Francis Bello, "The Information Theory," *Fortune,* December 1953, p. 137.

were the first to emphasize communication from a mathematical perspective, and in so doing they developed cybernetics. Wiener coined the term *cybernetics* (introduced in Chapter 4) to cover information theory plus "the study of messages as a means of controlling machinery and society, the development of computing machines and other such automata, certain reflections upon psychology and the nervous system, and a tentative new theory of scientific method."[17] He derived the term from the Greek word *kubernetes,* which means "steersman" or "governor." His stated purpose for cybernetics was "to develop a language and techniques that will enable us indeed to attack the problem of control and communication . . ."[18] Automatic-feedback control mechanisms have been the primary technique used to attain this purpose.

Much has happened since information theory and cybernetics were introduced by Wiener and Shannon. One information theorist has noted, "In the past 20 years, information theory has been made more precise, has been extended, and has been brought to the point where it is being applied in practical communication systems."[19] A great impetus to this development has come from computer technology and organizational systems analysis. Computers and systems go hand in hand with information theory and cybernetics. The impact that information theory has had on the study, analysis, and practice of organizational communication is somewhat analogous to the tremendous influence that quantitative techniques have had on management decision making.

Interpersonal Communication

The opposite extreme to information theory is the interpersonal approach to communication. Whereas information theory is very mathematically oriented, interpersonal communication is very behaviorally oriented. In the interpersonal approach, the major emphasis is on transferring information from one person to another. Communication is looked upon as a basic method of effecting behavior change, and it incorporates the psychological processes (perception, learning, and motivation) on the one hand and language on the other. Listening sensitivity and nonverbal communications are also closely associated with this approach.

The often posed riddle that asks, "Is there a noise in the forest if a tree crashes to the ground but no one is there to hear it?" demonstrates some of the important aspects of interpersonal communication.[20] From a communications perspective the answer to the riddle is "No." There are sound waves but no sound because no one perceives it. There must be both a sender and a receiver in order for interpersonal communication to take place. The sender is obviously important to communication, but so is the neglected receiver who gives feedback to the sender.

[17]Norbert Wiener, *The Human Use of Human Beings*, 2d ed., rev., Doubleday & Company, Inc., Garden City, N. Y., 1954, p. 15. Originally published in 1950 by Houghton Mifflin Company.
[18]Ibid., p. 17.
[19]Gallager, op. cit., pp. 1–2.
[20]Peter F. Drucker, *Management*, Harper & Row, Publishers, New York, 1974, p. 483.

The importance of feedback cannot be overemphasized because effective interpersonal communication is highly dependent on it. Sigband comments on the interpersonal process and the important role of feedback thus:

> ... it permits expressive action on the part of one or more persons and the conscious and unconscious perception of such action. Perhaps one of the most important factors in this network is . . . feedback [which] is vital if the originator and receiver are to secure some level of effectiveness in the communication process.[21]

Gellerman states that "the nub of the entire communication problem" is the following:

> The sender, to be certain that his message will be accepted by the receiver, must be prepared to let the receiver influence him. He must even be prepared to let the receiver alter or modify the message in ways that make it more acceptable to the receiver. Otherwise it may not be understood, or it may not be accepted, or it may simply be given lip service and ignored.[22]

Besides feedback, other variables, such as trust, expectations, values, status, and compatibility, greatly influence the interpersonal aspects of communication. For example, there are many research studies that show that people who do not trust one another do not communicate.[23] This finding, of course, has significant implications for superior-subordinate relations in an organization. If the subordinate does not trust the boss, there will be ineffective communication. The same is true of the other variables mentioned. People perceive only what they expect to perceive; the unexpected may not be received at all. The growing "value gap" discussed in Chapter 4 can play havoc with interpersonal communication; so can status differentials and incompatibilities of any sort. Giving attention to and doing something about these interpersonal variables can spell the difference between effective and ineffective communication.

Interpersonal communication plays a central role in the organizational communication process and is directly relevant to the study of organizational behavior. It is not given further attention in this chapter but, as indicated earlier, is really a major portion of Parts Three and Four, especially Chapter 11, on perception, and Chapter 15, on group dynamics.

ORGANIZATIONAL COMMUNICATION PROCESS

The organizational process approach to communication represents the middle ground between information theory on the one hand and interpersonal commu-

---

[21]Norman B. Sigband, *Communication for Management,* Scott, Foresman and Company, Glenview, Ill., 1969, p. 8.

[22]Gellerman, op. cit., p. 46.

[23]For example, see Glen Mellinger, "Interpersonal Trust as a Factor in Communication," *The Journal of Abnormal and Social Psychology,* May 1956, pp. 304–309.

nication on the other. Traditionally, the formal organization structure was viewed as a network over which there were linear information flows. For example, Hicks and Gullett note that the organization structure provides the

> . . . paths of inputs that form intricate circuits of communication. An organizational communication network is analogous to a telephone system: information flows in certain restricted patterns or paths through the entire system.[24]

Especially in classical organization structures, the communication process consisted simply of the following:

1 Instructions and commands to do or not do are always communicated down the chain of command, and only from one person to others directly below him in the hierarchy.

2 Reports, inquiries, and requests are always communicated up the chain of command, and only to the one person directly above the communicator in the hierarchy.

3 Subgroups do not communicate directly with other subgroups at their level on the chart, but instead communicate up the chain of command until the message arrives at an office where both subgroups share a supervisor, then down the chain of command to the recipient subgroup.

4 The staff plays the role of communication gadfly—i.e., it is given free rein to collect and disseminate nonauthoritative information in its role as an extension of the boss.[25]

This traditional view of organizational communication has been very influential through the years, but it has also been very limiting. Philip Tompkins interestingly notes that the purely structural view of organizational communication is like a bikini, "what it reveals is interesting, but what it conceals is vital."[26] The vital part that is concealed by this view is the dynamic, personal aspects of organizational communication.

The Shannon-Weaver Model of Organizational Communication

One of the first widely accepted comprehensive models of the communication process was the Shannon and Weaver model. Since they were information theorists, the model stressed the transmission of information. Figure 9-2 shows this model. The major parts of the model can be summarized as follows:

1 *Information Source.* This is the logical beginning of the communication process. The source consists of raw information and includes some form of intent and purpose on the part of the sender. Accounting, statistics, and

---

[24]Hicks and Gullett, op. cit., p. 488.

[25]Eugene Walton, *A Magnetic Theory of Organizational Communication,* U.S. Naval Ordnance Test Station, China Lake, Calif., 1962.

[26]Philip K. Tompkins, "Organizational Communication: A State-of-the-Art Review," in G. Richetto (ed.), *Conference on Organizational Communication,* George C. Marshall Space Flight Center, Huntsville, Ala., 1967.

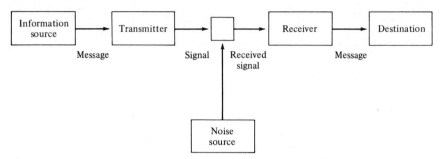

Figure 9-2   A model of the communication process. (*Source: Claude E. Shannon and Warren Weaver,* The Mathematical Theory of Communication, *The University of Illinois Press, Urbana, 1949, pp. 5 and 98.*)

computer data are examples of raw information which must be given meaning and purpose in the information source.

2   *Transmitter.*   The transmitter encodes the data into a message and sends it on to the receiver. The major form of encoding is language, which can be defined as any systematic pattern of signs, symbols, or signals. The raw data from the source are encoded into a meaningful language, e.g., the accounting, statistics, and computer data are translated into a message. This message is then transmitted by means of sound waves, electrical impulses, light waves, or pieces of paper.

3   *Noise.*   Noise is any interference that takes place between transmission and reception. It can be electrical static, semantic problems with the language, or deliberate distortion of the message. Noise is a "black box" concept. Any communication problem that cannot be fully explained can be categorized as noise.

4   *Receiver.*   Under this step of the model, the communication has passed from the sender side of the process to the receiver side. Decoding of the message now takes place. An interpretation must be made and understanding must be gained of the accounting, statistical, or computer information. Besides knowledge requirements, perception and listening enter the reception phase of the process model.

5   *Destination.*   Just as the information source is a requirement for the communication process to begin, a destination is necessary in order for the process to be completed. In the organization, the accounting, statistical, or computer information is most likely destined to go to line managers to assist them in accomplishing their unit's objectives or to top managers for use in evaluating performance.

Although the Shannon and Weaver model extended the classical structural approach to organizational communication by recognizing that it was a process, it still stressed linear information flows and was too static. As was pointed out in the discussion of the definition of communication, the process involves behaviors; it is a personal process. For example, receiver acceptance and expectations are vital to organizational communication. Merely sending and receiving information, i.e., transmission, is a necessary but insufficient condition for communication to take place in an organization.

The Berlo Dynamic Process Model

The first widely recognized model that presented communication as a dynamic, interactive process was proposed by David Berlo. He countered the linear, step-by-step information approach as follows:

> If we accept the concept of process, we view events and relationships as dynamic, on-going, ever-changing, continuous. When we label something as a process, we also mean that it does not have *a* beginning, *an* end, a fixed sequence of events. It is not static, at rest. It is moving. The ingredients within a process interact; each affects all the others.[27]

Figure 9-3 summarizes the Berlo model.

Organizational Communication as a Transactional Process

Contemporary theory and research have extended the Berlo dynamic process. For example, Wenburg and Wilmont present communication as a transactional process. The prefix "trans" (intended to denote "mutually" and "reciprocally") is stressed instead of "inter" (intended to denote "in-between"). They state in the process approach to communication, "All persons are engaged in sending (encoding) and receiving (decoding) messages *simultaneously.* Each person is constantly *sharing* in the encoding and decoding process, and each person is *affecting* the other."[28]

The remainder of the chapter assumes this dynamic, transactional view of organizational communication. It is a personal, not merely a linear information, process.

SUPERIOR-SUBORDINATE COMMUNICATION

Traditionally one of the dominant themes of organizational communication has been the so-called "downward" system. However, when a personal communi-

[27]David Berlo, *The Process of Communication,* Holt, Rinehart and Winston, Inc., New York, 1960, p. 24.
[28]John R. Wenburg and William W. Wilmont, *The Personal Communication Process,* John Wiley & Sons, Inc., New York, 1973, p. 5.

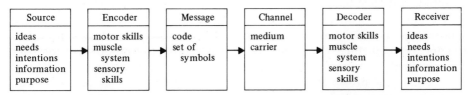

Source	Encoder	Message	Channel	Decoder	Receiver
ideas needs intentions information purpose	motor skills muscle system sensory skills	code set of symbols	medium carrier	motor skills muscle system sensory skills	ideas needs intentions information purpose

Figure 9-3 The Berlo model of communication. (*Source: Adapted from David K. Berlo,* The Process of Communication, *Holt, Rinehart and Winston, Inc., New York, 1960, pp. 30–32.*)

cation perspective replaces a linear information flow perspective, the downward system is more accurately portrayed as superior-subordinate communication. There are personal linkages, not just information flows, in the downward system.

The Purposes and Methods of Superior-Subordinate Communication

Katz and Kahn have identified five general purposes of superior-subordinate communication in an organization:

1   To give specific task directives about job instructions
2   To give information about organizational procedures and practices
3   To provide information about the rationale of the job
4   To tell subordinates about their performance
5   To provide ideological-type information to facilitate the indoctrination of goals[29]

Most organizations, in the past and also to a large extent today, have concentrated on and accomplished only the first two of these purposes. In general, superior-to-subordinate communication on job performance and the rationale-ideological aspects of jobs have been badly neglected. Tompkins, after an extensive review of the research literature, concludes that "widespread ineffectiveness is the rule, probably because of a variety of causes."[30]

A communicaton system that only gives specific directives about job instructions and procedures and fails to provide information about job performance or rationale-ideological information about the job has a negative organizational impact. This type of downward orientation promotes an authoritative atmosphere which tends to inhibit the effectiveness of the upward and horizontal systems of communication. Communicating to personnel the rationale for the job, the ideological relation of the job to the goals of the organization, and information about job performance, if properly handled, can greatly benefit the organization. As Katz and Kahn point out, "If a man knows the reasons for his assignment, this will often insure his carrying out the job more effectively; and if he has an understanding of what his job is about in relation to his subsystem, he is more likely to identify with organizational goals."[31] This does not imply that management should tell assembly-line workers that their jobs are extremely important to the success of the company, that the company would fold without their putting on a bolt right or welding a fender properly. Obviously, this type of communication can backfire. The workers would justifiably reason: "Who are they trying to kid? My job isn't *that* important. It is just another hypocritical con job by management." What is meant is that *full* information about the job, its ramifications for the rest of the

[29]Daniel Katz and Robert L. Kahn, *The Social Psychology of Organizations*, John Wiley & Sons, Inc., New York, 1966, p. 239.
[30]Tompkins, op. cit., p. 9.
[31]Katz and Kahn, op. cit., p. 242.

organization, and the quality of the employee's performance in it should be an important function of superior-subordinate communication.

Traditional downward communication systems rely on many types of media to disseminate information. Some examples of written media are organizational handbooks, manuals, magazines, newspapers, and letters sent to the home or distributed on the job; bulletin board items, posters, and information displays; and standard reports, descriptions of procedures, and memos. Examples of oral media utilized in the system include direct verbal orders or instructions from superiors, speeches, meetings, closed-circuit television sets, public address systems, and telephones. In addition, computerized information systems are becoming the major contributor to the downward flow of communication.

The numerous types of media give an indication of the avalanche of information that is descending on personnel from the downward system. Quality of information has often been sacrificed for quantity. Some organizations have tried to solve their downward communication problems by creating special departments whose goals are to make information reports more readable; to process information faster; and to prune information reports for brevity.[32] Besides the quantity and quality difficulties, much of downward communication becomes lost, distorted, misinterpreted, or ignored by organizational participants. One study of the communication efficiency of 100 representative business and industrial firms found that

> ... there is tremendous loss of information—37 percent—between the Board of Directors and the Vice-Presidential level. General supervisors got 56 percent of the information; plant managers 40 percent; and general foremen received only 30 percent of what had been transmitted downward to them. An average of only 20 percent of the communication sent downward through the five levels of management finally gets to the worker level.[33]

These problems point out that just because there is a very active downward flow of information, it does not mean that it is accurate or that it is received, understood, or accepted by subordinates.

Toward More Effective Superior-Subordinate Communication

To improve the effectiveness of superior-subordinate communication, more attention must be given the receiver and the use of multimedia techniques. Tompkins notes:

> The studies seem to suggest that management is ill-advised to depend on one-message campaigns or upon the written medium alone. Communication

---

[32]"The Crisis in Corporate Controls," *Dun's Review*, July 1963, p. 61. Also see "An Avalanche," an illustrative case based upon the above, in Fred Luthans, *Cases, Readings, and Review Guide for Principles of Management*, John Wiley & Sons, Inc., New York, 1969, p. 137.

[33]Ralph G. Nichols, "Listening Is Good Business," *Management of Personnel Quarterly*, Winter 1962, p. 4.

effectiveness can better be achieved by careful analysis of the intended receiver, by use of a combination of media and methods (giving the oral medium prominence), by careful monitoring of feedback, and by a continual effort to communicate.[34]

Most studies show that combined oral and written methods are most effective and that oral only is better than written only.

The biggest problem, however, is ignoring the importance of the receiver. This problem, of course, is symptomatic of taking a linear (in this case downward) information flow perspective as opposed to a personal process perspective. After an extensive review of the literature, Donald Roberts concludes that the downward flow of information can affect receivers in the following ways:

> **1** People's interpretations of communications follow the path of least resistance.
>
> **2** People are more open to messages which are consonant with their existing image, their beliefs and values.
>
> **3** Messages which are incongruent with values tend to engender more resistance than do messages which are incongruent with rational logic.
>
> **4** To the extent that people positively value need fulfillment, messages which facilitate need fulfillment are more easily accepted than messages which do not.
>
> **5** As people see the environment changing, they are more open to incoming messages.
>
> **6** The total situation affects communication; a message interpreted as congruent in one situation may be interpreted as incongruent in another.[35]

If managers understand these impacts of communication on subordinates and do something about it, communication can become more effective. Obviously, there is much more to superior-subordinate communication than merely the downward flow of information.

SUBORDINATE-INITIATED COMMUNICATION

Just as the downward system becomes superior-subordinate communication from a personal perspective, the upward system becomes subordinate-initiated communication in the personal view. In the traditional view, the classical organization structure formally provided for vertical information flows, downward and upward. However, in practice, except for feedback controls, the downward system completely dominated the upward system. Whereas the downward system is highly directive—giving orders, instructions, information, and procedures—the upward system is characteristically nondirective in

---

[34]Tompkins, op. cit., p. 9.

[35]Donald F. Roberts, "The Nature of Communication Effects," in Wilbur Schramm and Donald F. Roberts (eds.), *The Process and Effects of Mass Communication,* rev. ed., University of Illinois Press, Urbana, Ill., 1971, pp. 368–371.

nature. While bureaucratic authority facilitates a directive atmosphere, a free, participative supervisory approach is necessary for subordinate-initiated communication. Traditionally, bureaucratic authority has prevailed over the more participative styles, with the result that subordinate-initiated communication has often been outwardly stifled, badly misused, or conveniently ignored by management.

Research on Subordinate-initiated Communication

Research has generally verified the ineffectiveness of subordinate-initiated communication in organizations. One study asked the managers of twenty-four industrial plants to rank the ten most important morale factors of any employee group. The workers were then asked to do the same thing. Interestingly, the managers named the following bottom three factors: in the eighth place, full appreciation of work done; in the ninth, feeling "in" on things; and in the lowest place, sympathetic help on personal problems. The workers, on the other hand, ranked these same three factors as the first, second, and third most important.[36] The fact that the managers were completely wrong about the morale factors gives evidence that there was no communication from the workers to the managers.

In another study, fifty-eight superior-subordinate pairs, representing all functional areas from upper-management levels of five companies, were interviewed to determine the extent of mutual understanding and agreement on four factors of the subordinates' jobs: (1) duties, (2) requirements, (3) future changes, and (4) obstacles. After analyzing statistical results, the researchers concluded that ". . . [the subordinate] and his boss do not agree, or differ more than they agree, in almost every area. Also, superior and subordinate very often disagree about priorities—they simply don't see eye to eye on which are the most important and the least important tasks for the subordinate."[37] Once again these results do not speak very highly of the effectiveness of subordinate-initiated communication. Even when subordinates do communicate upward, the content is often meaningless because they send up only what they think the boss wants to hear or reports that are distorted or manipulated so that they contain only information that makes the subordinates look good. "Full and objective reporting is difficult, regardless of the organizational situation; no individual is an objective observer of his own performance and problems."[38]

Methods of Improving the Effectiveness of Subordinate-initiated Communication

The hierarchical structure is about the only formal method that the classical approach used to communicate upward and, as has been pointed out, in practice this has not worked out well. Other techniques and channels for

[36]Nichols, op. cit.

[37]Norman R. F. Maier, L. Richard Hoffman, John J. Hooven, and William H. Read, *Superior-Subordinate Communication in Management*, American Management Association, New York, 1961, p. 9.

[38]Katz and Kahn, op. cit., p. 246.

subordinate-initiated communication are necessary.[39] The following are some possible ways to promote more effective subordinate-to-superior communications:

1 *The grievance procedure.* Provided for in most collective bargaining agreements, the grievance procedure allows employees to make an appeal upward beyond their immediate superior. It protects individuals from arbitrary action by their direct superior and encourages communication about complaints.

2 *The open-door policy.* Taken literally, this means that the superior's door is always open to subordinates. It is a continuous invitation for subordinates to come in and talk about anything that is troubling them. Unfortunately, in practice the open-door policy is more fiction than fact. The boss may slap the subordinate on the back and say, "My door is always open to you," but in many cases both the subordinate and the boss know the door is really closed. It is a case where the adage that actions speak louder than words applies.

3 *Counseling, attitude questionnaires, and exit interviews.* The personnel department can greatly facilitate subordinate-initiated communication by conducting nondirective, confidential counseling sessions, periodically administering attitude questionnaires, and holding meaningful exit interviews for those who leave the organization. Much valuable information can be gained from these forms of communication.

4 *Participative techniques.* Participative-decision techniques can generate a great deal of communication. This may be accomplished by either informal involvement of subordinates or formal participation programs such as the junior boards, union-management committees, and suggestion boxes.

5 *The ombudsperson.* A largely untried but potentially significant technique to enable management to obtain more subordinate-initiated communication is the use of an ombudsperson. The concept has been used primarily in Scandinavia to provide an outlet for persons who have been treated unfairly or in a depersonalized manner by large, bureaucratic government. It has more recently gained popularity in American state governments, military posts, and universities. Although it is just being introduced in a few business organizations, if set up and handled properly, it may work where the open-door policy has failed. As business organizations become larger and more depersonalized, the ombudsperson may fill an important void which exists under these conditions.

Overall, subordinates can basically supply two types of information: first, personal information about ideas, attitudes, and performance, and secondly, more technical feedback information about performance, a vital factor for the control of any organization. The personal information is generally derived from what subordinates tell their superiors. Some examples of such information are:

1 What the persons have done
2 What those under them have done
3 What their peers have done

[39]Flippo, op. cit., pp. 389–392.

4 What they think needs to be done

5 What their problems are

6 What the problems of the unit are

7 What matters of organizational practice and policy need to be reviewed[40]

The other type of upward information, feedback for control purposes, is necessary if the organization is to survive. As Scott and Mitchell point out, "Decision centers utilize information feedback to appraise the results of the organization's performance and to make any adjustments to insure the accomplishment of the purposes of the organization."[41] The role that feedback communication plays in the control process will be examined in the next chapter.

INTERACTIVE COMMUNICATION IN ORGANIZATIONS

The classical hierarchical organization structure gives only formal recognition to vertical communication. Nevertheless, most of the classical theorists saw the need to supplement the vertical with some form of horizontal system, as Fayol did with his gangplank concept. Horizontal communication is required to make a coordinated effort in achieving the overall organizational goal. The horizontal requirement becomes more apparent as the organization becomes larger, more complex, and more subject to dramatic change. The modern organization structures presented in Chapter 7, e.g., the free form and matrix, recognize the need by formally incorporating horizontal flows into the structure. However, similar to vertical (downward and upward) flows in the organization structure, the real key to horizontal communication is found in people and behaviors. Because of the personal aspects of communication, the terminology "interactive" seems more appropriate than "horizontal." The horizontal flows of information (even in a matrix structure) are only part of the communication process that takes place across an organization.

The Extent and Implications of Interactive Communication

Most management writers today stress the important but overlooked role that interactive communication plays in organizations. In most cases the vertical communication process dominates the horizontal. For example, one observational study found that 17 percent of the total communications of a line-production manager in one plant were sent horizontally and 22 percent were received from a horizontal source. In another plant in the same study, 41 percent of the production manager's communications were sent horizontally and 40 percent were received from a horizontal source.[42] Obviously, the exact amount of horizontal communication is highly contingent upon the situation.

---

[40]Katz and Kahn, op. cit., p. 245.

[41]Willian G. Scott and Terence R. Mitchell, *Organization Theory*, rev. ed., Richard D. Irwin, Inc., Homewood, Ill., 1972, p. 147.

[42]Henry A. Landsberger, "The Horizontal Dimension in Bureaucracy," *Administrative Science Quarterly*, December 1961, p. 315.

One potentially significant research finding is that the nature of the productive or technological process will influence the type of communication that occurs. For example, Simpson found that communications of first-line supervisors were mainly horizontal because of the mechanized assembly-line nature of their work.[43] The assembly-line type of operation discouraged and even inhibited vertical communication, but it encouraged horizontal communication. The reason is that an assembly-line job is highly structured and largely dependent upon the speed of the line. Thus, there is little need for directives, instructions, or orders from above, but there is a necessity to communicate along the line to get the job done.

Just as in other aspects of organizational communication, there are many behavioral implications contained in the interactive process. Communication with peers, i.e., those persons of relatively equal status on the same level of an organization, provides needed social support for an individual. People can more comfortably turn to a peer for social support than they can to those above or below them. The result can be good or bad for the organization. If the support is couched in terms of task coordination to achieve overall goals, interactive communication can be good for the organization. On the other hand, "if there are no problems of task coordination left to a group of peers, the content of their communication can take forms which are irrelevant to or destructive of organizational functioning."[44] In addition, interactive communication among peers may be at the sacrifice of vertical communication. Persons at each level, giving social support to one another, may freely communicate among themselves but fail to communicate upward or downward.

The Purposes and Methods of Interactive Communication

Just as there are several purposes for vertical communication in an organization there are also varied reasons for the need for interactive communication. Based on several research studies, Gerald Goldhaber has summarized four of the most important purposes for interactive communication:

> **1** *Task coordination.* The department heads may meet monthly to discuss how each department is contributing to the system's goals.
> **2** *Problem solving.* The members of a department may assemble to discuss how they will handle a threatened budget cut; they may employ brainstorming techniques.
> **3** *Information sharing.* The members of one department may meet with the members of another department to give them some new data.
> **4** *Conflict resolution.* Members of one department may meet to discuss a conflict inherent in the department or between departments.[45]

[43]Richard L. Simpson, "Vertical and Horizontal Communication in Formal Organizations," *Administrative Science Quarterly,* September 1959, p. 195.
[44]Katz and Kahn, op. cit., p. 244.
[45]Gerald M. Goldhaber, *Organizational Communication,* William C. Brown Company Publishers, Dubuque, Iowa, 1974, p. 121.

The examples for each of the major purposes of interactive communication are mainly departmental or interdepartmental meetings. Such meetings and the system of committees that exist in most organizations have been the major methods of interactive communication. In addition, most organizations' procedures require written reports to be distributed across departments. The quantity, quality, and human implications discussed in relation to the vertical communication process are also inherent in the traditional methods of interactive communication.

Because of the failure of the classical structures to meet the needs of interactive communication, the informal organization and groups have filled the void. Informal contacts with others on the same level are a primary means of interactive communication. Chapter 15 will explore some of the dynamics of informal and group communication.

SUMMARY

At every level of modern society, communication is a problem. One of the problems when applied to organizations has been the failure to recognize that communication involves more than just linear information flows: it is a personal process that involves behavior exchanges. Knowledge of both information theory and interpersonal approaches is a necessary background for understanding the organizational communication process.

A purely structural view of organizational communication is no longer adequate. The Shannon-Weaver model was the first to recognize that communication is a process, but the Berlo model added a dynamic interactive dimension. The contemporary view is that communication is a transactional process. The three major dimensions of organizational communication from a personal, transactional perspective are superior-subordinate, subordinate-initiated, and interactive processes. Each has varied purposes and methods. The downward system is generally adequate in the superior-subordinate process, but better techniques are needed to improve the upward and horizontal systems. All three processes in organizations can greatly benefit from increased attention given to the personal aspects of communication.

CASE: DOING MY OWN THING

Rita Lowe had worked for the same boss for eleven years. Over coffee one day, her friend, Sara, asked her, "What is it like to work for old Charlie?" Rita replied, "Oh, I guess it's okay. He pretty much leaves me alone. I more or less do my own thing." Then Sara said, "Well, you've been at that same job for eleven years. How are you doing in it? Does it look like you will ever be promoted? If you don't mind me saying so, I can't for the life of me see what you do has anything to do with the operation." Rita replied, "Well, first of all, I really don't have any idea of how I am doing. Charlie never really tells me, but I've always taken the attitude that no news is good news. As for what I do and how it contributes to the operation around here, Charlie mumbled something when I started the job about being important to the operation, but that was it. We really don't communicate very well."

1   Analyze Rita's last statement, "We really don't communicate very well." What is the status of superior-subordinate communication in this incident? Katz and Kahn identified five purposes of the superior-subordinate communication process. Which ones are being badly neglected in this case?

2   In the chapter, communication was said to be a personal process. Does this incident verify this contention? Be specific in your answer.

3   Are there any implications in this incident for subordinate-initiated communication and for interactive communication?

SELECTED REFERENCES

Athanassiades, John C.: "The Distortion of Upward Communication in Hierarchical Organizations," *Academy of Management Journal,* June 1973, pp. 207–226.

Berlo, David K.: *The Process of Communication,* Holt, Rinehart and Winston, Inc., New York, 1960.

Brenner, Marshall H., and Norman B. Sigband: "Organizational Communication—An Analysis Based on Empirical Data," *Academy of Management Journal,* June 1973, pp. 323–339.

Davis, Keith: *Human Behavior at Work,* 4th ed., McGraw-Hill Book Company, New York, 1972, chaps. 20 and 21.

Farace, Richard, and Donald MacDonald: "New Directions in the Study of Organizational Communication," *Personnel Psychology,* Spring 1974, pp. 1–15.

Goldhaber, Gerald M.: *Organizational Communication,* William C. Brown Company Publishers, Dubuque, Iowa, 1974.

Greenbaum, Howard H.: "The Audit of Organizational Communication," *Academy of Management Journal,* December 1974, pp. 739–754.

Hall, Edward T.: *The Silent Language,* Fawcett Publications, Inc., Greenwich, Conn., 1959.

Hall, Jay: "Communication Revisited," *California Management Review,* Spring 1973, pp. 56–67.

Harriman, Bruce: "Up and Down the Communications Ladder," *Harvard Business Review,* September–October 1974, pp. 143–151.

Hicks, Herbert G., and C. Ray Gullett: *The Management of Organizations,* 3d ed., McGraw-Hill Book Company, New York, 1976, Chaps. 25 and 26.

Katz, Daniel, and Robert L. Kahn: *The Social Psychology of Organizations,* John Wiley & Sons, Inc., New York, 1966, chap. 9.

Lee, M. Baline, and William L. Zwerman: "Developing a Facilitation System for Horizontal and Diagonal Communications in Organization," *Personnel Journal,* July 1975, pp. 400–401.

Nichols, Ralph B.: "Listening Is Good Business," *Management of Personnel Quarterly,* Winter 1962, pp. 2–9.

Roberts, Karlene H., and Charles A. O'Reilly, III: "Failures in Upward Communication in Organizations: Three Possible Culprits," *Academy of Management Journal,* June 1974, pp. 205–215.

Roberts, Karlene H., Charles A. O'Reilly, III, Gene E. Bretton, and Lyman W. Porter: "Organizational Theory and Organizational Communication: A Communication Failure?" *Human Relations,* May 1974, pp. 501–524.

Schramm, Wilber: "The Nature of Communication between Humans," *The Process and Effects of Mass Communication,* rev. ed. (Wilber Schramm and Donald F. Roberts, eds.), University of Illinois Press, Urbana, Ill., 1971, pp. 3–53.

Stull, James B.: "The Benefits of Open Communication," *Supervisory Management,* July 1975, pp. 18–22.

Tompkins, Philip K.: "Organizational Communication: A State-of-the-Art Review," in G. Richetto (ed.), *Conference on Organizational Communication,* George C. Marshall Space Flight Center, Huntsville, Alabama, 1967.

Wenberg, John R., and William W. Wilmont: *The Personal Communication Process,* John Wiley & Sons, Inc., New York, 1973.

Chapter 10

The Control Process

Control is the third and final organization and management process that is given detailed attention. Along with the other two processes, decision making and communication, control interacts with structure and technology to constitute the formal organization system. The first section of this chapter clears up some common misconceptions about control. The second section defines control and points out the importance of both feedforward and feedback. The third section presents the three basic elements of the control process: standards and objectives, measurement and evaluation, and corrective control decisions. The fourth section is concerned with some modern management techniques of control, including the budgetary process in general and the newer, specific approaches of PPBS, real-time techniques, PERT/Cost, management audit, and feedforward techniques. The remaining sections analyze the behavioral implications of the organizational control process.

MISCONCEPTIONS ABOUT CONTROL

There is a great deal of misunderstanding about the nature of organizational control. Some of the misconceptions stem from the negativism attached to the common usage of the term. The American cultural value of individual freedom is supposedly threatened by any form of control. Highly simplified, the argument goes that freedom is good and control is bad. Despite this widely held value, the daily life of every American is highly controlled from waking to the ringing of the alarm clock in the morning to watching the 10 or 11 o'clock news at night. Inside as well as outside the organization, today's employees have many rules to follow—where to park, when to punch the time clock or report to the office, how to comply with safety regulations, and what to wear are just a few examples. In addition, there is the controlling atmosphere inherent in the superior-subordinate authority relationship which exists in every formal organization.

The behavioral implications of control are given specific attention later in the chapter, but for now it can be said that control per se is not categorically "bad" for the individual. Although they do not readily admit it, most people probably prefer some degree of control over their lives because it gives them some stability and contributes to their general welfare and safety. Yet, the negative connotation of control still exists and is amplified by the ways in which controls have been traditionally set, implemented, and used in formal organizations.

Another confusing aspect of control is its conceptual relationship to the other organization and management processes. As in this book, control is almost always presented last in the conceptual framework for the management processes. This ordering implies that control occurs after the other processes have been performed. For example, in the dynamic management process model presented in Chapter 3 there was an ordered sequence of decision making, communication, and control. As pointed out there, this is not necessarily the order in which the processes are performed. Whereas decision making most often precedes control in an organization, control may also precede and affect the decisions that are made. Similarly, it may precede or follow the communication process. Thus, even though presented last, control does not necessarily take that position in a realistic management process.

DEFINITION OF CONTROL

Despite the many misconceptions about the nature of control, surprisingly there is general agreement about its definition. Fayol's definition, which he gave in 1916, set a precedent that has been followed through the years and is commonly accepted today. In the very last section of his book, he states:

> In an undertaking, control consists in verifying whether everything occurs in conformity with the plan adopted, the instructions issued and principles established. It has for object to point out weaknesses and errors in order to rectify them and prevent recurrence. It operates on everything, things, people, actions.[1]

[1]Henri Fayol, *General and Industrial Management*, translated by Constance Storrs, Sir Isaac Pitman & Sons, London, 1949, p. 107.

Hicks and Gullett define control in reference to the practice of management in more direct terms: "Controlling is the process by which management sees if what did happen was what was supposed to happen. If not, necessary adjustments are made."[2] Johnson, Kast, and Rosenzweig point out the important role that the systems concept plays in control: "We shall define control as that function of the system which provides adjustments in conformance to the plan; the maintenance of variations from system objectives within allowable limits."[3] The cybernetic system concept, discussed in earlier chapters, is an important conceptual base for the organizational control process. Automatic-feedback control mechanisms play a significant role in controlling the modern organization. The general systems approach emphasizes feedback, which is an inherent part of any control process. Control decisions are traditionally based upon the feedback which is obtained from accounting information in the upward system of communication in an organization.

The new emphasis is also on the feedforward aspects of control. This feedforward approach recognizes that the feedback process alone is not enough for effective control. The input variables of a system are controlled in a feedforward system. Koontz and Bradspies note that "a shift must be made away from emphasis on quickly available data on final results to quickly available data on those input variables that lead to final results. It is a means of seeing problems as they develop and not looking back—always too late— to see why a planning target was missed."[4]

The very existence of the control process implies that the decision-making and communication processes (feedforward and feedback) are not perfect. The tremendous complexity of the modern organization, combined with certain psychological dependencies of personnel on order and stability, makes the control process a necessity. For example, because of an organization's size and complexity, planning decisions do not always work out in practice. Moreover, the organizational communication process can easily break down. A control process is required to anticipate and point out these types of difficulties and to try to get them corrected. In addition, many of the problems at which the control process is aimed are human in nature. McFarland contends, for example: "In the absence of control, an individual tends to allow results to stray from plans or orders. Anarchy is more than he can stand, for it permits him to work so poorly that it may trouble his conscience."[5] The behavioral impact of control is much more far-reaching than is implied by this statement. Yet, the key to interpreting McFarland's statement is the word *absence*. The absence of any organizational controls would probably lead to anarchy and

[2]Herbert G. Hicks and C. Ray Gullett: *The Management of Organizations,* 3d ed., McGraw-Hill Book Company, New York, 1976, p. 497.

[3]Richard A. Johnson, Fremont E. Kast, and James E. Rosenzweig, *The Theory and Management of Systems,* 3d ed., McGraw-Hill Book Company, New York, 1973, p. 74.

[4]Harold Koontz and Robert W. Bradspies, "Managing through Feedforward Control," *Business Horizons,* June 1972, pp. 25–36.

[5]Dalton E. McFarland, *Management,* 4th ed., The Macmillan Company, New York, 1974, p. 393.

psychological problems because people have learned to depend on various controls in their daily lives. The argument in the behavioral approach to management is not whether controls are to exist but rather how they are to be set and used in the modern organization. The control process per se is necessary for the attainment of objectives and ultimately for the very survival of the organization.

BASIC ELEMENTS OF CONTROL

Inherent in the definition of control are three basic elements. First, control sets the standards and objectives which serve as the guide for performance. Second, control measures and evaluates inputs and performance according to the standards and objectives. Third, control takes corrective action in the form of a control decision. Sometimes control is mistakenly equated with only one of the three elements. The control process includes all three elements and is very broad in scope.

With the wide agreement about the definition of control and its elements, on the surface there would appear to be few problems in applying control to the modern organization. Unfortunately, there is much controversy plus many problems and unanswered questions, when it comes to setting up, implementing, and using organizational control. The following questions point to some of the relevant problem areas in control that are currently facing management:

1   When and where should a review of performance take place?
2   Who should make the appraisals?
3   What standard should be used for evaluation?
4   To whom should the results of evaluation be reported?
5   How may the entire process be completed promptly, fairly, and at reasonable expense?[6]

The following discussion attempts to clarify some of these questions and to provide some behavioral insights into the three major elements of control.

Objectives and Standards

The objectives-and-standards phase of the control process is closely related to the management function of planning. Koontz and O'Donnell note that "every objective, every goal of the many planning programs, every activity of these programs, every policy, every procedure, and every budget become standards against which actual or expected performance might be measured."[7] Control standards and objectives are set for each organizational unit and range from a small work group at the bottom to the governing board at the top.

---

[6]William H. Newman, Charles E. Sumner, and E. Kirby Warren, *The Process of Management,* 3d ed., Prentice-Hall, Inc., Englewood Cliffs, N. J., 1972, p. 582.

[7]Harold Koontz and Cyril O'Donnell, *Principles of Management,* 6th ed., McGraw-Hill Book Company, New York, 1976, p. 657.

Traditionally, control units were structurally defined and assigned as a budget area. Recently, because of behavioral influence, the trend has been toward identifying control units by area of responsibility. The responsibility units are often expressed as profit centers. This type of "responsibility accounting" can be traced back to Sloan's profit-centered concept of decentralization, which he installed in General Motors in the 1920s. The philosophy and practice of responsibility-centered control are now beginning to be implemented in most modern organizations. The controllable variables are distinguished from the uncontrollable ones when standards are being set for performance. For example, overhead items (heat, light, water, and depreciation) or union wage rates cannot generally be controlled by middle- or lower-level unit managers. Therefore, these uncontrollable variables would be excluded from their standards for performance.

Some management writers do not mention objectives in the control process, and others equate objectives with standards. Here, objectives are treated as separate from standards, but both play an integral part in the control process. The following graphic presentation of the conceptual levels of the first control element may help to clarify how objectives differ from standards.

Standard $\longrightarrow$ Objective $\longrightarrow$ Goal $\longrightarrow$ Purpose

Accordingly, standards are set to provide a measuring point or yardstick for progress in attaining unit objectives. These objectives are aimed at overall organizational goals which must ultimately accomplish a purpose. For example, in a business organization, a standard may be a cost or sales figure; an objective may be rate of return on investment or share of the market; a goal may be total profit or social responsibility; and purpose may be survival in a free enterprise economy. Thus, standards are used to control objectives, objectives are used to control goals, and goals are used to control purpose. Obviously, all the conceptual levels of control are important to the survival (purpose) of the organization, but the practical mechanics of control are focused primarily on standards.

Setting standards for control is essentially a two-step procedure. Management must first decide what input needs or performance level is required to attain the unit objectives. Appropriate criteria are then selected which express the input needs or performance level decided upon. In practice, the standards may be expressed in either physical, financial, or intangible terms.

Meaurement and Evaluation

Once standards have been set, the next phase of the control process is to measure and evaluate inputs and performance. Measurement for inputs and outcomes may take the form of either personal observation or sophisticated managerial accounting procedures. Evaluation of performance depends chiefly on management by exception or appraisal by results.

Personal Observation   Personal observation is the most widely used method of measuring in the control process. It is relied upon especially when controlling human performance. For example, a skilled supervisor is "able to judge output by observing the pace of his workers; quality can be evaluated by personally inspecting the work in progress; and an estimate of morale and attitudes results from seeing employees, listening to their spontaneous remarks, and obtaining responses to questions."[8]

Not everyone is capable of obtaining and using observation to measure performance effectively. What reality is, what the visual sense picks up, and what the perceptual interpretation is may be three completely different things, as Chapter 11, on perception, will discuss in detail. The complex psychological process of perception greatly influences the use of personal observation as a measuring technique. In addition, the other psychological processes of learning and motivation strongly affect observation. Besides having a complicating psychological impact, personal observation is very time-consuming. Despite these real and potential problems, most management writers maintain that personal observation is one of the best ways to control people. As Koontz and O'Donnell note, "although many scientific devices aid in making sure that people are doing that which has been planned, the problem of control is still one of measuring activities of human beings."[9]

Managerial Accounting   Traditionally, accounting theory and practice concentrated on providing information for external users. In recent years, the emphasis in accounting has shifted to internal or management usage. Managerial accounting generates much objective information, and it has become a major method of measurement in the control process.

The American Accounting Association's Committee on Management Accounting defined its approach as follows:

> Management accounting is the application of appropriate techniques and concepts in processing the historical and projected economic data of an entity to assist management in establishing a plan for reasonable economic objectives and in the making of rational decisions with a view toward achieving these objectives.[10]

This statement brings out the comprehensive nature of management accounting. Besides providing information for measurement purposes, managerial accountants are also beginning to enter into the evaluative aspects of control. A publication on managerial accounting stresses that "at the minimum, the accounting system must provide the means to evaluate the appropriateness of

[8]Henry L. Sisk, *Principles of Management*, 2d ed., South-Western Publishing Company, Cincinnati, 1973, p. 649.

[9]Koontz and O'Donnell, op. cit., p. 671.

[10]"Report of Committee on Management Accounting," *The Accounting Review*, April 1959, p. 210.

the information needed and in no case should the accountant be merely the passive supplier of untreated data."[11]

Closely related to the managerial accountants are the computer technologists and systems analysts who supply much measurement information but who are also assuming a larger evaluative role. Formerly, these staff specialists provided control information and advice only to line executives who then made the evaluations. Despite the trends toward broader participation in evaluation, the guiding principle in this area continues to be management by exception and appraisal by results.

Management by Exception   Management by exception can be traced back to Jethro's often-quoted advice to Moses in the Bible. Jethro said that only exceptional matters should be brought to the attention of Moses. Management by exception was also advocated by Frederick W. Taylor in the scientific management movement. One of the more recent comprehensive treatments given management by exception comes from Lester Bittel's book on the subject. He stated that management by exception is "a system of identification and communication that signals the manager when his attention is needed; conversely, it remains silent when his attention is not required."[12]

Management by exception is a vitally important evaluation aspect of control in the modern organization. As organizations continue to grow in size and complexity, this aspect increases in relevance. By design or default, management by exception becomes a reality in the modern organization. Computerization and systems design are also compatible with this method of management. A properly designed cybernetic system will red-flag exceptions that require evaluation.

There are many advantages to controlling by exception. A partial list would show that it saves time, concentrates effort, reduces distractons, gives broader coverage, reduces the frequency of decision making, makes more use of knowledge and data, identifies critical problem areas, and stimulates communication.[13] On the other hand, if management by exception slips into being management by crisis, it may become disastrous for the organization.

Dependency upon a management-by-crisis approach is a sign of the breakdown of effective management. It is a mark of confusion and an admission of incompetence. Management by crisis is quite different from management by exception. Yet, some managers believe they are managing by exception when in fact they are managing by crisis. In the latter case, the crisis situations tend to become the rule rather than the exception. A typical example of management by crisis is a "drive" on a given problem. If an organization is in a financial squeeze, the solution under management by crisis is to have an

---

[11]*A Statement of Basic Accounting Theory,* American Accounting Association, Evanston, Ill., 1966, p. 40.
[12]Lester R. Bittel, *Management by Exception,* McGraw-Hill Book Company, New York, 1964, p. 5.
[13]Ibid., pp. 9–19.

economy drive. More often than not, the drive may initially save a few dollars but end up wasting thousands. Peter Drucker cites the following illustration:

> "For four weeks we cut inventories," a case-hardened veteran of management by crisis once summed it up. "Then we have four weeks of cost-cutting, followed by four weeks of human relations. We just have time to push customer service and courtesy for a month. And then the inventory is back where it was when we started. We don't even try to do our job. All management talks about, thinks about, preaches about, is last week's inventory figure or this week's customer complaints. How we do the rest of the job they don't even want to know."[14]

In actual practice, there is sometimes only a fine line separating management by exception from management by crisis. There is a subtle but very real difference between the two. Management by exception can be, and often is, a very effective approach to controlling the modern organization. On the other hand, if management by exception turns into management by crisis in practice, the organization is headed for a breakdown in planning and control.

Appraisal by Results A relatively new approach to evaluation in the control process is appraisal by results. Usually associated with management by objectives, this approach to control concentrates on ends rather than means and is diagnostic rather than punitive in character. The person or unit is evaluated according to the results obtained. In addition, the evaluation is concerned with the reasons why the person or unit did or did not meet the standards or accomplish the objectives that were set in the first phase of the control process.

Many organizations combine management by exception with appraisal by results. For example, General Electric developed key result areas which were derived from the question, "Will continued failure in this area prevent the attainment of management's responsibility for advancing General Electric as a leader in a strong, competitive economy, even though results in all other key result areas are good?" The eight key result areas determined in this way were: profitability, market position, productivity, product leadership, personnel development, employee attitudes, public responsibility, and balance between short-range and long-range goals.[15] Concentrating on these control points allows the manager to manage by exception but still appraise by results.

Controlling results emphasizes the role of the external (open-systems) environment. Drucker makes the point that results in business organizations exist *only* on the outside and it is much more difficult to control these outside

[14]Peter F. Drucker, *The Practice of Management,* Harper & Row, Publishers, Incorporated, New York, 1954, p. 128.
[15]Robert W. Lewis, "Measuring, Reporting and Appraising Results of Operations with Reference to Goals, Plans and Budgets," in *Planning, Managing and Measuring the Business, A Case Study of Management Planning and Control at General Electric Company,* Controllership Foundation, Inc., New York, 1955, pp. 30–31.

variables than it is the inside variables. He notes that even the most internally efficient buggy-whip companies are not in business today.

> It is of little value to have the most efficient engineering department if it designs the wrong product. The Cuban subsidiaries of U. S. companies were by far the best run and, apparently, the most profitable—let alone the least "troublesome"—of all U. S. operations in Latin America. This was, however, irrelevant to their expropriation. And it mattered little, I daresay, during the period of IBM's great expansion in the fifties and sixties how "efficient" its operations were; its basic entrepreneurial idea was the right, the effective one.[16]

In the long run, control of outside, environmental variables such as technological developments, economic conditions, social values, and the political/legal climate will affect the very survival of the organization. A contingency approach to management, as outlined in Chapter 3, can help in this control effort.

Being diagnostic, appraisal by results does not automatically reward conformance with standards or punish deviation from standards. This diagnostic characteristic, plus the fact that appraisal by results is environmentally and behaviorally oriented, does not mean that it is an easy or, to use Douglas McGregor's term, a "soft" approach to control. On the contrary, appraisal by results is a very demanding and stringent approach. If the appropriate philosophic base exists and is carefully implemented into practice, appraisal by results combines the behavioral, contingency, and more traditional aspects of management into an effective evaluation approach in controlling the modern organization.

Corrective Control Decisions

The third and final element of the control process is corrective action taken in the form of a control decision. Merely setting standards and measuring and evaluating inputs and performance do not achieve control. A control decision must be made in order for the control process to be complete. The third phase occurs in the same place as the first phase—the decision-making center of the dynamic management process. For example, suppose that a deviation from standards is detected by the measuring devices. An evaluation may lead to one of the following conclusions: The standards were set wrong; there is a need to "tighten up" and obtain conformance between standards and inputs or performance; new motivational techniques are needed to gain compliance with standards; or maintenance of the current deviation should be attempted. Each of these possible conclusions requires a corresponding control decision. If the first conclusion is adopted, the decision will be to reexamine present standards and/or make new ones. With the second conclusion, the decision may be to reprimand or fire the personnel involved and put on more pressure. The third

---

[16]Peter F. Drucker, *Management,* Harper & Row Publishers, New York, 1974, p. 497.

conclusion may lead to a decision that installs a new wage-incentive plan or supervisory style. For the fourth conclusion, the decision would be to maintain the status quo and continue to do things as they have been done in the past.

In effect, the manager who is trying to control is like the captain of a ship.[17] The captain receives information on the location and bearing of his ship and then adjusts his course in order to arrive at the planned destination. In a similar manner, the manager receives feedforward or feedback information about the inputs or performance of his unit and then makes a control decision that will accomplish the unit's objectives.

TECHNIQUES OF CONTROL

Many general techniques of control have already been mentioned in the measurement and evaluation section. Now attention will be given to some specific techniques of control. Starting with the scientific management techniques for output and cost controls at the turn of the century, control techniques through the years have included standardized accounts and cost systems, sophisticated budgeting and nonbudgeting techniques, and ingenious costing techniques. In addition, a wealth of information has been generated from mathematical and computerized information and other techniques.

Budgetary Technique

The common budget is the most widely used technique of organizational control. A budget is simply a plan containing quantitative measures which are used to control organizational performance. The quantitative measures of a budget may be expressed in either physical, nonfinancial terms or financial terms. Examples of nonfinancial budgets include labor and machine-hour budgets, product budgets, and materials budgets. Common financial budgets include capital expenditure, cash, and balance-sheet budgets. The great majority of budgets are expressed in monetary rather than physical units.

The financial budgeting process involves three basic steps: expressing in dollars the anticipated results of plans in a future period; coordinating these dollar estimates into a well-balanced program; and comparing actual performance with the estimated balanced program.[18] This approach is analogous to the three principal elements of the entire control process. The first step of budgeting assists in setting the desired standards for performance; the second step emphasizes that coordination between the various control units is needed to ensure attainment of the objectives and goals of the organization; and the third step aids in evaluating inputs or performance via appraisal by results.

Financial budgeting offers many unique advantages as a method of control. Newman, Summer, and Warren cite four especially important advantages. They are, in brief, the following:

[17]This analogy is made in Newman et al., op. cit., p. 597.
[18]Ibid., pp. 602–603.

    1 Budgets use a single common denominator—dollars—for many diverse actions and things.

    2 Budgets mainly use records and systems that are required for other purposes and are already in existence.

    3 For a business organization, the budget deals directly with one of its primary goals—making a profit.

    4 Budgets stimulate and bring life to other good management practices.[19]

The budget technique should not be thought of as a panacea for all the control problems of an organization. There are many drawbacks, especially, as the last part of the chapter shows, its impact on human behavior. In addition, there are many effective nonbudgetary techniques which contribute to organizational control. They include various statistical, reporting, and auditing programs and break-even and ratio analysis. Some of the newer techniques combine both budgetary and nonbudgetary concepts. PPBS, PERT/Cost, real-time techniques, management audit, and feedforward techniques represent specialized control methods which will supplement, if not eventually replace, traditional budgeting in the organizations of the future.

PPBS

Program budgeting, or, more specifically, PPBS (Planning-Programming-Budgeting-System), is a relatively new but popular control technique. Perhaps the best way to explain PPBS is to say that it combines program budgeting with systems analysis. A program is a results-oriented plan for the future. A program budget is a financial expression of a future plan. Although in theory there is no direct link between PPBS and systems, "in practice, the basic ideas of systems analysis and the approaches which lead to successful planning, programming, and budgeting are the same."[20] Thus, at least in practice, PPBS can be thought of as a systems approach to programmed budgeting.

    Over a decade ago, then President Johnson announced in a news conference that he was directing each department and agency of the federal government to introduce what he called "a revolutionary new system" of planning the government's many programs and drawing up its budget. The President said, "This system will permit us to find the most effective and the least costly alternative to achieving American goals."[21] The system was hailed by some public administration experts as potentially the most significant management improvement in the history of American government.[22] Over the years, PPBS has not generally lived up to these expectations. The approach generally worked well in defense, particularly in the Air Force, which could group a few activities into programs aimed at a limited number of large

    [19]Ibid., p. 613.

    [20]David I. Cleland and William R. King, *Systems Analysis and Project Management*, McGraw-Hill Book Company, New York, 1968, p. 114.

    [21]*New York Times*, Aug. 26, 1965, p. 17.

    [22]Bertram M. Gross and Michael Springer, "A New Orientation in American Government," *The Annals of the American Academy of Political and Social Science*, May 1967, p. 9.

weapons systems. But when PPBS was imposed on other areas of the federal government, particularly the domestic agencies such as Health, Education, and Welfare (HEW), which had different situations from those of defense, the approach ran into some real problems. One high-level federal administrator who lived under PPBS observed that "inordinate amounts of time and money went into techniques for moving data mechanically among accounting frameworks" and "complexity killed PPBS with top management."[23] The contingency implications are clear—PPBS or any other control techniques cannot be applied, categorically, to all situations.

Although the federal government is the most publicized user of PPBS, state and local governments and business, educational, and health care organizations are also trying out the technique. Cleland and King assert that many of the basic ideas for PPBS came, in fact, from the business world and were subsequently borrowed by government planners.[24] There is little doubt that PPBS is difficult to apply to traditionally organized and managed operations, but it has some promise of being an effective technique for controlling many of today's more complex organizations. It is particularly relevant to the organizations described in Chapter 7, i.e., the project, matrix, and free-form designs.

PERT/Cost

Chapter 3 briefly mentioned PERT (Program Evaluation and Review Technique). First used on complex defense projects, the major emphasis was on time scheduling, or PERT/Time. A few years later, the cost variable was added to the PERT approach to planning and control. Thus, PERT/Cost became an extension or expansion of the PERT/Time technique. PERT/Cost integrates time data with corresponding cost data and permits comparing time-cost alternative courses of action.

There are numerous advantages to a PERT/Cost technique of control. Some of the most obvious are the following:

    1 It greatly facilitates the assessment of project status in relation to financial planning.

    2 It highlights the interrelationships of time and costs and the financial effects on the project of possible changes in resources and/or schedules.

    3 It permits evaluation of progress from multiple sources of information.

    4 It provides a single set of reports for appraising both the financial and the physical status of a project.[25]

On the other hand, there are many practical limitations and disadvantages of PERT/Cost. Although the technique facilitates planning and control, it makes

    [23]Robert W. Fri, "How to Manage the Government for Results," *Organizational Dynamics,* Spring 1974, pp. 20–22.

    [24]Cleland and King, op. cit., p. 114.

    [25]Peter P. Schoderbek, "PERT/COST: Its Values and Limitations," *Management Services,* January–February 1966, p. 29.

some of the other managerial functions, such as coordination, more difficult. Because PERT/Cost is expressed in financial terms, it is often perceived and used as a traditional budget—with all the accompanying problems. These, plus problems associated with cost estimates, uncertainties, and allocations, leave the PERT/Cost technique as something less than a perfect control device. Yet, on balance, PERT/Cost can add a new dimension to organizational control. Its future looks bright in light of the growth of complex, project-oriented organizations.

Real-Time Techniques

With the increasing use of computers, many control systems are beginning to receive *immediate* feedforward or feedback information. This immediacy is labeled "real time." The control systems with such real-time capability are "usually set up in mathematical form on computers, attempt to direct decision making by recording and reporting actual occurrences as they take place. In real-time systems, decisions are programmed into the system (closed-loop controls) or require judgmental action (open-loop controls)."[26] The reservation systems used by the airlines, motels, and hotels and the inventory control systems used in an increasing number of retail stores and supermarkets are closed-loop real-time control systems. In real time, the airlines know almost exactly what the passenger status of each plane is, and the motel and hotel chains know what the occupancy levels of the various facilities are across the country. In the case of the retail outlet, when an item is sold, it is recorded at the cash register, tabulated, and fed back to the central processing unit. Restocking will also be fed into the central unit. In this way, a continuous, "real-time" inventory is maintained.

An example of an open-loop real-time control technique would be the SAGE-BUIC system of the Air Force. The acronyms stand for Semi-Automatic Ground Environment, and Back-Up Intercept Control. This method of air defense uses interconnected computers to set up a technologically sophisticated control system. A SAGE-BUIC system receives real-time inputs from a worldwide network of sensors, and after processing, both attack warning and optimum defensive action are provided to commanders. This gives commanders the option of initiating the defensive action recommended by the computer or directing an alternate course of action.[27] SAGE-BUIC demonstrates how computers can be combined with human judgment when used as an organizational control technique.

Management Audit

A completely different technique from those discussed so far is the management audit. Defined very broadly, *management audit* is "a comprehensive and

---

[26]John G. Hutchinson, *Management Strategy and Tactics,* Holt, Rinehart and Winston, Inc., New York, 1971, p. 284.
[27]Fremont E. Kast and James E. Rosenzweig, *Organization and Management,* 2d ed., McGraw-Hill Book Company, New York, 1974, pp. 489–490.

constructive examination of an organizational structure of a company, institution, or branch of government, or of any component thereof, such as a division or department, and its plans and objectives, its means of operation, and its use of human and physical facilities."[28] This definition indicates the all-encompassing nature of management audits. In simpler terms, this type of audit is concerned with the overall management of an organization.

The management audit begins where traditional accounting audit techniques leave off. The traditional external audit is a check to determine whether the "acceptable principles of accounting" were used in compiling the financial records and reports of an organization. The internal audit goes a step further and makes sure that the presently used accounting practices conform not only to generally accepted principles but also to internal organization policies and procedures. The management audit includes both traditional external and internal audits and more. It critically analyzes every aspect of the organization and its operations.

Because it is so comprehensive, there have been very few specific guidelines that help in conducting a management audit. John Burton suggests the following framework:

First, the criteria for a management audit must be considered.
Second, standards of managerial performance must be developed.
Third, a method of reporting must be established.
Fourth, it is necessary to develop management auditing procedures and standards of documentation to support the report given.[29]

Operating under this type of framework, management may choose to conduct a self-audit or to call in an outside agency or consulting firm. The American Institute of Management (AIM) has been a particularly active outside agency that conducts management audits. Through answers to a 300-item questionnaire and public records, AIM evelutes the management of an organization. Ten categories are given specific attention in the AIM audit. They are: economic function, corporate structure, health of earnings, service to stockholders, research and development, directorate analysis, fiscal policies, production efficiency, sales vigor, and executive evaluation.[30] Points are assigned and results are compared with those of previous years and those of similar organizations.

As with the other control techniques, the management audit does not solve all the control problems facing the modern organization. Nevertheless, with the growing separation between ownership and control in American corporations and the public's demand for increased accountability in all kinds of organizations, private and public, the management audit will undoubtedly assume a

[28]William P. Leonard, *The Management Audit,* Prentice-Hall, Inc., Englewood Cliffs, N. J., 1962, p. 35.
[29]John C. Burton, "Management Auditing," *Journal of Accountancy,* May 1968, p. 41.
[30]Jackson Martindell, "The Management Audit," *The Corporate Director,* December 1962, pp. 1–4.

bigger role in the future. Similar to corporations that meet the present requirements for an external audit of their financial performance, the government may respond to public demands by requiring that an annual management audit of its performance be conducted by an outside agency. Internally, the management audit helps to control the organization by making a very comprehensive, results-oriented evaluation. The valuable information generated by such an audit assists management in making control decisions.

Feedforward Control Techniques

The introductory comments on the meaning of control pointed out that new emphasis is being given to controlling inputs, not just "after the fact" controls. The techniques discussed so far all have feedforward implications but have traditionally been used to provide feedback about performance. However, both PERT and real-time techniques can have direct use for controlling inputs, and the others at least have indirect use for controlling inputs. Koontz and Bradspies suggest the following guidelines to improve feedforward control:[31]

1 Thorough planning and analysis are required. Planning, of course, is vital to all aspects of control but applied to inputs, they must be identified and related to desired end results.

2 Careful discrimination must be applied in selecting input variables. Since it is impossible to identify all input variables, it is essential that the critical ones be identified and monitored.

3 The feedforward system must be kept dynamic. New and/or unanticipated inputs must be controlled on an on-going basis.

4 A model of the control system should be developed. At minimum a simple schematic drawing but more likely a computer programmable mathematical model can be used to account for a larger number of input variables and evaluate their impact.

5 Data on input variables must be regularly collected and assessed. The real-time techniques can greatly aid in data collection and computerized models can aid the assessment.

6 Feedforward control requires action. The system should provide the manager enough lead time to take appropriate action and correct the potential or existing problems.

Figure 10-1 shows a typical inventory control process. The key for feedforward control is to monitor and feedforward information on the critical input variables that lead to the desired inventory level. Potential problems can be identified and the control process can begin to anticipate rather than just react.

BEHAVIORAL IMPLICATIONS OF CONTROL

The behavioral approach to management has probably expressed more concern about control than about any of the other management processes. Much of this

[31]Koontz and Bradspies, op. cit., pp. 35–36.

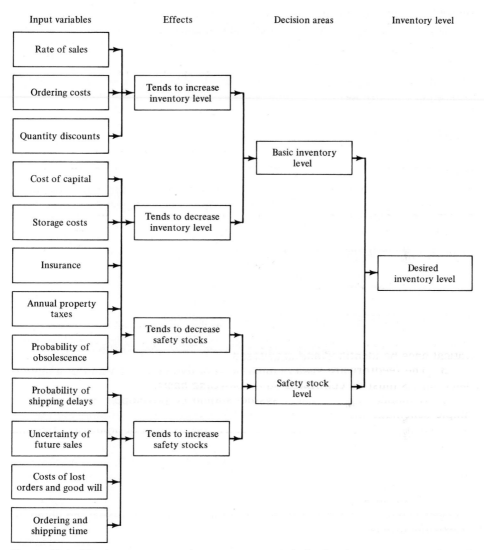

Figure 10-1 The inventory control process: an analysis for feedforward control. (*Source: Harold Koontz and Robert W. Bradspies, "Managing through Feedforward Control,"* Business Horizons, *June 1972, p. 33.*)

concern is a carry-over from the assumption that any form of control restricts individual freedom. The introductory discussion attempted to modify this totally negative attitude toward control. Some forms and degrees of control are essential and are even desired by most people. On the other hand, organizational controls, when put into practice, often create a situation where personnel attempt to work against, rather than with, the control system. In a typical control process, personnel frequently try to reap the rewards of good results for themselves but shift the blame for poor results to someone else. The N. I. H. factor (not invented here) seems to go into effect whenever anything goes wrong. Voich and Wren list some specific behavioral opposition to control as: ". . . disagreement with standards, reporting procedures (including the amount, nature, and frequency of reports), cost allocations pertaining to the control systems, and, in some cases, the need for control itself."[32]

Although there is undoubtedly justifiable criticism of the design, implementation, and use of control, there seems to be no legitimate argument against the need for control itself. As Haimann and Scott point out, "An individual's perception of freedom is not necessarily maximized by an absence of control."[33] They maintain that controls create more predictability in a person's own behavior and in the behavior of other relevant persons in the situation. The individual tends to equate predictability with freedom.

In summary, there is nothing behaviorally wrong with the control process per se. The key to organizational effectiveness is to obtain an optimum mix composed of freedom *and* control. Both are necessary, and too much of either may have a detrimental effect on organizational performance. What the exact mix turns out to be depends upon many variables. Retracing the three elements of the control process in terms of their direct impact on behavior should help clarify this analysis.

The Impact of Standards and Objectives on Behavior

A fundamental assumption in the behavioral approach to management is that humans generally react negatively to standards imposed from above. Beginning with the findings of the bank wiring room phase of the Hawthorne studies, there has been much evidence supporting this assumption. For example, basing his conclusions upon extensive research findings on the effects of incentive systems used in industry, William F. Whyte stated that full effort is received from "probably less than 10 per cent of the work force. In the sorts of situations we have been describing, the other nine-tenths of the force will refuse, more or less, to respond in full measure."[34] While many factors contribute to this situation, part of the problem lies in the negative reaction to imposed standards.

Why do standards bother organizational personnel? The first chapter suggested that the bank wirers at Hawthorne restricted output because of their fear of unemployment, because they believed management would raise the standard, because they felt they were protecting slower coworkers, and because tacit approval was given by management. In most respects, these same reasons still hold true today. Some other possibilities for the negative reaction are the following:

> **1** There may be a lack of understanding of standards because they are imposed without any accompanying explanation of their need and value.

---

[32]Dan Voich, Jr., and Daniel A. Wren, *Principles of Management,* The Ronald Press Company, New York, 1968, p. 263.

[33]Theo Haimann and William G. Scott, *Management in the Modern Organization,* Houghton Mifflin Company, Boston, 1970, p. 445.

[34]William F. Whyte, *Money and Motivation,* Harper & Row, Publishers, Incorporated, New York, 1955, p. 49.

2   Regardless of how carefully standards have been set and flexibility built in, unexpected conditions may make accomplishing the standard difficult or impossible but the person or persons involved get blamed for the poor performance.[35]

Furthermore, often the control standard has become a symbol for all the dysfunctional characteristics of modern bureaucratic organizations. Standards may represent impersonality, abstract rules, and even oppression to organizational personnel.

Nevertheless, standards and objectives are a necessary part of the control process, and in the end, the survival of an organization may depend on how they are set, implemented, and used. Miles and Vergin suggest three ways to make control standards more compatible with human behavior:

1   Standards must be established in such a way that they are recognized as legitimate. This requires that the method of deriving standards must be understood by those affected, and that standards must reflect the actual capabilities of the organizational process for which they are established.

2   The individual organization member should feel that he has some voice or influence in the establishment of his own performance goals. Participation of those affected in the establishment of performance objectives helps establish legitimacy of these standards.

3   Standards must be set in such a way that they convey "freedom to fail." The individual needs assurance that he will not be unfairly censured for an occasional mistake or for variations in performance which are outside his control.[36]

These points indicate that the key to overcoming the difficulties and obtaining a positive response to control standards depends on human inputs. The person or persons who are going to be affected and evaluated by the standard or objective should have an input into how it is formulated, implemented, and utilized. If the people concerned have this opportunity, they will tend to respond more positively; if they do not, there may be a negative reaction.

The Impact of Measurement and Evaluation on Behavior

Organizational personnel may also be dissatisfied with the way they are measured and evaluated under traditional control procedures. The following suggests some reasons for dissatisfaction:

1   Control measures may not be timely enough.

2   Control measures only get at the surface; they don't begin to measure all that is being done.

3   Control measures only concentrate on deviations; they don't account for effort.[37]

Typical of the reactions from personnel which express displeasure with

[35]Sisk, op. cit., pp. 690–691.
[36]Raymond E. Miles and Roger C. Vergin, "Behavioral Properties of Variance Controls," *California Management Review,* Spring 1966, p. 59.
[37]Sisk, op. cit., pp. 691–692.

traditional control measures and evaluation is the manager of a repair-parts department who stated, "We've no kick about the goals you set. The trouble with the controls is, we don't get credit for the work we do." Another example is the member of the maintenance department who commented, "You can't measure the breakdown that didn't happen."[38]

The key to obtaining a positive reaction to measurement and evaluation is closely tied to the way the standards were set in the first phase of the control process. If the affected person has helped set the standards and if performance is accurately measured against those standards, the reaction will tend to be more positive. Obviously, there are a lot of if's in measurement and evaluation, but a positive impact can be, and is being, accomplished in some modern control systems.

The Impact of Corrective Control Decisions on Behavior

Whether a small child in the home or an adult employee in a formal organization, people in general dislike being corrected. When the measurement and evaluation reveal that there is a deviation between standards and performance, the people affected sense a threatening and ego-damaging implication that they personally are at fault, so they often react by blaming the control system. Newman, Summer, and Warren note that some persons "find it difficult to accept the facts of life, and so develop a sense of frustration. Because a frustrated person needs some relief, it is only natural for him to put part of the blame on the mechanism that tells him he is not as good as he thinks he ought to be."[39] In other words, the control mechanism is blamed for any real or imagined personal failures. Besides their threatening nature and the danger of ego deflation, corrective control decisions openly expose an individual's failures to peers, superiors, and subordinates. This exposure may badly undermine the person's need for social support.

Corrective decisions are a necessary part of the control process. The clue to obtaining a positive reaction lies in the sensitivity and empathy that are required when correcting a person. Chapter 12, on learning, emphasizes that if a change in behavior is deemed necessary, reward is more effective than punishment. Positive control of behavior is more effective than negative control. When the control process indicates that inputs or performance is not in accordance with standards, the corrective decision should not only show that something is going wrong; it should also point out why this happened and what is necessary to correct the situation. Furthermore, not all control decisions are corrective in purpose. As noted earlier, decisions may be made to anticipate or to motivate or maintain the status quo.

THE IMPACT OF BUDGETS ON HUMAN BEHAVIOR

Budgets are the target of much criticism from behaviorally oriented management writers. The budget is often pictured as a straitjacket for human behavior

---

[38]Newman et al., op. cit., p. 626.
[39]Ibid., p. 627.

and is said to allow no room for initiative, flexibility, or freedom. Most of the research support for this view comes from a classic study on the effect of budgets on supervisory personnel, conducted by Chris Argyris. The study consisted of field research on three small plants, supplemented by other research findings. Major attention was given to the impact that manufacturing budgets have on first-line supervisors. The exploratory approach led Argyris to conclude that at least four human problems can result from budgets:

>   1   Budget pressure tends to unite the employees against management, and tends to place the factory supervisor under tension. This tension may lead to inefficiency, aggression, and perhaps a complete breakdown on the part of the supervisor.
>   2   The finance staff can obtain feelings of success only by finding fault with factory people. These feelings of failure among factory supervisors lead to many human relations problems.
>   3   The use of budgets as "needlers" by top management tends to make each factory supervisor see only the problems of his own department.
>   4   Supervisors use budgets as a way of expressing their own patterns of leadership. When this results in people getting hurt, the budget, in itself a neutral thing, often gets blamed.[40]

Argyris believes that the reason why budgets have such a negative impact on behavior stems from their pressuring effect on humans. Budgets become devices which pressure individuals into joining groups. A group formed in this way often has objectives which are contrary to the organizational objectives. Argyris described the pattern as follows:

>   1   First, the individuals sense an increase in pressure.
>   2   Then they begin to see definite evidences of the pressure. They not only feel it; they can point to it.
>   3   Since they feel this pressure is on them personally, they begin to experience tension and general uneasiness.
>   4   Next, they usually "feel out" their fellow workers to see if they too sense the pressure.
>   5   Finding out that others have noted the pressure, they begin to feel more at ease. It helps to be able to say, "I'm not the only one."
>   6   Finally, they realize that they can acquire emotional support from each other by becoming a group. Furthermore, they can "blow their top" about this pressure in front of their group.[41]

In summary, individuals being pressured by a budget can join a group and thereby reduce the pressure, relieve the tension, and make themselves more secure.

Standards and objectives, measurement and evaluation, corrective control decisions, and budgets do not have to have a negative effect on behavior. The

[40]Chris Argyris, "Human Problems with Budgets," *Harvard Business Review*, January–February 1953, p. 108.
[41]Ibid., p. 100.

next section explores some approaches that may lead to a positive behavioral impact from the organizational control process.

BEHAVIORAL APPROACHES TO CONTROL

Behavioral approaches are only beginning to have an influence on the organizational control process. Up to the last few years, the approach to controlling the organization seemed to follow what Roethlisberger called "the vicious-cycle syndrome." By this he meant that "the breakdown of rules begot more rules to take care of their breakdown or the breakdown of close supervision encouraged the use of still closer methods of supervision and as a result, the continuous search and invention of new control systems to correct for the limitations of previous ones."[42]

Behaviorally oriented management theorists have urged that controls break out of this vicious cycle. Their appeal has led practitioners to take a hard look at the way they are currently controlling their organizations. Consequently, although little if any change in the *number* of controls has occurred, there has been a general change in attitudes toward control and, in particular, toward the way in which controls are set and used.

Behavioral Trends in Control

Several important behavioral trends in control are emerging. Some of the more important are movements toward:

1 Participative budgeting
2 Diagnostic rather than punitive responses during evaluation
3 Goals set on an individual basis
4 A coaching, rather than a directive, role for superiors
5 Supplying control information to people on the firing line
6 Measurement of employee attitudes[43]

In addition, many articles on control in professional journals are beginning to analyze behavioral implications. For example, one article described a budgeting system as a hierarchical combination of a goal-setting machine and a goal-achieving machine. Basing his findings on behavioral science research, the author cautiously concluded that:

1 Goals significantly affect performance.
2 Participation in goal setting of itself has little discernible direct effect on the goal levels set.
3 Monetary incentives encourage the setting of less-difficult goals when the reward depends strictly on goal achievement.

[42]Fritz J. Roethlisberger, "Contributions of the Behavioral Sciences to a General Theory of Management," in Harold Koontz (ed.), *Toward a Unified Theory of Management,* McGraw-Hill Book Company, New York, 1964, p. 54.

[43]Edmund P. Learned and Audrey T. Sproat, *Organization Theory and Policy,* Richard D. Irwin, Inc., Homewood, Ill., 1966, p. 85.

4 Inadequate extrinsic rewards may result in the setting of difficult goals and higher performances.[44]

These conclusions are contrary to a simplistic "human relations" approach to control. They point out the complexity of the process and the need for further research on the behavioral aspects of control.

Human Resource Accounting

New, specific behavioral approaches, such as human resource or human asset accounting, are slowly beginning to affect organizational control. Human resource accounting formally recognizes the monetary value of human resources in an organization. For example, if a good employee leaves the organization, its assets are reduced by a certain dollar amount. There are also definite replacement costs associated with employee turnover. Although most accounting systems have detailed cost data on the use of paper cups for dispensing drinking water, they generally do not generate or analyze employee replacement costs. Figure 10-2 shows some of the indirect and direct costs that should be recognized in employee replacement analysis and control.

Analogous to replacement, when a good employee joins the organization, the assets will increase by the value of the new employee. Likert suggests that the following types of variables be considered when calculating the value of new or existing human resources: level of intelligence and aptitudes; level of training; quality of leadership; and quality of decision making, communication, and control.[45] Conflict can be of both positive and negative value in calculating the worth of human assets. "If bickering, distrust and irreconcilable conflict become greater, the human enterprise is worth less; if the capacity to use differences constructively and engage in cooperative teamwork improves, the human organization is a more valuable asset."[46]

Human resource accounting gives unprecedented recognition to the value of humans in organizations. Traditionally, this human value has been badly neglected. The new direction of emphasis has led to the entire accounting function's becoming more behaviorally oriented. In the past, accounting controls, in terms of both design and use, were greatly influenced by the public function of the auditor.[47] In other words, balance sheets and operating statements were geared to the stockholders and the government, not to the internal organizational control process. In the last few years, this situation has been changing. As explained in an article in a professional accounting magazine:

A school of behavioral accountants has sprung up in the last decade that believes

[44]Roger L. M. Dunbar, "Budgeting for Control," *Administrative Science Quarterly,* March 1971, p. 94.

[45]Rensis Likert, *The Human Organization,* McGraw-Hill Book Company, New York, 1967, p. 148.

[46]Ibid., p. 149.

[47]Eliot D. Chapple and Leonard R. Sayles, *The Measure of Management,* The Macmillan Company, New York, 1961, p. 70.

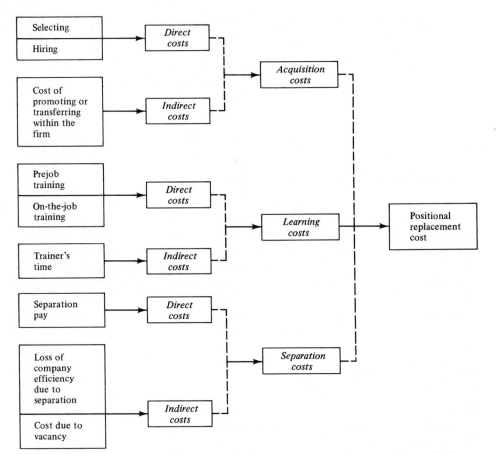

Figure 10-2 Employee replacement costs. (*Source: Eric G. Flamholtz, "Human Resource Accounting: Measuring Positional Replacement Costs,"* Human Resource Management, Spring 1973, p. 11.)

their responsibility extends beyond the classification and transmission of information to include the effect of this information on the users' behavior. These accountants are attempting to improve the effectiveness of accounting reports by applying the findings of behavioral science. They are interested not only in the behavior of report users, but also that of the persons who prepare reports and others who may be directly affected, such as those being reported on.[48]

The Need for Self-Control

Although the techniques of control are becoming more behaviorally oriented and although there is a movement toward techniques such as participative

[48]Robert K. Elliott, "Aspects of Behavioral Accounting," *World*, Fall 1970, p. 17.

budgeting and human resource accounting, if the control process is to be fully compatible with the human being, a sense of self-control must ultimately be developed. This self-control becomes especially relevant to a highly dynamic, complex environment. As David Hawkins notes in an article titled "Behavioral Implications of Generally Accepted Accounting Principles,"

> Until such research is available we will have to rely on the many studies in management control for our direction. One important conclusion of these studies that we could well work with now is that control systems with behavioral attributes which allow and encourage responsible management by self-control, rather than command through inflexible rules, are the most appropriate in times of change within complex business environments.[49]

The creation of self-control in organizational participants goes back to Douglas McGregor's Theory Y assumption that traditional external controls are not the only method of obtaining the effort needed to attain organizational goals. Instead, McGregor thought, and research has tended to verify, that a person will exercise self-direction and self-control toward objectives to which he is committed.[50] Obtaining this commitment for self-control is a major challenge facing modern management.

SUMMARY

There are many misconceptions about control. For example, the layperson usually views it as limiting freedom. Thus, a negative connotation is attached to it. In reality, of course, people need and even desire controls in their daily lives. As a management process, control is necessary to help attain goals, and it ultimately contributes to the survival of the organization.

The management control process consists of three basic elements: (1) standards and objectives, (2) measurement and evaluation, and (3) corrective action. The first phase is closely associated with the planning function. The standards and objectives that are set reflect the performance levels and criteria for management plans. Management can measure and evaluate inputs and performance against standards and objectives in several ways. Measurement largely depends on personal observation and managerial accounting, whereas evaluation can be made on the basis of exceptions or results. In addition, general budgetary techniques are widely used, and newer, more specialized approaches, such as PPBS, PERT/Cost, real-time techniques, management audits, and feedforward techniques are becoming more prevalent. The last phase of the control process occurs when a corrective control decision is made.

[49]David F. Hawkins, "Behavioral Implications of Generally Accepted Accounting Principles," *California Management Review*, Winter 1969, p. 21.

[50]Douglas McGregor, *The Human Side of Enterprise*, McGraw-Hill Book Company, New York, 1960, p. 47.

All three elements of control have a significant impact on human behavior in organizations. The behavioral theorists have aimed a great deal of criticism at the ways in which management has traditionally controlled. The problem is not with control per se but rather with how controls have been set and used in practice. Recently, there has been a definite trend toward making controls more behaviorally compatible through such techniques as participative budgeting and human resource accounting. The ultimate goal is to create self-control among organizational participants.

QUESTIONS FOR DISCUSSION AND REVIEW

1 Explain the statement, "The existence of the control process implies that the decision-making and communication processes are not perfect."
2 What is the difference between feedforward and feedback control? Give an example of feedforward control.
3 What are the three basic elements of the control process? Briefly describe the major facets of each element.
4 How does PPBS differ from traditional budgeting approaches?
5 What are some of the human problems resulting from budgets?
6 Justify human resource accounting.

CASE: LAKE INDUSTRIES

Lake Industries is a small textile mill in northern Wisconsin that manufactures woolen clothing. For many years they have had a reputation for high-quality, long-lasting sportswear. Most of their employees were hired right after World War II. Most had fought in the war, returned home, and gone to work for Lake, the biggest employer in the small town. In recent years, these employees have begun to retire and are being replaced by young men and women from Milwaukee, the largest city in the state, which is 50 miles south. The labor pool in town dried up many years ago and Milwaukee people who cannot find jobs at home migrate north to fill the openings at Lake Industries.

In recent years the quality of the clothing has badly deteriorated. The materials are still the best that money can buy, but the workmanship on the clothes is very sloppy and getting worse. Customers in the immediate region are beginning to cut back on their purchases of Lake Industries apparel, and the hard-earned reputation is beginning to crumble. The chief operating executive has held several meetings with his staff, and the problem seems to be that the production controls are breaking down. The older production supervisors complain that the new, younger workers refuse to be controlled, and spot checks with rank-and-file employees (old and young) indicate that the existing quality control has seemed to become an end in itself. Many of the old-timers mention that self-controls have been replaced by tight, bureaucratic controls in recent years. The chief executive is determined to turn the situation around. He feels that the company will have to start from scratch and reexamine the whole concept of control and institute some new control techniques to improve the quality of their clothes.

    1   What do you think are some of the problems contributing to the quality deterioration of this company's products?

    2   Analyze the finding that the "older production supervisors complain that the new, younger workers refuse to be controlled." What does this have to say about the control process at Lake? What about the statement that "self-controls have been replaced by tight, bureaucratic controls"?

    3   What would be involved in the reexamination of the whole concept of control at Lake? What control techniques studied in this chapter may help this company's control problems?

SELECTED REFERENCES

Benke, Ralph Louis, Jr.: "Human Behavior and Control," *Managerial Planning,* July–August 1975, pp. 18–23.

Bittel, Lester R.: *Management by Exception,* McGraw-Hill Book Company, New York, 1964.

Child, John: "Strategies of Control and Organizational Behavior," *Administrative Science Quarterly,* March 1973, pp. 1–17.

Daugherty, William, and Donald Harvey: "Some Behavioral Implications of Budgeting Systems," *Arizona Business,* April 1973, pp. 3–7.

Emery, James C.: *Organizational Planning and Control Systems,* The Macmillan Company, New York, Macmillan & Co., Ltd., London, 1969.

Flamholtz, Eric G.: "Human Resource Accounting: Measuring Positional Replacement Costs," *Human Resource Management,* Spring 1973, pp. 8–16.

Giglioni, Giovanni B., and Arthur G. Bedeian: "A Conspectus of Management Control Theory: 1900–1972," *Academy of Management Journal,* June 1974, pp. 292–305.

Koontz, Harold, and Robert W. Bradspies: "Managing through Feedforward Control," *Business Horizons,* June 1972, pp. 25–36.

Likert, Rensis: "Human Resource Accounting," *Personnel,* May–June 1973, pp. 3–24.

Lorange, Peter, and Michael S. Scott Morton: "A Framework for Management Control Systems," *Sloan Management Review,* Fall 1974, pp. 41–46.

Lyden, Fremont J.: "Control, Management, and Planning: An Empirical Examination," *Public Administration Review,* November–December 1974, pp. 625–628.

Machin, John: "Measuring the Effectiveness of an Organization's Management Control Systems," *Management Decision,* Winter 1973, pp. 260–279.

McMahon, J. Timothy, and G. W. Perritt: "Toward a Contingency Theory of Organizational Control," *Academy of Management Journal,* December 1973, pp. 624–635.

Moberg, Dennis J., and James L. Koch: "A Critical Appraisal of Integrated Treatments of Contingency Findings," *Academy of Management Journal,* March 1975, pp. 109–123.

Myers, M. Scott, and Vincent S. Flowers: "A Framework for Measuring Human Assets," *California Management Review,* Summer 1974, pp. 5–16.

Reimann, Bernard C., and Anant R. Negandhi: "Strategies of Administrative Control and Organizational Effectiveness," *Human Relations,* July 1975, pp. 475–486.

Sayles, Leonard: "The Many Dimensions of Control," *Organizational Dynamics,* Summer 1972, pp. 21–31.

Stroud, Bill L.: "Common Fallacies in Monitoring and Control," *Managerial Planning,* July–August 1974, pp. 18–21.

Tosi, Henry L., Jr.: "The Human Effects of Budgeting Systems on Management," *MSU Business Topics,* Autumn 1974, pp. 53–63.

Part Three

Understanding Human Behavior

Chapter 11

The Perceptual Process

This chapter gives an overview of the psychological process of perception. As discussed in Chapter 5, perception is a major cognitive input and explanation of behavior. Some management writers, such as Athos and Coffey, give perception a major role in behavior. They feel that behavior is largely a product of the way people perceive themselves and their world around them at any given moment.[1] In this book, perception is but one variable to be considered in understanding organizational behavior. The environment (both situation and consequent) plus the other psychological processes (learning and motivation) and personality are also important to a study of human behavior. However, the fact that perception is only one of several important variables in human behavior should not detract from its importance to the study of organizational behavior. For the most part, although much of the material on perception is basic psychological knowledge, it has largely been overlooked or not translated for use by the management field. All topics covered in the chapter are concerned with understanding organizational behavior and its many direct applications to organization and management practice.

The first major section presents a theoretical discussion of the general nature and significance of the perceptual process. The relationship between

---

[1]Anthony G. Athos and Robert E. Coffey, *Behavior in Organizations*, 2d ed., Prentice-Hall, Inc., Englewood Cliffs, N.J., 1975, p. 149.

sensation and perception is clarified and some of the important perceptual subprocesses are discussed. The second section covers the various aspects of perceptual selectivity. Both external factors (intensity, size, contrast, repetition, motion, novelty, and familiarity) and internal ones (motivation, personality, and learning) are included. The third section takes up the role that perceptual set plays in the workplace and presents the results and analysis of a specific perceptual study in industry. The next section is concerned with perceptual organization. The principles of figure-ground, grouping, constancy, and context are given primary emphasis. The topic of the last section is social perception. Stereotypes and the halo effect are given major attention.

THE NATURE AND IMPORTANCE OF PERCEPTION

Along with learning and motivation, perception is a primary psychological process. In terms of the S⟷O⟶B⟶C model presented in Chapter 5, perception is a cognitive process which involves the O's selecting, organizing, and interpreting the S. The key to understanding perception is to recognize that it is a unique interpretation of the situation, not an exact recording of the situation. Stated more eloquently:

> The cognitive map of the individual is not, then, a photographic representation of the physical world; it is, rather, a partial, personal construction in which certain objects, selected out by the individual for a major role, are perceived in an individual manner. Every perceiver is, as it were, to some degree a nonrepresentational artist, painting a picture of the world that expresses his individual view of reality.[2]

In short, perception is a very complex cognitive process that yields a unique picture of the world that may be quite different from reality.

Recognition of the difference between the perceptual world and the real world is vital to the understanding of organizational behavior. Harold Leavitt notes that "if one's concern as a supervisor or counselor or committee member is to try to effect some change in the behavior of other people, and if in turn people's present behavior is determined largely by their perceptions of their environments, then it is critical that one seek to understand their perceptions if one is to understand the circumstances under which their behavior might change."[3] He cites the example of the universal assumption made by managers that subordinates always want promotions when, in fact, many subordinates really feel psychologically *forced* to accept a promotion. Managers seldom attempt to find out, and sometimes subordinates themselves do not know, whether the promotion should be offered. In other words, the perceptual world of the manager is quite different from the perceptual world of the subordinate,

[2]David Krech, Richard S. Crutchfield, and Egerton L. Ballachey, *Individual in Society,* McGraw-Hill Book Company, New York, 1962, p. 20.

[3]Harold J. Leavitt, *Managerial Psychology,* The University of Chicago Press, Phoenix Books, Chicago, 1958, p. 355.

and both may be very different from reality. If this is the case, what can be done about it from a management standpoint? The best answer seems to be that better understanding of the concepts involved should be developed. Direct applications and techniques should logically follow complete understanding. The rest of the chapter is devoted to providing a better understanding of the psychological process of perception.

SENSATION VERSUS PERCEPTION

There is usually a great deal of misunderstanding about the relationship between sensation and perception. Berelson and Steiner make the following profound statement: "(1) All knowledge of the world depends on the senses and their stimulation, but (2) the facts of raw sensory data are insufficient to produce or to explain the coherent picture of the world as experienced by the normal adult."[4] If this is true, then the study of perception should clarify the relationship between perception and sensation.

The Senses

Psychologists are not in full agreement as to the differences and similarities between sensation and perception. The physical senses are considered to be vision, hearing, touch, smell, and taste. There are many other so-called sixth senses. However, none of these sixth senses is fully accepted. The five senses are constantly bombarded by numerous stimuli that are both outside and inside the human body. Examples of outside stimuli include light waves, sound waves, mechanical energy of pressure, and chemical energy from objects that smell and taste. Inside stimuli include energy generated by muscles, food passing through the digestive system, and glands secreting behavior-influencing hormones. These examples indicate that sensation deals chiefly with very elementary behavior that is largely determined by physiological functioning. In this way, the human being uses the senses to experience color, brightness, shape, loudness, pitch, heat, cold, odor, and taste.

Definition of Perception

Perception is much more complex and much broader than sensation. The perceptual process involves a complicated interaction of selection, organization, and interpretation. Although perception largely depends upon the senses for raw data, the cognitive process may filter, modify, or completely change these data. A simple illustration may be seen by looking at one side of a stationary object, e.g., a statue or a tree. By slowly turning the eyes to the other side of the object, the person probably *senses* that the object is moving. Yet, the person *perceives* the object as stationary. The perceptual process overcomes the sensual process and the person "sees" the object as stationary. In other words, the perceptual process adds to, and subtracts from, the "real"

[4]Bernard Berelson and Gary A. Steiner, *Human Behavior,* Harcourt, Brace & World, Inc., New York, 1964, p. 87.

sensory world. Some organizational examples which point out the difference between sensation and perception are the following:

1   The purchasing agent buys a part that she thinks is best, not the part that the engineer says is the best.
2   A subordinate's answer to a question is based on what he heard the boss say, not on what the boss actually said.
3   The same worker may be viewed by one supervisor as a very good worker and by another supervisor as a very bad worker.
4   The same widget may be viewed by the inspector to be of high quality and by a customer to be of low quality.

These are only representative of the thousands of everyday examples where perception plays a crucial part in organizational life.

Subprocesses in Perception

The existence of several subprocesses gives evidence of the complexity of perception.[5] The first important subprocess is the *stimulus* or *situation* that is present. Perception begins when a person is confronted with a stimulus or a situation. This confrontation may be with the immediate sensual stimulation or with the total physical and sociocultural environment. An example is the employee who is confronted with his supervisor or with the total formal organizational environment. Either one or both may initiate the workings of his perceptual process. In other words, this represents the S$\longleftrightarrow$O in the model of Chapter 5.

In addition to the S$\longleftrightarrow$O interaction are the internal processes of registration, interpretation, and feedback. During the registration phenomenon the physiological (sensory and neural) mechanisms are affected; the physiological ability to hear and see will affect perception. Interpretation is the most significant cognitive aspect of perception. The other psychological processes will affect this interpretation. For example, in an organization, employees' interpretations of a situation are largely dependent upon their learning and motivation and their personality. The fourth subprocess is feedback. Kimble and Garmezy explain that "most perceptual acts produce stimuli that are of value in interpreting the perceptual event."[6] An example would be the kinesthetic feedback (sensory impressions from muscles) that helps assembly-line workers perceive the speed of materials moving by them on the line. An example of psychological feedback that may influence an employee's perception is the supervisor's raised eyebrow or change in voice inflection. The behavioral termination of perception is the reaction or response, either overt or covert, which is necessary if perception is to be considered a behavioral event and thus a psychological process. As a result of perception, an employee may move rapidly or slowly (overt) or develop an attitude (covert).

[5]See Gregory A. Kimble and Norman Garmezy, *Principles of General Psychology*, 2d ed., The Ronald Press Company, New York, 1963, p. 314.
[6]Ibid.

All of these perceptual subprocesses are compatible with the $S \longleftrightarrow O \longrightarrow B \longrightarrow C$ model presented in Chapter 5. The stimulus or environmental situation is part of the S; registration, interpretation, and feedback occur within the complex O; and reaction is the B. The subprocesses of registration, interpretation, and feedback are internal and unobservable, but the situation and reaction recognize that perception is a behavioral process. Perceptual selectivity and organization, which are next discussed, play a key role in the cognitive aspects of perception.

PERCEPTUAL SELECTIVITY

There are numerous stimuli constantly confronting everyone all the time. At this very moment, the noise of the air conditioner or furnace, the sound of other people talking and moving, and outside noises from cars, planes, or street repair persons are a few of the stimuli aimed at the hearing sense alone. There are literally hundreds of other stimuli affecting the other senses, plus the impact of the total environmental situation. With all this stimulation impinging upon people, how and why do they select out only a very few stimuli at a given time? Part of the answer can be found in the principles of perceptual selectivity.

External Attention Factors

Various external and internal attention factors affect perceptual selectivity. The external factors consist of outside environmental influences such as intensity, size, contrast, repetition, motion, and novelty and familiarity.

Intensity   The intensity principle of attention states that the more intense the external stimulus, the more likely it will be perceived. A loud noise, strong odor, or bright light will be noticed more than a soft sound, weak odor, or dim light. Advertisers use intensity to gain the consumer's attention. Examples include bright packaging and TV commercials that are slightly louder than the regular program. Supervisors may yell at their subordinates to gain attention. This last example also shows that other, more complex psychological variables may overcome the simple external variable. By speaking loudly, the supervisor may actually be turning the subordinates off instead of gaining their attention. These types of complications enter into all aspects of the perceptual process. As with the other psychological concepts, a given perceptual principle cannot stand alone in explaining complex human behavior. The intensity principle is only one small factor in the perceptual process, which is only a part of the cognitive processes, which are only a part of what goes into human behavior. Yet, for convenience of presentation and for the development of basic understanding, these small parts can be effectively isolated for study and analysis.

Size   Closely related to intensity is the principle of size. It says that the larger the object, the more likely it will be perceived. The largest machine "sticks out" when personnel view a factory floor. The maintenance engineering staff may pay more attention to a big machine than to a smaller one, even though the smaller one costs as much and is as important to the operation. A 6-foot 4-inch, 250-pound supervisor may receive more attention from his subordinates than a 5-foot 10-inch, 160-pound supervisor. In advertising, a full-page spread is more attention-getting than a few lines in the classified section.

Contrast   The contrast principle states that external stimuli which stand out against the background or which are not what people are expecting will receive their attention. Plant safety signs which have black lettering on a yellow background or white lettering on a red background are attention-getting. In a similar manner, when the 6-foot 4-inch, 250-pound supervisor mentioned above is placed next to a 5-foot 4-inch, 130-pound supervisor, the smaller one will probably receive as much notice as the bigger one. A worker with many years' experience hardly notices the deafening noise on the factory floor of a typical manufacturing operation. However, if one or more of the machines should come suddenly to a halt, the person would immediately notice the silence.

The contrast principle can be demonstrated by the experience of some companies with training hard-core unemployed workers. In designing hard-core training programs, some firms have found that they have more success when they conduct the initial sessions in the unemployable person's own environment. The familiar location relieves some of the tension and creates a more favorable learning atmosphere. However, at some point the unemployable person must make the transition to the organization environment. A regular, quiet classroom in the organization does not seem to be enough. One company learned that when the entire training of the hard-core trainees was conducted in a clean, quiet factory classroom, their subsequent performance was very poor. Fortunately, the company did not jump to the conclusion that the workers were "no good" or untrainable. Instead, through rational behavioral analysis, the company discovered that the poor performance was due to the extremely loud noises that occurred on the assembly line. The workers were not accustomed to the noise because their training had taken place under nice, clean, and quiet conditions. When placed on the noisy factory floor, the contrasting din drew all their attention and adversely affected their performance. To solve this problem, the company conducted the training sessions right next to the noisy factory floor. By the end of the training sessions, the workers were used to the noise and they performed very well when subsequently placed on the job.

Repetition   The repetition principle states that a repeated external stimulus is more attention-getting than a single one. The explanation is, "A stimulus that is repeated has a better chance of catching us during one of the periods when our attention to a task is waning. In addition, repetition increases our sensitivity or alertness to the stimulus."[7] Thus, a worker will generally "hear"

[7] Clifford T. Morgan and Richard A. King, *Introduction to Psychology,* 3d ed., McGraw-Hill Book Company, New York, 1966, p. 343.

better when directions for a dull task are given more than once. This principle partially explains why supervisors have to give directions over and over again for even the simplest of tasks. Workers' attention for a boring task may be waning and the only way they hear directions for the task is when the supervisors repeat themselves several times. Advertisers trying to create a unique image for nondifferentiated products, such as aspirins, soaps, and deodorants, rely heavily on repetitious advertising.

Motion The motion principle says that people will pay more attention to moving objects in their field of vision than they will to stationary objects. Workers will notice materials moving by them on a conveyor belt but they may fail to give proper attention to the maintenance needs of the stationary machine next to them. In addition, the assembly-line workers may devote their entire attention to the line of slowly moving materials they are working on and fail to notice the relatively nice working conditions (pastel-colored walls, music, and air conditioning). Advertisers capitalize on this principle by creating signs which incorporate moving parts. Las Vegas at night is an example of advertisement in motion.

Novelty and Familiarity The novelty and familiarity principle states that either a novel or a familiar external situation can serve as an attention getter. New objects or events in a familiar setting or familiar objects or events in a new setting will draw the attention of the perceiver. Job rotation is an example of this principle. Changing workers' jobs from time to time will tend to increase the attention they give to the task. Being a polisher one week and a painter the next week may not motivate workers, but it will increase their attention until they become accustomed to the new job. The same is true for the newly trained hard-core workers placed on their first job assignments. The work environment is a completely novel experience for them. If supervisors use familiar street jargon in communicating with the employees, they may receive more attention from them. However, once again, this approach could backfire unless properly handled.

Internal Set Factors

The concept of a set is an important cognition in selectivity. It can be thought of as an internal form of attention getting and is largely based on the individual's complex psychological makeup. People will select out stimuli or situations from the environment that appeal to and are compatible with their learning and motivation and with their personality. Although these aspects are given specific attention in the next three chapters, a very brief discussion here will help in the understanding of perception.

Learning and Perception Although interrelated with motivation and personality, learning may play the biggest single role in developing perceptual set. Read the phrase in the triangle below. It may take several seconds to realize

there is something wrong. Because of familiarity with the phrase from prior learning, the person is perceptually set to respond "Turn off the engine." This illustration shows that learning affects set by creating an *expectancy* to perceive in a certain manner. As pointed out in Chapter 5, such expectancies are a vital element in the cognitive explanations of behavior. This view states simply that people see and hear what they expect to see and hear. This can be further demonstrated by pronouncing the following words very slowly:

M-A-C-T-A-V-I-S-H
M-A-C-D-O-N-A-L-D
M-A-C-B-E-T-H
M-A-C-H-I-N-E-R-Y

If the last word was pronounced "Mac-Hinery" instead of the more conventional "machinery," the reader was caught in a verbal response set.

There are many other illustrations that are commonly used to demonstrate the impact of learning on the development of perceptual set. Figure 11-1 is found in many introductory psychology textbooks. What is perceived in this picture? If one sees an attractive, apparently wealthy young woman, the perceiver is in agreement with about 60 percent of the people who see the picture for the first time. On the other hand, if an ugly, poor old woman is seen, the viewer is in agreement with about 40 percent of first viewers. Obviously, two completely distinct women can be perceived in Figure 11-1. Which woman

Figure 11-1 Ambiguous picture of a young woman and an old woman. (*Source: Edwin G. Boring, "A New Ambiguous Figure,"* American Journal of Psychology, *July 1930, p. 444. Also see Robert Leeper, "A Study of a Neglected Portion of the Field of Learning—The Development of Sensory Organization,"* Journal of Genetic Psychology, *March 1935, p. 62. Originally drawn by cartoonist W. E. Hill and published in* Puck, *November 6, 1915.*)

Old woman   Young woman

Figure 11-2 Clear picture of the young and old woman. (*Source: Robert Leeper, "A Study of a Neglected Portion of the Field of Learning—The Development of Sensory Organization,"* Journal of Genetic Psychology, *March 1935, p. 62.*)

is seen supposedly depends on whether the person is set to perceive young, beautiful women or old, ugly women. How did the reader come out?

How Figure 11-1 is perceived can be radically influenced by a simple learned experience. When first shown a clear, unambiguous picture of a beautiful young woman (Figure 11-2) and then shown Figure 11-1, the person will almost always report seeing the young woman in Figure 11-1. If the clear picture of the old woman is seen first (Figure 11-2), the viewer will subsequently report seeing the old woman in Figure 11-1.

In addition to the young woman–old woman example, there is a wide variety of commonly used illusions that effectively demonstrate the impact that learned set has on perception. An illusion may be thought of as a form of perception that badly distorts reality. Figures 11-3 and 11-4 show some of the most frequently used forms of perceptual illusion. The two three-pronged objects in Figure 11-3 are drawn contrary to common perceptions of such

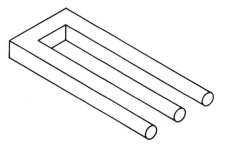
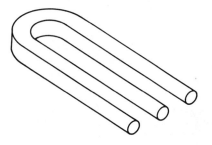

Figure 11-3 Common illusions.

objects. In (*a*) of Figure 11-4, the length of the nose (from the tip to the *X*) is exactly equal to the vertical length of the face. In (*b*), the height of the hat is exactly equal to the width of the brim. Both shapes in (*c*) are exactly the same size, and in (*d*), the lines *AX, CX, CB,* and *XD* are of equal length.

Figure 11-5 brings out the role that learned set plays in perception even more than Figure 11-4 does. The three men in Figure 11-5 are drawn exactly equal in height. Yet, the men are perceived as of different heights because the viewer has learned that the cues found in the picture normally imply depth and distance. A lot of what the human "sees" in the world is a result of past experience and learning. Even though the past experience may not be relevant to the present situation, it is nevertheless used by the perceiver.

Perceptual Set in the Workplace

Perceptual set has many direct implications for organizational behavior. The young woman–old woman illustration demonstrates that the same stimulus may be perceived two completely different ways (young and beautiful or old and

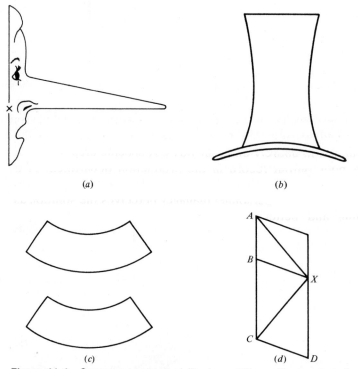

(*a*)   (*b*)

(*c*)   (*d*)

Figure 11-4 Common perceptual illusions. (*These illusions are found in almost all introductory psychology textbooks. For example, see Gregory A. Kimble and Norman Garmezy, General Psychology, 2d ed., The Ronald Press Company, New York, 1963, pp. 324–325. The face is from N. L. Munn and E. P. Johnson,* Student's Manual to Accompany Psychology, *2d ed., Houghton Mifflin Company, Boston, 1951.*)

Figure 11-5 The role that learning plays in perception.

ugly) because of the way the individual is set to perceive. Numerous instances of this situation occur in a modern organization. Participants may perceive the same stimulus or situation in entirely different ways. A specific organizational example might be a poor output record in the production department of a manufacturing plant. The engineer perceives the solution to this problem as one of improved machine design. The personnel manager perceives the solution as one of more training and better wage incentives. The department head perceives the solution to be more effective organizing, planning, and controlling. On the other hand, the workers may perceive the low output with pleasure because it is a way of "getting back" at their supervisor, whom they dislike. For the purpose of this discussion, it is not important who is right or wrong in this example; rather, the point is that all the relevant personnel perceive the *same* situation in completely *different* ways.

Another common example is the differences in perception that occur between the union and management. Stagner and Rosen believe that perceptual differences are a major explanation for industrial disputes. The same "facts" in a dispute are perceived quite differently by union members and by management.

Thus, to a union steward, the "fact" may be that a change in machine layout has created a safety hazard, whereas the foreman may deny that the safety hazard is a fact. Differences in job duties, calling for a pay increase, may seem obvious to workers, but the plant manager may honestly deny that any differences exist; and, for him, they do not exist.[8]

A Perceptual Study in Industry   Among the many instances of differences in perception in organization life, of particular relevance in recent years has been the black worker who comes from a different cultural and often disadvantaged educational background. This person is perceived in many completely different ways. One supervisor or white coworker may perceive a disadvantaged black worker as a no-good, defiant troublemaker who does not deserve a break. At the same time, another supervisor or white coworker may perceive the same black person as a decent human being who has been discriminated against and educationally deprived and is deserving of a break.

Using the facts regarding differing perceptions as a starting point, a survey was conducted to gather information through which to analyze how black workers are perceived by business managers.[9] Practically all the 184 Lincoln and Omaha, Nebraska companies which filled out the confidential questionnaire had black employees. The major finding of the study was that black workers currently on the job were generally perceived by managers to be relatively good workers. This finding has interesting implications. If black workers are perceived as good workers, what is the problem? Why is the unemployment rate so much higher for blacks than for whites? Why are most blacks generally relegated to lower-level jobs? The answers to these complex questions may lie in how the word *qualification* is perceived.

What is the meaning of *qualification*? How is it perceived by white managers? How is it perceived by blacks? Although difficult to define operationally, "qualification" usually means an accepted quality, accomplishment, or level of standard which permits a person to perform acceptably in a job. This elusive concept has been shown to be the single most important concern of the entire business community when analyzing the employment of blacks. For example, in an extensive American Management Association study, it was found that in almost every survey response in which the executive discussed the question of the employment of blacks, the word "qualified" appeared as some part of the statement.[10] If managers perceive the performance of their presently employed black workers favorably, why are they so "hung up" on the black person's qualifications? Has the staffing process found, chosen, and placed all so-called qualified blacks? Or, as many blacks think, has "qualification" taken on the same meaning as "law and order"? Both *qualification* and *law and order* are righteous terms, but as far as many in the black community

[8]Ross Stagner and Hjalmar Rosen, *Psychology of Union Management Relations*, Wadsworth Publishing Company, Inc., Belmont, Calif., 1965, p. 19.

[9]Fred Luthans, "Training for Qualification: The Black Worker's Dilemma," *Training and Development Journal*, October 1968, pp. 3–7.

[10]Jack G. Gourlay, "The Black Salaried Worker," *AMA Research Study 70*, American Management Association, New York, 1965, p. 12.

are concerned, there are negative hidden meanings. Many blacks are convinced that *qualification,* even for low-level jobs, really means "white," "superior skills," or "advanced education."

One purpose of the survey study was to attempt to determine how managers really do perceive employee qualifications. The managers were asked, in an open-ended question, to specify the two major factors holding back the employment of blacks. Thus, the managers could express in their own words what they meant by "qualification." The following shows the three most frequently cited problems and summarizes the typical comments regarding them.

   1 Training (58 responses). "It is much better to hire a skilled or trained person that is qualified for the job rather than to hire a black that is untrained. The biggest problem for blacks is lack of training."
   2 Education (44 responses). "Those employers who try to hire black employees are faced with the very real problem of finding sufficiently qualified candidates. This is a problem of education. School counselors could put a greater effort into helping to keep black students in school at least through high school levels, and possibly help with expenses if the student would want additional education."
   3 Motivation and desire (40 responses). "I have found that most black workers have plenty of ability, but my experience has shown these workers have a decided lack of desire."[11]

Forty-four additional responses indicated that there were too few qualified applicants but failed to give a particular reason for this situation. Lack of dependability was mentioned by seventeen managers, absenteeism and turnover by nine, and transportation difficulties by six.

The conclusion from this study is that respondents seem to perceive qualification to mean appropriate training, education, and motivation. It is interesting to note that no one answered that prejudice or color of skin was holding back the employment opportunities of blacks. The managers did not perceive, or at least were not willing to admit in a confidential questionnaire, that, for many blacks, qualification means being white, well educated, and highly skilled.

There are many obvious limitations to a study of this kind, but one in particular is that it assumes that all black workers are a single entity. In truth, of course, each black employee is just as unique an individual as is each employee of any other color. Yet, in reality this blanket perception does exist. Managers tend to discuss and perceive black workers as a single mass instead of as a group of distinct individuals whose skin happens to be black. This was brought out in the study by the fact that not one respondent objected to treating the black worker as an overall classification. It is hoped that someday this blanket perception will disappear. As the upcoming generations, who will have

[11]Luthans, op. cit., p. 5.

different perceptual sets, replace the older generations, a new "color-blind" perception may become a reality.

Motivation and Perception Besides the learned aspects of perceptual set, motivation also has a vital impact on perceptual selectivity. The primary motives of sex and hunger could be used to demonstrate the role that motivation plays in perception.

In traditional American culture, the sex drive has been largely suppressed, with the result being an unfulfilled need for sex. Accordingly, any mention of sex or a visual stimulus dealing with sex is very attention-getting to the average American. The picture of a scantily clad or naked female is readily perceived by the virile American male. On the other hand, as nudity becomes increasingly commonplace in magazines, motion pictures, live entertainment, and fashions, the female anatomy slowly begins to lose its appeal as an attention getter. In a culture where the female breasts are always exposed, such a sight draws no attention from the males of that culture. Analogously, however, if there is a great need for food in the culture, the mention, sight, or smell of food is given a great deal of attention.

The secondary motives also play an important role in developing perceptual set. A person who has a relatively high need for power, affiliation, or achievement will be more attentive to the relevant situational variables. An example is the worker who has a strong need for affiliation. When such a worker walks into the lunch room, the table where several coworkers are sitting tends to be perceived and the empty table or the one where a single person is sitting tends to get no attention. Although very simple, the lunch room example points out that perception may have an important impact on motivation as well as motivation having an impact on perception.

Another example is the role of motivation in the perception of the members of a top-management committee. One committee member may be self-oriented and perceive the problem being discussed as personally threatening. Another member may be interaction-oriented and perceive the same problem in terms of whether it is discussed in a relaxed, friendly way; the content is not important. A third member of the committee may be task-oriented and solely concerned with the content of the problem and bringing it to an immediate solution.[12] Chapter 13 will give detailed attention to the process of motivation, some of which is directly related to perception.

Personality and Perception Closely related to learning and motivation is the personality of the perceiving person, which affects what is attended to in the confronting situation. Leavitt reported on a senior executive whose biggest problem with young managers was their tendency to avoid making little, unpleasant decisions. The young managers did not pay attention to disciplining

---

[12]Bernard M. Bass and George D. Dunteman, "Behavior in Groups as a Function of Self, Interaction, and Task Orientation," *Journal of Abnormal and Social Psychology*, May 1963, pp. 419–428.

people, to digging through boring and repetitive records, or to writing unpleasant letters.[13] These unpleasant tasks were not compatible with the personalities
of the young managers. The tedious tasks were given attention by the older
executive because his personality makeup had "hardened" over the years.

The growing "value gap" mentioned in Chapter 4 definitely contributes to
differing perceptions. An example can be found in the perceptions of modern
movies. Older people tend to be either disgusted or do not understand some of
the popular movies of the 1970s, such as *Shampoo,* starring Warren Beatty.
The author observed about a dozen couples (all over 35) who walked out after
the first fifteen minutes of this movie. Those in the twenty-five–thirty-five age
group tend to perceive these movies as kind of "naughty but neat." As one
thirty-year-old commented after seeing *Shampoo* "We never saw anything that
good at the fraternity stag parties." The young, college-age people tend to
perceive this type of movie as "where it's at." They tend to get neither
"up-tight" nor titillated over a movie like *Shampoo.* There are, of course,
individual differences in all age categories, and the above example tends to
stereotype (this is discussed later in the chapter) people by age. Yet it does
show how personalities, values, and even age may affect the way people
perceive the world around them.

PERCEPTUAL ORGANIZATION

The discussion of perceptual selectivity was concerned with the external and
internal variables that gain an individual's attention. This section focuses on
what takes place in the perceptual process once the information from the
situation is received. This aspect of perception is commonly referred to as
perceptual organization. An individual seldom perceives patches of color or
light or sound. Instead, the person will perceive organized patterns of stimuli
and identifiable whole objects in the situation. For example, when a male
college student is shown a football, he does not normally perceive it as the
color brown or as grain-leather in texture or as the odor of leather. Rather, he
perceives a football which has, in addition to the characteristics named, a
potential for giving the viewer fun and excitement as either a participant or a
spectator. In other words, the person's perceptual process *organizes* the
incoming information into a meaningful whole, which in this case is a football.

Figure-Ground

Figure-ground is usually considered to be the most basic form of perceptual
organization. The figure-ground principle simply means that perceived objects
stand out as separable from their general background. It can be effectively
demonstrated as one is reading this paragraph. In terms of light-wave stimuli,
the reader is receiving patches of irregularly shaped blacks and whites. Yet the
reader does not perceive it this way. The reader perceives black letters, words,

[13]Leavitt, op. cit., p. 31.

and sentences printed against a white background. To say it another way, the reader perceptually organizes incoming stimuli into recognizable figures (words) that are seen against a ground (white page).

Another interesting figure-ground illustration is shown in Figure 11-6. At first glance, one probably perceives a jumble of black, irregular shapes against a white background. Only when the white letters are perceptually organized against a black background will the words FLY and TIE literally jump out with clarity. This illustration shows that perceptual selectivity will influence perceptual organization. The viewer is set to perceive black on white because of the black words (figures) throughout the book. However, in Figure 11-6 the reverse is true. White is the figure and black is the ground.

Perceptual Grouping

The grouping principle of perceptual organization states that there is a tendency to group several stimuli together into a recognizable pattern. This principle is very basic and seems to be largely inborn. There are certain underlying uniformities in grouping. When simple constellations of stimuli are presented to people, they will tend to group them together by closure, continuity, proximity, or similarity.

Closure   The closure principle of grouping is closely related to the gestalt school of psychology. A basic gestalt principle is that a person will sometimes perceive a whole when one does not actually exist. The person's perceptual process will close the gaps which are unfilled from sensory input. In the formal organization, participants may either see a whole where none exists or not be able to put the pieces together into a whole that does exist. An example of the first case is the department head who perceived complete agreement among the

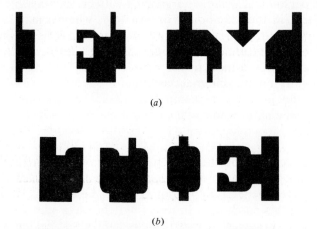

(a)

(b)

Figure 11-6   Illustrations of figure-ground. (*Sources:* (a) *Warner Brown and Howard Gilhousen*, College Psychology, *Prentice-Hall, Inc., Englewood Cliffs, N.J., 1949, p. 330;* (b) *Jerome Kagan and Ernest Havemann*, Psychology: An Introduction, *Harcourt, Brace & World, Inc., New York, 1968, p. 166.*)

members of her department on a given project when, in fact, there was opposition from several members. The department head in this situation closed the existing gaps and perceived complete agreement when, in fact, it did not exist. An example of the other side of the coin is the adage of not being able to see the forest (whole) because of the trees (parts). High degrees of specialization have often resulted in functionally oriented managers losing sight of the whole organization's objectives. Specialists may get so caught up in their own little area of interest and responsibility that they lose sight of the overall goal. They cannot close their part together with the other parts to perceive the whole.

Continuity   Continuity is closely related to closure. Some psychologists do not even bother to make a distinction between the two grouping principles. However, there is a slight difference. Closure supplies *missing* stimuli and the continuity principle says that a person will tend to perceive *continuous* lines or patterns. This type of continuity may lead to inflexible, or noncreative, thinking on the part of organizational participants. Only the obvious, continuous patterns or relationships will be perceived. For example, a new design for some productive process or product may be limited to obvious flows or continuous lines. New, innovative ideas or designs may not be perceived. Continuity can greatly influence the systems design of an organizational structure.

Proximity   The principle of proximity or nearness states that a group of stimuli that are close together will be perceived as a whole pattern of parts belonging together. For example, several employees in an organization may be identified as a single group because of physical proximity. Several workers who work on a particular machine may be perceived as a single whole. If the output is low and the supervisor reports a number of grievances from the group, management may perceive all the workers on the machine as one troublemaking group when, in fact, some of the workers are loyal, dedicated employees. Yet, the fact remains that often departmental or work groups are perceived as a single entity because of physical proximity.

Similarity   The principle of similarity states that the greater the similarity of the stimuli, the greater is the tendency to perceive them as a common group. Similarity is conceptually related to proximity but in most cases predominates over proximity. In an organization, all employees who wear blue (white) collars may be perceived as a common group when, in reality, each blue- (white-) collar worker is a unique individual. Similarity also applies to the black worker study discussed earlier. There is a tendency to perceive all black-skinned employees as a single unit.

Perceptual Constancy

Constancy is one of the more sophisticated forms of perceptual organization. It gives a person a sense of stability in a changing world. Constancy permits the individual "to interpret the kaleidoscopic variability of proximal stimuli in such a manner that these same stimuli more or less accurately reflect the constancies of the real world—the stability and unchangeability of objects and people, the consistency of the three-dimensionality of our everyday world."[14] When compared with figure-ground and grouping, learning plays a much bigger role in the constancy phenomenon.

The size, shape, color, brightness, and location of an object are fairly constant regardless of the information received by the senses. Kendler points out that "perceptual constancy does not result from ignoring any particular cue; it results from responding to *patterns* of cues."[15] These patterns of cues are for the most part learned, but each situation is different and there are interactions between the inborn and learned tendencies within the entire perceptual process.

If constancy were not at work, the world would be very chaotic and disorganized for the individual. An organizational example would be the worker who must select a piece of material or a tool of the correct size from a wide variety of materials and tools at varying distances from his work station. Without perceptual constancy, the sizes, shapes, and colors of objects would change as he moved about and would make his job almost impossible.

Perceptual Context

The highest, most sophisticated form of perceptual organization is context. It gives meaning and value to simple stimuli, objects, events, situations, and other persons in the environment. The principle of context can be simply demonstrated by the well-known doodles shown in Figure 11-7 (answers are found in footnote 16). The visual stimuli by themselves are meaningless. Only when the doodles are placed in a verbal context do they take on meaning and value to the perceiver.

The formal organization environment provides the primary context in which workers and managers do their perceiving. Thus, a verbal order, a suggestion, a raised eyebrow, or a pat on the back takes on unique meaning and value when placed in the context of the formal organization. The discussion of the formal organization structure (Chapters 6 and 7) and processes (Chapters 8, 9, and 10) is the major context in which organizational participants perceive.

Perceptual Defense

Closely related to context is perceptual defense. A person may build a defense against (block or refuse to recognize) stimuli or situational events in the context which are personally or culturally unacceptable or threatening. Accordingly,

---

[14]Merle J. Moskowitz and Arthur R. Orgel, *General Psychology,* Houghton Mifflin Company, Boston, 1969, p. 168.

[15]Howard H. Kendler, *Basic Psychology,* 2d ed., Appleton-Century-Crofts, Inc., New York, 1968, p. 162.

[16]Answers to doodles in Figure 11-7 are (*a*) the start of a "rat race"; (*b*) two mice in a beer can; (*c*) a column of ants marching through spilled whiskey.

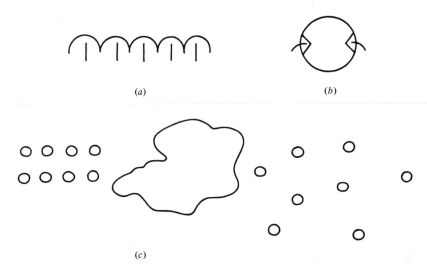

(a)   (b)

(c)

Figure 11-7   Doodles: illustration of the role that context plays in perception.

perceptual defense may play an influential role in understanding union-management or supervisor-subordinate relationships.

Although there is some conflicting evidence, most studies verify the existence of a perceptual defense mechanism. Two examples are the studies by Bruner and Postman,[17] who found barriers to perceiving personally threatening words, and by McGinnies,[18] who raised identification thresholds for critical, emotionally toned words. In a study directly relevant to organizational behavior, Haire and Grunes describe how people may react to a perceptual defense that is activated in them when they are confronted with a fact that is inconsistent with a preconceived notion.[19] In this study, college students were presented with the word *intelligent* as a characteristic of a factory worker. This was counter to their perception of factory workers, and they built defenses in one of the following ways:

    1 *Denial.* A few of the subjects denied the existence of intelligence in factory workers.

    2 *Modification and distortion.* This was one of the most frequent forms of defense. The pattern was to explain away the perceptual conflict by joining intelligence with some other characteristic, e.g., "He is intelligent, but doesn't possess initiative to rise above his group."

    3 *Change in perception.* Many of the students changed their perception of the worker because of the intelligence characteristic. Most of the change, however, was very subtle, e.g., "cracks jokes" became "witty."

    [17]Jerome S. Bruner and Leo Postman, "Emotional Selectivity in Perception and Reaction," *Journal of Personality,* September 1947, pp. 69–77.
    [18]Elliott McGinnies, "Emotionality and Perceptual Defense," *Psychological Review,* September 1949, pp. 244–251.
    [19]Mason Haire and Willa Freeman Grunes, "Perceptual Defenses: Processes Protecting an Organized Perception of Another Personality," *Human Relations,* vol. 3, no. 4, 1950, pp. 403–412.

4 *Recognition, but refusal to change.* A very few subjects explicitly recognized the conflict between their perception of the worker and the characteristic of "intelligent" that was confronting them. For example, one subject stated, "The traits seem to be conflicting . . . most factory workers I have heard about aren't too intelligent."[20]

From this study, the general conclusion is that people may learn to avoid perceiving certain conflicting, threatening, or unacceptable aspects of the context.

David Lawless has summarized the above and other relevant experiments into three explanations of perceptual defense:

1 Emotionally disturbing information has a higher threshold for recognition (i.e., we do not perceive it readily) than neutral or nondisturbing information. This is why a chain of events may be seen differently by those who are not personally involved than by those who are involved, so that warning signs of trouble are often not seen by those who will be most affected by the trouble.

2 Disturbing information and stimuli are likely to bring about substitute perceptions which are distorted to prevent recognition of the disturbing elements. In this way the manager can perceive that his workers are happy when actually they are disgruntled. Then when a grievance committee is formed or a strike takes place, he cannot perceive his "happy" workers participating willingly and concludes that it is because they have fallen victim to some agitator and that things in the shop are still basically fine.

3 Emotionally arousing information actually does arouse emotion even though the emotion is distorted and directed elsewhere. Kicking the cat, snarling at the wife and kids, cutting someone off for trying to pass you on the right while driving home, or browbeating an underling all offer a sense of relief and a good substitute for perceiving that the people "upstairs" think you are an idiot.[21]

Such findings as the above help explain why some people, especially supervisors and subordinates in an organization, have a "blind spot." (They do not "see" or they consistently misinterpret certain events or certain situations.)

SOCIAL PERCEPTION

Although context and perceptual defense are closely related to social perception, this section gives recognition to social perception per se. The social aspects of perception are given detailed coverage because they play such an important role in organizational behavior. Social perception is directly concerned with how one individual perceives other individuals. Formal organization participants are constantly perceiving one another. Managers are perceiv-

[20]Ibid., pp. 407–411.
[21]David J. Lawless, *Effective Management*, Prentice-Hall, Inc., Englewood Cliffs, N.J., 1972, pp. 36–37.

ing workers, workers are perceiving managers, line personnel are perceiving staff personnel, staff personnel are perceiving line personnel, superiors are perceiving subordinates, subordinates are perceiving superiors, and on and on. There are numerous complex factors which enter into such social perception, but the primary factors are found in the psychological processes and personality.

Characteristics of Perceiver and Perceived

Zalkind and Costello provide a better understanding of social perception by summarizing research findings on some specific characteristics of the perceiver and the perceived. A profile of the perceiver is as follows:

1 Knowing oneself makes it easier to see others accurately.
2 One's own characteristics affect the characteristics he is likely to see in others.
3 The person who accepts himself is more likely to be able to see favorable aspects of other people.
4 Accuracy in perceiving others is not a single skill.[22]

These four characteristics greatly influence how a person perceives others in the environmental situation.

There are also certain characteristics of the person being perceived which influence social perception. Research has shown that:

1 The status of the person perceived will greatly influence others' perception of him.
2 The person being perceived is usually placed into categories to simplify the viewer's perceptual activities. Two common categories are status and role.
3 The visible traits of the person perceived will greatly influence the perception of him.[23]

These characteristics of the perceiver and the perceived suggest the extreme complexity found in social perception. Learning, motivation, and personality all enter into social perception. Besides these psychological factors, sociological concepts such as status and role further complicate the situation. In addition, there are two general categories of problems or errors that creep into social perception: stereotyping and halo effect.

Stereotyping

A common error which results in many perceptual problems is the tendency to stereotype. This means that the perceiver sees the person perceived as belonging to a *single* class or category. Besides this categorization, a stereotype

---

[22]Sheldon S. Zalkind and Timothy W. Costello, "Perception: Some Recent Research and Implications for Administration," *Administrative Science Quarterly*, September 1962, pp. 227–229.
[23]Ibid., p. 230.

also implies general agreement on the attributed traits and the existence of a discrepancy between attributed traits and actual traits.[24]

The term *stereotype* is derived from the typographer's word for a printing plate made from previously composed type. In 1922, Walter Lippmann applied the word to perception. Since then, stereotyping has become a frequently used term to describe perceptual errors. In particular, it is employed in analyzing ethnic prejudice. Not commonly acknowledged is the fact that stereotyping may attribute favorable *or* unfavorable traits to the person being perceived. Secord and Backman explain that

> Stereotyping is not simply the assignment of favorable or unfavorable traits to a class of persons as a function of whether the observer has a positive or negative attitude toward the person category. Most stereotypes have both favorable and unfavorable traits, and more prejudiced individuals assign both in greater degree.[25]

Most often a person is put into a stereotype because the perceiver knows only the overall category to which the person belongs. However, because each individual is unique, the real traits of the person will generally be quite different from those the stereotype would suggest.

Stereotyping greatly influences social perception in a formal organization. Common stereotyped groups include managers, supervisors, union members, workers, and all the various functional and staff specialists, e.g., accountants and engineers. There is a consensus about the traits possessed by the members of these categories. Yet, in reality, there is often a discrepancy between the agreed-upon traits of each category and the actual traits of the members. In other words, not all engineers carry slide rules and are cold and calculating, nor are all personnel managers do-gooders who are trying to keep workers happy.

In a research study, Haire found that individuals will both perceive and be perceived according to whether they are identified with a union or a management group. "Thus, 74 percent of the subjects in the managerial group chose the word 'honest' as description of Mr. A, *when he was identified as a manager.* The same managerial subjects, however, chose the word 'honest' to describe Mr. A only 50 percent of the time when he was identified as a representative of the union."[26] There are numerous other research studies and common, everyday examples which point out the stereotyping that occurs in formal organizations.

Halo Effect

The halo error in social perception is very similar to stereotyping. Whereas in stereotyping the person is perceived according to a single category, under the

---

[24]Paul F. Secord and Carl W. Backman, *Social Psychology,* 2d ed., McGraw-Hill Book Company, New York, 1974, pp. 20–30.

[25]Ibid., p. 30.

[26]Mason Haire, "Role-Perception in Labor-Management Relations: An Experimental Approach," *Industrial and Labor Relations Review,* January 1955, p. 208.

halo effect the person is perceived on the basis of one trait. Halo is often discussed in personnel management when a rater makes an error in appraising a person's total personality and/or performance on the basis of a single trait such as intelligence, appearance, dependability, or cooperativeness. Whatever the single trait is, it may override all other traits in forming the perception of the person. Examples of halo effect are the extremely attractive woman secretary who is perceived by her male boss as being an intelligent, good performer, when, in fact, she is a poor typist and quite dense, and the good typist who is also very bright but is perceived by her male boss as a "secretary" but not a potential manager with the ability to cope with important responsibilities. Bruner and Tagiuri note three conditions where the halo effect is most marked: (1) when the traits to be perceived are unclear in behavioral expressions; (2) when the traits are not frequently used by the perceiver; and (3) when the traits have moral implications.[27]

Many research studies have pointed out how halo effect can influence perception. For example, a study by Asch found that when two persons were described as having identical personalities except for one trait, the character qualities in one list included the trait "warm" and in the other list, the trait "cold"—two completely different perceptions resulted.[28] In other words, one trait blinded the perceiver to all other traits in the perceptual process. Grove and Kerr also documented the impact of halo effect when they studied employee perceptions in a company that was in receivership. Although the company paid relatively high wages and provided excellent working conditions and at least average supervision, the employees did not perceive these favorable factors. The insecurity produced an inverse halo effect so that insecurity dominated over the pay and conditions of the job.[29] The results of this study make the point that "when there's one important 'rotten' attitude, it can spoil the 'barrel' of attitudes."[30] As with all the other aspects of the psychological process of perception discussed here, the halo effect has important implications for the study and eventual understanding of organizational behavior.

SUMMARY

Perception is one of the major psychological processes. Through complex cognitive subprocesses, the human makes an interpretation of stimulus situations. Both selectivity and organization go into perceptual interpretations. Externally, selectivity is affected by intensity, size, contrast, repetition,

[27]Jerome S. Bruner and Renato Tagiuri, "The Perception of People," in Gardner Lindzey (ed.), *Handbook of Social Psychology*, Addison-Wesley Publishing Company, Inc., Cambridge, Mass., 1954, p. 641.

[28]S. E. Asch, "Forming Impressions of Personalities," *Journal of Abnormal and Social Psychology*, July 1946, pp. 258–290.

[29]Byron A. Grove and Willard A. Kerr, "Specific Evidence on Origin of Halo Effect in Measurement of Employee Morale," *Journal of Social Psychology*, August 1951, pp. 165–170.

[30]Timothy W. Costello and Sheldon S. Zalkind, *Psychology in Administration,* Prentice-Hall, Inc., Englewood Cliffs, N.J., 1963, p. 35.

motion, novelty, and familiarity. Internally, it is influenced by the individual's motivation, learning, and personality. After the stimulus situation is filtered by the selective process, the incoming information is organized into a meaningful whole. Figure-ground is the most basic form of perceptual organization. Another basic form is the grouping of constellations of incoming stimuli by closure, continuity, proximity, and similarity. The constancy, context, and defensive aspects of perceptual organization are more complex. The social context in particular plays an important role in understanding human behavior in organizations.

QUESTIONS FOR DISCUSSION AND REVIEW

1   How does sensation differ from perception?
2   Give some examples of the external factors that affect perceptual selectivity.
3   Explain how perceptual constancy works.
4   What does stereotyping mean? Why is it considered to be a perceptual problem?
5   What effect can the perceptual process have on organizational behavior?

CASE: SPACE UTILIZATION

Sherman Adder, assistant plant manager for Frame Manufacturing Company, was chairman of the ad hoc committee for space utilization. The committee was made up of the various department heads in the company. The plant manager of Frame had given Sherman the charge to see if the various office, operations, and warehouse facilities of the company were being optimally utilized. The company was beset by rising costs and the need for more space. However, before okaying an expensive addition to the plant, the plant manager wanted to be sure that the currently available space was being utilized properly.

Sherman opened up the first committee meeting by reiterating the charge of the committee. Then Sherman asked the members if they had any initial observations to make. The first to speak was the office manager. He stated, "Well, I know we are using every possible inch of room that we have available to us. But when I walk out into the plant I see a lot of open spaces. We have people piled on top of one another, but out in the plant there seems to be plenty of room." The production manager quickly replied, "We do not have a lot of space. You office people have the luxury facilities. My supervisors don't even have room for a desk and a file cabinet. I have repeatedly told the plant manager we need more space. After all, our operation determines whether this plant suceeds or fails, not you people in the front office pushing paper around." Sherman interrupted at this point and said, "Obviously we have different interpretations of the space utilization around here. Before further discussion I think it would be best if we have some objective facts to work with. I am going to ask the industrial engineer to provide us with some statistics on plant and office layout before our next meeting. Today's meeting is adjourned."

1 What perceptual principles are evident in this case?

2 What concept was brought out when the production manager labeled the office personnel a bunch of "paper pushers"? Can you give other organiztional examples of this concept?

3 Do you think that Sherman's approach to getting "objective facts" from statistics on plant and office layout will affect the perceptions of the office and production managers? How does such information affect perception in general?

SELECTED REFERENCES

Anderson, Carl R., and Frank T. Paine: "Managerial Perceptions and Strategic Behavior," *Academy of Management Journal,* December 1975, pp. 811–823.

Costello, Timothy W., and Sheldon S. Zalkind: *Psychology in Administration,* Prentice-Hall, Inc., Englewood Cliffs, N.J., 1963, part I.

Dubin, Robert, Lyman W. Porter, Eugene F. Stone, and Joseph E. Champoux: "Implications of Differential Job Perceptions," *Industrial Relations,* October 1974, pp. 265–273.

Kimble, Gregory A., and Norman Garmezy: *Principles of General Psychology,* 2d ed., The Ronald Press Company, New York, 1963, chaps. 11–13.

Leavitt, Harold J.: *Managerial Psychology,* The University of Chicago Press, Phoenix Books, Chicago, 1958, chap. 3.

Renwick, Patricia A.: "Perception and Management of Superior-Subordinate Conflict," *Organizational Behavior and Human Performance,* June 1975, pp. 444–456.

Stagner, Ross, and Hjalmar Rosen: *Psychology of Union-Management Relations,* Wadsworth Publishing Company, Belmont, Calif., 1970, chap. 10.

Taylor, Ronald N.: "Perception of Problem Constraints," *Management Science,* September 1975, pp. 22–29.

Zalkind, Sheldon S., and Timothy W. Costello: "Perception: Some Recent Research and Implications for Administration," *Administrative Science Quarterly,* September 1962, pp. 218–235.

Chapter 12

The Learning Process

Learning is an extremely important psychological process. It was presented in Chapter 5 as being a vital element in understanding, prediction, and control of organizational behavior. Many behavioral scientists believe that learning is the single most important concept in the study of human behavior, and few would challenge the statement that learning is involved in almost everything that everyone does. Learning definitely affects human behavior in organizations. There is little organizational behavior that is not either directly or indirectly affected by learning. For example, a worker's skill, a manager's attitude, a supervisor's motivation, and a secretary's mode of dress are all learned. Costello and Zalkind conclude:

> Every aspect of human behavior is responsive to learning experiences. Knowledge, language, and skills, of course; but also attitudes, value systems, and personality characteristics. All the individual's activities in the organization—his loyalties, awareness of organizational goals, job performance, even his safety record—have been learned, in the largest sense of that term.[1]

Learning, of course, is also involved in the consequences of organizational

[1]Timothy W. Costello and Sheldon S. Zalkind, *Psychology in Administration*, Prentice-Hall, Inc., Englewood Cliffs, N.J., 1963, p. 205.

behavior. The $S \longleftrightarrow O \longrightarrow B \longrightarrow C$ model of Chapter 5 had feedback loops from the C to both the O and the S. These feedback loops represent learning. The purpose of this chapter is to present an overview of the learning process which will contribute to the better understanding, prediction, and control of organizational behavior.

The first section defines learning and the second summarizes the major theoretical approaches. The third section briefly covers the important learning concepts of classical and operant conditioning. The fourth section presents the learning principles of acquisition-learning curves, extinction, spontaneous recovery, generalization, and discrimination. The reinforcement principle is given major attention in the fifth section. Included is a discussion of the law of effect, types of reinforcement, and schedules of reinforcement. The next-to-last section is devoted to the effect of punishment on learning, and the last section deals with other less understood learning phenomena such as higher-order conditioning, escape-avoidance learning, and selective learning.

DEFINITION OF LEARNING

Learning is a term frequently used by a great number of people in a wide variety of contexts. Yet, despite its diverse use, there is, surprisingly, general agreement on a formal definition. Although there may be slight variations, practically all behavioral scientists would agree on the following definition: *Learning is a relatively permanent change in behavior that results from reinforced practice or experience.* There are four points in this definition that need emphasis:[2]

1 Learning involves a change, though not necessarily an improvement, in behavior. Learning generally has the connotation of improved performance, but under this definition bad habits, prejudice, stereotypes, and work restriction are also learned.

2 The change in behavior must be relatively permanent in order to be considered learning. This qualification rules out behavioral changes resulting from fatigue or temporary adaptations as being learning.

3 Some form of practice or experience is necessary for learning to occur. This qualification rules out behavioral change that is the result of physical maturation. For example, the ability to walk is largely based on physical maturation and would not be considered learning.

4 Finally, it should be stressed that the practice or experience must be reinforced in some way in order for learning to occur. If reinforcement does not accompany the practice or experience, the behavior will eventually disappear.

It should also be remembered that learning is only a concept, a psychological process. As McGehee has pointed out,

[2]See Gregory A. Kimble and Norman Garmezy, *Principles of General Psychology,* 2d ed., The Ronald Press Company, New York, 1963, pp. 133–134.

No one of you has ever seen "learning." You have seen people in the process of learning, you have seen people who behave in a particular way as a result of learning, and some of you (in fact, I guess the majority of you) have "learned" at some time in your life. In other words we infer that learning has taken place if an individual behaves, reacts, responds as a result of experience in a manner different from the way he formerly behaved.[3]

Applying the conceptual definition of learning to the study of organizational behavior would have direct implications in the following areas:

1   Knowing something intellectually or conceptually one never new before.
2   Being able to do something one couldn't do before—behavior or skill.
3   Combining two knowns into a new understanding of a skill, piece of knowledge, concept, or behavior.
4   Being able to use or apply a new combination of skills, knowledge, concept, or behavior.
5   Being able to understand and/or apply that which one knows—either skill, knowledge, or behavior.[4]

The above discussion of the definition of learning serves only as a starting point for the theory and concepts of learning covered in the rest of the chapter.

LEARNING THEORY

The most basic purpose of any theory is to fully explain the phenomena in question. When theories become perfected, they have universal application and should be able to predict and control. Thus, a perfected theory of learning would have to be able to explain all aspects of learning (how, when, and why), have universal application (for example, to children, college students, managers, and workers), and predict and control learning situations. To date, no such theory of learning exists. Although there is general agreement on the definition of learning, there is much disagreement on the theory behind it. This does not mean that no attempts have been made to develop a theory of learning. In fact, the opposite is true. The two most widely recognized theoretical approaches follow the cognitive and behavioristic models discussed in Chapter 5.

Tolman felt that learning consisted of a *relationship between cognitive environmental cues and expectation.* He developed and tested this theory through highly controlled experimentation. He was one of the first to use the now famous white rat in psychological experiments. He found that a rat could learn to run through an intricate maze with purpose and direction toward a goal (food). Tolman observed that at each choice point in the maze, expectations were established. In other words, the rat learned to *expect* that certain cognitive

---

[3]William McGehee, "Are We Using What We Know about Training?—Learning Theory and Training," *Personnel Psychology,* Spring 1958, p. 2.
[4]Leslie E. This and Gordon L. Lippitt, "Learning Theories and Training," *Training and Development Journal,* April 1966, p. 3.

cues associated with the choice point might eventually lead to food. If the rat actually received the food, the association between the cue and the expectancy was strengthened and learning occurred.

Tolman's theory is sometimes criticized as being too narrow. Yet, it had a great impact on the early human relations movement. Industrial training programs in the 1940s and 1950s drew heavily on Tolman's ideas.[5] Programs were designed to strengthen the relationship between cognitive cues (supervision, organizational and job procedures) and worker expectations (incentive payments for good performance). The theory was that the worker would learn to be more productive by building an association between taking orders or following directions and expectancies of monetary reward for this effort. Today, many of Tolman's ideas have been extended in the expectancy theories of motivation which are having a tremendous impact on the study and application areas of organizational behavior. Chapter 17 gives specific attention to these expectancy theories and their applications to managing people.

Although Tolman's work has had a tremendous influence on motivation, except for a few instances such as Osgood's demonstration of how expectancy theory can be applied to the difficult problem of avoidance learning[6] and Rotter's development of a social-learning theory,[7] his major contribution has been to serve as a prod and devil's advocate for the more popular behavioristic learning theorists.[8]

The classical behaviorists such as Pavlov and Watson attributed learning to the association or connection between stimulus and response. The more modern behaviorists, such as Skinner, give more attention to the role that consequences play in learning or the R-S connection. The emphasis on the connection (S-R or R-S) has led some to label these the "connectionist" theories of learning. The S-R deals with classical or respondent conditioning and the R-S with instrumental or operant conditioning. An understanding of these two conditioning processes is vital to the study of learning.

Classical Conditioning

Pavlov's classical conditioning experiment with dogs as subjects is undoubtedly the single most famous study ever conducted in the behavioral sciences. A simple surgical procedure permitted Pavlov to measure accurately the amount of saliva secreted by a dog. When he presented a piece of meat (unconditioned stimulus) to the dog in the experiment, Pavlov noticed a great deal of salivation (unconditioned response). On the other hand, when he merely rang a bell (neutral stimulus), the dog had no salivation. The next step taken by Pavlov was to accompany the meat with the ringing of the bell. After doing this several

[5]George S. Odiorne, *Training by Objectives,* The Macmillan Company, New York, 1970, p. 243.

[6]Charles E. Osgood, "Can Tolman's Theory of Learning Handle Avoidance Training," *Psychological Review,* May 1950, pp. 133–137.

[7]Julian B. Rotter, *Social Learning and Clinical Psychology,* Prentice-Hall, Inc., Englewood Cliffs, N.J., 1954.

[8]Robert C. Bolles, *Learning Theory,* Holt, Rinehart and Winston, Inc., New York, 1975, p. 90.

times, Pavlov rang the bell without the meat. This time, the dog salivated to the bell alone. The dog had become classically conditioned to salivate (conditioned response) to the sound of the bell (conditioned stimulus). This classical experiment was a major breakthrough and has had a lasting impact on the understanding of learning.

Classical conditioning experimentation has been a major source of support for the S-R theories of learning. Since Pavlov's original experiments in the late 1800s, psychologists have classically conditioned everything from the flatworm to the human being. The overall conclusion from this vast amount of research is stated by Bass and Vaughan as follows:

> In all probability, any response in an organism's behavioral repertoire can be conditioned if an unconditioned stimulus can be found that regularly produces the response and if this unconditioned stimulus can be paired in training with a conditioned stimulus.[9]

Despite the theoretical possibility of the widespread applicability of classical conditioning, most psychologists agree that it represents only a very small part of total human learning. Skinner in particular felt that classical conditioning explained only respondent (reflexive) behaviors. These are the involuntary responses that are elicited by a stimulus. Skinner felt that the more complex, but common, human behaviors could not be explained by classical conditioning alone. He felt that most human behavior affects, or operates on, the environment. The latter type of behavior is learned through operant conditioning.

Operant Conditioning

Operant conditioning is primarily concerned with learning that occurs as a *consequence* of behavior. It is not concerned with the eliciting causes of behavior as is classical or respondent conditioning. The specific differences between classical and operant conditioning may be summarized as follows:

1   In classical conditioning a change in the stimulus (unconditioned stimulus to conditioned stimulus) will elicit a particular response. In operant conditioning one particular response out of many possible ones occurs in a given stimulus situation. The stimulus situation serves as a cue in operant conditioning. It does not elicit the response but serves as a cue to emit the response. The critical aspect of operant conditioning is what happens as a consequence of the response. The strength and frequency of classically conditioned behaviors are mainly determined by the frequency of the eliciting stimulus (the environmental event that precedes the behavior). The strength and frequency of operantly conditioned behaviors are mainly determined by the consequences (the environmental event that follows the behavior).

2   During the classical conditioning process, the unconditioned stimulus,

[9]Bernard M. Bass and James A. Vaughan, *Training in Industry: The Management of Learning,* Wadsworth Publishing Company, Inc., Belmont, Calif., 1966, p. 15.

serving as a reward, is presented every time. In operant conditiong the reward will occur only if the organism performs the correct response. The organism must operate on the environment in order to receive a reward. The response is instrumental in obtaining the reward.

Operant conditioning has a much greater impact on human learning than does classical conditioning. Operant conditioning also explains, at least in very general terms, much of organizational behavior. For example, it might be said that employees work eight hours a day, five days a week, in order to feed, clothe, and shelter themselves and their families. Working (conditioned response) is only instrumental in obtaining the food, clothing, and shelter. Some significant insights can be directly gained from this kind of analysis. The consequences of organizational behavior can change the environmental situation and largely affect subsequent employee behaviors. In other words, the analysis of the consequences of organizational behavior can help accomplish the goals of prediction and control.

In summary, it can be said that operant conditioning is the basis for modern behaviorism and consists of the following:

    1 a series of assumptions about behavior and its environment;
    2 a set of definitions which can be used in objective, scientific description of behavior and its environment;
    3 a group of techniques and procedures for the experimental study of behavior in the laboratory; and
    4 a large body of facts and principles which have been demonstrated by experiment.[10]

These four points show that operant conditioning leads to a very comprehensive approach to the study of behavior. Chapter 20 will discuss in detail and apply to organizational behavior most of these aspects of operant conditioning.

PRINCIPLES OF LEARNING

There are many widely recognized principles of learning. Reinforcement is probably the single most important one for explaining, predicting, and controlling human behavior in organizations. However, before reinforcement is examined in detail, the less-known principles of acquisition-learning curves, extinction, spontaneous recovery, generalization, and discrimination are briefly explored. Figure 12-1 summarizes in graphic form some of these principles.

Acquisition-Learning Curves

Figure 12-1 clearly shows the principle of acquisition. There is a gradually increasing strength of response for each repeated trial. As represented, this

[10]G. S. Reynolds, *A Primer of Operant Conditioning*, Scott, Foresman and Company, Glenview, Ill., 1975, p. 1.

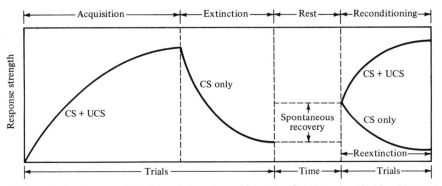

Figure 12-1 Some principles of learning. (*Source: Gregory A. Kimble, Norman Garmezy, and Edward Ziegler*, General Psychology, *4th ed., copyright © 1974, The Ronald Press, New York, p. 228. Used with permission.*)

mainly applies to classical conditioning, but operant conditioning also follows an acquisition curve. The acquisition curve can be thought of as a learning curve where the vertical axis represents measured performance and the horizontal axis represents the amount of practice or experience, which is usually expressed in time or number of trials. Figure 12-2 summarizes the four general types of learning curves.

Decreasing Returns Curve The curve in (*a*) of Figure 12-2 is negatively accelerating and is commonly referred to as the *curve of decreasing returns.* The acquisition curve in Figure 12-1 is of this type. This curve shows the most common way in which acquisition takes place. The learning of most mental and motor tasks exhibits a decreasing returns pattern. There is an initial spurt of learning, which then begins to slow down and finally reaches a point where there is practically no learning progress. Learning to perform most of the specialized, routine-type jobs found in modern organizations would tend to follow the decreasing returns learning curve.

Increasing Returns Curve The curve in Figure 12-2 (*b*) is essentially the opposite of (*a*). It shows a positively accelerating curve that produces increasing returns. The (*b*) is a rarer learning curve than (*a*) and will usually occur only when a person is learning a completely unfamiliar mental or motor task. Many of the staff positions in an organization, e.g., engineers and marketing researchers, may experience an increasing return on certain tasks. The same holds true of workers learning very highly skilled lower-level jobs. In both cases, it has been found that initial learning may progress very slowly, but after a time, the learning will take giant strides.

S Learning Curve The learning curve in Figure 12-2 (*c*) is commonly referred to as the *S curve.* This curve is really a combination of the decreasing and increasing returns curves. Theoretically, all learning would probably follow

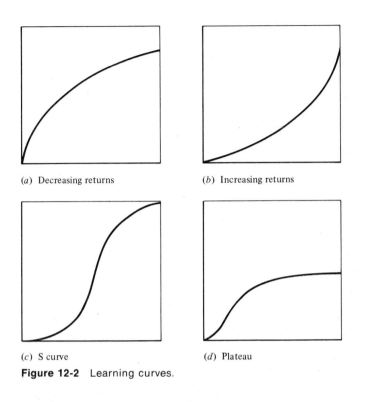

(*a*) Decreasing returns   (*b*) Increasing returns

(*c*) S curve   (*d*) Plateau

Figure 12-2   Learning curves.

an S curve if the person brings absolutely no relevant experience to the learning situation. In reality, of course, this is not the case. An S curve would most likely result when a person attempts to learn a relatively difficult, unfamiliar task that requires insight. For example, learning, when applied to many of the highly skilled jobs in a technical industry, might follow the S pattern.

Learning Plateau   The curve in Figure 12-2 (*d*) shows the plateau principle of acquisition. Many learning situations seem to progress satisfactorily but then reach a point where nothing new is learned. This leveling off in learning is called a *plateau*. The learning of many relatively simple tasks follows this pattern. Most lower-level and "dead end" jobs in modern organizations have personnel who are in a learning plateau. Something must spur people on in order to get them on an accelerated path again. Behavioral techniques are needed to break organizational personnel out of plateau learning situations. Some of the newer techniques that may help are given attention in the last part of the book.

Value of Learning Curves   Not all human learning can be neatly fitted into one of the learning curves discussed here. On the other hand, the curves do represent in a general way the major patterns of acquisition, with the learning of certain types of tasks following certain types of curves. Kagan and

Havemann summarize the applicability of the curves to the learning of specific types of tasks as follows:

> **1** The more unfamiliar the task to be learned, the more likely it is that progress will be slow at the start and will then increase.
> **2** In most learning of complicated skills, there is at least one period, short or long, in which each new trial produces an improvement of equal size.
> **3** As we approach the ultimate limit of learning, progress slows down, and it takes many trials to produce even a small amount of improvement.[11]

Extinction

The principle of extinction is closely related to reinforcement. In classical conditioning, if the conditioned stimulus is not reinforced by the unconditioned stimulus, the conditioned response will weaken and eventually disappear or become extinct. For example, in the Pavlov experiment, if the meat is withheld when the bell is rung, the drops of saliva will slowly decrease and will eventually become extinct with just the sound of the bell. In operant conditioning, if the response is not reinforced by the consequence, the response will become extinct. Thus, the extinction principle simply means that if a response is not reinforced, it will eventually disappear.

The principle of extinction has important implications for understanding and controlling human behavior. More detailed attention will be given to it in the discussion of reinforcement, but an example can demonstrate its impact. Workers may be continually rewarded, by bonus and praise, for learning a new skill in a training program. However, when the newly trained workers are placed on the job, they may never be rewarded for performing the skill. Their work record may slowly decline, and their newly acquired skill may even become extinct.

Besides the inadvertent use of extinction, it can be deliberately used as an effective strategy for decreasing undesirable behaviors as well. When a behavior is not reinforced (this does *not* mean punishing but instead just ignoring the behavior), it will weaken and decrease in subsequent frequency. Such an extinction strategy does not have the side-effect problems associated with punishment (these are discussed later in the chapter). In other words, extinction has the same effect on behavior as does punishment but without the problems of punishment. For example, suppose a supervisor wants to decrease the complaints from a subordinate. When the subordinate comes to the supervisor with a complaint, the supervisor could do one of three things: (1) give attention and listen carefully to the complaint, (2) give the subordinate "heck" for always complaining, or (3) ignore the person and not listen to the complaint. The most likely extinction strategy would be the last one. The first is probably reinforcing and the second is probably punishing. If the third approach is used and the complaining behavior does decrease in subsequent frequency, the extinction strategy has worked.

---

[11]Jerome Kagan and Ernest Havemann, *Psychology,* Harcourt, Brace & World, Inc., New York, 1968, p. 90.

Spontaneous Recovery

Figure 12-1 shows another interesting learning principle, called *spontaneous recovery.* The graph in the figure indicates that if people experience a sequence of nonreinforced conditioned responses and then take a rest, immediately thereafter they will return to a more intense level of conditioned response even though no reinforcement has taken place. This jump in response strength following rest is called *the principle of spontaneous recovery.* This principle suggests that the conditioned response does not totally disappear during extinction, but instead is suppressed or becomes inhibited.

Figure 12-1 shows that, following spontaneous recovery, the slope of the relearning curve accelerates if the conditioned stimulus in classical, or the response in operant, conditioning is reinforced. In a parallel manner, the slope of the extinction curve also accelerates downward if there is no reinforcement. An example of spontaneous recovery occurring in an organizational situation would be the spurt in an employee's job performance immediately following his vacation or layoff. Management could take advantage of spontaneous recovery by consciously attempting to reinforce positive responses and nonreinforce undesirable responses immediately following the spurt in performance occurring after a rest. By doing this, management would be taking advantage of the steep relearning and extinction curves which follow spontaneous recovery.

Generalization

The common meaning of generalization is applicable to the learning principle of the same name. Simply, the generalization principle states that a new, but similar, stimulus or stimulus situation will produce a response that is the same as that produced by the original stimulus. In classical conditioning, generalization occurs when a conditioned response that has been elicited by a conditioned stimulus is given a new but similar stimulus which produces the same conditioned response. The more the new stimulus is like the conditioned stimulus, the more probable it is that the new stimulus will produce the same conditioned response. This latter relationship is commonly called the *generalization gradient,* which is hypothetically depicted in Figure 12-3. Stimulus generalization can also occur in operant conditioning. A response that is reinforced in the presence of a certain cue may generalize. Similar cues may emit the behavior. In addition, response generalization may occur. For example, in a common Skinner box,[12] if an animal's conditioned response of pressing the bar with its paw is prevented, a similar response, such as pushing the bar with its nose or tail, may take place. The latter response is an example of response generalization which is instrumental in obtaining the desired consequence.

The principle of generalization has important implications for human learning. Without generalization, the person would find it extremely difficult to adapt to any new situation. However, because of generalization, people do not have to completely relearn each of the new tasks or situations which constantly

[12]This is a box containing a lever that dispenses food that is widely used in learning experiments with animals.

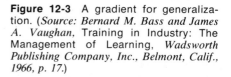

Figure 12-3 A gradient for generaliza-
tion. (*Source: Bernard M. Bass and James
A. Vaughan*, Training in Industry: The
Management of Learning, *Wadsworth
Publishing Company, Inc., Belmont, Calif.,
1966, p. 17.*)

confront them. It allows the organizational participant to adapt to overall
changing conditions and specific new or modified job assignments. The
individual, no matter at what level in the organization, can borrow from past
learning experiences to adjust more smoothly to new learning situations.

Besides the positive contributions that result from generalization, there are
also certain negative implications for learning. Generalization may lead a
person to counterproductive behaviors. For example, an accountant may make
an entry in a similar, but incorrect, account in a management information
report. This one error may lead the report reader to generalize to all accounting
data and take erroneous actions. Another example of the possible negative
impact of generalization is the case of hiring and training the hard-core
unemployed. One or a few bad experiences with hard-core workers may lead
management to generalize that "they" are untrainable and poor risks. The one
bad apple generalizes to the whole barrel. The implications of the word *they*
point out the potentially harmful behavioral consequences that may result from
stimulus generalization. The latter example also emphasizes the close relationship between the learning principle of generalization and the perceptual
principles presented in the last chapter. Once again, the difficulty is illustrated
in isolating one psychological process for study without recognizing that it
affects, and is affected by, the other psychological processes.

Discrimination

In recent times, the word *discrimination* has taken on the connotation of race
prejudice. Technically, of course, the word has a much broader meaning.
Applied to learning, discrimination is essentially opposite to generalization.
Whereas generalization is a reaction to *similar* stimuli or responses, discrimination is a reaction to *differences,* as can be simply demonstrated by a Pavlovian
type of experiment. A light can be added to the experiment of the dog being
classically conditioned to the sound of a bell. If the experiment is set up so that
the dog gets food only when the bell rings and the light is on and gets no food

when the bell rings and the light is off, the dog will soon learn to discriminate between the two stimuli. The dog will respond only to the bell–light-on stimulus and not to the bell–light-off stimulus.

An example of the principle of discrimination operating in an organizational situation is the supervisor who distinguishes between two equally productive workers. The supervisor responds positively to only one of the high producers, having learned to discriminate between them. One of the workers produces a great quantity of items but pays no attention to quality and has a lot of rejects. The other worker also produces a great quantity but has virtually no rejects as the result of being quality-conscious. At first the supervisor may respond positively to both workers; but when the presence of the sloppy worker does not lead to desirable consequences for the supervisor's responses, the supervisor learns to discriminate between the two workers. Positive response is given only to the quality-conscious high producer. It is interesting to note that this discrimination may also modify the sloppy worker's behavior. If the worker is not reinforced by the supervisor for high-quantity–low-quality performance, it will eventually become extinct. On the other hand, if no discrimination is made and the supervisor reinforces the high-quantity–low-quality performance, it will continue unabated.

In an analogous manner, discrimination also occurs in operant conditioning. A response that is reinforced in the presence of one stimulus situation but not in the presence of another will lead to stimulus discrimination. The behavior will be emitted only in the presence of the stimulus that led to a desirable consequence and will not be emitted when this stimulus is changed or absent. This leads to what is called *stimulus control.* Even though behavior is a function of its consequences in operant conditioning, the discriminative stimulus cue can control the behavior. The behavior will be emitted only in the presence of the stimulus situation that in the past has led to a desirable consequence. Once again, this does *not* mean that this discriminative stimulus causes the behavior. Instead, it controls the behavior by serving as a cue to either emit or not emit the behavior.

Stimulus control also has many implications for organizational development. If environmental cues can be so arranged as to emit more productive behaviors in an organization, many of the goals of organizational development can be accomplished. Chapter 21 is specifically devoted to organization development.

THE REINFORCEMENT PRINCIPLE

Reinforcement has played a central role in the learning theories, concepts, and principles discussed thus far in the chapter. Most learning experts agree that reinforcement is the single most important principle of learning. Yet, there is much controversy over its theoretical explanation. The first major theoretical treatment given to reinforcement in learning and the theory that still dominates today is Thorndike's classic law of effect.

The Law of Effect

In Thorndike's own words, the law of effect is simply stated thus:

> Of several responses made to the same situation, those which are accompanied or closely followed by satisfaction [reinforcement] . . . will be more likely to recur; those which are accompanied or closely followed by discomfort [punishment] . . . will be less likely to occur.[13]

From a strictly empirical standpoint, most behavioral scientists, even those of a cognitive orientation, generally accept the validity of this law. It has been demonstrated time after time in highly controlled learning experiments and is directly observable in everyday learning experiences. Desirable or reinforcing consequences will increase the strength of a response and increase its probability of being repeated in the future. However, there is disagreement when Thorndike's law is carried a step further and used as an overall theory of learning.

As a theory of learning, the law of effect would say that reinforcement is *always* necessary in order for learning to occur. The critics of this theory point out the existence of latent learning (no outward expression of performance), which is not accounted for by the law of effect. Latent learning situations seem *not* to require reinforcement. Thus, the law of effect is controversial as a theoretical explanation of learning. Despite the theoretical controversy, however, the law does effectively show the importance of reinforcement to the learning process.

Theoretical attempts besides the law of effect have failed to fully explain reinforcement. However, as with the failure to develop a generally accepted theory of learning, the lack of a meaningful theory of reinforcement does not detract from recognizing its extreme importance. As Kendler notes, "Controversies about theoretical issues are common in all sciences. The important point to understand is that, in spite of the fact that the nature of reinforcement is not fully comprehended, behavior nevertheless can be modified by controlling reinforcement."[14]

Definition of Reinforcement

The term *reinforcement* is conceptually related to the psychological process of motivation, which is covered in the next chapter. There is a temptation to equate reinforcement with motivation. Although this is sometimes deliberately or nondeliberately done, this book treats them separately. Motivation is a basic psychological process and is broader and more complex than is implied by the learning principle of reinforcement as used here. In addition, the need states that are so central to motivation are cognitive in nature; they are unobservable

---

[13]Edward L. Thorndike, *Animal Intelligence,* The Macmillan Company, New York, 1911, p. 244.
[14]Howard H. Kendler, *Basic Psychology,* 3d ed., W. A. Benjamin, Inc., Menlo Park, Calif., 1974, p. 179.

inner states. Reinforcement, on the other hand, is environmentally based. Reinforcers are external, environmental events that follow a response. In general terms, motivation is an internal explanation of behavior and reinforcement is an external explanation of behavior. Thus, the perspectives and explanations of behavior from motivation and reinforcement are different.

An often-cited circular definition of reinforcement says that it is anything the person finds rewarding. This definition is of little value because the words *reinforcing* and *rewarding* are used interchangeably but neither one is operationally defined. A more operational definition can be found by reverting back to the law of effect. With this law, reinforcement can be defined as anything that both increases the strength of response and tends to induce repetitions of the behavior that preceded the reinforcement.

Rewards, on the other hand, are simply the presentation of something that is subjectively deemed to be desirable. A reward is given by a person who thinks it is desirable. Reinforcement is functionally defined. Something is reinforcing only if it strengthens the response preceding it and induces repetitions of the response. For example, a manager may ostensibly reward an employee who found an error in a report by publicly praising the employee. Yet, upon examination it is found that the employee is embarrassed and harassed by coworkers and decreases error-finding behavior in the future. In this example, the "reward" is *not* reinforcing. Even though there is this technical difference between a reward and a reinforcer, the terms are often used interchangeably and will be in this book.

Besides clearing up the differences between reinforcers and rewards, to better understand reinforcement it is necessary to make the distinctions between positive and negative, extrinsic and intrinsic, and primary and secondary reinforcers.

Positive and Negative Reinforcers

There is much confusion surrounding the terms *positive* and *negative reinforcement* and between *negative reinforcement* and *punishment.* First of all, it must be understood that reinforcement, positive or negative, strengthens the response and increases the probability of repetition. But the positive and negative reinforcers accomplish this impact on behavior in completely different ways. Positive reinforcement strengthens and increases behavior by the *presentation* of a desirable consequence. Negative reinforcement strengthens and increases behavior by the *termination* or *withdrawal* of an undesirable consequence. Giving praise to an employee for the successful completion of a task could be an example of a *positive* reinforcer (if this does in fact strengthen and subsequently increase this task behavior). On the other hand, a worker is *negatively* reinforced for getting busy when the supervisor walks through the area. Getting busy terminates being "chewed-out" by the supervisor.

Negative reinforcement is more complex than positive reinforcement but should not be equated with punishment. In fact, they have an opposite effect on behavior. Negative reinforcement strengthens and increases behavior while punishment weakens and decreases behavior. However, both are considered to be forms of negative control of behavior.[15] Negative reinforcement is really a form of social blackmail, because the person will behave a certain way or be punished. The discussion of escape and avoidance learning at the end of the chapter will help clarify this aspect of negative reinforcement. In addition, the specifics of punishment are also given detailed attention later in the chapter.

Extrinsic and Intrinsic Reinforcers

The distinction between extrinsic and intrinsic reinforcers is not as clear as the difference between positive and negative reinforcers. One recent study concluded that "among industrial and organizational psychologists in general, as well as those most likely to be reporting and reading motivational research, the concept intrinsic and extrinsic convey a variety of divergent connotations. In no instance did a majority of the respondents agree on any particular definition of either of these terms."[16] Some of the representative definitions include the following:

> Intrinsic rewards are those "mediated by the person himself" while extrinsic rewards are "externally mediated . . . ; i.e., . . . mediated by someone other than the employee himself."[17]

> Intrinsic factors are "those directly related to the actual performance of the job" and extrinsic factors are "those related to the environment in which the job is being performed."[18]

> "All the intrinsic factors are internal *feelings,* while extrinsic factors are external situations."[19]

Obviously, there is a need for operational definitions of these terms. In general, however, it can be said that an extrinsic reinforcer has no direct relationship to the behavior itself. It is external and often artificial. An example of how extrinsic reward works would be the money given for a good idea in a suggestion plan. The money may reinforce a worker's putting suggestions into a box, but the money is not a natural outgrowth of this behavior. Intrinsic rewards, on the other hand, are a more natural consequence of a behavior. They create a cognitive expected relationship to the behavior itself. Organizational examples of intrinsic rewards include craftsmanship, successful comple-

---

[15]Fred Luthans and Robert Kreitner, *Organizational Behavior Modification,* Scott, Foresman and Company, Glenview, Ill., 1975, p. 112.

[16]Lee Dyer and Donald F. Parker, "Classifying Outcomes in Work Motivation Research: An Examination of the Intrinsic-Extrinsic Dichotomy," *Journal of Applied Psychology,* August 1975, p. 457.

[17]E. L. Deci, "The Effects of Contingent and Non-Contingent Rewards and Controls on Intrinsic Motivation," *Organizational Behavior and Human Performance,* vol. 8, 1971, pp. 218–219.

[18]S. D. Saleh and T. G. Grygier, "Psychodynamics of Intrinsic and Extrinsic Job Orientation," *Journal of Applied Psychology,* vol. 53, 1969, p. 446.

[19]P. F. Wernimong, "A Systems View of Job Satisfaction," *Journal of Applied Psychology,* vol. 56, 1972, p. 173.

tion of a difficult project, acquisition of a new skill, and performance up to capacity.[20]

The extrinsic and intrinsic concepts of reinforcement are closely related to the motivation process. For example, in an organization, money may be considered as a type of incentive in the motivation process or as an extrinsic reinforcer in the learning process. By the same token, giving a job challenge, growth, recognition, and responsibility may be considered types of motivators or intrinsic reinforcers. In general, the extrinsic reinforcers are more closely associated with the behavioristic approach and the intrinsic reinforcers are more associated with the cognitive approach. The humanistic and cognitive approaches stress the importance of the intrinsic over the extrinsic reinforcers. For example, Bass and Vaughan suggest four specific ways to make training more intrinsically rewarding to employees:

1   Stress the future utility or value of the activity or material to be learned.
2   Provide feedback during the learning experience, showing the extent to which the trainees are progressing toward the final training objectives.
3   Relate the learning activity to interesting, meaningful materials already studied outside the training program.
4   Maintain suspense as to the conclusion of a particular line of thought until all the relevant facts have been considered.[21]

The implication is that the intrinsic reinforcers are more effective than the extrinsic. For example, Mitchell and Nebeker state that "a number of authors have presented data indicating that intrinsic factors are better motivators than extrinsic ones."[22] One highly publicized laboratory study conducted by Edward L. Deci concluded that the use of extrinsic reinforcers would actually decrease intrinsic motivation of subjects working on tasks.[23] This finding gives support to the cognitive position, but Deci's findings are the subject of much recent criticism.[24] At present, the definitional problem needs to be cleared up and more research is needed before any sound conclusions can be drawn concerning the application of extrinsic and intrinsic rewards to organizational behavior.

Primary and Secondary Reinforcers

Besides making a distinction between extrinsic and intrinsic rewards, many discussions of learning divide reinforcement into primary and secondary

[20]Costello and Zalkind, op. cit., p. 214.
[21]Bass and Vaughan, op. cit., p. 58.
[22]T. R. Mitchell and D. M. Nebeker, "Expectancy Theory Predictions of Academic Effort and Performance," *Journal of Applied Psychology*, vol. 57, 1973, p. 62.
[23]Deci, op. cit., and E. L. Deci, "Effects of Externally Mediated Rewards on Intrinsic Motivation," *Journal of Personality and Social Psychology*, vol. 18, 1971, pp. 105–115.
[24]Barnet D. Feingold and Michael Mahoney, "Reinforcement Effects on Intrinsic Interest: Undermining the Overjustification Hypothesis," *Behavior Therapy*, vol. 6, 1975, 367–377. Also see: Fred Luthans, Mark Martinko, and Tom Kess, "An Analysis of the Impact of Contingent Monetary Rewards on Intrinsic Motivation," *Proceedings of the Midwest Division, Academy of Management*, 1976, pp. 209–221.

categories. A primary reinforcer is innately satisfying to people and directly reduces their primary motivational drives. An example is the unconditioned stimulus of food in classical conditioning. The unconditioned stimulus is an unlearned reward for the organism. Primary rewards are largely used in simple learning situations. Food and candy are effective reinforcers in basic conditioning, such as in teaching children to do simple tasks or in behavior therapy for mental patients. In more complex human learning situations like those in modern organizations, secondary rewards are much more frequently used and are more effective than the primary rewards.

A secondary reinforcer results from previous association with a primary reinforcer. Whereas the primary reward is innately satisfying, the secondary reward must be learned. Starting in infancy, many neutral stimuli acquire reinforcing properties. A mother who feeds her infant milk (primary reward) soon becomes a secondary reinforcer herself. These learned secondary rewards play a vital role in understanding the more complex aspects of human behavior.

Numerous social stimuli serve as secondary reinforcers for human behavior.[25] Four of the more common forms relevant to organizational behavior are the following:

1 *Attention.* The mere visual stimulus of paying attention by looking at or responding to another human being is reinforcing. Managers giving their full attention to subordinates' ideas will reinforce participative behavior on the part of subordinates.

2 *Approval.* A visual stimulus of one person's affirmative nod or smile is reinforcing to another person. The same is true of a verbal stimulus indicating approval. A manager nodding his or her head or voicing approval of a suggestion from a subordinate would reinforce the subordinate's behavior.

3 *Affection.* Visual, verbal, and physical expressions of affections are an important form of reinforcement for human beings. A manager who expresses genuine affection for a subordinate will reinforce the subordinate's efforts to please the boss.

4 *Tokens.* Various types of tokens are probably the most consciously used type of secondary reinforcement for human behavior. Money is the best example. The adage that a person cannot eat money interestingly points out that money is not a primary reinforcer. Yet, money remains an extremely important reinforcer because many people believe that another adage, "Money will buy everything except possibly happiness," is true. Outstanding performance is reinforced by raises and bonuses in an organization.

When each of these four secondary reinforcers is applied as a consequence and the behavior strengthens and increases, they are positive reinforcers. By the same token, their counterparts of lack of attention, disapproval, dislike, and docking of pay may act as negative reinforcers by strengthening and increasing

[25]See Arthur W. Staats and Carolyn K. Staats, *Complex Human Behavior,* Holt, Rinehart and Winston, Inc., New York, 1963, p. 54.

behavior by their termination, or these can be punishing by their presentation. In the punishing case, presenting these as a consequence would weaken the behavior and decrease its subsequent frequency.

TECHNIQUES OF ADMINISTERING REINFORCEMENT

The preceding discussion was primarily concerned with the theoretical basis and categories of reinforcement. The role of reinforcement in the study of organizational behavior cannot be overemphasized. It plays a central role in general organization areas such as training, adaptation to change, and operational performance. Modification of certain specific aspects of organizational behavior, such as tardiness or participation, also depends upon reinforcement. Reinforcement will increase the strength of desired organizational behavior and the probability of its being repeated. Costello and Zalkind summarize the research findings on the impact of reinforcement on organizational behavior as follows:

> **1** Some type of reinforcement (reward or knowledge of successful performance) is necessary to produce change.
> **2** Some types of rewards are more effective for use in the organization than are others.
> **3** The speed with which learning takes place and also how lasting its effects will be is determined by the timing of reinforcement.[26]

The last point brings out the importance of administering reinforcement.

During the acquisition phase of classical conditioning experiments, every conditioned response is reinforced. This seldom occurs in reality. Human behavior in organizations or everyday life is generally reinforced on an intermittent or random basis. The exact pattern and timing of the reinforcement have a tremendous impact on the resulting behavior. In other words, how the reward is administered can greatly influence the specific organizational behavior that takes place. The four major techniques of administering rewards are fixed ratio, fixed interval, variable ratio, and variable interval.

Fixed Ratio Schedule

If a schedule is administered on a ratio basis, reinforcement is given after a certain *number* of responses. If the schedule is a fixed ratio, the exact number of responses is specified. A fixed ratio that reinforces after every response is designated as 1:1. The 1:1 fixed ratio is generally used in basic conditioning experiments, and almost every type of learning situation must begin with this schedule. However, as learning progresses, it is more effective to shift to a fixed ratio of 2:1, 4:1, 8:1, and even up to 20:1. To illustrate the extreme, Skinner was able to obtain responses from rats at a fixed ratio of 192:1.

[26]Costello and Zalkind, op. cit., p. 193.

Administering reward under a fixed ratio schedule tends to produce a high rate of response which is characterized as vigorous and steady. The person soon determines that reinforcement is based on the number of responses and performs the responses as quickly as possible in order to receive the reward. A common example of how the fixed ratio schedule is applied to industrial organizations is the piece-rate incentive system. Production workers are paid on the basis of how many pieces they produce (number of responses). Other things being equal, the worker's performance responses should be energetic and steady. In reality, of course, other things are not always equal and a piece-rate incentive system may not lead to this type of behavior. Nevertheless, knowledge of the effects of the various methods of administering reward would be extremely valuable in analyzing employee-incentive systems.

Fixed Interval Schedule

The other most common way to administer reward is on a fixed interval basis. Under this schedule, reinforcement is given after a specified period of *time,* which is measured from the last reinforced response. The length of time that can be used by this schedule varies a great deal. In the beginning of practically any learning situation, a very short interval is required. However, as learning progresses, the interval can be stretched out. Skinner was able to make pigeons respond when rewards were as much as 45 minutes apart, and more recently, experiments have successfully expanded the interval to several hours.

Behavior resulting from a fixed interval method of reinforcing is quite different from that exhibited by a fixed ratio. Whereas under fixed ratio there is a steady, vigorous response pattern, under fixed interval there is an uneven pattern that varies from a very slow, unenergetic response immediately following reinforcement to a very fast, vigorous response immediately preceding reinforcement. This type of behavior pattern can be explained by the fact that the person figures out that another reward will not immediately follow the last one. Therefore, the person may as well relax a little until it is time to be rewarded again. A common example of administering reward on a fixed interval schedule is the payment of employees by the hour, week, or month. Monetary reinforcement comes at the end of a period of time. In practice, however, even though people are paid by the hour, they receive their reward only weekly, biweekly, or monthly. Whether for pigeons or humans, this time interval is generally too long to be an effective form of reinforcement for the work-related behavior.

Variable or Intermittent Schedules

Both ratio and interval schedules can be administered on a variable or intermittent basis. This means that the reinforcement is given in an irregular or unsystematic manner. In variable ratio, the reward is given after a number of responses, but the exact number is randomly varied. When the variable ratio is expressed as some number, say 50, this means that on the *average* the organism is reinforced after 50 responses. However, in reality the ratio may randomly vary between 1:1 to 1:100. In other words, each response has a chance of being reinforced regardless of the number of reinforced or nonreinforced responses that have preceded it.

The variable interval schedule works basically the same as the variable ratio except that reward is given after a randomly distributed length of time rather than after a number of responses. A 50-minute variable interval schedule means that on the *average*, the individual is reinforced after 50 minutes, but the actual reinforcement may be given anywhere from a few seconds to several hours.

Behavior under Variable Schedules   Both variable ratio and variable interval schedules tend to produce stable, vigorous behavior. The behavior under variable schedules is similar to that produced by a fixed ratio schedule. Under the variable schedules, the person has no idea when reward is coming, so the behavior tends to be steady and strong. It logically follows that the variable schedules are very resistant to extinction.

Variable schedules are not very effective in highly controlled learning experiments and are seldom used. On the other hand, they are the way in which many real-life, everyday learning situations are reinforced. Although primary reinforcers for humans are administered on a relatively fixed basis, e.g., food is given three times a day at mealtimes and organization compensation plans are on either a fixed ratio or an interval basis, most of the other human behavior that takes place is reinforced in a highly variable manner. For example, practically all the social rewards are administered on a variable basis. Attention, approval, and affection are generally given as rewards in a very random fashion.

Examples of Variable Schedules   Variable reinforcement schedules play the most important role in most organizational behavior situations. Although piece-rate or day-rate payments for job performance appear on the surface to be fixed schedules, by paying on a biweekly or monthly basis, the supposedly fixed schedule becomes in reality no reinforcement for day-to-day job behaviors at all. Unfortunately, in most cases, all the weekly or monthly paycheck does is reinforce walking up to the pay window or opening the pay envelope. Consequently, organizational participants' job behaviors largely depend upon variably administered social rewards from supervisors and coworkers.

The variable schedule can be administered on a formal basis by an organization. The most common example is its application to the sales people who work on a commission. The salesperson's reinforcement (commission for a sale) is highly variable on either a ratio or an interval basis. The salesperson experiences a variable ratio when the commission depends upon the number of customers contacted, but a variable interval when it depends upon when the salesperson last called on the customer.

Administration of Reinforcement in Perspective

The fixed ratio and interval and the variable ratio and interval are not the only methods of administering reward. Many other possible combinations exist.

However, these four schedules are the way most learning situations are reinforced, and they greatly affect both the modification and extinction of organizational behavior. Staats and Staats note, "Not only do these intermittent schedules produce characteristically different rates of maintenance of the response, but, in addition, once reinforcement has been discontinued, different extinction rates are also produced."[27] Much of the learning and resulting behavior of every worker, supervisor, salesperson, engineer, and executive is determined by when and how they are reinforced.

In general, the timing of the reward should be kept as close to the desired response as possible, not two weeks or a month away, as in the case of the paycheck. In addition, ratio schedules are generally more desirable than interval schedules because they tend to produce steady, strong responses, and variable schedules are generally preferable to fixed schedules because they are more resistant to extinction. Understanding and then applying what is known about the administration of reinforcement can be of great assistance to modern human resource managers. In fact, one of the most important functions of all managers may well be the way they administer reinforcement to their people. Chapter 20 carries this discussion further by giving specific attention to behavioral-change strategies for modern human resource management.

THE EFFECT OF PUNISHMENT

Punishment is one of the most used, but least understood and badly administered, aspects of learning. Whether in rearing children or dealing with subordinates in an organization, parents and supervisors often revert to punishment instead of reward in order to modify or change behavior. Punishment is commonly thought to be the reverse of reward but equally effective in altering behavior. Costello and Zalkind dispel this widely held view as follows:

> Reward tends to increase the probability of response's future occurrence; the effect of punishment cannot be said, unequivocally, to decrease its probability. . . . If we are seeking a way to find punishment to be the opposite of reward, perhaps the answer can be found by saying the impact of reward on behavior is simple (it reinforces it); the impact of punishment on behavior is complex.[28]

In other words, punishment is a very complex phenomenon and must be carefully defined and used.

The Definition of Punishment

The meaning of *punishment* was mentioned in the discussion of extinction and negative reinforcement. To reiterate, punishment is anything which weakens behavior and tends to decrease it in subsequent frequency. The punishment

[27]Staats and Staats, op. cit., p. 65.
[28]Costello and Zalkind, op. cit., p. 215.

process can take either of two forms: (1) there can be the application of an undesirable or noxious consequence or (2) there can be the withdrawal or termination of a desirable or rewarding consequence. In either case, in order for punishment to occur, there is a weakening and decrease in the behavior which preceded its application or withdrawal. Just because a supervisor gives a "tongue lashing" to a subordinate and thinks this is punishment, it is not necessarily that unless the behavior that preceded the "tongue lashing" weakens and decreases. In many cases when supervisors think they are punishing employees, they are in fact reinforcing them because they are giving attention, and attention tends to be very reinforcing. This explains the common complaint that supervisors often make: "I call Joe in, give him heck for goofing-up, and he goes right back out and goofs-up again." What is happening is that the supervisor thinks Joe is being punished when operationally what is obviously happening is that the supervisor is reinforcing Joe's undesirable behavior by giving him attention and recognition.

Administering Punishment

Opinions on administering punishment range all the way from the one extreme of dire warnings never to use it to the other extreme that it is the only effective way to modify behavior. As yet, research has not been able to support either view consistently. However, there is little doubt that the use of punishment tends to result in many undesirable side effects. Neither children nor adults like to be punished. The punished behavior tends to be only temporarily suppressed rather than permanently changed, and the punished person tends to get anxious or "up-tight" and resentful of the punisher. The following summarizes some of the major difficulties in the use of punishment and some ways to more effectively administer it:

1 Punishment is effective in modifying behavior if it forces the person to select a desirable alternative behavior that is then reinforced.

2 If the above doesn't occur, then the behavior will be only temporarily suppressed and will reappear when the punishment is removed. Furthermore, the suppressed behavior may cause the person to become fearful and anxious.

3 Punishment is much more effective when applied at the time the undesirable behavior is actually performed than at a later time.

4 Punishment must be administered with extreme care so that it doesn't become a reward for undesirable behavior. The termination of punishment is reinforcing just as the termination of reinforcement is punishing.[29]

These four points should be considered when administering punishment in an organization. The persons administering punishment must always provide an acceptable alternative to the behavior that is being punished. If they do not, the undesirable behavior will tend to reappear and will cause fear and anxiety

[29]Howard H. Kendler, *Basic Psychology*, 2d ed., Appleton-Century-Crofts, New York, 1968, pp. 290–291.

in the person being punished. The punishment must always be administered as close in time to the undesirable behavior as possible. Calling persons into the office to give them a reprimand for breaking a rule the week before is not effective. All the reprimand tends to do at this time is punish them for getting caught. It has little effect on the rule-breaking behavior. The fourth point above calls attention to the care that must be exercised so that what is intended as punishment does not in fact act as a reward for the recipient. A supervisor who shouts at a worker may be rewarding this individual's position as the informal leader of a work-restricting group. The same is true of the example given in the last section on punishment turning into rewarding attention. It is very easy for supervisors or managers to use punishment but very difficult for them to effectively administer punishment so as to modify or change undesirable behavior. A simple rule of thumb for managers should be: Always attempt to reinforce instead of punish in order to change behavior. As discussed earlier, the use of an extinction strategy (nonreinforcement) is usually more effective in decelerating undesirable behaviors than is punishment because the bad side effects do not accompany extinction. Chapter 20 will get into these behavioral-change strategies in more depth.

OTHER LEARNING PHENOMENA

Classical and operant conditioning dominate most discussions of learning. One reason is that conditioning and its basic principles are adaptable to highly controlled experimentation; therefore, much is known about them, and they are widely accepted. However, there is more to learning than just conditioning and the basic principles discussed so far. Unfortunately, however, not as much is known about other learning phenomena. Yet, the following questions concerning learning are still relevant to the understanding of behavior:

1 Is learning a sudden or gradual process?
2 When learning occurs, what exactly is learned?
3 How many kinds of learning are there?
4 Is learning without awareness possible?[30]

These are only four questions, but there are many, many others that need to be answered in order to fully understand the learning process.

It is not the purpose or within the scope of this chapter to analyze all learning phenomena in detail. The attempt here is only to give a basic understanding of the learning process as it affects human and, specifically, organizational behavior. The remainder of the chapter considers a few selected learning phenomena that are most relevant to this purpose.

Higher-Order Conditioning

Higher-order conditioning is probably the most logical place to start in analyzing learning phenomena beyond simple classical conditioning. Pavlov went beyond

[30]See Kimble and Garmezy, op. cit., p. 179.

the simple conditioning of the dogs to salivate to the sound of a bell. He next paired a black square with the bell. After a number of trials with this pairing, the dogs salivated to the black square alone. The original conditioned stimulus (bell) had become a reinforcing unconditioned stimulus for the new conditioned stimulus (black square). When the dogs responded to the black square, they became what is known as *second-order conditioned.* Pavlov was able to obtain no higher than third-order conditioning with his dogs.

Most behavioral scientists agree that humans are capable of being conditioned higher than the third order. The exact number is not important but the potential implications of higher-order conditioning for human learning and behavior should be recognized.[31] For example, it can explain how learning can be transferred to stimuli other than those used in the original conditioning by going a step beyond the principle of generalization. The existence of higher-order conditioning shows the difficulty of tracing back to find the exact cause of a certain behavior. Another important implication concerns the principle of reinforcement. Higher-order conditioning implies that reinforcement can be acquired. A conditioned stimulus becomes reinforcing under higher-order conditioning. It substantiates, and perhaps offers a plausible explanation for, the secondary rewards which play such an important role in organizational behavior.

Escape-Avoidance Learning

Another learning phenomenon which is of particular interest to the study of organizational behavior is escape-avoidance learning. It goes a step beyond simple conditioning by the use of negative reinforcement. The discussion of negative reinforcement indicated the complexity inherent in this form of learning. A simple escape learning experiment involves shocking a rat in a Skinner box. Only pressing the bar will terminate the shock. The rat must learn to press the bar to escape the pain from the shock. Once escape is learned, avoidance can also be learned. In the Skinner box, a light may be timed to go on 10 seconds before the shock is administered. The rat can learn to avoid the shock altogether by running over to press the bar whenever the bulb lights up.

Humans learn escape-avoidance in much the same way as the rat in the Skinner box. For example, workers in an organization may learn to escape a boring job with no challenge by forming into informal groups or by playing games during working hours. After the quitting whistle blows, the punishment stops and the employees return to being very active, serious-minded individuals. In another situation a worker may learn to avoid an unpleasant confrontation with a supervisor by knowing the time of day when the supervisor makes rounds. The worker is either conveniently gone or too busy to have any interaction with the supervisor, thus avoiding a punishing situation. People come to work on time to *avoid* being "chewed out" by the boss. Supervisors get their reports in on time to *avoid* being punished by their boss. Middle managers conform to established policies to *avoid* being punished by top management,

---

[31]Ibid., p. 146.

and top management tries to look good on the balance sheet to *avoid* getting into trouble with the board of directors. In other words, organizational participants are exhibiting many avoidance behaviors and are under negative control. A major goal for organizational development would be to somehow turn this situation around so that organizational participants perform appropriate behaviors because they are *positively* reinforced for doing so.

Selective Learning

The introductory part of the chapter said that there were two major theoretical explanations for learning: behavioristic connectionist approaches and cognitive approaches. The discussion so far on classical and operant conditioning, the principles of learning, and even higher-order and escape-avoidance learning is largely of the behavioristic orientation. In this last section some of the more cognitive dimensions are given attention.

One of the important cognitive approaches involves selective learning. In selective learning the person must not only associate stimulus and response and response and consequence experiences but must also determine which things to connect in the mind.[32] Under selective learning, the human chooses from a wide variety of possible learning mechanisms. For example, the individual does not have a simple choice, say, between classical and operant conditioning. Rather, selective learning involves a complex interaction between thinking, emotion, perception, and motivation. In other words, there are many cognitions that come into play in selective learning. As is true regarding the other theories of learning, there is not general agreement as to what exactly goes on in such a cognitive learning process, but whatever it is can be called *selective learning.* Other names attached to this complex cognitive type of learning include *insightful learning* and *perceptual learning.* These latter types give a little different emphasis, but they are fundamentally the same as what is here called selective learning. Although controversy and lack of knowledge exist, some learning theorists argue that a form of learning like selective learning takes place, and that it is much more complex than merely strengthening stimulus-response or response-consequence connections.

Selective learning can be experimentally demonstrated by maze learning, or the term can be used to describe some of the very complicated learning tasks which occur in an organization. An employee faced with a problem-solving type of situation may be using a selective learning process. Basic conditioning and the principles of learning are relegated to a supplementary role in selective learning. A worker faced with a job requiring a new skill, an office manager challenged by a new filing system, a systems analyst confronted by a new computer language, and a top executive who must explain the new budgeting system to the board of directors may be using the selective learning process to accomplish their tasks.

[32]Norman R. F. Maier, *Psychology in Industry,* 3d ed., Houghton Mifflin Company, Boston, 1965, p. 379.

SUMMARY

Learning is a major psychological process that has been largely neglected in the study of organizational behavior. The definition of learning (a relatively permanent change in behavior that results from reinforced practice or experience) is widely agreed upon, but the theoretical foundation is not. Despite the controversy surrounding learning theory, there are many accepted principles of learning. Principles such as learning curves, extinction, spontaneous recovery, generalization, and discrimination are largely derived from experimentation and the analysis of classical and operant conditioning. In addition, more concepts dealing with higher-order conditioning, escape-avoidance learning, and selective learning are also widely recognized.

Reinforcement is the single most important concept in the learning process and is most relevant to the study of organizational behavior. Based on the classic law of effect, reinforcement can be operationally defined as anything that increases the strength of response and that tends to induce repetitions of the behavior that preceded the reinforcement. Rewards may be either positive or negative, extrinsic or intrinsic, or primary or secondary. They may be administered on a fixed ratio or interval or on a variable ratio or interval basis. The effective administration of reinforcement is one of the most critical challenges facing modern management.

QUESTIONS FOR DISCUSSION AND REVIEW

1 Do you agree with the statement, "Learning is involved in almost everything that everyone does"? Explain.
2 What is the difference between classical and operant conditioning?
3 Apply three of the learning principles to the modern workplace.
4 What is the difference between positive and negative reinforcement? What is the difference between negative reinforcement and punishment?
5 What are some common forms of secondary reinforcers relevant to organizational behavior?
6 Why is the administration of reinforcement so vitally important to learning and management practice?

CASE: CONTRASTING STYLES

Henry Adams has been a production supervisor for eight years. He came up through the ranks and is known as a tough, but hard-working, supervisor. Jerry Wake has been a production supervisor for about the same length of time and also came up through the ranks. Jerry is known as a nice, hard-working guy. Over the past several years these two supervisors' sections have been head and shoulders above the other six sections on hard measures of performance (number of units produced). This was true despite the almost opposite approaches the two took in handling their workers. Henry explained his approach as follows:

"The only way to handle workers is to come down hard on them whenever they make a mistake. In fact, I call them together every once in a while and give them heck whether they deserve it or not, just to keep them on their toes. If they are doing a good job, I tell them that's what they're getting paid for. By taking this approach, all I have to do is walk through my area, and people start working like mad."

Jerry explained his approach as follows:

"I don't believe in that human relations stuff of being nice to workers. But I do believe that a worker deserves some recognition and attention from me if he or she does a good job. If people make a mistake, I don't jump on them. I feel that we are all entitled to make some errors. On the other hand, I always do point out what the mistake was and what they should have done, and as soon as they do it right I let them know it. Obviously, I don't have time to give attention to everyone doing things right, but I deliberately try to get around to people doing a good job every once in a while."

Although Henry's section is still right at the top along with Jerry's section in units produced, personnel records show that there has been three times more turnover in Henry's section than in Jerry's section, and the quality control records show that Henry's section has met quality standards only twice in the last six years but Jerry's has missed attaining quality standards only once in the last six years.

    1 Both of these supervisors have similar backgrounds. On the basis of learning, how can you explain their opposite approaches to handling people?
    2 What are some of the examples of punishment, positive reinforcement, and negative reinforcement found in this case? What schedule of reinforcement is Jerry using? If Jerry is using a reinforcement approach, how do you explain his statement, "I don't believe in that human relations stuff of being nice to people"?
    3 How do you explain the performance, turnover, and quality results in these two sections of the production department?

SELECTED REFERENCES

Bolles, Robert C.: *Learning Theory,* Holt, Rinehart and Winston, Inc., New York, 1975.

Hilgard, Ernest R.: *Theories of Learning,* 4th ed., Prentice-Hall, Inc., Englewood Cliffs, N.J., 1975.

Kagan, Jerome, and Ernest Havemann: *Psychology: An Introduction,* Harcourt, Brace & World, Inc., New York, 1968, part II.

Keller, Fred S.: *Learning: Reinforcement Theory,* Random House, Inc., New York, 1969.

Kendler, Howard H.: *Basic Psychology,* 2d ed., Appleton-Century-Crofts, Inc., New York, 1968, chaps. 7 and 9.

Kimble, Gregory A., and Norman Garmezy: *Principles of General Psychology,* 2d ed., The Ronald Press Company, New York, 1963, part III.

Lawson, Tom E.: "Gagne's Learning Theory Applied to Technical Instruction," *Training and Development Journal,* April 1974, pp. 32–40.

Luthans, Fred, and Robert Kreitner: *Organizational Behavior Modification,* Scott, Foresman and Company, Glenview, Ill., 1975.

Mawhinney, Thomas C.: "Operant Terms and Concepts in the Descriptions of Individual Work Behavior: Some Problems of Interpretation, Application, and Evaluation," *Journal of Applied Psychology,* December 1975, pp. 704–712.

McGehee, William: "Are We Using What We Know About Training?— Learning Theory and Training," *Personnel Psychology,* Spring 1958, pp. 1–12.

Premack, David: "Reinforcement Theory," *Nebraska Symposium on Motivation,* David Levine (ed.), University of Nebraska Press, Lincoln, Nebr., 1965, pp. 123–188.

Reif, William E.: "Intrinsic versus Extrinsic Rewards: Resolving the Controversy," *Human Resource Management,* Summer 1975, pp. 2–10.

Reynolds, G. S.: *A Primer of Operant Conditioning,* Scott, Foresman and Company, Glenview, Ill., 1975.

Schneier, Craig Eric: "Behavior Modification in Management: A Review and Critique," *Academy of Management Journal,* September 1974, pp. 528–548.

This, Leslie E., and Gordon L. Lippitt: "Learning Theories and Training," *Training and Development Journal,* May 1966, pp. 10–18.

Chapter 13

The Basic Motivational Process

Motivation is the third and last psychological process that is given detailed attention in the study of human behavior. Many people equate the causes of behavior with motivation. Chapter 5 and the two preceding chapters emphasized that the explanation of behavior is much broader and more complex than just motivation. However, motivation should never be underrated. Along with perception and learning, it is presented here as being a very important process in understanding behavior. On the other hand, it must be remembered that motivation should not be thought of as the only explanation of behavior. It interacts with and acts in conjunction with the other psychological processes and personality. It must also be remembered that, like the other psychological processes and personality, motivation cannot be seen. All that can be seen are behaviors. Motivation is a hypothetical construct that is used to help explain behavior; it should not be equated with the behavior.

This chapter presents motivation as a basic psychological process in the understanding of human behavior. As in the case of learning, the more applied aspects of motivation are covered in Parts Four and Five of this book. Approaches to job satisfaction and work motivation are given attention in Chapter 17 and some specific techniques to motivate workers and managers are found in applications-oriented Chapters 19, 20, and 21. This chapter provides a necessary foundation for these dynamics and applications of motivation.

The first section of the chapter traces the historical development of the study of motivation. A brief discussion of hedonism is followed by the major historical concepts: instincts, unconscious motivation, and drive theory. The second section clarifies the meaning of motivation by defining the relationship between its various parts. The need——→drive——→goal cycle is defined and analyzed. The rest of the chapter is devoted to an overview of the various types of human motives. The discussion is broken down into the three generally recognized categories of motives: primary, general, and secondary. The motives within the general and secondary categories are given major attention, and a summary of supporting research findings on these motives is included.

HISTORICAL DEVELOPMENT

The study of motivation can be traced back to the writings of the ancient Greek philosophers. More than twenty-three centuries ago, they presented hedonism as an explanation of human motivation. Hedonism says that a person seeks out comfort and pleasure and avoids discomfort and pain. Many centuries later, hedonism was still a basic assumption in the prevailing economic and social philosophies of such famous men as Adam Smith, Jeremy Bentham, and John Stuart Mill. They all explained motivation in terms of people trying to maximize pleasure and minimize pain.

Early psychological thought was also influenced by hedonism. Psychologists in the 1800s and even in the early 1900s assumed that humans consciously and rationally strive for hedonistic pleasure and avoidance of pain. William James, who is often called the father of American psychology, was one of the first to question this assumption. In his classic *Principles of Psychology,* he gave recognition to two additional important historical concepts in the study of motivation: instincts and unconscious motivation. Later, using the scientific perspective of early behaviorists, Clark Hull formulated the drive theory of motivation.

Instincts

James did not feel that the human is always consciously rational. He thought that much of human behavior is instinctively based. A partial list of the unlearned instincts that James believed influence behavior included crying, locomotion, curiosity, imitation, sociability, sympathy, fear of dark places, jealousy, and love. These and many other instincts were thought by James to be present in every person. William McDougall, the pioneering social psychologist, further developed the instinctual theory of behavior. In his social psychology book of 1908, he defined an instinct as "an innate disposition which determines the organism to perceive or to pay attention to any object . . . and to act or have an impulse to action which finds expression in a specific mode of behavior." The key assumption of those who advocated the instinctual approach was that there is an unlearned *predisposition* to behavior.

Starting in the 1920s, the instinctual view of human motivation came under heavy attack. The behaviorists, who dealt with observable behavior in only a scientific manner, in particular completely disagreed with the theory of largely unobservable, almost mystical instinct. The other schools of thought also questioned some of the extreme instinctual views. This severe criticism has carried over so that today the term *instinct* is seldom used in academic discussions of human behavior. Although modern psychologists recognize that some human motives seem to be unlearned, they are not willing to accept the extreme instinctual views, especially the idea of predisposed behaviors, that were advocated by James and McDougall.

There is too much evidence that humans do not have simplistic, innate predispositions toward behavior. Animals have certain such instincts but humans do not. While some psychologists recognize a sucking instinct, most do not admit to any human instincts whatsoever. Instead, behavior is explained by complex cognitive causes and by environmental consequences. As presented in Chapter 5, behavior consists of the environment interacting with the complex human being and the environmental consequences. Instincts are an insufficient explanation for behavior because: "(1) people differ in the strength of their motivational dispositions, and (2) at any one time the relevant behavior may not correspond to the strengths of the persisting dispositions."[1]

Unconscious Motivation

Implicit in James's emphasis on instincts is the whole question of unconscious motivation. However, it was Sigmund Freud, not James, who openly recognized the importance of the unconscious and made it a vital part of the study of human motivation. In fact, many students of Freud argue that this was his greatest contribution. In light of Freud's many significant contributions, this accolade indicates how important unconscious motivation can be to the study of human behavior.

The existence of unconscious motivation implies that humans are not consciously aware of all their desires. The presence of an unconscious explains why people cannot always verbalize their motivation to attain certain goals or even tell what their goals are. Freud uncovered this phenomenon while analyzing his clinical patients. He found that in many ways a person is like an iceberg: only a small part is conscious and visible, the rest is beneath the surface. This below-the-surface concept is the unconscious.

In contrast to their rejection of instincts, many contemporary psychologists accept the existence and importance of the unconscious. On the other hand, for the most part they do *not* agree with Freud's explanation of the unconscious. Like James, Freud attempted to equate unconscious motives with instincts. He felt that the unconscious motives are primarily sexual and aggressive in nature and, even though unconscious, they greatly influence everyday behavior. He pointed out that these motives are revealed in dreams, slips of speech (the so-called Freudian slip), and lapses of memory.

[1] Ernest R. Hilgard and Richard C. Atkinson, *Introduction to Psychology*, 4th ed., Harcourt, Brace & World, Inc., New York, 1967, p. 140.

The Impact of Unconscious Motivation

The Freudian explanation of motivation has a devastating effect on human pride. People like to picture themselves as being consciously rational and in complete control of their own behavior. Now, if Freud was right, this was an illusion. Was it true that sexual and aggressive motives locked in the mysterious unconscious were determining people's behavior? In general such fears have been put to rest.

Psychologists generally recognize that a human possesses a degree of unconscious motivation, but not in the Freudian sense. Instead of the view that sexual and aggressive instincts dominate behavior, the more modern view is that normal behavior contains some consciously unexplainable motives, but that these are largely based on learning and not on instinct. For example, Morgan and King give three reasons why all motives cannot be consciously explained:

1   Several drives and goals may be intertwined in any given bit of behavior; it is not always possible to identify correctly the motive or motives behind an act.

2   Habits of which the person is generally unaware may develop.

3   Some motives are formed under unpleasant circumstances and are repressed.[2]

The third point on repression is the most complex explanation of unconscious motivation. Repression was believed by Freud to be vital to understanding abnormal personalities. A form of defense mechanism, repression disguises real motives by "perceiving them as different from what they really are, or by refusing to recognize them at all."[3]

Although instincts and the unconscious are important to a historical analysis of motivation, they play a relatively minor role in the modern study of motivation. On the other hand, although instincts are a dead issue, unconscious motivation is still open for discussion, debate, and more research. Currently, not much is known about the unconscious, but it may still prove to be an important element in the better understanding of human behavior. However, the major historical foundation for the study and understanding of motivation comes from the work of Clark Hull on drive theory.

Early Drive Theories

The drive theories of motivation evolved from the dissatisfaction with the instinctual view of motivation. The drive theorists were greatly influenced by early behaviorists who stressed the need for a scientific perspective. By the 1930s motivation was considered to be an important aspect of behavior, but no scientifically based theory could explain it. Clark Hull (1884–1952) was finally able to synthesize the preceding thinking into a scientifically based theory of

---

[2]Clifford T. Morgan and Richard A. King, *Introduction to Psychology*, 3d ed., McGraw-Hill Book Company, New York, 1966, p. 235.

[3]Ibid., p. 236.

motivation. Hull proposed that motivation was a product of drive times habit (Effort = D × H). The drive concept in particular was motivationally based. To Hull, drive was the energizing influence which determined the intensity of behavior. The habit concept reflected the behavioristic (learning) influence on Hull. Later, to counteract the emphasis given to the past by habit, Hull added the futuristic concept of incentive to his equation (Effort = D × H × I). This incentive factor had cognitive properties and served as a forerunner of expectancy theories of motivation.

Hull's theory generated a tremendous amount of research in the 1940s and 1950s. Unfortunately, most of this research was conducted on rats in the laboratory and few generalizations to human motivation are possible. Hull's students did extend the original concepts, but it is now generally recognized that most of Hull's concepts were wrong. Nevertheless, the scientific research tradition initiated by Hull and his followers, plus his emphasis on both the cognitive (drive and incentive) and learning (habit) aspects associated with motivation, are extremely important contributions to the modern study of motivation. Drive theory serves as a theoretical basis for the motivational cycle of needs——→drives——→goals.

THE MEANING OF HUMAN MOTIVATION

Today, virtually all people—lay people and scholars—have their own definition of motivation. Usually one or more of the following words are included in the definition: desires, wants, wishes, aims, goals, needs, drives, motives, and incentives. Technically, the term *motivation* can be traced to the Latin word *movere,* which means to move. This meaning is evidenced by the following formal definition given by Berelson and Steiner: "A motive is an inner state that energizes, activates, or moves (hence 'motivation'), and that directs or channels behavior toward goals."[4] Sanford and Wrightsman describe a motive, in a less formal sense, as follows: "A motive is a restlessness, a lack, a yen, a force. Once in the grip of a motive, the organism does something. It most generally does something to reduce the restlessness, to remedy the lack, to alleviate the yen, to mitigate the force."[5] The key to understanding motivation, it appears, lies in the meaning and relationship between needs, drives, and goals.

The Motivation Cycle

Figure 13-1 graphically depicts the motivation cycle. Needs set up drives to accomplish goals; this is what motivation is all about. In a systems sense, motivation consists of the three interacting and interdependent elements of needs, drives, and goals.

[4]Bernard Berelson and Gary A. Steiner, *Human Behavior,* Harcourt, Brace & World, Inc., New York, 1964, p. 240.
[5]Fillmore H. Sanford and Lawrence S. Wrightsman, Jr., *Psychology,* 3d ed., Brooks/Cole Publishing Company, Belmont, Calif., 1970, p. 189.

NEEDS ——————————→	DRIVES —————————————→	GOALS
(Deprivation)	(Deprivation with direction)	(Reduction of drives)

Figure 13-1   The motivation process.

   1   *Needs.* The best one-word definition of a need is *deficiency.* In the homeostatic sense, needs are created whenever there is a physiological *or* psychological imbalance. For example, a need exists when a cell in the body is deprived of food and water or when the human personality is deprived of other persons who serve as friends or companions.
   2   *Drives.* With a few exceptions,[6] drives or motives (the two terms will be used interchangeably) are set up to alleviate needs. A drive can be simply defined as a deficiency with direction. Similar to Hull's use of the term, drives are action-oriented and provide an energizing thrust toward goal accomplishment. They are at the very heart of the motivational process. The examples of the needs for food and water are translated into the hunger and thirst drives, and the need for friends becomes a drive for affiliation.
   3   *Goals.* At the end of the motivation cycle is the goal. A goal in the motivation cycle can be defined as anything which will alleviate a need and reduce a drive. Thus, attaining a goal will tend to restore physiological or psychological balance and will reduce or cut off the drive. Eating food, drinking water, and obtaining friends will tend to restore the homeostatic balance and reduce the corresponding drives. Food, water, and friends are the goals in these examples.

Refinements of the Motivation Process

Before examining the individual motives, a couple of points about the motivation process need further refinement. First, it should be repeated that motivation, like perception and learning, is a hypothetical construct which is defined in terms of antecedent conditions and consequent behavior. No one has actually observed motivation or isolated it under a microscope. Motives such as hunger, sex, power, and achievement cannot be seen. Only the behavioral manifestations of these motives are observable. Restlessness, walking, running, and talking can be observed and so can eating food, drinking water, and winning a new friend. Yet, the corresponding motives can only be inferred from watching this behavior. As Sanford and Wrightsman note, "We can see [a person] seek a restaurant, we can see him eat, and we can see a decrease in restlessness. We infer, with considerable confidence, that a hunger motive was in full operation. But we have not directly observed hunger."[7]

---

   [6]The most frequently cited exception is the need for oxygen. A deficiency of oxygen in the body does not automatically set up a corresponding drive. This is a fear of high-altitude pilots. Unless their gauges show an oxygen leak or the increased intake of carbon dioxide sets up a drive, they may die of oxygen deficiency without a drive ever being set up to correct the situation. The same is true of the relatively frequent deaths of teen-agers parked in "lovers' lanes." Carbon monoxide leaks into their parked autos and they die from oxygen deficiency without its ever setting up a drive (opening the car door).
   [7]Sanford and Wrightsman, op. cit., p. 191.

Types of Motivated Behavior   A point that needs emphasis is that motives can be expressed in several types of behavior. Kimble and Garmezy's description of three such types of motivated behavior[8] may be summarized thus:

1 *Consummatory behavior.* This is the most obvious form of motivated behavior because it directly satisfies the need in question. Examples of consummatory behavior with the corresponding drives would include eating (hunger), drinking (thirst), joining a small club (affiliation or status), and running for political office (power).

2 *Instrumental behavior.* Similar to its meaning in learning, this type of motivated behavior is instrumental in satisfying the need in question. Walking to the grocery store and joining the company bowling league are behavioral expressions of the hunger and affiliation motives. But this behavior is only instrumental in obtaining food and friends. The instrumental behavior does not directly satisfy the need as does consummatory behavior. A complicating factor is that the same behavior may be instrumental for one person but consummatory for another.[9]

3 *Substitute behavior.* This type of motivated behavior is the most complex and difficult to explain. The reason is that it is indirect or substitutive in nature and on the surface seems to have little relevance to the need in question. An example comes from the hunger study by Keys.[10] Much of the behavior of the semistarved human subjects in the study seemed to be substitute rather than consummatory or instrumental in obtaining food. Another example is the worker who has a strong affiliation need but produces above the informal performance norm. In a way, substitute behavior is a "black box" concept, i.e., it is known to be motivated behavior but it can't be fully explained.

The existence of intrumental and substitute behavior points out the difficulty in trying to predict and control behavior that will result from a given need. By the same token, it is impossible always to infer what motive is behind given observable behavior. In the earlier example, the man's eating behavior in the restaurant may or may *not* be based upon the hunger motive. Maybe he was having an extramarital affair (sex), and the restaurant provided an out-of-the-way meeting place. Another possibility is that the restaurant has a prestigious reputation and he wanted to be seen there (status). There are numerous other possible motives behind the eating behavior in the restaurant. Hilgard and Atkinson summarize five reasons for the difficulty in inferring motives from behavior:

1 The expression of human motives differ from culture to culture and from person to person within a culture.

[8]Gregory A. Kimble and Norman Garmezy, *General Psychology*, 3d ed., The Ronald Press Company, New York, 1968, pp. 378–379.

[9]An example is sexual behavior. For a prostitute, sexual behavior may be instrumental in satisfying the hunger motive, but for the married couple, it may be consummatory.

[10]See A. Keys et al., *The Biology of Human Starvation*, vols. I and II, The University of Minnesota Press, Minneapolis, 1950.

2 Similar motives may be manifested through unlike behavior.
3 Unlike motives may be expressed through similar behavior.
4 Motives may appear in disguised forms.
5 Any single act of behavior may express several motives.[11]

Relationship between the Variables Another complexity is the relationship between the variables in the motivation cycle. In Hull's formula for motivation there was a multiplicative relationship between drive, habit, and incentive. If any of the variables in Hull's formula was zero, e.g., there was no drive present, there would be no motivation. In the motivational cycle presented here, there is not such a multiplicative relationship between needs, drives, and goals. But drives will not be set up unless there is a need, and motivation involves, but not necessarily in a multiplicative relationship, all three variables. This, of course, indicates that motivation is extremely complex in nature and meaning. There is certainly not a simple relationship between motivation and behavior. Yet, despite this complexity, it is helpful to classify the various types of motives for study and analysis. For the purposes of this book, the primary, general, and secondary categories seem most appropriate.

PRIMARY MOTIVES

Psychologists do not totally agree on how to classify the various human motives, but, as was brought out in the discussion of instincts, they would acknowledge that some motives are unlearned and physiologically based. Such motives are variously called physiological, biological, unlearned, or primary. The last term is used here because it is more comprehensive than the other terms. On the other hand, the use of the term *primary* does not imply that this group of motives always takes precedence over the general and secondary motives.

Although the precedence of primary motives is implied in the motivation theories of Maslow and others,[12] there are many situations where general and secondary motives predominate over primary motives. Common examples include celibacy among priests and fasting for a religious or political cause. In both cases, learned secondary motives are stronger than unlearned primary motives. In this regard, Figure 13-2 presents some interesting speculation as to what percentage of the population would perform varying degrees of antisocial acts in the face of starvation. The figure shows that scarcely anyone who was starving would murder someone in order to obtain food unless this person lived in a cannibalistic society. In this last situation, under proper conditions cannibals would kill other people and eat them without hesitation because they have learned that this is culturally acceptable. On the other hand, practically every hungry person in a noncannibalistic society would be willing to violate

[11]Hilgard and Atkinson, op. cit., pp. 141–142.
[12]See Abraham Maslow, *Motivation and Personality*, Harper & Brothers, New York, 1954. His hierarchical theory of motivation is discussed in detail in Chapter 17.

Figure 13-2   Approximate Percentage of the Population Showing Various Behaviors under Starvation Conditions

Activities induced by starvation	Percentage of population succumbing to pressure of starvation
Cannibalism (in non-cannibalistic societies)	Less than one third of 1%
Murder of members of the family and friends	Less than 1%
Murder of other members of one's group	Not more than 1%
Murder of strangers who are not enemies	Not more than 2 to 5%
Infliction of various bodily and other injuries on members of one's social group	Not more than 5 to 10%
Theft, larceny, robbery, forgery, and other crimes against property which have a clearcut criminal character	Hardly more than 7 to 10%
Violation of various rules of strict honesty and fairness in pursuit of food, such as misuse of rationing cards, hoarding, and taking unfair advantage of others	From 20 to 99%, depending upon the nature of the violation
Violation of fundamental religious and moral principles	Hardly more than 10 to 20%
Violation of less important religious, moral, juridical, conventional, and similar norms	From 50 to 99%
Surrender or weakening of most of the aesthetic activities irreconcilable with food-seeking activities	From 50 to 99%
Weakening of sex activities, especially coitus	From 70 to 90% during prolonged and intense starvation
Prostitution and other highly dishonorable sex activities	Hardly more than 10%

Source: Pitirim A. Sorokin, *Man and Society in Calamity*, E. P. Dutton & Co., Inc., New York, © 1942, p. 81. Renewal © 1970, by Helen P. Sorokin. Published by E. P. Dutton & Co., Inc., and used with their permission.

relatively unimportant societal values (to lie and cheat) in order to obtain food.

Two criteria are necessary in order for a motive to be included in the primary classification: It must be *unlearned,* and it must be *physiologically* based. Thus defined, the most commonly recognized primary motives include hunger, thirst, sleep, avoidance of pain, sex, and maternal concern. Some psychologists break the primary drives down into more finite categories. Berelson and Steiner use the following subclassifications for primary motives:

   1 *Positive or supply motives.* This type is a direct result of homeostatic deficiency of the cells. Examples would be hunger, thirst, and sleep.
   2 *Negative or avoidance motives.* This type results from the presence of physically harmful or potentially harmful noxious stimulation. An example would be pain.

3   *Species-maintaining motives.* This type results from the reproduction system that stimulates mating, produces children, and cares for the children. Examples would be sex and maternal.[13]

GENERAL MOTIVES

A separate classification for general motives is not always given. Yet, such a category seems necessary because there are a number of motives which lie in the gray area between the primary and secondary classifications. To be included in the general category, a motive must be unlearned but not physiologically based. Although not all psychologists would agree, the motives of competence, curiosity, manipulation, activity, and affection seem best to meet the criteria for this classification. An understanding of these general motives is important to the study of human behavior—especially in organizations. They are more relevant to organizational behavior than are the primary motives.

The Competence Motive

Robert W. White is most closely associated with the competence motive. He questioned the approaches to motivation that are based solely on the primary drives. For example, the primary drives cannot explain exploration, manipulation, and activity. White proposed a new conceptualization based upon the assumption that all organisms, animal or human, have a capacity to interact effectively with their environment. He called this common capacity *competence.* "It receives substantial contributions from activities which, though playful and exploratory in character, at the same time show direction, selectivity, and persistence in interacting with the environment."[14] Thus defined, the competence motive is the most inclusive general drive. The other general drives of curiosity, manipulation, and activity can be considered as more specific competence drives.

White built an entire theory of motivation around competence. He was convinced that people strive to have control or competence over their environment. People need to know what they are doing and be able to make things happen. White determined that the critical age for competence development is between six and nine years old. During this age period, the children cut the apron strings and venture out into the world on their own. They develop needs to cross the street by themselves, to ride a bike, play baseball, roller-skate, and read. These needs are manifested by the drive for competence or mastery over the environment. The successes and failures that youngsters experience in this critical age period will have a lasting impact on the intensity of their competence motive.

This motive has interesting implications for job design in an organization. It says that people may be motivated by the challenge of trying to master the

---

[13]Berelson and Steiner, op. cit., p. 242.

[14]Robert W. White, "Motivation Reconsidered: The Concept of Competence," *Psychological Review,* September 1959, p. 329.

job or to become competent in the job. But once the job is mastered, which most highly specialized jobs in modern organizations are in a very short period of time, competence motivation will disappear. The discussion of job design in Chapter 19 draws from knowledge of the competence motive.

Curiosity, Manipulation, and Activity Motives

Early psychologists noted that the animals used in their experiments seemed to have an unlearned drive to explore, to manipulate objects, or just to be active. This was especially true if monkeys were used as subjects and if they were placed in an unfamiliar or novel situation. These observations and speculations about the existence of curiosity, manipulation, and activity motives in monkeys were later substantiated through experimentation.[15] In this case, psychologists feel completely confident in generalizing the results of animal experiments to humans. It is generally recognized that human curiosity, manipulation, and activity are quite intense, and anyone who has reared or been around small children will quickly support this generalization.

Although these drives often get the small child into trouble, curiosity, manipulation, and activity, when carried forward to adulthood, can be very beneficial. If these motives are stifled or inhibited, the total society might become very stagnant. The same is true on an organizational level. If employees are not allowed to express their curiosity, manipulation, and activity motives, the organization will eventually suffer, given today's dynamic environment.

The Affection Motive

Love or affection is a very complex form of general drive. Part of the complexity stems from the fact that in many ways love resembles the primary drives and in other ways it is similar to the secondary drives. In particular, the affection motive is closely associated with the primary sex motive on the one hand and the secondary affiliation motive on the other. For this reason, affection is sometimes placed in all three categories of motives, and some psychologists do not even recognize it as a separate motive.

Affection merits specific attention because of its growing importance to the modern world. There seems to be a great deal of truth to the adages, "Love makes the world go around" and "Love conquers all." In a world suffering from intra- and interpersonal and national conflict and where quality of life is becoming increasingly important to modern society, the affection motive takes on added importance in the study of human behavior. It is given academic respectability mainly because of the extensive basic research done on primates by Harry F. Harlow at the University of Wisconsin.[16]

Harlow's findings suggest that monkeys have an intense, unlearned drive

---

[15]See Robert A. Butler, "Discrimination Learning by Rhesus Monkeys to Visual Exploration Motivation," *Journal of Comparative and Physiological Psychology,* vol. 46, 1953, pp. 95–98; and Robert A. Butler, "Incentive Conditions Which Influence Visual Exploration," *Journal of Experimental Psychology,* July 1954, pp. 19–23.

[16]See Harry F. Harlow, "The Nature of Love," *American Psychologist,* December 1958, pp. 673–685.

to receive warmth, comfort, and support. Through the years, Harlow has introduced many variations and refinements, but the same results continue to emerge. However, the big question remaining to be answered is whether a baby monkey's unlearned drive for warmth, comfort, and support can be generalized to apply to human love or affection. At this time such a generalization may not be justified. Yet, Harlow's findings provide some interesting insights and a sound beginning for the better understanding of the human motive for love.

SECONDARY MOTIVES

Whereas the general drives seem relatively more important than the primary ones to the study of human behavior in organizations, the secondary drives are unquestionably the most important. As a human society develops economically and becomes more complex, the primary, and to a lesser degree the general, drives give way to the learned secondary drives in motivating behavior. With some glaring exceptions that are yet to be eradicated, the motivations of people living in the economically developed Western world are not dominated by hunger or thirst. This situation is obviously subject to change; for example, the "population bomb" may alter certain human needs. But for now, modern Western societies are largely populated by "men of full-blown human complexity, men who love and strive and hate and fight, men who create and destroy, men who shape the world and make human history."[17] In such a world, the learned secondary motives predominate.

Secondary motives are closely tied to the learning concepts discussed in the last chapter. In particular, the learning principle of reinforcement is conceptually and practically related to motivation. The relationship is obvious when reinforcement is divided into primary and secondary motives. Although some writers regard reinforcement and motivation as being equivalent, as was pointed out in the last chapter, they are treated separately in this book. Once again, however, it should be emphasized that although the various behavioral concepts can be separated for study and analysis, in reality concepts like reinforcement and motivation do not operate as separate entities in producing human behavior. The interactive effects are always present.

A motive must be learned in order to be included in the secondary classification. Numerous important human motives meet this criterion. Some of the more important ones are power, achievement, and affiliation, or, as they are commonly referred to today, *n Pow, n Ach,* and *n Aff.* In addition, especially in reference to organizational behavior, security and status are also important secondary motives. Each of these five motives is conceptually unique and has different intensities, but they all share the commonality of being learned.

The Power Motive

The power motive is discussed first because it has been formally recognized and studied for a relatively long time. The leading advocate of the power motive was Alfred Adler. In 1911, Adler officially broke his close ties with

[17]Sanford and Wrightsman, op. cit., p. 208.

Sigmund Freud and proposed an opposite theoretical position. Where Freud stressed the impact of the past and sexual, unconscious motivation, Adler substituted the future and a person's overwhelming drive for superiority or power. In Adler's words:

> Now I began to see clearly in every psychical phenomenon the *striving for superiority.* . . . All our functions follow its direction; rightly or wrongly they strive for conquest, surety, increase. . . Whatever premises all our philosophers and psychologists dream of—self preservation, pleasure principle, equalization—all these are but vague representations, attempts to express the great upward drive . . . *the fundamental fact of our life.*[18]

To explain the power need—the need to manipulate others or the drive for superiority over others—Adler developed the concepts of inferiority complex and compensation. He felt that every small child experiences a sense of inferiority. When this feeling of inferiority is combined with what he sensed as an innate need for superiority, the two rule all behavior. The person's life style is characterized by striving to compensate for the feelings of inferiority which are combined with the innate drive for power.

Although modern psychologists do not generally accept the tenet that the power drive is inborn and so dominating, in recent years it has prompted renewed interest. The quest for power is readily observable in modern American society. The politician is probably the best example, and the Watergate scandal makes a fascinating study in striving for and use of power in government and politics.[19] However, in addition to politicians, anyone in a responsible position in business, government, education, or the military may also exhibit a significant need for power. It has significant implications for organizational leadership and the informal, political aspects of organizations. Chapter 18, on "Leadership and Power," will examine in detail the dynamics of power in the study of organizational behavior.

The Achievement Motive

Whereas recognition and discussion of the power motive have been going on for a long time, there is a noted absence of any research back-up. The opposite is true of the achievement motive. Although given only relatively recent attention, more is known about achievement than about any other motive because of the tremendous amount of research that has been devoted to it. The Thematic Apperception Test (TAT) has proved to be a very effective tool in researching achievement. The TAT can effectively identify and measure the achievement motive. It works in the following manner:

> One picture in the TAT shows a young man plowing a field while the sun is about ready to sink in the west. The person taking the test is supposed to tell a story about

---

[18]Alfred Adler, "Individual Psychology," translated by Susanne Langer, in Carl Murchison (ed.), *Psychologies of 1930,* Clark University Press, Worcester, Mass., 1930, pp. 398–399.
[19]Max Ways, "Watergate as a Case Study in Management," *Fortune,* November 1973, pp. 109–111, 196–201.

what he sees in the picture. By telling a story he will project his major motives. For example, the test taker may respond that the man in the picture is sorry the sun is going down because he still has more land to plow and he wants to get the crops planted before it rains. Such a response indicates high achievement. A low achiever might answer that the man is happy that the sun is finally going down so he can go into the house, relax, and have a cool drink.

The research approach to achievement has become so effective that it is often cited by psychologists as a prototype of how knowledge and understanding can be accomplished in the behavioral sciences.

Characteristics of High Achievers   David C. McClelland, a Harvard psychologist, is most closely associated with the achievement motive. Beginning in 1947, McClelland thoroughly investigated and wrote about all aspects of *n Ach* (achievement).[20] Out of this extensive research has emerged a clear profile of the characteristics of the high achiever. Very simply, the achievement motive can be expressed as a desire to perform in terms of a standard of excellence or to be successful in competitive situations. The specific characteristics of a high achiever can be summarized as follows:[21]

   1   *Moderate risks.* Taking moderate risks is probably the single most descriptive characteristic of the person possessing high *n Ach.* On the surface it would seem that a high achiever would take high risks. However, once again research gives a different answer from common sense. The ring-toss game can be used to demonstrate risk-taking behavior. It has been shown that when ring tossers are told that they may stand anywhere they want to toss the rings at the peg, low and high achievers behave quite differently. Low achievers will tend to stand either very close and just drop the rings over the peg, or very far away and wildly throw the rings at the peg. In contrast, high achievers will almost always carefully calculate the exact distance from the peg that will challenge their own abilities. People with high *n Ach* will not stand too close because there would then be no test of their ability simply to drop the ring over the peg. By the same token, they will not stand ridiculously far away because luck and not skill would determine whether the ring lands on the peg. In other words, low achievers take either a high or a low risk and high achievers take a moderate risk. This seems to hold true both for the simple children's game and for important adult decisions or activities.
   2   *Immediate feedback.* Closely connected to high achievers' taking moderate risks is their desire for immediate feedback. People with high *n Ach* prefer activities which provide immediate and precise feedback information on how they are progressing toward a goal. Some hobbies and vocations offer such feedback and others do not. High achievers generally prefer hobbies, such as woodworking or mechanics, which provide prompt, exact feedback, and they

   [20]David C. McClelland et al., *The Achievement Motive,* Appleton-Century-Crofts, Inc., New York, 1953; and David C. McClelland, *The Achieving Society,* D. Van Nostrand Company, Inc., Princeton, N.J., 1961.
   [21]For an expanded summary of the characteristics of the high achiever, see Saul W. Gellerman, *Motivation and Productivity,* American Management Association, New York, 1963, chap. 12.

shy away from the coin-collecting type of hobby which takes years to develop. Likewise, the high achievers tend to gravitate toward, or at least are more satisfied in, job careers, such as sales or certain management positions, which are frequently evaluated by specific performance criteria. On the other side of the scale, high *n Ach* persons will generally not be found, or will tend to be frustrated, in research and development or teaching vocations where performance feedback is very imprecise, vague, and long-range.

3 *Accomplishment.* High achievers find accomplishing a task intrinsically satisfying in and of itself, or they do not expect or necessarily want the accompanying material rewards. A good illustration of this characteristic is high achievers' attitude toward money. They definitely like to earn a lot of money, but not for the usual reasons of wanting money for its own sake or for the material benefits that it can buy. Rather, high n Ach people look at money as a form of feedback or measurement of how they are doing. Given the choice between a simple task with a good payoff for accomplishment and a challenging task with the same or even lower payoff for accomplishment, other things being equal, high achievers generally choose the latter.

4 *Preoccupation with the task.* Once high achievers select a goal, they tend to be totally preoccupied with the task until it is successfully completed. They cannot stand to leave a job half finished and are not satisfied with themselves until they have given maximum effort. This type of dedicated commitment often reflects on their outward personalities, which frequently have a negative effect on those who come in contact with them. High achievers often strike others as being unfriendly and "loners." They may be very quiet and may seldom brag about their accomplishments. They tend to be very realistic about their abilities and do not allow other people to get in the way of their goal accomplishments. Obviously, with this type of approach high achievers do not always get along well with other people. Typically, high achievers make excellent salespersons but seldom good sales managers.

Development of the Achievement Motive   Contrary to common belief, only about 10 percent of the population are actually high achievers. Similar to the other secondary motives, achievement seems to be developed at an early age. The child's independence training appears to be largely responsible for the development of achievement. One study empirically determined that the amount, timing, and type of independence that young children receive have the greatest impact on their later drive for achievement.[22] For instance, mothers of high achievers reported that they expected their children to obey traffic lights, entertain themselves, earn their own spending money, and choose their own clothes at a significantly younger age than did the mothers of low achievers. Another interesting finding was that mothers who gave physical rewards (hugging and kissing) for independence had sons who scored twice as high on the *n Ach* test as did the sons of mothers who did not give physical rewards for independence. An overall conclusion based on research that investigated the development of achievement is that "the relatively demanding parent who

[22]M. R. Winterbottom, "The Relation of Childhood Training in Independence to Achievement Motivation," reported in McClelland et al., *The Achievement Motive*, op. cit., pp. 297–304.

clearly instigates self-reliance in the child and who then rewards independent behavior is teaching the child a need for achievement."[23]

Achievement and Economic Development McClelland was not satisfied with just looking at the impact that achievement has on individual behavior. He broadened his research to encompass the effect that achievement motivation has on entire societies and the economic rise and fall of civilizations. His revealing studies of this broad area consistently find a positive relationship between the level of achievement motivation and the level of economic development of a given society.

Although there is a distinct time lag, a society whose populace generally exhibits high *n Ach* will experience economic growth and prosperity, whereas a society consisting of low achievers will economically decline and eventually collapse.[24] This conclusion is supported by many empirical studies. Typical was the study conducted on ancient Greece. The researchers determined the level of achievement of a given period in Greek history by examining the literature of the time. The economic activity was judged according to the areas of trade controlled by the Greeks. When the two variables were analyzed, it was found that a high level of achievement preceded a period of economic growth and a low achievement level was the forerunner of economic decline. A similar analytical approach has been applied to different periods of history and to a wide variety of societies around the world.

Achievement Motivation in Perspective The full impact of the research findings on the achievement motive is yet to be felt. Probably the fundamental question is whether a high degree of achievement motivation is of beneficial value to an individual, organization, or society. Traditionally, high achievers have been portrayed as American folk heroes. Yet, from a "normal" personality standpoint, some of their characteristics are of questionable desirability. McClelland himself makes the following observations on his dealings with high achievers over the years:

> Some psychologists think that because I've done so much on n Ach I must like the kind of people who have strong needs for achievement. I don't. I find them bores. They are not artistically sensitive. They're entrepreneurs, kind of driven—always trying to improve themselves and find a shorter route to the office or a faster way of reading their mail. . . [25]

Not only are high achievers not necessarily heroes, they also are not unique to the American middle class. McClelland shatters this myth by commenting as follows:

[23]Sanford and Wrightsman, op. cit., p. 212.
[24]McClelland, *The Achieving Society,* op. cit.
[25]"To Know Why Men Do What They Do: A Conversation with David C. McClelland and T. George Harris," *Psychology Today,* January 1971, p. 36.

No, this is neither capitalist nor white, neither Western nor middle class. The Ethiopian people of the Gurage are fabulously high in n Ach. So are some tribes of American Indians, we've found, and the Biafran, or Ibo people. . . Communist states like Poland and Russia now score very high in the achievement motive, and they seem to have passed it on to China. Why not? In Poland, for instance, plant managers work under a quota system for output that demands solutions to problems and provides very clear feedback.[26]

Under current societal values in this country, there seems little doubt that everyone needs a degree of achievement motivation to get along, but how much? The question becomes greatly amplified when applied to organizations and societies. Is *n Ach* the breakthrough for attaining objectives and economic development? Can an underdeveloped organization or entire country train its people to have high *n Ach* and become prosperous?

From psychoanalytic influence it has been generally assumed that motives such as achievement are developed only in childhood and, once formed, nothing much can be done to alter them. Some very interesting preliminary studies by McClelland have begun to undermine this traditional assumption. For the past decade McClelland and his research group have been attempting to develop achievement motivation in adults. Their achievement development course has four primary goals:

    1 To teach participants how to think, talk and act like a person with high achievement.
    2 To stimulate participants to set higher, but carefully planned and realistic work goals for themselves over the next two years.
    3 To give the participants knowledge about themselves.
    4 To create a group esprit de corps from learning about each other's hopes and fears, successes and failures, and from going through an emotional experience together, away from everyday life, in a retreat setting.[27]

So far, McClelland has given the achievement course to executives in a large American firm and in several Mexican firms, and to businessmen in India. Except for one Mexican case, it was demonstrated statistically that, after two years, those who had taken the achievement course made more money, were promoted faster, and expanded their businesses faster than comparable people who had not taken the course or who had taken some other management course.[28] For example, in India he subjected a group of fifty-two entrepreneurs to the concentrated achievement-motivation course. Follow-ups were conducted over the next six to ten months on those who had completed the training. Two-thirds of the subjects were unusually active in the post-training period. Some had actually started new businesses and others had investigated new

[26]Ibid., p. 70.
[27]David C. McClelland, "That Urge to Achieve," *Think*, November–December 1966, p. 22.
[28]Ibid.

product lines, increased profits, or expanded their present organizations. For example, one banker became less conservative in his money-lending practices, and the owner of a small radio store opened a paint and varnish factory after completion of the training program. After a detailed analysis, McClelland concluded that the course appeared to have doubled the natural rate of unusual entrepreneurial activity in the group studied.[29]

The preliminary results obtained by McClelland seem to indicate that achievement training can potentially play a future role in getting disadvantaged Americans as well as underdeveloped countries into the mainstream of modern affluency. The potential for organization development also appears to be great. Whether such achievement training is right or wrong, good or bad, will be decided, it is hoped, by the persons affected.

The Affiliation Motive

Affiliation plays a very complex but vital role in human behavior. Sometimes affiliation is equated with social motives and/or group dynamics. As presented here, the affiliation motive is not so broad as is implied by the definition of social motives nor so comprehensive or complex as is implied by the definition of group dynamics. The study of affiliation is further complicated by the fact that some behavioral scientists believe that it is an unlearned motive. Their position is partially supported by the work of Harlow on the affection motive in monkeys. Few would debate that "some form of social contact appears necessary for the normal physical and personality development of the human infant; and total isolation is virtually always an intolerable situation for the human adult—even when physical needs are provided for."[30]

Autobiographical accounts of hermits, prisoners, and castaways support this conclusion on the importance of social interaction. The following pattern evolves from the reports of persons who have been deprived of other human beings:

1   The "pain" of isolation increases with time, but then decreases sharply.
2   Those who are isolated tend to think, dream, and occasionally hallucinate about people.
3   Isolates who keep occupied with distracting activities seem to suffer less than those who do not.[31]

Despite the evidence which suggests the inherent nature of affiliation, the majority of psychologists still classify the motive as one of the important secondary drives. In the few isolated cases where children have been taken away from human contact, for example, by being confined in an attic, the

[29]David C. McClelland, "Achievement Motivation Can Be Developed," *Harvard Business Review*, November–December 1965, p. 20.
[30]Berelson and Steiner, op. cit., p. 252.
[31]Stanley Schachter, *The Psychology of Affiliation*, Stanford University Press, Stanford, Calif., 1959, pp. 6–8.

children do not express an affiliation drive. Such cases point to the fact that affiliation is probably learned; but because it is normally so intense, it appears on the surface to be an inherent human motive.

Research on the Affiliation Motive   In contrast to achievement, not much research has been done directly on affiliation. Although affiliation was formally recognized at the beginning of the century (for example, Trotter specifically mentioned gregariousness along with self-preservation, nutrition, and sex as the four most important instincts in the life of man[32]), not much is really known about it even today. About the most promising research effort so far has been conducted by Stanley Schachter. Gellerman comments on the Schachter research as follows:

> Schachter has pursued the affiliation motive further toward its origins than anyone else; yet it is clear that he has made only a beginning. In many ways his research raises more questions than it answers. Even so seemingly commonplace a trait as wanting to be with someone else turns out, on analysis, to be quite complex.[33]

"Misery Loves Company"   The best-known, most interesting, and potentially most significant research by Schachter was his study of the relationship between anxiety (fear) and affiliation.[34] The study was built around testing the folk hypothesis that misery loves company. Undergraduate females who did not know one another were used as subjects in the study. The experiment began by bringing Dr. Zilstein, a sinister-looking, stereotyped doctor from a horror movie, to the front of the room to talk to the women subjects. Behind the doctor was a conglomeration of devices containing many electric wires, knobs, and switches. The weird-looking doctor explained to the wide-eyed women that they were going to participate in an experiment that would test the effects of electric shock on human subjects. The terrified subjects found little consolation in the doctor's parting comment that although the shock would be quite painful, no permanent damage would result.

The purpose of the preliminaries in the experiment was to create fear in the subjects. Told that there would be a short delay while the electrical equipment was set up, the frightened subjects were asked whether they perferred to wait with the other subjects or by themselves. The results were overwhelmingly that the subjects would rather wait with the others. On the other hand, a control group of subjects who were not in the fear condition preferred to wait alone. Such a result substantiates that misery really does love company.

"Misery Loves Company That Is Miserable"   An important refinement of the misery study was then to divide the experimentally created miserable

[32]W. Trotter, *Instincts of the Herd in Peace and War,* The Macmillan Company, New York, 1916. His views were published in essay form ten years before publication of the book.
[33]Gellerman, op. cit., p. 115.
[34]Schachter, op. cit.

subjects into two groups. One of the anxious groups was asked whether they preferred to wait alone or with other subjects in the same state, i.e., those who were also going to participate in the shock experiment. The other group of miserable subjects was given the choice of waiting alone or with some coeds in a different state, i.e., students who were waiting out in the hall to talk with their advisors. Some interesting results came out of this second phase of the study. A majority of the subjects in the first group chose to wait with other subjects in their same state. In contrast, not a single subject in the second group chose to wait with students not in their same state. This finding adds a qualification to the adage. Misery doesn't love just any company, misery only loves company that is miserable.

Analysis of Results   Schachter suggests several possible explanations for the results of his misery study. Briefly, the logical reasons are as follows:

1   *Escape.* The subjects may have wanted to band together to formulate a plan for getting out of the terrifying experiment, the idea being that there is strength in numbers.

2   *Indirect anxiety reduction.* Possibly the subjects just wanted to get together to talk about the weather or whatever to get their minds off the upcoming ordeal.

3   *Cognitive clarity.* The subjects perhaps wanted to clarify in their own minds what the experiment was all about. For example, they may have wanted to make sure that Dr. Zilstein said that the shock would be extremely painful.

4   *Self-evaluation or social comparison.* It is possible that the subjects just wanted to see if everyone else in the experiment was as scared as they were. The subjects wanted to evaluate their own opinions and feelings.

5   *Direct anxiety reduction.* A final possibility is that the subjects merely wanted another miserable human being with them. They didn't have to talk about escape, the weather, or what the experiment was about. Under this explanation, they didn't even have to look at the other subjects as they do in social comparison.

Each of the above statements represents a plausible explanation for the results of the misery study. However, to determine the best explanation more scientifically, Schachter carried his study one more step. When asking the subjects whether they wanted to wait alone or with others in the same state, he added a further choice variation. With some of the subjects he stipulated that they could communicate while waiting, and to others he stated that they could not communicate while waiting. The result of this phase was that being able to communicate or not made little difference to the subjects. The subjects did not care one way or the other if they could talk. Although they definitely wanted to wait with miserable counterparts, they did not necessarily want to talk and exchange ideas. This finding makes it possible to rule out escape, indirect anxiety reduction, and cognitive clarity as explanations for "Misery loves company that is miserable." Each of these three goals requires verbal communication, but social comparison and direct anxiety reduction do not. Social comparison requires nonverbal communication, and direct anxiety reduction calls for no form of communication in the usual sense. The mere presence of another human being is all that is necessary for direct anxiety reduction. This is what Schachter thinks is the best explanation of why the subjects had an intense drive to affiliate.

Implications of the Schachter Study　　Relatively lengthy treatment has been given to Schachter's study because it contains some interesting implications for certain kinds of human behavior. For example, the misery study provides a scientifically based explanation of why people tend to group together during any kind of crisis situation. Another example is the problem faced by a military leader in combat. When his men come under enemy fire, there is always a tendency for them to bunch up, a formation that of course compounds the danger. The misery study also has direct implications for understanding human behavior in organizations. It provides some insights as to why workers join unions and contributes to the understanding of group dynamics. To reduce their anxieties, which may have been created by a feeling of insecurity or a dead-end job, workers may be motivated to join with others who are in a similar miserable situation.

To draw too many generalizations from Schachter's research is at this time unwarranted. As the Gellerman quote noted, Schachter probably raises more questions than he answers. For example, studies relating affiliation with hunger come up with more complicated results. Affiliation tends to correlate positively with hunger up to a point, but then to taper off. Researchers have also found that anxiety created by embarrassing and normally inhibiting activities tends to decrease the affiliation motive. There are enough of these kinds of exceptions to stop one from generalizing that any strong drive will increase the affiliation drive. Although Schachter has made a good start and provides some interesting insights for human and organizational behavior, much more research on affiliation is badly needed. Chapter 15, on group dynamics, will provide further insights into the social interaction phenomena.

The Security Motive

Security is a very intense motive in a fast-paced, highly technological society such as is found in modern America. The typical American can be insecure in a number of areas of everyday living—being liable for payments on a car or house; keeping the lover's or spouse's affections; staying in school; getting into graduate, law, or medical school; or obtaining and/or keeping a good job. Job insecurity, in particular, has a great effect on organizational behavior.

On the surface, security appears to be much simpler than other secondary motives, for it is largely based on fear and is avoidance-oriented. Morgan and King note: "The feeling involves being able to hold on to what one has, being sure that one will be able to fare as well in the future as in the past. Conversely, insecurity is a haunting fear that 'things may not last,' that one may lose what he now has."[35] Briefly, humans have a learned security motive to protect themselves from the contingencies of life and actively try to avoid situations which would prevent them from satisfying their primary, general, and secondary motives.

Complexity of the Security Motive In reality, security is much more complex than it appears on the surface. There is the simple, conscious security motive described above, but there seems also to be another type of security motive that is much more complicated and difficult to identify. Gellerman notes that this special drive for security is largely unconscious but that it greatly influences the behavior of many people. He explains that "the hazards against which they seek to protect themselves are vague, pervasive, and fearsome; usually they have an underlying conviction that the environment is at best capricious and at worst malicious."[36] The simple, conscious security motive is typically taken care of by insurance programs, personal savings plans, and fringe benefits at the place of employment. On the other hand, the more complex, unconscious security motive is not so easily fulfilled but may have a greater and more intense impact on human behavior. Although much attention has been given to the simple security motive, much more understanding is needed on the role of the unconscious, complex security motive.

Development of the Security Motive Similar to the other secondary motives, the desire for security seems to be largely developed in childhood. The intensity of the security motive in adults largely depends upon their experiences as children. For example, people who have identified with security-conscious parents as children may carry their concern over to adulthood; or, as children, people may have been reared in an economic and social atmosphere of unpredictability which makes them very security-conscious as adults. Gellerman notes that a person whose security motive developed as a result of the latter childhood circumstances is apt to be an adult who is very likable, noncompetitive, patient, and slow to complain. "Other people tend not to expect too much of him and therefore seldom find fault with his work, and—what is more important—he is rather pleasant to have around."[37]

Another, essentially opposite example of security development is the child who experiences overprotection and overindulgence. Under these conditions, the child grows up thinking that the world is a very nice place in which to live. This person feels that someone will grant every wish the person makes and that no hard work or initiative is required. As an adult, this person tends to have an air of sublime assurance and an attitude of unruffled calm regardless of the pressure.[38]

Both the child who experiences the world as uncontrollable and the one

[35]Morgan and King, op. cit., p. 234.
[36]Gellerman, op. cit., p. 156.
[37]Ibid., p. 157.
[38]Ibid., pp. 157–158.

who experiences it as benevolent will tend to have an intense security motive as an adult. These security-conscious individuals are most satisfied with, and tend to gravitate into, jobs which are secure, pleasant, and predictable. This type of analysis can contribute much to the better understanding of individual differences in organizational behavior.

The Status Motive

Along with security, the status or prestige motive is especially relevant to a dynamic society. The modern affluent person is often pictured as a status seeker. Such a person is accused of being more concerned with material symbols of status—the right clothes, the right car, the right address, and a swimming pool or an executive sandbox—than with the more basic, human-oriented values in life. Although the symbols of status are inferred to be a unique by-product of modern society, the fact is that status has been in existence since there have been two or more persons on the earth.

Determination of Status   Status can be simply defined as the *relative* ranking that a person holds in a group, organization, or society. Under this definition, any time two or more persons are together, a status hierarchy will evolve, even if it is an equal status. The symbols of status only attempt to represent the relative ranking of the person in the status hierarchy. The definition also corrects the common misconception that *status* means *high status*. Everyone has status, but it may be high or low depending on how the relative positions are ranked.

How are status positions determined? Why is one person ranked higher or lower than another? Secord and Backman say that status evolves from the capacity of people for rewarding those with whom they interact, the extent to which they are seen as receiving rewards, the types of costs they incur, and their investments (past history or background).[39] The sociologist Talcott Parsons summarizes several sources of status:[40]

1   *Membership in a family.* In previous eras, an individual could be born into a high-status (nobility) or low-status (serfs) family. Today, certain family names may still confer status in a locale but this is becoming less important than it once was.

2   *Personal qualities.* Physical characteristics (handsome or beautiful versus ugly) and personality may confer status. Age, race, and sex may also be a determinant of status.

3   *Achievements.* Educational attainment (M.D. or Ph.D.) or professional accomplishments (C.P.A. or C.L.U.) may be a source of status. A worker's skill or a person's athletic ability may also confer status.

4   *Possessions.* Material wealth such as a lot of money, real estate, or a

[39]Paul F. Secord and Carl W. Backman, *Social Psychology*, 2d ed., McGraw-Hill Book Company, New York, 1974, pp. 274–276.

[40]Talcott Parsons, *Essays in Sociological Theory*, rev. ed., The Free Press, New York, 1964, pp. 75–76.

yacht may be a source of status. These possessions can become status symbols.

  5 *Authority and power.* Those who hold formal positions of authority and power in a company or a civic club or a crime ring may be given more status than those below them.

Each of these above factors is hedged by saying they "may contribute to status" because, in the final analysis, status determination will always depend upon the prevailing cultural values and societal roles.

  Status-determining factors generally have quite different meanings depending on the values of a particular culture. An example of the impact of cultural values on status is the personal qualities of people. In some cultures, the older persons are, the higher is their status. However, in other cultures, once a person reaches a certain age, the status goes downhill with age. It must be remembered that such cultural values are highly volatile and change with the times and circumstances. There are also many subcultures in a given society which may have values different from the prevailing values of society at large and correspondingly different statuses.

  Cultural roles have a big impact on status determination as well as on values. As indicated in Chapter 2's discussion of sociological concepts, a role represents expectations of a position. A level of status is accorded to each role in a society. Status is a significant input but is also inferred from roles such as those of parent or child, student or teacher, general or private, and manager or worker.

  Development of the Status Motive   The drive to attain higher status is fairly intense for most people. Like the other secondary motives, it seems to start developing at an early age. A frequent misconception is that the status-conscious person is always the Horatio Alger type who comes from a poverty-stricken background. Gellerman tries to dispel this notion by claiming that "it is not poverty itself but the individual's sense of justice—of whether his status is in line with what he deserves—that determines whether he will accept the status he was born to."[41] In other words, a person's specific background is important only to the extent that it affects the expectations of what his status should be. If people do not accept their present status, they will have a strong drive to attain a higher one and all the accompanying symbols that go with it.

  Relation to Level of Aspiration   The status motive is closely linked to what psychologists call the level of aspiration. This is the level at which people set their sights, their goals. For the high jumper in track and field it may be a 7-foot jump, or for the aspiring young executive it may be a salary of $50,000 per year. All the secondary motives have an input into what this level of aspiration will be, and the person's successes and failures will tend to raise or lower it. The level of aspiration can be translated into status levels. The 7-foot-high jumpers

[41]Gellerman, op. cit., p. 153.

are a very high-status group among track and field athletes and their followers, and the same holds true for $50,000-a-year young executives.

SUMMARY

Like perception and learning, motivation is a basic psychological process. The key to understanding motivation lies in the need, drive, goal sequence, or cycle. The motivation process involves needs (deprivations) which set drives in motion (deprivations with direction) to accomplish goals (anything which alleviates a need and reduces a drive). The drives or motives may be classified into primary, general, and secondary categories. The primary motives are unlearned and physiologically based. Common primary motives include hunger, thirst, sleep, avoidance of pain, sex, and maternal concern. The general motives are also unlearned but are not physiologically based. Competence, curiosity, manipulation, activity, and affection are examples of general motives. Secondary motives are learned and are most relevant to the study of organizational behavior. The needs for power, achievement, affiliation, security, and status are major motivating forces in the behavior of organizational participants.

QUESTIONS FOR DISCUSSION AND REVIEW

1   Do humans have instincts? Explain your answer.
2   Briefly define the three classifications of motives. What are some examples of each?
3   What are the characteristics of high achievers?
4   What relevance does Schachter's research on the affiliation motive have for the study of organizational behavior?
5   How is status defined? What are some determinants of status?

CASE: STAR SALESPERSON

While growing up, Jerry Slate had always been rewarded by his parents for showing independence. When he started school, he was successful both inside and outside the classroom. He was always striving to be things like traffic patrolperson and lunch room monitor in grade school. Yet, his mother worried about him because he never got along well with other children his own age. When confronted with this, Jerry would reply, "Well, I don't need them. Besides, they can't do things as well as I can. I don't have time to help them, I'm too busy improving myself." Jerry went on to do very well in both high school and college. He was always at or near the top of his class academically and was a very good long-distance runner for the track teams in high school and college. In college he shied away from joining a fraternity and lived in an apartment by himself. Upon graduation he went to work for a large insurance company and soon became one of their top salespersons. Jerry was very proud of the fact that he had been one of the top five salespersons in six out of the eight years he was with the company.

At the home office of the insurance company, the executive committee which was in charge of making major personnel appointments was discussing the upcoming vacancy of the sales manager's job for the Midwest region. The personnel manager gave the following report:

> Gentlemen and women, as you know, the Midwest region is lagging far behind our other regions as far as sales goes. We need a highly motivated person to take that situation over and turn it around. After an extensive screening process, I am recommending Jerry Slate be offered this sales manager position. As you know, Jerry has an outstanding record with the company and is highly motivated. I think he is the person for the job.

1   Do you agree with the personnel manager? Why or why not?

2   Based on Jerry's background, what motives discussed in the chapter would appear to be very intense in Jerry? What motive(s) would appear to be very low? Give specific evidence from the case for each motive.

3   What type of motivation is desirable for sales positions? What type of motivation is desirable for managerial positions?

SELECTED REFERENCES

Berelson, Bernard, and Gary S. Steiner: *Human Behavior,* Harcourt, Brace & World, Inc., New York, 1964, chap. 6.

Gellerman, Saul W.: *Motivation and Productivity,* American Management Association, New York, 1963, part II.

Hilgard, Ernest R., and Richard D. Atkinson: *Introduction to Psychology,* 4th ed., Harcourt, Brace & World, Inc., New York, 1967, chaps. 5 and 6.

Kimble, Gregory A., and Norman Garmezy: *Principles of General Psychology,* 3d ed., The Ronald Press Company, New York, 1968, chap. 13.

Lawler, Edward E., III: *Motivation in Work Organizations,* Brooks/Cole Publishing Company, Monterey, Calif., 1973.

McClelland, David C.: *The Achieving Society,* D. Van Nostrand Company, Inc., Princeton, N. J., 1961.

Schacter, Stanley: *The Psychology of Affiliation,* Stanford University Press, Stanford, Calif., 1959.

Varga, Koroly: "n Achievement, n Power and Effectiveness of Research and Development," *Human Relations,* August 1975, pp. 571–590.

Chapter 14

Personality Development and Theory

The three preceding chapters gave attention to the psychological processes of perception, learning, and motivation. This chapter puts the processes together into a *whole person* system. Such a psychological system can be called *personality*. The human being operates as a whole, not as a series of distinct parts. To use a very simple analogy: The various psychological processes may be thought of as pieces of a jigsaw puzzle and personality as the completed puzzle picture. However, as D. E. James warns,

> Analogies are often misleading and many psychologists would say that the jig-saw concept may be inadequate. Perhaps it is better to consider the individual aspects of a person's make-up as bricks and personality as the whole house, built of bricks but held together with cement.[1]

As indicated in the quote, personality is probably more accurately portrayed as something over and above the psychological building blocks. Contrary to mathematical logic, personality seems to be a case where the whole is greater than the sum of the parts. This, of course, has implications from gestalt psychology discussed in Chapter 2 and the synergistic effect in systems analysis discussed in Chapter 7.

[1]D. E. James, *Introduction to Psychology*, Constable & Co., Ltd., London, 1968, p. 219.

The primary purpose of this chapter is to develop a basic understanding of human personality. Such understanding is vital to the study and analysis of organizational behavior. Similar to the chapter on motivation, this chapter offers only a few *direct* applications of its content to organization and management. It attempts to be more education- than applications-oriented, and it serves as the natural conceptual conclusion to the human behavior part of the book.

The first section of the chapter defines and clarifies the concept of personality. The next section is devoted to personality development and includes discussions of some well-known stages of development formulated by Freud, Erikson, Piaget, and Argyris. The third section breaks down the determinants of personality development into biological, cultural, family, and situational categories. Some of the more important research findings on the determinants of personality are included. The last section gives a brief overview of the major theories of personality structure. Particular attention is given to the type, trait, and self theories.

THE DEFINITIONAL CONTROVERSY

About forty years ago Gordon Allport found no less than fifty different definitions of personality. He categorized these definitions into five areas and labeled them as follows:

1 *Omnibus.* These definitions view personality as the "sum-total," "aggregate," or "constellation" of properties or qualities.

2 *Integrative and configurational.* Under this view of personality, the organization of personal attributes is stressed.

3 *Hierarchical.* These definitions specify the various levels of integration or organization of personality.

4 *Adjustment.* This view emphasizes the adjustment (adaptation, survival, and evolution) of the person to the environment.

5 *Distinctiveness.* The definitions for this category stress the uniqueness of each personality.[2]

Drawing from these five approaches, Allport offered his own definition of personality: "Personality is the dynamic organization within the individual of those psychophysical systems that determine his unique adjustments to his environment."[3]

Unfortunately, Allport's analysis did not lead to universal agreement on the meaning of personality. Much of the controversy can be attributed to the fact that laypersons and behavioral scientists define personality from different perspectives. Laypersons tend to equate personality with social success (good, popular, or "a lot of personality") and to describe personality by a single

[2]Gordon W. Allport, *Personality,* Henry Holt and Company, Inc., New York, 1937, pp. 43–47.
[3]Ibid., p. 48.

dominant characteristic (strong, weak, shy, or polite). When it is realized that more than 4,000 words in the dictionary can be used to describe personality this way, the definitional problem becomes staggering. The academicians, on the other hand, take a different perspective. For example, the descriptive-adjective approach used by the layperson plays only a small part. However, scholars cannot agree on a definition of personality because they operate from different theoretical bases. As long as there is disagreement on the theory of personality, there will be disagreement on its definition.

THE COMPREHENSIVE MEANING OF PERSONALITY

The word *personality* has an interesting derivation. It can be traced to the Latin words *per sonare*, which translates as "to speak through." The Latin term was used to denote the masks worn by actors in ancient Greece and Rome. This Latin meaning is particularly relevant to the contemporary analysis of personality. Common usage of the word *personality* emphasizes the role which the person (actor) displays to the public. The academic definitions of personality are concerned more directly with the person (actor) than with the role played. Probably the most meaningful approach would be to include both the person and the role, as Floyd Ruch does in his definition. He states that the human personality includes:

1 External appearance and behavior or social stimulus value
2 Inner awareness of self as a permanent organizing force
3 The particular pattern or organization of measurable traits, both "inner" and "outer"[4]

More simply, in this book *personality* will mean how people affect others, how they understand and view themselves, and their pattern of inner and outer measurable traits.

How people affect others primarily depends upon their external appearance (height, weight, facial features, color, and other physical aspects) and behavior (vulgar, friendly, courteous, and so on). The role concept is closely tied to these aspects of personality. A very large, friendly worker will have a different impact on other people than a very small, courteous manager. Obviously, all the ramifications of perception enter into these aspects of personality.

People's attempts to understand themselves are called the *self-concept* in personality theory. The self is a unique product of many interacting parts and may be thought of as the personality viewed from within. The last part of the chapter analyzes this self-concept in more detail.

The pattern of measurable traits adds an important dimension to the understanding of the human personality. As explained by Ruch, the traits are

[4]Floyd L. Ruch, *Psychology and Life*, 6th ed., Scott, Foresman and Company, Chicago, 1963, p. 353.

... *dimensions* of personality because they can be measured on a mathematical *continuum*. . . . The basic problem in describing a given individual is not deciding which traits he does or does not possess, but finding *how much* of each trait he possesses and, equally important, how the traits *interact* in the total pattern of his personality.[5]

The trait theories of personality are covered in the last part of the chapter.

In summary, the personality is a very diverse and complex psychological concept. It incorporates all the psychological processes studied so far and more. As defined above, personality is concerned with external appearance and behavior, self, and measurable traits. Probably the best concluding statement on the meaning of personality was given by Kluckhohn and Murray when they said that to some extent, a person's personality is like all other people, like some other people, like no other people.[6]

THE DEVELOPMENT OF PERSONALITY

Study of and research on the development of personality is one of the most rapidly growing areas in behavioral analysis. It is concerned with "the processes by which the child gradually acquires patterns of overt behavior, thinking, problem solving, and above all, the motives, emotions, conflicts, and ways of coping with conflicts that will go to make up his adult personality."[7]

The development approach is actually a form of personality theory but, in contrast to most personality theories, it is highly research-oriented. Modern developmental psychology does not get into the argument of heredity versus environment or maturation versus learning. As previously pointed out, the human system consists of both physiological *and* psychological interacting parts. Therefore, heredity, environment, maturation, and learning *all* contribute to the human personality.

The study of personality development can be divided into two separate but closely allied approaches. One approach attempts to identify specific physiological and psychological stages that occur in the development of the human personality. The other approach has tried to identify the important determinants of personality. The "stages" approach has been theoretical in nature, whereas the search for major determinants has been more empirical.

STAGES OF PERSONALITY DEVELOPMENT

There are many well-known stage theories of personality development. Most deal with psychosocial development rather than directly with personality development. As with most aspects of personality, there is little agreement

[5]Ibid., p. 354.

[6]Clyde Kluckhohn and H. A. Murray, "Personality Formation: The Determinants," in C. Kluckhohn and H. A. Murray (eds.), *Personality*, Alfred A. Knopf, Inc., New York, 1948, p. 35.

[7]Jerome Kagan and Ernest Havemann, *Psychology*, Harcourt, Brace & World, Inc., New York, 1968, p. 536.

among psychologists about the exact stages. In fact, a number of today's psychologists contend there are *no* identifiable stages. They argue that personality development is a continuous process and that the sequence is based solely upon the learning opportunities available. The more prevalent view that does support stages in personality development is generally explained in the following manner: ". . . socialization is not a haphazard accumulation of bits of behavior but entails, instead, some orderly development. That is true at least to the degree that some complex social behavior patterns are sequential."[8]

Freudian Stages

Once again, Sigmund Freud is found in the vanguard. Although the analysis of stages of development can be traced as far back as the ancient Greeks, it was Freud who first formulated a meaningful stage theory. He felt that a child progresses through four identifiable stages of psychosexual development: oral, anal, phallic or Oedipus, and genital. These stages were believed to be the main driving forces behind the personality.

To most persons, the Freudian stages often seem silly or even bizarre. In addition, modern psychologists are generally not in agreement with the Freudian stages. However, they do give Freud credit for providing some valuable insights and for initiating the meaningful study of personality development. The major disagreement centers on Freud's terminology and the degree to which he carried the stages rather than on the possibility that he was totally wrong. For example, with regard to Freud's choice of words, Mischel notes:

> Without having at hand a suitable set of learning concepts and terms for personality development, Freud relied on his own preference for a "body language": he preferred to say "oral" rather than "dependent," "anal" rather than "compulsive," "genital" rather than "mature."[9]

Unfortunately, when one assesses Freud's contribution to the understanding of personality development, the sexually oriented terms seem to overshadow the underlying concepts.

Neo-Freudian Stages

Besides the controversy on terminology, the major disagreement with Freud is the heavy emphasis he placed on the sexual and biological factors in the developing personality. This criticism seems to be more legitimate. Among others, Erik Erikson felt that relatively more attention should be given to the social rather than the sexual adaptations of the individual. He identified eight psychosocial stages:[10]

---

[8]Walter Mischel, *Introduction to Personality*, Holt, Rinehart and Winston, Inc., New York, 1971, p. 227.

[9]Ibid., p. 43.

[10]Erik Erikson, *Childhood and Society*, 2d ed., W. W. Norton & Company, Inc., New York, 1963. Also see Mischel, op. cit., pp. 39–41.

Stage of development	Age
1. Mouth and senses	0–1
2. Eliminative organs and musculature	1–2
3. Locomotion and the genitals	3–5
4. Latency	6–puberty
5. Puberty and adolescence	
6. Early adulthood	
7. Young and middle adulthood	
8. Mature adulthood	

Erikson asserted that a psychosocial crisis occurs within each of the above stages, and in order to have a normal, fulfilling personality, each crisis should be optimally resolved. Probably the most widely known crisis identified by Erikson is the identity experience of adolescents. He believes that the optimum outcome of this teen-age crisis is the reintegration of past with present goals. For purposes of the study of organizational behavior, the most relevant stage is that of the young and middle adult. Typical organizational participants in the midst of their productive years are in this stage. In Erikson's thinking, the crisis that this person faces is one of generativity versus stagnation. The best outcome for personality fulfillment would be an attitude of *production* and concern with the world and future generations. Put another way, according to Erikson young and middle-aged adults who solve their psychosocial crises by being productive will develop the healthiest personalities. The employing organization should permit and take advantage of this productivity.

Erikson's approach is representative of the neo-Freudian stage theories. As indicated by the stages he identified, he did not totally reject, but rather changed the emphasis of, modified, and extended, the ideas of Freud.

Cognitive Stages

The cognitive stage theories of personality development make a more complete break with Freudian ideas. The work of the Swiss psychologist Jean Piaget probably best represents the cognitive approach.[11] In contrast to Freud, Piaget was convinced that the conscious, not the instinctive unconscious, was the critical variable in the developing personality. It is sometimes said that whereas Freud discovered the unconscious, Piaget "discovered" the conscious. In addition to the break from Freud, Piaget is often credited with being the first to offer a successful challenge to the prevailing behaviorist perspective in modern American child psychology. He based his theories and extensive research (thirty books and 100 articles) on children subjects, whereas the behaviorists seldom used children as subjects in their research. He felt that the behavioristic approach to learning was too narrow and superficial. He felt that learning was more broadly concerned with development and would only occur when the child had the necessary cognitive structures for assimilating new information.

[11]Jean Piaget, "The General Problems of the Psychobiological Development of the Child," in J. M. Tanner and Bärbel Inhelder (eds.), *Discussions on Child Development,* International Universities Press, Inc., New York, 1960, pp. 3–27.

Piaget identified four major stages of cognitive or intellectual development:

Stage of development   **Age**
1. Sensorimotor   0–2
2. Preoperational   2–7
3. Concrete operational   7–11
4. Formal operational   11 and above

In the initial stage, infants acquire knowledge or cognition about their surrounding environment through simple, sensorimotor manipulations. When only a few months old, children begin to repeat acts which produce reward or some other interesting outcome. As children approach two years of age, they start to solve simple problems and to realize they are in a world of objects separate from themselves that they can control and affect. Thus, at about age two children's intellectual capacities shift from a strict sensorimotor level to more of a conceptual or operational level. It is during this preoperational stage that children begin to use symbols and language in their thought processes and to develop a concept of class or category.

At about age seven children enter the concrete stage of cognitive development. They are now able to understand concepts such as conservation, which can be simply demonstrated as follows:

> Water is first poured into two identical, flat containers. Children in either the preoperational or concrete-operational stages will readily acknowledge that the two containers contain equal amounts of water. Then the water in one of the flat containers is poured into a tall container *in front of the child.* When asked which container has more water, children in the preoperational stage will generally say the tall container, but children who are in the concrete stage will say that there is the same amount of water in both the flat and tall containers.

This demonstration indicates that only children who have reached the concrete stage of operational development will understand concepts such as conservation (the mass of an object remains constant no matter how much the form changes).

Empirical research has generally given support to the stages identified by Piaget. Recent studies have implied that certain social and political attitudes may be dependent upon the stage of cognitive development. Such findings have significant implications for organizational behavior. For instance, determining organizational participants' stages of cognitive development may greatly help in explaining their behavior.

The final formal operational stage of cognitive development is most relevant to the study of organizational behavior. This is the developmental stage reached by most of the mature, intelligent adults found in today's organizations. Organizational participants in this stage of conceptualization need not depend upon the manipulation of concrete objects. They have the capacity symbolically to analyze, reason, imagine, and evaluate events. However, it must be remembered that the cognitive stages cannot be totally equated with personality stages any more than can Freud's psychosexual stages. Both the cognitive and psychosexual stage theories only partially contribute to the understanding of the complex human personality.

IMMATURITY TO MATURITY

In a departure from the strict stage approach, Chris Argyris has identified specific dimensions of the human personality as it develops. Argyris proposes that the human personality, rather than going through precise stages, progresses along a continuum from immaturity as an infant to maturity as an adult. However, at any age, people can have their degree of development plotted according to the seven dimensions shown in Figure 14-1.

Argyris carefully points out that the model below does not imply that all persons reach or strive for all dimensions on the mature end of the continuum. He further explains that:

 1 The seven dimensions represent only one aspect of the total personality. Much also depends upon the individual's perception, self-concept, and adaptation and adjustment.
 2 The seven dimensions continually change in degree from the infant to the adult end of the continuum.
 3 The model, being only a construct, cannot predict specific behavior. However, it does provide a method of describing and measuring the growth of any individual in the culture.
 4 The seven dimensions are based upon latent characteristics of the personality which may be quite different from the observable behavior.[12]

In contrast to the stage theories of Freud, Erikson, and Piaget, Argyris's immaturity-maturity model of personality is specifically directed to the study and analysis of organizational behavior. He assumes that the personalities of

[12]Chris Argyris, *Personality and Organization*, Harper & Brothers, New York, 1957, pp. 51–53.

Figure 14-1 The Immaturity-Maturity Continuum

IMMATURITY CHARACTERISTICS	MATURITY CHARACTERISTICS
Passivity————————————→	Activity
Dependence————————————→	Independence
Few ways of behaving————————→	Diverse behavior
Shallow interests ————————————→	Deep interests
Short-time perspective————————→	Long-time perspective
Subordinate position————————————→	Superordinate position
Lack of self-awareness————————→	Self-awareness and control

Source: Adapted from Chris Argyris, *Personality and Organization*, Harper & Brothers, New York, 1957, p. 50.

organizational employees can be generally described by the mature end of the continuum. This being the case, in order to obtain full expression of their personalities, the formal organization should allow for activity rather than passivity, independence rather than dependence, long- rather than short-time perspective, occupation of a position higher than that of peers, and expression of deep, important abilities.[13] Argyris argues that too often the exact opposite occurs. The mature organizational participant becomes frustrated, anxious, and in conflict with the modern formal organization. In other words, Argyris sees a basic incongruence between the needs of the mature personality and the nature of the formal organization. This incongruency hypothesis has been mentioned in earlier chapters and will be expanded upon in the discussion of conflict in Chapter 16.

MAJOR DETERMINANTS OF PERSONALITY

What determines personality? Of all the complexities and unanswered questions in the study of human behavior, this question may be the most difficult. The problem lies in the fact that the psychological processes that have been discussed so far in the book, plus many other variables, *all* contribute to personality. However, for ease of study and analysis, the determinants of personality can perhaps best be summarized into four broad categories: biological, cultural, family, and situational.

Biological Contributions

The study of the biological contributions to personality can be divided into several major approaches: heredity, the brain, biofeedback, and physical stature.

The Role of Heredity   The impact of heredity on the human personality is a very active but still unsettled area of study. One problem is that geneticists face a major obstacle in scientifically gathering information on the human being. Animal scientists can conduct highly controlled breeding experiments but geneticists studying human heredity cannot. Through research on animals, it has been clearly shown that both physical and psychological characteristics can be transmitted through heredity.[14] However, in the case of humans, who cannot be subjected to the necessary controls, the evidence is much less conclusive. Although studies of twins permit some control over the critical variables, they have generally proved to be inadequate.[15] Yet, despite these problems, with the recent breakthroughs in genetics, e.g., discovery of the double-helix model of DNA, there are potential ways of altering and controlling behaviors. This is called *genetic engineering.* Genetics experts feel that some

[13]Ibid., p. 53.
[14]Louis Kaplan, *Foundations of Human Behavior,* Harper & Row, Publishers, Incorporated, New York, 1965, p. 24.
[15]Ibid., pp. 25–26.

human behavior is at least partly affected by heredity. For example, Charles Shaw lists such items as strength of sex drive, aggressiveness, sensitivity, verbal and mathematical abilities, musical ability, the craving for alcohol and drugs, and intelligence as being at least partly determined by genetic endowment.[16] Especially the impact of heredity on intelligence has created much controversy. The *Wall Street Journal* reported that the heredity versus environmental impact on IQ is "the most furious controversy to rock the educational world since the days of John Dewey 70 years ago."[17] Geneticists have been, joined by some educational psychologists such as Arthur Jensen in claiming that intelligence is largely inherited. This, of course, has implications for racial differences, which adds emotional fuel to the controversy. The major issue of the controversy is how intelligence is measured. Until this is fully answered, the controversy and emotional debates will continue. In the meantime, there seems little doubt that the role of heredity in behavior will receive increased attention in the coming years.

The Role of the Brain   The second biological approach is to concentrate on the role that the brain plays in personality. Similar to the geneticists, the physiologists have been unable to supply precise information on the contributions of the brain, but also, as in genetics, some promising inroads are being made. The most recent and exciting possibilities come from the work done with electrical stimulation of the brain (ESB). Preliminary results from ESB research indicate that better understanding of human personality and behavior may come from the study of the brain.

To date, ESB has been conducted primarily on animal subjects. Electrodes are implanted in the animal's brain. Depending upon the area that is stimulated, either a pleasurable or a painful sensation is experienced. In rats, about 60 percent of the brain has been determined to be neutral, 35 percent pleasurable, and 5 percent painful. Several years ago a spectacular demonstration of ESB was conducted by José Delgado. He implanted a radio-controlled electrode in the pleasure area of a bull's brain. When stimulated, the bull could be stopped in the middle of a ferocious charge.[18]

Work with ESB on human subjects is just beginning. However, the research results are, in general, similar to those on animals. There seem to be definite pleasurable and painful areas in the human brain. This being true, it may be possible physically to manipulate personality through ESB. Some business firms are reportedly investigating ESB as a method of reducing executive tensions and stimulating creative thinking.[19] There is the possibility, though admittedly far out, that future people may possess a little button that

[16]Charles R. Shaw, *When Your Child Needs Help,* William Morrow & Company, Inc., New York, 1972.

[17]Jerry E. Bishop, "The Argument Over Heredity and I.Q.," *Wall Street Journal,* June 20, 1973, p. 14.

[18]José Delgado, *Physical Control of the Mind,* Harper & Row, Publishers, Incorporated, New York, 1969, pp. 166–168.

[19]*Newsweek,* June 12, 1971, p. 65.

literally "turns them on" or "off" depending on their mood. This possibility does not mean that the basic human personality can be altered by ESB or that some diabolical plot to take over the world with ESB can be implemented.

Research so far indicates that it is not possible to substitute one entire personality for another through ESB. Instead, ESB seems to work in a manner similar to hypnosis. It can give pleasure or pain, and it seems to influence some of the conscious and unconscious characteristics of the personality, but it cannot alter the basic personality structure. As far as someone's using ESB to take over the world, one doctor who works with ESB notes, "Anyone influential enough to get an entire population to consent to having electrodes placed in its heads would already have achieved his goal without firing a single volt."[20]

Biofeedback Similar to the work on electrical stimulation of the brain have been some of the widely publicized and spectacular results of biofeed-back training (BFT). Up to recent years, physiologists and psychologists felt that certain biological functions such as brainwave patterns, gastric secretions, and fluctuations in blood pressure and skin temperature were beyond conscious control. Now some scientists and many quasi-scientists believe that these involuntary functions can be consciously controlled through biofeedback. In BFT the individual learns the internal rhythms of a particular body process through electronic signals fed back from equipment that is wired to the body area (e.g., skin, brain, or heart). From this biofeedback the person can learn to control the body process in question.

Newsweek reported that BFT has been used to alleviate migraine head-aches by diverting blood from the throbbing region to other parts of the body; cerebral palsy patients have learned to control muscle spasms by listening to clicks from a feedback machine wired to their body; people with dangerously irregular heart rhythms have learned to modify them by watching blinking lights that tell them when the heart is functioning properly; and, on the lighter side, a person can control an electric train through brain waves.[21] Such results have snowballed to the point that the implication is that there has been uniform success with BFT. Such is not the case. Researchers have found BFT to have mixed results.[22] Many individuals who have tried BFT are unable to control the process in question or fail to experience the intended benefits. Most behavioral scientists are still taking a "wait and see" approach to BFT. For example, Hilgard and Bower note that "the evidence to date suggests that 'alpha control' may be little more than inexplicit control of eye-movement or eye-focusing," but they do add that "despite these critical remarks, it should be noted that this research has been significant in altering our conceptions of self-control,

---

[20]Ibid., p. 67.

[21]*Newsweek*, Oct. 14, 1974, pp. 76–77.

[22]Thomas B. Mulholland, "Occipital Alpha Revisited," *Psychological Bulletin*, September 1972, pp. 176–182; and D. A. Paskewitz and M. T. Orne, "Visual Effects on Alpha Feedback Training," *Science*, vol. 181, 1973, pp. 360–363.

awareness, and the nature of 'private events.' "[23] Similar to many other areas of the behavioral sciences, more research is needed on biofeedback before any definitive conclusions can be drawn. But its potential impact is extremely interesting for the future.

Physical Characteristics and Rate of Maturing   Another biologically based approach is to analyze the effects of physical characteristics and rate of maturing on personality. Despite the tremendous potential offered by the study of genetics, the brain, and biofeedback, this approach has already proved to be a significant contributor to the human personality. An individual's external appearance, which was said to be a vital ingredient of the personality, is biologically determined. The fact that a person is tall or short, fat of skinny, handsome or ugly, or black or white will influence the person's effect on others and, in turn, will affect the self-concept.

There are entire theories of personality based upon body build. Sheldon's classic theory, which correlated certain body builds (endomorphic, mesomorphic, and ectomorphic) with specific personality traits, is an example. However, most modern psychologists do not go so far as Sheldon in recognizing the importance of physical attributes. There are too many exceptions for such a theory to be meaningful. On the other hand, practically all would agree that physical characteristics have at least some influence on the personality. The prevailing attitude is expressed by Paul Mussen as follows: ". . . a child's physical characteristics may be related to his approach to the social environment, to the expectancies of others, and to their reactions to him. These, in turn, may have impacts on personality development."[24] This same reasoning is applied to the rate of maturation. A rapidly maturing boy or girl will be exposed to different physical and social situations and activities than will a slowly maturing child. This differing rate of maturation will be reflected in the personality.

Cultural Contribution

At least traditionally, the culture is usually considered to make a more significant contribution to personality than the biological factors. Chapter 12 was concerned with learning as a psychological *process*. Nothing was said about what was learned—the *content*. Yet, in terms of personality development, the content is probably as important as the process. Culture is the key concept in analyzing the content of learning. The prevailing culture pretty much dictates *what* a person will learn.

As indicated in Chapter 2, culture is a major tenet of anthropology. Anthropologists, using cross-cultural analysis, have clearly demonstrated the important role that culture plays in the development of the human personality.

[23]Ernest R. Hilgard and Gordon H. Bower, *Theories of Learning,* 4th ed., Prentice-Hall, Inc., Englewood Cliffs, N.J., 1975, pp. 559–560.

[24]Paul H. Mussen, *The Psychological Development of the Child,* Prentice-Hall, Inc., Englewood Cliffs, N.J., 1963, pp. 60–61.

The methods by which an infant is fed and toilet-trained and makes the transition from adolescence to adulthood are all culturally determined. As indicated by the discussion of the stage theories, such cultural events contribute significantly to the personality. The culture largely determines attributes toward independence, aggression, competition, and cooperation. As noted by Mussen,

> . . . each culture expects, and trains, its members to behave in the ways that are acceptable to the group. To a marked degree, the child's cultural group defines the range of experiences and situations he is likely to encounter and the values and personality characteristics that will be reinforced and hence learned.[25]

For example, Western cultures generally reward a person for being independent and competitive while Oriental cultures do not. It follows that a person reared in a Western culture has a different personality from a person reared in an Oriental culture. Even a person who is biologically of Western descent but is brought up in an Oriental culture will have an Oriental type of personality, and vice versa.

Despite the importance of the cultural contribution to personality, a linear relationship cannot be established between personality and a given culture. One problem stems from the existence of numerous subcultures within a given culture. For example, the Protestant Ethic may be an overall value of Western culture. However, there are extreme differences among socioeconomic classes, ages, and geographic regions. The point is that it is wrong to assume that all workers or managers in Western societies possess the Protestant Ethic. On the other hand, this does not rule out the fact that culture affects personality. The difficulty comes when broad generalizations are made. When analyzing organizational behavior, the *relevant* cultural impact must be recognized. Workers are not influenced by the same culture as managers are, and technical, skilled workers are affected by a different culture from unskilled workers. These and many other differences must be taken into account when analyzing the impact of culture on organizational behavior.

Contribution from the Family and Social Group

Whereas the culture generally prescribes and limits what a person can be taught, it is the family, and later the social group, which selects, interprets, and dispenses the culture. Thus, it is the family and the social group which probably have the most significant impact on personality development.

Socialization Process The contribution of the family and social group in combination with the culture is commonly referred to in the behavioral sciences as the *process of socialization.* Mussen defines socialization as "the process by which an individual infant acquires, from the enormously wide range of behavioral potentialities that are open to him at birth, those behavior

[25]Ibid., p. 62.

patterns that are customary and acceptable according to the standards of his family and social group."[26] Socialization starts with the initial contact between a mother and her new infant. After infancy, other members of the immediate family (father, brothers, sisters, and close relatives or friends) and the social group (peers, school friends, and members of the work group) play influential roles in the socialization process. This process takes place throughout a person's life.

Identification Process The parents play an especially important part in the identification process which is important to the person's early development. Usually, the parent of the same sex as the child will serve as the model for the child's identification. The process can be examined from three different perspectives.

> *First,* identification can be viewed as the similarity of behavior (including feelings and attitudes) between child and model.
> *Second,* identification can be looked at as the child's motives or desires to be like the model.
> *Third,* it can be viewed as the process through which the child actually takes on the attributes of the model.[27]

From all three perspectives, the identification process is fundamental to the understanding of personality development.

Home Environment There is a substantial amount of empirical evidence to indicate that the overall home environment created by the parents is critical to personality development. For example, children with markedly institutional upbringing (orphans) or children reared in a cold, unstimulating home have a much greater potential to be socially and emotionally maladjusted than children raised by parents in a warm, loving, and stimulating environment. The key variable is not the parents per se, but rather the type of atmosphere that is generated for the child. As explained by Mussen:

> Children between the ages of four and six from democratic homes are more stable, less argumentative, more sensitive to praise and blame, more socially successful, and more considerate than children from authoritarian homes. Overattention or overindulgence at home also leads to many kinds of maladaptive, infantile behavior—for instance, crying easily, dawdling, lack of independence and persistence, withdrawal, and high dependence on adults.[28]

Clinical case histories of maladjusted children and adults also show the important role that the parents play. The most common element in histories of maladjusted persons is that of friction between their mother and father.[29]

[26]Ibid., p. 65.
[27]Mischel, op. cit., p. 312.
[28]Mussen, op. cit., pp. 72–73.
[29]Ibid., p. 73.

Research Study on Parental Influence   A classic study by James Abegglen effectively points of the impact of the parents on the personalities of very successful executives.[30] He conducted a detailed case study of twenty executives who had risen from a lower-class childhood to hold top-ranking positions with business firms. Data were accumulated from interviews which at first focused on personal and job histories and then on the use of eight thematic apperception cards (pictures from which subjects report what they see). It was found that fifteen of the twenty executives, while children, had what Abegglen called a separation trauma with their fathers. Two fathers had died during the childhood of the subjects, two subjects had lived with their mothers following a divorce, six of the fathers had been in severe business and financial difficulties, and in five cases the fathers were seriously ill. The fathers were blamed by the sons for the hardships suffered by the family. They were described as inept, sometimes hostile, and usually inadequate. The mother, on the other hand, was generally viewed as being economically and morally stable but not "motherly" in the affection sense.

The results obtained by Abegglen indicate that a classic Freudian "reaction formation" had taken place. The normal positive identification process between father and son had been blocked. Instead, the son negatively identified with his father and strove to be the opposite from him. This negative identification turned out to be a major motivating force throughout the son's life. The high needs for achievement and low needs for affiliation exhibited by the subjects can be traced back to the negative identification in childhood. Thus, the father and mother (who transmitted values that were conducive to upward striving) seemed to have had a great deal of influence on the personalities of this group of business executives.

The Abegglen study has potentially significant implications for the study of organizational behavior. For instance, the case histories of organizational participants might provide much insight into their behavior. Yet, as with most studies of this nature in the behavioral sciences, broad generalizations or grandiose conclusions are unwarranted. Gellerman, in evaluating the Abegglen study, cautions that

> . . . intriguing as Abegglen's findings are, it must be remembered that they were drawn from a small and highly select group. He has demonstrated that an early reaction-formation can lead to a lifelong pattern of achievement striving and upward mobility; but so can other kinds of psychological relationships. Sons who are disappointed in their fathers are not destined to corner the market in successful careers![31]

Birth-Order Data   Besides parents, siblings (brothers and sisters) contribute to personality. So far, studies of birth order have produced some very

---

[30]James C. Abegglen, "Personality Factors in Social Mobility: A Study of Occupationally Mobile Businessmen," *Genetic Psychology Monographs*, August 1958, pp. 101–159.
[31]Saul W. Gellerman, *Motivation and Productivity*, American Management Association, New York, 1963, p. 147.

interesting but inconclusive results. An offshoot of Schachter's affiliation study, reported in the last chapter, found that first born and only children in a family have a stronger need to affiliate than do children born later. The conclusion drawn from Schachter's research is that "first-born children, at least in our society, are probably more anxious; more dependent on others, especially in anxious situations; and more inclined to go along with the group than are other children."[32] There is other research evidence, although it is far from being conclusive, that indicates firstborns may be more serious, less carefree, and more likely to be a problem than later-borns. [33]

Staunch advocates of birth-order data claim it is possible to describe major personality characteristics based solely upon the position in the family constellation. For example, Toman gives specific personality sketches for the oldest and the youngest brother of one or more brothers (OBB and YBB, respectively); and the oldest and youngest brother of sisters (OBS and YBS, respectively). These four types have equivalent female counterparts for a total of eight combinations. Toman even makes suggestions, based upon numerous empirical cases, as to the kind of worker each type will be. For example, he states that the OBB is a good worker and independent; YBB fakes independence and tends to be an irregular worker; the OBS, who is also said to be a "true ladies' man" who adores women, is a responsible worker; and the YBS, who is adored and loved by women, is not a very regular or systematic worker but is capable of great accomplishments.[34] On the surface, there seems to be a great deal of truth to these descriptions and possible implications for management. For example, if found to correlate with employment variables, birth order may take on added significance in the selection process. At the present time, however, birth-order data, like astrology charts, make a lot of surface sense but need much more scientific research before any definitive conclusions can be drawn.

Other Relevant Persons Besides parents and siblings, other relevant persons (relatives, peers, neighbors, teachers, coworkers, or even matinee idols), individually or in a group, as in the case of peers and coworkers, can and generally do greatly contribute to the human personality. In some cases these relevant others reinforce, in other cases modify, and in still other cases directly conflict with the family influence. In a world characterized by increased mobility, education, and independence combined with the decline of the traditional family unit, relevant others are having a much greater impact on personality development than in the past. In previous generations not only the parents but also grandparents and aunts and uncles greatly influenced the personality development of children. Today, in many cases, children seldom see their grandparents or other relatives. Grandmother and grandfather live in Sun City and Aunt Mary and Uncle Joe have moved to California. All that is

[32]Bernard Berelson and Gary A. Steiner, *Human Behavior,* Harcourt, Brace & World, Inc., New York, 1964, p. 74.
[33]Ibid., p. 73.
[34]Walter Toman, "Birth Order Rules All," *Psychology Today,* December 1970, pp. 46–49.

left is the nuclear family (parents and children). Dad travels a lot with his job and mother also has a career outside the home. In such a world relevant "others" and even television start to influence the child's personality development. All indications are that in the future, the balance will tip further away from the family and toward relevant others. Most of today's parents are already keenly aware of this shift.

Situational Contributions

The preceding discussion has indicated that, in order of relative importance, biological factors, culture, and the family determine the human personality. The historical nature of personality development has been emphasized from the beginning of the chapter. The immediate situation or social context was not specifically given attention. Yet, the adage that "it all depends on the situation" seems to have direct relevance to the complex human personality.

The importance that developmental history plays in personality should never be slighted, but it should also be recognized that the immediate situation may predominate. As the SOBC model in Chapter 5 showed, it is the situation interacting with the human being (including the individual's personality) that are vital antecedents to behavior. An example is the worker whose developmental history has shaped a personality which incorporates a high need for power and achievement. However, when placed into a highly bureaucratized work situation, this individual may become frustrated and react apathetically and/or aggressively. Thus, on the surface this worker appears lazy and/or a troublemaker. Yet, the developmental history would predict that the individual would be a very hard worker, striving to get ahead. The countless potential combinations of the situation and the human being make it virtually impossible always to predict accurately from the developmental history alone the ways in which the personality will be behaviorally expressed. The interaction is too complex, and when the role of consequences is included, it becomes obvious that the developmental aspects of personality fall way short of understanding, predicting, and controlling human behavior.

Research on the Situational Impact A very significant study by Stanley Milgram gives support to the important role that the situation plays in the human personality. He conducted a series of tightly controlled experimental studies that used almost a thousand adult subjects.[35] These subjects were not students and ranged from twenty to fifty years of age and came from a wide variety of occupations (unskilled, skilled, white-collar, sales, business, and professional). Each experimental session consisted of a naïve subject, an accomplice, and the experimenter. The experimenter explained that the subject would be part of a learning experiment to test the effect of punishment on memory. After a rigged drawing on roles to be played, the naïve subject always became the teacher and the accomplice the learner in the experiment. The

[35]Stanley Milgram, "Some Conditions of Obedience and Disobedience to Authority," *Human Relations,* February 1965, pp. 57–76.

learner (accomplice) was then taken to the next room and strapped into a sinister-looking "electric chair" that the subject could see through a glass partition. The experimenter carefully explained that the teacher (naïve subject) would administer increasing levels of shock to the learner whenever a mistake was made. The shock generator had clearly marked voltage levels that ran from 15 to 450 volts and printed descriptions that ranged from "Slight Shock" to "Danger: Severe Shock." To convince the naïve subjects of the authenticity of the shock device, they were given a real shock from the 45-volt switch.

For control purposes, accomplices' responses to the shocks were broadcast from a premade tape, and of course they did not actually receive any shocks. Starting with what the subject believed to be a 75-volt shock, the victim began to grunt and moan. As the succeeding shocks increased in voltage, the cries became louder and more desperate. The victim pleaded with the subject to have mercy and to stop the experiment. Whenever the subject would hesitate to administer more shock, the experimenter would prod him on by saying, "You have no other choice, you must go on!" Finally, the victim refused to give any more answers and the naïve subject was told by the experimeter to give the maximum voltage shock. Contrary to common or expert opinion, almost two-thirds of the subjects went ahead and administered what they thought was a very dangerous, severe shock that might even lead to death. Milgram, who was obviously disturbed by his findings, stated:

> With numbing regularity good people were seen to knuckle under the demands of authority and perform actions that were callous and severe. Men who are in everyday life responsible and decent were seduced by the trappings of authority, by the control of their perceptions, and by the uncritical acceptance of the experimenter's definition of the situation, into performing harsh acts.[36]

Implications of the Milgram Study Compared to the developmental aspects of personality, relatively little attention has been given to the situational impact. Yet, Milgram's research suggests the very powerful role that the situation may play in the human personality. In fact, he calls for a theory that would provide a definition and typology of situations. He believes that if such guidance were available, certain definable properties of situations could be transformed into psychological forces in the individual.[37] In other words, studying the situational determinants may be of as much value as studying case histories. To prove the point, Milgram put leading advocates of the case history approach to the test. Forty psychiatrists from a prestigious medical school were asked to predict the behavior of the subjects in the shock experiment. The highly trained experts did a very poor job. They estimated that only about one-tenth of one percent would administer maximum shock, when in fact almost two-thirds did so.

The Milgram research certainly does not completely rule out the impor-

[36]Ibid., p. 75.
[37]Ibid.

tance of the developmental aspects of personality. Rather, it demonstrates that the situation may potentially have a very big impact on the behavioral expression of the personality, even to the point where it seems to override what the developmental history would predict. The experimenter in the Yale psychological laboratory where the studies were conducted produced a situation where people violated their moral codes. They were obedient to scientific authority. When the setting was moved to a run-down commercial building under the guise of Research Associates of Bridgeport, those who obeyed to the end dropped to 48 percent.

The results of Milgram's studies have produced a strong emotional reaction from academicians and the public. Critics claim that Milgram was unethical and doubt that the subjects really believed that they were administering such severe shock. Milgram answers the ethical charge by saying that every precaution was taken and all subjects were carefully debriefed. He supported those who disobeyed and assured those who obeyed that their behavior was perfectly normal and that other subjects had shared their conflicts. Follow-up questionnaires found that almost everyone said the experiment had been worthwhile and only 1 percent were sorry they had participated. As for the other charge questioning the validity of the study, Milgram has data from direct observation, interviews, and questionnaires to support his claim that subjects accepted the experiment at face value. He feels that not one subject suspected the deception.

In his most recent book, *Obedience to Authority,* Milgram expounds on some of his original findings and discusses the follow-up on the modifications and variations. The following summarizes some of the finer points and variations on obedience to authority:

1 Obedience decreases when the victim is in the same room as the teacher, and decreases farther when the teacher must touch the victim directly to administer the shock. The modern state, of course, is designed for impersonality, where switches can be pulled and bombs dropped without anyone ever seeing the victim.

2 Obedience drops sharply when the experimenter is absent. To commit acts they would otherwise consider immoral, people must have authority beside them.

3 Obedience drops when the subject is in a group of rebellious peers. Rebels awaken the subject to the possibility of disobedience and, in this case, to its benign results. The group offers social support for the decision to disobey.

4 By contrast, obedience increases when the subject is merely an accessory to the crime, when he does not have to pull the shock lever himself. In this case, 37 subjects out of 40 stay in the experiment to the end.[38]

The findings of Milgram's study have implications for explaining the behavior during some of the highly publicized war atrocities (for example, at

[38]See *Psychology Today,* June 1974, p. 77.

Auschwitz in World War II and My Lai in the Vietnam war). In fact, the studies are sometimes called the "Eichmann experiments" after the Nazi war criminal. Some of the anxieties of Milgram and the implications of the study have also been captured in a fictionalized television drama, *The Tenth Level.* Besides the emotional impact the studies have on people, Milgram's work does have significant implications for understanding organizational behavior. Although this chapter has been primarily concerned with the impact of the situation on personality, in the broader sense the Milgram study reinforces the importance that the situation also has on overall human behavior. As stated by Milgram,

> A situation exerts an important press on the individual. It exercises constraints and may provide push. In certain circumstances it is not so much the kind of person a man is, as the kind of situation in which he is placed, that determines his actions.[39]

The situational importance described by Milgram is recognized in the conceptual framework used for this book.

THEORIES OF PERSONALITY

So far, the discussion has centered on the meaning and development of personality, but realistically, of course, these factors cannot be separated from the general theory of personality. However, for the purposes of this chapter, it is convenient to separate them.

Just as all people have their own definition of personality, practically all laypersons and scholars have their own theory of personality. The diversity is attributable to the extreme complexity of the unique, whole-person conceptualization of the personality. Because of the wide range of opinion, it is difficult to organize a meaningful discussion. However, the most logical breakdown seems to be into psychoanalytic, type, trait, and self theories of personality.

Psychoanalytic Theories

Sigmund Freud has been presented as one of the foremost pioneers in many areas of psychological thought, and personality theory is no exception. Freud's theory, based upon the concepts of id, ego, and superego and discussed in detail in Chapter 5, is historically the most significant and probably the best-known theory of the structure of personality. But similar to his ideas about personality development, the id, ego, and superego theory served only as a point of departure for further refinement, modification, and extension. The work of Carl Jung, one of Freud's colleagues, is an example.

Usually classified as a neo-Freudian, Jung carried Freud's concept of the unconscious one step further. He believed that a collective unconscious exists in the personality which is deeper and more unknown to the person than the personal unconscious conceived by Freud. Jung went so far as to say that the

---

[39]Milgram, op. cit., p. 72.

collective unconscious includes the cumulative experiences of *all* past generations, even those of primitive ancestors. Perhaps a more significant contribution than the concept of the collective unconscious (which is thought-provoking and novel but which relies heavily on mysticism rather than on science) is his work on introversion and extroversion. Jung felt that these two opposing attitudes or modes of reaction exist in every person but that one will dominate the other.

Many colleagues and contemporaries of Freud besides Jung contributed historically important psychoanalytic ideas about personality theory. In addition, all the other historical schools (structuralism, functionalism, behavioralism, and gestaltism) made contributions. Yet, Freud's theory of personality has had the greatest and most long-lasting impact.

Type Theories

The type theories represent an attempt to put some degree of order into the chaos of personality theory. Both layperson and scholar would feel more comfortable if they could place personalities into clearly identifiable categories. This is a basic aim of any scientific endeavor. The search for personality types has generally taken the following three approaches:

1 The physique or body-type theories have concentrated on determining a relationship between features of the face or body and personality. Sheldon's body types, mentioned in the discussion of the biological determinants of personality development, is the most widely known body-type theory.

2 The physiological theories have concentrated on the relationship between body chemistry or endocrine balance and personality. Typically, certain chemical substances are correlated with temperament.

3 The third way to type personalities is in terms of behavior or psychological factors. Jung's introvert and extrovert types are an example. However, as Jung himself pointed out, the introvert-extrovert typology turns out to be more in the nature of a continuum than discretely separate types.

The continuum reference made by Jung generally applies to the other type theories as well. They tend to oversimplify the very complex human personality. It is doubtful that any truly meaningful personality type theories can ever be developed.

Trait Theories

Another approach to putting some degree of order into personality theory has been the search for identifiable traits. A personality trait can be defined as an "enduring attribute of a person that appears consistently in a variety of situations."[40] In combination, such traits distinguish one personality from another. The two most widely known trait theories come from the classic work of Gordon Allport and Raymond Cattell.

[40]Gregory A. Kimble, Norman Garmezy, and Edward Zigler, *General Psychology*, 4th ed., The Ronald Press Company, New York, 1974, p. 298.

Allport's Trait Theory   Allport bases his theory on the distinction between common traits and personal dispositions. Common traits are used to compare people. For example, the theoretical, economic, esthetic, social, political, and religious categories in Allport's *Scale of Values Test* are primarily used for comparative purposes. However, besides the common traits, there are traits which are completely unique. These unique traits Allport calls *personal dispositions.* They can be cardinal (most pervasive), central (unique and limited in number), or secondary (peripheral). Allport's emphasis on personal dispositions is a departure from the more traditional common-trait approach. He gives more recognition to the complexity and uniqueness of the human personality.

Cattell's Trait Theory   Cattell takes a different approach from Allport. As was pointed out in the introductory discussion in this chapter, many thousands of words can be used to describe personality. By eliminating overlapping meanings, Cattell was able to come up with 171 words that can be used to describe personality traits. He then made a distinction between what he called *surface traits* and *source traits.* He determined thirty-five surface traits by finding clusters of traits that correlated. Some examples are wise–foolish, affectionate–cold, sociable–seclusive, and honest–dishonest. Such traits lie on the surface of the personality and are largely determined by the underlying source traits. Using factor analysis, Cattell was able to determine twelve source traits. Examples include affectothymia (good nature and trustfulness) versus sizothymia (critical and suspicious attitudes); ego strength (maturity and realism) versus emotionality and neuroticism (immaturity and evasiveness); dominance versus submissiveness; and surgency (cheerfulness and energy) versus desurgency (depressed and subdued feelings).[41]

The Value of Trait Theories   Overall, the trait theories seem to make more sense than the type theories. The type theories unrealistically attempt to place personalities into discrete, discontinuous categories. The trait theories, on the other hand, give recognition to the continuity of personalities. The trait theorists have also contributed personality tests and factor-analysis techniques to the behavioral sciences. The major drawback of these theories is that they are very descriptive rather than analytical and are a long way from being comprehensive theories of personality.

Self Theories

The psychoanalytic, type, and trait theories represent the more traditional approaches to explaining the complex human personality. Of the many other theories, the one that has received the most recent emphasis and that is probably most relevant to the study of organizational behavior is the self theory of personality. It seems to hold the most promise of unifying the wide divergence currently found in personality theory.

[41]Raymond B. Cattell, *The Scientific Analysis of Personality,* Aldine Publishing Company, Chicago, 1965. First published in 1965 by Penguin Books, Inc., Baltimore.

Elements of the Self-Concept   Self theories attempt to integrate the various parts of the personality structure into a meaningful whole. Carl Rogers is most closely associated with this approach. He defined the self or self-concept as an "organized, consistent conceptual gestalt composed of perceptions of the characteristics of the 'I' or 'me' and the perceptions of the relationships of 'I' or 'me' to others and to various aspects of life, together with the values attached to these perceptions."[42] The distinction made between "I" and "me" is vitally important to the understanding of the self-concept.

The "I" is the *personal* self, the self that one believes oneself is and strives to be. It consists of the individual's psychological processes (perception, learning, and motivation) which, in combination, result in a unique whole.

The "me" represents the *social* self. The "me" is the way a person appears to others and the way this person thinks he or she appears to others. The "me" is explained in more explicit terms by Knowles and Saxberg as follows:

> When I know what other people expect, I can try to integrate myself with the social situation by being a "normal" person in that situation as this is defined by others. This part of me is the part I want to and find myself willing to set forth in my behavior or what, because it is my habitual way, I want to be. The role that I play is therefore a reflection of my inner self. . . . It is also a mirror image of what I believe others expect from me. . . . [43]

This explanation points out that the "me" is closely tied to the role expectations that others have of the self.

Impact of the Self-Concept   The self-concept (both "I" and "me") gives the individual a sense of meaningfulness and consistency. Gellerman notes that "the average individual is not particularly well acquainted with himself, so to speak, but he remains quite faithful to his not-so-accurate image of himself and thereby acquires some consistency."[44] People's self-concepts will also have a direct effect on their behavior. Thus, in analyzing organizational behavior, it would be beneficial to remember that because each self-concept is unique, the application of various reinforcement, motivation, and leadership techniques will have different effects on different people. For example, monetary reward for performance, a security-oriented motivation technique, or an authoritarian leadership style applied to a worker with a self-concept of independence, intelligence, security, and confidence, may be ineffective. On the other hand, the same reward for performance, motivational technique, and leadership style applied to a worker with a self-concept of dependence, unintelligence, insecurity, and indecisiveness may be effective. This simple example points out the

[42]Carl R. Rogers, "A Theory of Therapy, Personality, and Interpersonal Relationships, as Developed in the Client-centered Framework," in S. Koch (ed.), *Psychology: A Study of a Science,* vol. 3, McGraw-Hill Book Company, New York, 1959, p. 200.

[43]Henry P. Knowles and Borje O. Saxberg, *Personality and Leadership Behavior,* Addison-Wesley Publishing Company, Reading, Mass., 1971, p. 78.

[44]Gellerman, op. cit., p. 184.

potential applicability that the self theory of personality may have to the study of organizational behavior and the need for contingency application of reinforcement, motivation, and leadership techniques.

SUMMARY

Personality represents the "whole person" concept. It includes perception, learning, motivation, and more. Definitionally, people's external appearance and behavior, inner awareness of self, and pattern of measurable traits make up their personalities. Classic stage theories of personality development by Freud, Erikson, and Piaget make significant contributions, but the seven-dimension continuum of immaturity-maturity by Argyris is of more relevance to the study of organizational behavior. Determining the inputs into personality may be the most complex and difficult task in the study of human behavior, but a comprehensive approach would have to include biological, cultural, family, and situational factors.

A universally accepted personality theory does not currently exist. The historically significant theories were dominated by the psychoanalytic ideas of Freud. The traditional type and trait theories attempted to put some order into the existing diversity. Both approaches made a contribution but fell far short of providing an overall theory of personality. The type theories unrealistically tried to force personalities into discrete, discontinuous categories, and the trait theories were helpfully descriptive but not meaningfully analytical. The more recent self theories try to integrate the various complex parts of the personality into a more meaningful whole. The self-concept seems to have the best chance for unifying personality theory and is most relevant to the study of organizational behavior.

QUESTIONS FOR DISCUSSION AND REVIEW

1 Critically analyze the statement that "the various psychological processes could be thought of as pieces of a jigsaw puzzle and personality as the completed puzzle picture."
2 What is the comprehensive definition of personality? Briefly give examples of each of the major elements.
3 What are the various factors in the biological contributions to personality? The cultural contributions? The family contributions? The situational contributions?
4 How do the type theories differ from the trait theories?
5 What are the major elements of the self-concept? How can this analysis contribute to the better understanding of organizational behavior?

CASE: CHEERLEADER VERSUS ACTIVIST

Liz Case grew up in a Midwestern town of 25,000 people. She was the third generation of the Case family in this town. Her grandparents, who had come from Germany, were retired, but they took care of her younger brother and her whenever her mother and dad had to go some place—like a wedding or a funeral. Neither of Liz's parents had attended college, but once her father took an IQ test and scored almost in the genius category. They always encouraged her to do well in school and saved their money so she could go to State University. Liz also worked during the summers to save money for college. She did very well academically in high school and was a varsity cheerleader. She went on to State University, joined a sorority, majored in English, and took a job with Landis and Smith Advertising Agency. Liz, now 37 years old, has been with L&S for 15 years and has a good work record.

One of Liz's coworkers is Todd Long. Todd grew up in a suburb of Los Angeles. His parents both attended U.C.L.A., and he had seen his grandparents, who were retired military people, only a few times. While growing up, Todd's parents were gone a lot. His mother had arranged for babysitters while she finished her degree at U.C.L.A. It was always assumed that when Todd graduated from high school he too would go on to U.C.L.A. Todd was not particularly active in extracurricular activities but graduated in the top 10 percent of his high school class. At U.C.L.A. he majored in journalism and was very active in the student movement in the late 1960s. Upon graduation he cut his hair and went to work for L&S. Todd, now 27, has been employed by L&S for five years and has a very good work record.

The job of copy editor is now open, and Liz and Todd are the two top candidates. The head of L&S, Stacy McAdams, made it clear that "this job requires a good personality. He or she will be in contact with all the people in the office, and we need someone who can get along well with others and still be able to coordinate the work and meet our critical deadlines."

1   Based on the brief sketches of the two people in this incident, what do you think their personalities are like? Use the determinants of personality and give an example of each determinant that can be found in the incident.

2   Who do you think will get the job? You can discuss the male/female implications; but based solely upon personalities that you outlined in the first question, who do you think *would* get the job? Who do you think *should* get the job?

3   What does the boss mean by saying that a "good" personality is required? Is there such a thing? Do you feel that personality makes much of an input into these types of staffing decisions? Should it have an input? Why?

SELECTED REFERENCES

Argyris, Chris: *Personality and Organization,* Harper & Brothers, New York, 1957, chap. 2.

Argyris, Chris: "Personality and Organization Theory Revisited," *Administrative Science Quarterly,* June 1973, pp. 141–167.

Brown, Barbara B.: "The Anatomy of a Phenomenon: Me and BFT," *Psychology Today,* August 1974, pp. 48–56, 74, 78–84, 88–96, 102–107, 110–112.

Cattell, Raymond B.: *The Scientific Analysis of Personality,* Aldine Publishing Company, Chicago, 1965.

Delgado, José M. R.: *Physical Control of the Mind,* Harper & Row, Publishers, Incorporated, New York, 1969.

Hall, Calvin S., and Gardner Lindzey: *Theories of Personality,* John Wiley & Sons, Inc., New York, 1957.

Kagan, Jerome, and Ernest Havemann: *Psychology: An Introduction,* Harcourt, Brace & World, Inc., New York, 1968, chap. 12.

Knowles, Henry P., and Borje O. Saxberg: *Personality and Leadership Behavior,* Addison-Wesley Publishing Co., Inc., Reading, Mass., 1971.

Mischel, Walter: *Introduction to Personality,* Holt, Rinehart and Winston, Inc., New York, 1971.

Mussen, Paul H.: *The Psychological Development of the Child,* Prentice-Hall, Inc., Englewood Cliffs, N.J., 1963.

Ruch, Floyd L.: *Psychology and Life,* 6th ed., Scott, Foresman and Company, Chicago, 1963, chap. 13.

Part Four

The Dynamics of Organizational Behavior

Chapter 15

Group Dynamics
and Informal Organization

The chapters in Parts Two and Three were devoted chiefly to the situational and major human variables that make an input into organizational behavior. The first two chapters in this part are more concerned with the dynamic outcomes of organizational behavior. This chapter approaches organizational behavior dynamics from the perspective of the group and the informal organization. The first section examines the way groups are formed, the various types of groups, and the findings from research on groups. The second section discusses the committee form of organization as a special, practical case of group dynamics. The positive and negative attributes of committees are analyzed. The third and last section focuses on the dynamics of the informal organization. The status, power, and communication implications of the informal organization are stressed.

GROUP DYNAMICS

Chapter 2 introduced the group as an important unit of sociological analysis that contributes much to the understanding of organizational behavior. This is especially true when the dynamics of the group are analyzed. Group dynamics is concerned with the interactions and forces between group members in a social situation. When the concept is applied to the study of organizational behavior, the focus is on the dynamics of members of formal or informal groups in the organization.

Just as there is no one definition of the group itself, there is no universal agreement on what is meant by group dynamics. Although Kurt Lewin popularized the term in the 1930s, through the years different connotations have been attached to the term. One normative view is that group dynamics describes *how* a group *should* be organized and conducted. Democratic leadership, member participation, and overall cooperation are stressed. This view of group dynamics is given attention in Chapter 18, on the dynamics of leadership. Another view of group dynamics is that it consists of a set of *techniques*. Here, role playing, brainstorming, buzz groups, leaderless groups, group therapy, sensitivity training, transactional analysis, and the Johari window are equated with group dynamics. Some of these techniques are covered in Chapter 21, on organization development. A third view is the closest to Lewin's original conception. Group dynamics is viewed from the perspective of the internal nature of groups, how they form, their structure and processes, and how they affect individual members, other groups, and the organization.[1] The following sections are devoted to this third view of group dynamics.

The Dynamics of Group Formation

Why do individuals form into groups? Before discussing some very practical reasons, it would be beneficial to examine briefly some of the major theories of group formation. The most basic theory explaining affiliation is propinquity. This interesting word simply means that individuals affiliate with one another because of spatial or geographical proximity. The theory would predict that students sitting next to one another in class, for example, are more likely to form into a group than students sitting at opposite ends of the room. In an organization, employees who work in the same area of the plant or office or managers with offices close to one another would more probably form into groups than those who are not physically located together. There is some research evidence to support the propinquity theory,[2] and on the surface it has a great deal of merit for explaining group formation. The drawback is that it is not analytical and does not begin to explain some of the complexities of group formation. Some theoretical and practical reasons need to be explored.

Theories of Group Formation   A more comprehensive theory of group formation than merely propinquity comes from George Homans. His theory is based on activities, interactions, and sentiments.[3] These three elements are

[1]Joe Kelly, *Organizational Behaviour,* rev. ed., Richard D. Irwin, Inc., and The Dorsey Press, Homewood, Ill., 1974, p. 306.

[2]Leon Festinger, Stanley Schachter, and Kurt Back, *Social Pressures in Informal Groups: A Study of Human Factors in Housing,* Stanford University Press, Stanford, Calif., 1963. First published by Harper & Brothers in 1950.

[3]George C. Homans, *The Human Group,* Harcourt, Brace & World, Inc., New York, 1950, pp. 43–44.

directly related to one another. The more activities persons share, the more numerous will be their interactions and the stronger will be their sentiments; the more interactions between persons, the more will be their shared activities and sentiments; and the more sentiments persons have for one another, the more will be their shared activities and interactions. The Homans theory lends a great deal to the understanding of group formation and process. The major element is interaction. Persons in a group interact with one another, not in just the physical propinquity sense, but also to solve problems, attain goals, facilitate coordination, reduce tension, and achieve a balance.[4] Participants in an organization interacting in this manner tend to form into powerful groups.

There are many other theories that attempt to explain group formation. Most often they are only partial theories, but they are generally additive in nature. One of the more comprehensive is a balance theory of group formation proposed by Theodore Newcomb.[5] The theory states that persons are attracted to one another on the basis of similar attitudes toward commonly relevant objects and goals. Once a relationship is formed, it strives to maintain a symmetrical balance between the attraction and the common attitudes. If an imbalance occurs, an attempt is made to restore the balance. If the balance cannot be restored, the relationship dissolves. Both propinquity and interaction play a role in balance theory.

The approach to group formation receiving the most recent emphasis is exchange theory.[6] It is based upon reward-cost outcomes of interaction. A minimum positive level (rewards greater than costs) of an outcome must exist in order for attraction or affiliation to take place. Rewards from interactions gratify needs while costs incur anxiety, frustration, embarrassment, or fatigue. Propinquity, interaction, and common attitudes all have roles in exchange theory.

Practicalities of Group Formation Besides the theoretical explanations for group formation, there are some very practical reasons for joining and/or forming a group. For instance, employees in an organization may form a group for economic, security, or social reasons. Economically, workers may form a group to work on a project that is paid for on a group-incentive plan or form a union to demand higher wages. For security, joining a group provides the individual with a united front in combating indiscriminant, unilateral treatment. The adage that there is strength in numbers applies in this case. The most important practical reason why individuals join or form groups is, however, that groups tend to satisfy the very intense social needs of most people. Workers, in particualr, generally have a very strong desire for affiliation. This

[4]William G. Scott, *Organization Theory*, Richard D. Irwin, Inc., Homewood, Ill., 1967, p. 83.

[5]Theodore M. Newcomb, *The Acquaintance Process*, Holt, Rinehart and Winston, Inc., New York, 1961.

[6]John W. Thibaut and Harold H. Kelley, *The Social Psychology of Groups*, John Wiley & Sons, Inc., New York, 1959.

need is met by belonging to a group. Research going as far back as the Hawthorne studies has found the affiliation motive to have a major impact on human behavior in organizations. Chapter 13 discussed this motive in detail.

Types of Groups

There are numerous types of groups. The theories of group formation that were just discussed are partly based upon the attraction between two persons—the simple dyad group. Of course, in the real world groups are usually much more complex than the dyad. There are small and large groups, primary and secondary groups, membership and reference groups, in- and out-groups, and formal and informal groups. Each type has different characteristics and impacts on its members. The differences between small and large and primary and secondary groups were covered in the discussion of sociological concepts in Chapter 2. Kolasa makes the distinction between membership and reference and in- and out-groups as follows:

> Membership groups are those to which the individual actually belongs, while a reference group is one with which he identifies or to which he would like to belong. . . The in-group represents a clustering of individuals holding prevailing values in a society or, at least, having a dominant place in social functioning. . . The out-groups are the conglomerates looked upon as subordinate or marginal in the culture.[7]

All these types of groups have relevance to the study of organizational behavior, but the formal and informal types are most directly applicable.

There are many formally designated groups and committees in the modern organization. Two very common examples are the command and task groups.[8] A command group consists of a superior and the immediate subordinates. The membership and structure of command groups are formally determined and are represented on the organization chart. The superior is granted formal authority over the other members of the command group. The task group is formally designed to work on a specific project or job. Its interaction and structure are formally designed to accomplish the task. Committees as a type of formal group in an organization are given detailed attention in the next section of the chapter.

There are also numerous informal groups in the organization. Interest and friendship are common examples.[9] Although interest groups may also be formally designated, generally they are established on an informal basis according to common interests or attitudes in the manner described by

---

[7]Blair J. Kolasa, *Introduction to Behavioral Science for Business,* John Wiley & Sons, Inc., New York, 1969, pp. 451–452.

[8]See Leonard R. Sayles, "Work Group Behavior and the Larger Organization," in *Research in Industrial Human Relations,* Industrial Relations Research Association, Publication no. 17, Harper & Brothers, New York, 1957, pp. 131–145.

[9]Ibid.

Newcomb's balance theory. Common interests range from sports (an informal group gets together to bet on sports events) to hatred of management (an informal group unites to restrict output). Friendship groups are a more common kind of informal group. Persons join this type of group in the manner described by exchange theory—the rewards of the friendship group outweigh the costs. Organizational participants join and form friendship groups in order to satisfy their needs for affiliation. Most often, formal organizational arrangements do not satisfy the important social needs. The dynamics of informal groups are examined in more detail in the last section of the chapter.

Implications from Research on Group Dynamics

Starting with the Hawthorne studies, there has been an abundance of significant research on groups which has implications for organizational behavior and management. Besides the Hawthorne studies, the widely known studies that relate group dynamics to human performance in an organizational setting include the Lippitt and White leadership studies, which are covered in Chapter 18; the Coch and French study on overcoming resistance to change; Van Zelst's study of two groups of carpenters and bricklayers;[10] Trist and Bamforth's study of British coal mining;[11] and William F. Whyte's research of the restaurant industry.[12] In addition, there are numerous research studies on group dynamics which indirectly contribute to the better understanding of organizational behavior. Donnelly, Gibson, and Ivancevich briefly summarize these research findings as follows:

> Groups are ubiquitous.
> Groups influence an employee's perceptions and attitudes.
> Groups influence the productivity of employees.
> Groups aid an individual in satisfying unfulfilled needs.
> Groups facilitate communications.[13]

In addition to the classical studies of groups in organizations, one experiment in particular, which is fairly well known within the confines of social psychology but not in the study of organizational behavior, also seems to have significant implications for management.[14]

The Schachter Checkerboard Study Stanley Schachter and his associates tested the effect that group cohesiveness and induction had on productivity

---

[10]Raymond H. Van Zelst, "Sociometrically Selected Work Teams Increase Production," *Personnel Psychology*, Autumn 1952, pp. 175–185.

[11]E. L. Trist and K. W. Bamforth, "Some Social and Psychological Consequences of the Longwall Method of Coal Getting," *Human Relations*, vol. 4, no. 1, 1951, pp. 3–38.

[12]William F. Whyte, *Human Relations in the Restaurant Industry*, McGraw-Hill Book Company, 1948.

[13]James H. Donnelly, Jr., James L. Gibson, and John M. Ivancevich, *Fundamentals of Management*, rev. ed., Business Publications, Inc., Austin, Tex., 1975, p. 202.

[14]Stanley Schachter, Norris Ellertson, Dorothy McBride, and Doris Gregory, "An Experimental Study of Cohesiveness and Productivity," *Human Relations*, vol. 4, no. 3, 1951, pp. 229–239.

under highly controlled conditions. College coeds were used as subjects. *Cohesiveness* was defined as the average resultant force acting on members to remain in a group. The researchers assumed that by making the group appear attractive or not attractive, the subjects would correspondingly feel high or low cohesiveness. About half the subjects were told by the experimenter that they would be members of an extremely congenial group and that "there is every reason to expect that the other members of the group will like you and you will like them." The other half of the subjects were told by the experimenter that, because of scheduling difficulties, it was impossible to assemble a congenial group and that "there is no particular reason to think that you will like them or that they will care for you." In this manner, high and low cohesive groups were created by the experimenter.

All the subjects were told that their task was to make cardboard checker-boards. It was to be a three-person, assembly-line operation consisting of cutting out pieces of cardboard, mounting and pasting them on heavier stock, and painting them through a stencil. For control purposes, all subjects were made cutters, but they thought they would pass on the cut boards to the other two members of their group (the paster and painter) in another room.

The subjects were informed that they could write notes to their pasters and painters. Of course, the experimenter intercepted all the notes from the subjects and gave them prewritten notes. These notes were used to test the impact of positive and negative induction. In the first 16 minutes of the experiment, each subject received five notes from her nonexistent paster and painter which made no attempt to influence productivity. In the remaining 16 minutes of the experiment, half the subjects who believed they were members of high cohesive groups and half the subjects who thought they were members of low cohesive groups received six positive notes. These notes urged increased production, for example, "Time's running out, let's really make a spurt—Paster." The other half of the high and low cohesive subjects received negative notes urging them to slow down production. An example of a negative note was: "Let's try to set a record—let's be the slowest subjects they ever had—Painter."

Through the manipulations of cohesiveness and induction just described, the following experimental groups were created:

1   High cohesive, positive induction (Hi Co, + Ind)
2   Low cohesive, positive induction (Lo Co, + Ind)
3   High cohesive, negative induction (Hi Co, − Ind)
4   Low cohesive, negative induction (Lo Co, − Ind)

Thus, the independent variables in the experiment were cohesiveness and induction and the dependent variable was productivity. Figure 15-1 summarizes the results. Although Schachter's experiment did not obtain a statistically significant difference in productivity between the high and low cohesive groups

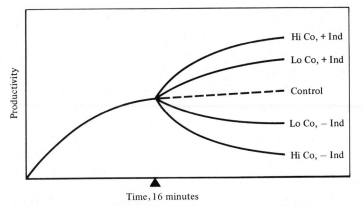

Figure 15-1   The "pitchfork" results from the Schachter checkerboard study. *(Source: Adapted from Stanley Schachter et al., "An Experimental Study of Cohesiveness and Productivity,"* Human Relations, *vol. 4, no. 3, 1951, pp. 229–239.)*

that were positively induced, a follow-up study which used a more difficult task did.[15]

Implications of the Schachter Study   The results of Schachter's study contain some very interesting implications for the study of organizational behavior. The "pitchfork" productivity curves in Figure 15-1 imply that highly cohesive groups have very powerful dynamics, both positive and negative, for the organization. On the other hand, the low cohesive groups are not so powerful. However, of even more importance to the organization is the variable of induction. Performance depends largely on how the high or low cohesive group is induced.

At least for discussion purposes, leadership may be equated with induction. If this is done, the key variable for the subjects' performance in the Schachter experiment becomes leadership. A highly cohesive group that is given positive leadership will have the highest possible productivity. On the other side of the coin, a highly cohesive group that is given poor leadership will have the lowest possible productivity. A highly cohesive group is analogous to a time bomb in the hands of management. The direction in which the highly cohesive group goes, breaking production records or severely restricting output, depends on how it is led. The low cohesive group is much safer in the hands of management. Leadership will not have a serious negative or positive impact on this group. However, the implication is that if management wishes to maximize productivity, it must build a cohesive group and give it proper leadership.

The above discussion does not imply that passing notes to college coeds cutting out checkerboards in a classroom laboratory setting can be made

[15]Leonard Berkowitz, "Group Standards, Cohesiveness, and Productivity," *Human Relations,* vol. 7, no. 4, 1954, pp. 509–519.

equivalent to leading personnel in the modern, complex organization. This, of course, cannot and should not be attempted. On the other hand, there are some interesting insights and points of departure for organizational behavior analysis that can come out of laboratory investigations such as Schachter's experiment. For instance, the results of Schachter's study can be applied in retrospect to the work of Frederick W. Taylor or the Hawthorne studies. Taylor accounted only for the *Hi Co, − Ind* productivity curve when he advocated "breaking up the group." If his scientific management methods could be considered as *+ Ind,* the best productivity he could obtain would be that of the *Lo Co, + Ind.* In other words, in light of the Schachter study, Taylor's methods could only possibly yield second-best productivity. In the Hawthorne studies, both the relay room women and the bank wirers were highly cohesive work groups. As was brought out in Chapter 1, a possible explanation of why one highly cohesive work group (relay workers) produced at a very high level and the other highly cohesive group (bank wirers) produced at a very low rate is the type of induction (supervision) that was applied. The complex role that leadership plays in group dynamics is explored further in Chapter 18.

COMMITTEE ORGANIZATION

Any discussion of group dynamics within the context of organizational behavior would not be complete without thorough analysis of the committee form of organization. The committee is the most important type of formally designated group found in today's organizations. Unfortunately, these committees are often described in the following manner:

A camel is a horse designed by a committee.
The best committee is a five-person committee with four members absent.
In a committee, minutes are taken but hours are wasted.
A committee is a collection of the unfit appointed by the unwilling to perform the unnecessary.

Although these remarks are jokes, they represent the widespread negativism attached to the committee form of organization.

Despite the attacks, all indications are that the use and perceived value of committees in organizations is still increasing. Most committees seem to serve as a focal point for the exchange of different viewpoints and information, but some are making major decisions. There is an indication that the use of committees is directly related to the size of the organization. One survey found that 94 percent of the firms with over 10,000 employees had formal committees, while only 64 percent of the companies with fewer than 250 employees utilized committees.[16] With today's organizations becoming increasingly large and complex, the committee form of organization will undoubtedly become more important and more widely used in the future.

[16]"Committees on Trial," *Harvard Business Review,* May–June 1960, p. 8.

The Nature and Functions of Committees

There are many definitions of committees. Haimann and Scott say that "a committee is a group of people who function collectively."[17] Koontz and O'Donnell state that "a committee is a group of persons to whom, as a group, some matter is committed."[18] These and most other definitions stress the idea that committees consist of groups that are formed to accomplish specific objectives. They can be conducted in either a formal or an informal manner. Most often, committees have specified duties and authority. Some committees meet on an ad hoc basis to solve some specialized problem and then disband. Committees may be referred to as teams, commissions, boards, groups, or task forces.

Committees are found in all types of organizations. There is a myriad of committees in government, educational, religious, and business organizations. For example, the board of directors is a type of committee present in all corporate forms of organization. Other prevalent types in business are the finance, executive, operations, bonus, audit, and grievance committees. Although they are more frequent at the top of the pyramid, there is usually some type of formal committee on every level of the organization.

Committees perform many different functions. They may act in a service, advisory, coordinating, informational, or final decision-making capacity. In the decision-making function, a committee acts in a line capacity and is usually termed a *plural executive*. Many companies are moving toward the plural-executive concept rather than a single executive head. One top executive noted: "There is a tendency to include more than a single man in the role of chief executive in order to provide greater breadth. I suspect that this will become more and more popular in larger and more complex companies."[19] Union Carbide is typical of this trend. The company's major policy evolves from the office of the president. This office is composed of the president and three executive vice presidents. The quadrumvirate serves as the central point of management authority in the company. This type of group management is becoming increasingly common.

Positive Attributes of Committees

Committee action has many advantages over individual action. Perhaps the greatest attribute of the committee group is the combined and integrated judgment which it can offer. It is the adage that two heads are better than one. To speak optimistically, committee members bring with them a wide range of experience, knowledge, ability, and personality characteristics. This agglomeration lends itself to the tremendous amount of diverse knowledge that is required to solve modern organizational problems. An averaging of personali-

---

[17]Theo Haimann and William G. Scott, *Management in the Modern Organization,* Houghton Mifflin Company, Boston, 1970, p. 280.

[18]Harold Koontz and Cyril O'Donnell, *Management,* 6th ed., McGraw-Hill Book Company, New York, 1976, p. 403.

[19]"More Room at the Top?" *Dun's Review,* March 1967, p. 29.

ties and a source of creative ideas are also needed by today's organizations. The committee form of organization can contribute a great deal to these requirements; but, as Chapter 8 pointed out in presenting the group decision techniques of Delphi and the Nominal Group Technique (NGT), the interacting group may also inhibit individual creativity. On the other hand, as the Chapter 8 discussion noted, at least at some point the interactive, group dynamics effects as found in a committee can be beneficial to group problem solving. The third step of NGT (full group discussion and analysis of individual ideas and/or solutions) accounts for the value of the interactive effect.

Committees can be a very effective organizational device to help reduce conflict and promote coordination between departments and specialized sub-units. Through committee discussion, each member can empathize with the others' purposes and problems. In effect, committees foster horizontal communication. An example is the interdepartmental meeting where each member receives information and insights about the others' departments. The production department is informed of delivery dates being promised by sales, and sales gets a first-hand look at the problems it may be creating for production scheduling and inventory. As Chapter 9 pointed out, the committee is about the only formalized vehicle for horizontal communication in most traditional forms of organization structure.

From a human standpoint, the biggest advantage of committees may be the increased motivation and commitment derived from participation. By being involved in the analysis and solution of committee problems, individual members will more readily accept and try to implement what has been decided. A committee can also be instrumental in human development and growth. Group members, especially the young and inexperienced, can take advantage of observing and learning from other members with much experience or with different viewpoints and knowledge. A committee provides the opportunity for personal development that individuals would never receive on their own.

Negative Attributes of Committees

The last section pointed out some definite advantages of committees. Traditionally, management theorists stressed the negative aspects. The classical theorist Luther Gulick wanted to limit the use of committees to abnormal situations because he thought they were too dilatory, irresponsible, and time-consuming for normal administration.[20] Urwick was an even harsher critic. He listed no less than fourteen faults of committees, the main ones being that committees are often irresponsible, are apt to be bad employers, and are costly.[21] Thus, the classicists tended to emphasize the negative, but the more

---

[20]Luther Gulick, "Notes on the Theory of Organization," in Luther Gulick and L. Urwick (eds.), *Papers on the Science of Administration,* Institute of Public Administration, New York, 1937, p. 36.

[21]Lyndall F. Urwick, *Committees in Organization,* reprint from the *British Management Review* by Management Journals, Ltd., 1933, p. 14; and *The Elements of Administration,* Harper & Row, Publishers, Incorporated, New York, 1943, pp. 71–72.

modern view recognizes that committees have both positive and negative attributes.

One very practical disadvantage is that committees are indeed time-consuming and costly. Anyone who has participated in committee meetings can appreciate the satirical definition, cited earlier, that a committee takes minutes but wastes hours. The nature of a committee is that everyone has an equal chance to speak out, but this takes a great deal of time and time costs money. A $25,000-per-year executive costs almost $15 per hour. Therefore, a five-person committee of this caliber costs the organization $75 per hour. Added to this figure may be transportation, lodging, and staff back-up costs.

Most often, cost is discussed with regard to committee versus individual action. Taking another approach, it can be argued that committees are actually *less* expensive when compared with a series of repetitious conferences. In terms of work hours, a committee meeting where an executive meets with five others for one hour represents six work hours. On the other hand, if the same executive meets for one hour with each of the five people individually, the expended time turns out to be ten work-hours. Assume that the executive makes $25,000 ($15 per hour) per year, and that the five others average $12,000 ($7 per hour). For the one-hour committee meeting the cost would be about $50, but for the five individual conferences the total cost would be about $110, over twice as much. The point of this elementary cost analysis is that one cannot automatically condemn all committees as being excessively expensive. The nature and purpose must be considered when assessing cost. Furthermore, it is difficult, if not impossible, to quantify for cost purposes the advantages of a committee in terms of member motivation and quality of decision or problem solution.

From an organization standpoint, there are some potential problems inherent in committees. The most obvious is divided responsibility. Urwick made the analogy that a committee is like a corporation with "neither a soul to be damned nor a body to be kicked."[22] This is saying that, in a committee, there is group or corporate, but no individual, responsibility or accountability. Thus, critics argue, the committee in reality turns out to have no responsibility or accountability. In fact, individuals may use the committee as a shield to avoid personal responsibility for bad decisions or mistakes. One solution to this problem is to make all committee members responsible, and another is to hold the chairman responsible. Both approaches have many obvious difficulties. For example, if the entire committee is held responsible for a wrong decision, what about the individual members who voted against the majority? Holding them accountable for the committee's decision could have disastrous effects on their morale, but holding only those who voted for a particular decision responsible would create an inhibiting effect that would destroy the value of committee action.

Besides being time-consuming, costly, and having divided responsibility,

[22]Urwick, *The Elements of Administration*, op. cit., p. 72.

committees may reach decisions that are products of excessive compromise, logrolling, and one-person or minority domination. The comment that the camel is a horse designed by a committee points out this limitation. It represents the reverse of the advantages of integrated group judgment and the pooling of specialized knowledge. Where unanimity is either formally required or an informal group norm, the difficulties are compounded. The final decision may be so extremely watered down or "compromised to death" that the horse actually does turn out to be a camel. The strength of committee action comes through a synthesis and integration of divergent viewpoints, not through a compromise of the least common denominator. One way to avoid the problem is to limit the committee to serving as a forum for the exchange of information and ideas. Another possibility is to let the chairperson have the final decision-making prerogative. Yet, these solutions are not always satisfactory because, when the committee is charged with making a decision, considerable social skill and a willingness to cooperate fully must exist if good, quality decisions are to evolve. Committees should be subjected to the same intensive research that has been conducted on small groups. Much can be learned from behavorial science research on the small group, but more effort needs to be directed specifically at the formal organization committee as a form of group dynamics.

INFORMAL ORGANIZATION

The informal organization plays a significant role in the dynamics of organizational behavior. The major difference between the formal and informal organization is that the formal organization, as discussed in Part Two, has officially prescribed goals and relationships while the informal one does not. More specifically, Argyris points out four major areas where the formal and informal organization differ:[23]

1   *Interpersonal relations.* In the formal organization the relationships between people are prescribed whereas in the informal the relationships largely depend on people's needs.

2   *Leadership.* Leaders are assigned and designated in the formal and emerge and are chosen in the informal.

3   *Behavioral control.* Formal organizations control employee behavior through reward and punishment while informal groups control members with need fulfillment.

4   *Dependency.* Because of the formal leaders' capacity to reward and punish, subordinates are more dependent than are members of an informal group.

Yet, despite these differences, it is a mistake to think of the formal and informal groups as two distinctly separate organizational entities. The two coexist and are inseparable. Every formal organization has an informal organization and

[23]Chris Argyris, *Leadership and Interpersonal Behavior,* Holt, Rinehart and Winston, Inc., New York, 1961, p. 331.

every informal organization eventually evolves into some degree of formal organization. As pointed out by Blau and Scott,

> It is impossible to understand the nature of a formal organization without investigating the networks of informal relations and the unofficial norms as well as the formal hierarchy of authority and the official body of rules, since the formally instituted and the informally emerging patterns are inextricably intertwined. The distinction between the formal and the informal aspects of organization life is only an analytical one and should not be reified; there is only one actual organization.[24]

Status, Roles, and Power in the Informal Organization

The informal organization largely evolves from the different status positions of the participants. There are four generally recognized status positions in a group or organization:

1　Group leader
2　Member of the primary group
3　Fringe status
4　Out status[25]

Figure 15-2 graphically depicts these status positions.

Closely related to status are the roles in the informal system of the organization. As indicated in Chapter 2, a role is an expectation that people have of a position. The informal roles in an organization vary widely and are highly volatile. Figure 15-3 summarizes some of the general informal roles that are found in a modern organization. These roles are not intended to be

[24]Peter M. Blau and W. Richard Scott, *Formal Organizations,* Chandler Publishing Company, San Francisco, 1962, p. 6.
[25]Haimann and Scott, op. cit., p. 432.

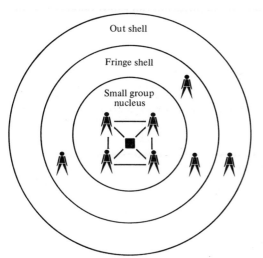

Figure 15-2　Relationship of status positions in an informal organization. *(Source: Adapted from Theo Haimann and William G. Scott,* Management in the Modern Organization, *Houghton Mifflin Company, Boston, 1970, p. 433.)*

Figure 15-3   Informal Roles Found in Organizations

Task-oriented: the role of "getting the job done" and known as those who "deliver the goods"

Technique-oriented: the masters of procedure and method

People-oriented: the role of patron saint and good samaritan to people in need

Nay-sayers: those who counterbalance the "yes" persons, who have thick skins and can find fault with anything

Yea-sayers: those who counterbalance the nay-sayers, the "yes" persons who circumvent opposition

Rule-enforcers: the "people of the book" who are stereotype bureaucrats

Rule-evaders: the "operators," those who know how to get the job done "irrespective"

Rule-blinkers: the people who are not against the rules but don't take them seriously

Involved: those who are fully immersed in their work and the activities of the organization

Detached: slackers who either "go along for the ride" or "call it quits" at the end of regular hours

Regulars: those who are "in," who accept the values of the group and are accepted by the group

Deviants: those who depart from the values of the group—the "mavericks"

Isolates: the true "lone wolves," they are further from the group than deviants

Newcomers: they know little and must be taken care of by others; they are "seen but not heard"

Old-timers: those who have been "around" a long time and "know the ropes"

Climbers: those who are expected to "get ahead," not necessarily on the basis of ability but on the basis of potential

Stickers: those who are expected to stay put, who are satisfied with life and their position in it

Cosmopolitans: those who see themselves as members of a broader professional, cultural, or political community

Locals: those who are rooted to the organization and local community

Source: Adapted from Bertram M. Gross, *Organizations and Their Managing*, The Free Press, New York, 1968, pp. 242–248.

stereotypes or meant to imply that each participant has only one role. The same person may have one role in one situation (e.g., a member of a middle-management work group) and another role in another situation (e.g., informal leader of the dissident group on a new project).

To point out the power of the informal organization, the classic Milo study conducted by Melville Dalton remains the best illustration.[26] Part *(a)* in Figure 15-4 represents the formal organization at Milo. Through the use of intimates, interviews, diaries, observation, and socializing, Dalton was able to construct the informal organization chart shown in *(b)* of Figure 15-4. This informal chart shows the actual power as opposed to the formally designated power and influence of the various managers at Milo.

As with the formal organization structures discussed in Chapters 6 and 7, the informal organization has both functions and dysfunctions. In contrast to formal organization analysis, the dysfunctional aspects of informal organiza-

[26]Melville Dalton, *Men Who Manage*, John Wiley & Sons, Inc., New York, 1959.

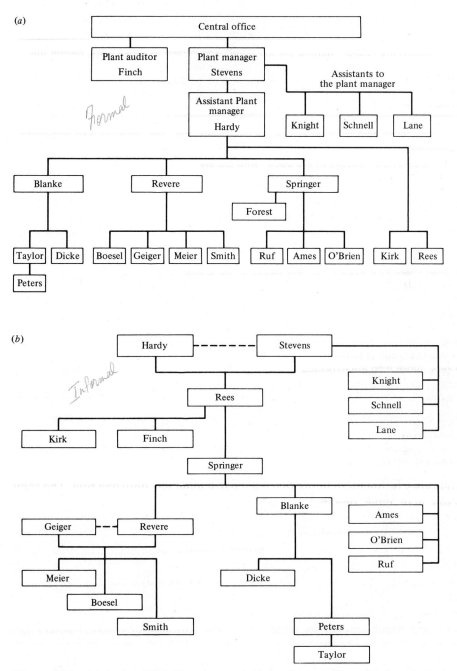

Figure 15-4 *(a)* A simplified formal organization chart of Milo. *(b)* An informal organization chart of Milo. *(Source: Melville Dalton,* Men Who Manage, *John Wiley & Sons, Inc., New York, 1959, pp. 21–22. Used with permission.)*

tion have received more attention than the functional. For example, conflicting objectives, restriction of output, conformity, blocking of ambition, inertia, and resistance to change are frequently mentioned dysfunctions of the informal organization.[27] More recently, however, organizational analysis has begun to recognize the functional aspects as well. For example, Keith Davis notes the following very practical benefits that can be derived from the informal organization:

    1 It blends with the formal organization to make a workable system for getting the work done.
    2 It lightens the workload of the formal manager and fills in some of the gaps of his abilities.
    3 It gives satisfaction and stability to work groups.
    4 It is a very useful channel of communication in the organization.
    5 Its presence encourages a manager to plan and act more carefully than he would otherwise.[28]

Because of the inevitability and power of the informal organization, the functions should be exploited in the attainment of objectives rather than futilely combated by management. As Haimann and Scott emphasize:

It is folly for management to suppose that the functioning of the formal system alone can provide the entire range of satisfaction necessary for high spirit among employees. The informal organization has a positive contribution to make in this respect. As such, it should be nurtured by management.[29]

This is especially true with regard to the informal communication system of an organization.

Informal Communication System

The term *grapevine* is commonly used to refer to the informal communication system in an organization. It can be traced back to the Civil War period when telegraph lines were strung from tree to tree like a grapevine. Messages sent over this haphazard system often became garbled, and any false information or rumor that came along was therefore facetiously said to come from the grapevine.[30] The negative connotation of the grapevine, carried over to modern times, seems to have the following pattern: The informal communication system is equated with the grapevine; the grapevine is equated with rumor; and rumor is viewed as being bad for the organization. In management practice, the next step in the above sequence is to interpret the informal system of communication as being bad for the organization. Although admittedly the

---

[27]Ross Webber, *Management*, Richard D. Irwin, Inc., Homewood, Ill., 1975, p. 518.
[28]Keith Davis, *Human Behavior at Work*, 4th ed., McGraw-Hill Book Company, New York, 1972, pp. 257–259.
[29]Haimann and Scott, op. cit., p. 435.
[30]Davis, op. cit., p. 261.

informal system is often misused and has potential dangers, most organization theorists now agree that there are also many positive functions.

Negative and Positive Aspects of the Grapevine   The informal system of communication can spread false rumors and destructive information *or* it can effectively supplement the formal channels of communication discussed in Chapter 9. It can quickly disseminate pertinent information that assists the formal systems to attain goals. However, whether the informal system turns out negative or positive for the organization largely depends on the goals of the person doing the communicating. Like any communication, the entire informal system has a highly personal orientation and, as pointed out earlier, personal goals may or may not be compatible with organizational goals. The degree of compatibility that does exist will have a major impact on the effect that the grapevine has on organizational goal attainment. The negative viewpoint is expressed by John Miner thus:

> There is very little that can be done to utilize the grapevine purposefully as a means of goal attainment. As a result, rumors probably do at least as much to subvert organizational goals as to foster them. They may well stir up dissension. They are contrary to fact.[31]

Research does not completely support this position. For example, Robert Hershey conducted a study of six companies that analyzed the accuracy of thirty rumors which dealt with transfers, procedural changes, promotions, relocation, reorganization, profit sharing, retirement, pay raises, and union disaffiliation. Sixteen of these rumors proved to be groundless, nine turned out to be accurate, and five were partially accurate.[32] Thus, in this study only slightly more than half the rumors were false. Several other studies have found the grapevine to be even more accurate. Studies at a U.S. Naval Ordnance Test Station and a major public utility found about 80 percent accuracy.[33] In other words, it seems to be a mistake to equate the entire informal communication system with false rumors. A more logical criticism of informal communication is the point made by Scott about irresponsibility. He stated:

> Since the origin and direction of the flow of information on the grapevine is hard to pinpoint, it is difficult to assign responsibility for false information or morale-lowering rumors. The speed at which the grapevine is capable of transmitting information makes control of invalid messages troublesome.[34]

On the other hand, the speed factor that Scott talks about may also work to the advantage of the organization. Since the informal system is so personally based

---

[31]John B. Miner, *Personnel Psychology,* The Macmillan Company, New York, 1969, p. 259.

[32]Robert Hershey, "The Grapevine—Here to Stay But Not Beyond Control," *Personnel,* January–February 1966, p. 64.

[33]Eugene Walton, "How Efficient Is the Grapevine," *Personnel,* vol. 28, 1961, pp. 45–49.

[34]Scott, op. cit., p. 172.

and directed, it tends to be much faster than the formal downward system of information flows. Important, relevant information that requires quick responsive action by lower-level personnel may be more effectively handled by the informal system than by the formal system. As pointed out in Chapter 9, the informal system is a major way that the necessary requirements for interactive and subordinate-initiated communication are accomplished. The formal horizontal and upward systems are often either inadequate or completely ineffective. The informal system is generally relied upon to coordinate the units horizontally on a given level and to provide valuable upward information about subordinate performance, ideas, and attitudes.

Types of Informal Communication   Since an informal organization structure will always coexist with a formal structure, there will be an informal communication system in every formal organization. Keith Davis has depicted the ways in which the informal communication networks may be arranged. Figure 15-5 shows four possible informal communication networks. The cluster chain, which research shows to be the most prevalent form of informal communication,

> . . . means that most people in management acted as passive receivers, and only a few (10 to 30 per cent in most cases) re-communicated the information originally to another person. . . . There was no established, consistent group of communicators, but some persons tended more than others to be active in communication.[35]

[35]Keith Davis, "Communication within Management," *Personnel*, November 1954, p. 215.

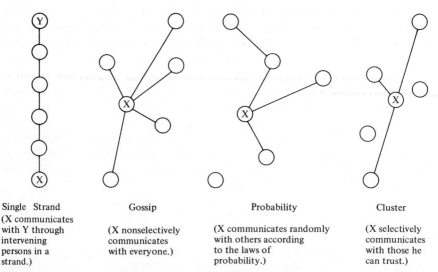

| Single Strand (X communicates with Y through intervening persons in a strand.) | Gossip (X nonselectively communicates with everyone.) | Probability (X communicates randomly with others according to the laws of probability.) | Cluster (X selectively communicates with those he can trust.) |

Figure 15-5   Informal communication networks in an organization. *(Source: Adapted from Keith Davis, "Management Communication and the Grapevine,"* Harvard Business Review, *September–October, 1953, p. 45.)*

Management cannot directly establish a certain type of informal network, but it can indirectly influence the outcome of informal communication. Research has indicated certain predictable patterns of informal communication. For example:

1 People talk most when the news is recent.
2 People talk about things that affect their work.
3 People talk about people they know.
4 People working near each other are likely to be on the same grapevine.
5 People who contact each other in the chain of procedure tend to be on the same grapevine.[36]

Briefly, management must recognize that just as the informal organization is inevitable, so is the informal communication system. It should not be narrowly equated with false rumors. Rather, it should be recognized that the grapevine is accurate, it is fast, and it carries much information that is needed to supplement the formal systems of communication in an organization. Today's managers should attempt to manage and make use of the informal system to help them attain organization objectives.

SUMMARY

Groups and the informal organization represent two important dynamics of organizational behavior. Group formation, types, and processes, and the structure and functions of the informal organization, all are of particular relevance to the study of organizational behavior. Group formation can be theoretically explained by propinquity; as a relationship between activities, interactions, and sentiments; as a symmetrical balance between attraction and common attitudes; and as a reward-cost exchange. Participants in an organization also form into groups for very practical economic, security, and social reasons. Many different types of formal and informal groups are found in modern organizations. Command and task groups and all types of committees are common examples of formally designated groups. Committees in particular are playing an increasingly important role in modern organizations. Although they can be time-consuming and costly and conducive to divided responsibility and excessive compromise, they can improve decisions through combined and integrated judgment, reduce conflict, facilitate coordination, and increase motivation and commitment through participation.

An informal organization structure coexists with every formal structure. Not formally designated, the informal structure is determined by various group-status positions and roles. Traditionally, only the dysfunctional aspects of informal organization were emphasized. More recently, the functional aspects are also recognized. A good example is the informal communication system which can either spread false rumors and cause destructive conflict or

[36]Ibid., p. 217.

become an effective supplement to the formal systems of communication. Management in the future must be able to understand and, when possible, take advantage of group dynamics and informal organization.

QUESTIONS FOR DISCUSSION AND REVIEW

1 Briefly discuss the major theoretical explanations for group formation. Which do you think is most relevant to the study of organizational behavior? Defend your choice.
2 What implications does the Schachter checkerboard study have for the study of organizational behavior?
3 How can the disadvantages of committees be overcome?
4 What are some functions of the informal organization? What are some of the dysfunctions?
5 Give some specific examples of the informal roles found in Figure 15-3 from your own experiences.

CASE: THE SCHOOLBOY ROOKIE

Kent Sikes was a junior at State University. After spring semester he went back to his home town and took a summer job in the biggest factory in town. He was told to report to the warehouse supervisor the first day at work. The supervisor assigned him to a small group of men who were responsible for loading and unloading the boxcars that supplied the materials and carried away the finished goods of the factory.

After two weeks on the job, Kent was amazed how little work the men in his crew accomplished. It seemed that they were forever standing around and talking or, in some cases, even going off to hide when there was work to be done. Kent often found himself alone unloading a boxcar while the other members of the crew were off messing around some place else. When Kent complained to his coworkers, they made it very plain that if he did not like it he could quit, but if he complained to the supervisor he would be sorry. Although Kent was deliberately excluded from any of the crew's activities such as taking breaks together or a Friday afternoon beer after work at the tavern across the street, finally toward the end of the summer he went up to one of the older members of the crew and said, "What gives with you guys anyway? I am just trying to do my job. The money is good and I just don't give a hang about this place. I will be leaving to go back to school in a few weeks, and I wish I could have got to know you all better, but frankly I am sure glad I'm not like you guys." The old worker replied, "Son, if you were here as long as I have been, you would be just like us."

1 Using some of the theories, explain the possible reasons for the group formation of this work crew. What types of groups exist in this case?
2 Place this work group in the Schachter study. What role does the supervisor play in the performance of this group?

3 What are the major informal roles of the crew members and Kent? What status position did Kent have with the group? Why?

4 Why wasn't Kent accepted by the group? Do you agree with the old worker's last statement in the case? Why or why not?

SELECTED REFERENCES

Cartwright, Dorwin, and Alvin Zander (eds.): *Group Dynamics,* 2d ed., Row, Peterson & Company, Evanston, Ill., 1960.

Dalton, Melville: *Men Who Manage,* John Wiley & Sons, Inc., New York, 1959, chaps. 3 and 4.

Filley, A. C.: "Committee Management: Guidelines from Social Science Research," *California Management Review,* Fall 1970, pp. 13–20.

Homans, George C.: *The Human Group,* Harcourt, Brace & World, Inc., New York, 1950.

Kelly, Joe: *Organizational Behaviour,* rev. ed., Richard D. Irwin, Inc., and The Dorsey Press, Homewood, Ill., 1974, chap. 8.

Olmstead, Michael S.: *The Small Group,* Random House, Inc., New York, 1959.

Schein, Edgar H.: *Organizational Psychology,* 2d ed., Prentice-Hall, Inc., Englewood Cliffs, N.J., 1970.

Thibaut, John W., and Harold H. Kelley: *The Social Psychology of Groups,* John Wiley & Sons, Inc., New York, 1959.

Tsaklanganos, Angelos A.: "Informal Organization: A Managerial Myth Revisited," *Marquette Business Review,* Winter 1973, pp. 167–173.

Chapter 16

The Dynamics of Conflict

An understanding of the concept and ramifications of conflict has become a vital part of the study of organizational behavior. The most obvious and relevant conflict is that between the human being and the formal organization. Argyris would say that given the mature, adult human being and the nature of the bureaucratic, formal organization, conflict is inevitable. This basic incongruency thesis provides a great deal of insight into the study of organizational behavior, but it is not enough. Like the other concepts discussed in this book, conflict is very complex. Conflict can mean many different things to many different people and can range in intensity from a minor difference of opinion to war between nations.

The discussion of group dynamics and informal organization in the last chapter provides many insights into the study of conflict in organizational behavior. For example, Kelly notes that conflict occurs when the group faces a novel problem or task; when new values are imported from the social environment into the group; or when members' extra-group roles are different from their intra-group roles.[1] Yet, even though these and many other examples indicate the inherent conflict found in groups, its presence does not necessarily

---

[1]Joe Kelly, *Organizational Behaviour*, rev. ed., Richard D. Irwin, Inc., and The Dorsey Press, Homewood, Ill., 1974, p. 565.

imply a negative impact for organizational behavior. Citing Georg Simmel's classic essay called "Conflict," Lewis Coser explains that

> ... groups require disharmony as well as harmony, dissociation as well as association; and conflicts within them are by no means altogether disruptive factors. Group formation is the result of both types of processes. Far from being necessarily dysfunctional, a certain degree of conflict is an essential.[2]

This positive view of conflict found in group processes can also be found when analyzing conflict from the perspective of individuals and the organization.

This chapter first examines conflict from the perspective of the individual. Intraindividual concepts such as frustration, goal conflict, and role conflict are initially given attention, and then interpersonal conflict is discussed within the framework of the Johari window. Strategies for conflict resolution are presented. The last part of the chapter examines conflict from the perspective of the organization. The chapter concludes by presenting some of the major assumptions and strategies in the management of organizational conflict.

INTRAINDIVIDUAL ASPECTS OF CONFLICT

A smooth progression of the need-drive-goal motivational cycle, discussed in Chapter 13, and living up to one's role expectations does not always occur in reality. Within every individual there are usually (1) a number of competing needs and roles; (2) a variety of different ways that drives and roles can be expressed; (3) many types of barriers which can occur between the drive and the goal; and (4) both positive and negative aspects attached to desired goals. These complicate the human adaptation process and often result in conflict. Ways of analyzing intraindividual forms of conflict are the frustration paradigm, goals, and roles.

Conflict from Frustration

Frustration occurs when a motivated drive is blocked before reaching a desired goal. Figure 16-1 graphically shows what happens. The barrier may be either overt (outward, physical) or covert (inward, mental-sociopsychological). An example of a frustrating situation might be that of the thirsty person who comes up against a stuck door and is prevented from reaching a water fountain. Figure 16-2 illustrates this simple frustrating situation. Frustration normally triggers defense mechanisms in the person. Traditionally, psychologists felt that frustration always leads to the defense mechanism of aggression. On becoming frustrated, it was thought that a person would react by physically or symbolically attacking the barrier. In the example in Figure 16-2, the person would react by kicking and/or cursing the jammed door.

More recently, aggression has come to be viewed as only one possible reaction. Frustration may lead to any of the defense mechanisms used by the

[2]Lewis Coser, *The Functions of Social Conflict*, The Free Press, Glencoe, Ill., 1956, p. 31.

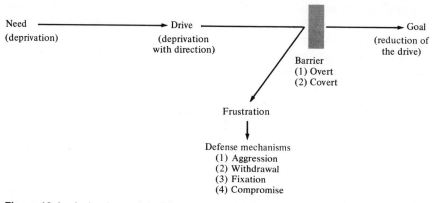

Figure 16-1   A simple model of frustration.

human organism. Although there are many such mechanisms, they can be summarized into four broad categories: aggression, withdrawal, fixation, and compromise. In the illustration of Figure 16-2, backing away from the door and pouting would be an example of withdrawal; pretending the door is not jammed and continually trying to open it would be an example of fixation; and substituting a new goal (a cup of coffee already in the room) or a new direction (climbing out the window) would be an example of compromise.

Although the thirsty person frustrated by the stuck door is a very uncomplicated example, the same frustration model can be used to analyze more complex behavior. One example would be a black individual who comes from a disadvantaged educational and economic background but who still has intense needs for pride and dignity. A goal that may fulfill the individual's needs

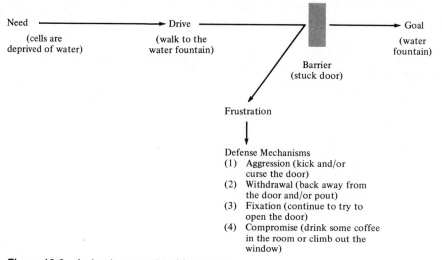

Figure 16-2   A simple example of frustration.

is meaningful employment. The drive set up to alleviate the need and accomplish the goal would be to search for a good job. The black person in this example who meets barriers (prejudice, discrimination, lack of education, and nonqualification) may become frustrated. Possible reactions to this frustration may be aggression (riot or hate), withdrawal (apathy and unemployment), fixation (pretending the barriers do not exist and continuing to search unsuccessfully for a good job), or compromise (finding expression of pride and dignity in something other than a good job, such as in a militant group).

The frustration model can be useful in the analysis not only of behavior in general but also of specific aspects of organizational behavior. Figure 16-3 summarizes some behavioral reactions to frustration that may occur in the formal organization. These examples generally imply that there is a negative impact on the individual's performance and on the organization as a result of frustration. Although research indicates this is generally true, it cannot be automatically assumed. There are some cases where frustration may actually result in a positive impact on individual performance and organizational goals. An example is the worker or manager who has high needs for competency and achievement and has a self-concept that includes confidence in being able to do a job well. A person of this type who is frustrated on the job may react in a traditional defensive manner, but the frustration may result in improved performance. The person may try harder to overcome the barrier or may overcompensate, or the new direction or goal sought may be more compatible with the organization's goals. In addition, it should be remembered that defense mechanisms per se are not bad for the individual. They play an important role in the psychological adjustment process and are "unhealthy" only when they dominate the individual's personality. Reactions to frustration are also influenced by external factors. For example, group norms, such as those that exist in a professional setting, may dictate that the accepted reaction to frustration is to try harder to overcome the barriers.[3] Obviously, examples such as the above are the exceptions, but they do point out that, in certain situations, frustration can lead to positive as well as negative organizational behavior. However, in general, a major goal of management in cases of conflict should be to eliminate the barriers (imagined, real, or potential) that are or will be frustrating to their employees.

Goal Conflict

Another common source of conflict for an individual is a goal which has both positive and negative features or the existence of two or more competing goals. Whereas in frustration a single motive is blocked before the goal is reached, in goal conflict two or more motives block one another. For ease of analysis, three separate types of goal conflict are generally identified:

[3]See Abraham K. Korman, *Industrial and Organizational Psychology*, Prentice-Hall, Inc., Englewood Cliffs, N.J., 1971, pp. 170–171.

Figure 16-3   Examples of Reactions to Frustration

Adjustive reactions	Psychological process	Illustration
Compensation	Individual devotes himself to a pursuit with increased vigor to make up for some feeling of real or imagined inadequacy	Zealous, hard-working president of the Twenty-Five Year Club who has never advanced very far in the company hierarchy
Conversion	Emotional conflicts are expressed in muscular, sensory, or bodily symptoms of disability, malfunctioning, or pain	A disabling headache keeping a staff member off the job, the day after a cherished project has been rejected
Displacement	Redirecting pent-up emotions toward persons, ideas, or objects other than the primary source of the emotion	Roughly rejecting a simple request from a subordinate after receiving a rebuff from the boss
Fantasy	Day-dreaming or other forms of imaginative activity provide an escape from reality and imagined satisfactions	An employee's day-dream of the day in the staff meeting when he corrects the boss' mistakes and is publicly acknowledged as the real leader of the industry
Identification	Individual enhances his self-esteem by patterning his own behavior after another's, frequently also internalizing the values and beliefs of the other; also vicariously sharing the glories or suffering in the reversals of other individuals or groups	The "assistant-to" who takes on the vocabulary, mannerisms, or even pomposity of his vice-presidential boss
Negativism	Active or passive resistance, operating unconsciously	The manager who, having been unsuccessful in getting out of a committee assignment, picks apart every suggestion that anyone makes in the meetings
Projection	Individual protects himself from awareness of his own undesirable traits or unacceptable feelings by attributing them to others	Unsuccessful person who, deep down, would like to block the rise of others in the organization and who continually feels that others are out to "get him"
Rationalization	Justifying inconsistent or undesirable behavior, beliefs, statements, and motivations by providing acceptable explanations for them	Padding the expense account because "everybody does it"

   1   *Approach-approach* conflict, where the individual is motivated to approach two or more positive but mutually exclusive goals.
   2   *Approach-avoidance* conflict, where the individual is motivated to approach a goal and at the same time is motivated to avoid it. The single goal contains both positive and negative characteristics for the individual.

Figure 16-3 (cont.)

Adjustive reactions	Psychological process	Illustration
Reaction-formation	Urges not acceptable to consciousness are repressed and in their stead opposite attitudes or modes of behavior are expressed with considerable force	Employee who has not been promoted who overdoes the defense of his boss, vigorously upholding the company's policies
Regression	Individual returns to an earlier and less mature level of adjustment in the face of frustration	A manager having been blocked in some administrative pursuit busies himself with clerical duties or technical details more appropriate for his subordinates
Repression	Completely excluding from consciousness impulses, experiences, and feelings which are psychologically disturbing because they arouse a sense of guilt or anxiety	A subordinate "forgetting" to tell his boss the circumstances of an embarrassing situation
Fixation	Maintaining a persistent nonadjustive reaction even though all the cues indicate the behavior will not cope with the problems	Persisting in carrying out an operational procedure long since declared by management to be uneconomical as a protest because the employee's opinion wasn't asked
Resignation, apathy, and boredom	Breaking psychological contact with the environment; withholding any sense of emotional or personal involvement	Employee who, receiving no reward, praise, or encouragement, no longer cares whether or not he does a good job
Flight or withdrawal	Leaving the field in which frustration, anxiety, or conflict is experienced, either physically or psychologically	The salesman's big order falls through and he takes the rest of the day off; constant rebuff or rejection by superiors and colleagues pushes an older worker toward being a loner and ignoring what friendly gestures are made

Source: Timothy W. Costello and Sheldon S. Zalkind, *Psychology in Administration: A Research Orientation,* Prentice-Hall, Inc., Englewood Cliffs, N.J., © 1963, pp. 148–149. Reprinted by permission.

3 *Avoidance-avoidance* conflict, where the individual is motivated to avoid two or more negative but mutually exclusive goals.

To varying degrees, each of these forms of goal conflict exists in the modern formal organization.

Approach-Approach Conflict This type of goal conflict probably has the least impact on organizational behavior. Research from the behavioral sciences concludes that "the choice between two positive goals naturally becomes more difficult and takes longer when they are seen of equal value, but in any case it remains relatively easy to make a selection."[4] For example, if both personal and organizational goals are attractive to organizational participants, they will usually make a choice rather quickly and thus eliminate their conflict. A more specific example would be the young person who is faced with two excellent job opportunities or the executive who has the choice between two very attractive offices in which to work. Such situations often cause the person some anxiety but are quickly resolved and the person does not "starve between two haystacks."

Approach-approach conflict can be analyzed in terms of Leon Festinger's well-known Theory of Cognitive Dissonance.[5] In simple terms, dissonance is the state of psychological discomfort or conflict created in people when they are faced with two or more goals or alternatives to a decision. Although these alternatives occur together, they do not belong or fit together. The theory states that the person experiencing dissonance will be highly motivated to reduce or eliminate it and will actively avoid situations and information which would likely increase it. For example, the young person faced with two equally attractive job opportunities would experience dissonance. According to Festinger's theory, this young person would actively try to reduce the dissonance. The individual may cognitively rationalize that one job is really better than the other one, and once the choice is made be sincerely convinced that it was the right choice and actively avoid any evidence or argument to the contrary.

Approach-Avoidance Conflict   This type of goal conflict is most relevant to the analysis of organizational behavior. Normally, organizational goals have both positive and negative aspects for organizational participants. Accordingly, the organizational goal may arouse a great deal of conflict within a person and may actually cause the person to vacillate anxiously at the point where approach equals avoidance.

Figure 16-4 shows some possible gradients for approach and avoidance. X represents the point of maximum conflict where the organism may come to a complete stop and vacillate. In order for the organism to progress beyond X, there must be a shift in the gradients so that there is a greater strength of response for approach than for avoidance. The slopes of the gradients shown in Figure 16-4 approximate those obtained from animals who are first trained to approach food at the end of a runway and are then shocked while feeding there. "The pull toward a positive goal increases with nearness, but only slightly; while the tendency to retreat from a negative goal rises very steeply as it is approached."[6]

The approach-avoidance gradients for humans will not always resemble

    [4]Bernard Berelson and Gary A. Steiner, *Human Behavior,* Harcourt, Brace & World, Inc., New York, 1964, p. 271.
    [5]Leon Festinger, *A Theory of Cognitive Dissonance,* Stanford University Press, Stanford, Calif., 1957.
    [6]Berelson and Steiner, op. cit., p. 273.

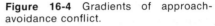

Goal Near X Far **Figure 16-4** Gradients of approach-
(+, −) Distance from the goal avoidance conflict.

that found in Figure 16-4. The slopes may be different for different people and different goals. In general, however, it is safe to assume that the positive aspects of a given organizational goal are stronger and more salient at a distance (in time and/or space) than are the negative aspects. On the other hand, as a person gets nearer to the goal, the negative aspects become more pronounced, and at some point the individual may hesitate or fail to progress any further. For example, managers engaged in long-range planning typically are very confident of a goal (plan) they have developed for the future. Yet, as the time gets near to commit resources and implement the plan, the negative consequences seem to appear much greater than they did in the developing stage. The manager or managers involved may reach the point where approach equals avoidance. The result is a great deal of internal conflict which may cause indecision, ulcers, or even neurosis. Such conflict and its aftermath are very common among decision makers and people in responsible positions in modern, complex organizations. The following almost unbelievable health report on executives in one randomly selected successful firm is indicative of the situation.[7]

   1 *Executive vice president,* aged fifty, had had three attacks and a stroke. He was retired on full pay and shortly afterward committed suicide.

   2 *Treasurer* trembles each time the president talks to him and has developed a skin disease.

   3 *Employee relations director* feels he cannot live up to the job, has had a nervous breakdown, and is under constant treatment by a psychiatrist.

   4 *Vice president marketing* had had a heart attack while playing with his children after "a record game of golf."

   5 *Vice president planning* had become a manic-depressive and had to be moved to another location—to a "soft job."

   [7]Ernest Dale and Lyndall Urwick, *Staff in Organization,* McGraw-Hill Book Company, New York, 1960, pp. 17–18.

6 *Vice president finance* had been fired after a disagreement with the president; he had overdrawn on his charge accounts with local firms because of the pressure his wife had been exerting on him to live beyond his means.

7 *Director of purchasing* suddenly dropped dead of a heart attack.

8 *Regional manager* suddenly dropped dead of a heart attack.

Obviously, the above is not necessarily representative of all executive personnel, but it does make the point that the stress and internal conflict in executives are certainly more severe than in the population as a whole. On the other hand, the approach-avoidance type of conflict can often be resolved in the manner of cognitive dissonance, or the gradients are shifted by the individual so that either the positive or the negative aspects clearly outweigh the other.

Avoidance-Avoidance Conflict   Analogous to approach-approach conflict, this type of conflict does not have a great deal of impact on organizational behavior. Avoidance-avoidance conflict is usually easily resolved. A person faced with two negative goals may not choose either of them and may simply leave the situation. If this can be done, the conflict is quickly resolved. In some situations, however, the person is unable to leave. This would be true of persons in nonvoluntary organizations, such as inmates in a prison, patients in a hospital, or draftees in the armed services. To a lesser extent, most personnel in modern organizations are also restricted from leaving. An example is the worker who detests his supervisor and has too much pride to accept unemployment compensation. This worker cannot easily resolve his avoidance-avoidance conflict in a time when jobs are very scarce.

Goal Conflict in Perspective   There are a few instances where all three types of goal conflict might benefit the organization. Approach-approach conflicts can be mildly distressing for a person but represent the best of both worlds. Approach-avoidance conflicts arising over organizational goals may force very careful planning and forecasting of exact positive and negative outcomes. Even avoidance-avoidance may stimulate the person involved to examine and try to improve the problems causing the conflict. Yet, on balance, except for approach-approach conflicts, management should attempt to resolve goal conflicts. In particular, a major management effort should be devoted to building compatibility, not conflict, between personal and organizational goals.

Role Conflict

The concept of role has been pointed out as being a basic unit of analysis in the behavioral sciences. Closely related to the concept of norms (the "oughts" of behavior), *role* was defined in Chapter 2 as a position that has expectations evolving from established norms. Persons living in a contemporary Western society assume a succession of roles throughout life. A typical sequence of social roles would be that of child, son or daughter, teen-ager, college student, boyfriend or girlfriend, husband or wife, father or mother, and grandfather or grandmother. Each of these roles has recognized expectations which are acted out like a role in a play.

Besides progressing through a succession of roles such as those just mentioned, the adult in modern society fills numerous roles at the same time. It is not uncommon for the adult middle-class male to be simultaneously playing the roles of husband, father, provider, son (to elderly parents), worker or manager, student (in a night program), coach of a Little League baseball team, church member, member of a social club, bridge partner, poker club member, officer of a community group, and weekend golfer. Although all the roles which individuals bring into the organization are relevant to their behavior, in the study of organizational behavior the organizational role is the most important. Roles such as assembly-line worker, clerk, supervisor, salesperson, engineer, systems analyst, department head, vice president, and chairperson of the board often carry conflicting demands and expectations. The classic example of an organizational role in constant conflict is that of the first-line supervisor.

Role Conflict in Supervisors   The first-line supervisor is often described as the "person in the middle." One set of expectations of this role is that the supervisor is part of the management team and should have the corresponding values and attitudes. A second set of expectations is that the supervisor came from, and is still part of, the workers' group and should have their values and attitudes. Still a third set of expectations is that supervisors are a separate link between management and the work force and should have their own unique set of values and attitudes. Conflict arises because supervisors themselves, like the workers and managers, do not know which set of expectations they should follow.

The typical supervisor often experiences intrarole as well as interrole conflict. Intrarole conflict is inherent in the following description of the supervisor's job: "It is thus abundantly clear that the foreman's job necessitates a 'management slant.' But at the same time, he should be able to see the job from the worker's point of view."[8] This dual membership in both the management and rank-and-file groups is a source of anxiety and intrarole conflict. The interrole conflict, on the other hand, is candidly expressed by one supervisor as follows: ". . . the supervisor is a 'bumping post.' . . . He's a 'bumping post' because he's in the middle; he has to take it from both ends; and those running the place don't give him any credit for it."[9]

The first-line supervisor obviously represents the extreme case of organizational role conflict. Yet, to degrees, varying with the individual and the situation, every other position in the modern organization also experiences both intrarole and interrole conflict. Staff engineers are not sure of their real authority. The clerk in the front office does not know whether to respond to a

[8]John P. Foley, Jr., and Anne Anastasi, *Human Relations and the Foreman*, National Foremen's Institute, Inc., Chicago, 1951, p. 25.

[9]William F. Whyte and Burleigh Gardner, "The Position and Problems of the Foreman," *Applied Anthropology*, Spring 1945, p. 19.

union-organizing drive. The examples are endless. The question is not that role conflict exists—it does, and it seems inevitable. Rather, the key for organizational analysis is to determine how role conflict can be resolved and/or effectively managed.

Role Conflict: The Lesser of Two Evils   Filley and House conclude, after an extensive review of research literature on organizational role conflict, that it has undesirable consequences but may be the lesser of two evils.[10] An example would be the classic interrole conflict between the staff engineer and the line supervisor. This conflict could easily be resolved by granting the engineer final decision-making authority. Yet, this "solution" to role conflict may create more problems than it solves. In this situation, from the perspective of organizational goals, it is probably preferable to have interrole conflict rather than to have formal decision-making authority lie with the staff engineer. Filley and House also report that research indicates that the extent of the undesirable effects from role conflict depends upon four major variables:

1   Awareness of role conflict
2   Acceptance of conflicting job pressures
3   Ability to tolerate stress
4   General personality makeup[11]

Role conflict cannot be wished or completely planned away. As with the other forms of individual conflict already discussed, the approach that management should take is to recognize the existence of role conflict, attempt to understand its causes and ramifications, and then try to manage it as effectively as possible.

INTERPERSONAL CONFLICT

Besides the intraindividual aspects of conflict, the interpersonal aspects of conflict are also an important dynamic of organizational behavior. The interrole conflict discussed in the last section certainly has interpersonal implications, and so does organizational conflict, discussed in the next section. But this section is specifically concerned with analyzing the conflict that results from two or more persons interacting with one another. Kelly notes, "Conflict situations inevitably are made up of at least two individuals who hold polarized points of view, who are somewhat intolerant of ambiguities, who ignore delicate shades of grey, and who are quick to jump to conclusions."[12] A more analytical treatment of interpersonal conflict can be gained from examining some different ways that the "self" interacts with others.

[10]Alan C. Filley and Robert J. House, *Managerial Process and Organizational Behavior*, Scott, Foresman and Company, Glenview, Ill., 1969, p. 315.
   [11]Ibid.
[12]Kelly, op. cit., p. 563.

The Johari Window

One increasingly popular framework for analyzing the dynamics of the interaction between self and others is the Johari window. Developed by Joseph Luft and Harry Ingham (thus the name *Johari*), this model can be used to analyze interpersonal conflict. As Figure 16-5 shows, the model helps identify several interpersonal styles, shows the characteristics and results of these styles, and suggests ways of interpreting the conflicts that may develop between self and others.

In simple terms, the self can be thought of as "me" and others can be thought of as "you" in two-person interaction. There are certain things that the person knows about himself or herself and certain things that are not known. The same is true of others. There are certain things the person knows about the other and certain things that are not known about the other. The following summarizes the four cells in the Johari window:

1 *Open self.* In this form of interaction the person knows about himself or herself and about the other. There would generally be openness and compatibility and little reason to be defensive. This type of interpersonal relationship would tend to lead to little, if any, interpersonal conflict.

2 *Hidden self.* In this situation the person understands himself or herself but does not know about the other person. The result is that the person remains hidden from the other because of the fear of how the other might react. The person may keep his or her true feelings or attitudes secret and will not open up to the other. There is potential interpersonal conflict in this situation.

3 *Blind self.* In this situation the person knows about the other but not about himself or herself. The person may be unintentionally irritating to the other. The other could tell the person but may be fearful of hurting the person's feelings. As in the "hidden self," there is potential interpersonal conflict in this situation.

4 *Undiscovered self.* This is potentially the most explosive situation. The person does not know about himself or herself and does not know about the other. In other words, there is much misunderstanding, and interpersonal conflict is almost sure to result.

	The person knows about the other	The person does not know about the other
The person knows about him or herself	1 Open self	2 Hidden self
The person does not know about him or herself	3 Blind self	4 Undiscovered self

Figure 16-5 The Johari window. *(Source: Adapted from Joseph Luft, "The Johari Window," Human Relations Training News, vol. 5, no. 1, 1961, pp. 6–7.)*

The Johari window only points out possible interpersonal styles. It does not necessarily describe but rather helps analyze possible interpersonal conflict situations.

One way of decreasing the "hidden self" and increasing the "open self" is through the processes of self-disclosure. By becoming more trustful of the other and disclosing information about oneself, the potential for conflict may be reduced. On the other hand, such self-disclosure is a risk for the individual, and the outcome must be worth the cost. To decrease the "blind self" and at the same time increase the open self, the other must give and the person must use feedback. The National Training Laboratory (NTL) recommends seven guidelines for providing feedback for effective interpersonal relations:

1   Be descriptive rather than judgmental.
2   Be specific rather than general.
3   Deal with things that can be changed.
4   Give feedback when it is desired.
5   Consider the motives for giving and receiving feedback.
6   Give feedback at the time the behavior takes place.
7   Give feedback when its accuracy can be checked with others.[13]

Following these seven guidelines can help decrease the potential for interpersonal conflict.

Strategies for Interpersonal Conflict Resolution

In addition to the self-disclosure and feedback approaches to interpersonal conflict reduction there are three basic strategies titled according to the outcomes: lose-lose, win-lose, and win-win.

Lose-Lose   A lose-lose approach to conflict resolution is where both parties lose. Filley, House, and Kerr point out that this approach can take several forms.[14] One of the more common approaches is to compromise or take the middle ground in a dispute. A second approach is to pay off one of the parties in the conflict. These payments often take the form of bribes. A third approach is to use an outside third party or arbitrator. A final type of lose-lose strategy appears when the parties in a conflict resort to bureaucratic rules or existing regulations to resolve the conflict. In all four of these approaches, both parties in the conflict lose. It is sometimes the only way that conflicts can be resolved, but it is generally less desirable than the win-lose or, especially, the win-win strategy.

Win-Lose   A win-lose strategy is a very common way of resolving conflict in American society. In a competitive type of culture, as is generally found in America, one party in a conflict situation attempts to marshal its forces to win

[13]*National Training Laboratories' Summer Reading Book,* NTL Institute for Applied Behavioral Science, Bethel, Maine, 1968.
[14]Alan C. Filley, Robert J. House, and Steven Kerr, *Managerial Process and Organizational Behavior,* 2d ed., Scott, Foresman and Company, Glenview, Ill., 1976, pp. 166–167.

and the other party loses. The following list summarizes some of the characteristics of a win-lose situation:

    1   There is a clear we-they distinction between the parties.
    2   Parties direct their energies toward each other in an atmosphere of victory
and defeat.
    3   Parties see the issue from their own point of view.
    4   The emphasis is on solutions rather than on the attainment of goals,
values, or objectives.
    5   Conflicts are personalized and judgmental.
    6   There is no differentiation of conflict-resolving activities from other group
processes, nor is there a planned sequence of those activities.
    7   The parties take a short-run view of the issues.[15]

Examples of win-lose strategies can be found in superior-subordinate
relationships, line-staff confrontations, union-management relations, and many
other conflict situations found in today's organizations. The win-lose strategy
can have both functional and dysfunctional consequences for the organization.
It is functional in the sense of creating a competitive drive to win and can lead
to cohesiveness and esprit de corps among the individuals or groups in the
conflict situation. On the dysfunctional side, a win-lose strategy ignores other
solutions such as a cooperative, mutually agreed-upon outcome; there are
pressures to conform which may stifle a questioning, creative atmosphere for
conflict resolution; and highly structured power relationships tend to rapidly
emerge. The biggest problem, however, with a win-lose strategy is that
someone always loses. Those who suffer the loss may learn something in the
process, but losers also tend to be bitter and vindictive. A much healthier
strategy is to have both parties of a conflict situation win.

    Win-Win   A win-win strategy of conflict resolution is probably the most
desirable from a human and organizational standpoint. Energies and creativity
are aimed at solving the problems rather than beating the other party. It takes
advantage of the functional aspects of win-lose and eliminates many of the
dysfunctional aspects. The needs of both parties in the conflict situation are
met and both parties receive rewarding outcomes. After a review of relevant
literature, Filley, House, and Kerr conclude that "win-win decision strategies
are associated with better judgments, favorable organization experience, and
more favorable bargains."[16] Although it is often difficult to accomplish a
win-win outcome of an interpersonal conflict, this should be a major goal of the
management of conflict.

ORGANIZATIONAL CONFLICT

So far, the chapter has concentrated on intraindividual and interpersonal
conflict. This individual perspective of conflict takes place within the organiza-

    [15]Ibid., p. 167.
    [16]Ibid., p. 177.

tional setting, and that is why it is so important to the study of organizational behavior. However, now attention is directed at organizational conflict per se, but it must be remembered that both intra- and interpersonal conflict are inherent in organizational conflict.

Structural Conflict

Individuals in the organization have many conflicting organizational cross-pressures operating on them. Bass notes the following examples:

> The boss wants more production; subordinates want more consideration. Customers demand faster deliveries; peers request schedule delays. Consultants suggest change; subordinates resist change. The rule book prescribes a formula; the staff says it will not work.[17]

More conceptually, Litterer suggests four causes of organizational conflict: (1) an incompatible goals situation, (2) the existence of incompatible means or incompatible resource allocations, (3) a problem of status incongruities, and (4) a difference in perceptions.[18] These sources of organizational conflict result largely from the dynamics of individual and group interactions and psychological processes.

In the classical organization there are four structural areas where conflict is most pronounced:

1 *Hierarchical conflict.* There may be conflict between the various levels of the organization. The board of directors may be in conflict with top management, middle management may be in conflict with supervisory personnel, or there may be general conflict between management and the workers.

2 *Functional conflict.* There may be conflict between the various functional departments of the organization. Conflict between the production and marketing departments in an industrial organization is a classic example.

3 *Line-staff conflict.* There may be conflict between the line and staff. It often results from situations where staff personnel do not formally possess authority over line personnel.

4 *Formal-informal conflict.* There may be conflict between the formal and informal organizations. For example, the informal organization's norms for performance may be incompatible with the formal organization's norms for performance.

The hierarchical, functional, and line-staff forms of organizational conflict were covered extensively in Chapter 6, on classical organization structure, and the dynamics of the formal-informal conflict situation were analyzed in the last chapter.

---

[17]Bernard M. Bass, *Organizational Psychology,* Allyn and Bacon, Inc., Boston, 1965, pp. 324–325.

[18]Joseph A. Litterer, "Managing Conflict in Organizations," *Proceedings of the 8th Annual Midwest Management Conference,* Southern Illinois University, Business Research Bureau, 1965. Reprinted in Max S. Wortman and Fred Luthans, *Emerging Concepts in Management,* The Macmillan Company, 1969, pp. 192–194.

Modern organization design also contains potential conflict situations. The project and matrix organizations in particular have structurally created conflict. The project manager with responsibility but no authority and the manager in a matrix structure with a functional boss and a project boss present two obvious conflict situations. But the existence of conflict in modern organization design also indicates that it can be healthy. In some cases the modern designs may actually try to promote conflict to benefit the organization.

The Role of Conflict in Today's Organizations

Traditionally, the approach to organizational conflict was very simple and optimistic. It was based on the following assumptions:

1 Conflict is by definition avoidable.
2 Conflict is caused by troublemakers, boat rockers, and prima donnas.
3 Legalistic forms of authority such as "going through channels" or "sticking to the book" are emphasized.
4 Scapegoats are accepted as inevitable.[19]

Management relied on formal authority and classical organization restructuring to solve their "conflict problem." Individual managers often became hypocritical in order to avoid conflicts from above or below. They developed blind spots to the existence of conflict, created ingenious delaying tactics to avoid conflict, and reverted to the extensive use of defense mechanisms as pseudosolutions to conflict.[20]

Starting with the wide acceptance of the Argyris basic incongruency thesis, the behavioral approach to management began to reexamine its assumptions about conflict. Today, conflict has become one of its most vital subjects. This development has, at least indirectly, been caused by the overall societal concern for conflict on national, organizational, group, and individual bases. The outcome has been a new set of assumptions about conflict which are almost the exact opposite of the traditional assumptions:

1 Conflict is inevitable.
2 Conflict is determined by structural factors such as the physical shape of a building, the design of a career structure, or the nature of a class system.
3 Conflict is integral to the nature of change. *Stimulus to change - wise mgr who sees the necessity, but often the conflict itself leads to change.*
4 A minimal level of conflict is optimal.[21]

Based on these assumptions, the management of organizational conflict has taken a new approach. Representative are Litterer's three basic strategies to reduce organizational conflict.[22] First, buffers can be erected between conflicting parties. The classic example of this strategy was described by Whyte in his study of the restaurant industry. To reduce the conflict between

19Kelly, op. cit., p. 555.
20Bass, op. cit., pp. 326–327.
21Kelly, op. cit., p. 555.
22Litterer, op. cit., p. 195.

the cooks and runners which was caused by status incongruency—the runners were giving orders to the higher-status chefs—the runners were told to place their order slips on a hook. This hook created a buffer between the conflicting parties and the conflict was reduced. A second strategy is to help the parties in the conflicting situation develop better insights into themselves and how they affect others. The organizational development techniques discussed in Chapter 21 can be used to implement this strategy. A third strategy is to redesign the organization structure in order to reduce the conflict. This, of course, was the major strategy taken by the traditional approach to the management of conflict. However, besides trying to reduce conflict, the new approach also tries to contain it and, if at all possible, use it to obtain the objectives of the organization.

Conflict can lead to innovation and change; it can energize people to activity, develop protection for something else in the organization (in the divide-and-conquer sense), and be an important element in the systems analysis of the organization.[23] Such factors indicate that conflict can be managed to work for, rather than against, goal attainment in the modern organization.

SUMMARY

The dynamics of conflict plays a vital role in the modern analysis of organizational behavior. Conflict can be viewed from intraindividual, interpersonal, or organizational perspectives. Frustration, goal conflict, and role conflict are the major conceptual categories of intraindividual conflict. Frustration occurs when goal-directed behavior is blocked. Goal conflict can come about from approach-approach, approach-avoidance, or avoidance-avoidance situations. Role conflict results from a clash in the expectations of the various roles possessed by an individual. Interpersonal conflict was examined within the framework of the Johari window styles (open, hidden, blind, and undiscovered) and the three major strategies of interpersonal conflict resolution (lose-lose, win-lose, win-win). The broader organizational perspective of conflict can be found in both the classical (hierarchical, functional, line-staff, and formal-informal) and modern (project and matrix) structures. Traditionally, the management of organizational conflict was based on simplistic assumptions. Formal authority and classical restructuring were used in attempts to eliminate it. The more modern approach is to assume the inevitability of conflict, recognize that it is not always bad for the organization, and try to manage it effectively rather than merely try to eliminate it.

QUESTIONS FOR DISCUSSION AND REVIEW

1   What is frustration? What are some of its manifestations? How can the frustration model be used to analyze organizational behavior?

[23]Ibid., p. 192.

2 Explain approach-avoidance conflict. Give a realistic organizational example of where it may occur.

3 In an organization, when may role conflict be the lesser of two evils?

4 Briefly summarize the four "selfs" in the Johari window. What implications does each have for interpersonal conflict?

5 How do the traditional assumptions about organizational conflict differ from the modern assumptions? What implications do these new assumptions have for management of today's organizations?

CASE: DRINKING UP THE PAYCHECK

James Emery was the father of four children. He had been raised in a hard-working immigrant family. Needs for achievement and power were developed while growing up. Now he found himself in a low-paying, dead-end, assembly-line job with a large manufacturing firm. It was all he could do to get through the day, so he started daydreaming on the job. On pay-day he would often go to the tavern across the street and generally spend a lot of money. The next day he would not only be hung-over but would become very depressed because he knew that his wife could not make ends meet and his children often went without the basic essentials.

One day he could not take it any longer. At first he thought of going to his boss for some help and advice, but he really did not understand himself well enough, and he certainly did not know or trust his boss enough to openly discuss his problems with him. Instead he went to his union steward and told him about his financial problems and how much he hated his job. The steward told James exactly what he wanted to hear. "This darn company is the source of all of your problems. The working conditions are not suited for a slave, let alone us. The pay also stinks. We are all going to have to stick together when our present contract runs out and get what we deserve—better working conditions and more money."

1 Explain James's behavior in terms of the frustration model.

2 Cite a specific example of role conflict in this case.

3 What style from the Johari window can explain James's relationship with his boss? With his union steward?

4 What type of conflict resolution strategy is the union steward suggesting? Do you think the real problems facing James are working conditions and pay? Why or why not?

5 What, if anything, can be done to help the James Emerys of the world? Keep your answer in terms of human resource management.

SELECTED REFERENCES

Brooker, W. Michael A.: "Eliminating Intergroup Conflicts . . . through Interdepartmental Problem Solving," *S.A.M. Advanced Management Journal,* Spring 1975, pp. 16–25.

Derr, C. Brooklyn: "Conflict: A Neglected Resource," *The Conference Board Record,*
    March 1975, pp. 39–42.
Kelly, Joe: "Make Conflict Work for You," *Harvard Business Review,* July–August
    1970, pp. 103–113.
Mayer, Richard J.: "Communication and Conflict in Organizations," *Human Resource
    Management,* Winter 1974, pp. 2–10.
Nightingale, Donald: "Conflict and Conflict Resolution," in *Organizational Behavior
    Research and Issues,* George Strauss et al. (eds.), Industrial Relations Research
    Association, University of Wisconsin, Madison, Wis., 1974, pp. 141–163.
Scott, William G.: *The Management of Conflict,* Richard D. Irwin, Inc., Homewood, Ill.,
    1965.
Thamhain, Hans J.: "Conflict Management in Project Life Cycles," *Sloan Management
    Review,* Spring 1975, pp. 31–50.

Chapter 17

The Motivation to Work

The concept and application of motivation are probably more closely associated with the behavioral approach to management than any other single topic covered in this book. Chapter 13 spelled out the basic motivational process and examined the major motives that lead to the better understanding of human behavior. This chapter uses this as background information and is specifically concerned with work motivation. It is included in the dynamics of organizational behavior part of the book because work motivation has direct implications for the consequences of performance and satisfaction. The chapter first looks at traditional human relations approaches to motivation. The remainder of the chapter presents and analyzes the major content and process models of work motivation. Maslow's hierarchy of needs and Herzberg's two-factor theory are the two content models given attention. In the process approach, the expectancy models of Vroom and Porter and Lawler are given the most attention. Lawler's more recent refinement of the Porter-Lawler model and Smith and Cranny's simpler model are also discussed. Finally, Adams's equity theory is presented and analyzed in the additive sense for better understanding of the cognitive process of work motivation, and a brief examination is made of attribution theory and locus of control for the future development of the cognitive approach. Particular attention is devoted to the research evidence supporting or not supporting each of these models and the implications they have for the actual practice of human resource management.

TRADITIONAL HUMAN RELATIONS
APPROACH TO MOTIVATION

Chapter 13 presented motivation as a basic psychological process consisting of needs, drives, and goals. Only indirect attempts were made to apply this elemental psychological process to the practice of management. Yet, the traditional human relations approach to management generally failed to recognize the importance of this underlying psychological process. It sacrificed understanding of the variables and basic process involved for quick, stop-gap measures. The approach was based on three simple additive assumptions:

1 Personnel primarily are economically motivated and secondarily desire security and good working conditions. (A nonauthoritarian type of supervision is considered as part of conditions.)
2 Provision of the above rewards to personnel will have a positive effect on their morale.
3 There is a positive correlation between morale and productivity.

With these three assumptions, the motivational problem facing management was relatively clear-cut and easy to solve. All management had to do was devise monetary incentive plans, ensure security, and provide good working conditions; morale would be high and maximum productivity would result. It was as simple as one, two, three. Human relations experts, industrial psychologists, and industrial engineers supported this approach, and personnel managers then implemented it in practice.

Unfortunately, this human relations approach to motivation did not work out in practice. Although no harm was done and some good actually resulted in the early stages of organizational development, it soon became evident that such a simplistic approach fell far short of providing a meaningful solution to the complex motivational problems facing management. The three assumptions were at first questioned and, eventually, for the most part became invalidated by research and experience.

The major fault of the traditional approach is that the assumptions overlook far too many facts. Human motivation is much more complex and diverse than is suggested by the economic, security, working-conditions approach. Moreover, morale turned out to be a very elusive concept. Seldom operationally defined, it became a catch-all word and scapegoat for all the human problems facing management. If management could not explain a problem, it was a morale problem. Finally, as systematic research began to accumulate, the relationship between morale and productivity grew less clear. The positive correlation between them became more of an issue than an automatic assumption. Starting as far back as 1955, Brayfield and Crockett in an extensive review of the literature up to that time concluded that there was very little, if any, relationship between job satisfaction and performance.[1] About a decade later Victor Vroom analyzed the results of twenty studies and

[1]A. H. Brayfield and W. H. Crockett, "Employee Attitudes and Employee Performance," *Psychological Bulletin,* vol. 52, 1955, pp. 396–424.

found a very low (.14) median correlation between satisfaction and performance.[2]

Today, the satisfaction-performance controversy still rages on. Many
articles in contemporary organizational behavior journals attempt to present
evidence on the direction of causality between satisfaction and performance.
Three generally recognized points of view have emerged:

> **1** The view that satisfaction leads to performance, a position generally
> associated with early human relations concepts,
> **2** The view that the satisfaction-performance relationship is moderated by a
> number of variables, a position which gained acceptance in the fifties and continues
> to be reflected in current research, and
> **3** The view that performance leads to satisfaction, a recently stated posi-
> tion.[3]

Each of the above views currently has mixed support in theory and
research, but one thing is certain. The human relations position was much too
simplistic. The motivation to work is very complex, and the traditional
explanations only began to scratch the surface. There are a number of internal
and environmental variables that affect the motivation to work. The theories
and research reviewed in this chapter take a definite step in the direction of
better understanding.

MODERN THEORIES OF WORK MOTIVATION

As human problems facing management began to mount, the limitations of the
traditional human relations approach to motivation began to surface. Starting
around the beginning of the 1960s, the behavioral approach to management
started to search earnestly for a new theoretical foundation and to attempt to
devise new techniques for motivation. As Chapter 1 indicated, McGregor's
Theory Y served as the transition to the modern approach. McGregor also
adapted the humanistic psychologist Abraham Maslow's hierarchy of needs
concept to work motivation. Next came the two-factor theory of Frederick
Herzberg. Instead of Maslow's five levels, Herzberg felt there were only two
factors—hygiene/maintenance factors and motivators. He emphasized the role
of satisfaction and stimulated a great amount of research and controversy.
Because of the lack of research support for the two-factor theory, Victor
Vroom proposed an alternative expectancy theory of work motivation. Since
Vroom there have been refinements of the expectancy model (by Porter and
Lawler, and Lawler) and considerable interest in a related cognitive process
approach called *equity theory*. Figure 17-1 graphically depicts the theoretical
development of work motivation.

Figure 17-1 shows three major lines of theoretical development. The
content models go as far back as the turn of the century, when the pioneering

[2]Victor H. Vroom, *Work and Motivation,* John Wiley & Sons, Inc., New York, 1964, p. 183.

[3]Donald P. Schwab and Larry L. Cummings, ''Theories of Performance and Satisfaction: A
Review,'' *Industrial Relations,* October 1970, p. 409.

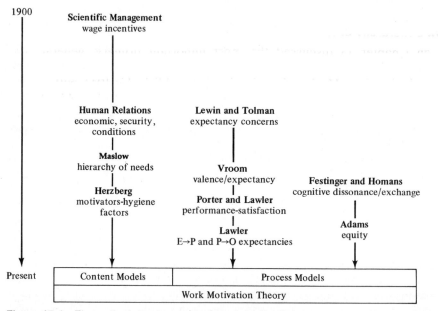

Figure 17-1 Theoretical development of work motivation.

scientific managers such as Frederick W. Taylor, Frank Gilbreth, and Henry L. Gantt proposed sophisticated wage incentive models to motivate workers. Next came the human relations movement, and then the content models of Maslow and Herzberg. The more recent developments have come from process models. Most work has been done on expectancy models, but recently equity theory has received attention. These process models are cognitively based—and, of course, there are many other cognitive models that exist in psychology (e.g., attribution theory, covered at the end of the chapter)—but these are the ones so far that have had the biggest influence on work motivation. Figure 17-1 purposely shows that at present there is a lack of integration or a synthesis of the various models. At present a group of content models can be identified and a group of process models can be identified, but there does not exist an overall theory of work motivation.

THE CONTENT THEORIES OF WORK MOTIVATION

The content theories of motivation attempt to determine what it is that motivates people at work. At first it was felt to be money only (scientific management) and then a little later it was felt to be also working conditions, security, and perhaps a democratic style of supervision (human relations). More recently, the content of motivation has been deemed to be the so-called "higher-level" needs or motives, such as esteem and self-actualization (Maslow) and responsibility, recognition, achievement, and growth (Herzberg). A thorough understanding of the two major content models contributes to the understanding of work motivation.

Maslow's Hierarchy of Needs

Although Chapter 13 discussed the most important primary, general, and secondary needs of humans, it did not relate them within a theoretical framework. Abraham Maslow, in a classic paper published in 1943, outlined the elements of an overall theory of motivation.[4] Drawing chiefly from his clinical experience, he thought that a person's motivational needs could be arranged in a hierarchical manner. In essence, he believed that once a given level of need became satisfied, it no longer served to motivate. The next higher level of need had to be activated in order to motivate the individual.

Maslow identified five levels in his need hierarchy (see Figure 17-2). They are, in brief, the following:

1 *Physiological needs.* The most basic level in the hierarchy, the physiological needs, generally corresponds to the unlearned primary needs discussed in Chapter 13. The needs of hunger, thirst, sleep, and sex are some examples. According to the theory, once these basic needs are satisfied, they no longer motivate. For example, a starving man will strive for a carrot held out in front of him. However, after he eats his fill of carrots and another carrot is held out, he will not strive to obtain it. Only the next higher level of needs will motivate him.

2 *Safety needs.* This second level of needs is roughly equivalent to the security need discussed in Chapter 13. Maslow stressed emotional as well as physical safety. The whole organism may become a safety-seeking mechanism. Yet, like the physiological needs, once these safety needs are satisfied, they no longer motivate.

3 *Love needs.* This third or intermediate level of needs loosely corresponds to the affection and affiliation needs covered in Chapter 13. Like Freud, Maslow seems guilty of poor choice of wording to identify his levels. His use of the word *love* has many misleading connotations, such as sex, which is actually a physiological need. Perhaps a more appropriate word describing this level would be *belongingness.*

4 *Esteem needs.* The esteem level represents the higher needs of humans. The needs for power, achievement, and status can be considered to be part of this level. Maslow carefully pointed out that the esteem level contains both self-esteem and esteem from others.

5 *Need for self-actualization.* This level represents the culmination of all

[4]A. H. Maslow, "A Theory of Human Motivation," *Psychological Review*, July 1943, pp. 370–396.

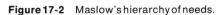

Figure 17-2 Maslow's hierarchy of needs.

the lower, intermediate, and higher needs of humans. People who have become self-actualized are self-fulfilled and have realized all of their potential. Self-actualization is closely related to the self-concept discussed in Chapter 14. In effect, self-actualization is the person's motivation to transform perception of self into reality.

Maslow did not intend that his need hierarchy should be directly applied to work motivation. In fact, he did not delve into the motivating aspects of humans in organizations until about twenty years after he originally proposed his theory.[5] Despite this lack of intent on Maslow's own part, others, such as McGregor, popularized the Maslow theory in management literature. The need hierarchy has had a tremendous impact on the modern management approach to motivation.

In a very rough manner, Maslow's need hierarchy theory can be converted into the content model of work motivation shown in Figure 17-3. If Maslow's estimates are applied to an organization example, the lower-level needs of personnel would be generally satisfied (85 percent of the basic needs and 70 percent of the security needs), but only 50 percent of the belonging needs, 40 percent of the esteem needs, and a mere 10 percent of the self-actualization needs would be met.

On the surface, the content model shown in Figure 17-3 and the estimated percentages given by Maslow seem logical and applicable to the motivation of humans in today's organizations. Maslow's need hierarchy has often been uncritically accepted by management textbooks and by practitioners. Unfortunately, the little research that has been conducted lends little, if any, support to the theory. Maslow himself provided no research back-up. About a decade after publishing his original paper, Maslow did attempt to modify his position by saying that gratifying the self-actualizing need of growth-motivated individuals can actually increase rather than decrease this need. He also hedged on some of his other original ideas, e.g., that higher needs may emerge after the

[5]A. H. Maslow, *Eupsychian Management,* Richard D. Irwin, Inc., and The Dorsey Press, Homewood, Ill., 1965.

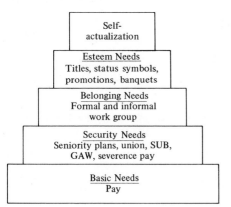

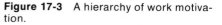

Figure 17-3 A hierarchy of work motivation.

long deprivation or suppression of lower needs instead of only when the lower needs are satisfied.[6] He stressed that human behavior is multidetermined and multimotivated.

Despite Maslow's attempts to refine and hedge on his need hierarchy theory, the direct attempts to test the theory have come up with, at best, inconclusive results. In one study of female clerks in an insurance company, Beer concluded that the Maslow model is open to question as an overall theory of work motivation. However, he did find the Maslow model to be a fairly reliable way of measuring priority needs of workers.[7] In another study which gathered data from managers at American Telephone and Telegraph over a five-year period, little support was found for the model when need changes were correlated with need strengths.[8] The same was true of another longitudinal study. Little support was found for the hypothesis that changes in satisfaction of needs in one level correlated negatively with changes in the importance of needs in the next higher level.[9] The most recent and comprehensive study by Wahba and Birdwell also does not support the Maslow model.[10] They reviewed 22 studies and found two primary clusters of needs instead of Maslow's five, and they found no support for the contention that satisfaction of one level of need will be positively associated with the activation of the next higher level of needs. However, they did find in 18 of the 22 studies that the strength of the self-actualization need was associated with a deprivation of that need.

The research studies cited above certainly make the point that Maslow is not the final answer in work motivation. Yet, the model does make a significant contribution in terms of making management aware of the diverse needs of humans at work. The number and names of the levels are not important nor, as the studies show, is the hierarchical concept. What is important is the fact that humans in the workplace have diverse motives, some of which are "high level." In other words, such needs as esteem and self-actualization are important to the content of work motivation. The exact nature of these needs and how they relate to motivation are not clear.

Herzberg's Two-Factor Theory of Motivation

Herzberg extended the work of Maslow and developed a specific content theory of work motivation. In the 1950s, he conducted a motivational study on

[6]Also see Mahmoud A. Wahba and Lawrence G. Birdwell, "Maslow Reconsidered: A Review of Research on the Need Hierarchy Theory," *Proceedings of the Academy of Management*, 1973, pp. 514–520.

[7]Michael Beer, *Leadership, Employee Needs, and Motivation,* Ohio State University, College of Commerce and Administration, Bureau of Business Research, Monograph no. 129, Columbus, 1966, p. 68.

[8]Douglas T. Hall and Khalil E. Nougaim, "An Examination of Maslow's Need Hierarchy in an Organizational Setting," *Organizational Behavior and Human Performance*, February 1968, pp. 12–35.

[9]Edward E. Lawler and J. Lloyd Suttle, "A Causal Correlational Test of the Need Hierarchy Concept," *Organizational Behavior and Human Performance*, April 1972, pp. 265–287.

[10]Wahba and Birdwell, op. cit.

about two hundred accountants and engineers employed by firms in and around Pittsburgh, Pennsylvania. He used the critical incident method of obtaining data for analysis. The professional subjects in the study were given the following directions by an interviewer:

> Think of a time when you felt exceptionally good or exceptionally bad about your job, either your present job or any other job you have had. This can be either the "long-range" or the "short-range" kind of situation, as I have just described it. Tell me what happened.[11]

Responses obtained from this critical incident method were interesting and fairly consistent. Reported good feelings were generally associated with job experiences and job content. An example was the accounting supervisor who felt good about being given the job of installing new computer equipment. He took pride and was gratified in knowing that the new equipment made a big difference in the overall functioning of his department. Reported bad feelings, on the other hand, were generally associated with the surrounding or peripheral aspects of the job—the job context. An example of these feelings was related by an engineer whose first job was to keep tabulation sheets and manage the office when the boss was gone. It turned out that his boss was always too busy to train him and became annoyed when he tried to ask questions. The engineer said that he felt frustrated in this job context and that he felt like a flunky in a dead-end job. Tabulating these reported good and bad feelings, Herzberg concluded that job satisfiers were related to job content and job dissatisfiers were allied to job context. The satisfiers were labeled *motivators* and the dissatisfiers were called *hygiene factors.* Taken together, they became known as Herzberg's *two-factor theory of motivation.*

Herzberg's theory is closely related to Maslow's need hierarchy. The hygiene factors, like the medical term, are preventive and environmental in nature, and they are roughly equivalent to Maslow's lower-level needs (see Figure 17-4). These hygienic factors prevent dissatisfaction, but they do not lead to satisfaction. In effect, they bring motivation up to a theoretical zero level and are a necessary "floor" to prevent dissatisfaction, and they serve as a take-off for motivation. By themselves, the hygiene factors do not motivate. Only the motivators (see Figure 17-4) motivate humans on the job. They are roughly equivalent to Maslow's higher-level needs. According to the Herzberg theory, an individual must have a job with a challenging content in order to be truly motivated.

Herzberg's two-factor theory cast a new light on the content of work motivation. Up to this point, management had generally concentrated on the hygienic factors. When faced with a morale problem, the typical solution was higher pay, more fringe benefits, and better conditions. However, as pointed out earlier, this simplistic solution did not work. Management is often

---

[11]Frederick Herzberg, Bernard Mausner, and Barbara Bloch Snyderman, *The Motivation to Work*, 2d ed., John Wiley & Sons, Inc., New York, 1959, p. 141.

Figure 17-4 Herzberg's Two-Factor Theory

Hygiene factors	Motivators
Company policy and administration	Achievement
Supervision, technical	Recognition
Salary	Work itself
Interpersonal relations, supervisor	Responsibility
Working conditions	Advancement

perplexed because they are paying high wages and salaries, have an excellent fringe-benefit package, and great working conditions, but their employees are still not motivated. Herzberg's theory offers an explanation for this dilemma. By concentrating only on the hygienic factors, management is not motivating its personnel.

There are probably very few workers or managers who do not feel they deserved the raise they received. On the other hand, there are many dissatisfied workers and managers who did not get a raise. This simple observation points out that the hygiene factors seem to be important in preventing dissatisfaction but do not lead to satisfaction. Herzberg would be the first to say that hygienic factors are absolutely necessary to maintain the human resources of an organization. However, as in the Maslow sense, once "the belly is full" of hygiene factors, which is the case in most modern organizations, dangling any more in front of employees will not motivate them. Only a challenging job which has the opportunities for achievement, recognition, responsibility, advancement, and growth will motivate personnel.

Criticism of Herzberg's Theory

Although Herzberg's two-factor theory became very popular as a textbook explanation of work motivation and was widely accepted by practitioners in the middle 1960s, it came under heavy attack by most academicians. Victor Vroom was in the vanguard of the attack. In 1964, he stated that the two-factor conclusion was only one of many that could be interpreted from Herzberg's research findings. "One could also argue that the relative frequency with which job-content or job-contextual features will be mentioned as sources of satisfaction and dissatisfaction is dependent on the nature of the content and context of the work roles of the respondents."[12] Vroom cited the classic study of the assembly-line worker, by Walker and Guest, to support his interpretation.[13] In response to this and other criticism, Herzberg cites the results of an impressive number and diversity of replications of his original Pittsburgh study which supported his position.[14] He included studies which were conducted on

[12]Vroom, op. cit., p. 128.

[13]Charles R. Walker and Robert H. Guest, *The Man on the Assembly Line*, Harvard University Press, Cambridge, Mass., 1952.

[14]Frederick Herzberg, *Work and the Nature of Man*, The World Publishing Company, Cleveland, 1966.

agricultural administrators, professional women, hospital maintenance personnel, nurses, manufacturing supervisors, food handlers, scientists, engineers, teachers, technicians, assemblers, accountants, military officers, and managers about to retire, plus cross-cultural studies conducted in Finland, Yugoslavia, Hungary, and Russia. He also obtained some support from those who analyzed the existing evidence from a wide variety of studies[15] and from further reexamination by himself and his colleagues.[16]

Analysis of the "Herzberg Controversy"

The two keys to the "Herzberg controversy" lie in the different theoretical interpretations made and the research methodology that is used. For example, Nathan King outlined no less than five different versions of the two-factor theory.[17] Briefly summarized, these are:

   1   Theory I states that all motivators combined contribute more to job satisfaction than to job dissatisfaction and that all hygienes combined contribute more to job dissatisfaction than to job satisfaction.
   2   Theory II states that all motivators combined contribute more to job satisfaction than do all hygienes combined, and conversely, that the hygienes contribute more to job dissatisfaction than do the motivators.
   3   Theory III states that each motivator contributes more to satisfaction than to dissatisfaction (and conversely, that each hygiene contributes more to dissatisfaction than to satisfaction).
   4   Theory IV states that each principle hygiene contributes more to job dissatisfaction than does any motivator, and conversely, that each principal motivator contributes more to job satisfaction than does any hygiene.
   5   Theory V states that only motivators determine job satisfaction and only hygienes determine job dissatisfaction.

King analyzed each of the five versions in light of existing research and concluded that Theories I and II have not been adequately tested to eliminate subjects' defensive biases and that Theories III, IV, and V, although supported by Herzberg-type studies, merely reflect experimenter biases and are thus invalid. A follow-up study of female office workers that specifically tested all five theories found no support for any of them.[18]

   Inherent in King's analysis of the five versions of the two-factor theory is the other key factor in the "Herzberg controversy"—the type of research methodology that is used. When researchers depart from the critical incident

[15]Valerie M. Bockman, "The Herzberg Controversy," *Personnel Psychology*, Summer 1971, pp. 155–189.
   [16]Benedict S. Grigaliunas and Frederick Herzberg, "Relevancy in the Test of Motivation-Hygiene Theory," *Journal of Applied Psychology*, February 1971, pp. 73–79.
   [17]Nathan A. King, "A Clarification and Evaluation of the Two-Factor Theory of Job Satisfaction," *Psychological Bulletin*, July 1970, p. 18.
   [18]L. K. Waters and Carrie Wherry Waters, "An Empirical Test of Five Versions of the Two-Factor Theory of Job Satisfaction," *Organizational Behavior and Human Performance*, February 1972, pp. 18–24.

method used by Herzberg, they generally obtain results which are quite different from those the two-factor theory would predict.[19] These studies find that there is not always a clear distinction between factors that lead to satisfaction and those that lead to dissatisfaction. One study even used Herzberg's same methodology and obtained results different from what his theory would predict.[20] There seem to be job factors that lead to both satisfaction and dissatisfaction. These findings tend to invalidate a strict interpretation of the two-factor theory.

In spite of the seemingly legitimate criticism, few would question that Herzberg contributed substantially to work motivation. He extended the Maslow need hierarchy concept and made it more applicable to work motivation. Herzberg also drew attention to the importance of job content factors in work motivation, which previously had been badly neglected and often totally overlooked. The job design technique of job enrichment is also one of Herzberg's contributions. Overall, he added much to the better understanding of job content factors and satisfaction but, like his predecessors, fell short of a comprehensive theory of work motivation. His model describes only some of the content of work motivation—it does not adequately describe the complex human motivational process in modern organizations.

THE PROCESS THEORIES OF WORK MOTIVATION

The content models attempted to identify what it was that motivated people at work (e.g., self-actualization or responsibility); they tried to specify correlates of motivated behavior. The process theories, on the other hand, are more concerned with identifying the variables that go into motivation and, more importantly, how they relate to one another. As Figure 17-1 pointed out, the expectancy models make the most significant contribution to understanding the cognitive processes involved in work motivation. After these are examined, equity theory will also be presented and analyzed as a major process model of work motivation.

Vroom's Expectancy Theory of Motivation

Expectancy theory has its roots in the cognitive concepts of pioneering psychologists Kurt Lewin and Edward Tolman. However, the first to formulate an expectancy theory of work motivation was Victor Vroom in 1964. Contrary to most critics, Vroom proposed his expectancy theory as an alternative to the

---

[19]See Marvin D. Dunnette, John P. Campbell, and Milton D. Hakel, "Factors Contributing to Job Satisfaction and Job Dissatisfaction in Six Occupational Groups," *Organizational Behavior and Human Performance,* May 1967, pp. 143–174; C. L. Hulin and P. A. Smith, "An Empirical Investigation of Two Implications of the Two-Factor Theory of Job Satisfaction," *Journal of Applied Psychology,* October 1967, pp. 396–402; and C. A. Lindsay, E. Marks, and L. Gorlow, "The Herzberg Theory: A Critique and Reformulation," *Journal of Applied Psychology,* August 1967, pp. 330–339.

[20]Donald P. Schwab, H. William DeVitt, and Larry L. Cummings, "A Test of the Adequacy of the Two-Factor Theory as a Predictor of Self-report Performance Effects," *Personnel Psychology,* Summer 1971, pp. 293–303.

content models, which he felt were inadequate explanations of the complex process of work motivation. At least in academic circles, his theory has become the most widely accepted explanation for work motivation and serves as the theoretical foundation for the research on performance-satisfaction.

Figure 17-5 graphically summarizes the Vroom model. As shown, the model is built around the concepts of valence, expectancy, and outcomes; the basic assumption is that "The choices made by a person among alternative courses of action are lawfully related to psychological events occurring contemporaneously with the behavior."[21] Vroom's concept of force is basically equivalent to motivation and is shown to be the algebraic sum of the products of valences multiplied by expectancies.

Meaning of Valence By "valence" Vroom means the strength of an individual's preference for a particular outcome. Other terms that might be substituted for *valence* include *incentive, attitude,* and *expected utility.* In order for the valence to be positive, the person must prefer attaining the outcome to not attaining it. A valence of zero occurs when the individual is indifferent toward the outcome; the valence is negative when the individual prefers not

[21]Vroom, op. cit., pp. 14–15.

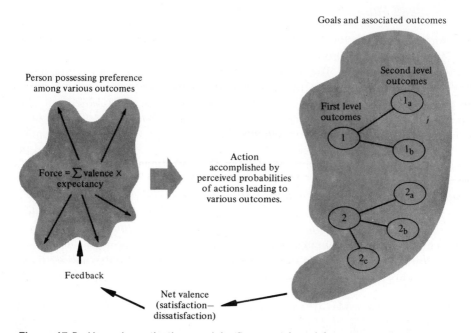

Figure 17-5 Vroom's motivation model. *(Source: Adapted from Marvin D. Dunnette, "The Motives of Industrial Managers,"* Organizational Behavior and Human Performance, *May 1967, p. 178. Dunnette developed the model from Victor H. Vroom,* Work and Motivation, *John Wiley & Sons, Inc., New York, 1964.)*

attaining the outcome to attaining it. Another major input into the valence is the instrumentality of the first-level outcome in obtaining a desired second-level outcome.

> For example, assume that an individual desires promotion and feels that superior performance is a very strong factor in achieving that goal. His first-level outcomes are then superior, average, or poor performance. His second-level outcome is promotion. The first-level outcome of high performance thus acquires a positive valence by virtue of its expected relationship to the preferred second-level outcome of promotion.[22]

In this example, the person would be motivated toward superior performance because of the desire to be promoted. The superior performance (first-level outcome) is seen as being instrumental in obtaining promotion (second-level outcome).

Meaning of Expectancy   The major variable besides valence in the Vroom motivational process is expectancy. Although at first glance the expectancy concept may seem to be the same as the instrumentality input into valence, it is actually quite different. "Expectancy differs from instrumentality in that it relates *efforts* to first-level outcomes where instrumentality relates first- and second-level outcomes to each other."[23] In other words, expectancy is the probability (ranging from 0 to 1) that a particular action or effort will lead to a particular *first-level* outcome. *Instrumentality* refers to the degree to which a first-level outcome will lead to a desired *second-level* outcome. In summary, the strength of the motivation to perform a certain act will depend on the algebraic sum of the products of the valences for the outcomes (which include instrumentality) times the expectancies.

Implications of the Vroom Model for Organizational Behavior   Vroom's theory departs from those of Maslow and Herzberg in that it depicts a process of cognitive variables that reflects individual differences in work motivation. It does not attempt to describe what the content is or what the individual differences are. Everyone has a unique combination of valences and expectancies. Thus, the Vroom theory indicates only the conceptual determinants of motivation and how they are related. It does not provide specific suggestions on what motivates humans in organizations, as did the Maslow and Herzberg models.

Although the Vroom model does not directly contribute much to the techniques of motivating personnel in an organization, it is of value in

---

[22]J. G. Hunt and J. W. Hill, "The New Look in Motivation Theory for Organizational Research," *Human Organization*, Summer 1969, p. 104.
[23]Ibid.

understanding organizational behavior. For example, it can clarify the relationship between individual and organizational goals.

> Thus instead of assuming that satisfaction of a specific need is likely to influence organizational objectives in a certain way, we can find out how important to the employees are the various second-level outcomes (worker goals), the instrumentality of various first-level outcomes (organizational objectives) for their attainment, and the expectancies that are held with respect to the employees' ability to influence the first-level outcomes.[24]

From the above, suppose workers are given a certain standard for production. By measuring the workers' output, management can determine how important their various personal goals (second-level outcomes such as money, security, and recognition) are; the instrumentality of the organizational goal (the first-level outcome, such as the production standard) for the attainment of the personal goals; and the workers' expectancies that their effort and ability will accomplish the organizational goal. If output is below standard, it may be that the workers do not place a high value on the second-level outcomes; or they may not see that the first-level outcome is instrumental in obtaining the second-level outcomes; or they may think that their efforts will not be able to accomplish the first-level outcome. Any one, or a combination, of these possibilities will result in a low level of motivation to produce. The Vroom model is designed to help management understand and analyze the workers' motivation and identify some of the relevant variables; it does not provide specific solutions to motivational problems.

Research Results on the Vroom Model To develop his model, Vroom depended largely upon prior research. Since the model has been proposed, almost every issue of the academic journals in organizational behavior have reported the results of research on the expectancy model. Although not all studies directly test the Vroom model (some are more concerned with the Porter-Lawler type of model that is discussed next), some definite conclusions can begin to be drawn concerning its validity and predictability. Filley, House, and Kerr draw the conclusion from the numerous studies (from 1969 to 1974 there were more than 32 studies) that

> **1** In general, each variable pertinent to value/expectancy theory has been found to have significant predictive powers in some studies, but not in others.
> **2** The most consistently positive findings involve the expectancy that performance will result in extrinsic rewards, and that intrinsic satisfaction will result from the work itself. These variables show rather consistent, statistically significant associations (although usually of low or moderate magnitude) with effort and performance.
> **3** Weighting the expectancy that performance leads to rewards by the value

---

[24]Ibid., p. 105.

placed on extrinsic rewards does not improve power of prediction over that obtained by using the unweighted expectancy that performance leads to rewards.

4 The theory is limited to conditions where subjects have the requisite ability, accurate role perceptions, and accurate perceptions of contingent rewards.

5 The better controlled the study (in longitudinal analyses and laboratory investigations) the more support will generally be shown for the theory. The superiority of such carefully controlled approaches over cross-sectional studies suggests that cross-sectional tests result in underestimates of the theory's predictive validity.[25]

In other words, there is some support, especially relative to the content theories, of the validity of the expectancy theory of motivation. On the other hand, even the most ardent supporters of this approach recognize the need for even more research, especially for a study that tests all relevant variables and not just bits and pieces.

Importance of the Vroom Model Probably the major reason Vroom's model has emerged as an important modern theory of work motivation and has generated so much research is that he does not take a simplistic approach. Both Maslow and Herzberg oversimplified human motivation. Yet, their theories remain extremely popular with practicing managers because the concepts are easy to understand and to apply to their own situations. On the other hand, the Vroom theory recognizes the complexities of work motivation, but it is relatively difficult to understand and apply. Thus, from a theoretical standpoint the Vroom model seems to be a step in the right direction, but it does not give managers much practical help in solving their motivational problems. This is not necessarily a criticism of the expectancy model because, as Porter, Lawler, and Hackman have pointed out:

> . . . the expectancy model is just that: a model and no more. People rarely actually sit down and list their expected outcomes for a contemplated behavior, estimate expectancies and valences, multiply, and add up the total, unless, of course, they are asked to do so by a researcher. Yet people *do* consider the likely outcomes of their actions, do weigh and evaluate the attractiveness of various alternatives, and do use these estimates in coming to a decision about what they will do.[26]

The expectancy model is like marginal analysis in economics. Businesspersons do not actually calculate the point where marginal cost equals marginal revenue, but it is still a useful concept for the theory of the firm. The expectancy model attempts only to mirror the complex motivational process; it

[25]Alan C. Filley, Robert J. House, and Steven Kerr, *Managerial Process and Organizational Behavior*, 2d ed., Scott, Foresman and Company, Glenview, Ill., 1976, pp. 200–201. Also see: R. J. House, H. J. Shapiro, and M. A. Wahba, "Expectancy Theory as a Predictor of Work Behavior and Attitude: A Reevaluation of Empirical Evidence," *Decision Sciences*, December 1974, pp. 54–77.

[26]Lyman Porter, Edward E. Lawler, III, and J. Richard Hackman, *Behavior in Organizations*, McGraw-Hill Book Company, 1975, p. 58.

does not attempt to describe how motivational decisions are actually made or to solve actual motivational problems facing a manager.

The Porter and Lawler Model:
Implications for Performance and Satisfaction

The introductory comments in the chapter pointed out the controversy that has existed since the human relations movement over the relationship between satisfaction and performance. The content theories implicitly assume that satisfaction leads to improved performance and that dissatisfaction detracts from performance. The Herzberg model is, at best, a theory of job satisfaction, but still it does not deal with the relationship of satisfaction to performance. The Vroom model also largely avoids the relationship between satisfaction and performance. Although satisfactions make an input into Vroom's concept of valence and the outcomes have performance implications, it was not until Porter and Lawler refined and extended Vroom's model that the relationship between satisfaction and performance was dealt with directly by a motivation model.

Porter and Lawler start with the premise that motivation (effort or force) does not equal satisfaction and/or performance. Motivation, satisfaction, and performance are all separate variables and relate in different ways from what was traditionally assumed. Figure 17-6 depicts the multivariable model that is used to explain the complex relationship that exists between motivation, performance, and satisfaction. As shown in the model, boxes 1, 2, and 3 are basically the same as the Vroom equation. Importantly, however, Porter and Lawler point out that effort (force or motivation) does not directly lead to performance. It is mediated by abilities/traits and role perceptions. More important in the Porter and Lawler model is what happens after the perfor-

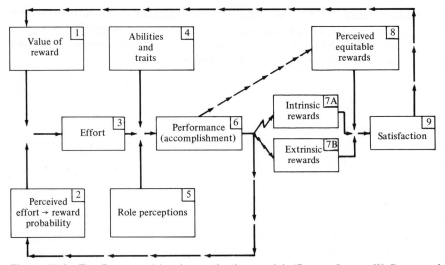

Figure 17-6 The Porter-and-Lawler motivation model. *(Source: Lyman W. Porter and Edward E. Lawler, III,* Managerial Attitudes and Performance, *Richard D. Irwin, Inc., Homewood, Ill., 1968, p. 165. Used with permission.)*

mance. The rewards that follow and how these are perceived will determine satisfaction. In other words, the Porter and Lawler model suggests—and this is a significant turn of events from traditional thinking—that performance leads to satisfaction.

Variables in the Porter-Lawler Model

Similar to the Vroom model, the Porter and Lawler model is an expectancy-based theory of motivation. The future-oriented expectancy theories emphasize the anticipation of response-outcome connections and depend heavily upon cognitive concepts such as value/valence and perception. Porter and Lawler explain their choice for the expectancy approach as follows:

> The emphasis in expectancy theory on rationality and expectations seems to us to describe best the kinds of cognitions that influence managerial performance. We assume that managers operate on the basis of some sort of expectancies which, although based upon previous experience, are forward-oriented in a way that does not seem to be as easily handled by the concept of habit strength.[27]

A clearer understanding of the model can be gained by a more detailed examination of the major variables in the model.

Effort   In the model, as in the daily language, "effort" refers to the amount of energy exerted by an employee on a given task. However, contrary to the common usage of the word, effort is not the same as performance. As used in the model, effort is more closely associated with motivation than with performance. The amount of effort depends upon the interaction between the value of the reward and the perceived effort-reward probability. It is roughly equivalent to Vroom's use of the term *force.*

The value placed on a reward depends on its degree of attractiveness and desirability. Friendship, promotion, pay, recognition, and praise are assigned different values by different people. For example, one person may feel threatened and insecure with a promotion. The perceived effort-reward probability is the other major input into effort. This variable refers to the employees' perception of the probability that differential rewards depend upon differential amounts of effort. In interactive combination, these two variables (value of reward and perception of effort-reward probability) determine the amount of effort that will be exerted. If employees place a high value on a reward, and if they perceive a high probability that their effort will lead to this reward, then they will exert a great quantity of effort. But, once again, it should be noted that this effort will not directly lead to a particular level of performance.

Performance   Performance represents the pragmatic result that organizations are able to measure objectively. Effort precedes performance, but the two cannot be equated. A discrepancy between effort and performance may result

---

[27]Lyman W. Porter and Edward E. Lawler, III, *Managerial Attitudes and Performance,* Richard D. Irwin, Inc., Homewood, Ill., 1968, pp. 12–13.

from the employees' abilities and traits and/or their role perceptions. Performance depends not only on the amount of effort exerted but also on the persons' abilities (e.g., job knowledge and skill) and the way they perceive the role they should take. The way the job is defined, the direction of efforts, and the level of effort thought to be necessary for effective performance all go into the role perception. In other words, even though the employees exert a great amount of effort, if they have little ability and/or an inaccurate role perception, the resulting performance may end up being ineffective. A good illustration would be the athletes who give a great deal of effort but, because of a lack of ability and/or because they perceive the situation incorrectly and misdirect that effort, turn out losers rather than winners. This ineffective performance occurred in spite of the amount of effort that was exerted by the athletes.

Rewards   Initially, Porter and Lawler included only a single reward variable in their model. However, empirical testing showed that it should more accurately be divided into extrinsic and intrinsic categories. Chapter 12 pointed out the difference between extrinsic and intrinsic rewards and the difficulty of operationalizing these concepts. As used in the Porter-Lawler model, both are desirable outcomes. However, Porter and Lawler feel that the intrinsic rewards are much more likely to produce attitudes about satisfaction that are related to performance. In addition, the perceived equitable rewards vitally affect the performance-satisfaction relationship. They reflect the fair level of rewards that the individual feels should be granted for a given level of performance. The perception of equitable rewards can be directly affected by self-rated performance, as indicated by the diagonally directed short arrows in the model in Figure 17-6.

Satisfaction   As was pointed out, satisfaction is not the same as motivation. Satisfaction is an attitude, an internal cognitive state. Motivation is a process, and that is why the content models, especially Herzberg's, have more to do with satisfactions than with the complex process of motivation. In the content models, job satisfaction was deemed to be the sum of various content factors such as responsibility and growth potential. In Porter and Lawler's model, satisfaction is only one of the variables and is derived from the extent to which actual rewards fall short, meet, or exceed the person's perceived equitable level of rewards. Therefore, if actual rewards meet or exceed perceived equitable rewards, the individual will be satisfied. On the other hand, if actual rewards are below what is perceived to be equitable, the individual will be dissatisfied. This explanation of satisfaction makes two important departures from traditional thinking about satisfaction. First, the model recognizes that satisfaction is determined only in part by actual rewards received. It depends also on what a person feels the organization *should* reward for a given level of performance. Second, and of greater importance, the model recognizes satisfaction to be more dependent on performance than performance is on satisfaction. Only through the less direct feedback loops will satisfaction affect performance. This, of course, makes a 180-degree turn from the traditional analysis of the satisfaction-performance relationship.

Research on the Porter-Lawler Model   The model in Figure 17-6 was meant only to be the conceptual scheme to guide and structure a comprehensive research study that Porter and Lawler were conducting. They ran a correlational study that investigated the relationship between managerial attitudes toward pay and managerial performance. Based on the responses to 563 questionnaires filled out by managers in seven organizations, Porter and Lawler concluded that, taken as a whole, their model was validated by the study. They note that "those variables presumed to affect performance turned out to show relations to performance, and those variables presumed to result from performance also typically were related to performance."[28] Although they are careful to point out that the correlational study does not prove or show the direction of cause and effect, they are confident that the major hypothesis of performance causing satisfaction is supported by their data. Many follow-up studies have generally substantiated this conclusion.[29]

Others have expressed concern that the relationship between performance and satisfaction is extremely complex and feel that the role of rewards should be given more attention. For example, Greene concludes that, ". . . (1) rewards constitute a more direct cause of satisfaction than does performance and (2) rewards based on current performance (and not satisfaction) cause subsequent performance."[30] This represents more of an operant position on the role that rewarding consequences play in subsequent performance. Chapter 12 introduced the operant approach and Chapter 20 will apply it to human resource management. The end of the chapter offers some observations of the role that operant, behavioristic concepts can play in motivation, but for now it can be said that there are definitely some operant implications inherent in the highly cognitive, expectancy models of motivation.

Implications for Management Practice   Although the Porter and Lawler model is more applications-oriented than the Vroom model, it is still quite complex and has proved to be a difficult way to bridge the gap to actual management practice. To Porter and Lawler's credit, they have been very conscious of putting their theory and research into practice. They recommend

[28]Porter and Lawler, op. cit., pp. 159–160.

[29]For example, see David G. Kuhn, John W. Slocum, Jr., and Richard B. Chase, "Does Job Performance Affect Employee Satisfaction?," *Personnel Journal*, June 1971, pp. 455–459 and 485; Jay R. Schuster, Barbara Clark, and Miles Rogers, "Testing Portions of the Porter and Lawler Model Regarding the Motivational Role of Pay," *Journal of Applied Psychology*, June 1971, pp. 187–195; and D. O. Jorgenson, M. D. Dunnette, and R. D. Pritchard, "Effects of the Manipulation of a Performance-Reward Contingency on Behavior in a Simulated Work Setting," *Journal of Applied Psychology*, vol. 57, 1973, pp. 271–280.

[30]Charles N. Greene, "The Satisfaction Performance Controversy," *Business Horizons*, October 1972, p. 40. Also see David J. Cherrington, H. Joseph Reitz, and William E. Scott, Jr., "Effects of Contingent and Noncontingent Reward on the Relationship between Satisfaction and Task Performance," *Journal of Applied Psychology*, December 1971, pp. 531–536.

that practicing managers should go beyond traditional attitude measurement and attempt to measure variables such as the values of possible rewards, the perceptions of effort-reward probabilities, and role perceptions.[31] These variables, of course, can help managers better understand what goes into employee effort and performance. Giving attention to the consequences of performance, Porter and Lawler also recommend that organizations should critically reevaluate their current reward policies. They stress that management should make a concentrated effort to measure how closely levels of satisfaction are related to levels of performance.[32] These types of recommendations have been verified in a few studies. For example, one study of piece-rate workers found that those with high effort-performance probability perceptions were significantly higher producers than those with low probability perceptions.[33] Such a finding could aid the actual practice of management. Some specifics of the reward applications can also be found in the recent book by Porter, Lawler, and Hackman.[34] The Porter and Lawler model has definitely made a significant contribution to the better understanding of work motivation and the relationship between performance and satisfaction, but, to date, it has not had nearly the impact on management practice that the content models have had.

The Lawler Expectancy Model: A Refinement

Since the original Porter-Lawler model, Lawler has proposed several refinements on his own. In particular, he feels that there are actually two types of expectancies: the E → P expectancy and P → O expectancies. Both of these make an input into effort or motivation. There is a multiplicative relationship among the expectancy factors. The Lawler equation for motivation would be:

$$\text{Effort} = (E \rightarrow P) \times \Sigma \; [(P \rightarrow O)(V)]$$

Verbalized, this means that the effort → performance expectancy is multiplied by the sum of products of all performance → outcome expectancies times valences. Graphically, this equation can be represented in the model shown in Figure 17-7.

As shown in Figure 17-7, the first expectancy (E → P) is the person's estimate of the probability (from 0 to 1) of accomplishing the intended performance. The second expectancy (P → O) involves the person's estimation (from 0 to 1) of the likelihood that performance will lead to particular outcomes. An example of an E → P expectancy (shown in Figure 17-7) would be the salesperson who estimates that there is a good probability (say, .7) of being able to sell 100 widgets. The outcomes of this level of performance (the

---

[31]Porter and Lawler, op. cit., p. 183.

[32]Ibid., pp. 183–184.

[33]Donald P. Schwab and Lee D. Dyer, "The Motivational Impact of a Compensation System on Employee Performance," *Organizational Behavior and Human Performance*, April 1973, pp. 215–225.

[34]Porter, Lawler, and Hackman, op. cit., especially chap. 12.

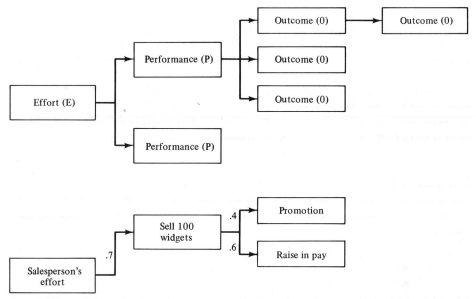

Figure 17-7   The Lawler expectancy model of motivation. *(Source: Adapted from Edward E. Lawler, III, Motivation in Work Organizations, Brooks/Cole Publishing Company, Monterey, Calif., 1973, p. 50.)*

P → O expectancies) may be a probability of .4 for a promotion or of .6 for a raise in pay.

Lawler feels that the single most important determinant of the E → P expectancy is the objective situation. In addition, the person's self-esteem, past experiences in similar situations, and communications from others are some of the major inputs into the person's perception of the situation. The person's perception of the P → O expectancies is influenced by many of the same things as the E → P expectancy. In addition, the attractiveness of outcomes, the belief of who controls the outcomes (the person himself or herself or others, which is known as *locus of control,* which is discussed at the end of the chapter), and the E → P expectancy will all have an impact on the person's P → O expectancies.

This more complex expectancy model of work motivation is a step toward better understanding but compounds the problems of translation into practice. Lawler himself does provide some insights into the use of the model to help explain how pay motivates behavior. After reviewing a number of studies, he concludes that:

   1   Beliefs about the degree to which pay depends upon performance are positively related to job performance.
   2   Where pay depends upon performance, statements about the importance of pay are related to job performance.
   3   Job performance is most strongly related to a multiplicative combination of important attitudes and P → O beliefs.

4 P → O beliefs seem to be more strongly related to future performance than to either present or past performance.[35]

Despite these insights for the practical administration of pay plans, the fact remains that, in Lawler's own words,

> If we try to predict a person's behavior using our model, and if we gather complete data on all his or her perceptions of existing relationships, we still might predict behavior incorrectly because our model would be too complex to allow for valid predictions.[36]

The Smith and Cranny Model: A Simplified Process

In contrast to the comparatively complex Porter-and-Lawler and Lawler expectancy models, industrial psychologists Patricia Smith and C. J. Cranny propose a more simplistic three-way relationship between effort, satisfaction, and reward. Each variable in the corners of the triangle in Figure 17-8 has causal effects on the others, either individually or in combination. In other words, an increase in pay (reward) may lead to increased satisfaction, or a satisfied, cooperative worker may lead to increased pay. However, as in the other expectancy models, the real key to the Smith and Cranny model lies in the concept of effort. Performance is affected only by effort, not by reward or by satisfaction. As shown in Figure 17-8, performance is at the heart of the

[35]Edward E. Lawler, III, *Pay and Organizational Effectiveness*, McGraw-Hill Book Company, New York, 1971, p. 139.

[36]Edward E. Lawler, III, *Motivation in Work Organizations*, Brooks/Cole Publishing Company, Monterey, Calif., 1973, p. 60.

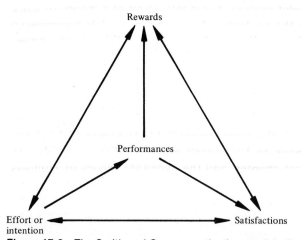

Figure 17-8   The Smith and Cranny motivation model. *(Source: Patricia Cain Smith and C. J. Cranny, "Psychology of Men at Work,"* Annual Review of Psychology, *vol. 19, 1968, p. 469.)*

model and can influence rewards and satisfactions but can itself be influenced only by effort or intention.

Whereas the Porter-and-Lawler and Lawler models can be criticized for using technical jargon and making application difficult for the practitioner, Smith and Cranny's model does not have this problem. They recognize but do not get involved with the complexity of the work motivation process. But they do incorporate some of the same concepts as the Porter-and-Lawler and Lawler expectancy models.

The Smith and Cranny model is much easier for practitioners to understand and apply. It leaves the complex expectancy and valence antecedents of effort out of the model. In other words, the Smith and Cranny model has a different purpose from the previously discussed expectancy models. The psychological jargon and complexities are left out. Smith and Cranny stress that management's job is to administer rewards, but that these alone do not have a direct impact on performance. Taking a systems viewpoint, Smith and Cranny emphasize the interrelationships and interdependencies between effort, satisfaction, and reward. Yet, it is effort, not reward or satisfaction, that directly affects performance. They cite many research studies that have been conducted on work motivation, plus the basic psychological research done on the impact of intention or expectancies on task performance, to support their model.[37]

Although the Smith and Cranny model effectively relates the important variables of work motivation and has practical implications for management, it does fall short of the theoretical goals of full understanding, prediction, and control. It is a model of relationships rather than a comprehensive theory of work motivation. The model certainly helps clarify some of the complexities raised by the Vroom, Porter and Lawler, and Lawler expectancy models and thus helps students and practicing managers grasp and focus on the important, relevant variables and their relationships, but it falls short of a theory of work motivation. Fortunately, both the content and expectancy models discussed so far, as well as the equity theory discussed next, are additive in the better *understanding* of work motivation.

Equity Theory of Work Motivation

Equity theory has been around for just as long as the expectancy theories of job motivation. However, only recently has equity as a process of motivation received widespread attention in the management field. As Figure 17-1 indicated, its roots can be traced back to Festinger's cognitive dissonance theory, which was discussed in the last chapter, and the exchange theory of Homans and others, which was discussed in Chapter 15. As a theory of work motivation, credit for equity theory is usually given to J. Stacy Adams. Simply put, the theory argues that a major input into job performance and satisfaction is the degree of equity (or inequity) that people perceive in their work situation. In

[37]Patricia Cain Smith and C. J. Cranny, "Psychology of Men at Work," *Annual Review of Psychology*, vol. 19, 1968, pp. 469–477.

other words, it is another cognitively based motivation theory, and Adams depicts a specific process of how this motivation occurs.

Using the terminology of "Person" (any individual for whom equity or inequity exists) and "Other" (any individual with whom person is in a relevant exchange relationship or with whom person compares himself or herself), Adams states that, "Inequity exists for person whenever he perceives that the ratio of his outcomes to inputs and the ratio of other's outcomes to other's inputs are unequal."[38]

Schematically, inequity occurs when

$$\frac{\text{Person's outcomes}}{\text{Person's inputs}} < \frac{\text{other's outcomes}}{\text{other's inputs}}$$

or

$$\frac{\text{Person's outcomes}}{\text{Person's inputs}} > \frac{\text{other's outcomes}}{\text{other's inputs}}$$

and equity occurs when

$$\frac{\text{Person's outcomes}}{\text{Person's inputs}} = \frac{\text{other's outcomes}}{\text{other's inputs}}$$

Both the inputs and outputs of person and other are based upon the person's perceptions. Age, sex, education, social status, organizational position, qualifications, and how hard the person works would be examples of perceived input variables. Outcomes would primarily be rewards such as pay, status, promotion, or intrinsic interest in the job. In essence, the ratio is based upon the person's *perception* of what the person is giving (inputs) and receiving (outcomes) versus the ratio of what the relevant other is giving and receiving. This cognition may or may not be the same as someone else's observation of the ratios or the actual, realistic situation.

If the person's perceived ratio is not equal to the other's, he or she will strive to restore the ratio to equity. This "striving" to restore equity is used as the explanation of work motivation. The strength of this motivation is in direct proportion to the perceived inequity that exists. Adams suggests that such motivation may be expressed in several forms. To restore equity, the person may alter the inputs or outcomes, cognitively distort the inputs or outcomes, leave the field, act on the other, or change the other.[39]

It is important to note that inequity does not come about only when the person feels cheated. For example, Adams has studied the impact that perceived overpayment has on inequity. His findings suggest that workers

---

[38]Stacy Adams, "Inequity in Social Exchange," in L. Berrowitz (ed.), *Advances in Experimental Social Psychology*, Academic Press, New York, 1965. Reprinted in Richard M. Steers and Lyman W. Porter, *Motivation and Work Behavior*, McGraw-Hill Book Company, 1975, p. 141.
[39]Ibid., pp. 144–151.

prefer equitable payment to overpayment. A worker on a piece-rate incentive system who feels overpaid will reduce his or her productivity in order to restore equity. More likely, however, is the case of people feeling underpaid (outcome) or overworked (input) in relation to others in the workplace. In the latter case there would be motivation to restore equity that may be dysfunctional from an organizational standpoint.

To date, research that has specifically tested the validity of Adams's equity theory has been fairly supportive. Citing a comprehensive review of relevant research, Filley, House, and Kerr conclude the following about equity theory:[40]

1   Overpaid hourly or salaried employees will increase their contribution by producing more as a means of reducing inequity. There are mixed findings but the better controlled studies show support for this proposition.
2   Overpaid piece-rate employees will produce higher quality and lower quantity than equitably paid employees. This is strongly supported by the findings.
3   Underpaid hourly or salaried employees will produce less to achieve a contribution-reward balance. There are mixed findings but some at least preliminary support.
4   Underpaid piece-rate employees will produce a high volume of low quality output because production of low quality output permits increasing rewards without substantially increasing contributions. There are only two studies that test this proposition but both support it.

Armed with this type of research back-up, there is little question that equity theory can make a contribution to better understanding of the work motivational process. But, like the expectancy models, equity theory has not yet reached the important goals of prediction and control for the actual practice of human resource management.

FUTURE DEVELOPMENT OF WORK MOTIVATION THEORY

In Chapter 5 two major theoretical orientations for human behavior in general were identified: cognitive and behavioristic. Motivation, because it deals with internal need states and energizers of behavior, is largely cognitively based. The models discussed in this chapter are largely cognitive models. The future development of work motivation theory will undoubtedly involve further cognitive development, but the theory must also come to grips with the important role that contingent consequences play in human behavior. A brief look at these two thrusts for the further development of work motivation can help set the perspective for the future.

[40]Filley, House, and Kerr, op. cit., pp. 207–208. Also see: P. S. Goodman and A. Friedman, "An Examination of Adams' Theory of Inequity," *Administrative Science Quarterly,* vol. 16, 1971, pp. 271–288; and Charles S. Telly, Wendell L. French, and William G. Scott, "The Relationship of Inequity to Turnover Among Hourly Workers," *Administrative Science Quarterly,* March 1971, pp. 164–172. The latter study supports equity theory in regard to turnover while the others deal with compensation.

Attribution Theory and Locus of Control

One important cognitive input for the future development of work motivation may come from attribution theory and its offshoot, locus of control. Unlike the other motivation theories, attribution theory is more a theory of the relationship between person perception and interpersonal behavior than it is a theory of individual motivation. It is mainly concerned with the cognitive processes by which an individual interprets behavior as being caused by (or attributed to) certain parts of the relevant environment.[41] It is concerned with the "why" questions of motivation and behavior. Since most causes, attributes, or "whys" are not directly observable, the person must depend upon cognitions, particularly perception. The attribution theorist assumes humans are rational and are motivated to identify and understand the causal structure of their relevant environment. It is this search for attributes that characterizes attribution theory.

Although attribution theory has roots in all the pioneering cognitive theorists' work (e.g., Lewin and Festinger), the founder is generally recognized to be Fritz Heider. Heider believed that both internal (personal attributes such as ability, effort, and fatigue) and external (environmental attributes such as rules or the weather) forces combine additively to determine behavior. He stressed that it is the *perceived*, not the actual determinants, that are important to behavior. People will behave differently if they perceive internal attributes from the way they behave if they perceive external attributes. It is this concept of differential ascriptions that has very important implications for work motivation.

Usually referred to as *locus of control*, work behavior may be explained by whether employees perceive their outcomes as controlled internally or externally. Employees who perceive internal control feel that they personally can influence their outcomes through their own ability, skills, or effort. Employees who perceive external control feel that their outcomes are beyond their own control; they feel that external forces control their outcomes. Importantly, this perceived locus of control may have a differential impact on their performance and satisfaction. For example, studies by Rotter and his colleagues suggest that skill versus chance environments differentially affect behavior.[42] In addition, in a recent study, Mitchell and his colleagues have directly assessed the impact of locus of control or internal-external (I-E) characteristics in work settings. In a study of 900 employees in a public utility it was found that internally controlled employees are generally more satisfied with their jobs, are more likely to be in managerial positions, and are more satisfied with a participatory management

---

[41]H. H. Kelly, "Attribution Theory in Social Psychology," in D. Levine (ed.), *Nebraska Symposium on Motivation*, vol. 15, University of Nebraska Press, Lincoln, Nebr., 1967, p. 193. Also see Bernard Weiner, *Theories of Motivation*, Rand McNally & Company, Chicago, 1972, chap. 5.

[42]Julian B. Rotter, Shephard Liverant, and Douglas P. Crowne, "The Growth and Extinction of Expectancies in Chance Controlled and Skilled Tasks," *The Journal of Psychology*, July 1961, pp. 161–177.

style than are employees who perceive external control.[43] Such research seems extremely important for the future development and understanding of work motivation. This is especially true in the increasingly turbulent organizational and social environments that employees will probably face in the future.

Behavioristic Implications for Work Motivation

As has been noted, the whole concept of motivation and the models discussed in this chapter are largely cognitively based. The refinements of the expectancy models (e.g., Porter and Lawler, Lawler, and Smith and Cranny) do have rewards and contingent consequences play an increasingly important role. However, it must be remembered that a purely operant perspective (discussed in Chapter 12) largely ignores the cognitive antecedents (for example, assignment of valences or determining expectancies) and instead concentrates on the impact that contingent consequences have on subsequent behavior. Instead of polarizing the two approaches (expectancy on the one extreme and reinforcement on the other), there seems to be a need to bring these two approaches together and synthesize them. The Porter and Lawler model is a step in this direction, and the concept of locus of control also has elements of both expectancy and reinforcement approaches. But for now it should be remembered that the internal approach, as discussed in this chapter, is only one explanation of behavior. As was concluded at the end of the discussion of each model, the cognitive models are a long way from the goals of prediction and control. Chapter 20 will present and analyze the external approach. The latter approach, when combined with this chapter, can help lead to all three goals of understanding, prediction, and control of organizational behavior.

SUMMARY

Work motivation and its dynamics were covered in this chapter. The simplistic human relations assumptions and approach have proved to be inadequate in terms of both theoretical explanation and management practice. The modern approach to work motivation can be divided into content and process approaches. The Maslow and Herzberg models attempt to identify specific content factors in the individual (in the case of Maslow) or in the job environment (in the case of Herzberg) that motivate employees. Although such a content approach has surface logic, is easy to understand, and can be readily translated into practice, the research evidence points out some definite limitations. There is very little research support for the theoretical basis and predictability for either model. The trade-off for simplicity sacrifices true understanding of the complexity of work motivation. On the positive side, however, the content models have given emphasis to important content factors

---

[43]Terence R. Mitchell, Charles M. Smyser, and Stan E. Weed, "Locus of Control: Supervision and Work Satisfaction," *Academy of Management Journal,* September 1975, pp. 623–631.

that were largely ignored by the human relationists, and the Herzberg model is useful as an explanation for job satisfaction.

The process theories provide a much sounder theoretical explanation of work motivation. The expectancy model of Vroom and the extensions and refinements provided by Porter and Lawler and Lawler help explain the important cognitive variables and how they relate to one another in the complex process of work motivation. The Porter-and-Lawler model also gives specific attention to the important relationship between performance and satisfaction. Porter and Lawler propose that performance leads to satisfaction, instead of the human relations assumption of the reverse. A growing research literature is generally supportive of these expectancy models as theoretical explanations. However, in a manner opposite to that of the content models, because these expectancy models are relatively complex and difficult to translate into actual practice, they have generally failed to meet the goals of prediction and control of organizational behavior. The Smith and Cranny model more clearly delineates the relationship between the relevant variables but sacrifices theoretical explanation of the complexities involved. Finally, equity theory was presented, in the additive sense of better understanding of work motivation. A process theory—the equity model based upon perceived input-outcome ratios—lends increased understanding to the complex cognitive process of work motivation but has the same limitation as the expectancy models for prediction and control in the practice of human resource management. Attribution theory and locus of control, as a potentially important contribution to the cognitive development of work motivation theory, and recognition of the external, operant, reinforcement approach were discussed in terms of the future of work motivation.

QUESTIONS FOR DISCUSSION AND REVIEW

1 In your own words, briefly explain Maslow's theory of motivation. Relate it to work motivation.
2 What is the major criticism of Herzberg's two-factor theory of motivation? Do you think it has made a contribution to the better understanding of motivation in the workplace? Defend your answer.
3 In Vroom's model, what do valence, expectancy, and force mean? How do these variables relate to one another and to work motivation? Give realistic examples.
4 In your own words, briefly explain the Porter-and-Lawler model of motivation. How do performance and satisfaction relate to one another? What is involved in Lawler's refinement?
5 Explain the Smith and Cranny model of motivation. What can managers do to affect the performance of organizational personnel?
6 Briefly give an example of an inequity that a manager of a small business may experience. How would the manager strive to attain equity in the situation you describe?
7 What is attribution theory? How can analysis of locus of control be applied to workers and managers?

CASE: WHAT DO THEY WANT?

Mike Riverer is vice president of manufacturing and operations of a medium-sized pharmaceutical firm in the Midwest. Mike has a Ph.D. in chemistry but has not been directly involved in research and new-product development for twenty years. He was from the school of "hard knocks" when it came to managing operations, and he ran a "tight ship." The company did not have a turnover problem, but it was obvious to Mike and other key management personnel that the hourly people were only putting in their eight hours a day. They were not working anywhere near their full potential. Mike was very upset with the situation because, with rising costs, the only way that the company could continue to prosper was to increase the productivity of their hourly people.

Mike called in his personnel manager and laid it on the line. "What is it with our people anyway? Your wage surveys show that we pay near the top in this region, our conditions are tremendous, and our fringes choke a horse. Yet, these people still are not motivated. What in the world do they want?" The personnel manager replied, "I have told you and the president time after time that money, conditions, and benefits are not enough. Employees also need other things to motivate them. Also, I have been conducting some random confidential interviews with some of our hourly people, and they tell me that they are very discouraged because, no matter how hard they work, they get the same pay and opportunities for advancement as their coworkers who are just scraping by." Mike then replied, "Okay, you are the people expert; what do we do about it? We *have* to increase their performance."

1 Explain the "motivation problem" in this organization in terms of the content models of Maslow and Herzberg. What are the "other things" that the personnel manager is referring to in speaking of things besides money, conditions, and fringe benefits that are needed to motivate employees?

2 Explain the motivation of the employees in this company in terms of one or more of the process models. On the basis of the responses from the confidential interviews, what would you guess are some of the expectancies, valences, and outcomes of the employees in this company? How about Mike? Do you think Mike is internally or externally controlled?

3 How would you respond to Mike's last question and statement if you were the personnel manager in this company?

SELECTED REFERENCES

Adams, J. Stacy: "Inequity in Social Exchange," in *Advances in Experimental Social Psychology,* L. Berkowitz (ed.), Academic Press, New York, 1965.

Behling, Orlando, and Mitchell B. Shapiro: "Motivation Theory: Source of Solution or Part of the Problem?" *Business Horizons,* February 1974, pp. 59–66.

Behling, Orlando, and Frederick A. Starke: "The Postulates of Expectancy Theory," *Academy of Management Journal,* September 1973, pp. 373–388.

Goodman, P. S., and A. Friedman: "An Examination of Adams' Theory of Inequity," *Administrative Science Quarterly,* September 1971, pp. 271–288.

Greene, Charles N.: "The Satisfaction-Performance Controversy," *Business Horizons,* October 1972, pp. 31–41.

Herzberg, Frederick: "Motivation-Hygiene Profiles," *Organizational Dynamics,* Fall 1974, pp. 18–29.

House, R. J., H. J. Shapiro, and M. A. Wahba: "Expectancy Theory as a Predictor of Work Behavior and Attitude: A Reevaluation of Empirical Evidence," *Decision Sciences,* December 1974, pp. 54–77.

House, R. J., and L. A. Wigdor: "Herzberg's Dual-Factor Theory of Job Satisfaction and Motivation: A Review of the Evidence and a Criticism," *Personnel Psychology,* Winter 1967, pp. 369–389.

Kesselman, Gerald A., Eileen L. Hagen, and Robert J. Wherry, Sr.: "A Factor Analytic Test of the Porter-Lawler Expectancy Model of Work Motivation," *Personnel Psychology,* Winter 1974, pp. 569–579.

Lawler, Edward E., III, and J. Lloyd Suttle: "Expectancy Theory and Job Behavior," *Organizational Behavior and Human Performance,* June 1973, pp. 482–503.

Leidecker, Joel K., and James J. Hall: "Motivation: Good Theory—Poor Application," *Training and Development Journal,* June 1974, pp. 3–7.

Mitchell, Terence R., Charles M. Smyser, and Stan E. Weed: "Locus of Control: Supervision and Work Satisfaction," *Academy of Management Journal,* September 1975, pp. 623–631.

Porter, Lyman W., and Edward E. Lawler, III: *Managerial Attitudes and Performance,* Richard D. Irwin, Inc., Homewood, Ill., 1968.

Reinharth, Leon, and Mahmoud A. Wahba: "Expectancy Theory as a Predictor of Work Motivation, Effort Expenditure, and Job Performance," *Academy of Management Journal,* September 1975, pp. 520–537.

Schwab, Donald P., and Larry Cummings: "Theories of Performance and Satisfaction: A Review," *Industrial Relations,* October 1970, pp. 408–430.

Schwab, Donald P., and Marc J. Wallace, Jr.: "Correlates of Employee Satisfaction with Pay," *Industrial Relations,* February 1974, pp. 78–89.

Sheridan, John E., and John W. Slocum, Jr.: "The Direction of the Causal Relationship between Job Satisfaction and Work Performance," *Organizational Behavior and Human Performance,* October 1975, pp. 159–172.

Starke, Frederick A., and Orlando Behling: "A Test of Two Postulates Underlying Expectancy Theory," *Academy of Management Journal,* December 1975, pp. 703–714.

Steers, Richard M.: "Effects of Need for Achievement on the Job Performance–Job Attitude Relationship," *Journal of Applied Psychology,* December 1975, pp. 678–682.

Steers, Richard M., and Lyman W. Porter (eds.), *Motivation and Work Behavior,* McGraw-Hill Book Company, New York, 1975.

Vroom, Victor H.: *Work and Motivation,* John Wiley & Sons, Inc., New York, 1964.

Wahba, Mahmoud A., and Lawrence G. Birdwell: "Maslow Reconsidered: A Review of Research on the Need Hierarchy Theory," *Proceedings of Academy of Management,* 1973, pp. 514–520.

Wahba, Mahmoud A., and Robert J. House: "Expectancy Theory in Work and Motivation: Some Logical and Methodological Issues," *Human Relations,* January 1974, pp. 121–147.

Chapter 18

Leadership and Power

This chapter is the appropriate conclusion to the dynamics of organizational behavior part of the book. There is a close relationship—a dynamic relationship—betweeen groups, conflict, work motivation, and leadership and power. The first third of the chapter deals with the classical background and major theoretical perspectives of leadership. The second third presents and analyzes the various styles of leadership and supervision. Particular attention is given to the research evidence on the impact of style on satisfaction and performance. The last third of the chapter is devoted to power. Although there is a distinction between leadership and power, the two concepts go hand in hand. For example, David McClelland has noted that,

> ... managers are primarily concerned with influencing others ... [and] a high need for Power. ... Thus, leadership and power appear as two closely related concepts, and if we want to understand better effective leadership, we may begin by studying the power motive in thought and action.[1]

Power is defined and the sources of power are presented and critically analyzed.

[1]David C. McClelland, "The Two Faces of Power," *Journal of International Affairs*, vol. 24, no. 1, 1970, p. 31.

THE BACKGROUND AND CLASSIC STUDIES
ON LEADERSHIP

Leadership has probably been written about, formally researched, and informally discussed more than any other single topic. Throughout history, it has been recognized that the difference between success and failure, whether in a war, a business, a protest movement, or a basketball game, can be largely attributed to leadership. Yet, despite all the attention given to it and its recognized importance, leadership still remains pretty much of a "black box" or unexplainable concept. It is known to exist and to have a tremendous influence on human performance, but its inner workings and specific dimensions cannot be precisely spelled out. Despite these inherent difficulties, a review of some of the widely known classic studies on leadership can help set the stage for the analysis of modern theories and styles of leadership.

Lippitt and White Leadership Studies

A pioneering leadership study conducted in the late 1930s by Ronald Lippitt and Ralph K. White under the general direction of Kurt Lewin at the University of Iowa has had a lasting impact. Lewin is recognized as the father of group dynamics and an important cognitive theorist. In the initial studies, hobby clubs for ten-year-old boys were formed. Each club was submitted to three different styles of leadership—authoritarian, democratic, and laissez faire. The authoritarian leader was very directive and allowed no participation. This leader tended to give individual attention when praising and criticizing but tried to be friendly or impersonal rather than openly hostile. The democratic leader encouraged group discussion and decision. He tried to be "objective" in his praise or criticism and to be one of the group in spirit. The laissez faire leader gave complete freedom to the group; he essentially provided no leadership.

Under experimental conditions, the three leadership styles were manipulated to show their effects on variables such as satisfaction and frustration-aggression. Controls in the experiment included the following:

    1 *Characteristics of the boys.* All the boys had about the same intellignece and social behaviors.
    2 *Types of activities performed.* Each of the clubs made similar things, such as masks, model airplanes, murals, and soap carvings.
    3 *The physical setting and equipment.* The experiments were conducted in the same rooms and used identical equipment for all the clubs.
    4 *The physical characteristics and personality of the leader.* The leaders assumed a different style as they shifted every six weeks from group to group.[2]

These controls were employed so that the experimenters could state with some

---

[2]All specific references made to the styles-of-leadership study are drawn from Kurt Lewin, Ronald Lippitt, and Ralph K. White, "Patterns of Aggressive Behavior in Experimentally Created 'Social Climates,'" *Journal of Social Psychology*, May 1939, pp. 271–276.

degree of assurance that the styles of leadership were causing the changes in the dependent variables of satisfaction and frustration-aggression.

Results of the Studies   Some of the results were clear-cut and others were not. One definite finding was the boys' overwhelming preference for their democratic leader. In individual interviews, nineteen of the twenty boys stated they liked the democratic leader better than the authoritarian leader. Interestingly, the only boy who preferred the autocratic leader was the son of an army officer stationed with the university R. O. T. C. unit. The boy commented that the leader who had the authoritarian role "was the strictest, and I like that a lot."[3] The other nineteen boys did not consider strictness a virtue. They said the autocrat "didn't let us do what we wanted to do," or "we just had to do things; he wanted us to get it done in a hurry."[4] They liked the democratic leader because "he never did try to be the boss, but we always had plenty to do."[5] The boys also chose the laissez faire leader over the autocratic one in seven out of ten cases. For most of the boys, even confusion and disorder were preferable to strictness and rigidity.

Unfortunately, the effects that styles of leadership had on productivity were not directly examined. The experiments were primarily designed to examine patterns of aggressive behavior. However, an important by-product was the insight that was gained into the productive behavior of a group. For example, the researchers found that the boys subjected to the autocratic leader reacted in one of two ways: either aggressively or apathetically. Through filming and recording detailed observations, Lippitt's original 1937 study found hostility was thirty times as frequent in the autocratic as in the democratic group. Also, aggression ("hostility" and "joking hostility") was eight times as prevalent. In a second experiment performed a year later, one of five autocratic groups had the same aggressive reaction. The other four had extremely nonaggressive, "apathetic" patterns of behavior. Both the aggressive and apathetic behaviors were deemed to be reactions to the frustration caused by the autocratic leader. The researchers also pointed out that the apathetic groups exhibited outbursts of aggression when the autocratic leader left the room or when a transition was made to a freer leadership atmosphere. The laissez faire leadership climate actually produced the greatest number of aggressive acts from the group. The democratically led group fell between the one extremely aggressive group and the four apathetic groups under the autocratic leaders.

Implications of the Studies   Sweeping generalizations on the basis of the Lippitt and White studies are dangerous. Preadolescent boys making masks and carving soap are a long way from adults working in a complex, formal organization. Furthermore, from the viewpoint of modern behavioral science

[3]Ibid., p. 284.
[4]Ibid.
[5]Ibid.

research methodology, many of the variables were not controlled. Neverthe-less, these leadership studies have extremely important historical significance. They were the pioneering attempts to determine, experimentally, what effects styles of leadership have on the group. As with the Hawthorne studies, the Lippitt and White studies are too often automatically discounted or at least deemphasized because they were experimentally crude. The values of the studies were that they were the first to analyze leadership from the standpoint of scientific methodology and, more important, they showed that different styles of leadership can produce different, complex reactions from the same or similar groups.

Ohio State Leadership Studies

In 1945, the Bureau of Business Research at Ohio State University initiated a series of studies on leadership. An interdisciplinary team of researchers from psychology, sociology, and economics developed and used the Leader Behav-ior Description Questionnaire (LBDQ) to analyze leadership in numerous types of groups and situations.[6] Studies were made of Air Force commanders and members of bomber crews; officers, noncommissioned personnel, and civilian administrators in the Navy Department; manufacturing foremen; executives of regional cooperatives; college administrators; teachers, principals, and school superintendents; and leaders of various student and civilian groups.

The Ohio State studies started with the premise that no satisfactory definition of leadership existed. They also recognized that previous work had too often assumed that "leaderhip" was synonymous with "good leadership." The Ohio State group was determined to study leadership, regardless of definition or whether it was effective or ineffective.

In the first step, the LBDQ was administered in various leadership situations. In order to examine the leader's behavior, the answers to the questionnaire were then subjected to factor analysis. The outcome was amazingly consistent. The same two dimensions of leadership behavior contin-ually emerged. They were *consideration* and *initiating structure.* For example, one of the first studies conducted by Halpin and Winer examined fifty-two bomber crews.[7] The leadership behaviors of the commanders were described by 300 crew members. It was found that consideration accounted for 49.6 percent of the common-factor variance. This consideration factor meant that a friendly, trusting, respectful, and warm relationship existed between the bomber commander and his crew. Close behind consideration was the dimen-sion of initiating structure. This factor accounted for 33.6 percent of the common-factor variance. *Initiating structure* meant that the leader organized and defined the relationship between himself and the members of his crew. "He

[6]Ralph M. Stogdill and Alvin E. Coons (eds.), *Leader Behavior: Its Description and Measurement,* Ohio State University, Bureau of Business Research, Columbus, 1957.

[7]Andrew W. Halpin and B. James Winer, "A Factorial Study of the Leader Behavior Descriptions," in ibid., pp. 39–51.

tends to define the role which he expects each member of the crew to assume, and endeavors to establish well defined patterns of organization, channels of communication, and ways of getting jobs done."[8] Combined, consideration and initiating structure accounted for 83.2 percent of the common-factor variance in this study.

The same two factors were found in many follow-up studies encompassing many kinds of leadership positions and contexts. The researchers carefully emphasize that the studies show only *how* leaders carry out their leadership position. Initiating structure and consideration are very similar to the time-honored military commander's functions of mission and concern with the welfare of the men. In simple terms, the Ohio State factors are task or goal orientation (initiating structure) and recognition of individual needs (consideration). The two dimensions are separate and distinct from one another.

The value of the Ohio State studies is their empirical determination of the functions of leadership. These studies were the first to point out and emphasize the importance of *both* task direction and consideration of individual needs in assessing leadership behavior. This two-dimensional approach lessened the gap between the strict task orientation of the scientific management movement and the human relations emphasis which was popular up to recent times.

Early Michigan Studies on Leadership Styles

At about the same time the Ohio State studies were being conducted, the Office of Naval Research granted a contract to the University of Michigan Survey Research Center. The purpose of the grant was to determine the "principles which contribute both to the productivity of the group and to the satisfaction that the group members derive from their participation."[9] To accomplish this objective, a study was initiated in 1947 at the home office of the Prudential Insurance Company, Newark, New Jersey.

The Michigan group tried to avoid the methodological difficulties of other pioneering research such as the Hawthorne studies. The researchers were particularly critical of the failure of the Hawthorne studies to develop quantitative measures for variables affecting supervisors and workers. In the Prudential study, systematic measurement was made of the perceptions and attitudes of supervisors and workers. These variables were then related to measures of performance. The research design also included a high degree of control over nonpsychological variables that might influence morale and productivity. Thus, certain factors, such as type of work, working conditions, and work methods, were controlled.

Twelve high-low productivity pairs were selected for examination. Each pair represented a high-producing section and a low-producing section, with the other variables, such as type of work, conditions, and methods, being the same

[8]Ibid., pp. 42–43.

[9]Rensis Likert, "Foreword," in Daniel Katz, Nathan Maccoby, and Nancy C. Morse, *Productivity, Supervision and Morale in an Office Situation*, University of Michigan, Survey Research Center, Ann Arbor, 1950.

in each pair. Nondirective interviews were conducted with the 24 section supervisors and 419 clerical-type workers. Results showed that supervisors of high-producing sections were significantly more likely

1   To receive general, rather than close, supervision from their supervisors;
2   To like the amount of authority and responsibility they have in their jobs;
3   To spend more time in supervision;
4   To give general, rather than close, supervision to their employees; and
5   To be employee-oriented, rather than production-oriented.[10]

The low-producing section supervisors had essentially opposite characteristics and techniques. They were found to be close, production-centered supervisors. Another important, but sometimes overlooked, finding was that employee satisfaction was *not* directly related to productivity.

The general, employee-centered supervisor, described above, has been the standard-bearer for the traditional human relations approach to leadership. The results of the Prudential studies are always cited when human relations advocates are challenged to prove their theories. The studies have been followed up with hundreds of similar studies in a wide variety of industrial, hospital, governmental, and other organizations. Thousands of employees, performing unskilled to highly professional-scientific tasks, have been analyzed. In 1961, Rensis Likert, the director of The Institute for Social Research of the University of Michigan, presented the results of the years of research in *New Patterns of Management.*[11] Although there were some variations and refinements, the "new patterns" were essentially the same as those found in the Prudential studies.

THEORIES OF LEADERSHIP

The Lippitt and White, Ohio State, and Michigan studies are three of the historically most important leadership studies for the study of organizational behavior. Unfortunately, they are still heavily depended upon, and leadership research has not surged ahead from this relatively auspicious beginning. Before analyzing the current status of leadership research, it is important to look at the theoretical development that has occurred through the years.

There are several distinct theoretical bases for leadership. At first leaders were felt to be born, not made. This so-called "great man" theory of leadership implied that some individuals were born with certain traits that allowed them to emerge out of any situation or period of history to become a leader. This evolved into what is now known as the "trait theory" of leadership. Another approach was to give greater attention to followers. The trait approach is mainly concerned with identifying personality traits of the leader. Because of

---

[10]Ibid., p. 62.

[11]Rensis Likert, *New Patterns of Management,* McGraw-Hill Book Company, New York, 1961.

the dissatisfaction with this approach, and stimulated by research such as the Ohio State studies, emphasis switched from the individual leader to the group being led. In the group approach, leadership is viewed more in terms of the leader's behavior and how such behavior affects and is affected by the group of followers. Finally, besides the leader and the group, the situation began to receive increased attention in leadership theory. The situation was initially called *Zeitgeist* (a German word meaning "spirit of the times"), and the leader is viewed as a product of the times, the situation. The person with the particular qualities or traits that a situation requires will emerge as the leader. Such a view has much historical support for a theoretical base fot leadership and serves as the base for today's situational, and now, contingency, theories of leadership. Finally, very recently, some of the expectancy concepts of motivation that were discussed in the last chapter began to be adapted to leadership. Called the "path-goal" theory of leadership, this latest approach is a step toward synthesizing motivational and leadership concepts. The following will examine in detail these major theoretical bases of leadership.

Trait Theories of Leadership

The scientific analysis of leadership started off by concentrating on leaders themselves. The vital question that this theoretical approach attempted to answer was, what characteristics or traits make a person a leader? The earliest trait theories, which can be traced back to the ancient Greeks and Romans, concluded that leaders were born, not made. This "great man" theory of leadership said that a person was born either with or without the necessary traits for leadership. Famous figures in history, for example Napoleon, were said to have had the "natural" leadership abilities to rise out of any situation to be a great leader.

Eventually, the "great man" theory gave way to a more realistic trait approach to leadership. Under the influence of the behavioristic school of psychological thought, acceptance was given to the fact that leadership traits are not completely inborn but can also be acquired through learning and experience. Attention turned to the search for universal traits possessed by leaders. Numerous physical, mental, and personality traits were researched from about 1930 to 1950. The results of this voluminous research effort were generally very disappointing. Only intelligence seemed to hold up with any degree of consistency. One summary of leadership research found intelligence in ten studies, initiative in six, extroversion and sense of humor in five, and enthusiasm, fairness, sympathy, and self-confidence in four.[12] When combined with studies on physical traits, the conclusion seems to be that leaders are bigger and brighter than those being led, but not too much so.

When the trait approach is applied to organizational leadership, the result is even cloudier. One of the biggest problems is that all managers think they know what the qualities of a successful leader are. Kelly notes,

[12]Joe Kelly, *Organizational Behaviour,* rev. ed., Richard D. Irwin, Inc., Homewood, Ill., 1974, p. 363.

This optimistic if somewhat naïve attitude springs from the belief that a manager is a person who has some of the following characteristics (which and how many depends upon the prejudices of the individual making the selection): analytical, intelligent, not too bright, keen, enthusiastic, aggressive, capable of maintaining smooth interpersonal relationships, persuasive, dominant, personally acceptable, tactful, extraverted, well-balanced, needing to succeed, ambitious, etc.[13]

Obviously, almost any adjective can be used to describe a successful leader. Recognizing these semantic limitations and realizing that there is no cause-and-effect relationship between observed traits and successful leadership, Keith Davis summarizes four of the major traits which seem to have an impact on successful organizational leadership:[14]

1 *Intelligence.* Research generally shows that the leader has higher intelligence than the average intelligence of his followers. Interestingly, however, the leader cannot be exceedingly much more intelligent than his followers.

2 *Social maturity and breadth.* Leaders tend to be emotionally stable and mature and to have broad interests and activities. They have an assured, respectful self-concept.

3 *Inner motivation and achievement drives.* Leaders have relatively intense motivational drives of the achievement type. They strive for intrinsic rather than extrinsic rewards.

4 *Human relations attitudes.* A successful leader recognizes the worth and dignity of his followers and is able to empathize with them. In the terminology of the Ohio State leadership studies, he possesses consideration, and in the Michigan studies terminology, he is employee- rather than production-centered.

The above represents only one among many possible lists of important organizational leadership traits. Although one can find some research evidence to support the traits on Davis's list and others, to date none are conclusive. Research findings do not begin to agree on which traits are generally found in leaders or even which ones are more important than others. Similar to the trait theories of personality, the trait approach to leadership has provided some descriptive insight but has little analytical or predictive value.

Group Theories of Leadership

The group theories of leadership have their roots in social psychology. Homans's exchange theory, in particular, serves as an important basis for this approach. Presented in Chapter 15, this simply means that the leader provides more benefits/rewards than burdens/costs for followers. There must be a positive exchange between the leader and followers in order for group goals to be accomplished. Chester Barnard applied such an analysis to managers and subordinates in an organizational setting almost forty years ago. More recently

[13]Ibid., pp. 363–364.

[14]Keith Davis, *Human Behavior at Work*, 4th ed., McGraw-Hill Book Company, New York, 1972, pp. 103–104.

Hollander and Julian articulate the social exchange view of leadership as follows:

> . . . the person in the role of leader who fulfills expectations and achieves group goals provides rewards for others which are reciprocated in the form of status, esteem, and heightened influence. Because leadership embodies a two-way influence relationship, recipients of influence assertions may respond by asserting influence in return. . . . The very sustenance of the relationship depends upon some yielding to influence on both sides.[15]

The above quote emphasizes that leadership is an exchange process between the leader and followers and also involves the sociological concept of role expectations. Social psychological research can be used to support the exchange and role concepts applied to leadership. In addition, the original Ohio State studies and follow-up studies through the years, especially the dimension of giving consideration to followers, gives support to the group perspective of leadership. A thorough review of research to date indicates that leaders who take into account and support their followers have a positive impact on attitudes, satisfaction, and performance.[16] However, these findings are tempered by the fact that there are many other variables in the leadership process (for example, the leader's traits and situational variables). All three seem to have an impact on satisfaction and performance and, similarly to the case of motivation, the direction of causality is not clear. The research evidence does not make clear whether the traditionally assumed case that a certain style of leadership (e.g., supportive of the group) leads to or causes satisfaction and performance or the reverse is correct.[17] The analysis of leadership styles in the middle of the chapter will pursue this question further.

Situational Theories of Leadership

After both the trait and group approaches proved to fall short of an adequate overall theory of leadership, attention turned to the situational aspects of leadership. Starting in the 1940s, social psychologists began the search for situational variables that impact on leadership roles, skills, and behavior and on followers' performance and satisfaction. Numerous situational variables were identified but no overall situational theory pulled it all together. Then, about a decade ago, Fred Fiedler proposed a situationally based model for leadership effectiveness. A brief review of his research techniques and findings is

[15]Edwin P. Hollander and James W. Julian, "Contemporary Trends in the Analysis of Leadership Processes," *Psychological Bulletin*, vol. 71, 1969, pp. 387–397. Reprinted in Richard M. Steers and Lyman W. Porter, (eds.), *Motivation and Work Behavior*, McGraw-Hill Book Company, New York, 1975, p. 349.

[16]Alan C. Filley, Robert J. House, and Steven Kerr, *Managerial Process and Organizational Behavior*, 2d ed., Scott, Foresman and Company, Glenview, Ill., 1976, pp. 219–222.

[17]See Charles N. Greene, "A Longitudinal Analysis of Relationships among Leader Behavior and Subordinate Performance and Satisfaction," *Academy of Management Proceedings*, 1973, pp. 433–440, and Steven Kerr and Chester Schriesheim, "Consideration, Initiating Structure, and Organizational Criteria: An Update of Korman's 1966 Review," *Personnel Psychology*, Winter 1974, pp. 555–568.

necessary to fully understand his contingency theory of leadership effectiveness.

ASO and LPC Scores Fiedler developed a unique operational technique to measure leadership style. Measurement is obtained from scores which indicate the Assumed Similarity between Opposites (ASO) and Least Preferred Coworker (LPC). ASO calculates the degree of similarity between leaders' perceptions of their most and least preferred coworkers. LPC calculates the degree to which the leaders favorably perceive their worst coworkers. The two measurements, which can be used interchangeably, relate to leadership style in the following manner:

1 *The human relations or "lenient" style* is associated with the leader who does not discern a great deal of difference between the most and least preferred coworkers (ASO) *or* who gives a relatively favorable description of the least preferred coworker (LPC).

2 *The task-directed or "hard-nosed" style* is associated with the leader who perceives a great difference between the most and least preferred coworkers (ASO) and gives a very unfavorable description of the least preferred coworker (LPC).

Fiedler's Findings Through the years the performance of both laboratory groups and numerous real groups (basketball teams, fraternity members, surveying teams, bomber crews, infantry squads, open-hearth steel employees, and farm-supply service employees) was correlated with the leadership styles described above. The results were somewhat encouraging, but no simple relationships between leadership style as determined by the leaders' ASO and LPC scores and group performance developed. Eventually Fiedler concluded that more attention would have to be given to situational variables. He became convinced that leadership style in *combination* with the situation determines group performance.

Fiedler's Contingency Model of Leadership

To test the hypothesis he had formulated from previous research findings, Fiedler developed what he called a *contingency model of leadership effectiveness*. This model contained the relationship between leadership style and the favorableness of the situation. Situational favorableness was described by Fiedler in terms of three empirically derived dimensions:

1 The *leader-member relationship*, which is the most critical variable in determining the situation's favorableness;

2 The degree of *task structure*, which is the second most important input into the favorableness of the situation; and

3 The leader's *position power* obtained through formal authority, which is the third most critical dimension of the situation.[18]

[18]Fred E. Fiedler, *A Theory of Leadership Effectiveness*, McGraw-Hill Book Company, New York, 1967, pp. 143–144.

Situations are favorable to the leader if all three of the above dimensions are high. In other words, if the leader is generally accepted by followers (high first dimension), if the task is very structured and everything is "spelled out" (high second dimension), and if a great deal of authority and power is formally attributed to the leader's position (high third dimension), the situation is very favorable. If the opposite exists (if the three dimensions are low), the situation will be very unfavorable for the leader. Fiedler was convinced that the favorableness of the situation in combination with the leadership style determines effectiveness.

Through the manipulation of research findings, Fiedler was able to discover that under very favorable *and* very unfavorable situations, the task-directed or "hard-nosed" type of leader was most effective. However, when the situation was only moderately favorable or unfavorable (the intermediate range of favorableness), the human relations or lenient type of leader was most effective. Figure 18-1 summarizes this relationship between leadership style and the favorableness of the situation.

Why is the task-directed type of leader successful in very favorable situations? Fiedler offered the following explanation:

> In the very favorable conditions in which the leader has power, informal backing, and a relatively well-structured task, the group is ready to be directed, and the group expects to be told what to do. Consider the captain of an airliner in its final landing approach. We would hardly want him to turn to his crew for a discussion on how to land.[19]

[19]Ibid., p. 147.

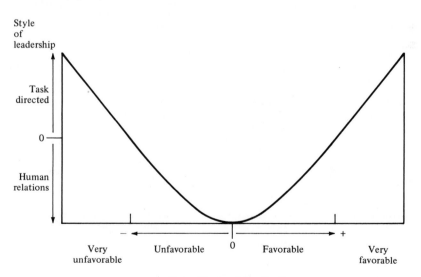

Favorableness of the situation

Figure 18-1 Fiedler's model of leadership. (*Source: Adapted from Fred E. Fiedler,* A Theory of Leadership Effectiveness, *McGraw-Hill Book Company, New York, 1967, pp. 142–148.*)

As an example of why the task-oriented leader is successful in a highly unfavorable situation, Fiedler cited

> . . . the disliked chairman of a volunteer committee which is asked to plan the office picnic on a beautiful Sunday. If the leader asks too many questions about what the group ought to do or how he should proceed, he is likely to be told that "we ought to go home."[20]

The leader who makes a wrong decision in this highly unfavorable type of situation is probably better off than the leader who makes no decision at all. Figure 18-1 shows that the human relations leader is effective in the intermediate range of favorableness. An example of such situations is the typical committee or a unit which is staffed by professionals. In these situations, the leader may not be wholly accepted by the other members of the group, the task may be generally vague and not completely structured, and little authority and power may be granted to the leader. Under such circumstances, the model predicts that a human relations, lenient type of leader will be most effective.

Research Support of the Contingency Model   As is true of any widely publicized theoretical breakthrough, Fiedler's model has stimulated a great deal of research. Also, as is true of most theories in the social-behavioral sciences, the results are mixed and a controversy has been generated. Fiedler himself recognizes that his model must be able to explain and predict if it is to be a valid theory for leadership.

On the basis of thirty studies in a wide variety of teams and organizations, e.g., Navy teams, chemical research teams, shop departments, supermarkets, heavy machinery plant departments, engineering groups, hospital wards, public health teams, and others, Fiedler concludes that "the theory is highly predictive and that the relations obtained in the validation studies are almost identical to those obtained in the original studies."[21] With one exception which Fiedler explains away, the model correctly predicted the correlations that should exist between LPC scores of the leader (which determines the style) and performance in relation to the identified favorableness of the situation. For example, his studies show that in very unfavorable and very favorable situations, there is a negative correlation between the leader's LPC score and performance (i.e., the task-oriented leader performs best). In a moderately favorable and moderately unfavorable situation, there is a positive correlation between the leader's LPC score and performance (i.e., the human relations–oriented leader is more effective).

Critical Analysis of the Contingency Model   Although there is not nearly as much criticism of Fiedler's work as there is, for example, of Herzberg's

---

[20]Ibid.

[21]Fred Fiedler and Martin M. Chemers, *Leadership and Effective Management,* Scott, Foresman and Company, Glenview, Ill., 1974, p. 83.

motivation theory, some researchers do not wholly agree with Fiedler's interpretations or conclusions. For example, Graen and his colleagues and Ashour have been critical of the procedures and statistical analysis of the studies used to support the validity of the model.[22] Some of these criticisms have been answered by Fiedler's colleagues in a follow-up study which used large samples and appropriate statistical tests.[23]

Most of the justifiable criticism comes from Fiedler's extension of the model to the actual practice of human resource management. Based on the model, Fiedler suggests that management would be better off to engineer positions so that the requirements fit the leader instead of the more traditional way of selecting and developing leaders to fit into existing jobs.[24] Although appealing and with significant potential implications for selection and development of managerial personnel and job design, the evidence is not yet sufficient to justify the implementation of this suggestion to human resource management policy and practice. On the other hand, even the critics would admit that Fiedler has provided one of the major breakthroughs for leadership theory and practice. Further research, especially leading to an understanding of what behavior is actually represented by the LPC response and specifying how the situational moderators will change as the leader asserts influence on subordinates,[25] should put Fiedler's contingency approach on firmer ground so that it can actually guide the future practice of human resource management. In addition, Fiedler has set an important precedent for the development of contingency models, not just for leadership, but for other management concepts and techniques as well.[26]

Path-Goal Leadership Theory

The most recent widely recognized theoretical development for leadership uses the expectancy framework from motivation theory. This is a healthy development because leadership is closely related to motivation on the one hand (discussed in the last chapter) and power on the other (discussed in the last part of this chapter). Any theory which attempts to synthesize the various concepts seems to be a step in the right direction.

Although Georgopoulos and his colleagues at the University of Michigan's

---

[22]George Graen, K. Alvares, V. B. Orris, and J. A. Martella, "Contingency Model of Leadership Effectiveness: Antecedent and Evidential Results," *Psychological Bulletin*, vol. 74, 1970, pp. 285–296; George Graen, James B. Orris, and Kenneth M. Alvares, "Contingency Model of Leadership Effectiveness: Some Experimental Results," *Journal of Applied Psychology*, June 1971, pp. 196–201; and Ahmed Ashour, "The Contingency Model of Leadership Effectiveness: An Evaluation," *Organizational Behavior and Human Performance*, June 1973, pp. 339–355.

[23]Martin M. Chemers and George J. Skrzypek, "Experimental Test of the Contingency Model of Leadership Effectiveness," *Journal of Personality and Social Psychology*, November 1972, pp. 172–177.

[24]Fred E. Fiedler, "Engineer the Job to Fit the Manager," *Harvard Business Review*, September–October 1965, pp. 115–122.

[25]Filley, House, and Kerr, op. cit., p. 261.

[26]See Fred Luthans, *Introduction to Management: A Contingency Approach*, McGraw-Hill Book Company, New York, 1976, for a contingency framework for management as a whole.

Institute for Social Research used path-goal concepts and terminology over two decades ago in analyzing the impact of leadership on performance, the modern development is usually attributed to Martin Evans and Robert House in separate papers.[27] In essence, the path-goal theory attempts to explain the impact that leader behavior has on subordinate motivation, satisfaction, and performance. The theory incorporates four major types or styles of leader behavior.[28] Briefly summarized these are:

1 *Directive leadership.* This style is similar to the Lippitt and White authoritarian leader. Subordinates know exactly what is expected of them and specific directions are given by the leader. There is no participation by subordinates.

2 *Supportive leadership.* Self-explanatory; the leader is friendly and approachable and shows a genuine human concern for subordinates.

3 *Participative leadership.* This leader asks for and uses suggestions from subordinates but still makes the decisions.

4 *Achievement-oriented leadership.* This leader sets challenging goals for subordinates and shows confidence in them to attain these goals and perform well.

The path-goal theory—and here is how it differs in one respect from Fiedler's contingency model—suggests that these various styles can be and actually are used by the same leader in different situations.[29] Two of the situational factors that have been identified so far are the personal characteristics of subordinates and the environmental pressures and demands facing subordinates. With respect to the first situational factor, the theory asserts that,

> . . . leader behavior will be acceptable to subordinates to the extent that the subordinates see such behavior as either an immediate source of satisfaction or as instrumental to future satisfaction.[30]

And with respect to the second situational factor, the theory states that,

> . . . leader behavior will be motivational (e.g., will increase subordinate effort) to the extent that (1) it makes satisfaction of subordinate needs contingent on effective performance, and (2) it complements the environment of subordinates by providing the coaching, guidance, support, and rewards which are necessary for effective performance and which may otherwise be lacking in subordinates or in their environment.[31]

[27]Basil S. Georgopoulos, Gerald M. Mahoney, and Nyle W. Jones, "A Path-Goal Approach to Productivity," *Journal of Applied Psychology,* December 1957, pp. 345–353; Martin G. Evans, "The Effect of Supervisory Behavior on the Path-Goal Relationship," *Organizational Behavior and Human Performance,* May 1970, pp. 277–298; and Robert J. House, "A Path-Goal Theory of Leader Effectiveness," *Administrative Science Quarterly,* September 1971, pp. 321–338.

[28]Robert J. House and Terence R. Mitchell, "Path-Goal Theory of Leadership," *Journal of Contemporary Business,* Autumn 1974, pp. 81–97.

[29]Ibid.

[30]Ibid., in Steers and Porter, op. cit., p. 386.

[31]Filley, House, and Kerr, op. cit., p. 254.

Using one of the four styles contingent upon the situational factors as outlined above, the leader attempts to motivate subordinates, in turn leading to their satisfaction and performance. This is specifically done by:

1 recognizing and/or arousing subordinates' needs for outcomes over which the leader has some control,

2 increasing personal payoffs to subordinates for work-goal attainment,

3 making the path to those payoffs easier to travel by coaching and direction,

4 helping subordinates clarify expectancies,

5 reducing frustrating barriers, and

6 increasing the opportunities for personal satisfaction contingent on effective performance.[32]

In other words, by doing the above the leader attempts to make the path to goals as smooth as possible for subordinates. But to accomplish this path-goal facilitation, the leader must use the appropriate style contingent on the situational variables present.

As is true of the expectancy theory of motivation, there has been a recent surge of research on the path-goal theory of leadership. So far, the research has generally been supportive of the theory. For example, a sampling of the research findings, most of which have been made in the last couple of years, indicates that:[33]

1 Studies of seven organizations have found that *leader directiveness* is (1) positively related to satisfactions and expectancies of subordinates engaged in ambiguous tasks, and (2) negatively related to satisfactions and expectancies of subordinates engaged in clear tasks.

2 Studies involving ten different samples of employees found that *supportive leadership* will have its most positive effect on satisfaction for subordinates who work on stressful, frustrating, or dissatisfying tasks.

3 In a major study in an industrial manufacturing organization, it was found that in nonrepetitive ego-involving tasks, employees were more satisfied under *participative leaders* than under nonparticipative leaders.

4 In three separate organizations it was found that for subordinates performing ambiguous-nonrepetitive tasks, the higher the *achievement orientation of the leader,* the more subordinates were confident that their efforts would pay off in effective performance.

Not all studies that have tested path-goal are as clear and supportive as the above, but there does seem to be a great deal of early support, and the theory certainly warrants continued research and refinement. Both the Fiedler contingency model and the path-goal approach take into consideration all three important variables in leadership: the leader, the group, and the situation.

Leadership as an Influence System

A truly meaningful and comprehensive approach to leadership would seem to have to incorporate the leader, the group, and the situation. Just as the Smith

[32]House and Mitchell, op. cit., in Steers and Porter, op. cit., pp. 385–386.

[33]Filley, House, and Kerr, op. cit., pp. 256–260.

and Cranny model in the last chapter clarified some of the complexities of modern motivation theory, an influence system model can clarify some of the complexities of modern leadership theory. Figure 18-2 depicts the heart of leadership to be influence and consists of the systems interaction of the leader, the group, and the situation. Each of the three major subsystems influences, and is influenced by, the other. Thus, the leader influences the group and the group influences the leader; the leader influences the situation and the situation influences the leader; and the group influences the situation and the situation influences the group. This influence-system model seems most accurately to depict what the leadership process is all about. The next part of the chapter will relate this model and the other theoretical background to the actual styles of leadership and supervision that are used in the practice of human resource management.

LEADERSHIP STYLES

The classic leadership studies discussed at the beginning of the chapter and the various leadership theories all have direct implications for what style the manager or supervisor uses in human resource management. The terminology "style" is roughly equivalent to the leader's behavior. It is the *way* in which the leader influences followers. The following discussion will first explore the implications for style from the classic studies and the theories, and then it will present the most recent approaches that deal directly with style.

Style Implications from the Classic Studies and the Modern Theories

Chapter 1 discussed the major historical contributions to the behavioral approach to management. Most of this discussion either indirectly or directly had implications for leadership style. For example, the Hawthorne studies

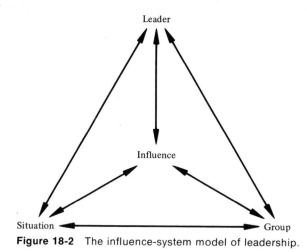

Figure 18-2 The influence-system model of leadership.

were interpreted in terms of their implications for supervisory style, and Douglas McGregor's Theory X represents the old, authoritarian style and his Theory Y represents the enlightened, humanistic style of leadership. Also, the studies at the beginning of this chapter were concerned with style. The Lippitt and White study analyzed the impact of autocratic, democratic, and laissez faire styles, and the Prudential studies conducted by the Michigan group found the employee-centered supervisor to be more effective than the production-centered supervisor. The Ohio State studies identified consideration (a supportive type of style) and initiating structure (a directive type of style) as being the major functions of leadership. Both the trait and the group theories have indirect implications for style, and the human relations and task-directed styles play a direct role in Fiedler's contingency theory. The path-goal conceptualization depends heavily upon directive, supportive, participative, and achievement-oriented styles of leadership.

The various styles discussed so far can be incorporated into the following continuum:

Boss-centered		**Subordinate-centered**
Theory X	←————————————————————→	Theory Y
autocratic	←————————————————————→	democratic
production-centered	←————————————————————→	employee-centered
close	←————————————————————→	general
initiating structure	←————————————————————→	consideration
task-directed	←————————————————————→	human relations
directive	←————————————————————→	supportive
directive	←————————————————————→	participative

Although the above represents only a rough approximation of the various styles for ease of presentation and a brief summary, the styles may be substituted for the boss-centered → subordinate-centered terminology used in Figure 18-3. The verbal descriptions and the relationship between authority and freedom found in Figure 18-3 give an overall rough summary of the characteristics of the various styles of leadership. This depiction can serve as background for a more detailed examination of the specific application of styles to the practice of human resource management.

Managerial Grid Styles

One very popular approach to identifying leadership styles of practicing managers is the use of Robert R. Blake and Jane S. Mouton's managerial grid. Figure 18-4 shows that the two dimensions of the grid are concern for people along the vertical axis and concern for production along the horizontal. These two dimensions, of course, are equivalent to the consideration and initiating structure functions identified by the Ohio State studies and the employee-centered and production-centered styles used in the Michigan studies.

The five basic styles identified in the grid represent varying combinations

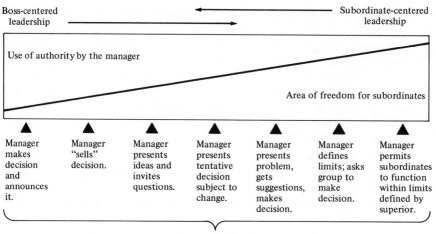

Boss-centered leadership

Subordinate-centered leadership

Use of authority by the manager

Area of freedom for subordinates

| Manager makes decision and announces it. | Manager "sells" decision. | Manager presents ideas and invites questions. | Manager presents tentative decision subject to change. | Manager presents problem, gets suggestions, makes decision. | Manager defines limits; asks group to make decision. | Manager permits subordinates to function within limits defined by superior. |

Range of behavior

Figure 18-3 A continuum of leadership behavior. (*Source: Robert Tannenbaum and Warren H. Schmidt, "How to Choose a Leadership Pattern,"* Harvard Business Review, *March–April 1958, p. 96. Used with permission.*)

of concern for people and production. The 1, 1 manager has minimum concern for people and production and is sometimes labeled the "impoverished" style. The opposite is the 9, 9 manager. This individual has maximum concern for people and production. Practically all managers feel this is the best style of

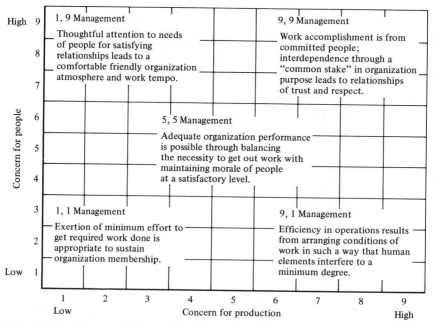

Figure 18-4 The managerial grid. (*Source: Robert R. Blake and Jane S. Mouton, "Managerial Façades,"* Advanced Management Journal, *July 1966, p. 31. Used with permission.*)

management, but Blake and Mouton carefully point out that the best style will depend on the situation. The 5, 5 manager is the "middle-of-the-roader," and the other two styles represent the extreme concerns for people (1, 9, "country club" manager) and production (9, 1, "task" manager). Where a manager falls on the grid can be determined by a questionnaire developed by Blake and Mouton and the results can play an important role in organization development (OD). Chapter 21 will discuss this grid approach to OD.

Reddin's Three-Dimensional Model

Blake and Mouton's grid identifies the style of a manager but does not directly relate it to effectiveness. William J. Reddin, a Canadian professor and consultant, has added the third dimension of effectiveness to his model. Besides incorporating the effectiveness dimension, he also builds in the situational impact on the appropriate style. Figure 18-5 shows the relatively elaborate 3-D leader effectiveness model.

The center grid in Figure 18-5 represents the four basic leadership styles. These are basically the same as the styles identified by Blake and Mouton. Importantly, where Reddin goes beyond the Blake and Mouton grid, each of the four styles can be effective or ineffective depending on the situation. The four styles on the upper right are effective (they achieve the output require-

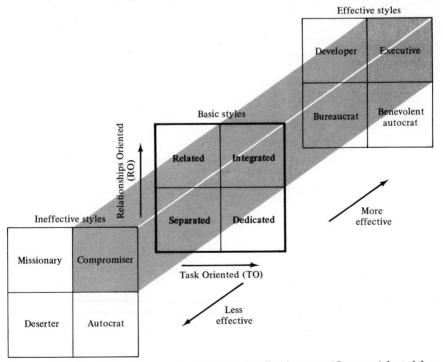

Figure 18-5 Reddin's 3-D model of leadership effectiveness. (*Source: Adapted from W. J. Reddin,* Managerial Effectiveness, *McGraw-Hill Book Company, New York, 1970, p. 230. Used with permission.*)

ments of the manager's job and/or attain the goals of the position) and the four styles on the lower left are ineffective. Very briefly, these eight styles can be summarized as follows:[34]

Effective Styles

1 *Executive.* This style gives a great deal of concern to both task (TO) and people (RO). A manager using this style is a good motivator, sets high standards, recognizes individual differences, and utilizes team management.

2 *Developer.* This style gives maximum concern to people (RO) and minimum concern to the task (TO). A manager using this style has implicit trust in people and is mainly concerned with developing them as individuals.

3 *Benevolent Autocrat.* This style gives maximum concern to the task (TO) and minimum concern to people (RO). A manager using this style knows exactly what he or she wants and how to get it without causing resentment.

4 *Bureaucrat.* This style gives minimum concern to both task (TO) and people (RO). A manager using this style is mainly interested in the rules and wants to maintain and control the situation by their use but is seen as conscientious.

Ineffective Styles

1 *Compromiser.* This style gives a great deal of concern to both task (TO) and people (RO) in a situation that requires only emphasis on one or neither. This style of manager is a poor decision maker; the pressures affect him or her too much.

2 *Missionary.* This style gives maximum concern to people (RO) and minimum concern to the task (TO) where such behavior is inappropriate. This manager is typically the "do gooder" who values harmony as an end in itself.

3 *Autocrat.* This style gives maximum concern to the task (TO) and minimum concern to the people (RO) where such behavior is inappropriate. This manager has no confidence in others, is unpleasant, and is interested only in the immediate job.

4 *Deserter.* This style gives minimum concern to task (TO) and people (RO) in a situation where such behavior is inappropriate. This manager is uninvolved and passive.

Reddin has developed a sixty-four item forced-choice test that managers can take to identify their styles. It has become a very popular technique to use in training programs and executive development seminars. The test can help managers make a self-diagnosis of their strengths and weaknesses. It is emphasized that a style per se can be effective or ineffective depending on the situation. Reddin's 3-D approach incorporates all three theoretical bases (leader, group, and situation) and stresses that the manager should have an adaptive style that leads to effectiveness.

[34]William J. Reddin, "Managing Organizational Change," *Personnel Journal,* July 1969, p. 503.

Likert's Four Systems of Management

Both the Blake and Mouton and Reddin 3-D approaches are highly descriptive and at this time lack empirically validated research back-up. In contrast, evolving from the many years of research by the Michigan group, Rensis Likert proposes four basic systems or styles of organizational leadership. Figure 18-6 summarizes these four styles.

The manager who operates under a system 1 approach is very authoritarian and actually tries to exploit subordinates. The system 2 manager is also authoritarian but in a paternalistic manner. This benevolent autocrat keeps strict control and never delegates to subordinates, but he or she "pats them on the head" and "does it for their best interests." The system 3 manager uses a consultative style. This manager asks for and receives participative input from subordinates but maintains the right to make the final decision. The system 4 manager uses a democratic style. This manager gives some direction to subordinates but provides for total participation and decision by consensus and majority.

To give empirical research back-up to which style is most effective, Likert and his colleagues asked thousands of managers to describe, on an expanded version of the format shown in Figure 18-6, the highest- and lowest-producing departments with which they have had experience. Quite consistently, the high-producing units are described according to systems 3 and 4, and the low-producing units fall under systems 1 and 2. This response occurs irrespective of the manager's field of experience or whether the manager is in a line or staff position.[35]

The Impact of Intervening Variables and Time   An important refinement of Likert's work is the recognition of three broad classes of variables that affect the relationship between leadership and performance in a complex organization.[36] Briefly summarized, these are:

1 *Causal variables.* These are the independent variables that determine the course of developments and results of an organization. They include only those variables that are under control of management; e.g., economic conditions are *not* causal variables in this sense. Examples would include organization structure and management's policies and decisions and their leadership styles, skills, and behavior.

2 *Intervening variables.* These reflect the internal climate of the organization. Performance goals, loyalties, attitudes, perceptions, and motivations are some important intervening variables. They affect interpersonal relations, communication, and decision making in the organization.

3 *End-result variables.* These are the dependent variables, the outcomes

---

[35]Rensis Likert, *The Human Organization,* McGraw-Hill Book Company, New York, 1967, pp. 3 and 11.
[36]Ibid., pp. 26 and 29.

Figure 18-6 Likert's Systems of Management Leadership

Leadership variable	System 1 (exploitive autocratic)	System 2 (benevolent autocratic)	System 3 (participative)	System 4 (democratic)
Confidence and trust in subordinates	Has no confidence and trust in subordinates	Has condescending confidence and trust, such as master has to servant	Substantial but not complete confidence and trust; still wishes to keep control of decisions	Complete confidence and trust in all matters
Subordinates' feeling of freedom	Subordinates do not feel at all free to discuss things about the job with their superior	Subordinates do not feel very free to discuss things about the job with their superior	Subordinates feel rather free to discuss things about the job with their superior	Subordinates feel completely free to discuss things about the job with their superior
Superiors seeking involvement with subordinates	Seldom gets ideas and opinions of subordinates in solving job problems	Sometimes gets ideas and opinions of subordinates in solving job problems	Usually gets ideas and opinions and usually tries to make constructive use of them	Always asks subordinates for ideas and opinions and always tries to make constructive use of them

Source: Adapted from Rensis Likert, *The Human Organization*, McGraw-Hill Book Company, New York, 1967, p. 4. Used by permission.

of the organization. Examples would be productivity, service, costs, quality, and earnings.

Importantly, Likert points out that there is not a direct cause-and-effect relationship between, for example, leadership style (a causal variable) and earnings (an end-result variable). The intervening variables must also be taken into consideration. For example, moving to a system 1 style of management may lead to an improvement in profits but a deterioration of the intervening variables (i.e., attitudes, loyalty, and motivation decline). In time, these intervening variables may lead to a decrease in profits. Thus, although on the surface it appeared that system 1 was causing profits, because of the impact on the intervening variables, in the long run system 1 may lead to a decrease in profits. The same can be said for the application of a system 4 style. In the short run, profits may dip; but because of the impact on intervening variables, there will be an increase in profit over time. Obviously, the time lag between intervention and the impact on end-result variables becomes extremely important to Likert's scheme. Based upon some research evidence, Likert concludes that, "Changes in the causal variables toward System 4 apparently require an appreciable period of time before the impact of the change is fully manifest in corresponding improvement in end-result variables."[37]

An Example of Time Lag   Likert's "time-lag" helps explain the following relatively common sequence of events. A system 1 manager takes over an operation and immediately gets good performance results. In the meantime, however, the intervening variables are declining. Because the system 1 manager is getting results, he is promoted. A system 4 manager now takes over the operation. Because of the time lag, the intervening variables, which were affected by the system 1 manager, now start to impact on performance. Under the system 4 manager, performance starts to decline but the intervening variables start to improve. However, top mangement sees that when the system 4 manager took over, performance started to decline. The system 4 manager is replaced by a system 1 manager to "tighten up" the operation. The intervening variables affected by the system 4 manager now start to affect performance and the cycle repeats. Figure 18-7 graphically depicts this situation. In other words, the cause-and-effect relationships that appear on the surface may be very misleading because of the time-lag impact of the intervening variables. As in the example, top-management evaluations often credit the wrong manager (the system 1 manager in this case) for improving performance and unjustly blame the wrong manager (the system 4 manager in the example) for poor performance. Some organizations are caught up in this never-ending cycle of rewarding and punishing the wrong managers because of the time-lag effect of intervening variables.

[37]Ibid., pp. 80–81.

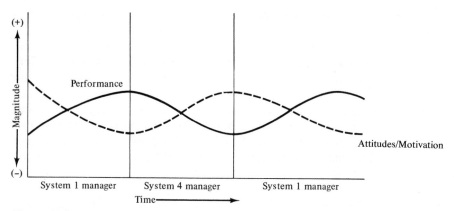

Figure 18-7 Hypothetical example depicting Likert's time-lag impact of intervening variables on performance.

Analysis of Likert's Approach   Likert and his colleagues are still actively involved in further development, research, and application of the system 4 style of management. For example, some predictive models are being developed to forecast what impact current causal and intervening variables will have on future outcome variables such as profit. Likert's survey instruments are being widely used in the diagnostic phase of organizational development. The concept and practice of human resource accounting, which Likert has helped develop and of which he is a leading advocate, are also closely tied into this discussion. Chapter 10 covered this important development for the control of modern organizations.

One of the major criticisms of Likert's work is the overdependence on survey questionnaire measures for gathering data to develop the theory and application of system 4 management. Sole dependence on Likert scale (continuums of dimensions as shown in Figure 18-6) questionnaire responses is not enough. Today there is increasing criticism of data gathered only by questionnaires and interviews. Multiple measures of behaviorally oriented variables in organizations are needed. More use of archival information (existing records kept by every organization for other use, e.g., government reports, personnel records, and performance data) and data gathered through observation are needed. Although ethical standards must always be maintained, subject awareness must be minimized to increase the reliability and validity of data that are gathered for research purposes. Both questionnaires and interviews have a great deal of subject awareness or intrusiveness. Archives and some naturalistic observational techniques minimize subject awareness and are called *unobtrusive measures.*[38] Not only Likert's work but much of the research reported in this book is based upon intrusive measures, i.e., questionnaires and interviews. What is needed is to supplement these measures with unobtrusive measures. By the use of multiple measures the chance of getting better, more accurate,

[38]Eugene J. Webb, Donald T. Campbell, Richard D. Schwartz, and Lee Sechrest, *Unobtrusive Measures: Nonreactive Research in the Social Sciences,* Rand McNally & Company, Chicago, 1966.

and valid data is increased tremendously. The research designs presented in Chapter 2 can all benefit from the use of multiple measures.

Besides the measurement problems inherent in Likert's scheme is the implication of the universality of the system 4 approach. Although Likert carefully points out that ". . . differences in the kind of work, in the traditions of the industry, and in the skills and values of the employees of a particular company will require quite different procedures and ways to apply appropriately the basic principles of system 4 management,"[39] he still implies that system 4 will *always* be more effective than system 1. The situational/contingency leadership theories and research findings would, of course, counter this generalization.

The Vroom-Yetton Normative Model

The Blake and Mouton, Reddin, and Likert approaches to leadership are all directly or by implication prescriptive. In addition, to varying degrees they try to take into consideration the situation (Blake and Mouton and Likert in passing and Reddin as a vital part of his approach). But none of these approaches spell out exactly *how* a manager should act or what decision should be made in a given situation. Vroom and Yetton attempt to provide a specific, normative (how decisions "ought" to be made in given situations) model that a leader could actually use in making effective decisions.[40]

The Vroom-Yetton model was first developed several years ago and has since been modified. The latest model contains five leadership styles, seven situation dimensions, fourteen problem types, and seven decision rules. The leadership styles consist of variations of autocratic, consultative, and group styles and the situational dimensions are of two general types: (1) the way in which problems affect the quality and acceptance of a decision, and (2) the way in which the problems affect the degree of participation. The seven situational dimensions are stated in the form of yes-no questions and the answers can quickly diagnose the situation for the leader.

Vroom and Yetton use a decision tree to relate the situation to the appropriate leadership style. Figure 18-8 shows the approach. The seven situational questions are listed at the top. Starting at the left, the manager would answer each question above the box in the decision tree until it led to the appropriate style. In this way the manager could determine the appropriate style based on the given confronting situation. Vroom and Yetton also point out that the fourteen problem types (the combinations of the seven situational variables listed as 1 through 14 in the decision tree) could actually have more than one acceptable leadership style. In order to be acceptable, the style must meet the criteria of seven decision rules that protect quality and acceptance. If more than one style remains after the test of both quality and acceptance (and many do), the third most important aspect of a decision—the amount of

[39]Rensis Likert, *The Human Organization*, op. cit., p. 192.

[40]Victor H. Vroom and Philip W. Yetton, *Leadership and Decision-Making*, University of Pittsburgh Press, Pittsburgh, Pa., 1973, chap. 3.

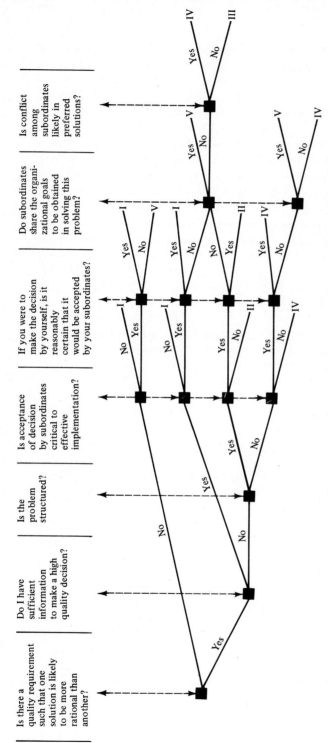

Column headers (left to right):

- Is there a quality requirement such that one solution is likely to be more rational than another?
- Do I have sufficient information to make a high quality decision?
- Is the problem structured?
- Is acceptance of decision by subordinates critical to effective implementation?
- If you were to make the decision by yourself, is it reasonably certain that it would be accepted by your subordinates?
- Do subordinates share the organizational goals to be obtained in solving this problem?
- Is conflict among subordinates likely in preferred solutions?

I You solve the problem or make the decision yourself, using information available to you at that time. **II** You obtain the necessary information from your subordinate(s), then decide on the solution to the problem yourself. You may or may not tell your subordinates what the problem is in getting the information from them. The role played by your subordinates in making the decision is clearly one of providing the necessary information to you, rather than generating or evaluating alternative solutions. **III** You share the problem with relevant subordinates individually, getting their ideas and suggestions without bringing them together as a group. Then *you* make the decision that may or may not reflect your subordinates' influence. **IV** You share the problem with your subordinates as a group, collectively obtaining their ideas and suggestions. Then *you* make the decision that may or may not reflect your subordinates' influence. **V** You share a problem with your subordinates as a group. Together you generate and evaluate alternatives and attempt to reach agreement (consensus) on a solution. Your role is much like that of a chairperson. You do not try to influence the group to adopt "your" solution and you are willing to accept and implement any solution that has the support of the entire group.

Figure 18-8 Vroom-Yetton normative leadership model. (*Source: Adapted from Victor H. Vroom, "A New Look at Managerial Decision Making,"* Organizational Dynamics, *vol. 1, no. 4, 1973, pp. 67 and 70.*)

time—is used to determine the single style that "ought" to be used in the given situation. The styles shown at the ends of the various branches on the decision tree reflect the single best style that should be used in light of the way the situation was diagnosed by answers to the questions at the top.

The Vroom-Yetton model is a fitting conclusion to the discussion of leadership in this chapter. The progression has been from theory to styles to specific prescription. Vroom has used a self-report and standardized problem method of testing his model on over a thousand managers going through training and development programs. These managers were asked to recall a problem they had encountered and to indicate which of the five styles they used to solve it. In the other approach the managers were given standardized problem cases and asked which style could best be used to solve it. One of the major conclusions that Vroom draws from these data is that there are bigger differences *within* managers than there are *between* managers.[41] The managers report using all styles, depending on the situation. Such a finding has implications for contingency management. If true, it means that managers can adapt; they are not so set in one style that they cannot change when confronted with another situation.

Despite the surface logic of the model and the fact that it does give precise answers to practicing managers, the research conducted so far is far from sufficient to validate it and justify its use in actual practice. On the other hand, it certainly is a step in the right direction of bridging the gap from theory to practice and can serve as a prototype for the actual practice of contingency management.

THE MEANING AND DYNAMICS OF POWER

As indicated in the introductory comments of the chapter, there is a close relationship between leadership and power. Especially when leadership is defined as influencing others, much can be learned about leadership by understanding power, and vice versa. In this last part of the chapter the meaning of power is examined, the sources and types of power are identified, and the use of power in organizations is analyzed.

The Meaning of Power

In Chapter 13 the power motive was defined as the need to manipulate others and have superiority over them. Taken from this definition of the need for power, power itself can be defined as an ability to get an individual or group to do something—to get the person or group to change in some way. The person who possesses power has the ability to manipulate or change others. Such a definition of power distinguishes it from authority and influence.

Authority legitimates power. Authority is the *right* to manipulate or

[41]Victor H. Vroom, "A New Look at Managerial Decision Making," *Organizational Dynamics*, vol. 1, no. 4, 1973, p. 77.

change others. Power need not be legitimate. Chapter 7 made the distinction between top-down classical, bureaucratic authority and Barnard's concept of bottom-up authority based upon acceptance. Influence is usually conceived as being narrower than power. It involves the ability on the part of a person to alter another person or group in specific ways, such as in their satisfaction and performance. Influence is more closely associated with leadership than is power, but both obviously are involved in the leadership process. Therefore, authority is different from power because of its legitimacy and influence is narrower than power but is so conceptually close that the two terms can be used interchangeably.

The above points out that an operational definition for power is lacking and, because of its vagueness, the concept of power has been largely ignored in the study of organizational behavior. Hicks and Gullett point out the problems with the study of power when they say, "Because power is not well understood, is often extremely subtle or obscure, springs from multiple sources, is highly dynamic, has multiple causes and effects, is multidimensional, and is particularly difficult—if not impossible—to quantify, positivists have tended to ignore it."[42] Yet, by looking at the sources and types of power and the organizational use of it, much can be learned about leadership in particular and organizational behavior in general.

Sources and Types of Power

The most widely recognized categories of the sources of power come from French and Raven.[43] They identify the following bases of power:

1 *Reward power.* The person having this power has the ability to reward. Managers frequently have reward power in that they can give merit increases or incentive pay and promotions to their subordinates. In operant terms this means the person has the power to administer positive reinforcers. In expectancy terms this means that the person has the power to provide positive valences and the other person perceives this ability.

2 *Coercive power.* The person having this power has the ability to threaten and/or punish. Managers frequently have coercive power in that they can fire or demote subordinates or dock their pay. They can also directly or indirectly threaten an employee that these punishing consequences will occur. In operant terms this means the person has the power to administer punishers or to negatively reinforce (terminate punishing consequences, which is a form of negative control). In expectancy terms this means that power comes from the expectation on the part of the other persons that they will be punished if they will not conform to the powerful person's desires.

3 *Legitimate power.* This power stems from the internalized values of the other persons which give the legitimate right to the person to influence

[42]Herbert G. Hicks and C. Ray Gullett, *Organizations: Theory and Behavior,* McGraw-Hill Book Company, New York, 1975, p. 238.

[43]John R. P. French, Jr., and Bertram Raven, "The Bases of Social Power," in *Studies in Social Power,* D. Cartwright (ed.), Institute for Social Research, Ann Arbor, Mich., 1959.

them. This, of course, could be labeled authority rather than power. The other persons have the obligation to accept this power. Such legitimate power can come from cultural values, acceptance of the social structure, or the designation of a legitimizing agent. Managers generally have legitimate power because employees believe in private property law values and in the hierarchy where higher positions have been designated to have power over lower positions.

4 *Referent power.* This type of power comes from the feeling or desire on the part of the other persons to identify with the person wielding power. The other persons want to identify with the powerful person regardless of the outcomes. A manager who desires to have referent power must be attractive to subordinates so that they want to identify with the manager regardless of whether the manager gives rewards or punishers.

5 *Expert power.* Managers have expert power to the extent that the other employees attribute knowledge and expertise to them. The experts are seen to have knowledge or ability only in well-defined areas. In an organization engineers may have expert power in their area of specialization but not outside of it. For example, the engineers are granted power on production problems but not on personnel problems. The same hold true for other staff experts such as accountants and computer technologists.

French and Raven recognize that there may be other sources of power, but these are the major ones. They also point out that the five sources are interrelated (e.g., the use of coercive power by managers may reduce their referent power) and the same person may use different types of power under different circumstances and at different times.

Research on Power

There has been some research devoted to the French and Raven categories of power. Schopler reviewed several studies that directly tested the bases of power and found that coercive power induces greater resistance than reward power; users of reward power are liked better than those depending on coercive power; conformity to coercive power increases with the strength of the potential punishment; as the legitimacy of a punishing act increases, the conformity increases; and expertness on one task increases the ability to exert influence on a second task.[44] Schopler does point out that the interdependence of the bases of power may contaminate the findings.

Of more direct relevance to organizational behavior are the studies that have related the bases of a manager's power or control to satisfaction and performance. On the basis of five organizational studies (branch office, college, insurance agency, production work units, and utility company work group) the following conclusions were drawn on each of the French and Raven bases of power:[45]

[44]John Schopler, "Social Power," in *Advances in Experimental Social Psychology,* vol. 2, Leonard Berkowitz (ed.), Academic Press, New York, 1965, pp. 177–218.
[45]Jerald G. Bachman, David G. Bowers, and Philip M. Marcus, "Bases of Supervisory Power: A Comparative Study in Five Organizational Settings," in *Control in Organizations,* Arnold S. Tannenbaum (ed.), McGraw-Hill Book Company, New York, 1968, p. 236.

1 *Expert power* was most strongly and consistently correlated with satisfaction and performance.

2 *Legitimate power* along with expert power was rated as the most important basis of complying with a supervisor's wishes but was an inconsistent factor in organizational effectiveness.

3 *Referent power* was given intermediate importance as a reason for complying and in most cases was positively correlated with organizational effectiveness.

4 *Reward power* was also given intermediate importance for complying but had inconsistent correlations with performance.

5 *Coercive power* was by far the least prominent reason for complying and was actually negatively related to organizational effectiveness.

The conclusion from research so far is that the nonformal bases of power (expert and referent) impact most favorably on organizational effectiveness. However, such a conclusion should be interpreted with caution because, like the Likert studies, the studies on power are almost all based on questionnaire responses and may reflect the cultural values of the respondents instead of the actual uses of power in an organization. The most recent study by Patchen, which generally substantiates the findings reported above, warns that, "It is possible that some respondents were reluctant to talk about such modes of influence [as rewards and coercion]."[46] The challenge for the future will be to use other measures in the research of power.

The Use of Power in an Organization

The French and Raven bases of power point out that some types of power may have a positive impact on organizational effectiveness and others may not. In general, the research on power follows the findings in leadership styles reported earlier in the chapter. The important implication is that leadership and power approaches and uses can be good or bad for the organization.

In society as a whole, "power" generally has a negative connotation. The commonly used term *power hungry* reflects this negative feeling about power. McClelland cites the characteristics of the evils of power as follows:

> . . . is associated with heavy drinking, gambling, having more aggressive impulses, and collecting "prestige supplies" like a convertible or a Playboy Club Key. People with this personalized power concern are more apt to speed, have accidents, and get into physical fights. If . . . possessed by political officeholders, especially in the sphere of international relations, the consequences would be ominous.[47]

McClelland feels that this negative use of power is associated with personal power. He feels that it is primitive and has negative consequences.

The contrasting other face of power is social power. It is characterized by

[46]Martin Patchen, "The Locus and Basis of Influence on Organizational Decisions," *Organizational Behavior and Human Performance,* April 1974, p. 216.
[47]McClelland, op. cit., p. 36.

a "concern for group goals, for finding those goals that will move men, for helping the group to formulate them, for taking some initiative in providing members of the group with the means of achieving such goals, and for giving group members the feeling of strength and competence they need to work hard for such goals."[48] This social power points out that the leader is often in a precarious position of walking the fine line between exhibiting personal dominance and the more socializing use of power.

Power is inevitable in organizations. One of Adolf Berle's several "laws" of power is that power invariably fills any vacuum in human organization.[49] How power is used and what type of power is used will vitally affect organizational goals. In French and Raven's terms, the use of expert and referent power in organizations may be more effective than traditionally used legitimate and coercive power. In McClelland's terms, social power may be of greater value to the organization than is traditionally used personal power. Research gives some indication that such conclusions are valid. But once again, the use of the various types of power depends on the situation. Contingency models of power are needed. A challenge for the future will be to better understand power and how it is contingently related to varying situations.

SUMMARY

This chapter presented and analyzed various theoretical and practical aspects of leadership and power. The classic research studies on leadership set the stage for the theoretical development of leadership. The trait theories concentrate on the leaders themselves but, with the possible exception of intelligence, really do not come up with any agreed-upon traits of leaders. The group theories emphasize the importance of the followers, but these are also only partial theories. The most recent breakthroughs for leadership theory are situationally based. In particular, Fiedler's contingency model makes a significant contribution to leadership theory and potentially to the practice of human resource management. The path-goal approach is the latest contribution to leadership theory. It incorporates expectancy motivation concepts. Both the Fiedler and path-goal approaches recognize the leader, the group, and the situation. All three of these variables need to be incorporated into an understanding of the leadership process. They can be related in an influence systems model.

There are many style implications in the classic leadership studies and modern theories. More directly, however, is the attention given to leadership styles in Blake and Mouton's managerial grid, Reddin's 3-D model, and Likert's four systems. Each of these is of value in relation to the actual practice of human resource management. The grid and 3-D models are mainly valuable to let managers describe their styles, and Likert's work has implications for organizational effectiveness. Likert's recognition of intervening variables and their time-lag effects has significant implications for practice. Finally, the

[48]Ibid., p. 41.

[49]Adolf A. Berle, *Power*, Harcourt, Brace & World, Inc., New York, 1969, p. 37.

Vroom and Yetton model can actually prescribe exactly what style to use in a given situation. All of these approaches to style need more and better research in order to make meaningful contributions to the actual practice of human resource management in the future.

The last part of the chapter discussed power. Closely related to leadership, there are five widely recognized types of power that are identified by French and Raven: reward, coercive, legitimate, referent, and expert. Research to date points out that nonformal power (expert and referent or social) may be more effective than the more traditional (coercive and legitimate or personal) sources of power in an organization. However, as in the case of leadership, more and better research is needed to truly understand and effectively use power in a modern, complex organization.

QUESTIONS FOR DISCUSSION AND REVIEW

1 Briefly summarize the findings of the three classical leadership studies.
2 How do the group theories differ from the trait theories of leadership?
3 What are the three critical situational variables identified by Fiedler? If these are very favorable, what is the most effective style to use?
4 In simple terms, what is the path-goal theory of leadership? What is the leader's function in this conceptualization?
5 Briefly identify the major styles from Blake and Mouton's grid, from Reddin's 3-D model, and from Likert's four systems. Which are more effective or less effective?
6 Briefly summarize the French and Raven sources of power. Which one(s) does research say is (are) more effective than the others?

CASE: IF IT IS GOOD ENOUGH FOR US, IT IS GOOD ENOUGH FOR THEM

Jesse White was a training specialist for the personnel department of a large company. His boss, Rose O'Brien, called him in one day and said that she had just come back from an executive committee meeting. She had been given charge of developing a leadership training program for all middle-management personnel in the firm. She told Jesse that he would be in charge of the project. Jesse wanted to know what the objectives of the program were supposed to be. Rose replied that the top management of the company were concerned that the styles that they were using now and in the past were not being used by the middle managers. For example, the executive vice president was concerned that the younger lower/middle managers were too idealistic about how to treat people. The others had all agreed with this observation. Then the vice president for finance added that it was their styles that had taken this company to the top of the industry, and if it was good enough for them it should be good enough for the middle managers. Rose then said, "I have to follow orders, so what I would like you to do is first get a good understanding of the modern theoretical basis for leadership. Then find out what styles of leadership the president and the vice presidents are using in their present jobs. Based upon the theory and what you find out about their present styles, design a program that I can present to the executive committee for middle-management leadership training."

1 Do you agree with the approach outlined by Rose to set up the training program? If you were Jesse, what would be some important theoretical considerations that would go into your program? What techniques would you use to determine the top managers' present styles?

2 Based on the comments of the executive vice president and the vice president for finance, what styles do you feel you would find for the top managers? For the middle managers? How would you be able to justify a program that was different from the styles of the top managers?

3 What types of power do the people in this incident exhibit? What power implications are there for Rose? For Jesse?

SELECTED REFERENCES

Ashour, Ahmed Sakr: "The Contingency Model of Leadership Effectiveness: An Evaluation," *Organizational Behavior and Human Performance,* June 1973, pp. 339–355.

Berle, Adolf A.: *Power,* Harcourt, Brace & World, Inc., New York, 1969.

Chapman, J. Brad, and Fred Luthans: "The Female Leadership Dilemma," *Public Personnel Management,* May–June 1975, pp. 173–179.

Clarly, Thomas C., and Robert A. Luke, Jr.: "Organizational and Individual Power," *Training and Development Journal,* April 1975, pp. 41–51.

Fiedler, Fred E.: *A Theory of Leadership Effectiveness,* McGraw-Hill Book Company, New York, 1967.

Fiedler, Fred E.: "How Do You Make Leaders More Effective? New Answers to an Old Puzzle," *Organizational Dynamics,* Autumn 1972, pp. 3–18.

Fiedler, Fred E., and Martin M. Chemers: *Leadership and Effective Management,* Scott, Foresman and Company, Glenview, Ill., 1974.

Francis, Elton L.: "How Are You Using Your Power?" *Supervisory Management,* September 1975, pp. 3–8.

Franklin, Jack L.: "Power and Commitment: An Empirical Assessment," *Human Relations,* October 1975, pp. 737–753.

French, John R. P., Jr., and Bertram Raven: "The Bases of Social Power," in D. Cartwright (ed.), *Studies in Social Power,* Institute for Social Research, Ann Arbor, Mich., 1959.

Halal, William E.: "Toward a General Theory of Leadership," *Human Relations,* April 1974, pp. 401–416.

Helmich, Donald L., and Paul E. Erzen: "Leadership Style and Leader Needs," *Academy of Management Journal,* June 1975, pp. 397–402.

Hicks, Herbert G., and C. Ray Gullett: *Organizations: Theory and Behavior,* McGraw-Hill Book Company, 1975.

Hill, Walter A.: "Leadership Style: Rigid or Flexible?" *Organizational Behavior and Human Performance,* February 1973, pp. 35–47.

House, Robert J., and Terence R. Mitchell: "Path-Goal Theory of Leadership," *Journal of Contemporary Business,* Autumn 1974, pp. 81–97.

Justis, Robert R.: "Leadership Effectiveness: A Contingency Approach," *Academy of Management Journal,* March 1975, pp. 160–167.

Larson, Lars L., and Kendrith M. Rowland: "Leadership Style and Cognitive Complexity," *Academy of Management Journal,* March 1974, pp. 37–45.

Likert, Rensis: *The Human Organization: Its Management and Value,* McGraw-Hill Book Company, New York, 1967.

McClelland, David C.: "The Two Faces of Power," *Journal of International Affairs,* vol. 24, no. 1, 1970, pp. 29–47.

Nebeker, Delbert M., and Terence R. Mitchell: "Leader Behavior: An Expectancy Theory Approach," *Organizational Behavior and Human Performance,* February 1974, pp. 355–367.

Oates, David: "Managers and the Need for Power," *Management Review,* December 1975, pp. 35–38.

Stinson, John E., and Thomas W. Johnson: "The Path-Goal Theory of Leadership: A Partial Test and Suggested Refinement," *Academy of Management Journal,* June 1975, pp. 242–252.

Stogdill, Ralph M.: "The Evolution of Leadership Theory," *Academy of Management Proceedings,* 1975, pp. 4–6.

Tannenbaum, Robert, and Warren H. Schmidt: "How to Choose a Leadership Pattern," *Harvard Business Review,* May–June 1973, pp. 162–180.

Vroom, Victor H., and Philip W. Yetton: *Leadership and Decision-Making,* University of Pittsburgh Press, Pittsburgh, Pa., 1973.

Part Five

Applications for Human Resource Management

Chapter 19

Selection, Job Design, and Appraisal

This chapter is concerned with three of the most important areas of application in human resource management. The first third of the chapter is devoted to selection. Tests and interviews have traditionally been the major selection tools. However, because of legal interpretations on the use of tests, new selection techniques such as assessment centers are being developed and used. All three selection techniques (tests, interviews, and assessment centers) are presented and analyzed. The middle third of the chapter gives attention to the design of work. The controversy surrounding Frederick Herzberg's two-factor theory of motivation has carried over into job design. The pros, cons, and actual experience of using job enrichment is given major attention, and a proposed predictive contingency model is presented. The final third of the chapter covers appraisal. In recent years there have been some major changes in the purposes and techniques of performance appraisal. Management by objectives (MBO), which utilizes appraisal by results, is given primary attention and a relatively new technique called "behaviorally anchored rating scales" (BARS) is introduced and discussed.

SELECTION

Up to a few years ago, most organizations depended heavily upon tests and interviews to select personnel for either entry-level jobs or, internally, to select someone for transfer or promotion. Now many organizations have turned completely away from tests, and a growing number are foregoing interviews as well. What is the reason for this drastic turn of events? One answer lies in the changing social and legal climate. After examining the legal climate for testing, the nature and use of tests, interviews, and assessment centers will be presented and analyzed.

The Legal Climate for Testing

The Passage of the Civil Rights Act in 1964 did not spell the doom of testing. In fact, immediately after the passage of the act, testing experienced a boom period. According to Title VII of the act, employers could not discriminate on the basis of race, creed, sex, or national origin, but they could exclude anyone on the basis of how they scored on "an objective test that doesn't discriminate." Of course, all organizations that used tests in the selection process claimed that their tests met this criterion. Then in 1971 the U. S. Supreme Court ruled in the *Griggs v. Duke Power Company* case that in order to use a test as the basis of selection, the test had to be proved valid. In other words, the test had to measure what it was supposed to measure; it had to be able to predict successful job performance. In this case, Duke Power hired blacks as long as they could pass the selection tests. But when challenged in court, the company could not prove that the tests related to job performance (shoveling coal). The Court in an eight-to-zero vote decided that the test was discriminatory. The reaction across the country was dramatic. Instead of validating their tests, which they should have been doing all along if in fact the test was going to be an effective selection tool, a great number of organizations simply dropped testing.

The reasoning in dropping testing from the selection process seemed to be: "If we drop testing, this will prove we don't discriminate." The industrial psychologists, many of whose jobs were at stake, countered that it was not tests that discriminated but rather the people who used the test results. The latter reasoning has also come under attack in the academic community in relation to intelligence testing and racial differences (this was discussed in Chapter 14). In addition, there is vigorous enforcement of antidiscrimination policies and practices. The Equal Employment Opportunity Commission (EEOC), which is charged with enforcing the Civil Rights Act, went from a budget of $2.25 million and a handful of staff after passage of the act in 1964 to a $43 million budget and a staff of about 2,000. Many organizations have simply chosen to drop testing instead of taking on the powerful EEOC.

Today there is little question that testing is not used as much as it was several years ago as a selection device. Nevertheless, understanding the concept and types of tests is still useful to the study of organizational behavior. Testing has played a very important role in the past and, if validated, there is no reason why it cannot be a useful selection technique. The same goes for interviews. Every organization still uses interviews in one form or another, but they may go the same way as tests unless they have proven validity. In part, the assessment center approach has become important in the last few years because so far it has been judged to be compatible with EEOC requirements.

Testing: Types and Concepts

A *test* can be simply defined as a systematic procedure for comparing the behavior of two or more persons. With the qualifications discussed above (i.e., they are proved valid), tests can be used for selection but can also be used for evaluation, placement, promotion, transfer, and research. Besides the many uses of tests, there are also many ways to classify tests.

One way to differentiate tests is as individual versus group. Individual tests consist of one examiner and one person taking the test and have two major advantages. First, misinterpretations of directions and test items are held to a minimum, and second, the examiner's observation can supplement the information given and contribute additional information for the final evaluation. The Wechsler Adult Intelligence Scale (WAIS) is a good example of an individual test. In group tests, one examiner or psychometrist administers a test to two or more persons. The group tests have traditionally been used more frequently because they are more economical and less time-consuming.

Another way to classify tests is by speed versus power. A *speed test* has items of equal difficulty that are to be answered in a specified period of time. The object is to answer as many questions as possible in the allotted time. A *power test* has items of increasing difficulty and time is not a factor. Its purpose is to measure certain kinds of capability.

Perhaps the most familiar differentiation is seen in tests for aptitude versus achievement. An *aptitude test* is designed to measure potential ability, and it attempts to predict success. Experience or past achievement is not supposed to influence the outcome of the test. An *achievement test* also measures ability, but actual ability—not potential ability, as in the aptitude test. Achievement tests measure past learning and experience. In reality, of course, there is a fine line between aptitude and achievement tests. Often the only real difference between the two is how the test is interpreted and used. If the test is used to measure potential, it is an aptitude test. However, if the same test is used to judge how much has been learned, it may be considered an achievement test.

Intelligence Tests   A major factor in measuring individual differences is intelligence. An oddity is that intelligence-test results provide the only operational definition of intellectual capacity. In other words, about the only operational definition is that intelligence is what an intelligence test measures. This brings to mind a dog chasing its tail but does point out the complexity of operationally defining and measuring this elusive individual capacity.

The general intelligence test is normally scored according to the well-known intelligence quotient or IQ. Intelligence tests, such as the Stanford-Binet Intelligence Scale, determine the mental age of the person taking the test. The IQ is obtained by dividing the mental age (M. A.) by the person's actual or chronological age (C. A.) and multiplying the result by 100 (M. A./C. A. × 100).

An IQ of 100 is considered average. Widely used tests of mental abilities besides the Stanford-Binet are the Wechsler Adult Intelligence Scale, Otis Self-Administering Test of Mental Ability, Wonderlic Personnel Test, Miller Analogies Test, and the Concept Mastery Test.

Personality Tests The complexity associated with intelligence testing is compounded by trying to measure personality. Most of the problem can be traced to the difficulty of defining personality. As Chapter 14 pointed out, there is little agreement on a practical or analytical definition and almost no agreement on an operational definition. This glaring problem, of course, has contributed to the controversy surrounding testing and to its declining use as a selection tool.

There are two major ways of measuring and describing personality—the self-report personality inventories and the projective techniques. The self-report approach relies on paper-and-pencil tests that can usually be answered by "true" or "false." They are based on the assumption that the personality consists of a group of traits. The purpose of the tests is to measure traits such as masculinity-femininity, introversion-extroversion, dominance-submissiveness, and independence-dependence. The results are usually shown on an overall personality profile. The biggest problem with self-report personality tests is that they are designed and interpreted on the basis of a priori rather than empirical data and can be easily faked. An important exception is the highly regarded Minnesota Multiphasic Personality Inventory (MMPI), which has empirically validated dimensions and scales which identify those who are faking.

The other approach to testing personality is by projective means. In contrast to the self-report, projective tests attempt to assess the whole personality rather than a set of traits. The best-known projective tests are the word-association and Rorschach inkblot tests and the Thematic Apperception Test (TAT). Word-association tests are one of the oldest tests used in the behavioral sciences. Even Wilhelm Wundt, the founder of modern psychology, utilized the technique in his study of thought processes. Word associations are still widely used in assessing personality for clinical purposes.

The Rorschach and the TAT present a series of stimuli to the test taker. In the Rorschach, the stimuli consist of unstructured inkblots, whereas in the TAT a series of realistic pictures is presented. Subjects respond to the stimulus by telling a story about what they see. By doing this the test-takers project their personalities. Using some predetermined guides, a qualified psychologist or psychometrist will then interpret these projections and make conclusions about the individual's personality.

Interest Tests A third major category of tests traditionally used for selection are interest tests. Besides selection, however, these tests can be used in vocational counseling and are also adaptable to problems relating to job satisfaction. The two most commonly used interest tests are the Strong

Vocational Interest Blank (VIB) and the Kuder Preference Record. These two tests were originally designed to measure professional and semiprofessional occupational interests. The newer Minnesota Vocational Interest Inventory tests the interests for lower-level jobs in an organization.

Since interests are closely linked with personality, interest tests are plagued with some of the same problems as personality tests. For instance, responses can be easily faked. Furthermore, before maturity, most people's interests are not stabilized, and therefore results are often meaningless. Although the Strong VIB attempts to determine how successful people in various occupations answer the questions, most interest tests start off with preconceived notions of how a member of a given occupation *should* respond to the questions. In other words, except for a few tests like the Strong, interest tests are not empirically validated.

Test Validity   Validity has been mentioned throughout the discussion of testing. It is *the* key concept to the value of testing as a selection tool or for any of its other uses. Ignoring validity is the major reason testing is in the precarious situation it is today as a selection technique. It is not only the social and legal climate or the EEOC that has "done testing in." Rather, the real root of the problem is the long-standing refusal of organizations to validate their selection process. Miles suggests there are two reasons for this state of affairs: ignorance and no incentive to do so. "The costs of poor selection processes are, in the main, either hidden or borne by persons outside the organization, whereas the costs of carrying out the careful analysis and evaluation which experts argue should underlie a good selection program appear high and the returns uncertain."[1] Now with legislation and EEOC enforcement, tests that are used *must* be validated. Regardless of the legislative implications, the simple fact is that if a test is not valid, it is useless, can be dangerous and misleading, and *should not* be used.

Exactly what is this important concept? *Validity* simply means: Does the test measure what it is supposed to measure? There are many connotations attached to the term. *Face validity,* which most tests depend upon, is a pseudo type of validity and refers only to the surface appearance of the test. In someone's subjective judgment, the test *should* measure what it is supposed to measure. This is normative, as opposed to empirical, judgment. Under face validity, the results are not correlated with an outside criterion to determine if the test really does accomplish its intended purpose.

In *empirical validity* lies the crux of the testing concept. Most tests are used to predict. In order to make confident predictions, there must be a high degree of relationship (correlation) between the test results and an outside criterion that is relevant to what is being tested. For example, intelligence tests have a fairly good predictive ability for performance in school. The correlation between Stanford-Binet IQ scores and school grades is about +.60. However,

---

[1]Raymond E. Miles, *Theories of Management,* McGraw-Hill Book Company, New York, 1975, p. 169.

such validity coefficients must be carefully interpreted. Given the operational definition of intelligence, it may be that performance in school is a self-validating criterion. Generally speaking, tests are not, but should be, empirically validated. With the exception of the MMPI, personality tests are notoriously nonvalid. Only those psychometric devices that have been empirically validated make a valuable contribution to the selection process, and now only such are allowed by the force of law. It is the classic case where if those using tests for selection were doing what they were supposed to be doing all along, there would be no need for the legislation and resulting problems that have ensued.

Test Reliability   The other major concept of testing, but not nearly as important as validity, is reliability. In order for a test to be valid it must also be reliable. *Test reliability* refers to the *accuracy* of measurement and the *consistency* of results. Test reliability is not nearly as difficult to achieve as is validity. Normally, all that is required for a high degree of reliability is control over the testing conditions. As long as directions are clear, the environment is comfortable, the test is long enough, and ample time is given, there is no problem with test reliability. About the only aspect of test reliability that is difficult to control is the attitude and motivation of the person taking the test. If test-takers do not try to do their best, the test will not be reliable.

Even though tests are usually very reliable, it does not automatically follow that they will be valid. The test may be accurately and consistently measuring the wrong variables. The major challenge facing the use of tests in the future is not with reliability but with validity. It will be necessary to improve upon and empirically validate the tests that are, or will be, used for selection. If this is done, perhaps testing can make a comeback as an important selection tool.

Interviews

Interviews are often called the most used but least useful selection technique. Interviews can also be used for counseling employees and for gathering data for research. Simply defined, an *interview* is a conversation with a purpose. Analysis of the word itself implies a process of interaction. The interaction that takes place between the interviewer and the interviewee is a very complex phenomenon. In fact, it is so complex and imprecise that interviewing can best be considered an art rather than a science.

There is overwhelming evidence to suggest that interviews are even less valid than tests.[2] There are many reasons for this. A summary of the existing studies on interviewing finds the following problems:

[2]Eugene C. Mayfield, "The Selection Interview: A Re-evaluation of Published Research," *Personnel Psychology,* Autumn 1964, pp. 239–260; Donald P. Schwab, "Why Interview? A Critique," *Personnel Journal,* February 1969, pp. 126–129; and Enzo Valenzi and I. R. Andrews, "Individual Differences in the Decision Process of Employment Interviewers," *Journal of Applied Psychology,* August 1973, pp. 49–53.

1   In an unstructured interview, material is not consistently covered.

2   When interviewers obtain the same information, they are likely to weigh it differently. What is positive information to one interviewer may turn out to be negative to another.

3   Interviewers have great difficulty in reliably and validly assessing traits other than intelligence or mental ability.

4   Interviewers in unstructured interviews tend to make their decisions early in an interview, that is, before all the information is in.

5   Interviewers give more weight to negative information than to positive information.[3]

To make the interview more effective as a selection technique it should always be used in conjunction with other selection tools. A selection decision should never be made on the basis of an interview alone. In addition, there are certain techniques and procedures that can be used to improve the art of interviewing. Although interviews can be directive or nondirective and structured or unstructured, the interview should always be planned in advance. In the directive/structured interview a detailed guide should be prepared and the items asked should be empirically validated in the same way that test items are validated. For the nondirective/unstructured interview the overall atmosphere is important to its success. "The ideal usually sought is a permissive situation in which the respondent is encouraged to voice his frank opinions without fearing that his attitudes will be revealed to others and without the expression of any surprise or value judgment by the interviewer."[4] In the conduct of the interview, the interviewer must consciously play the role of a reporter, not an antagonist, a debater, or an evangelist. Another trick of the trade is to use a pause to slow down and pace the interview. The closing of the interview is also critical. When finishing the interview, an open-end question is useful to "clear the air" between interviewer and interviewee. It is important to the long-range objective of the organization that a good rapport exist when the interview is terminated. Desirably, the use of interviews as a selection tool can avoid the mistakes made by testing. At present, interviews are still widely used; but if selection decisions are going to be based on them, they are going to have to have proven validity. Justifiably, most employers would be reluctant to hire people without interviewing them. But unless the interview can be shown to have validity, this may be the case in the future.

Assessment Centers

In response to the problems with using tests for selection and the movement to expand the scope of selection by tying it into development, many organizations

---

[3]Lyman W. Porter, Edward E. Lawler, and J. Richard Hackman, *Behavior in Organizations,* McGraw-Hill Book Company, New York, 1975, p. 145.

[4]Claire Selltiz et al., *Research Methods in Social Relations,* rev. ed., Holt, Rinehart and Winston, Inc., New York, 1959, p. 575.

are beginning to use assessment centers. All the big companies, such as AT&T, IBM, Standard Oil, Sears, J. C. Penney, G. E., and Kodak, are already using assessment centers for selection and for identifying training and development needs, and hundreds of other organizations in both the public and private sectors are beginning to use them. William Byham, who, along with Douglas Bray of AT&T, is the most widely recognized expert on assessment centers, explains, "An assessment center is a formal procedure incorporating group and individual exercises for the identification of dimensions of managerial or sales success identified as important for a particular position or level of management."[5] In general, it can be said that the assessment center is limited in scope (to managerial and sales personnel, but it could also be used to select workers to be supervisors), and, depending on the objectives, the centers can greatly differ in terms of length, cost, content, staffing, and administration.

Figure 19-1 outlines the content and conduct of a typical two-day assessment center. At the end of the two days the assessors meet to thoroughly discuss their observations and the results of the exercises for each participant. A summary evaluation would then be used to select the individual for the entry-level position or for the internal promotion. Training and development needs are also a by-product of the center described in Figure 19-1.

There is little question that the assessment center is a much more comprehensive approach to selection than are tests and interviews. By use of the simulated exercises, the approach is also much more directly related to job performance than is a question on a personality test asking whether the job applicant likes to sleep with a light on or not. The big companies have given a great deal of effort and financial support for relating actual job dimensions to the exercises used in their assessment centers. Byham reports that almost three-fourths of the published research studies validate the assessment center technique for predicting success and those that don't use such small samples that the results can be discounted.[6]

Despite the relatively glowing reports on assessment centers from Byham and a few others, conclusions must be tempered somewhat by the fact that there are still many unanswered questions. Kelly focuses on some of these questions as follows:

1 Should the exercises relate to general problems or problems particular to the company?

2 What attributes of management should be assessed—oral communication skill, planning, decision making, personal acceptability?

3 Who are the major beneficiaries? The candidates, who get an insight into the nature of the job that lies ahead? The assessors, who get to know the "ins and

---

[5]William C. Byham, "The Assessment Center as an Aid in Management Development," *Training and Development Journal,* December 1971. Reprinted in Kenneth N. Wexley and Gary A. Yukl (eds.), *Organizational Behavior and Industrial Psychology,* Oxford University Press, New York, 1975, pp. 497–498.

[6]Ibid., p. 503.

Figure 19-1   A Typical Two-Day Assessment Center

Day 1   Orientation meeting

Management game—"Conglomerate." Forming different types of conglomerates is the goal with four-man teams of participants bartering companies to achieve their planned result. Teams set their own acquisition objectives and must plan and organize to meet them.

Background interview—A 1¹/₂ hour interview conducted by an assessor.

Group discussion—"Management Problems." Four short cases calling for various forms of management judgment are presented to groups of four participants. In one hour the group, acting as consultants, must resolve the cases and submit its recommendation in writing.

Individual fact-finding and decision-making exercise—"The Research Budget." The participant is told that he has just taken over as division manager. He is given a brief description of an incident in which his predecessor has recently turned down a request for funds to continue a research project. The research director is appealing for a reversal of the decision. The participant is given 15 minutes to ask questions to dig out the facts in the case. Following this fact-finding period, he must present his decision orally with supporting reasoning and defend it under challenge.

Day 2

In-basket exercise—"Section Manager's In-Basket." The contents of a section manager's in-basket are simulated. The participant is instructed to go through the contents, solving problems, answering questions, delegating, organizing, scheduling and planning, just as he might do if he were promoted suddenly to the position. An assessor reviews the contents of the completed in-basket and conducts a one-hour interview with the participant to gain further information.

Assigned role leaderless group discussion—"Compensation Committee." The Compensation Committee is meeting to allocate $8,000 in discretionary salary increases among six supervisory and managerial employees. Each member of the committee (participants) represents a department of the company and is instructed to "do the best he can" for the employee from his department.

Analysis, presentation, and group discussion—"The Pretzel Factory." This financial analysis problem has the participant role-play a consultant called in to advise Carl Flowers of the C. F. Pretzel Company on two problems: what to do about a division of the company that has continually lost money, and whether the corporation should expand. Participants are given data on the company and are asked to recommend appropriate courses of action. They make their recommendation in a seven-minute presentation after which they are formed into a group to come up with a single set of recommendations.

Source: William C. Byham, "The Assessment Center as an Aid in Management Development," *Training and Development Journal*, December 1971.

outs" of their subordinates' roles? The personnel people, who get experience with a new training and selection technique?

4   Is the assessment center the answer to the U. S. Supreme Court decision [*Griggs v. Duke Power*] which stated that job requirements and testing must have a demonstrable relationship to job performance?

5   Can the assessment centers be kept honest? The reports are not meant to be "go or no-go" documents which decide the fate of the candidate forever in his company. But the reports are carefully filed.[7]

[7]Joe Kelly, *Organizational Behaviour,* rev. ed., Richard D. Irwin, Inc., Homewood, Ill., 1974, pp. 409–410.

In other words, the assessment center is not the panacea for all selection problems, at least not yet. On the other hand, because of its comprehensive nature and because there are continued efforts to validate the procedure, it would seem to hold a great deal of potential for the future.

JOB DESIGN

Concern for the design of work goes as far back as the scientific management movement at the turn of the century. Frederick Taylor and his colleagues advocated the scientific design of jobs by use of techniques such as time and motion analysis. Through the years jobs have become more and more specialized. Automation in the 1950s and 1960s and cybernation in more recent times have contributed to the specialization of work. The often cited example of the person on the assembly line putting a nut on a bolt as the product moves by on the conveyor belt is all too common in today's manufacturing plants across the country. One young worker recently described his job in the ultramodern Lordstown, Ohio, assembly plant of General Motors as follows: "There's a lot of variety in the paint shop. You clip on the color hose, bleed out the old color, and squirt. Clip, bleed, squirt, think; clip, bleed, squirt, yawn; clip, bleed, squirt, scratch your nose."[8] The same types of specialized jobs are present in banks, offices, hospitals, schools, and every other type of modern organizational setting.

Starting in the 1950s some practicing managers around the country, such as the founder of IBM, Thomas Watson, became concerned about the specialization of work and began implementing job enlargement programs. Essentially these programs horizontally loaded the job (expanded the number of operations performed by the worker, i.e., made the job less specialized). Then in the 1960s and early 1970s, with the increasing concern for deteriorating employee productivity—which was felt to be largely the result of so-called "blue-collar blues" and "white-collar woes"—job design became the focus of attention for both academicians and practitioners of human resource management. Newspaper stories and TV news specials commonly had titles such as the following:

"Is the American Worker Alienated?"
"Today's Worker: Idealism's Gone"
"Is the Work Ethic Going Out of Style?"
"Boredom Spells Trouble"

A special HEW task force on *Work in America* reported that ". . . the productivity of the worker is low—as measured by absenteeism, turnover rates, wildcat strikes, sabotage, poor quality products, and a reluctance by workers to commit themselves to their work."[9] In addition, Gallup polls

[8]Barbara Garson, "Luddites in Lordstown," *Harper's*, June 1972, p. 69.
[9]*Work in America*, Report of a Special Task Force to the Secretary of Health, Education. and Welfare, The MIT Press, Cambridge, Mass., 1973, p. xvi.

regularly reported that a majority of people responded that "they could produce more each day if they tried." Job design seemed to provide a ready answer to the productivity problems and deteriorating human resources of organizations.

The reported successes of the early job enlargement programs,[10] plus the increasingly popular motivation theories of Maslow and Herzberg (discussed in Chapter 17), led to the job enrichment movement in job design.

Job Enrichment

Job enrichment represents an extension of the earlier, more simplified job rotation and job enlargement techniques of job design. Since it is a direct outgrowth of Herzberg's two-factor theory of motivation, the assumption is that in order to motivate personnel, the job must be designed to provide opportunities for achievement, recognition, responsibility, advancement, and growth. The technique entails "enriching" the job so that these factors are included. In particular, *job enrichment* is concerned with designing jobs that include a greater variety of work content; require a higher level of knowledge and skill; give the worker more autonomy and responsibility for planning, directing, and controlling his or her own performance; and provide the opportunity for personal growth and meaningful work experience. As opposed to job enlargement, which horizontally loads the job, job enrichment *vertically* loads the job (e.g., not necessarily more tasks to perform, but more responsibility and autonomy). Figure 19-2 gives some specific examples of job enrichment.

Although Herzberg provided the necessary impetus for the development of job enrichment, M. Scott Meyers, formerly of Texas Instruments, and Robert N. Ford of American Telephone and Telegraph assumed the role of proselytizers and implementers of the technique. The management at Texas Instruments (TI) undertook an extensive research study in an attempt to validate Herzberg's two-factor theory.[11] Satisfied with the outcome of this study, TI proceeded to enrich some of the jobs in the company. To implement the TI program, supervisors were trained to analyze subordinates' functions in terms of the potential for appealing to the hygiene or motivator factors. In addition, a formalized attitude measurement program structured around the motivation-hygiene factors was instituted for control purposes. At Texas Instruments, job enrichment became part of the management philosophy as well as a technique of job design.

The other leading advocate of job enrichment, Robert Ford, has been chiefly responsible for implementing the technique in the Bell System.[12] Taking

---

[10]Charles R. Walker, "The Problem of the Repetitive Job," *Harvard Business Review,* May 1950, pp. 54–58, reports on the IBM experience, and Maurice D. Kilbridge, "Reduced Costs Through Job Enlargement: A Case," *The Journal of Business,* October 1960, pp. 357–362, reports on the Maytag experience with job enlargement.

[11]M. Scott Meyers, "Who Are Your Motivated Workers?" *Harvard Business Review,* January–February 1964, pp. 73–88.

[12]Robert N. Ford, *Motivation through the Work Itself,* American Management Association, New York, 1969.

Figure 19-2 Examples of Job Enrichment

Old situation	Situation after job enrichment
Each employee rotated among all machines.	Each employee assigned to only two machines.
When machine failure occurred, operator called on maintenance group.	Each operator given training in maintenance; each conducts preventive and corrective maintenance on the two machines for which he is responsible.
Operator changes the slicing blade (the most important component of the machine) following a rigid rule contained in a manual.	Operator given authority to decide when to replace blade, based on his judgment.
Supervisor monitors operator and corrects unsatisfactory performance.	Performance feedback system developed that provides daily information on their work quality directly to operators.
Individual performs specialized task on units passing by him.	Three- to five-man teams build entire unit.
Supervisor decides who should do what.	Team decides who should do what.
Inspectors and supervisor test output and correct performance.	Team conducts own quality audits.

Source: Ross A. Webber, *Management*, Richard D. Irwin, Inc., Homewood, Ill., 1975, pp. 124–125. These examples were provided to Webber by David R. Sirota, Wharton School, University of Pennsylvania.

a similar validation approach to that of Texas Instruments, Ford, on the basis of research results, is convinced of the value of job enrichment. An often cited example of what can be accomplished with job enrichment is the Shareholder Relations Department of AT&T. After job enrichment was installed in this department of 120 correspondents, there was a 27 percent reduction in the termination rate and an estimated cost savings of $558,000 over a twelve-month period.[13] Encouraged by this kind of result, Ford implemented job enrichment in many areas of the huge Bell System.

Criticism of Job Enrichment

Although behavioral scientists have been critical of the Herzberg theory practically since it was first formulated in the late 1950s, it is only in recent years that management writers in the literature aimed at practitioners have raised questions about the value of job enrichment.[14] Up to this time, both management professors and practitioners had generally accepted Herzberg's theme that "job enrichment pays off."[15] However, as the criticism of the

[13]Robert Janson, "Job Enrichment: Challenge of the 70's," *Training and Development Journal*, June 1970, p. 7.

[14]For example see Thomas H. Fitzgerald, "Why Motivation Theory Doesn't Work," *Harvard Business Review*, July–August 1971, pp. 37–44; and more recently, William E. Reif and Fred Luthans, "Does Job Enrichment Really Pay Off?" *California Management Review*, Fall 1972, pp. 30–37.

[15]William J. Paul, Jr., Keith B. Robertson, and Frederick Herzberg, "Job Enrichment Pays Off," *Harvard Business Review*, March–April 1969, pp. 61–78.

two-factor theory began to grow and become more widely known, management professors and writers also started to question the effectiveness of job enrichment as a universally applicable technique of job design.

In general, the same criticisms leveled at the two-factor theory apply to job enrichment. However, of more direct consequence for management is that job enrichment may not be working out in actual practice as it was commonly thought to do. Even the "success stories" of job enrichment at Texas Instruments and Bell Telephone can be questioned. For example, a report to TI stockholders announced that the company aimed to have 10,000 employees involved in team-improvement efforts. On the surface, this looked very impressive, but as Mitchell Fein notes, the 10,000 figure represents only 16 percent of the total employment at Texas Instruments. Yet it is often falsely assumed that all TI personnel are on enriched jobs.[16] Not only is job enrichment not used throughout TI, but a recent survey of randomly selected large firms found only 5 of 125 respondents reported using any formal job enrichment.[17] In other words, the fad of job enrichment seems to be talked about more than it is actually being used. Not only the extent of use but also the reported successes of job enrichment can be questioned. Reporting on the overall success of the AT&T job enrichment program, Ford himself stated, "Of the nineteen studies nine were rated 'outstandingly successful,' one was a complete 'flop,' and the remaining nine were 'moderately successful.' "[18] Obviously, when assessing the job enrichment impact at AT&T the operational definition of "success" becomes critical. It is also interesting to note a seldom cited comment by Ford. He stated:

> No claim is made that these 19 trials cover a representative sample of jobs and people within the Bell System. For example, there were no trials among the manufacturing or laboratory employees, nor were all operating companies involved. There are more than a thousand different jobs in the Bell System, not just the nine in these studies.[19]

Yet, despite this brief interlude from bright optimism, Ford and many others have gone on to generalize that job enrichment has universal applicability to the problems facing modern human resource management. Unfortunately, this type of generalization does not seem entirely justified. To date, research evidence also indicates the following to be true:

Important

1   There seems to be a substantial number of workers who are not necessarily alienated from work but are alienated from the middle class values expressed by the job enrichment concept. For these workers, job content is not automatically

---

[16]Mitchell Fein, *Approaches to Motivation*, unpublished paper, Hillsdale, N. J., 1970, p. 20.
[17]Fred Luthans and William E. Reif, "Job Enrichment: Long on Theory, Short on Practice," *Organizational Dynamics*, Winter 1974, p. 31.
[18]Ford, op. cit., p. 188.
[19]Ibid., p. 189.

related to job satisfaction and motivation is not necessarily a function of job satisfaction. These "alienated from the middle class" workers are capable of finding need satisfaction outside the work environment. If they do experience satisfaction at work, it is not the result of job content or formal job design but instead, is due to their social interactions with other primary group members. Job enrichment may not motivate this type of worker.

    2 For some workers improved job design (job enrichment) does not seem to be an even trade for the reduced opportunity for social interaction. The present job may be considered unpleasant and boring, but social isolation is completely unbearable.

    3 The introduction of a job enrichment program may have a negative impact on many workers and result in feelings of inadequacy, fear of failure, and a concern for dependency. For many employees, low level competency, security, and relative independence are more important than the opportunity and potential for increased responsibility and growth in the enriched job.[20]

These points are not intended to negate the value of the enrichment technique, but they do show that, like assessment centers discussed in the last section on selection, job enrichment is not a panacea for all job design problems facing modern management. Job enrichment is a valuable motivational technique, but management must use it selectively and give proper recognition to the complex human and situational variables. The new contingency models are beginning to do this.

Contingency Models of Job Design

Repeatedly in this book so far, it has been suggested that the successful application of human resource management concepts and techniques is contingent on the situation. This, of course, is compatible with the contingency approach to management that was outlined in Chapter 3. In the initial applications of job enrichment, both academicians and practitioners tended to take an "all or nothing" approach. The advocates, such as Herzberg, Ford, and Meyers, suggested directly or implicitly that job enrichment had universal applicability, while the critics implied that it should never be used. Research evidence, on the other hand, suggests that job enrichment does have a positive impact on satisfaction and performance for some types of employees under certain conditions and not for others under different organizational environments. In other words, there is a need for contingency models of job design that will help predict when job enrichment will be successful and when simple, routine designs will be more successful.

    Figure 19-3 summarizes from the literature the variables that seem to be most important to the application of job enrichment. However, a comprehensive contingency model for job design that incorporates these variables and is predictive as well is shown in Figure 19-4. Based upon research findings, this model relates organizational design (open, organic or closed, mechanistic), job

---

[20]Reif and Luthans, op. cit., p. 36.

Figure 19-3 Critical Variables for Job Enrichment

The job(s) to be enriched
  —Organizational level
  —Autonomous work unit
  —Job control
  —Performance feedback
The employee on the enriched job
  —Skill level
  —Personal values
  —Need for "motivators"
The organization impact of the job enrichment program
  —Approval and support
  —Costs
  —Evaluation

Source: Fred Luthans and Edward Knod, "Critical Factors in Job Enrichment," *Atlanta Economic Review*, May–June 1974, p. 9.

design (simple, routine or enlarged), and employee characteristics (high or low growth needs). The model shows that of the eight possible combinations, cells 2 and 7 have congruence between the three variables. In other words, the contingency guideline for practice would be, if there is a mechanistic organization and the employees have low growth needs, a simple, routine job design should be used; and if there is an organic design and employees have high growth needs, a job enrichment design should be used. The model would also predict that, because cells 1 and 8 have congruence between the variables, there would be poor performance and dissatisfaction. In cells 3–6 the variables are contradictory. For these cells, Porter, Lawler, and Hackman note that,

> The prediction (which is not based firmly on existing theory or data) is that individuals will tend to respond to and act in accordance with *those cues which are congruent with their own need states.* Thus, high growth need individuals will tend to respond to cues provided by their jobs in cell 3 and to organizational cues in cell 5; low growth need people will tend to respond to the organization in cell 4 and to the job in cell 6.[21]

In any case, because of the contradictory relationship between the variables in cells 3–6, it is predicted that there will be poor performance and dissatisfaction.

The authors carefully point out that such "pure" categories as shown in Figure 19-4 seldom exist in reality and it is more useful to think of the cells in the model as end points on a continuum. They also point out that, to date, there are only empirical research data to support the predictions of cells 1, 2, and 7. Yet, despite the realistic limitations and the need for more empirical validation, this type of predictive model for job design is indicative of the real progress that is being made in the applications area of the field of organizational behavior.

[21]Porter, Lawler, and Hackman, op. cit., p. 310.

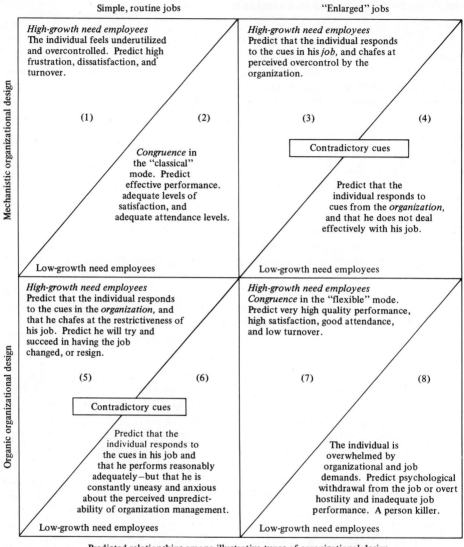

Predicted relationships among illustrative types of organizational design, job design, and employee characteristics.

Figure 19-4 Contingency model of job design. (*Source: Lyman W. Porter, Edward E. Lawler, and J. Richard Hackman*, Behavior in Organizations, *McGraw-Hill Book Company, New York, 1975, p. 309. Used with permission.*)

APPRAISAL

Performance appraisal represents a third important area of application for human resource management. Like the other applications areas of selection and job design, traditional appraisal of human resources was handled very ineffectively. Only recently have some important breakthroughs in the theory and practice of appraisal occurred.

The Purposes and Trends in Appraisal

In recent years the purposes of appraisal have greatly expanded. It used to be solely a means of differentiating between hourly employees for wage increases, transfers, promotions, and layoffs. Today appraisals are used not only for the above but also as a means of communication, motivation, and development of all employees in the organization. In addition, because of the extremely important value of employees (both pragmatically in cost terms and in the contribution they make to the success of the organization), the appraisal process is a major method of controlling the human assets. Such human controls are necessary if organizations are going to survive and grow in the coming years.

Figure 19-5 summarizes the specific trends that have taken place in appraisal. The former emphasis depended on narrowly based subjective ratings of personal traits. Figure 19-6 is meant in jest but is not too far from the truth on how appraisals were, and in many cases still are, made. The new emphasis is to objectively appraise performance. Porter, Lawler, and Hackman summarize the available research findings into the following characteristics of an ideal performance appraisal system:

    1   Measures are used that are inclusive of all the behaviors and results that should be performed.

    2   The measures used are tied to behavior and as far as possible are objective in nature.

    3   Moderately difficult goals and standards for future performance are set.

    4   Measures are used that can be influenced by an individual's behavior.

    5   Appraisals are done on a time cycle that approximates the time it takes the measures to reflect the behavior of the persons being evaluated.

    6   The persons being evaluated have an opportunity to participate in the appraisal process.

    7   The appraisal system interacts effectively with the reward system.[22]

Although the above represents the ideal, realistically there is no appraisal technique to date that can embody all of these characteristics. The two techniques of appraisal that come closest are management by objectives (MBO) and behaviorally anchored rating scales (BARS). These two techniques represent a significant point of departure from the traditional trait approaches and offer a great deal of potential for the future.

Management by Objectives (MBO)

MBO involves the process of setting objectives and appraising by results. The meaning of MBO ranges all the way from a simple budgeting process to an overall philosophy of management. Peter Drucker introduced the concept over twenty years ago. Today, in contrast to modern techniques such as job enrichment—which is talked about a lot but not widely used—MBO in one form or another is probably used by almost every large business organization and is being increasingly used in nonprofit organizations as well.

    [22]Ibid., p. 339.

Figure 19-5   Chart Summarizing Changing Emphasis in Performance Appraisal over the Years

Item	Former emphasis	Present emphasis
Terminology	Merit rating	Employee appraisal Performance appraisal
Purpose	Determine qualification for wage increase, transfer, promotion, layoff	Development of the individual; improved performance on the job
Application	For hourly paid workers	For technical, professional, and managerial employees
Factors rated	Heavy emphasis upon personal traits	Results, accomplishments, performance
Techniques	Rating scales with emphasis upon scores. Statistical manipulation of data for comparison purposes	Management by objectives, mutual goal setting, critical incidents, group appraisal, performance standards, less quantitative
Post-appraisal interview	Supervisor communicates his rating to employee and tries to sell his evaluation, seeks to have employee conform to his views	Supervisor stimulates employee to analyze himself and set own objectives in line with job requirements, supervisor is helper and counselor

Source: Dale S. Beach, *Personnel,* 3d ed., The Macmillan Company, New York, 1975, p. 336. Used with permission.

MBO is, of course, more than just an appraisal technique. In order to put the appraisal part of MBO into proper perspective, the setting-of-objectives part of MBO must first be understood.

Setting Overall Objectives   MBO takes a top-down approach. If MBO is implemented on an organization-wide basis, the top management team gets together to formulate overall objectives. The usual procedure is to first identify key results areas in the organization. A *key results area* is one that has the greatest impact on the overall performance of the organization. It may be sales volume or market share, production output, or quality of service. After the key results areas are identified, measures of performance are determined. Objectives are always stated so that they can be objectively measured. Finally, the actual objectives are agreed upon (usually with input from all members of the top management staff but with final authority vested in the chief operating executive). These objectives are results-oriented and are stated in objective, measurable terms with target dates and accompanying action plans that propose how the objectives will be accomplished.

Developing the Organization for an MBO System   After the overall objectives have been formulated, it is vital that the organization be prepared to now

Figure 19-6 Appraisal Form Using Personal Traits

Personal traits	Far exceeds job requirements	Exceeds job requirements	Meets job requirements	Needs some improvement	Does not meet minimum requirements
Quality	Leaps tall buildings with a single bound	Must take running start to leap over tall buildings	Can only leap over a short building or medium one with no spires	Crashes into buildings when attempting to jump over them	Cannot recognize buildings at all, much less jump over one
Timeliness	Is faster than a speeding bullet	Is as fast as a speeding bullet	Not quite as fast as a speeding bullet	Would you believe a slow bullet?	Wounds self with bullets when attempting to shoot gun
Initiative	Is stronger than a locomotive	Is stronger than a bull elephant	Is stronger than a bull	Shoots the bull	Smells like a bull
Adaptability	Walks on water consistently	Walks on water in emergencies	Washes with water	Drinks water	Passes water in emergencies
Communication	Talks with God	Talks with the angels	Talks to himself	Argues with himself	Loses those arguments

implement the system downward. What too often happens is that the chief executive, or someone who is close to the executive, gets sold on the idea of MBO. A memo to all personnel goes out that the organization *will* go onto an MBO system next Monday morning. This type of approach to implementing MBO is a sure way of effectuating a program that will not work. The people and the organization itself must be developed so that MBO can be successfully implemented. Such an organization development effort often involves using the techniques that will be discussed in Chapter 21. There may also be need for a reorganization to accommodate the MBO system. The needed development may take anywhere from a few weeks to several years, depending on the current stage of development of the human resources of the organization.

Setting Individual Objectives Once the overall objectives have been set and the organization is developed to the point of accommodating an MBO system, individual objectives are set. These individual objectives are determined by each superior-subordinate pair, starting at the top and going down as far as the system is to be implemented. The scenario for this process would be something like the following: The boss would contact each subordinate under him or her and say,

> "As you know, we have completed our MBO orientation and it is now time to set individual objectives. I would like you to develop by next Tuesday a proposed set of objectives for your area of responsibility. Remember that your set of objectives should be in line with the organization's overall objectives, which you have a copy of, and they should be able to contribute to the objectives of those that you interact with, namely, my objectives, the other units' objectives on your same level, and your subordinates' objectives. Your objectives should be stated in quantifiable, measurable terms and have a target date. I will also have some ideas and things written down that I think should be given top priority for your area of responsibility. We will sit down and have an open give-and-take session until we reach a mutually agreeable set of objectives for your area of responsibility."

As with the overall objectives, the set of individual objectives should also have action plans developed to spell out how the objectives are to be accomplished.

Appraisal by Results So far, only the setting-of-objectives part of MBO has been discussed. However, these objectives play a vital role in the appraisal part of MBO. The individuals will be appraised as to how they perform in accordance with the objectives that are set. These appraisals take place on both a periodic (at least every quarter in most MBO systems) and an annual basis. The appraisal sessions attempt to be diagnostic rather than purely evaluative. This simply means that why objectives were either attained or not attained is assessed, rather than having the sessions purely punitive if objectives are not met or rewarding if they are. The periodic reviews are conducted in order to evaluate progress toward the attainment of objectives, and they give the opportunity to make the necessary changes in objectives. Every organization is operating in such a dynamic environment that objectives set at the beginning of the period (usually the fiscal year) may be rendered obsolete in a few months because of changing conditions. Priorities and conditions are constantly changing, and these must be monitored in the periodic review sessions and the needed changes made. Constant revision of the individual objectives and, to a lesser degree, the overall objectives makes MBO a living system that is adaptable to change. At the annual review session, overall diagnosis and evaluation are made according to results attained, and the system starts over again. Figure 19-7 summarizes the parts of the typical MBO process.

Critical Analysis of MBO

There are some generally recognized problems that can occur in an MBO program. Webber summarizes these as: (1) distrust of the system, (2) resentment of a forced program, (3) resistance to paperwork and talk, (4) an overly narrow focus, (5) inconsistency between bottom-up and top-down plans, (6) evaluation not tied to MBO, and (7) inability to measure objectives.[23] Most of these problems can be overcome by careful implementation and proper administration of the program. Of more relevance, however, is the fact that, despite its widespread use in practicing organizations of every type across the

[23]Ross A. Webber, *Management*, Richard D. Irwin, Inc., Homewood, Ill., 1975, pp. 351–355.

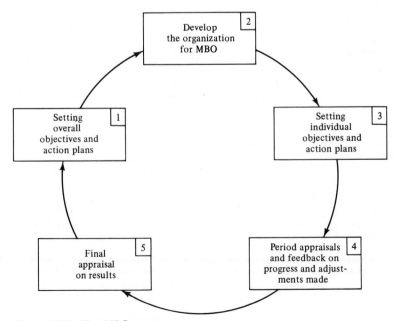

Figure 19-7   The MBO process.

country, there has been practically no meaningful research that directly evaluates the effectiveness of MBO. After reviewing in detail the existing studies on MBO programs,[24] Carroll and Tosi conclude,

> The research on organizational MBO programs indicates that the adoption of this approach can improve managerial performance, managerial attitudes, and organizational planning. This research also indicates that MBO programs require considerable time and effort expenditures for successful adoption, and unless they are given adequate support and attention and are well integrated into the organization, they will fail or not live up to expectations.[25]

Although only tentative conclusions such as the above can be made from research that directly evaluates MBO, the research on related aspects of goal setting, feedback on performance, and participation, which has been given relatively great attention in organizational psychology, may be generalized to MBO. For example, experimental studies by Locke and his colleagues have found that goal setting per se may have a very positive influence on performance.[26] There is also considerable evidence that objective feedback about performance or knowledge of results can improve performance.[27] The next chapter, on behavioral change strategies, will indicate that such feedback can be a very powerful positive reinforcer for organizational participants. The MBO periodic appraisals provide feedback closer to the actual behavior (at least quarterly) and give the supervisor the opportunity to positively reinforce subordinates' progress toward goals and goal accomplishment. Since MBO also

[24]See: H. H. Meyer, E. Kay, and J. R. P. French, "Split Roles in Performance Appraisal," *Harvard Business Review*, January–February 1965, pp. 123–129; John M. Ivancevich, James H. Donnelly, and Herbert L. Lyon, "A Study of the Impact of Management by Objectives on Perceived Need Satisfaction," *Personnel Psychology*, Summer 1970, pp. 139–151; A. P. Raia, "Goal Setting and Self-Control," *Journal of Management Studies*, vol. 2, 1965, pp. 34–53; J. D. Wickens, "Management by Objectives: An Appraisal," *Journal of Management Studies*, vol. 5, 1968, pp. 365–379; W. S. Wikstrom, "Management by—and with—Objectives," *National Industrial Conference Board*, Studies in Personnel Policy No. 212, 1968, pp. 1–21; and Stanley Sloan and David E. Schrieber, *Hospital Management . . . An Evaluation*, Monograph No. 4, Bureau of Business, University of Wisconsin, Madison, Wis., 1971.

[25]Stephen J. Carroll, Jr., and Henry L. Tosi, Jr., *Management by Objectives*, The Macmillan Company, New York, 1973, p. 16.

[26]See: Edwin A. Locke and Judith F. Bryan, "Performance Goals as Determinants of Level of Performance and Boredom," *Journal of Applied Psychology*, April 1967, pp. 120–139; Judith F. Bryan and Edwin A. Locke, "Goal Setting as a Means of Increasing Motivation," *Journal of Applied Psychology*, June 1967, pp. 274–277; Edwin A. Locke, "Toward a Theory of Task Motivation and Incentives," *Organizational Behavior and Human Performance*, May 1968, pp. 157–189; and Edwin A. Locke, Norman Cartledge, and Claramae S. Knerr, "Studies of the Relationship between Satisfaction, Goal-setting, and Performance," *Organizational Behavior and Human Performance*, March 1970, pp. 135–158.

[27]See: R. B. Zajonc, "The Effects of Feedback and Group Task Difficulty on Individual and Group Performance," *Technical Report 15*, University of Michigan, Ann Arbor, Mich., 1961; Ewart E. Smith and Stanford S. Knight, "Effects of Feedback on Insight and Problem-solving Efficiency in Training Groups," *Journal of Applied Psychology*, June 1959, pp. 209–211; and C. H. Hammer and S. Ringel, "The Effect of the Amount of Information Provided and Feedback of Results on Decision-making Efficiency," *Human Factors*, vol. 7, 1965, pp. 513–519.

has participation of subordinates in the goal-setting process, the literature going as far back as the human relations movement (e.g., the well-known Coch and French study which clearly demonstrated the positive impact that participation has on performance) can be used to support the effectiveness of MBO.

Overall, management by objectives, either as a specific technique for appraisal or as a complete system of management, seems to hold enough promise to continue its widespread application. It is readily adaptable and can be used in conjunction with other modern human resource management techniques such as job enrichment, discussed earlier, and organizational behavior modification, which is examined in the next chapter. MBO's greatest advantage is that it combines good, sound management techniques for decision making, communication, and control with basic behavioral requirements. Goal setting, feedback about performance, participative decision making, open two-way communication, and self-control are some of the very positive characteristics of MBO. This unique combination makes MBO worthy of careful consideration. Although there can be problems and more research is required, MBO, if carefully implemented and developed, seems to hold a great deal of promise for management in the future.

Behaviorally Anchored Rating Scales (BARS)

Besides MBO, the other performance appraisal technique which comes closest to the ideal described earlier is behaviorally anchored rating scales (BARS), sometimes called "behavioral expectancy scales." The BARS approach gets away from measuring subjective personal traits and instead measures observable, critical behaviors that are related to specific job dimensions. BARS takes advantage of many of the modern, effective approaches to the evaluation of personnel. First of all, behaviors, and not unobservable inner states of employees, are measured. Second, BARS is aimed at specific dimensions of job performance. This makes the technique much more compatible with EEOC requirements, which were discussed at the beginning of the chapter. Third, the people who are actually involved with the job participate in determining the job dimensions and the development of the scales. Such involvement greatly enhances acceptance of the technique. Fourth, because the evaluation is in terms of specific behaviors, the rater can give objective feedback on how the ratee performed and what specific behavior the ratee must exhibit to improve. Such feedback is much more effective than the vague, subjective feedback given in traditional rating methods. Finally, the technique is highly adaptable to evaluating "nonwidget" types of jobs. Most white-collar jobs and practically all jobs in nonprofit organizations, both of which are becoming increasingly important now and in the future, do not have number of widgets sold or produced as a measure of performance. BARS provides an effective way of measuring the performance on these types of jobs because it is critical behaviors and not the number of widgets that is evaluated.

One of the most important aspects of BARS is that the job dimensions and scales are developed from scratch for each job. Although the recommended steps vary slightly from author to author, the original procedure described by Smith and Kendall is usually followed.[28] The steps in developing BARS include the following:

1 *Identify performance measures.* Knowledgeable, relevant people, usually supervisors, staff personnel, and the jobholder, are asked to identify the important dimensions of the job in question. These dimensions may be the same or different from what traditional job analysis would turn up.

2 *Identify critical behaviors.* Through the use of critical incidents, the participants in step 1 are asked to identify the critical behaviors (both effective and ineffective) for the job dimensions identified in step 1. These are usually stated in a few short sentences or phrases and use the terminology of the job in question.

3 *Retranslation.* The critical behaviors identified in step 2 are next retranslated, usually by another group of participants. Each member of the group is asked to assign the various critical behaviors identified in step 2 to the job dimension that it best describes. Those critical behaviors that the majority assign to the job dimension that was intended are kept for further development. This retranslation process assures the reliability of the critical behaviors (consistent, accurate behaviors for the job dimensions).

4 *Scale development.* Those critical behaviors that survive the retranslation are next numerically scaled (usually from 1 to 7 or 1 to 9) to a level of performance that each is perceived to represent. The final value for each critical behavior is the average (to the nearest whole number) of values of those making the estimates.

5 *The BARS instrument.* The product of the preceding steps is a vertical scale (1 to 7 or 1 to 9) for each job dimension. Figure 19-8 shows an example for the job dimension "absorb and interpret policies" for interviewers and claims deputies in a state labor department. The nine behaviors on the scale are the critical behaviors that were retranslated, i.e., there was high rater agreement on these. They were assigned the values 1 through 9 according to the scaling procedure of step 4.

The research on BARS indicates mixed findings. Recent studies by Campbell and his colleagues and by Millard, Luthans, and Ottemann found that the BARS technique is more effective than traditional rating techniques in reducing the common errors of leniency, central tendency, and halo, but another study by Borman and Vallon found that BARS resulted in significantly higher ratings than a numerically anchored scale.[29] As for whether BARS does

[28]Patricia C. Smith and L. M. Kendall, "The Retranslation of Expectations: An Approach to the Construction of Unambiguous Anchors for Rating Scales," *Journal of Applied Psychology,* April 1963, pp. 149–155.

[29]J. P. Campbell, M. D. Dunnette, R. D. Arvey, and L. W. Hellervik, "The Development and Evaluation of Behaviorally Based Rating Scales," *Journal of Applied Psychology,* vol. 57, 1973, pp. 15–22; Cheedle W. Millard, Fred Luthans, and Robert L. Ottemann, "BARS: A New Breakthrough for Performance Appraisal," *Business Horizons,* in press; and W. C. Borman and W. R. Vallon, "A View of What Can Happen When Behavioral Expectation Scales Are Developed in One Setting and Used in Another," *Journal of Applied Psychology,* vol. 59, 1974, pp. 197–201.

Absorb and Interpret Policies—learns new policies and procedures with a minimum of instruction.

Interviewers and claims deputies must keep abreast of current changes and interpret and apply new information. Some can absorb and interpret new policy guides and procedures quickly with a minimum of explanation. Others seem unable to learn even after repeated explanations and practice. They have difficulty learning and following new policies. When making this rating, disregard job knowledge and experience and evaluate ability to learn on the job.

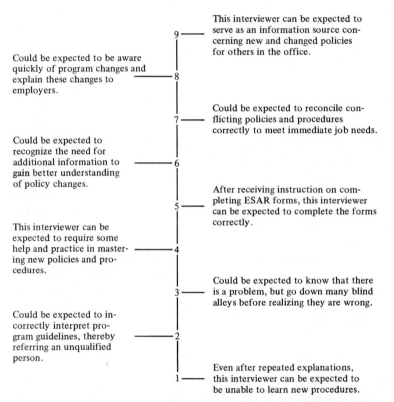

This interviewer can be expected to serve as an information source concerning new and changed policies for others in the office.

Could be expected to be aware quickly of program changes and explain these changes to employers.

Could be expected to reconcile conflicting policies and procedures correctly to meet immediate job needs.

Could be expected to recognize the need for additional information to gain better understanding of policy changes.

After receiving instruction on completing ESAR forms, this interviewer can be expected to complete the forms correctly.

This interviewer can be expected to require some help and practice in mastering new policies and procedures.

Could be expected to know that there is a problem, but go down many blind alleys before realizing they are wrong.

Could be expected to incorrectly interpret program guidelines, thereby referring an unqualified person.

Even after repeated explanations, this interviewer can be expected to be unable to learn new procedures.

Figure 19-8   An example of BARS. (*Source: Cheedle W. Millard, Fred Luthans, and Robert L. Ottemann, "BARS: A New Breakthrough for Performance Appraisal,"* Business Horizons, *in press.*)

in fact get at independent performance dimensions and whether the critical behaviors are reliable, a recent review of available studies concludes ". . . it is clear that research on BARS to date does not support the high promise regarding scale independence," and "In short, while BARS may outperform conventional rating techniques, it is clear that they are not a panacea for obtaining high interrater reliability."[30] Yet, despite the legitimate warnings that BARS is not a panacea, like MBO, the technique has such strong theoretical

[30]Donald P. Schwab, Herbert Heneman, III, and Thomas A. Decotiis, "Behaviorally Anchored Rating Scales: A Review of the Literature," *Academy of Management Proceedings,* 1975, p. 223.

and related research support (e.g., with respect to participation, feedback, and the whole external, behavioral approach to organizational behavior that is given detailed attention in the next chapter) that it seems to deserve continued use in performance appraisal and continued research and development for the future.

SUMMARY

This chapter examined three important areas of application for effective human resource management: selection, job design, and appraisal. Traditionally, there was heavy dependence on test results in the selection process. Today, because of legal interpretations and enforcement, organizations are required to validate their selection tests. Although they should have been validating their tests all along, many organizations have now simply chosen to drop their testing programs. Interviews are the other widely used traditional way of selecting people. Although it is commonly referred to as the most used but least useful selection technique, the art of interviewing can be improved by better planning and by employing certain skills. The newest, most comprehensive technique of selection which is directly related to job performance is the assessment center. This selection technique has proved to be fairly valid so far but also has some definite limitations. The new approach to job design is dominated by the concept of job enrichment. Some of the criticisms of Herzberg's two-factor theory of motivation carry over to job enrichment. There is a need for contingency models for job enrichment. The model that relates organization design, employee characteristics, and job design seems particularly promising in its ability to predict the impact on performance and satisfaction. The two most promising appraisal techniques are management by objectives (MBO) and behaviorally anchored rating scales (BARS). MBO includes the setting of objectives (both overall and individual) and appraisal by results. To date there is very little research directly on MBO that allows us to draw any valid generalizations, but there is much supporting research on goal setting, feedback, and participation, which are all at least indirectly related to MBO. The BARS technique is a departure from the highly subjective personal traits approach to performance appraisal. Specific behaviors that are related to job dimensions are rated in the BARS approach. Although the research to date is mixed, as with MBO there is enough related support to justify its present use and future development.

QUESTIONS FOR DISCUSSION AND REVIEW

1 What is the current legal status of the use of tests for selection? Do you think this is fair? Why or why not?
2 What is validity? How does it relate to reliability?
3 In your own words, what is an assessment center? Do you feel this is a good way to select people? Why or why not?

4 What is job enrichment? What are some critical variables that should be considered in the application of job enrichment?

5 What is MBO? What are some of the specific aspects of the MBO process? What do you see as some of the pros and cons of MBO?

6 What is involved in BARS? Would you rather be rated by a BARS approach or a traditional technique which measures personal traits? Why?

CASE: HOSPITAL CONSULTANT

You have been hired as a consultant for setting up a comprehensive human resource management program for General Hospital. After interviewing the personnel manager, you decide that major attention must be given to selection, job design, and appraisal. You find out that at present the hospital uses the following approaches:

1 *Selection.* A battery of personality, intelligence, and aptitude tests is used to hire hourly paid employees. There is no evidence that these tests have been validated. In addition, the personnel manager's assistant gives a short interview and the interviewee fills out a standard application blank. On the basis of the test scores, interview, and application blank, selection decisions are made. Managerial personnel are selected on the basis of an interview with the administrator.

2 *Job design.* Most jobs in the hospital have been designed along the lines of standard job descriptions supplied by the National Hospital Association. The jobs for the most part are very specialized and the job designs spell out step by step how each job is to be performed.

3 *Appraisal.* The hourly people have an annual appraisal made by their immediate supervisor. This amounts to the supervisor filling out a checklist of the employee's personal traits such as initiative and dependability. No formal evaluations are made of managerial employees. The latter are felt to be professionals and not in need of formal performance appraisals.

1 Based on the present selection, job design, and appraisal processes that are used by this hospital, what recommendations would you make and why? Be specific in your recommendations and your reasoning.

2 Comment on the last statement under "Appraisal." Do professionals need to be evaluated? Why or why not?

3 Would your answer to the first question change if this was a business organization rather than a hospital? How and why?

SELECTED REFERENCES

Anundsen, Kristin: "An Assessment Center at Work," *Personnel,* March–April 1975, pp. 29–36.

Bollmeier, Warren S., II, and Waino W. Suojanen: "Job Enrichment and Organizational Change," *Atlanta Economic Review,* May–June 1974, pp. 16–22.

Borman, Walter C., and Marvin D. Dunnette: "Behavior-based versus Trait-oriented

Performance Ratings: An Empirical Study," *Journal of Applied Psychology,* October 1975, pp. 561–565.

Bucalo, John P., Jr.: "The Assessment Center—A More Specified Approach," *Human Resource Management,* Fall 1974, pp. 2–13.

Byham, William C.: "The Assessment Center as an Aid in Management Development," *Training and Development Journal,* December 1971, pp. 10–21.

Carroll, Stephen J., and Henry L. Tosi, Jr.: *Management by Objectives,* The Macmillan Company, New York, 1973.

Donaldson, Lex: "Job Enlargement: A Multidimensional Process," *Human Relations,* September 1975, pp. 593–610.

Fein, Mitchell: "Job Enrichment Is Not Enough," *Atlanta Economic Review,* May–June 1974, pp. 28–31.

Ford, Robert N.: "Job Enrichment Lessons from AT&T," *Harvard Business Review,* January–February 1973, pp. 96–106.

Ford, Robert N.: *Motivation through the Work Itself,* American Management Association, New York, 1969.

Goodale, James G., and Ronald J. Burke: "Behaviorally Based Rating Scales Need Not Be Job Specific," *Journal of Applied Psychology,* June 1975, pp. 389–391.

Hackman, J. Richard: "Is Job Enrichment Just a Fad," *Harvard Business Review,* September–October 1975, pp. 129–138.

Howard, Ann: "An Assessment of Assessment Centers," *Academy of Management Journal,* March 1974, pp. 115–143.

Huck, James R.: "Assessment Centers: A Review of the External and Internal Validities," *Personnal Psychology,* Summer 1973, pp. 191–212.

Jablin, Fredric: "The Selection Interivew: Contingency Theory and Beyond," *Human Resource Management,* Spring 1975, pp. 2–9.

Keaveny, Timothy J., and Anthony F. McGann: "A Comparison of Behavioral Expectation Scales and Graphic Rating Scales," *Journal of Applied Psychology,* December 1975, pp. 695–703.

Kirchhoff, Bruce A: "MBO: Understanding What the Experts Are Saying," *MSU Business Topics,* Summer 1974, pp. 17–22.

Kraft, W. Philip, and Kathleen L. Williams: "Job Redesign Improves Productivity," *Personnel Journal,* July 1975, pp. 393–397.

Latham, Gary P., and Gary A. Yukl: "A Review of Research on the Application of Goal Setting in Organizations," *Academy of Management Journal,* December 1975, pp. 824–843.

Luthans, Fred, and Edward Knod: "Critical Factors in Job Enrichment," *Atlanta Economic Review,* May–June 1974, pp. 6–11.

Luthans, Fred, and William E. Reif: "Job Enrichment: Long on Theory, Short on Practice," *Organizational Dynamics,* Winter 1974, pp. 30–49.

Millard, Cheedle W., Fred Luthans, and Robert L. Ottemann, "BARS: A New Breathrough for Performance Appraisal," *Business Horizons,* in press.

Miner, John B.: "Psychological Testing and Fair Employment Practices: A Testing Program That Does Not Discriminate," *Personnel Psychology,* Spring 1974, pp. 49–62.

Mitchel, James O.: "Assessment Center Validity: A Longitudinal Study," *Journal of Applied Psychology,* October 1975, pp. 573–579.

Monczka, Robert M., and William E. Reif: "A Contingency Approach to Job Enrichment Design," *Human Resource Management,* Winter 1973, pp. 9–17.

Morse, John J.: "A Contingency Look at Job Design," *California Management Review,* Fall 1973, pp. 67–75.

Odiorne, George S.: *Management by Objectives,* Pitman Publishing Corporation, New York, 1965.

Orpen, Christopher: "The 'Correct' Use of Personality Tests: A View from Industrial Psychology," *Public Personnel Management,* May–June 1974, pp. 228–229.

Parke, E. Lauck, and Curt Tausky: "The Mythology of Job Enrichment: Self-Actualization Revisited," *Personnel,* September–October 1975, pp. 12–21.

Patz, Alan L.: "Performance Appraisal: Useful But Still Resisted," *Harvard Business Review,* May–June 1975, pp. 74–80.

Peterson, Donald J.: "The Impact of Duke Power on Testing," *Personnel,* March–April 1974, pp. 30–37.

Porter, Lyman, Edward Lawler, and J. Richard Hackman: *Behavior in Organizations,* McGraw-Hill Book Company, 1975.

Raia, Anthony P.: *Managing by Objectives,* Scott, Foresman and Company, Glenview, Ill., 1974.

Reif, William E., and Gerald Bassford: "What MBO Really Is," *Business Horizons,* June 1973, pp. 23–30.

Reif, William E., and Fred Luthans: "Does Job Enrichment Really Pay Off?" *California Management Review,* Fall 1972, pp. 30–37.

Robertson, David E.: "Employment Testing and Discrimination," *Personnel Journal,* January 1974, pp. 18–21.

Schoderbek, Peter P., and William E. Reif: *Job Enlargement: Key to Improved Performance,* University of Michigan, Ann Arbor, Mich., 1969.

Schwab, Donald P., Herbert G. Heneman, II, and Thomas A. Decotiis: "Behaviorally Anchored Rating Scales: A Review of the Literature," *Personnel Psychology,* Winter 1975, pp. 549–562.

Sharf, James C.: "How Validated Testing Eases the Pressures of Minority Recruitment," *Personnel,* May–June 1975, pp. 53–59.

Slusher, E. Allen: "A Systems Look at Performance Appraisal," *Personnel Journal,* February 1975, pp. 114–117.

Stone, Thomas H.: "An Examination of Six Prevalent Assumptions Concerning Performance Appraisal," *Public Personnel Management,* November–December 1973, pp. 408–414.

Villarreal, John J.: "Management by Objectives Revisited," *S.A.M. Advanced Management Journal,* April 1974, pp. 28–33.

Werther, William B., Jr.: "Beyond Job Enrichment to Employment Enrichment," *Personnel Journal,* August 1975, pp. 438–442.

Chapter 20

Applied Behavioral Analysis
and Change

Chapter 5 introduced the external approach to organizational behavior. The external approach emphasizes the important role that the environment plays in organizational behavior. In particular, the B——→C part of the S←——→O——→B——→C model recognizes the importance of consequences in the prediction and control of organizational behavior. Chapter 12 added some depth of understànding to the external approach by explaining learning concepts, especially reinforcement. With the exception of these two chapters, both the dynamics of organizational behavior and the specific applications for human resource management have been presented mainly from the internal perspective. For example, the chapters on group dynamics, conflict, motivation, and leadership deal with many intra- and interpersonal cognitive variables, and the preceding chapter, on selection, job design, and appraisal, is largely geared to improving employee attitudes and satisfactions.

This chapter is specifically devoted to an applied, external approach to the practice of human resource management. Observable behaviors and their direct impact on performance effectiveness are the focus of attention. The concepts and techniques presented in this chapter are not proposed as an alternative to the more traditional and widely accepted methods of human resource management presented in the preceding chapter and the next. Instead, the suggested techniques in this chapter are meant to supplement and to be used in combination with other human resources techniques.

The first part of the chapter builds on the material that was given in Chapters 5 and 12. Background information on the use of applied behavioral analysis and change is given. Then almost the entire chapter is devoted to a fairly detailed explanation and analysis of the organizational behavior modification—or simply O.B.Mod.—approach to human resource management. All the steps of O.B.Mod. (identify, measure, analyze, intervene, and evaluate) are given attention, but relatively more attention is given to the intervention strategies that can be used to change organizational behaviors. The last part of the chapter reports some actual experiences and research findings on the application of O.B.Mod. in practicing organizations. Finally, some of the possible ethical implications are presented and analyzed.

BACKGROUND FOR APPLIED BEHAVIORAL ANALYSIS AND CHANGE

As was brought out in Chapter 5, the external approach has its roots in behaviorism. Modern behaviorism stems from the significant distinction that B. F. Skinner made between respondent or reflexive behaviors that are the result of classical conditioning and operant behaviors that are the result of operant conditioning (see Chapter 12 for a detailed discussion of the difference). In an organization, very few of the behaviors of participants are the result of classical conditioning; the mechanistic S-R type of behaviorism is of little value to the analysis or change of organizational behaviors. Operant conditioning is a much better basis for the analysis and change of organizational behavior. Organizational behavior is largely a function of its consequences. This premise is the basis for the external approach. It is the overriding assumption in applied behavioral analysis and change.

Applied Behavioral Analysis in Other Settings

The basic principles of operant conditioning were developed by Skinner and his colleagues mainly with the use of lower-animal subjects under highly controlled laboratory conditions. The application of Skinner's principles as a behavioral change strategy for humans had its beginnings in the mental health field. Through the systematic management of antecedent and consequent environments, psychologists were able to dramatically change the behaviors of their patients (the mentally retarded, psychotics, and autistic children). For example, mentally retarded patients were systematically taught to take care of themselves, psychotically disturbed patients who had been silent for many years were shaped to the point where they carried on a conversation, and autistic children's self-destructive behaviors were eliminated. Such changes in behaviors were often attained with patients who had had years of traditional psychotherapeutic and medical treatments with no noticeable effect. Few would argue that applied behavioral analysis has had a tremendous impact on the treatment of mental patients in recent years.

The next major thrust of the application of Skinnerian behaviorism has been in education. In particular, applied behavior analysis has been used in both classroom instruction techniques and child management problems. For example, it has been successfully used in the acquisition of language and other intellectual skills and in the modification of undesirable behaviors of problem children in a classroom. Many of today's teachers systematically manage their classroom environment to accelerate desirable behaviors and decelerate undesirable behaviors. Although the approach is still controversial, most would agree with the conclusion of a comprehensive review of the literature on "Operant Conditioning in the Classroom Setting" that ". . . it appears that the entry of the behavior modifiers into the public-school classroom has shown that the techniques and designs developed for behavioral control in the laboratory are applicable in natural settings."[1]

The Application to Organizational Behavior

The natural extension of the application of behavior modification from mental hospitals and classrooms would be to the more complex, less controlled environment of work organizations. Only very recently has this been attempted. Although suggestions on the use of operant techniques in managing people can be found as far back as fifteen years ago,[2] only in the last few years have systematic theory, research, and application of the operant approach to human resource management been attempted. In one of the first comprehensive articles in 1969, Walter Nord pointed to the fact that the work of Skinner had been almost completely ignored by the field of management. He suggested how the operant model could be applied to training and personnel development, job design, compensation, and organization design, and in a follow-up article he described how attendance may be improved.[3] Shortly after, Luthans and White suggested the direct application of behavior modification to human resource management in general, and Adam and Scott reported research results on the application of behavioral conditioning to quality control.[4] With this start, the theoretical underpinnings and practical applications for an operant, external approach to human resource management called "organizational behavior

[1]Karl I. Altman and Thomas E. Linton, "Operant Conditioning in the Classroom Setting," *The Journal of Educational Research,* February 1971, reprinted in Roger Ulrich, Thomas Stachnik, and John Mabry (eds.), *Control of Human Behavior,* vol. 3, Scott, Foresman and Company, Glenview, Ill., 1974, p. 86. This volume contains many other classic studies on the applications of behavior modification to education. The other two volumes contain applications to other settings.

[2]Owen Aldis, "Of Pigeons and Men," *Harvard Business Review,* July–August 1961, pp. 59–63.

[3]Walter R. Nord, "Beyond the Teaching Machine: The Neglected Area of Operant Conditioning in the Theory and Practice of Management," *Organizational Behavior and Human Performance,* November 1969, pp. 375–401; and Walter R. Nord, "Improving Attendance through Rewards," *Personnel Administration,* vol. 33, no. 6, 1970, pp. 37–41.

[4]Fred Luthans and Donald White, "Behavior Modification: Application to Manpower Management," *Personnel Administration,* July–August 1971, pp. 41–47; and E. E. Adam and William E. Scott, "The Application of Behavior Conditioning to the Problems of Quality Control," *Academy of Management Journal,* June 1971, pp. 175–193.

modification" or "O.B.Mod." has been developed.[5]

Figure 20-1 briefly traces the theoretical paths that lead up to O.B.Mod. As shown, O.B.Mod. is the result of two separate paths of development. On the one path is the development of behaviorism into behavior modification and on the other is the development of the behavioral approach to management into organizational behavior. The combination of these two paths of development is *O.B.Mod.* The approach was introduced in the previous edition of this book but was given only minor attention. The first comprehensive treatment of all aspects of O.B.Mod. (theory, research, and application) appeared in a book by this title authored by Luthans and Kreitner.[6] The rest of this chapter summarizes the O.B.Mod. approach to human resource management.

ORGANIZATIONAL BEHAVIOR MODIFICATION

The basic premise of O.B.Mod. is that organizational behavior is a function of its consequences. As a specific approach to organizational behavior analysis and change, O.B.Mod. can be portrayed as a five-step problem-solving model. Figure 20-2 shows this model. It can be used in a step-by-step process to actually change performance-related behaviors of personnel in today's organizations. Thus, O.B.Mod. can be thought of as a technique of human resource management. The reader should be reminded that O.B.Mod. represents only one technique of human resource management. To be sure, it is a very powerful technique, but there are other techniques, such as assessment centers, job enrichment, management by objectives, and BARS, discussed in the last chapter, and organizational development techniques, discussed in the next, which can all be selectively used (desirably in a contingency framework) to effectively manage human resources. The following sections discuss the various steps of O.B.Mod., and then the experience with its application is reported and the ethical implications are analyzed.

Step 1: Identification of Critical Behaviors

In this first step the critical behaviors that make a significant impact on performance (e.g., making or selling widgets or service to clients or customers) are identified. In every organization, regardless of type or level, numerous

---

[5]See: Fred Luthans and Robert Kreitner, "The Role of Punishment in Organizational Behavior Modification (O.B. Mod.)," *Public Personnel Management*, May–June 1973, pp. 156–161; Fred Luthans and David Lyman, "Training Supervisors to Use Organizational Behavior Modification," *Personnel*, September–October 1973, pp. 38–44; Fred Luthans and Robert Ottemann, "Motivation vs. Learning Approaches to Organizational Behavior," *Business Horizons*, December 1973, pp. 55–62; Fred Luthans and Robert Kreitner, "The Management of Behavioral Contingencies," *Personnel*, July–August 1971, pp. 7–16; Fred Luthans and Mark Martinko, "An O.B.Mod. Analysis of Absenteeism," *Human Resource Management*, in press; and Fred Luthans, "An Organizational Behavior Modification (O.B.Mod.) Approach to O.D.," *Organization and Administrative Sciences*, Winter 1975/1976, pp. 47–53. For a comprehensive review of other related approaches see Craig E. Schneier, "Behavior Modification in Management: A Review and Critique," *Academy of Management Journal*, September 1974, pp. 528–548.

[6]Fred Luthans and Robert Kreitner, *Organizational Behavior Modification*, Scott, Foresman and Company, Glenview, Ill., 1975.

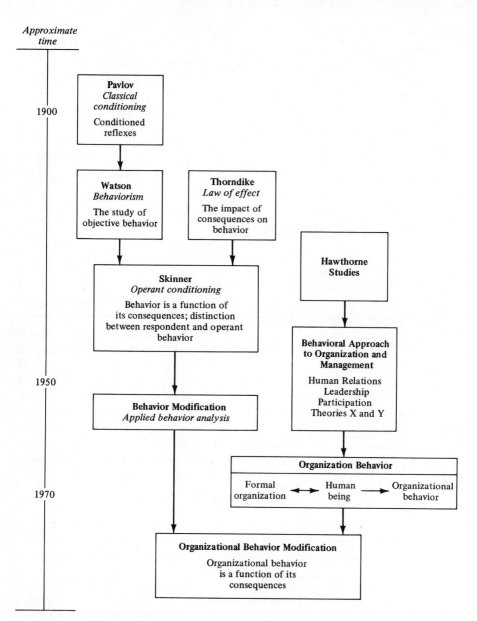

Figure 20-1 Historical development of organizational behavior modification. (*Source:* Organizational Behavior Modification, *by Fred Luthans and Robert Kreitner. Copyright © 1975 by Scott, Foresman and Company. Reprinted by permission of the publisher.*)

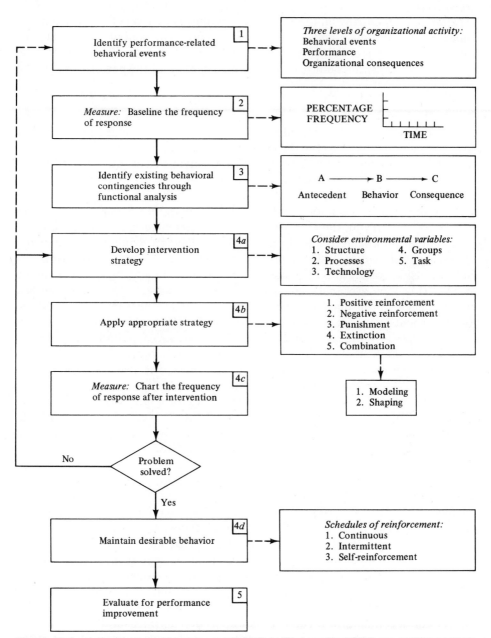

Figure 20-2 Behavioral contingency management. (*Source: Fred Luthans and Robert Kreitner, "The Management of Behavioral Contingencies,"* Personnel, *July–August 1974, p. 13.*)

behaviors are occurring all the time. Some of these behaviors have a significant impact on performance and some of them do not. The goal of the first step of O.B.Mod. is to identify the critical behaviors—that 5 to 10 percent of the behaviors that may account for up to 70 or 80 percent of the performance in the area in question.

Methods of Identifying Critical Behaviors   The process of identifying the critical behaviors can be carried out in a couple of ways. One approach is to have the person closest to the job in question, e.g., the immediate supervisor or the actual jobholder, determine the critical behaviors. This goes hand in hand with using O.B.Mod. as a problem-solving approach for the individual manager. Its advantages are that the person who knows the job best can most accurately identify the critical behaviors, and, by participating, that person may be more committed to carrying the O.B.Mod. process to its successful completion.

Another approach to identifying critical behaviors would be to conduct a systematic behavioral audit. The audit would use internal staff specialists and/or outside consultants. The audit would systematically analyze, e.g., in the manner that jobs are analyzed in the BARS technique discussed in the last chapter, each job in question. The advantages of the personal approach (the jobholder and/or the immediate supervisor making a vital input into the audit) can be realized by the audit. In addition, the advantages of staff expertise and consistency can be gained. Such an audit approach has been successfully used in the behavioral management program at Emery Air Freight.[7] Even if an outside audit identifies the critical behaviors, it is usually the supervisor of the area in question who performs the succeeding steps in O.B.Mod. In the future, if an entire organization sets up behavioral systems and takes an O.B.Mod. approach to total organization development,[8] there could be more involvement of staff specialists in the succeeding steps in O.B.Mod.

Guidelines for Identifying Critical Behaviors   Regardless of the method used, there are certain guidelines that can be helpful in identifying critical behaviors. First, only observable, countable behaviors are included. An employee's "bad attitude" and someone who "goofs off all the time" are unacceptable. Attitudes and a lack of motivation are unobservable inner states of people. Only observables—behaviors that can be seen (e.g., absenteeism or attendance, tardiness or promptness, complaints or constructive comments, and doing or not doing a particular task or procedure that leads to quantity and/or quality outcomes)—play a role in O.B.Mod. Something like "goofing off" is not acceptable because it is not operationally measurable. It could be broken down into observable, measurable behaviors such as not being at the

---

[7]"Performance Audit, Feedback, and Positive Reinforcement," *Training and Development Journal*, November 1972, pp. 8–13; and "At Emery Air Freight: Positive Reinforcement Boosts Performance," *Organizational Dynamics*, Winter 1973, pp. 41–50.

[8]An example of such a total organization development approach can be found in Luthans and Kreitner, *Organizational Behavior Modification*, op. cit., pp. 164–170.

work station, being tardy when returning from breaks, spending time at the water cooler, disrupting coworkers, and even flirting with the opposite sex. To be idenfified as a critical behavior there must be a positive answer to the two questions: (1) Can it be seen? and (2) Can it be measured?

Another helpful guideline for identifying critical behaviors is to work backward from an obvious performance deficiency. Just as not all behaviors contribute to performance (e.g., complaining behavior may have nothing to do with performance), not all performance problems can be traced to behaviors. For example, the cause of poor performance of a production unit in a manufacturing organization may be faulty machinery or poorly trained workers (they do not know the proper procedures) or unrealistically high production standards. Each of these possible causes is not, at least directly, a behavioral problem. The same is true of the person who does not have the ability to produce at an acceptable level. This is a selection problem, not a behavioral problem. However, after noting the possibility of nonbehaviorally related performance problems, it should be emphasized that in general such problems are the exception rather than the rule. Most organizations are not having problems with their technology or the ability of their people, but they have many behaviorally related performance problems. Desirable performance-related behaviors need to be strengthened and accelerated in frequency, and undesirable performance-related behaviors need to be weakened and decelerated in frequency. Like the initial step in any problem-solving process, the critical behaviors must be properly identified or the subsequent steps of O.B.Mod. become meaningless for attaining the overall goal of performance improvement.

Step 2: Measurement of the Behaviors

After the critical behaviors have been identified in step 1, they are next measured. A baseline frequency is obtained by determining (either by observing and counting or by extracting from existing records) the number of times that the identified behavior is occurring under present conditions. Often this baseline frequency is in and of itself very revealing. Sometimes it is discovered that the behavior identified in step 1 is occurring much less or much more frequently than anticipated. The baseline measure may indicate the problem is much smaller or bigger than was thought to be the case. In some instances the baseline measure may cause the "problem" to be dropped because its low (or high) frequency is now deemed not to need change. For example, attendance may have been identified in step 1 as a critical behavior that needed to be changed. The supervisor reports that her people "never seem to be here." The baseline measure, however, reveals that there is 96 percent attendance, which is deemed to be acceptable. In this example, the baseline measure rules out attendance as being a problem. The reverse, of course, could also have occurred. Attendance may have been a much bigger problem than anticipated.

The purpose of the baseline measure is to provide objective frequency data on the critical behavior. A baseline frequency count is an operational definition of the strength of the critical behavior under existing conditions. Such precise measurement is the hallmark of any scientific endeavor and separates O.B.Mod. from more subjective human resource management approaches such as participation. Although the baseline is established before the intervention to see what happens to the behavior as a result of the intervention, it is important to realize that measures are taken post-intervention as well. Busy managers may feel that they do not have time to objectively record behavioral frequencies, but, at least initially, they must record them in order to effectively use the O.B.Mod. approach. The following discussion of tally sheets and charting point out how to minimize the problems associated with this second step of O.B.Mod.

Tally Sheets   A tailor-made tally sheet should be designed for each behavior. A piece of notebook paper usually is sufficient. Figure 20-3 shows a typical talley sheet. As shown, the tallies usually record behavioral frequencies in relation to time. The frequencies are usually broken down in a yes-no type of format which greatly simplifies the job of the recorder. However, such an approach requires precise definitions of what constitutes a frequency. For example, say that the critical behavior is tardiness in returning from breaks. A decision must be made on what is considered tardy. Say that it is decided (and this may be different from situation to situation) that five minutes or over is tardy. The observer/recorder then has a definite guideline in checking "yes" or "no" for frequency of tardiness behavior.

The time dimension on the tally sheet can also follow some specific guidelines to simplify the observer/recorder's job. With some behaviors, such as attendance or complaints, it may be feasible to record every occurrence. However, with many other critical behaviors it would be so time-consuming to record every frequency that it would be practically impossible. On behaviors of

	Monday		Tuesday		Wednesday		Thursday		Friday	
Times	Yes	No	Yes	No	Yes	No	Yes	No	Yes	No

Employee:_____   Behavior:_____

Position:_____   Supervisor:_____

Figure 20-3   Typical tally sheet.

the latter type, time-sampling techniques can be effectively used. The approach is similar to the work-sampling techniques that have been successfully used by industrial engineers for years. An example of a time-sampling approach would be to randomly select a time per each working hour to observe the behavior. As in any sampling procedure, if the times are in fact random, confident generalizations can be made to the whole day.

Charting the Behaviors   The data collected on the tally sheets are transferred to a chart or graph like the one shown in Figure 20-4. As shown, the frequencies of behaviors are along the vertical and time is on the horizontal. Percentage rather than raw frequency is usually used. This usage again simplifies the recorder's job because it permits the recorder to miss a time or two during the day or even entire days without badly distorting the data.

Charting of critical behaviors is important to O.B.Mod. because it permits quick, accurate visual inspection of the frequency data. As Kreitner has noted,

> In effect, behavior charts are mini behavioral experiments complete with "before" and "after" measures for control purposes. Baseline data collected under normal conditions later act as a standard for evaluating interventions. Baseline data help answer the pivotal question: Has the intervention strengthened, weakened, or not affected the target behavior?[9]

The Role of the Observer/Recorder   The role assumed by the observer/recorder can be important not only to the measurement step but to the credibility and ethics of the entire approach. As Chapter 18 pointed out, there is a real need for accurate, observational measures of organizational behavior. This is true not only in the O.B.Mod. approach but for gathering data for any research purpose in organizational behavior. Questionnaire and interview data

[9]Robert Kreitner, "PM—A New Method of Behavior Change," *Business Horizons,* December 1975, p. 82.

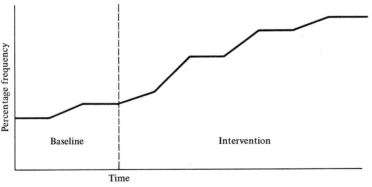

Figure 20-4   Charting critical behaviors.

were criticized in Chapter 18 as being highly reactive. However, the mere presence of an observer may also badly distort the behaviors being measured. For this reason, it is important that observational data be gathered as unobtrusively (inconspicuously) as possible.

Advocating the use of unobtrusive observational measures does not mean that hidden observers or hidden audio and/or video equipment should be used. Obviously, such practice gets into ethical and legal problems. With possibly a few exceptions (e.g., security), such hidden or deceptive approaches cannot be justified. On the other hand, straightforward observational techniques that use common sense can minimize the reactive effects of those being measured. The observer should be completely open to any questions that the person being observed may have. Most employees in modern organizations are not sensitive to being measured because industrial engineers and personnel specialists have been doing it for years. There have certainly been abuses of this in the past, but desirably the lessons have been learned and the abuses can be eliminated.

In addition to observational techniques of data collection, much data on typical critical behaviors (e.g., absenteeism, quantity, and quality data) are already being gathered for other purposes. All that recorders have to do is retrieve these data; they do not have to intrusively intervene. Finally, self-reporting procedures can be employed to gather the data. Having people reinforced for honestly and accurately keeping records on their own targeted behaviors will eliminate the need for an observer/recorder. In the Emery Air Freight program of behavioral management such self-reporting was successfully used.[10]

Step 3: Functional Analysis of the Behavior

Once the critical behavior has been identified and a baseline measure is obtained, a functional analysis is performed. As Chapters 5 and 12 brought out, both the antecedent (the S in the $S \longleftrightarrow O \longrightarrow B \longrightarrow C$ model) and the consequent (the C in the model) environments are vital to the understanding, prediction, and control of human behavior in organizations. In Figure 20-2 the functional analysis is referred to simply as $A \longrightarrow B \longrightarrow C$ or antecedent $\longrightarrow$ behavior $\longrightarrow$ consequence. The functional analysis brings out the problem-solving nature of O.B.Mod. Both the antecedent cues which emit the behavior and sometimes control it and the consequences which are currently maintaining the behavior must be identified and understood before an effective intervention strategy can be developed.

An example can demonstrate why the functional analysis is so important to O.B.Mod. In an actual case of an O.B.Mod. application, a production supervisor in a large manufacturing firm identified unscheduled breaks as a critical behavior affecting the performance of his department. It seemed that his people were frequently wandering off the job; and when they were not

---

[10]"Performance Audit, Feedback, and Positive Reinforcement," op. cit.; and "At Emery Air Freight," op. cit.

tending their machines, time was lost—and irrecoverable production. When a baseline measure of this critical behavior was obtained, he was proved to be right. The data indicated that unscheduled breaks (defined as leaving the job for reasons other than taking a scheduled break or to obtain materials, etc.) were occurring in his department on a relatively frequent basis. The functional analysis was performed to determine the antecedent(s) and consequence(s) of the unscheduled break behavior. It was found that the clock served as the antecedent cue for the critical behavior. The workers in this department started work at 8 A.M.; at 10 A.M. they had their first scheduled break; they had lunch at 12. They started again at 1 P.M. and had a break at 3 P.M. and quit at 5 P.M. The functional analysis revealed that almost precisely at 9 A.M., 11 A.M., 2 P.M., and 4 P.M. the workers were leaving their jobs and going to the rest room. In other words, the clock served as a cue for them to take an unscheduled break midway between starting time and the first scheduled break, between the first scheduled break and lunch, between lunch and the scheduled afternoon break, and between the afternoon break and quitting time. Importantly, the clock did not *cause* the behavior; it only served as a cue to emit the behavior. On the other hand, the behavior was under stimulus control of the clock because the clock dictated when the behavior would occur. The consequence, however, was what was maintaining the behavior. The critical behavior was a function of its consequences. The functional analysis revealed that the consequence of the unscheduled break behavior was escape from a dull, boring task (i.e., the unscheduled break behavior was being negatively reinforced) and/or meeting with coworkers and friends to socialize and have a cigarette (i.e., the unscheduled break behavior was being positively reinforced). Through this functional analysis the antecedents and consequences are identified so that an effective intervention strategy can be developed. The next section on the intervention step will reveal what the production supervisor actually tried in this case.

The functional analysis pinpoints one of the most significant practical problems of using an O.B.Mod. approach to change critical behaviors. Only the *contingent* consequences have an impact on subsequent behavior. The functional analysis often reveals that there are many competing contingencies for every organizational behavior. For example, a supervisor may be administering what he or she believes to be contingent punishment for the undesirable behavior of subordinates. However, what often happens is that the coworkers are providing a very rewarding consequence for the undesirable behavior. In many cases the persons who are supposedly being punished will allow the coworkers' rewards to be the contingent consequence, and their undesirable behavior will increase in subsequent frequency. In other words, the supervisor's punishment was not contingent; it had no impact on the subordinates' subsequent behavior. The functional analysis must make sure that the *contingent* consequences are identified, and the analyst must not be deluded by the consequences that on the surface appear to be affecting the critical behavior.

Step 4: Development of an Intervention Strategy

The first three steps in an O.B.Mod. approach are preliminary to the action step, the intervention. The goal of the intervention is to strengthen and accelerate desirable critical behaviors and/or weaken and decelerate undesirable critical behaviors. There are several strategies that can be used, but the main ones are positive reinforcement, punishment/positive reinforcement, and extinction/positive reinforcement.

Positive Reinforcement Strategy   Chapter 12 devoted considerable attention to the concept of reinforcement. A *positive reinforcer* was defined as a consequence which strengthens the behavior and increases its subsequent frequency. It was also brought out that negative reinforcement (the termination or withdrawal of an undesirable consequence) has the same impact on behavior (strengthens and increases subsequent frequency). Yet, positive and not negative reinforcement is recommended as an effective intervention strategy for O.B.Mod. The reason is that positive reinforcement represents a form of positive control of behavior while negative reinforcement and punishment represent forms of negative control of behavior. As Chapter 12 pointed out, negative reinforcement is actually a type of "blackmail" control of behavior; the person behaves in a certain way in order not to be punished. Most organizations today control participants in this manner. People come to work in order not to be fired and look busy when the supervisor walks by in order not to be punished. Under positive control, the person behaves in a certain way in order to receive the desired consequence. Under positive control people would come to work in order to be recognized for making a contribution to their department's goal of perfect attendance or would keep busy whether the supervisor was around or not in order to receive incentive pay or because they get self-reinforcement from doing a good job. Positive control through a positive-reinforcement intervention strategy is much more effective and long-lasting than negative control. It creates a much healthier and more productive organizational climate.

Identifying Positive Reinforcers   Chapter 12 carefully pointed out that a reward becomes a positive reinforcer only if because of its presentation the behavior increases in subsequent frequency. Thus, some of the commonly used organizational rewards are not necessarily positive reinforcers. This is why it is so vitally important that the measures initiated in step 2 be continued after the intervention. The objective measures are the only way to tell whether an intervention is in fact a positive reinforcer.

Chapter 12 presented the various conceptual categories of rewards (extrinsic/intrinsic and primary/secondary) and indicated the impacts that each tends to have on behavior. There are also available several techniques to help determine potential positive reinforcers.[11] The most accurate but often

[11]See: Luthans and Kreitner, *Organizational Behavior Modification,* op. cit., pp. 91–99.

difficult-to-accomplish method of identifying positive reinforcers is to empirically analyze each individual's history of reinforcement. Knowledge of what a particular person likes and dislikes gained through experience can help in this regard, and, of course, empirical evidence post-intervention from the charting in step 2 can be used to analyze the history of reinforcement. However, in cases where there is little or no experience with the individual prior to trying an intervention, several self-reporting techniques can be used.

The most straightforward technique is to simply ask what the person finds to be rewarding. Although the person may not always tell the truth, it is nonetheless a logical point of departure for identifying potential reinforcers. A more formal approach is to use test instruments. For example, Blood developed an ipsative test which identifies the relative importance of several possible job-related reinforcers.[12] Another possible method of identifying reinforcers is the use of contingency questionnaires.[13] The latter tests measure perceived performance-outcome probabilities and can help identify the important outcomes (reinforcers) for employees. Still another way to help identify possible reinforcers is through self-selection techniques: the workers are allowed to select their own reinforcers from a variety of stated possibilities sometimes called "smorgasbords" or "menus."

Contrived Reinforcers The various techniques discussed above can be used to help identify reinforcers for the positive-reinforcement intervention stratety. Although reinforcers are highly individualized, research and experience have shown that there are several rewards that most organizational participants find positively reinforcing. These can be classified as contrived and natural rewards. The contrived rewards are those that are brought in from outside the natural work environment and generally involve costs for the organization over and above the existing situation.[14] Examples would include the consumables, manipulatables, visual/auditory reinforcers, and tokens found in Figure 20-5. The two most widely used and effective contrived rewards would be money and feedback about performance.

The literature on the impact that feedback has on organizational participants was discussed in the last chapter. Feedback played an important role in the Emery Air Freight program and was found to have a positively reinforcing impact on employee performance.[15] There is little question that despite the tremendous amount of data being generated by computerized information systems in modern organizations, individuals still receive very little, if any, feedback about their performance. People generally have an intense desire to

[12]Milton R. Blood, "Intergroup Comparisons of Intraperson Differences: Rewards from the Job," *Personnel Psychology*, Spring 1973, pp. 1–9.

[13]For example, see: H. Joseph Reitz, "Managerial Attitudes and Perceived Contingencies between Performance and Organizational Response," *Academy of Management Proceedings*, 1971, pp. 227–238.

[14]Luthans and Kreitner, *Organizational Behavior Modification*, op. cit., p. 102.

[15]"Performance Audit, Feedback, and Positive Reinforcement," op. cit.; and "At Emery Air Freight," op. cit.

Figure 20-5 Classifications of On-the-Job Rewards

	Contrived on-the-job rewards				Natural rewards	
Consumables	**Manipulatables**	**Visual and auditory**	**Tokens**		**Social**	**Premack**
Coffee-break treats	Desk accessories	Office with a window	Money		Friendly greetings	Job with more responsibility
Free lunches	Wall plaques	Piped-in music	Stocks		Informal recognition	Job rotation
Food baskets	Company car	Redecoration of work environment	Stock options		Formal acknowledgment of achievement	Early time off with pay
Easter hams	Watches	Company literature	Movie passes		Invitations to coffee/lunch	Extended breaks
Christmas turkeys	Trophies	Private office	Trading stamps (green stamps)		Solicitations of suggestions	Extended lunch period
Dinners for the family on the company	Commendations	Popular speakers or lecturers	Paid-up insurance policies		Solicitations of advice	Personal time off with pay
Company picnics	Rings/tiepins	Book club discussions	Dinner and theater tickets		Compliment on work progress	Work on personal project on company time
After-work wine and cheese parties	Appliances and furniture for the home	Feedback about performance	Vacation trips		Recognition in house organ	Use of company machinery or facilities for personal projects
Beer parties	Home shop tools		Coupons redeemable at local stores		Pat on the back	Use of company recreation facilities
	Garden tools		Profit sharing		Smile	
	Clothing				Verbal or nonverbal recognition or praise	
	Club privileges					
	Special assignments					

Source: Fred Luthans and Robert Kreitner, *Organizational Behavior Modification*, Scott, Foresman and Company, Glenview, Ill., 1975, p. 101. Used with permission.

know *how* they are doing, especially if they have some degree of achievement motivation (see Chapter 13). Feedback, in and of itself, can potentially be very positively reinforcing and thus be an effective O.B.Mod. intervention strategy.[16] The supervisor faced with the problem of his people taking unscheduled breaks used such an intervention. In that case, he could not change the antecedent cue (he could not change time) and he could not change the consequence by preventing his people from going to the bathroom. What he did do was calculate the exact cost for each worker in the unit (in terms of lost group piece-rate pay) every time any one of them took an unscheduled break. This information regarding the relatively significant amount of lost pay when any one of them took an unscheduled break was fed back to the employees in his unit. After this feedback intervention, staying on the job increased in frequency and taking unscheduled breaks dramatically decreased. The feedback pointed out the contingency that staying on the job meant more money. At least in this case, the money proved to be a more contingent consequence than the competing contingencies of social rewards with friends at the rest room and withdrawing from the boring job. The feedback in this case merely clarified the monetary contingency, but feedback about performance can by itself be reinforcing.

Money as a Reinforcer   Despite the tendency in recent years to downgrade the importance of money as an organizational reward, there is ample evidence that money can be positively reinforcing for most people. The downgrading of money is partly the result of the motivation theories of Maslow and Herzberg plus the publicity from surveys which consistently place wages and salaries near the middle of the list of employment factors that are important to workers and managers. Although money was probably overemphasized in classical management theory and motivation techniques, the pendulum now has seemed to swing too far in the opposite direction. Money remains a very important but admittedly complex potential reinforcer.

In terms of Maslow's hierarchy, money is often equated only with the most basic level of needs. It is viewed in the material sense of buying food, clothing, and shelter. Yet money has a symbolic as well as an economic material meaning. It can provide power and status and can be a means to measure achievement. In the latter sense, money can be used as an effective positive-reinforcement intervention strategy.

Accepting the importance of money as a possible reinforcer does not mean that the traditional techniques for dispensing it are adequate. Starting with the scientific management movement at the turn of the century, numerous monetary incentive techniques have been developed. Flippo and Munsinger classify them in three broad categories:

[16]Studies showing the positive impact that feedback has on the performance of workers in industrial settings include L. Miller, *The Use of Knowledge of Results in Improving the Performance of Hourly Operators,* Behavioral Research Service, General Electric Company, 1965, and P. S. Hundal, "Knowledge of Performance as an Incentive in Repetitive Industrial Work," *Journal of Applied Psychology,* June 1969, pp. 224–226.

   1 *Base pay* or salary which is given for a job regardless of how it is
performed.
   2 *Variable pay* which gives recognition to individual differences on the job.
   3 *Supplementary pay* which is not directly related to the job or the
individual.[17]

The base-pay technique provides for minimum compensation for a particular job. Pay by the hour for workers and the base salary for managers are
examples. The technique does not reward for above-average, or penalize for
below-average, performance, and it is largely controlled by the job rather than
by the person performing the job. The variable-pay technique attempts to
reward according to individual or group differences and is thus more human-
than job-controlled. Seniority variable-pay plans recognize age and length-of-
service differentials, and merit and individual- or group-incentive plans attempt
to reward contingently on performance. Incentive plans pay personnel according to piece rate, bonus, or profit sharing. Supplementary monetary techniques
have nothing to do with the job or performance per se. The extensive
fringe-benefit package received by employees in most modern organizations is
an example.
   Further refined and newly developed variable-pay or contingent-pay plans
seem to be necessary to the effective use of money as a reinforcer. The base-
and supplementary-pay plans are adequate for their intended purposes, but the
variable-pay plans do not seem to have the desired effects. After an extensive
review of relevant research, Filley and House note,

> Although there seems to be little question that incentive programs frequently result
> in greater productivity, the effects of both individual and group plans have been
> shown to vary with such factors as the attitudes and background of employees, the
> nature of the task performed, informal work norms, and the size of the work
> group.[18]

In other words, monetary incentive plans have many complicating factors.
Edward Lawler supports this conclusion in his book devoted specifically to the
relationship between pay and organizational effectiveness. At the end of the
book he states that "... a pay plan must fit the characteristics of an
organization if it is to be effective; it must be individualized in terms of
organization size, management style, etc."[19] Webber suggests that in order for
money to be reinforcing, the individual must believe that:

   1 increased effort would lead to better performance,

   [17]Edwin B. Flippo and Gary Munsinger, *Management: A Behavioral Approach,* 3d ed., Allyn
and Bacon, Inc., Boston, 1975, p. 334.
   [18]Alan C. Filley and Robert J. House, *Managerial Process and Organizational Behavior,*
Scott, Foresman and Company, Glenview, Ill., 1969, p. 371.
   [19]Edward E. Lawler, *Pay and Organizational Effectiveness: A Psychological View,* McGraw-
Hill Book Company, 1971, p. 284.

    2 your employer can determine the improved performance,

    3 increased money will follow from this performance,

    4 you would value the additional money because it would satisfy your needs, and

    5 you would not have to unduly sacrifice satisfaction of other needs for security, affiliation, and so on.[20]

Analyses of the role of money, such as the points made by Lawler and Webber above, are usually couched in cognitive terms. However, from these cognitive explanations it is very clear that the real key for assessing the use of money as a reinforcer is not necessarily whether it satisfies inner needs but rather how it is administered. In order for money to be an effective positive-reinforcement intervention strategy for O.B.Mod., it must be administered contingently on the performing of the critical behavior.

As Chapter 12 pointed out, about the only reinforcing function that pay currently has in organizations is to reinforce employees for walking up to a pay window or opening an envelope every two weeks or month. With the exception of some piece-rate incentive systems and commissions paid to salespersons, pay is generally not contingent on the performance of critical behaviors. One experimental study clearly demonstrated that money contingently administered can be an effective intervention strategy.[21] A contingently administered monetary bonus plan significantly improved the punctuality of workers in a Mexican division of a large United States corporation. It should be pointed out, however, that the mere fact that money was valued by the Mexican workers in this study does not mean that it would have the same impact on all workers. For example, in a society with an inflationary economy and nonmaterialistic social values, money may be much less likely to be a potential reinforcer for critical job behaviors. Money certainly cannot be automatically dismissed as a positive reinforcer, but, because of its complexity, it may also turn out to be a reward but not a reinforcer. Only post-intervention measurement will determine if in fact money is an effective positive reinforcer for the critical behavior in question.

Natural Reinforcers Besides the contrived rewards which most human resource managers tend to depend upon, there are a host of overlooked natural reinforcers available in every organizational setting. Potentially very powerful, these are the rewards that exist in the natural occurrence of events.[22] Figure 20-5 categorized the natural rewards under social and Premack headings.

Social rewards such as recognition, attention, and praise tend to be very reinforcing for most people. In addition, few people become satiated (filled up)

---

[20]Ross A. Webber, *Management*, Richard D. Irwin, Inc., Homewood, Ill., 1975, p. 108.

[21]Jaime A. Hermann, Ana I. deMontes, Benjamin Dominguez, Francisco deMontes, and B. L. Hopkins, "Effects of Bonuses for Punctuality on the Tardiness of Industrial Workers," *Journal of Applied Behavioral Analysis,* Winter 1973, pp. 563–570.

[22]Luthans and Kreitner, *Organizational Behavior Modification,* op. cit., p. 103.

with social rewards. However, similarly to the contrived rewards, the social rewards must be administered on a contingent basis. For example, a pat on the back or verbal praise that is randomly administered (as was the case under the old human relations approach) can have more of a punishing, "boomerang" effect than of positive reinforcement. But genuine social rewards, contingently administered to the critical behavior, can be a very effective positive-reinforcement intervention strategy. The added benefit of such a strategy in contrast to the use of contrived rewards is that the cost of social rewards to the organization is absolutely nothing.

Premack rewards are derived from the work of psychologist David Premack.[23] Simply stated, the Premack principle is that high-probability behaviors can be used to reinforce low-probability behaviors. For example, if there are two tasks A and B, and the person prefers A over B, the Premack principle would say that the person should perform B first and then A. In this sequence, task A serves as a contingent reinforcer for completing task B, and the person will perform better on both tasks than if the sequence were reversed. In common practice, people often tend to do the task they like best first and put off the less desired task. This common sequence of doing things is in direct violation of the Premack principle and can contribute to ineffective performance.

As an O.B.Mod. intervention strategy, the Premack principle would suggest that a natural reinforcer could always be found. Certain job activities could always be used to reinforce other job activities. No matter how much employees dislike their jobs, there are going to be some things they like to do better than others. Premack sequencing would allow the more desired activities to reinforce less desired activities. The rewards listed under "Premack" in Figure 20-5 can be used to reinforce the less desirable activities on a job.

Punishment/Positive-Reinforcement Strategy The discussion so far has emphasized that the positive-reinforcement strategy is the most effective intervention for O.B.Mod. Yet realistically it is recognized that in some cases the use of punishment to weaken and decelerate undesirable behaviors cannot be avoided. This would be true of something like unsafe behaviors that need to be immediately decreased. However, as was pointed out in Chapter 12, so many negative side effects accompany the use of punishment that it should be avoided if at all possible. Punished behavior tends to be only temporarily suppressed; e.g., if a supervisor reprimands a subordinate for some undesirable behavior, the behavior will decrease in the presence of the supervisor but will surface again when the supervisor is absent. In addition, a punished person becomes very anxious and up-tight; reliance on punishment may have a disastrous impact on employee satisfaction. Perhaps the biggest problem with the use of punishment, however, is that it is very difficult for a supervisor to

[23]David Premack, "Reinforcement Theory," in David Levine (ed.), *Nebraska Symposium on Motivation,* University of Nebraska Press, Lincoln, Nebr., 1965, pp. 123–180.

switch roles from punisher to positive reinforcer. Some supervisors/managers rely on punishment so much in dealing with their subordinates that it is almost impossible for them to effectively administer positive reinforcement. This is a bad situation for the management of human resources because the use of positive reinforcement is a much more effective way of changing organizational behavior. If punishment is deemed to be necessary, the desirable alternative behavior (e.g., safe behavior) should be positively reinforced at the first opportunity. By using this combination strategy, the alternative desirable behavior will begin to replace the undesirable behavior in the person's behavioral repertoire. Punishment should never be used alone as an O.B.Mod. intervention. If punishment is absolutely necessary, it should always be used in combination with positive reinforcement.

Extinction/Positive Reinforcement A much more effective way to decrease undesirable behavior than by punishment is to use an extinction strategy. As Chapter 12 pointed out, extinction has the same impact on behavior as punishment (although it does not act as fast), but extinction does not have the negative side effects of punishment. Whereas punishment could be thought of as the application of a noxious or aversive consequence or the *deliberate withdrawal* of a positively reinforcing consequence, extinction can be simply defined as providing *no* consequence. Obviously, there is a fine line between extinction and the withdrawal of a positive-reinforcer type of punishment. In fact, there is such a fine distinction between the two that some behaviorists do not even deal with extinction. They simply operationally define anything which decreases behavior as punishment. But the important point for human resource management is that undesirable behavior can be decreased without the accompanying negative side effects of punishment. This can be done by simply ignoring the undesirable behavior, i.e., putting it on extinction.

In the functional analysis performed in step 3 of O.B.Mod., the consequences maintaining the critical behavior were identified. The extinction strategy would eliminate those consequences of critical behaviors that were to be decelerated. For example, if complaining was the targeted behavior and the functional analysis revealed that the supervisor's attention to the complaining behavior was maintaining it, the extinction strategy would be to have the supervisor ignore the complaints—not give them any attention. The supervisor may be able to avoid the complainer. Walking away from the person when he starts to complain may be punishing; but if handled properly, i.e., in a nonobvious manner, it could be an extinction strategy without the negative side effects. Again, as with any intervention strategy, whether it was effective in reducing the behavior can be known only by what happened to the frequency measures post-intervention. Also, similarly to the punishment strategy, extinction should be used only in combination with positive reinforcement. The desirable alternative behavior would be positively reinforced at the first opportunity. The positively reinforced behavior would begin to replace the undesirable behavior. In the example of the complaining behavior, when the person did not complain, the supervisor would notice and give attention to the person for constructive comments and noncomplaining behavior.

Because most organizational behaviors are being reinforced by intermittent schedules, which Chapter 12 pointed out are very resistant to extinction, the use of the extinction strategy may take time and patience. But as a long-range strategy for weakening undesirable behaviors and decelerating the frequency of occurrence, extinction can be effective. In general, the very simple rule of thumb to follow in employing an O.B.Mod. intervention strategy is to positively reinforce desirable behaviors and ignore (nonreinforce) undesirable behaviors. This simple guideline may have as big an impact on effective human resource management as any single thing the supervisor/manager can do. But once again it should be pointed out that understanding and using the other concepts and techniques discussed in previous chapters and the following chapter are also necessary for the complex, challenging job of effective human resource management.

Step 5: Evaluation to Assure Performance Improvement

A glaring weakness of most human resource management techniques is the absence of any systematic, built-in evaluation. For example, one comprehensive survey of 154 selected companies concluded that ". . . most organizations are measuring *reaction* to training programs. As we consider the more important and difficult steps in the evaluation process (i.e., *learning, behavior,* and *results*) we find less and less being done, and many of these efforts are superficial and subjective."[24] In another survey, it was concluded that the typical firm that uses job enrichment "believes it has benefited from improvements in employee performance and job satisfaction but has made little effort to formally evaluate the effectiveness of the program, depending on impressions and anecdotal evidence, rather than quantifiable data, for its conclusions."[25] Such haphazard evaluations of human resource management techniques have led to credibility problems. Today all programs dealing with people, whether they are government welfare programs or human resource management programs, are under the pressure of accountability. Donald Campbell has labeled the current climate of accountability the "experimenting society."[26] Human resource managers no longer have the luxury of just trying something new and different and hoping they can improve performance. Today there is pressure for everything that is tried to be *proved* to have value. Like the validity of selection techniques discussed in the last chapter, systematic evaluations of human resource management techniques should have been being done all along.

---

[24]Ralph F. Cantalanello and Donald L. Kirkpatrick, "Evaluating Training Programs—The State of the Art," *Training and Development Journal*, May 1968, p. 9.

[25]Fred Luthans and William E. Reif, "Job Enrichment: Long on Theory, Short on Practice," *Organizational Dynamics*, Winter 1974, p. 33.

[26]Carol Tavris, "The Experimenting Society: A Conversation with Donald T. Campbell," *Psychology Today*, September 1975, pp. 47–56.

O.B.Mod. attempts to meet the credibility and accountability problems head-on by including evaluation as an actual part of the process. In this last step of the model, the need for four levels of evaluation (reaction, learning, behavioral change, and performance improvement) is stressed. The *reaction level* simply refers to whether the people using the approach and those having it used on them like it or not. If O.B.Mod. is well received, if there is a positive reaction to it, there is a better chance of its being used effectively. If it is not well received, there is little chance of its being used effectively. Reaction is obviously important to the evaluation of the O.B.Mod. technique. The second level is learning. This is especially important when first implementing an O.B.Mod. approach. Do the people using the approach understand the theoretical background and underlying assumptions and the meaning and reasons for the steps in the model? If they do not, the model will again tend to be used ineffectively. The third level is aimed at behavioral change. Are behaviors actually being changed? The charting of behaviors gives objective data for this level of evaluation. The fourth and final level, performance improvement, is the most important. The major purpose of O.B.Mod. is not to just receive a favorable reaction, learn the concepts, and change behaviors. The importance of these dimensions is mainly that they contribute to the overriding purpose, which is to improve performance. "Hard" measures (e.g., quantity and quality data, turnover, absenteeism, customer complaints, employee grievances, length of patient stay, number of clients served, and rate of return on investment) and experimental methodology are used whenever possible to systematically evaluate the impact of O.B.Mod. on performance.

EXPERIENCE WITH THE APPLICATION OF O.B.MOD.

As pointed out earlier, O.B.Mod. and related operant-based approaches to human resource management are relatively new. Several years ago *Business Week* reported that a number of companies were either looking into or using behavior modification techniques, but to date only a very few experiences have been reported in the literature.[27] After a discussion of the Emery Air Freight program, the author's own experience with the application and research findings on O.B.Mod. will be presented.

The Emery Air Freight Experience

Reference has already been made to the Emery Air Freight program of feedback and positive reinforcement in the discussion of the steps of O.B.Mod. The Emery experience has been widely publicized in management practitioner-oriented magazines and training films.[28] Under the direction of Edward Feeney, who was then a vice president of Emery and now has his own

[27]"Where Skinner's Theories Work," *Business Week,* Dec. 2, 1972, pp. 64–65.
[28]Ibid.; "Performance Audit, Feedback, and Positive Reinforcement," op. cit.; and "At Emery Air Freight," op. cit. The film on the Emery experience is "Business, Behaviorism, and the Bottom-Line," CRM McGraw-Hill Films, Del Mar, Calif.

consulting firm aimed at implementing his program, it is reported that they were able to realize a $2 million savings over a three-year period.

The program at Emery is similar to the O.B.Mod. approach in that critical performance-related behaviors are identified and then strengthened by positive reinforcement and feedback. For example, it was determined that a critical behavior was whether the dock workers were utilizing the air-freight containers to the fullest advantage. The containers have to be full in order for Emery to make money. Because the employees on this job were extensively trained and because they were constantly reminded of the importance of full containers, both management and the workers estimated that the containers were being optimally utilized about 90 percent of the time. However, the performance audit team found the actual effective utilization to be 45 percent (this is essentially step 2 of O.B.Mod.). Through feedback and social reinforcers this situation was quickly turned around. This same type of approach was success-fully used in many other areas of the company and led to the $2 million savings claim.

Unfortunately, the way that this $2 million was saved is not reported. As far as can be determined, there was no methodologically sound evaluation to determine the direct impact of the Feeney program on the publicized results. In other words, all that exists in the body of knowledge is testimonial evidence that the Emery program worked to the tune of $2 million. What is not satisfactorily answered to date is whether these impressive results were due to the program or to some other factor such as the economy. The same criticism, of course, can be made of much of the literature reporting experiences in the applications of other human resource management techniques.

Field Research on O.B.Mod.

O.B.Mod. is being systematically researched by the author of this text and his colleagues, in particular, Robert Ottemann. The initial study was conducted in a medium-sized, light manufacturing firm located in a large city. Two groups (experimental and control) of nine production-type supervisors were used in the study. The experimental group received training (essentially on the five steps discussed earlier in the chapter) on the O.B.Mod. approach. The results showed that O.B.Mod. had a definite positive impact on reaction, behavior change, and performance (learning was not evaluated in this study). Question-naires administered to the trained supervisors indicated they liked the O.B. Mod. approach and the supervisors indicated their subordinates seemed to react positively. By the charts kept by each trainee (step 2) it was clearly shown that in all cases they were able to change critical behaviors. Examples of behavioral changes accomplished by the supervisors included decreasing the number of complaints, reducing the group scrap rate, decreasing the number of overlooked defective pieces, and reducing the assembly reject rate.[29]

The most important result of the study, however, was the significant

---

[29]These examples are reported in detail, including the charts, in Luthans and Kreitner, *Organizational Behavior Modification,* op. cit., pp. 153–157.

impact that the O.B.Mod. approach had on the performance of the supervisor's departments. By use of a pretest-posttest control group experimental design, it was found that the experimental group's (those supervisors who used O.B. Mod. in their departments) departments outperformed the control group's departments. Figure 20-6 shows the results. Statistical analysis revealed that the department production rates of supervisors who used O.B.Mod. increased significantly more than the department production rates of the control supervisors (those who were not using O.B.Mod.).[30]

A replication in a larger plant obtained almost identical results to those of the original study on all levels of evaluation (including learning).[31] The following summarize some typical cases of behavioral change that occurred in the production area of the larger manufacturing firm.

1   *Use of idle time.* One supervisor had a worker with a lot of idle time. Instead of using this time productively by helping others, the worker would pretend to look busy and stretch out the day. After getting a baseline measure and doing a functional analysis, the supervisor intervened by giving the worker social reinforcers (attention, praise, and recognition) contingent upon the worker's helping out at other jobs during idle time. Eventually the supervisor also reinforced the worker through more responsibility. This approach dramatically increased the worker's productive use of idle time.

[30]Robert Ottemann and Fred Luthans, "An Experimental Analysis of the Effectiveness of an Organizational Behavior Modification Program in Industry," *Academy of Management Proceedings,* 1975, pp. 140–142.
[31]Fred Luthans and Robert Ottemann are currently in the process of writing the results of the replication study.

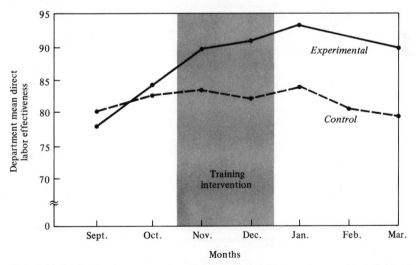

Figure 20-6   Performance results of experimental (those who received O. B. Mod. training) and control groups. *(Source: Robert Ottemann and Fred Luthans, "An Experimental Analysis of the Effectiveness of an Organizational Behavior Modification Program in Industry,"* Academy of Management Proceedings, *1975, p. 141.)*

2 *Low performer.* A production worker in one of the supervisor's departments was producing way below standard (80.3 percent of standard on a six-month baseline). The low performance was not deemed to be an ability, technical, training, or standards problem. After the functional analysis, the supervisor used an intervention of feedback and social reinforcers to increase the types of behaviors that would lead to higher output. This intervention resulted in a 93 percent performance level with no decrease in quality.

3 *Group quality.* One supervisor had a major problem with the quality of work in his department. The baseline measure verified this problem. After the functional analysis, the supervisor used feedback and social reinforcers on the group as a whole. Shortly after use of this intervention strategy the group attained the quality standard for the first time in three years.

4 *Group attendance.* Another supervisor felt he had an attendance problem in his department. The baseline measure revealed 92 percent attendance, which was not as big a problem as he had thought. However, he established the goal of 100 percent. After using daily feedback and social reinforcers on the group, 100 percent was attained very rapidly. An interesting anecdote told by the supervisor was that one of his workers was riding to work from a small town in a car pool early one morning when they hit a deer. The car was disabled by the accident. Coworkers who worked in other departments in the plant and rode in the car pool called relatives and went back home for the day. The worker in his department, however, because she did not want to spoil the 100 percent attendance record, hitchhiked to work by herself and made it on time.

5 *Problem with another department.* One supervisor felt the performance of his department was being adversely affected by the unrecoverable time of truck-lift operators who were not directly under his supervision. After obtaining baseline data and making a functional analysis, the supervisor decided to apply feedback and social reinforcers on the informal group leader and the supervisor of the truck-lift operators. This intervention substantially reduced the unrecoverable time affecting the operational performance of his department.

The five examples above are only representative of the type of behaviors that the supervisors using an O.B.Mod. approach were able to change. Cumulatively, such applied behavioral analysis and change were able to improve the performance of these supervisors' departments in both the original study and the follow-up. At present, such results cannot be generalized to other organizations or even other groups in the organizations studied. But the results so far certainly justify further research and application. Further replications and applications to other levels and other types of organizations are currently under way.

The Need for Other Research Methodologies

Besides the use of control group experimental methods described in the studies reported above, there is also a need for reversal and multiple-baseline designs to test the effectiveness of O.B.Mod.[32] The reversal, sometimes called the ABAB design, is performed in the following manner:

1 First a baseline measure is obtained on the individual or group behavior in question. (A)
2 Then an intervention is made and the behavior is measured until the change stabilizes. (B)
3 Then the intervention is withdrawn and baseline conditions are reestablished. (A)
4 Once the behavior under baseline conditions stabilizes, the intervention is made again. (B)

In this ABAB design the subject(s) serve as their own control. The problem of intersubject variability inherent in a control group design is eliminated. The drawback of this potentially powerful design, however, is that it assumes that the behaviors are capable of being reversed when returning to baseline conditions. Intermittent schedules which are resistant to extinction and the movement from the intervention to a self-reinforcing contingency may undermine this assumption. In addition, a very practical problem in using a reversal design is how to persuade results-minded management to return to baseline conditions if an intervention is working in the desired direction. Few managers are willing to sacrifice results in order to help prove a cause-and-effect relationship.

To get around some of the limitations of reversals, especially the practical problem of reversing desired results, a multiple-baseline design can be employed. In this design, baseline data are gathered across behaviors, individuals, or situations. The design is implemented as follows:

1 Baseline data are obtained on two or more behaviors (or individuals or situations).
2 An intervention is then made on one of the behaviors but baseline conditions are maintained on the other(s).
3 Once the behavior has stabilized after the intervention, the next behavior is given the intervention.
4 This continues until all the behaviors are brought under the intervention.

This design has advantages similar to the reversal and eliminates the practical problem of reversing the behavior but makes the assumption of noninterdependence. In some cases changing one behavior (or individual or situation) may cause the other to change. Despite some of the problems, both the reversal and multiple-baseline designs, especially when used in conjunction with more

[32]See Alan E. Kazdin, "Methodological and Assessment Considerations in Evaluating Reinforcement Programs in Applied Settings," *Journal of Applied Behavioral Analysis*, Fall 1973, pp. 517–531.

conventional control group designs, can greatly contribute to the evaluation of O.B.Mod. in the future.

ANALYSIS OF THE POSSIBLE ETHICAL ISSUES[33]

Skinner's work in general and some of the applications made in mental hospitals, clinics, classrooms, and especially prisons have generated emotional criticism and much controversy. Surprisingly, this concern has not yet seemed to carry over to the applications in management. To date there are only a few scattered criticisms, on ethical grounds, reported in the literature,[34] but there are probably many managers and potential managers who feel uneasy about using an O.B.Mod. type of an approach. Most would probably agree that it works but feel it is somehow wrong. Such concerns must be fully aired and constructively analyzed if O.B.Mod. is going to be a viable human resource management approach in the future. The ethical problems must be anticipated and discussed rather than simply reacted to.

Popular Criticism of Behavior Modification

Much of the popular criticism of Skinner's work revolves around his heavy dependence on the use of lower animals (especially the white rat) in developing the operant learning principles. The criticism that behavior modification tends to equate rats with humans is unfounded. The behaviorist would be the first to admit that rat and human behaviors are *not* the same. But at the same time they would point out that the *mechanism* of behavioral control is the same. From the operant perspective, all behaviors, animal and human, depend on their consequences. The transition that behaviorism has made from animals to the mentally retarded to children to normal adults has been sufficiently demonstrated by both empirical research and practical application.

Besides the "applied ratamorphism" charge, another problem stems from the villainous portrayal of behavior control in popular literature, television, and the movies. The simple fact is that although the behavior control techniques portrayed in popular movies like *A Clockwork Orange* may be entertaining (if sinister manipulation and sadistic punishment can be called entertaining) and theoretically possible, they have nothing to do with the approach discussed in this chapter. Aversive conditioning and severe forms of punishment have no more chance of being used in human resource management than any other preposterous diabolical scheme.

Legitimate Ethical Concerns

Getting the popular and spectacular but highly unreasonable ethical charges out of the way leaves the more legitimate ethical concerns surrounding control per

---

[33]The author is indebted to Professor Robert Kreitner for many of the thoughts expressed in this section.

[34]For example, see: M. Hammer, "The Application of Behavior Conditioning Procedures to the Problems of Quality Control: Comment," *Academy of Management Journal,* December 1971, pp. 529–532; and Fred Fry, "Operant Conditioning and O.B.Mod.: Of Mice and Men," *Personnel,* July–August 1974, pp. 17–24.

se, particularly individual freedom and dignity, and the question of who controls the controllers. First of all it should be recognized that control of behavior has, is, and will continue to exist regardless of whether it is purposeful or not. The primary concern should probably not be with control per se but instead with the beneficiary of the behavioral control. If behavioral control is misapplied for selfish purposes, the charge of being unethical seems legitimate. On the other hand, if the control is used for more effective management for the mutually beneficial consequences for both the person being controlled and the organization, it would seem to be on ethical grounds.

The individual-freedom-and-dignity issue popularized by Skinner's book *Beyond Freedom and Dignity* largely boils down to a philosophical discussion of relative ethics. The O.B.Mod. approach which emphasizes positive control and creating a reinforcing organization environment can increase rather than decrease an employee's freedom and dignity. This is especially true relative to the existing dependence on negative control found in most of today's organizations. The same can be said of the question of who controls the controllers. This is certainly not as big a problem in management application as it is in other applications. Whether in a public or private organization, the authority structure would always make the controller responsible to someone higher in the hierarchy. In addition, through countercontrol, subordinates can control their supervisors as well as be controlled by them. A major goal of O.B.Mod. is to create a mutually reinforcing environment so that participants may be self-reinforced for pursuing organizational objectives.

The Charge of Limited Application and Manipulation

Those who argue that applied behavior analysis and change can have only very limited application in a complex organizational setting must recognize that the underlying theory and mechanisms hold in very simple or in very complex environments. The previous section demonstrated how O.B.Mod. has been and can be applied in complex organizational settings. Certainly O.B.Mod. is not the only approach to effective human resource management, and there is a challenge for more research and broader application. This is why O.B.Mod. is exciting; it is relatively new in terms of application, and to date there is little research support, but it is built on a very well developed, sound theoretical base.

As far as being manipulative, the same charges could be made of the other techniques discussed in previous chapters. O.B.Mod. seems to be no more and no less manipulative than other human resource management approaches. If anything, in O.B.Mod. the environmental contingencies are manipulated, not the individual.

A Final Word on Ethical Implications

Issues such as measuring on-the-job behaviors cannot be automatically dismissed. However, such measurement is certainly not new with O.B.Mod. (industrial engineers have been doing this since the turn of the century), and, as discussed earlier, there are ways of obtaining behavioral data without contaminating the data or compromising the individual's privacy. In the final analysis, the ethical answer to O.B.Mod. or any other technique lies in the professional integrity of the manager using the approach and the mutual organizational and individual beneficiaries. O.B.Mod. should in no way attempt to be secretive or manipulative. If O.B.Mod. is to be an effective human resource management approach, it must be completely ethical from a societal, organizational, and individual standpoint.

SUMMARY

This chapter uses the O.B.Mod. model as an approach to applied behavioral analysis and change. The model consists of identifying critical performance-related behaviors; obtaining a baseline measure; functionally analyzing the antecedents and the consequences of the critical behavior; intervening by using a positive-reinforcement strategy to accelerate desirable critical behaviors and an extinction strategy to decelerate undesirable critical behaviors; and evaluating to ensure performance improvement. This is an applied, external approach to organizational behavior rather than an internal, motivational approach. O.B.Mod. represents only one, but potentially very powerful, approach to human resource management. It is given detailed attention so that the reader can gain some depth in an applied approach, but it should be recognized that the techniques covered in the other chapters are also important to effective human resource management in today's organizations.

QUESTIONS FOR DISCUSSION AND REVIEW

1 What are some methods that can be used to identify critical behaviors? What are some simple guidelines that can be used?
2 One of the quotes said, "In effect, behavior charts are mini behavioral experiments." Explain.
3 Why is positive reinforcement a more effective intervention strategy than punishment? What, if anything, is the difference between a punishment strategy and an extinction strategy?
4 What is the difference between contrived and natural rewards? Which is more effective to use as an O.B.Mod. intervention strategy? Why?
5 How do reversal and multiple-baseline designs differ from an experiment using a control group? What is the difference between reversals and multiple baselines? What are their strengths and weaknesses?
6 How, if possible, could you convince someone that an approach like O.B.Mod. is an ethical technique for human resource management?

CASE: UP THE PIECE RATE

Larry Ames had successfully completed a company training program on O.B.Mod. He liked the approach and started using it on the workers in his department. Following the O.B.Mod. model, he identified several critical behaviors, measured and analyzed them, and used a positive-reinforcement/extinction intervention strategy. His evaluation showed a significant improvement in the performance of his department. Over coffee one day he commented to one of the other supervisors "This contingent reinforcement approach really works. Before, the goody-goody people up in personnel were always telling us to try to understand and be nice to our workers. Frankly, I couldn't buy that. In the first place I don't think there is anybody who can really *understand* my people, let alone me. More important, though, is that under this approach I am only nice *contingently*—contingent upon good performance. That makes a lot more sense, and my evaluation proves that it works." The other supervisor commented, "You are being reinforced for using the reinforcement technique on your people." Larry said, "Sure am. Just like the trainer said: 'Behavior that is reinforced will strengthen and repeat itself.' I'm so reinforced that I am starting to use it on my wife and kids at home, and you know what? It works there, too."

The next week Larry was called into the department head's office and told, "Larry, as you know, your department has shown a substantial increase in performance since you completed the O.B.Mod. program. I have sent our industrial engineer down there to analyze your standards. I have received her report and it looks like we will have to adjust your rates upward by 10 percent. Otherwise we are going to have to pay too much incentive pay. I'm sure you can use some of the things you learned in that O.B.Mod. program to break the news to your people. Good luck, and keep up the good work."

1   Do you think Larry's boss, the department head, attended the O.B. Mod. program? Analyze the department head's action in terms of O.B.Mod.

2   What do you think will be Larry's reaction now and in the future? How do you think Larry's people will react?

3   Given the 10 percent increase in standards, is there any way that Larry could still use the O.B.Mod. approach with his people? With his boss? How?

SELECTED REFERENCES

Adam, Everett E., Jr.: "Behavior Modification in Quality Control," *Academy of Management Journal,* December 1975, pp. 662–679.

"At Emery Air Freight: Positive Reinforcement Boosts Performance," *Organizational Dynamics,* Winter 1973, pp. 41–50.

Beatty, Richard W., and Craig Eric Schneier, "A Case for Positive Reinforcement," *Business Horizons,* April 1975, pp. 57–66.

Berger, Chris J., L. L. Cummings, and Herbert G. Heneman, III: "Expectancy Theory and Operant Conditioning Predictions of Performance under Variable Ratio and Continuous Schedules of Reinforcement," *Organizational Behavior and Human Performance,* October 1975, pp. 227–243.

Fry, Fred: "Operant Conditioning and O.B.Mod.: Of Mice and Men," *Personnel,* July–August 1974, pp. 17–24.

Goldstein, Arnold P., and Melvin Sorcher: "Changing Managerial Behavior by Applied

Learning Techniques," *Training and Development Journal,* March 1973, pp. 36–39.

Heiman, Gary W.: "A Note on Operant Conditioning Principles Extrapolated to the Theory of Management," *Organizational Behavior and Human Performance,* April 1975, pp. 165–170.

Kazdin, Alan E.: "Methodological and Assessment Considerations in Evaluating Reinforcement Programs in Applied Settings," *Journal of Applied Behavioral Analysis,* Fall 1973, pp. 432–539.

Kreitner, Robert: "PM—A New Method of Behavior Change," *Business Horizons,* December 1975, pp. 79–86.

Latham, Gary P., Kenneth N. Wexley, and Elliott D. Pursell: "Training Managers to Minimize Rating Errors in the Observation of Behavior," *Journal of Applied Psychology,* October 1975, pp. 550–555.

Luthans, Fred: "An Organizational Behavior Modification (O.B.Mod.) Approach to O.D.," *Organization and Administrative Sciences* (in press).

Luthans, Fred, and Robert Kreitner: "The Management of Behavioral Contingencies," *Personnel,* July–August 1974, pp. 7–16.

Luthans, Fred, and Robert Kreitner: *Organizational Behavior Modification,* Scott, Foresman and Company, Glenview, Ill., 1975.

Luthans, Fred, and Robert Kreitner: "The Role of Punishment in Organizational Behavior Modification," *Public Personnel Management,* May–June 1973, pp. 156–161.

Luthans, Fred, and David Lyman: "Training Supervisors to Use Organizational Behavior Modification," *Personnel,* September–October 1973, pp. 38–44.

Luthans, Fred, and Robert Ottemann: "Motivation versus Learning Approaches to Organizational Behavior," *Business Horizons,* December 1973, pp. 55–62.

Luthans, Fred, and Donald D. White, Jr.: "Behavior Modification: Application to Manpower Management," *Personnel Administration,* July–August 1971, pp. 41–47.

Mawhinney, Thomas C.: "Operant Terms and Concepts in the Description of Individual Work Behavior: Some Problems of Interpretation, Application, and Evaluation," *Journal of Applied Psychology,* December 1975, pp. 704–712.

Nord, Walter R.: "Beyond the Teaching Machine: The Neglected Area of Operant Conditioning in the Theory and Practice of Management," *Organizational Behavior and Human Performance,* November 1969, pp. 375–401.

Organ, Dennis W., and Charles N. Greene: "The Perceived Purposefulness of Job Behavior: Antecedents and Consequences," *Academy of Management Journal,* March 1974, pp. 69–78.

Ottemann, Robert, and Fred Luthans: "An Experimental Analysis of the Effectiveness of an Organizational Behavior Modification Program in Industry," *Academy of Management Proceedings,* 1975, pp. 140–142.

Patten, Thomas H., Jr.: "Relating Learning Theory to Behavior Change in Organizations," *Human Resource Management,* Winter 1974, pp. 27–36.

Schneier, Craig Eric: "Behavior Modification in Management: A Review and Critique," *Academy of Management Journal,* September 1974, pp. 528–548.

Walter, Gordon A.: "Acted versus Natural Models for Performance-Oriented Behavior Change in Task Groups," *Journal of Applied Psychology,* June 1975, pp. 303–307.

Walter, Gordon A.,: "Effects of Video Tape Feedback and Modeling on the Behaviors of Task Group Members," *Human Relations,* March 1975, pp. 121–138.

Yukl, Gary A., and Gary P. Latham: "Consequences of Reinforcement Schedules and Incentive Magnitudes for Employee Performance: Problems Encountered in an Industrial Setting," *Journal of Applied Psychology,* June 1975, pp. 294–298.

Chapter 21

Organization Development

Organization development, or simply OD, has become associated with the applied aspects of organization behavior. OD is concerned mainly with the planned change of complex organizations. The development of an organization's human resources and its improved performance are the major aims of OD efforts. Many of the concepts and techniques (e.g., assessment centers, job enrichment, MBO, and O. B. Mod.) discussed in previous chapters could be considered part of OD. However, this chapter is directly concerned with the general issue of the management of change and with the widely recognized OD techniques.

After a general discussion of the impact of change, the overall characteristics of OD are explored. Then the three traditional OD techniques of sensitivity training, grid training, and survey-feedback are presented and analyzed. Next, a typology of OD interventions is given with particular attention devoted to the interpersonal/intergroup OD interventions of process consultation, third-party peacemaking, and team building. Finally, the last part of the chapter discusses the increasingly popular approach to interpersonal relations and development called "transactional analysis."

THE IMPACT OF CHANGE

Everyone today is keenly aware of and concerned about change. Kolasa summarizes the attitude toward change as follows:

We may not recognize it or otherwise be cognizant of it; we may oppose it or we may even try to accelerate it. No matter what our position may be, change makes its course in the evolution of human effort. Change may take place so slowly that it is not perceptible in one generation or even two, or it may occur with such rapidity that we are left somewhat breathless in the wake of the waves.[1]

There is little doubt of the dominant role that change has played in contemporary society, and this is nowhere more evident than in its organizations. All of today's organizations are vibrating from the external and internal forces of change.

External Forces for Change

There are many external forces bombarding the modern organization which make change inevitable. These forces can be categorized into three broad areas:

> **1** The highly competitive marketplace in the private, and also in many respects the public, sector of the economy
> **2** The tremendously accelerating rate of technological advance
> **3** The highly volatile changes that are occurring in both the physical and social environment.[2]

In order to remain competitive, organizations must forge ahead on all three fronts. Both private and public organizations cannot compete in today's marketplace by standing still or going backward. If they do, they go the way of the buggy-whip factory. They die in the long run. Change as a technological force was brought out in Chapter 4. It was emphasized that the technological impact on organizations has reached dramatic proportions. The computer alone, with all its ramifications, has been a major force for organizational change. The rapidly changing physical-ecological and social environment was also discussed in Chapter 4. Faced with limited physical resources and social pressures for equal-opportunity employment for minorities and women, environmental protection, employee safety, and quality, safe products, the modern organization faces a stiff challenge now and in the forseeable future to solve these problems. If it does not, it simply will not survive, at least in its present form. As has been repeatedly brought out in this book, the external, open-system environment has, is, and will have a tremendous impact on organizations and the behavior of their participants.

Internal Forces for Change

Many internal forces are also precipitating change in the modern organization. The most usual types of internal change have to do with machinery and

---

[1]Blair J. Kolasa, *Introduction to Behavioral Science,* John Wiley & Sons, Inc., New York, 1969, p. 348.

[2]James J. Donnelly, Jr., James L. Gibson, and John M. Ivancevich, *Fundamentals of Management,* rev. ed., Business Publications, Inc., Austin, Tex., 1975, pp. 269–270.

equipment; methods and procedures; work standards, personnel, and organizational adjustments; and interrelationships with those who hold power, authority, status, and responsibility.[3] This list shows that internal change affects both organizational and human variables. One of the best ways to understand the internal aspects of change is through the study of the organizational dynamics of change and human resistance to it.

Organizational Dynamics of Change   Change may affect and be affected by the major subsystems of the formal organization. Structurally, both the classical and modern approaches are all vitally concerned with change. The classical approach to the management of change relied on organizational principles such as unity of command, equal authority and responsibility, limited spans of control, and delegation of routine activities. As discussed in Chapter 3, this approach was too simplistic, and it generally ignored important behavioral variables. Yet this classical approach still plays a significant role in the analysis and management of change. As Harold Leavitt notes, "It is still a commonplace for consultants or organization planning departments to try to solve organizational problems by redefining areas of responsibility and authority or by redesigning the approved set of organizational channels."[4] The classical structural approach also depends on concepts like decentralization, departmentation, and line-staff arrangements to analyze and effect change. These structural concepts were fully discussed and analyzed in Chapter 6. In Chapter 7 modern structural concepts were examined. The project, matrix, free form, and systems organizational structures were presented as being most relevant and adaptable to change. They are specifically designed to manage change effectively.

The processes of decision making, communication, and control, plus technology, also play essential roles in the organizational dynamics of internal change. Each affects and is affected by change. The content of the earlier chapters on these subjects is directly applicable to the present discussion of change.

Human Resistance to Change   The role of human resistance to change is important to the study of organizational change. Human resistance to change is part of the dynamics of change. Resistance to change is a fact of organizational life and takes many forms. Some of the ways humans resist change in an organization were described by Paul Lawrence as follows:

1   Persistent reduction in output
2   Increase in the number of "quits" and requests for transfer

[3]Edgar G. Williams, "Changing Systems and Behavior," *Business Horizons*, August 1969, p. 54.
[4]Harold Leavitt, "Applied Organizational Change in Industry: Structural, Technological and Humanistic Approaches," in James March (ed.), *Handbook of Organizations*, Rand McNally & Company, Chicago, 1965, p. 1147.

    3 Chronic quarrels and sullen hostility
    4 Wildcat or slowdown strikes
    5 The expression of a lot of pseudological reasons why a change will not work[5]

Why do humans resist change? Traditionally, technological factors were given as the fundamental reason for resistance. However, in his classic original analysis, Lawrence pointed out that purely human and social factors also contribute to resistance. Fifteen years later, he still firmly believed this to be true. Some of the more common reasons why humans resist change follow:

    1 *Insecurity.* This is the most obvious reason why humans resist change. People are generally comfortable with the status quo. Change often is viewed as a threat to their security.
    2 *Economics.* A very practical reason why persons, especially in the lower levels of an organization, oppose change is that they are afraid of possible economic loss. Being replaced by a machine is a real threat to most workers. Today, with the increasing use of the computer. many middle managers are also beginning to experience the same fear.
    3 *Sociopsychological.* Although insecurity and economics are partly sociopsychological in nature, there are also perceptual, emotional, and cultural barriers to change. Perceptually wrong interpretations of the change may lead to resistance. Persons may react emotionally to a change by bringing fears and prejudices to the surface. Persons facing change in an organization are influenced by their cultural values which they bring to the situation with them.[6]

Despite the widespread resistance to change found at all levels of the modern organization, it should not be automatically assumed that participants will resist all change, or if they do resist, that it is inherently bad for the organization. As indicated above, resistance will occur when the change is viewed as a threat or barrier. If the change is not seen as endangering the person's security or economic position and does not erect sociopsychological barriers, there may be no resistance. In fact, change may be welcomed by a person because it may remove a threat or barrier. It is possible for both the individual and the organization to benefit from resistance. In most cases, however, an attempt should be made to overcome the resistance through effective management of change. This management of change has become known as "organization development."

CHARACTERISTICS OF ORGANIZATION DEVELOPMENT

Traditionally, the management of change and the development of human resources were handled in a variety of ways. Bennis identified eight types of

---

[5]Paul R. Lawrence, "How to Deal with Resistance to Change," *Harvard Business Review,* May–June 1954, reprinted with retrospective commentary in Gene Dalton and Paul Lawrence (eds.), *Organizational Change and Development,* Richard D. Irwin and The Dorsey Press, Homewood, Ill., 1970, p. 181.

[6]Williams, op. cit., pp. 55–56.

traditional change programs which management relied upon: (1) exposition and propagation, (2) elite corps, (3) human relations training, (4) staff, (5) scholarly consultation, (6) circulation of ideas, (7) developmental research, and (8) action research. Although recognizing that each of these change programs has some positive attributes, Bennis believes that inherent in each is some bias or flaw which weakens its effectiveness. As examples, he notes that graduates of human relations training programs often act like nonalumni shortly after returning to their organizational base; that the staff programs may be limited by the unresolved conflicts between line and staff; and that the elite strategy may focus on the individual and not the organization.[7]

Lawrence is also critical of the highly simplistic nature of traditional approaches to change. In the classic paper mentioned earlier, he recommended techniques like putting people's needs into the design of technological systems or making special efforts to help newly formed work groups to develop meaningful team relations quickly. However, in the retrospective analysis made fifteen years later, he was not so confident about these relatively simple solutions. He stated that "... they do not always enable management to prevent situations from developing in which some individuals win while others lose."[8]

OD: The Modern Approach to the Management of Change

The modern approach to the management of change and the development of human resources is called *organization development.* Although there is still not a generally agreed-upon definition, Bennis suggests that OD is

> ... a response to change, a complex educational strategy intended to change the beliefs, attitudes, values, and structure of organizations so that they can better adapt to new technologies, markets, and challenges, and the dizzying rate of change itself.[9]

Abstracting from the above type of definition and summarizing what the leaders in the OD movement emphasize, Filley, House, and Kerr suggest that several elements make up the modern OD approach to the management of change.[10] The following summarizes the major characteristics of OD.

1 *Planned change.* Bennis was one of the first to emphasize the need for systematic, planned change. This "planned" emphasis separates OD efforts from other kinds of more haphazard changes that are frequently occurring in modern organizations.

2 *Comprehensive change.* Most OD experts emphasize that OD efforts

[7]Warren G. Bennis, "Theory and Method in Applying Behavioral Science to Planned Organizational Change," *Journal of Applied Behavioral Science,* October–November–December 1965, p. 346.

[8]Lawrence, op. cit., p. 196.

[9]Warren G. Bennis, *Organization Development: Its Nature, Origins, and Prospects,* Addison-Wesley Publishing Company, Inc., Reading, Mass., 1969, p. 2.

[10]Alan C. Filley, Robert J. House, and Steven Kerr, *Managerial Process and Organizational Behavior,* 2d ed., Scott, Foresman and Company, Glenview, Ill., 1976, p. 488.

generally involve a "total system." The entire organization or an identifiable unit within it is the unit of analysis.

3 *Emphasis upon work groups.* Although some OD efforts are aimed at individual and organizational change, most are oriented toward groups. There is a sociological flavor to much of OD.

4 *Long-range change.* OD experts emphasize that the process takes months, or even in some cases years, to implement. Although there is pressure for quick results, the OD process is not intended to be a stopgap measure.

5 *Participation of a change agent.* Most OD experts stress the need for an outside, third-party "change agent" or catalyst. "Do-it-yourself" programs are discouraged.

6 *Emphasis upon intervention and action research.* The OD approach makes an active intervention in the ongoing activities of the organization. Action research attacks practical problems but differs from applied research in that the researcher (change agent) is involved in the actual change process in OD.

The desired organizational outcomes of OD efforts include increased effectiveness, problem solving, and adaptability. For human resource development, OD attempts to provide opportunities to be "human" and to increase awareness, participation, and influence. An overriding goal is to integrate individual and organizational objectives.[11]

Historical Development of OD

As with other behavioral approaches, it is difficult to pinpoint the precise beginning of OD. Wendell French and Cecil Bell, who have done the most work on the historical development of OD, feel that, "Organization development has emerged from applied behavioral science and social psychology and from subsequent efforts to apply laboratory training and survey-feedback insights into total systems."[12] Thus, the two major historical stems for OD are laboratory training and survey-feedback. The work of the pioneering social psychologist Kurt Lewin was instrumental in both approaches.

TRADITIONAL APPROACHES TO OD

Laboratory training applications to OD have two major techniques. One is the widely recognized t-group or sensitivity training approach, and the other is the very popular grid training. After a discussion of these two techniques, the survey-feedback stem of OD is presented and analyzed. These three techniques represent the traditional, but still widely used, approaches to OD.

Sensitivity Training

Sensitivity or t (training)-group training evolved from the group dynamics concepts of Kurt Lewin. The first specific sensitivity training session was held

---

[11]Ibid., pp. 489–490.
[12]Wendell L. French and Cecil H. Bell, Jr., *Organization Development*, Prentice-Hall, Inc., Englewood Cliffs, N. J., 1973, p. 29.

in 1946 on the campus of the State Teachers College in New Britain, Connecticut. The more widely recognized beginning was in 1947 at the National Training Laboratory in Bethel, Maine. Besides Lewin, Kenneth Benne, Leland Bradford, and Ronald Lippitt played important roles in the early sensitivity training effort.

Since the beginning at Bethel, sensitivity training has become a technique widely used by a variety of professionals (psychotherapists, counselors, educators, nurses, social workers, religious workers, and organizational trainers and consultants).[13] There are at least six major target populations to which laboratory training is aimed:

    1 Professional helpers with educational and consultative responsibilities (workers in religion, wives of corporation presidents, school superintendents, classroom teachers, juvenile court judges, and youth workers)
    2 Middle and top management
    3 Total membership of a given organization (Red Cross executives, a family, or a business organization)
    4 Laymen and/or professionals in a heterogeneous occupational group
    5 Children, youth, and college students
    6 Persons with different cultural and/or national backgrounds[14]

This list points out that sensitivity training has very diverse applications. However, for present discussion purposes, it is viewed in terms of its use as a technique of organizational development.

Goals of Sensitivity Training   There are many different goals that sensitivity training attempts to accomplish. Some training sessions stress the personal development aspects, others stress the ways to become a more effective group member, and still others stress both. Overall, the goals may be summarized as follows:[15]

    1 To make participants increasingly aware of, and sensitive to, the emotional reactions and expressions in themselves and others.
    2 To increase the ability of participants to perceive, and to learn from, the consequences of their actions through attention to their own and others' feelings.
    3 To stimulate the clarification and development of personal values and goals consonant with a democratic and scientific approach to problems of social and personal decision and action.
    4 To develop concepts and theoretical insights which will serve as tools in linking personal values, goals, and intentions to actions consistent with these inner factors and with the requirements of the situation.

---

[13]Leland Bradford, Jack R. Gibb, and Kenneth Benne (eds.), *T-Group Theory and Laboratory Method,* John Wiley & Sons, Inc., New York, 1964, p. ix.
[14]Kenneth Benne, Leland Bradford, and Ronald Lippitt, "The Laboratory Method," in Bradford et al., op. cit., pp. 19–22.
[15]Ibid., pp. 16–17.

5 To foster the achievement of behavioral effectiveness in transactions with the participants' environments.

Figure 21-1 relates and summarizes these major purposes. In a systems sense, the goals interact and are interdependent with one another.

Because of the rapid growth in popularity of sensitivity training and the tremendous emotional impact, both pro and con, that it has on people, many misconceptions exist. To clarify these misconceptions and at the same time to gain a better understanding of what sensitivity training is all about. Argyris lists the things which sensitivity training is *not:*[16]

1 Sensitivity training is not a set of hidden, manipulative processes by which individuals can be brainwashed into thinking, believing, and feeling the way someone might want them to without realizing what is happening to them.

2 Sensitivity training is not an educational process guided by a staff leader who is covertly in control and who by some magic hides this fact from the participants.

3 The objective of sensitivity training is not to suppress conflict or to get everyone to like one another.

4 Sensitivity training does not attempt to teach people to be callous and disrespectful of society and to dislike those who live a less-open life.

5 Sensitivity training is neither psychoanalysis nor intensive group therapy.

6 Sensitivity training is not necessarily dangerous, but it must focus on feelings.

7 Sensitivity training is not education for authoritarian leadership. Its

[16]Chris Argyris, "T-Groups for Organizational Effectiveness," *Harvard Business Review,* March–April 1964, pp. 68–70.

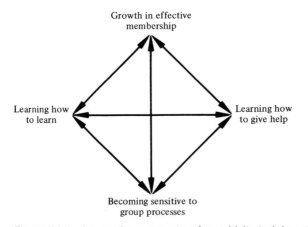

Figure 21-1 Interacting purposes of sensitivity training. *(Source: Leland P. Bradford, "Membership and the Learning Process," in Leland P. Bradford et al. (eds.), T-Group Theory and Laboratory Method, John Wiley & Sons, Inc., New York, 1964, p. 215. Used with permission.)*

objective is to develop effective, reality-centered leaders. The most sensitivity training can do is help individuals to see certain unintended consequences and costs of their leadership and to develop other leadership styles if they wish.

8 Sensitivity training does not guarantee change as a result of attendance at the training sessions.

Design and Conduct of Sensitivity Laboratories Sensitivity training may be designed as either a "stranger-lab" or a "cousin-" or "family-lab." In the stranger-labs, the participants are from different organizations and therefore do not know one another. The sequence of events runs something like this:[17]

1 In the beginning, there is a purposeful lack of directive leadership, formal agenda, and recognized power and status. This creates a behavioral vacuum which the participants fill with enormously rich projections of traditional behavior.

2 In the second phase, the trainer becomes open, nondefensive, and empathetic, and expresses his or her own feelings in a minimally evaluative way. However, the major impact on each participant comes from the feedback received from the here-and-now behavior of the other group members.

3 In the third phase, interpersonal relationships develop. The members serve as resources to one another and facilitate experimentation with new personal, interpersonal, and collaborative behavior.

4 The last phase attempts to explore the relevance of the experience in terms of "back home" situations and problems.

In the cousin-labs, the participants are from the same organization but not the same subunit, while in the family-labs they are all from the same subunit. These cousin- and family-labs are used more frequently in organizational development than the stranger-labs are. The conduct of these two labs may be the same as that described for the stranger-lab, but, more often, greater attention is given to intergroup linkages. Typically, in the cousin- and family-labs there is an interfacing of diagnostic surveys, interviews, and confrontation sessions dealing with a variety of policy, problem-solving, and interpersonal issues.[18]

Evaluation of Sensitivity Training Both the critics and the advocates of sensitivity training emotionally defend their position. George Odiorne, one of the leading critics, reported that he had incurred personal attacks from the other side. Personalized rebuttals to Odiorne's position typically take the following line of reasoning: "The very fact that you attack sensitivity training indicates that you are in favor of autocratic management and therefore *need* sensitivity training to straighten out your personal inadequacies."[19] Odiorne

[17]Andre Delbecq, "Sensitivity Training," *Training and Development Journal,* January 1970, p. 33.

[18]Ibid.

[19]George S. Odiorne, *Training by Objectives,* The Macmillan Company, New York, 1970, p. 51.

thinks that this type of argument, which sets itself above and immune to attacks, is a sure sign of weakness. The heated debate still continues. To date, not enough research evidence has accumulated to fully support either side.

One of the most comprehensive reviews of the research literature on sensitivity training was conducted by Dunnette and Campbell. They concluded that:

> Laboratory education has not been shown to bring about any marked change in one's standing on objective measures of attitudes, values, outlooks, interpersonal perceptions, self-awareness, or interpersonal sensitivity. In spite of these essentially negative results on objective measures, individuals who have been trained by laboratory education methods are more likely to be seen as changing their job behavior than are individuals in similar job settings who have not been trained.[20]

Although those who have gone through sensitivity training *seem* to be more open, to have better understanding of themselves and their effect on others, and to show improved communication and leadership skills, the results have not been proved by scientific research. In addition, many other important aspects of sensitivity training have undergone practically no research—good or bad. Dunnette and Campbell noted the lack of research on the effects of sensitivity training on a person's skills in analyzing information, facing up to and resolving interpersonal conflict, and deriving and implementing solutions to organizational problems.[21]

Although more recent interpretations of research findings are positive[22] as well as negative,[23] there is general agreement from everyone concerned that more scientific research on the effectiveness of sensitivity training is badly needed.

There is some evidence that practitioners are not too enthusiastic about using sensitivity training. A recent survey of personnel directors of large firms found that about twice as many respondents indicated that they would *not* recommend the use of sensitivity training as those who said they would recommend it.[24] However, despite the lack of research back-up to date and the apparent reluctance of many practitioners to recommend it, the use of sensitivity training can probably be justified in some situations with selected personnel. In other words, as with the other techniques discussed in this book, there is a need for developing some contingency guidelines for the use of

---

[20]Marvin D. Dunnette and John P. Campbell, "Laboratory Education: Impact on People and Organizations," *Industrial Relations*, October 1968, p. 23.

[21]Ibid.

[22]For example, see: Robert T. Golembiewski and Stokes B. Carrigan, "The Persistence of Laboratory-induced Changes in Organizational Styles," *Administrative Science Quarterly*, September 1970, pp. 330–340.

[23]For example, see: John H. DeMichele, "Measuring the Effectiveness of Laboratory Training in Organizational Development," *Academy of Management Proceedings*, 1972, pp. 47–48.

[24]William J. Kearney and Desmond D. Martin, "Sensitivity Training: An Established Management Development Tool?" *Academy of Management Journal*, December 1974, pp. 755–760.

sensitivity training. There is little question that sensitivity training has been subjected to many unwarranted generalizations and abuses. These problems must be corrected if sensitivity training is to be a truly effective organization development technique for the future.

Grid Training

Grid training is an outgrowth of the managerial grid approach to leadership discussed in Chapter 18 and is an instrumented approach to laboratory training. Benne explains the nature of the instrumented approach as follows:

> In the instrumented T-group, the trainer is removed from direct participation in the group. In his place, a series of self-administered instruments are introduced. The feedback provided by the compilation and analysis of the data provided by all members in responding to these instruments serves as a principal steering mechanism in the group's development and in the learnings which members achieve.[25]

A 9,9 position on Blake and Mouton's leadership grid shown in Chapter 18, indicating a maximum concern for both people and production, is an implied goal of grid training. A more comprehensive step-by-step approach is taken when grid training is used in OD. Whereas sensitivity training is more of a tool for OD, the grid training approach offers a complete plan for organization development. Blake and his colleagues explain that,

> The Grid helps to give businessmen a language system for describing their current managerial preferences. It also involves classroom materials and an educational program for designing more productive problem-solving relationships. Even more important, the program is meant to be taught and applied by line managers over a time span involving six overlapping phases.[26]

Summarized, the six phases of grid training for OD are the following:[27]

1 *Laboratory-seminar training.* The purpose of this first phase is to introduce the participants to the overall concepts and materials used in grid training. The seminars that are held are not like therapeutic sensitivity training. There is more structure and concentration on leadership styles than on developing self- and group insights.

2 *Team development.* This is an extension of the first phase. Members of the same department are brought together to chart how they are going to attain a 9,9 position on the grid. In this stage, what was learned in the orientation stage is applied to the actual organizational situation.

---

[25]Kenneth D. Benne, "History of the T-Group in the Laboratory Setting," in Bradford et al., op. cit., p. 129.

[26]Robert R. Blake, Jane S. Mouton, Louis B. Barnes, and Larry E. Greiner, "Breakthrough in Organization Development," *Harvard Business Review,* November–December 1964, p. 134.

[27]Ibid., pp. 137–138.

3 *Intergroup development.* Whereas the first two phases are aimed at managerial development, this phase marks the beginning of overall organization development. There is a shift from the micro level of individual and group development to a macro level of group-to-group organization development. Conflict situations between groups are identified and analyzed.

4 *Organizational goal setting.* In the manner of management by objectives, in this phase the participants contribute to and agree upon the important goals for the organization. A sense of commitment and self-control is instilled in participants.

5 *Goal attainment.* In this phase the participants attempt to accomplish the goals which they set in the fourth phase. As in the first phase, the participants get together, but this time they discuss major organizational issues and the stakes are for real.

6 *Stabilization.* In this final phase, support is marshaled for changes suggested earlier and an evaluation of the overall program is conducted.

These six phases of grid training may take from three to five years to implement, but in some cases they may be compressed into a shorter period of time.

Advocates of grid training are convinced of the validity of this approach. One research study on the technique led to the conclusion that ". . . managerial and team effectiveness *can* be taught by managers with outside assistance. Furthermore, it appears that this type of educational strategy can help to make significant contributions to organizational effectiveness."[28] In a later report where the grid program was carried to the lowest level of the firm, it was noted:

> . . . specific advantages have been shown in the gain in dollar savings. Plant-wide practical application of cooperative effort toward greater effectiveness is shown by: decreased time of plant units' tasks, such as unit shutdowns; increased use of capacities and energies of plant personnel through union-management agreed-upon arrangements . . . ; and a greater personal interest and involvement in the work.[29]

Despite the apparent favorable results, there are criticisms of nonrigorous methodology that is used on the grid studies.[30] Huse, after reviewing all relevant research on grid training, concluded that most programs either are not evaluated at all or depend on testimonial or anecdotal data with often contradictory results.[31] Despite the questionable research, one thing is certain. Grid training is widely used. A recent issue of *Organizational Dynamics* reported that,

---

[28]Ibid., p. 155.

[29]Robert R. Blake, Jane S. Mouton, Richard L. Sloma, and Barbara P. Loftin, "A Second Breakthrough in Organization Development," *California Management Review*, Winter 1968, p. 78.

[30]Dunnette and Campbell, op. cit., p. 21; and George Strauss, "Organizational Development: Credits and Debits," *Organizational Dynamics*, Winter 1973, p. 14.

[31]Edgar F. Huse, *Organization Development and Change*, West Publishing Co., St. Paul, Minn., 1975, pp. 159–163.

The Grid has been adopted in whole or in part by thousands of organizations. Almost 20,000 persons have participated in public Grids, while an additional 200,000 have attended in-company Grid learning sessions. In short, the Managerial Grid is the single most popular approach to organization development.[32]

A couple of years ago, Blake and Mouton's Scientific Methods, Inc., listed five executive grid seminars; fifty-four managerial grid seminars in the U. S., Mexico, Great Britain, Germany, and Japan; eleven managerial grid instructor development seminars in three different countries; 6 grid organization development seminars; and twenty-nine sales grid seminars in different parts of the world.[33] Blake and Mouton have even taken the grid approach to intimate relationships and marriage.[34] Continued use of the grid technique seems justified, but desirably more rigorous research will be forthcoming to evaluate its effectiveness for organization development.

Survey-Feedback

Besides laboratory training (sensitivity or grid) the other major thrust in the development of OD has come from survey research and feedback of the data. Once again Kurt Lewin had the original influence in survey-feedback, but for the last thirty years the approach is most closely associated with the University of Michigan's Institute for Social Research (ISR).

As the terminology indicates, this approach to OD surveys the unit of analysis (e.g., a work group, department, or whole organization) by use of questionnaires (sometimes supplemented by observations and interviews) and feeds back the data to those who generated them. The data are used in the action research sense of diagnosing problems and developing specific action plans to solve the problems. The questionnaire can be either tailor-made for each situation or, as more commonly in recent years, a standardized version thoroughly researched and developed by the ISR. A number of revisions have been made through the years, but the most recent ISR questionnaire provides data on the following areas.[35]

Leadership:
1 Managerial support
2 Managerial goal emphasis
3 Managerial work facilitation
4 Managerial interaction facilitation
5 Peer support

---

[32]"Using the Managerial Grid to Ensure MBO," *Organizational Dynamics,* Spring 1974, p. 55.

[33]Huse, op. cit., p. 159.

[34]Jane S. Mouton and Robert R. Blake, *The Marriage Grid,* McGraw-Hill Book Company, New York, 1971.

[35]See James C. Taylor and David G. Bowers, *Survey of Organizations: A Machine-Scored Standardized Questionnaire Instrument,* Institute for Social Research, University of Michigan, Ann Arbor, Mich., 1972, pp. 3–4.

    6 Peer goal emphasis
    7 Peer work facilitation
    8 Peer interaction facilitation

Organizational climate:
    9 Communication within company
  10 Motivation
  11 Decision making
  12 Control within company
  13 Coordination between departments
  14 General management

Satisfaction:
  15 Satisfaction with company
  16 Satisfaction with supervisor
  17 Satisfaction with job
  18 Satisfaction with pay
  19 Satisfaction with work group

Normally an external consultant will accumulate, present, and interpret the data for the group. The consultant will then, usually in a process consultation or team-building approach, (covered in the next section), help the group diagnose and solve their problems.

The ISR has conducted a relatively great amount of research over the years on their questionnaire instrument and survey-feedback as an OD intervention. After a detailed review of the research evidence on both, Huse concludes, the "questionnaire shows generally high reliability, but the assumption that it represents a complete 'metamodel' of organization needs to be rigorously checked" and "the available data seem to indicate that survey feedback can be an effective approach toward meeting both organizational goals and individual needs."[36] However, he does temper his conclusions with the observation that, "survey feedback comes out best in research done by the Institute for Social Research, the largest survey feedback organization in the world."[37]

A TYPOLOGY OF OD TECHNIQUES

As indicated, the two major stems in OD are laboratory training (sensitivity and grid) and survey-feedback. Both of these are important OD intervention strategies. However, today there are many other important interventions used in OD. Figure 21-2 gives a typology of the most widely recognized OD interventions according to the unit of analysis.

[36]Huse, op. cit., p. 174.
[37]Ibid., p. 172.

Figure 21-2 Types of Major OD Interventions

Unit of analysis	Major OD interventions
Intraindividual	Sensitivity training (therapeutic) Grid training (Phase 1)
Interpersonal (group) and intergroup (different groups are substituted for different individuals in intergroup applications)	Sensitivity training (family and cousin) Grid training (Phases 1, 2, and 3) Survey-feedback Process consultation Third-party peacemaking Team building
Total (system) organization	Grid training (all phases) Survey-feedback

As shown, sensitivity training can be used as a major OD intervention at both the intraindividual and interpersonal levels; survey-feedback is applied at both the interpersonal/intergroup and total-organization level; and grid training in its various phases or as a whole is applied to all three levels. Although there are other OD interventions that are sometimes used at the intraindividual (e.g., life and career planning, which helps individuals identify strengths and weaknesses in order to focus on their life and career objectives and how they can achieve them) and total-organization (e.g., technostructural interventions that strategically improve the technical or structural inputs) levels, most of the modern, widely used OD efforts are aimed at the interpersonal/intergroup level. Besides the sensitivity training, grid training, and survey-feedback techniques which have already been discussed, three of the most important interventions at the interpersonal/intergroup level are process consultation, third-party peacemaking, and team building.

Process Consultation

As the terminology suggests, the process consultation, or P-C, approach to OD is concerned with the processes that take place within a group or between groups and the role of the consultant. Edgar Schein, the leading writer and consultant on P-C, depicts the role of the outside consultant as helping "the client to perceive, understand, and act upon process events which occur in the client's environment."[38] The underlying assumption of P-C is that the process consultant can effectively help diagnose and solve important problems facing modern organizations. Schein points out that the consultant is mainly concerned with processes such as "the various human actions which occur in the normal flow of work, in the conduct of meetings, and in formal and informal encounters between members of the organization. Of particular relevance are the client's own actions and their impact on other people."[39] Specific areas that

[38]Edgar H. Schein, *Process Consultation: Its Role in Organization Development*, Addison-Wesley Publishing Company, Inc., Reading, Mass., 1969, p. 9.
[39]Ibid.

P-C is aimed at include communication, functional roles of group members, group problem solving and decision making, group norms and growth, leadership and authority, and intergroup processes.

Schein lists the following specific steps that the consultant would follow in a P-C program of OD:[40]

1 *Initiate contact.* This is where the client contacts the consultant with a problem that cannot be solved by normal organization procedures or resources.

2 *Define the relationship.* In this step the consultant and the client enter into both a formal contract spelling out services, time, and fees and a psychological contract. The latter spells out the expectations and hoped-for results of both the client and the consultant.

3 *Select a setting and method.* This step involves an understanding of where and how the consultant will do the job that needs to be done.

4 *Gather data and make a diagnosis.* Through a survey using questionnaires, observation, and interviews, the consultant makes a preliminary diagnosis. This data gathering occurs simultaneously with the entire consultative process.

5 *Intervene.* Agenda-setting, feedback, coaching, and/or structural interventions can be made in the P-C approach.

6 *Reduce involvement and terminate.* The consultant disengages from the client organization by mutual agreement but leaves the door open for future involvement.

There are two major advantages of a P-C approach to OD. First of all, P-C is aimed at important interpersonal and intergroup problems facing today's organizations. Second, although an outside consultant is used, with the accompanying advantages, the P-C approach is aimed at helping organizations help themselves. The disadvantages of P-C are that the participants are not as intensively involved in the process as in some of the other OD techniques and it generally takes two or three years of sustained involvement, which requires a great deal of commitment and cost. To date, although Chris Argyris has developed some innovative approaches to evaluating P-C[41] and there are some cases citing the effectiveness of P-C,[42] a rigorous research effort must be forthcoming before any generalizations on the effectiveness of P-C can be made.

Third-Party Peacemaking

A special case of process consultation is third-party peacemaking, which is specifically aimed at resolving interpersonal/intergroup conflict. Like P-C, it

---

[40]Ibid., pp. 79–131.

[41]See: Chris Argyris, *Organization and Innovation*, Richard D. Irwin, Inc., Homewood, Ill., 1965.

[42]For example, see: Schein, op. cit., pp. 126–129; and Gordon Lippitt, *Organization Renewal,* Appleton-Century-Crofts, New York, 1969.

examines the processes involved, makes a diagnosis of the reasons for the conflict, and through the third-party consultant facilitates a constructive confrontation and resolution of the conflict. The approach is based on the modern assumptions of conflict that were examined in detail in Chapter 16.

Richard Walton is most closely associated with third-party peacemaking. He feels that this approach may lead to constructive outcomes of conflict by: ensuring mutual motivation on the part of the principals; creating parity in their situational power; synchronizing their negative and positive moves; providing social support and process expertise that enhances openness; performing a translation function; and adjusting the tension to optimum levels.[43] The intervention made by the consultant can be either passive, with the consultant simply being present and available in the confrontation, or active, with the consultant taking the following types of steps:

1 Gather relevant data by interviewing the principles in the conflict.
2 Select the place and structure the context of the confrontation meeting.
3 Make a direct intervention in the process by doing actions such as the following:
   a refereeing the interaction process
   b initiating agenda
   c encouraging and participating in feedback
   d giving a diagnosis and prescription
   e assisting the principals to plan and prepare for further dialogue after the confrontation[44]

The advantage of third-party peacemaking is that it is a systematic approach to dysfunctional conflict resolution. The disadvantage is that the conflict can become worse if not handled properly. To prevent the problem from compounding, there must be a highly skilled consultant. Walton suggests that the profile for the ideal third-party peacemaker is one who has: (1) high professional expertise regarding social processes; (2) low power over the fate of the principals; (3) high control over the confrontation setting and processes; (4) moderate knowledge about the principals, issues, and background factors; (5) neutrality or balance with respect to substantive outcomes, personal relationships, and conflict-resolution methodology.[45] As with process consultation, there are testimonial cases that try to evaluate third-party consultation,[46] but as yet there is no rigorous research available.

Team Building

Both process consultation and third-party peacemaking are highly specialized OD interventions that are closely associated with a very few leading advocates

---

[43]Richard E. Walton, *Interpersonal Peacemaking: Confrontations and Third-Party Consultation*, Addison-Wesley Publishing Company, Inc., Reading, Mass., 1969, p. v.
[44]Ibid., pp. 148–150.
[45]Ibid., pp. 15–69.
[46]Ibid., pp. 15–69.

and practicing consultants. Of wider appeal and application is team building. Whereas sensitivity training "scares off" many managers because of the controversy surrounding it and the potentially powerful psychological implications inherent in it, team building is seen as accomplishing the same goals but without the potentially explosive problems. There is little question that team building has become an increasingly popular OD technique in recent years. French and Bell, in their book, go as far as to say that "Probably the most important single group of interventions are the team-building activities the goals of which are the improvement and increased effectiveness of various teams within the organization."[47]

As indicated in Figure 21-2, team building can be applied at either the interpersonal or the intergroup level. Most team building is used on family groups (those who work together on a day-to-day basis, e.g., a boss and the boss's immediate subordinates), but it can also be used on "start-up" teams, task forces, various committees, and interdepartmental (cousin-type) groups.

As an OD process, team building generally follows the classic change procedure originally formulated by Kurt Lewin:

1 *Unfreezing.* The first task is to make the team aware of the need for change. A climate of openness and trust is developed so that the group is ready for change.

2 *Moving.* Basically using a survey-feedback technique, the team makes a diagnosis of where they are and develops action plans to get to where they want to go.

3 *Refreezing.* Once the plans have been carried out and an evaluation has been made, the team starts to stabilize into more effective performance.

The above, of course, represents only a very general idea of what team building is all about and can also apply to the other OD techniques.

A typical team-building program actually used in a large industrial plant is described by Nielsen and Kimberly as follows:[48]

1 *Team skills workshop.* The production teams in this plant first went through a 2½-day workshop which mainly consisted of a series of experience-based exercises. The purpose of this first phase was essentially to unfreeze the various teams and get them ready to accept change.

2 *Data collection.* In a questionnaire survey, data were collected on organizational climate, supervisory behavior, and job content from all first-line supervisors in the program.

3 *Data confrontation.* The consultants presented the teams with the data gathered in step 2. The teams, with the consultant present, openly discussed problem areas, established priorities, and made some preliminary recommendations for change.

4 *Action planning.* Based on what went on in step 3, the teams then

[47]French and Bell, op. cit., p. 122.

[48]Warren R. Nielsen and John R. Kimberly, "The Impact of Organizational Development on the Quality of Organizational Output," *Academy of Management Proceedings,* 1973, pp. 528–529.

developed specific plans for the changes to be actually carried out on-the-job.

    5   *Team building.* The first four phases were preliminary to the actual team building. In this phase, each team met as a whole to identify barriers to effectiveness and developed ways of eliminating the barriers and agreed upon plans to accomplish the desired changes.

    6   *Intergroup building.* In this final phase there were 2-day meetings held between various teams which were interdependent in accomplishing goals. The purpose of this phase was to establish collaboration on shared goals and problems and to generalize the OD effort to the total organization.

This program took over a year to complete. The outside consultant in a team-building OD approach such as the above plays an important facilitative role but is not as central to the approach as in process consultation or third-party peacemaking.

    The advantages of team building are all those that are attributed to old-fashioned teamwork. The process can create a team effort under an open, participative climate. There can be improved communication and problem solving, and individual team members can experience psychological growth and improve their interpersonal skills. For example, one research study found that four trained teams reported significantly higher levels of group effectiveness, mutual influence, and personal involvement and participation than did the eight control groups.[49] Evaluation of the six-step program conducted by Neilsen and Kimberly also found that the program produced a positive impact on organizational performance (quality of output and profit but not quantity of output) and favorably affected the attitudes and perceptions of the members of the teams studied.[50] However, despite the potentially promising research that is just starting to emerge on the value of team building as an OD intervention, there is still a dearth of research on the effects that the technique has outside the team itself. After an extensive review of the relevant research, Friedlander and Brown conclude that, "It remains unclear what mechanisms operate in successful team development activities, or what critical conditions must be satisfied for successful generalization of learnings outside the team, or what effects group development has on actual task performance."[51] In other words, as with the other OD techniques discussed in this chapter and the other human resource applications discussed in the other chapters, more research is needed on team building, but its potential for the future seems very promising.

TRANSACTIONAL ANALYSIS

Transactional analysis, or TA, is given separate attention in this chapter because it is not part of the mainstream of OD. Most OD experts do not feel

---

[49]Frank Friedlander, "The Impact of Organizational Training Laboratories upon Effectiveness and Intervention of Ongoing Work Groups," *Personnel Psychology,* vol. 20, 1967, pp. 289–308.

[50]John R. Kimberly and Warren R. Nielsen, "Organizational Development and Change in Organizational Performance," *Administrative Science Quarterly,* June 1975, pp. 191–206.

[51]Frank Friedlander and L. Dave Brown, "Organization Development," *Annual Review of Psychology,* vol. 25, 1974, p. 329.

that TA is a full-blown intervention strategy, but rather treat it as a useful tool to help people better understand themselves and how they affect others. The application of TA is not limited to OD efforts. Similar to sensitivity training, TA has diverse applications in counseling and is widely used to analyze group dynamics and interpersonal communication. As an OD tool, Huse states that the purpose of TA is to "help the people involved better understand their own ego states and those of others, to understand the principles behind transactions and games, and to interact in more meaningful ways with one another."[52]

Eric Berne is usually credited with starting the TA movement with his best-selling book *Games People Play,* and Thomas Harris's book *I'm OK— You're OK* further popularized TA. More recent books by James and Jongeward are more relevant to OD applications.[53] TA is very popular today and has a wide appeal. In many respects it is a fad and is sometimes confused with the equally popular transcendental meditation (TM) movement. However, TA has been able to transcend the fad stage because it is based on a well-developed psychoanalytic theoretical base. A major reason for its popularity, and where Freud and other pioneering psychoanalytic theorists failed, is that it uses very understandable and everyday, relevant terminology. Everyone can readily relate to the concepts and practice of TA. The following sections give attention to the three major areas of transactional analysis: ego states, transactions, and strokes and games. The last section will comment on its application and value as an OD technique.

Ego States

Chapter 5 contained a discussion of the Freudian psychoanalytic model and Chapter 14 was devoted to the structure of personality. The ego plays a central role in the Freudian model. In the structure of the human personality, the ego represents reality, and it rationally attempts to keep the impulsive id and the conscience of the superego in check. The ego is a hypothetical construct because it is not observable; it is used to help explain the complex dynamics of the human personality. TA uses this psychoanalytic theory as background for identifying three important ego states: child, adult, and parent. These three ego states are roughly equivalent to the Freudian concepts of id (child), ego (adult), and superego (parent). A more detailed look at the three ego states is necessary to understand TA and how it can be used in OD.

Child (C) Ego State This is the state where the person acts as an impulsive child. This "child" state could be characterized by being either submissive and conforming (the dutiful child) or insubordinate, emotional, joyful, or rebellious (the "little brat"). In either case the child state is

[52]Huse, op. cit., p. 290.

[53]Muriel James and Dorothy Jongeward, *Born to Win,* Addison-Wesley Publishing Company, Inc., Reading, Mass., 1971; and Dorothy Jongeward and contributors, *Everybody Wins: Transactional Analysis Applied to Organizations,* Addison-Wesley Publishing Company, Inc., Reading, Mass., 1973.

characterized by very immature behavior. An example would be the employee who, when reprimanded by the boss for doing something known to be correct, responds by saying, "You know best. Whatever you say, sir." Another example would be the secretary who tells a coworker, "My boss makes me so mad sometimes I could scream" and then proceeds to break into tears. Both examples illustrate immature, childlike behaviors.

Adult (A) Ego State   In this state the person acts like a mature adult. In the adult state people attack problems in a "cool-headed," rational manner. They gather relevant information, carefully analyze it, generate alternatives, and make logical choices. In the adult state people do not act impulsively or in a domineering way. In dealings with other people, the adult state is characterized by fairness and objectivity. An example would be the sales manager who, when presented with a relatively high expense account by a subordinate, replies, "Well, this appears high, but we will have to look at the reasons for it. It may be that our other salespersons' expenses are too low to do the kind of job that needs to be done."

Parent (P) Ego State   In this state people act like domineering parents. Individuals can be either overly protective and loving or stern and critical. The parent state is also illustrated by those who give standards and rules for others. They tend to talk down to people and to treat others like children. An example would be the supervisor who comes up to a group of workers and says, "Okay, you guys, stop fooling around and get to work. You have to earn your keep around here."

Transactions between Ego States

It should be pointed out that people generally exhibit all three ego states, but one state may dominate over the other two. The strong inference, of course, is that the adult state is far superior to the child or parent state, at least for effective interpersonal relations. However, the TA authors generally stress that all three ego states are necessary for a healthy personality. More important than the ego state per se is how one ego state matches or conflicts with another ego state in interpersonal relations. As James and Jongeward note, "Anything that happens between people will involve a transaction between their ego states. When one person sends a message to another, he expects a response. All transactions can be classified as (1) complementary, (2) crossed, or (3) ulterior."[54] Analysis of these transactions is at the very heart of TA.

Complementary Transactions   Figure 21-3 shows three possible complementary transactions. As shown, transactions are complementary if the message sent or the behavior exhibited by one person's ego state receives the appropriate and expected response from the other person's ego state. For

---

[54]James and Jongeward, op. cit., p. 24.

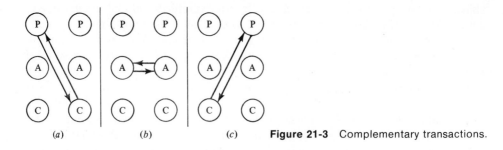

(a)   (b)   (c)   **Figure 21-3** Complementary transactions.

example, suppose that the two people interacting in Figure 21-3, are a boss and an immediate subordinate. In (a), the boss says, "Joe, I want you to be more careful in filling out a report on even the smallest accident. OSHA requirements are getting really tough, and we have to do better." The subordinate in case (a) replies, "Gee, boss, I really don't have time to fill out those dumb reports, but if you think I should, I will." In (b), the superior and subordinate both interact in an adult manner. For example, the boss says, "Joe, I would like your input on a report I am writing on how to improve the efficiency of the department." Joe responds by saying, "You bet, Jack. I have been gathering a lot of cost data over the past couple of months, and as soon as I analyze it, I would like to sit down with you and discuss it." In (c) the subordinate possesses the parent state and the boss represents the child state. Although rarer than the other two cases, an example might be the following dialogue:

Joe: Jack, I wish you would give more attention to maintenance around here. I can't do my job well unless you give me the proper support.

The boss: Heaven's sake! What do you want from me? You guys drive me up a wall. I can't take it anymore.

Once again it should be pointed out that although the adult-to-adult complementary transactions are probably most effective for organizational interpersonal relations, communication and understanding can also occur in the parent-child complementary transactions.

Crossed Transactions   A crossed transaction occurs when the message sent or the behavior exhibited by one person's ego state is reacted to by an incompatible, unexpected ego state on the part of the other person. There are many more possible crossed transactions than there are complementary transactions. Figure 21-4 shows one cross transaction that would typically occur in an organizational setting. As shown, the boss treats his subordinate as a child but the subordinate attempts to respond on an adult basis. The dialogue in this example might be as follows:

Boss: I have told you over and over that I want those reports in on time. You are either going to have to meet my deadlines or look for another job.

Subordinate: I did not realize that the timing of the reports was so critical. I will have to reorder my priorities.

Crossed transactions are the source of much interpersonal conflict in an

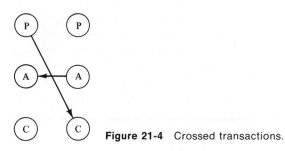

Figure 21-4 Crossed transactions.

organization. The result can be hurt feelings and frustrations on the part of the parties involved and possible dysfunctional consequences for the organization.

Ulterior Transactions The most complex are the ulterior transactions. These can be very subtle, but, like the crossed transactions, they are generally very damaging to interpersonal relations. As shown in Figure 21-5 the ulterior transactions always involve at least two ego states on the part of one person. The individual may say one thing (e.g., project an adult state, as indicated in Figure 21-5) but mean quite another (e.g., the parent state, as shown by the dashed line in Figure 21-5). Although there are many other possibilities besides the one shown in Figure 21-5, an example is this typical one in organizations, where the boss says, "My door is always open, come in so we can air your problems and together reach a rational solution" (adult state), when what he really means is: "Don't come whining to me with your troubles. Find an answer yourself. That is what you're getting paid for" (parent state). Obviously, these ulterior transactions are the most difficult to identify and deal with in transactional analysis.

Strokes and Games in TA

The three ego states and the three types of transactions are the basic elements of TA. In addition, however, there are other concepts and dynamics inherent in the TA approach. Two of the more important are strokes and games.

The Concept of Strokes TA experts feel that everyone has to have strokes. Using the common meaning of the word, this simply means that starting out as an infant and throughout one's life, a person needs cuddling,

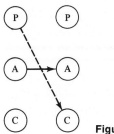

Figure 21-5 Ulterior transactions.

affection, recognition, and praise. Not everyone is turned on by the same strokes. (In the vernacular of TA this is stated as "different strokes for different folks.") But everyone needs them. It may be a simple "Good morning" or a pat on the back every once in a while. If people do not get such positive strokes, they will seek out negative strokes. The latter case may be the outgrowth of childhood experiences. People in this case tend to discount any attempts to give them positive strokes. Obviously, this TA concept of strokes is very closely related to the learning concept of reinforcement. For example, positive strokes could be thought of as social reinforcers.

The Games People Play   TA is also concerned with the ways that people structure their time. James and Jongeward suggest that people learn withdrawal, rituals or pastimes, games, activities, and intimacy to occupy their time.[55] The meanings of each of these are self-explanatory, and going into depth on each of them is beyond the scope of this discussion. However, a brief look at the games people play is especially relevant to some of the things that go on in modern organizations.

Eric Berne, who is most closely associated with the games aspect of TA and, of course, wrote the best-selling book *Games People Play,* which started the TA movement, defines a game as ". . . a recurring set of transactions, often repetitious, superficially plausible, with a concealed motivation; or, more colloquially, a series of moves with a snare, or 'gimmick.' "[56] Those involved in a game are usually not aware of it until the "snare" is drawing tight. The outcome of games is almost always a win-lose proposition. Normal as well as devious people commonly play games. Games that are frequently played in organizations include the following:

1   *"Blemish."* In this game the boss may continually dwell on one or a very few insignificant mistakes in an otherwise good report.
2   *"Yes, but . . ."* In this game the boss tacks on "Yes, but . . ." to every good answer or idea that the subordinate may have. By doing this the boss can maintain a superior position and keep subordinates in their place.
3   *"NIGYSOB."* This acronym stands for the game: "Now I've got you, you SOB." An example would be the subordinate who patiently waits until the exact, opportune time to "pull the rug" on his boss (e.g., publicly embarrass him for an obvious, stupid mistake). The motive for this game is usually revenge.

The above are only three examples of the games people play in organizations. Anyone who has spent some time working in an organization can readily identify many, many others.

Evaluation of TA as an OD Technique

As noted in the introductory comments on TA, most OD experts consider TA a tool rather than an intervention strategy for OD. Yet it is becoming increasingly

[55]Ibid., pp. 56–63.
[56]Eric Berne, *Games People Play*, Grove Press, Inc., New York, 1964, p. 48.

popular with management practitioners. Many companies in a wide variety of industries have sponsored TA programs for their managerial personnel and certain key positions such as customer service representatives. Questionnaire instruments which identify dominant ego states of people and exercises which help people understand and analyze their transactions with others have been developed.

When used as an OD approach, TA has attempted to develop more adult states in people and complementary transactions with others. TA is also used in certain phases of the interpersonal OD techniques of process consultation, third-party peacemaking, and team building. Unfortunately, the effectiveness of these TA efforts for OD is largely unknown.

To date, about the only evidence of the value of TA as an OD technique is the testimony of TA consultants and the results of a few questionnaire studies that asked participants how well they liked the TA program and whether they thought it did them any good back on the job. All the TA consultants, of course, give glowing testimony to the effectiveness of TA.[57] The same is true of the questionnaire studies. The participants are generally very positive about the TA program and feel that it has done some good back on the job.[58] However, as Huse notes, "Since the results of most of these programs are given in anecdotal or questionnaire-response form, the true value of TA and its long-term influence on employees, groups, or the larger social system have yet to be determined."[59] In other words, and the reader is probably getting tired of seeing this at the end of each section but it is nevertheless true for the relatively new and exciting applications for the field of organizational behavior, more research is needed on TA.

SUMMARY

Organizations today are faced with tremendous external and internal forces of change. A systematic, planned way of managing this change is through the process of organization development. The two major traditional paths of OD come from laboratory training (both sensitivity and grid) and survey-feedback. The more recent approach to OD is to utilize more specialized interpersonal techniques such as process consultation, third-party peacemaking, and team building. Finally, the increasingly popular transactional analysis is beginning to be used in organization development. However, like the other techniques and approaches, more rigorous research needs to be forthcoming before conclusions can be made on the effectiveness of TA as an OD technique.

QUESTIONS FOR DISCUSSION AND REVIEW

1 What are some of the major external and internal forces for change that are facing today's organizations?

[57]For example, see: Jongeward and contributors, op. cit.

[58]Ibid. In particular, see pp. 99–101; and Lynn Randall, "Red, White and Blue TA at 600 MPH"; Susan Sinclair, "TA Improves Customer Contacts"; and Kathy O'Brien Tiano, "Transactional Analysis Applied to Mountain Bell," which are all found in Jongeward, op. cit.

[59]Huse, op. cit., p. 291.

2 What are some of the major characteristics of organization development?

3 In your own words, briefly describe the three traditional approaches to OD. Discuss their major advantages and limitations.

4 In your own words, briefly describe the three major interpersonal/ intergroup OD techniques. What would be the major steps in a team-building approach to OD?

5 What are the three ego states in TA? Give an example of each of the three major transactions. What are strokes in TA? Give examples of some you have received in the last day or two. Can you describe any TA games you have been involved in lately?

CASE: CHANGE AT MIDSOUTH GAS AND ELECTRIC

Midsouth Gas and Electric is being challenged by almost unbelievable forces for change. For example, up to a few years ago the marketing department was charged with the responsibility of increasing the customers' use of gas and electricity; the power generation branch of the company had the "green light" on unlimited expansion with no worries about the effects of pollution from the power plant; and the personnel department used tests to hire the kind of people that "fit into the Midsouth family." Now all this has drastically changed. The company has launched into a public relations effort to have customers decrease their consumption of gas and electric; the power generation arm of the company is faced with extremely limited resources and is facing some very costly lawsuits from the government and conservationists unless it does something very quickly about its pollution problems; and under EEOC pressures the personnel department have eliminated their testing program and feel they must give preferential treatment to minorities and women.

Faced with this type of change, the chief executive of Midsouth feels that it is time that the company launched into a full-scale organization development program. The personnel of Midsouth are experiencing uncertainties, frustrations, and just plain confusion. Interdepartmental and interpersonal conflicts are running rampant throughout the company. All areas of organizational performance are beginning to decline. The future looks very bleak for Midsouth Gas and Electric.

1 You have been hired as a consultant to develop an organization development program for Midsouth. Weighing the pros and cons of the traditional and more specialized interpersonal/intergroup OD techniques, what kind of program would you propose? Why?

2 Could transactional analysis be used in the OD program for Midsouth? How?

3 Do you think that this company can turn itself around by the OD program you propose? What do you think the major problems will be? What do you think the major benefits will be?

SELECTED REFERENCES

Aplin, John C., Jr., and Duane E. Thompson: "Feedback: Key to Survey-based Change," *Public Personnel Management,* November–December 1974, pp. 524–530.

Beckhard, Richard: "Strategies for Large System Change," *Sloan Management Review,* Winter 1975, pp. 43–55.

Beer, Michael, and Edgar F. Huse: "A Systems Approach to Organization Development," *Journal of Applied Behavioral Science,* vol. 8, no. 1, pp. 79–101.

Bennett, Dudley: "Transactional Analysis in Management," *Personnel,* January–February 1975, pp. 34–44.

Blake, Robert R., and Jane S. Mouton: "An Overview of the Grid," *Training and Development Journal,* May 1975, pp. 29–37.

Bowers, David G., Jerome L. Franklin, and Patricia A. Pecorella: "Matching Problems, Precursors, and Interventions in OD: A Systematic Approach," *The Journal of Applied Behavioral Science,* October–November–December 1975, pp. 391–409.

Bradford, Leland P., Jack R. Gibb, and Kenneth D. Benne (eds.): *T-Group Theory and Laboratory Method,* John Wiley & Sons, Inc., New York, 1964.

Calhoon, Richard P., and Thomas H. Jerdee: "First-Level Supervisory Training Needs and Organizational Development," *Public Personnel Management,* May–June 1975, pp. 196–200.

Cooper, Cary L.: "How Psychologically Dangerous Are T-Groups and Encounter Groups?" *Human Relations,* April 1975, pp. 249–260.

Cushnie, William D.: "A Manager's Introduction to Transactional Analysis," *S. A. M. Advanced Management Journal,* Autumn 1975, pp. 37–45.

Ely, Donald D., and John T. Morse: "TA and Reinforcement Theory," *Personnel,* March–April 1974, pp. 38–41.

Friedlander, Frank, and L. Dove Brown: "Organization Development," *Annual Review of Psychology,* vol. 25, 1975, pp. 313–341.

French, Wendell: "Organization Development Objectives, Assumptions and Strategies," *California Management Review,* Winter 1969, pp. 23–32.

French, Wendell, and Cecil H. Bell, Jr.: *Organization Development,* Prentice-Hall, Inc., Englewood Cliffs, N. J., 1973.

Hand, Herbert H., Bernard D. Estafen, and Henry P. Sims, Jr.: "How Effective Is Data Survey and Feedback as a Technique of Organization Development? An Experiment," *The Journal of Applied Behavioral Science,* July–August–September 1975, pp. 333–347.

Hart, Howard A.: "The Grid Appraised—Phases 1 and 2," *Personnel,* July–August 1974, pp. 44–59.

Jongeward, Dorothy, and contributors: *Everybody Wins: Transactional Analysis Applied to Organizations,* Addison-Wesley Publishing Company, Inc., Reading, Mass., 1973.

Kahn, Robert L.: "Organizational Development: Some Problems and Proposals," *Journal of Applied Behavioral Science,* October–November–December 1974, pp. 485–501.

Kearney, William J., and Desmond D. Martin: "Sensitivity Training: An Established Management Development Tool?" *Academy of Management Journal,* December 1974, pp. 755–760.

Kimberly, John R., and Warren R. Nielsen: "Organizational Development and Change in Organizational Performance," *Administrative Science Quarterly,* June 1975, pp. 191–206.

Lawrence, Paul R.: "How to Deal with Resistance to Change," *Harvard Business Review,* January–February 1969, pp. 4–5, 8–12, and 166–176.

Lennung, Sven-Ake, and Ake Ahlberg: "The Effects of Laboratory Training: A Field Experiment," *The Journal of Applied Behavioral Science,* April–May–June 1975, pp. 177–188.

Lewis, John W., III: "Management Team Development: Will It Work for You?" *Personnel,* July–August 1975, pp. 11–25.

Lieberman, Morton: "Some Limits to Research on T-Groups," *The Journal of Applied Behavioral Science,* April–May–June 1975, pp. 241–249.

Lippitt, Ronald, and Gordon Lippitt: "Consulting Process in Action," *Training and Development Journal,* May 1975, pp. 48–54.

Luchsinger, V. P., and L. L. Luchsinger: "Transactional Analysis for Managers, or How to Be More OK with OK Organizations," *MSU Business Topics,* Spring 1974, pp. 4–12.

Maxwell, S. R., and M. G. Evans: "An Evaluation of Organizational Development: Three Phases of the Managerial Grid," *Journal of Business Administration,* Fall 1973, pp. 21–35.

Plovnick, Mark, Ronald Fry, and Irwin Rubin: "New Developments in OD Technology: Programmed Team Development," *Training and Development Journal,* April 1975, pp. 19–25.

Rettig, Jack L., and Matt M. Amano: "A Survey of ASPA Experience with Management by Objectives, Sensitivity Training and Transactional Analysis," *Personnel Journal,* January 1976, pp. 26–29.

Schein, Edgar H.: *Process Consultation: Its Role in Organization Development,* Addison-Wesley Publishing Company, Inc., Reading, Mass., 1969.

Selfridge, Richard J., and Stanley L. Sokolik, "A Comprehensive View of Organization Development," *MSU Business Topics,* Winter 1975, pp. 46–61.

Shirley, Robert C.: "A Model for Analysis of Organizational Change," *MSU Business Topics,* Spring 1974, pp. 60–68.

Strauss, George: "Organizational Development: Credits and Debits," *Organizational Dynamics,* Winter 1973, pp. 2–19.

Tichy, Noel M.: "How Different Types of Change Agents Diagnose Organizations," *Human Relations,* December 1975, pp. 771–799.

Walton, Richard E.: *Interpersonal Peacemaking: Confrontations and Third-Party Consultation,* Addison-Wesley Publishing Company, Inc., Reading, Mass., 1969.

Zenger, John H., and Dale E. Miller: "Building Effective Teams," *Personnel,* March–April 1974, pp. 20–29.

Chapter 22

Summary and Future Perspectives for Organizational Behavior

In this concluding chapter, each major part of the book is briefly summarized and some comments on the future of various aspects of organizational behavior are offered. The chapter ends with a look into the crystal ball of the future course of management as a whole.

SUMMARY AND FUTURE FOR THE FOUNDATION OF ORGANIZATIONAL BEHAVIOR

The purpose of the first part of the book was to lay a sound foundation for the study and analysis of organizational behavior. Included was a brief review of historical contributions, an overview of the behavioral sciences, a summary of the various approaches to management, and the presentation of a model for organizational behavior.

The first chapter laid the historical foundation for organizational behavior. Initially, the chapter gave attention to the evolution of the practice of management. Of particular importance to organizational behavior was the human relations movement. The Hawthorne studies provided the foundation for human relations and is usually considered to be the starting point for the behavioral approach to management. These famous studies certainly had methodological problems by today's standards, but the mere fact that they have remained so visible for over fifty years attests to their importance. Much can still be learned about organizational behavior from the Hawthorne studies. The last part of the chapter analyzed the transition from the old to the new in organizational behavior. McGregor's Theories X and Y can be used as contrasting assumptions between the old and the new, but the human resources model is an even better point of departure for the modern behavioral approach to management. The human resources model is an extension of McGregor's work. Theory Y is more closely aligned with a human relations model. The human resources approach, on the other hand, recognizes the complexities of human behavior in organizations and the need for a sound theoretical base supported by scientifically derived empirical research. In the future, such a perspective should dominate the behavioral approach to management.

The second chapter recognized the need to have a foundation in the behavioral sciences in order to study organizational behavior. One of the most important contributions from the behavioral sciences is the insistence on the use of scientific methodology in accumulating knowledge. Although case and survey designs can make some contributions to the body of knowledge in organizational behavior, more and better use of experimental designs is needed for the future. The remainder of the chapter examined the behavioral science disciplines of anthropology, sociology, psychology, and social psychology. Although psychology and social psychology will probably still dominate the field of organizational behavior, as they do in this book, sociology and, to a lesser extent, anthropology should be able to make significant future inputs.

The third chapter recognized the need to have a foundation in the field of management as a whole for the study of organizational behavior. There is a need to balance the behavioral science and management foundations for organizational behavior. Although each of the diverse approaches to management will continue to develop independently, e.g., the process approach can be made more dynamic, the contingency approach may turn out to be the path out of the existing management theory jungle. The contingency approach tries to accomplish three important goals for the field of management: (1) synthesize and unify the diverse theories of management; (2) integrate the environment into both the theory and practice of management; and (3) narrow the existing gap between management theory and management practice. The contingency approach attempts to accomplish these goals through an *if* (environmental variables)–*then* (management concepts and techniques) conceptual framework. In this approach, the appropriate management concept or technique that will lead to effective goal attainment is contingent on the environment. Such a contingency approach seems to hold a great deal of promise for the future development of the field of management. The behavioral approach, like the process, quantitative, and systems approaches, can fit into the contingency framework.

The fourth chapter built on the contingency perspective by giving specific attention to the environment. Along with history, behavioral science, and management, the environment makes an important input into the foundation for organizational behavior. Physical, sociocultural, and technological environments are making an increasingly significant impact on human behavior in general and organizational behavior in particular. Technology has received some attention in the study of organizational behavior in the past, but it is becoming increasingly clear that the physical and sociocultural environments are also very relevant. The sudden realization of the fact that physical resources are limited (e.g., the oil shortage) and of the implications of overpopulation (e.g., world starvation) plus the social upheavals of the 1960s and 1970s (e.g., changing attitudes and roles of minorities and women) have dramatically demonstrated that the organization is indeed an "open system." Organizations and the behaviors of their participants are greatly affected by the environment. All indications are that the environmental impact will be even greater in the future.

The last chapter in the introductory foundation presented a specific model for organizational behavior. The cognitive and behavioristic models have become the two major approaches to the study of human behavior. Although they are sometimes presented as being diametrically opposed, both approaches can contribute to the understanding, prediction, and control of organizational behavior. The $S \longleftrightarrow O \longrightarrow B \longrightarrow C$ organizational behavior model incorporates behavioristic and cognitive elements. The S (situation) and C (consequence) are external, environmentally based and the O (human organism) is internal, person-based inputs into B (organizational behavior). In the simplest sense, the $S \longleftrightarrow O$ interaction and particularly the $O \longrightarrow B$ relationship represent the cognitive approach and the $B \longrightarrow C$ relationship represents the behavioristic emphasis. The inclusion of the environmental situation (S) as an antecedent to behavior and its interaction with the cognitively based O (person), and the indirect feedback loops that go from the behavioristically based consequences (C) to O and S represent ways to integrate both cognitive and behavioristic approaches into a single model for organizational behavior. In the past, cognitive explanations have dominated the field of organizational behavior. In the future, with the increasing emphasis given to operant learning theory and applied behavioral analysis, there will be a more balanced input from the cognitive and behavioristic approaches. Obviously, both have something to contribute (the cognitive, especially to the understanding of organizational behavior, and the behavioristic, especially to the prediction and control of organizational behavior), and the $S \longleftrightarrow O \longrightarrow B \longrightarrow C$ model is a step toward integrating them for the future.

SUMMARY AND FUTURE FOR THE STRUCTURE AND PROCESSES OF ORGANIZATION

The second part of the book was concerned with the formal organization—the internal environment in which participants interact. Classical and modern structural elements and the management processes of decision making, communication, and control largely make up the formal organization system. It must be remembered, of course, that the external environment and the participants themselves (as individuals and in groups) are also part of the organizational system. But for purposes of study and analysis, it is helpful to separate the structure from the processes.

Chapter 6 examined classical organization theory and structure. The bureaucratic model and its extensions and modifications of centralization-decentralization, flat-tall, departmentation, and line-staff were given major attention. Today the dysfunctions of classical structure receive more attention in the literature than the functions. Yet the classical approach is still very much in evidence in practice and probably will be for the foreseeable future. It does not seem that this is necessarily a case where practice is lagging behind as much as it is a case where the classical approach simply retains value as a way of structuring some types of organizations. The classical approach still can be effectively used for large organizations that operate under relatively rigid constraints and relatively static environmental conditions, and in relatively early stages of development. However, such situations will become less likely for organizations in the future. Thus, it follows that there will be a decline of the classical approach in the future.

Chapter 7 presented the more modern theories of organization (behavioral, systems, and contingency) and some contemporary structural designs (project, matrix, and free-form). These theories and designs, in general, can help meet the modern challenges of complexity and change that are facing organizations now and will in the future. Yet the modern theories and structures are only the beginning of what will be needed for the future. Especially in terms of the actual designs that can be used in practice, there are presently very few viable alternatives to bureaucracy. There is a definite need for more and better structural designs to meet future organizational challenges.

Chapter 8 marked the beginning of the discussion of the management process elements of formal organization. The first part of this chapter on decision making discussed the various types of decisions. In the past, not much attention was given to the compatibility between personal and organizational decisions, and routine decisions received considerably more attention than basic decisions in both theory and practice. In the future, major goals for management decision making will have to be the compatibility of personal and organizational decisions and making the basic decisions as effective as the routine ones. The middle part of the chapter was concerned with the rationality of decision making. Traditional models of decision rationality will have diminishing value. As tomorrow's organizations increase in complexity and the external environment has a bigger impact, the social model and newly developed models should begin to replace the traditional models (e.g., the economic model) in the study and analysis of the rationality of decision making. The last part of the chapter presented some behaviorally oriented decision techniques. The quantitative techniques have been quite successful and are making definite progress toward a true science of management decision making. On the other hand, techniques aimed at more subjective, basic decisions that require creative solutions are lagging far behind. Although a few creative and participative techniques have been around for a long time and can be of some help in the future, the greatest potential for solving these difficult decision problems lies in the group problem-solving techniques of Delphi and NGT and in heuristic computer programming techniques.

Chapter 9 discussed the communication process. It was pointed out that the subject of communication is very diverse, but, most importantly, it is a personal process. Organizational communication was presented from this personal rather than a linear information flow perspective. Since organizational communication is so closely related to decision making and control, the future trends in the two elements will generally follow one another. In particular, there will be a further shift in emphasis in both theory and practice from the sending and transmission (which is relatively effective) to the receiving, feedback, and use of communication in organizations. From the personal perspective, relatively less attention will be given to superior-subordinate communication and more attention given to subordinate-initiated and interactive communication.

The process of control was covered in Chapter 10. It is safe to prophesy that both the theoretical and the practical aspects of control will take more note of the feedforward concept and techniques and of the behavioral implications. Instead of just lip service, theorists and practitioners will begin to seriously question how traditional controls are set and used by management. Management will be challenged to create and implement new concepts and techniques, such as feedforward, which will lend themselves to more effective control. All organizations today, and especially those in the public sector, are being challenged to be more accountable—to evaluate and control what they are doing. Often in the past, new programs or ventures were implemented without proper controls. Now, and probably more so in the future, environmental forces (social, political/legal, and economic) are demanding accountability and control. Under such pressures, the control process will become more important in the future than it has been in the past.

SUMMARY AND FUTURE OF THE STUDY
OF HUMAN BEHAVIOR

Part Three of the book was devoted to the understanding of human behavior. A chapter was devoted to each of the major psychological processes—perception, learning, and motivation. The last chapter in this part attempted to put all the processes together in terms of the theories and development of personality.

The general approach taken in these chapters was more educational than analytical. Thus, specific predictions for the future did not seem warranted. The purpose of the chapters was to provide some insights into, and an appreciation of, the complexities of the human being, so that, when the human is viewed in interaction with the environment, both antecedent and consequent, there will be a better understanding of organizational behavior. In the past, the understanding of the major variables of human behavior has not been part of the behavioral approach to management. In the future, an understanding of the basic elements, particularly the psychological processes of perception, learning, and motivation, plus personality, seems a prerequisite to the study and analysis of organizational behavior.

SUMMARY AND FUTURE OF THE DYNAMICS OF ORGANIZATIONAL BEHAVIOR

In Part Four of the book, the dynamic outcomes of organizational behavior were examined. In the first two chapters, the dynamics of organizational behavior were discussed in terms of group dynamics and informal organization and conflict. The last two chapters dealt with the theories and concepts of work motivation and leadership and power.

Although the dynamics of organizational behavior in the form of group dynamics and informal organization were brought to the surface almost a half-century ago in the Hawthorne studies, there is still much to be learned and to be translated into the study and practice of management. The power of the group and the informal organization can never be underestimated. It cannot be wished away or ignored by management. An important challenge for upcoming management will be to harness and channel the power and energy of the group and informal organization toward, instead of away from, organizational objectives.

The discussion of the dynamics of conflict in Chapter 16 pointed to another serious challenge facing management now and in the future. Just as group dynamics and the informal organization are inevitable, conflict is also a fact of organizational life. Old assumptions and approaches to the management of conflict are no longer adequate. In particular, the idea that conflict always affects the person and the organization negatively should be dispelled. However, the mere realization that conflict may benefit the person and organization does not diminish the need for new strategies and techniques of managing. All indications are that the management of conflict will increase in importance in the dramatically changing and complex world of tomorrow.

The first part of Chapter 17 described and evaluated the newest, most widely recognized theories of work motivation. The content theories of Maslow and Herzberg take on an almost historical perspective. The current and future analysis is more concerned with the processes of work motivation. The Maslow and Herzberg theories both made valuable contributions to answering the question of what motivates people in organizations, but they are too simplistic to be the final answer to the motivation problems facing human resource management. The models of Vroom and of Porter and Lawler and the recent refinements made by Lawler remain difficult to translate into practice.

The Smith and Cranny model was offered as an example of a conceptually sound and practically useful process model of work motivation. It recognizes the complexity of human motivation but can also more readily be adapted to the practice of management. Adams's equity theory and attribution theory and locus of control can make further additive contributions to the understanding of at least the cognitive dimensions of work motivation. There is little question that motivation problems will continue to dominate human resource management in the future. The newer process theories can lead to better understanding, which will desirably stimulate the development and use of specific techniques to help solve the problems. The techniques discussed in the last part of the book represent a good start in this direction.

The last chapter in the dynamics of organizational behavior stressed the importance of leadership and power. Although the more traditional approaches still contribute to the understanding of leadership, the contingency model seems to hold the most future promise for both theory development and improved practice. In addition, the relatively new path-goal theory of leadership can join with and take advantage of the developments taking place in the expectancy theories of motivation. In the final analysis, however, it is still most profitable to view leadership as an influence system consisting of the leader, the situation, and the group. As far as the style of leadership goes, the past models have been very prescriptive (e.g., Likert's emphasis on the value of system 4). In the future, normative models that also incorporate the situation should play a more important role. An example would be the Vroom-Yetton model, which spells out exactly how a manager should act in given situations. Although such an approach will probably never be able to identify all the possible contingencies, it is a step in the direction of the more effective practice of leadership. The last part of the chapter explored the dynamics of power. Power is closely related to leadership. More research is needed in the future to determine what impact the various types of power have on organizational effectiveness. Power is certainly going to receive increasing attention in the future study of organizational behavior.

SUMMARY AND FUTURE FOR HUMAN RESOURCE MANAGEMENT APPLICATIONS

The mere presence of the last part of the book is evidence of the increasing concern being given to applications in the field of organizational behavior. There has been an almost cyclical trend over the past fifty years in the behavioral approach to management. In the early human relations approach, emphasis was given to quick solutions to very difficult, complex human problems in organizations. There was little theoretical development or rigorous research in the human relations movement. Then, with the human resources perspective, theoretical understanding of the complexities of human behavior in organizations and the accompanying research back-up have dominated. Very recently there has been a reemphasis on application. The cycle has been completed, but this time around, sound theory and rigorous research provide the foundation for more effective application. The last part of the book presented and analyzed the newest and most effective techniques for the actual practice of human resource management. It should be emphasized again, however, that, unlike the human relations solutions, these applications are largely based upon and derived from the theories and research that were presented in the preceding parts of the book.

Chapter 19 presented the modern techniques for selection, job design, and appraisal. It was brought out that, mainly because of the legal and social climate of recent years, there is a mass movement away from the traditional use of tests in the selection process. If the tests were valid, as they should have been all along, they could still be an effective tool. There is no reason why valid testing instruments for selection cannot be developed for the future. In addition, however, there is a need to make interviews more valid if they are going to continue to be so widely used in the selection process. In addition, there is a need for totally new selection techniques. The recent use of assessment centers seems to be a step in the right direction. Job design was the second application area discussed in Chapter 19. The design of work has become a very visible area of concern with the general public. Media exposure of "blue-collar blues" and "white-collar woes" has become quite common. Job enrichment was initially proposed as the answer to job design problems, but the subsequent controversy surrounding Herzberg's two-factor theory of motivation has carried over to job enrichment as well. Much of the criticism of job design can be eliminated by empirically derived contingency models. The Porter, Lawler, Hackman model is a step in this direction. The final part of Chapter 19 dealt with performance appraisal. The MBO approach, although more rigorous research is needed to evaluate its effectiveness, seems justifiably popular. MBO combines the best of plan-organize-and-control techniques with participative, motivational concepts. In the future, it should play an even more important role in appraisal and as an overall approach to management. In addition to the relatively established MBO technique, there is room for new appraisal techniques such as BARS. The latter type of technique is needed to get away from the old, ineffective trait approaches to appraisal. Evaluating critical behaviors, not just subjective personality traits, is important to effective performance.

Chapter 20 was specifically devoted to behavioral analysis and change. Organizational behavior modification, or O.B.Mod., was discussed in depth. O.B.Mod. is essentially a five-step problem-solving technique aimed at more effective human resource management. Based on operant learning theory, O.B.Mod. assumes that organizational behavior is a function of its contingent consequences. O.B.Mod. is an external approach that systematically manages the environment (primarily by the contingent application of positive reinforcement). It does not try to directly affect the complex internal states of employees. In the past, the external approach to human resource management has been badly neglected. O.B.Mod. can be especially helpful in the prediction and control of organizational behavior. Along with the other techniques discussed in the preceding and following chapters, O.B.Mod. can play an important future role in more effective human resource management. The major goal of O.B.Mod. is not behavioral change per se but rather behavioral change that leads to performance improvement.

The third chapter of the part was concerned with the broader problem of the management of change. As the environment chapter in the introductory part of the book pointed out, change, with all its accompanying dynamics, is having and will continue to have a tremendous impact on the management of complex organizations. One way of meeting this challenge of change is through a systematic program of organizational development. Many specific OD techniques are available to help in the effort. The traditional sensitivity, grid, and survey-feedback OD techniques still have value, but the newer, interpersonal OD techniques such as process consultation, third-party peacemaking, and team building seem to hold more potential for the future. In addition, popularly accepted techniques such as transactional analysis, which are on the fringe of OD but have a sound theoretical base, can make a contribution to the more effective practice of human resource management.

THE FUTURE COURSE OF MANAGEMENT

Few would argue that the action and challenges today are found in the human side of management. Bigger and better facilities, more efficient use of accounting data and computerized information systems, broader applications of quantitative decision models, new and more appealing products and services, more effective marketing and distribution systems, and many other similar types of problems will remain important to managers in the future. Yet, despite these other important challenges, the understanding, prediction, and control of human resources should remain the single most important priority for managers in the future.

Human resources are of primary importance to the future course of management for two major reasons. The first is a very pragmatic reason. The cost of human resources is very significant. The operating budget of every type of organization is dominated by human costs. If dollars serve as any type of measure for giving relative emphasis, the management of human resources would come out on top. The second reason for giving human resources top priority in the future course of management is their underutilized potential. Compared with the management of human resources, the physical, technical side of management is very efficient. The simple fact is that human resources are not being used to anywhere near their full potential. Whereas a very small margin of increased effectiveness could be realized by giving increased emphasis to the physical and technical sides, tremendous gains can potentially be accomplished by giving increased attention to the human side of management.

The future of management seems clear. More attention will have to be given to the human aspects of management. The study of organizational behavior, as represented in this book, can help meet the important human challenges for management that lie ahead.

QUESTIONS FOR DISCUSSION AND REVIEW

1 What role do you feel organizational behavior will play in the future study of management?
2 What will organizations be like in the future? Discuss in terms of structure and processes.
3 Of what value are the application techniques for the future practice of human resource management?
4 What lies ahead for management as a whole? How does the study of organizational behavior, as represented in this book, help meet the future challenges?

SELECTED REFERENCES

Duncan, W. Jack: "Transferring Management Theory to Practice," *Academy of Management Journal,* December 1974, pp. 724–738.

Dunnette, Marvin D.: *Work and Nonwork in the Year 2001,* Brooks/Cole Publishing Company, Monterey, Calif., 1973.

Foss, Laurence: "Managerial Strategy for the Future: Theory Z Management," *California Management Review,* Spring 1973, pp. 68–81.

Greenwood, William T.: "Future Management Theory: A Comparative Evolution to a General Theory," *Academy of Management Journal,* September 1974, pp. 503–531.

Hart, David K., and William G. Scott: "The Organizational Imperative," *Administration and Society,* November 1975, pp. 259–285.

Hunt, J. G., and P. F. Newell: "Management in the 1980's Revisited," *Personnel Journal,* January 1971, pp. 35–43, 71.

Koontz, Harold: "On the Advancement of Management," *S. A. M. Advanced Management Journal,* October 1974, pp. 9–13.

Murray, Michael A.: "Comparing Public and Private Management: An Exploratory Essay," *Public Administration Review,* July–August 1975, pp. 364–371.

Preston, Lee E., and James E. Post: "The Third Managerial Revolution," *Academy of Management Journal,* September 1974, pp. 476–486.

Simon, William: "Management in the Future," *The Conference Board Record,* March 1973, pp. 44–47.

Toffler, Alvin: *Future Shock,* Random House, Inc., New York, 1970.

Toffler, Alvin (ed.): *The Futurists,* Random House, Inc., New York, 1972.

Young, Lewis H.: "A Scenario for Survival," *The Conference Board Record,* March 1975, pp. 61–64.

Name Index

Cleland, David I., 163, 168–169, 171–172, 175, 236–237
Coch, Lester, 367, 491
Coffey, Robert E., 255
Coleman, Charles, 147
Coleman, James C., 75, 99
Commoner, Barry, 77
Comte, Auguste, 25, 35–36
Cooley, Charles H., 38
Coons, Alvin E., 436
Cooper, Cary L., 555
Coser, Lewis, 385
Costello, Timothy W., 275, 277, 279–280, 295, 297, 300, 389
Coulson, C. A., 82
Cranny, C. J., 403, 424–425, 429–430, 448, 563
Crockett, W. H., 404
Crowne, Douglas P., 428
Crutchfield, Richard S., 256
Cummings, Larry L., 203, 405, 413, 432, 527
Cunniff, John, 188
Cushnie, William D., 555
Cyert, R. M., 191

Dale, Ernest, 5, 7, 22, 60–61, 130–131, 142, 391
Dalkey, N. C., 197, 199
Dalton, Gene, 532
Dalton, Melville, 145, 376–377, 383
Darwin, Charles, 25, 37
Daugherty, William, 251
Davies, J. H., 190
Davis, Keith, 81–83, 114, 175, 224, 378, 380–381, 440
Dean, Joel, 191
Debutts, Thomas C., 93
Dechert, Charles R., 85
Deci, E. L., 294–295
Decotiis, Thomas A., 493, 497
Delbecq, André, 175, 198–200, 203, 537
Delgado, Jose M. R., 343, 359
DeMichele, John H., 538
deMontes, Ana I., 515
deMontes, Francisco, 515
Derr. C. Brooklyn, 402
Deutsch, Karl W., 147
DeVitt, H. William, 413
Dewey, John, 44, 177–178, 343
Dewey, Richard, 76, 79, 105
Dickson, William J., 12–14, 17–18, 23, 38
Diebold, John, 85
Dominquez, Benjamin, 515
Donaldson, Lex, 496
Donham, Dean Wallace B., 12

Donnelly, James H., Jr., 367, 490, 530
Douglas, Jack D., 89
Drucker, Peter F., 84, 122, 132, 140, 175, 211, 233–234, 485
Dubin, Robert, 279
DuBois, Cora, 31, 34
Dunbar, Roger L. M., 247
Duncan, W. Jack, 566
Dunnette, Marvin D., 413–414, 421, 492, 495, 538, 540, 566
Dunteman, George D., 268
duPont, Pierre S., 6
Durant, William C., 4, 6, 21, 133
Durkheim, Emile, 35, 90, 99
Dyer, Lee C., 294, 422

Early, James, 184
Eckert, J. P., 86
Ehrlich, Paul R., 77–78
Eichmann, Adolf, 353
Elbing, Alvar O., 178
Ellertson, Norris, 367, 369
Elliott, Robert K., 248
Ely, Donald D., 555
Emerson, Harrington, 8
Emery, James C., 251
Erikson, Erik, 335, 338–339, 341, 357
Erzen, Paul E., 465
Estafen, Bernard D., 555
Evans, Martin G., 446, 556

Farace, Richard, 224
Faraday, Michael, 82
Faunce, William A., 91
Fayol, Henri, 6–7, 9, 53–54, 56, 59, 109, 177, 206–208, 221, 227
Fechner, Gustav, 25
Fein, Mitchell, 481, 496
Feingold, Barnet D., 295
Festinger, Leon, 364, 390, 425, 428
Fiedler, Fred E., 441–446, 449, 463–465
Filley, Alan C., 175, 394, 396–397, 416–417, 427, 441, 445–447, 514, 533–534
Fiore, Michael V., 168
Fisher, B. Aubrey, 209
Fitzgerald, Thomas H., 480
Flamholtz, Eric G., 248, 251
Fleming, Sir Alexander, 12
Flippo, Edwin B., 130, 206, 220, 513–514
Flowers, Vincent S., 114, 251
Foley, John P., Jr., 393
Ford, Henry, 5, 8–9, 11, 84

Subject Index